NEW WORLD
METAPHYSICS

NEW WORLD METAPHYSICS

Readings on the Religious Meaning of the American Experience

edited by

GILES GUNN

New York   Oxford
OXFORD UNIVERSITY PRESS
1981

Copyright © 1981 by Oxford University Press, Inc.

Library of Congress Cataloging in Publication Data

Main entry under title:

New World metaphysics.
1. Religious thought—United States—Addresses,
essays, lectures. 2. Religious thought—Modern
period, 1500–   —Addresses, essays, lectures.
3. United States—Civilization—Addresses, essays,
lectures. I. Gunn, Giles B.
BR515.N48   261   80-20233
ISBN 0-19-502873-2   AACR1
ISBN 0-19-502874-0 (pbk.)

Printing (last digit): 9 8 7 6 5 4 3 2 1

Printed in the United States of America

Permission to reprint material from the following selections is gratefully acknowledged:

From *Saga of Eric the Red,* by Courtesy of Barnes & Noble Books (Division of Harper and Row, Publishers, Inc.) from *The Northmen, Columbus and Cabot, 985–1503* 1906; reprinted 1959 by Olson, Julius E. (with Edward Gaylord Bourne, Editors).

From *De orbe novo,* by Peter Martyr d'Anghiera, translated by Francis Augustus MacNutt, G. P. Putnam's Sons. Copyright by Francis Augustus MacNutt, 1912. Reprinted by permission of G. P. Putnam's Sons.

From *The Histories of Gargantua and Pantagruel,* translated by J. M. Cohen (Penguin Classics, 1955) pp. 149–151, 159–160 Copyright © J. M. Cohen, 1955. Reprinted by permission of Penguin Books Ltd.

From *Utopia,* by Thomas More, edited and translated by H. V. S. Ogden. Reprinted by permission of AHM Publishing Corporation.

From *The Essays of Montaigne,* translated by E. J. Trechman. Reprinted by permission of Oxford University Press.

From *Of Plymouth Plantation,* by William Bradford, edited by Samuel Eliot Morison. Copyright 1952 by Samuel Eliot Morison. Reprinted by permission of Alfred A. Knopf, Inc.

For "Huswifery" and "Meditation One," in *The Poetical Works of Edward Taylor,* ed. Thomas H. Johnson (Princeton Paperback, 1966). Copyright Rockland, 1939; Princeton University Press, 1943, pp. 116 and 123. Reprinted by permission of Princeton University Press.

For *Narrative of the Captivity and Restauration of Mrs. Mary Rowlandson, 1682.* Reprinted with the permission of Charles Scribner's Sons from *Narratives of the Indian Wars, 1675–1699,* ed. Charles H. Lincoln, copyright 1913 Charles Scribner's Sons.

For Poems 258, 280, 465, 510, 564, 764, 870, and 1129 by Emily Dickinson. Reprinted by permission of the publishers and the Trustees of Amherst College from *The Poems of Emily Dickinson,* edited by Thomas H. Johnson, Cambridge, Mass.: The Belknap Press of Harvard University Press, Copyright © 1951, 1955 by the President and Fellows of Harvard College.

For Poems 564 and 985 by Emily Dickinson. From *The Complete Poems of Emily Dickinson,* edited by Thomas H. Johnson. Copyrght 1914, 1929, 1942 by Martha Dickinson Bianchi; copyright © 1957 by Mary L. Hampson. By permission of Little, Brown and Co.

From *The Souls of Black Folk* by W. E. B. DuBois. Copyright 1953 by W. E. Burghardt DuBois. Copyright © 1961, Fawcett Publications, Inc. Reprinted by permission of Fawcett Publications, Inc.

"The War Prayer" from *Europe and Elsewhere* by Mark Twain. Copyright 1923, 1951 by The Mark Twain Company. By permission of Harper and Row, Publishers, Inc.

From *The Sources of Religious Insight* by Josiah Royce. Reprinted with the permission of Charles Scribner's Sons from *The Sources of Religious Insight* by Josiah Royce, copyright 1912 The Trustees of Lake Forest University.

From *Winds of Doctrine* by George Santayana, J. M. Dent & Sons Ltd. Reprinted by permission of J. M. Dent & Sons Ltd.

"Coatesville" from *The Selected Writings of John Jay Chapman* edited with an Introduction by Jacques Barzun. Copyright © 1957 by Farrar, Straus & Cudahy, Inc. (now Farrar, Straus & Giroux, Inc.). Reprinted with the permission of Farrar, Straus & Giroux, Inc.

From "Puritanism as a Literary Force" by H. L. Mencken. Copyright 1917 by Alfred A. Knopf, Inc. and renewed 1945 by H. L. Mencken. Reprinted from *A Book of Prefaces,* by H. L. Mencken, by permission of Alfred A. Knopf, Inc.

From *A Theology for the Social Gospel* by Walter A. Rauschenbusch. Reprinted with permission of Macmillan Publishing Co., Inc. from *A Theology for the Social Gospel* by Walter A. Rauschenbusch. Copyright 1917 by Macmillan Publishing Co., Inc., renewed 1945 by Pauline E. Rauschenbusch.

From *The Faith of Modernism* by Shailer Mathews. Reprinted by permission of Robbert Elden Mathews.

For "Shine, Perishing Republic" by Robinson Jeffers. Copyright 1925 and renewed 1953 by Robinson Jeffers. Reprinted from *The Selected Poetry of Robinson Jeffers,* by permission of Random House, Inc.

From William Carlos Williams, *In the American Grain.* Copyright 1925 by James Laughlin. Reprinted by permission of New Directions.

From *The Modern Temper* by Joseph Wood Krutch, copyright 1929 by Harcourt Brace Jovanovich, Inc.; renewed 1957 by Joseph Wood Krutch. Reprinted by permission of the publisher.

"Proem: To Brooklyn Bridge" is reprinted from *The Bridge* by Hart Crane, with the permission of Liveright Publishing Corporation. Copyright 1933, © 1958, 1970 by Liveright Publishing Corporation.

For "Marina" from *Collected Poems 1909–1962* by T. S. Eliot, copyright, 1936, by Harcourt Brace Jovanovich, Inc.; copyright © 1963, 1964 by T. S. Eliot. Reprinted by permission of the publisher. Reprinted by permission of Faber and Faber Ltd from *Collected Poems 1909–1962* by T. S. Eliot.

"A Clean Well-Lighted Place" by Ernest Hemingway is reprinted with the permission of Charles Scribner's Sons, copyright 1933 Charles Scribner's Sons.

From *A Common Faith* by John Dewey. Copyright 1934 by Yale University Press. Reprinted by permission of Yale University Press.

For "The Idea of Order at Key West" by Wallace Stevens. Copyright 1936 by Wallace Stevens and renewed 1964 by Holly Stevens. Reprinted from *The Collected Poems of Wallace Stevens,* by Wallace Stevens, by permission of Alfred A. Knopf, Inc.

From *Beyond Tragedy* by Reinhold Niebuhr. Reprinted with the permission of Charles Scribner's Sons from *Beyond Tragedy* by Reinhold Niebuhr, copyright 1937 Charles Scribner's Sons.

From *Let Us Now Praise Famous Men* by James Agee. Copyright © renewed 1969 by Mia Fritsch Agee. Reprinted by permission of Houghton Mifflin Company.

For "The Gift Outright" and "The Most of It" from *The Poetry of Robert Frost* edited by Edward Connery Lathem. Copyright 1942 by Robert Frost. Copyright © 1969 by Holt, Rinehart and Winston. Copyright © 1970 by Lesley Frost Ballantine. Reprinted by permission of Holt, Rinehart and Winston, Publishers.

For "What Are Years?" by Marianne Moore. Reprinted with permission of Macmillan Publishing Co., Inc. from *Collected Poems* by Marianne Moore. Copyright 1941 by Marianne Moore, renewed 1969 by Marianne Moore.

For "The Old People" by William Faulkner. Copyright 1940, 1942, and renewed 1968, 1970 by Estelle Faulkner and Jill Faulkner Summers. Reprinted from *Go Down, Moses,* by William Faulkner, by permission of Random House, Inc.

For "The Loan" from *The Magic Barrel* by Bernard Malamud. Copyright © 1952,

1958 by Bernard Malamud. Reprinted with the permission of Farrar, Straus & Giroux, Inc.

For "Religion as a Dimension in Man's Spiritual Life" by Paul Tillich. Reproduced from *Man's Right to Knowledge* (2nd series), New York: Herbert Muschel, 1954, by permission of the Trustees of Columbia University in the City of New York.

For "Love Calls Us to the Things of This World" by Richard Wilbur from *Things of This World,* © 1956 by Richard Wilbur. Reprinted by permission of Harcourt Brace Jovanovich, Inc.

From *Radical Monotheism and Western Culture* by H. Richard Niebuhr. Copyright © 1943, 1952, 1955, 1960 by H. Richard Niebuhr. By permission of Harper & Row, Publishers, Inc.

For "A Blessing" by James Wright. Copyright © 1961 by James Wright. Reprinted from *The Branch Will Not Break,* by permission of Wesleyan University Press. "A Blessing" first appeared in *Poetry.*

From *The Fire Next Time* by James Baldwin. Copyright © 1963, 1962 by James Baldwin. Reprinted by permission of The Dial Press.

From *The Autobiography of Malcolm X.* Reprinted by permission of Grove Press, Inc. Copyright © 1964 by Alex Haley and Malcolm X. Copyright © 1965 by Alex Haley and Betty Shabazz.

For "The Abyss," copyright © 1963 by Beatrice Roethke, Administratrix for the Estate of Theodore Roethke from *The Collected Poems of Theodore Roethke.* Reprinted by permission of Doubleday & Company, Inc.

"The Making of a Rabbi" by Richard Rubenstein. First published in *Varieties of Jewish Belief,* edited by Ira Eisenstein (Reconstructionist Press). Reprinted by permission of Richard Rubenstein and Ira Eisenstein.

From "How Does God Function in Human Life?" by Schubert M. Ogden. Reprinted from the May 15, 1967 issue of *Christianity and Crisis,* copyright © 1967 by Christianity and Crisis, Inc. by courtesy of Schubert M. Ogden and Christianity and Crisis.

From *Armies of the Night* by Norman Mailer. Copyright © 1968 by Norman Mailer. Reprinted by arrangement with The New American Library, Inc., New York, N. Y.

For "Wilderness in America" by Henry G. Bugbee from *Journal of the American Academy of Religion,* vol. 42, no. 4 (December, 1974). Reprinted by permission of Henry G. Bugbee and the *Journal of the American Academy of Religion.*

For "Thanks-Offering for Recovery" from *Day by Day* by Robert Lowell. Copyright © 1975, 1976, 1977 by Robert Lowell. Reprinted by permission of Farrar, Straus and Giroux, Inc.

To Adam
my New-found Land

Preface

The idea for this anthology arose from my general dissatisfaction with the way American religion and American culture are still taught in the schools and discussed in the secondary literature. Students of American religion have been curiously blind to the massive cultural diffusion of religious creeds, sentiments, and assumptions, while students of American culture have just as frequently glossed over, or remained indifferent to, the crucial theological, liturgical, and eschatological propulsions of American civilization. There are numerous reasons for this: long-standing distrust of culture on the part of students of culture, a legacy of thought in America about the division between church and state, and a general intellectual suspicion about modes of analysis and interpretation that are necessarily interdisciplinary. Whatever the causes, the history of American religion has been oddly insensitive to what was most theologically problematic for the majority of our cultural spokesmen, and the history of American culture has paid little heed to what was most spiritually consequential to the majority of our religious leaders. In both cases, the decisive element was the symbolic meaning of America itself.

There are numerous signs that this myopia is rapidly diminishing. Historians of culture in America are now prepared to concede that American religious history may be one of the central ingredients in the study of American civilization, and American historians of religion are now willing to admit that theological beliefs and religious practices have often flowed in wider social, political, artistic, racial, and ethnic channels. The study of myths, images, and forms by which a national ideological consensus was developed, nurtured, and spread has now become a staple of American cultural history, and the study of social, political, and cultural structures of American religious life has now become a prominent feature of the history of American religion.

What one sees in all this is a new disposition to accept the fact that part of the story of religion *in* America concerns the religion *of* America, that the culture of American religion has to an important degree become the religion in American culture. To put this another way, America now appears distinctive from a religious as well as a cultural point of view precisely to the degree that it has provided the symbolic terms in which its various peoples have had to work out their own salvation, whether in fear and trembling, in outrage and dismay, in wonder and hope, or in madness and despair. Indeed, this sacralization of the symbolic meaning of America itself may, for better or worse, be the one constant in our spiritual history as a nation.

As this anthology attempts to show, this process of sacralization began long before the transmigration of Europeans to these shores and has been continually nourished by groups and individuals, from native American Indians and African slaves to East European, Latin

American, and Far Eastern immigrants, who initially felt alienated from or repelled by it. It is a process which has taken a nearly infinite variety of forms and moved in almost as many directions. But always its central thrust was, and remains, the same: to determine what it was the land held out to us and, as Robert Frost writes in "The Gift Outright," forthwith to find "salvation in surrender."

In the conception and preparation of this volume, I have received encouragement, assistance, and necessary criticism from many individuals. To name only the most obvious, they are William P. Moore, James Sellers, Martin E. Marty, William A. Clebsch, Rowland A. Sherrill, Errol M. McGuire, Preston M. Browning, Amanda Porterfield, Roland Delattre, John McDermott, Charles H. Long, Donald G. Mathews, Grant A. Wacker, Stephen Marini, John Wilson, and Janet Varner Gunn.

This project would never have been undertaken or completed without the belief in it of Oxford's two religion editors, Mr. Allen Kelley and Mr. Charles W. Scott. From the start Allen Kelley gave that kind of invaluable stimulus and challenge to my thinking that only a gifted editor can provide, and almost every page of commentary and a number of my selections and abridgments have profited from the exacting and intelligent editorial scrutiny of Charles Scott. As can rarely be said of the relation between author and editor, we three have been real collaborators.

Through the good offices of Ruel W. Tyson I was able to receive the research assistance of two skilled, patient, and generous individuals, Susan Jarvis and Sandra Alley. At a much later stage, Curtis Church of Oxford University Press gave invaluable support and advice as my copy editor. Funds for the preparation of the manuscript were made available through the generosity of the University Research Council of the University of North Carolina at Chapel Hill. Lastly, I wish to thank all the members of the Department of Religion at the University of North Carolina at Chapel Hill for providing a congenial environment in which to work out my ideas.

Hillsborough, North Carolina   G.G.
October 1980

Contents

CONTENTS

CONTENTS

Introduction

One interesting aspect of the intellectual and cultural history of America is that much of the most significant reflection inspired by America itself has been framed in religious rather than social, political, or philosophical terms. Paradoxically, this reflection has to a considerable extent been the work of secular, or at least theologically unorthodox, thinkers. Why have so many of the ideas provoked by and concerned with America found natural expression in religious modes? Why have so many discerning spiritual interpreters of America been identified as cultural rather than religious figures? Is there something characteristic of the collective experience of American culture that explains the inclination of representative thinkers and writers to see the meaning of America itself as inviting religious interpretation, or at least as problematic in a religious sense? Is it possible to differentiate between the culture of American religions and the religion of American culture?

This anthology cannot furnish any simple answers to these and similar questions. Nor does it assume that such questions have simple answers. But it does attempt to provide for the first time a representative collection of many of the primary source materials in which such questions are raised. *New World Metaphysics* is distinctive in several respects. First, it begins its chronicle of the spiritual life of America at a point long before the establishment of the first American colony—at a time when America was to Europeans more image than fact, more dream than reality. Second, it includes among the contributors to the religious meaning of American experience a range of individuals extending from Puritan clergymen to contemporary poets, from Renaissance adventurers to Romantic historians, from Revolutionary statesmen to modern novelists and critics. Third, it includes some signal contributions to this chronicle from members of such important minorities as native Americans and American blacks. Fourth, it gathers together in one volume an extremely diverse body of material: travel narratives, metaphysical treatises, political constitutions, biographical portraits, theological essays, autobiographical journals, personal diaries and letters, religious oratory, social history, lyric poetry, literary criticism, historical fiction, cultural commentary, and still more. Fifth, it attempts to highlight themes and issues religiously central to the meaning of America: the importance of the land, the character of its native inhabitants, the purpose of community, the problem of cultural identity, the destiny of the nation, the uses of the past, the centrality of Nature, the possibilities of personal and social regeneration.

This great welter of material is unified by the common quest for what can be called "a New World metaphysics." This term was first coined by Walt Whitman in *Democratic Vistas* to designate the spiritual foundations on which Whitman believed a new American literature—really a new American culture—must be based. The notion of a New World metaphysics need not be restricted, however, to Whitman's limited use of it as the basis of a democratic American philosophy, but can be extended to refer to any spiritual vision or ultimate "idea of order" inspired by reflection on the symbolic meaning of America. Considered in this light, the quest for a New World metaphysics is, and always has been, an essentially religious undertaking. This American quest is part of that more universal human effort to ferret out the true meaning of life and to develop a way of living in accordance with this understanding.

But what makes this interest, this concern, religious? Is not religion to be associated with specific convictions, such as belief in God or the divinity of man, specific rituals, such as prayer or confession, or specific feelings, such as adoration, awe, or absolute dependence? Such elements as these, cultural anthropologists and historians of religion have recently suggested, are merely the attributes of religion, its formal properties. The essence of religion, they generally agree, lies elsewhere, lies not in particular beliefs, rites, or feelings, but in a certain way of looking at things, a certain perspective on experience. At the heart of this perspective is a conviction that there is, or should be, an integral connection between the way life essentially is and the way one ought to live, between the inherent structure of reality and the values that make life worth living. According to this view, the religious perspective is comprised of two basic components which serve to

reinforce one another—a world view or metaphysic and a code of conduct or ethic. The metaphysic or world view is simply the fundamental view of the world implied by the actual nature of experience. The ethic or moral code is simply the mode of behavior which seems most consistent with, and responsive to, this fundamental view of things.

When we apply this understanding of religion to America, it becomes clear that the quest for a New World metaphysics is distinguished from other forms of cultural and philosophical inquiry not by its subject matter, nor by its method, but rather by its special obsession. As I will use the term, and as I think Whitman intended it to be understood, the quest for a New World metaphysics describes the intellectual activity of all those who, in response to materials of the American experience, have attempted to discern the idea of order or world view inherent in, or expressive of, that experience.

But when did the quest for a New World metaphysics begin? What forms has it taken? How has this quest evolved?

Whitman was certainly not the first American thinker to associate the development of a distinctive American culture with the creation of a new spiritual vision, nor was he the last. The correlation of the meaning of America with a new religious vision is at least as old as the idea of America itself. That idea was first formulated not at the time of the founding of the American republic, nor at the time of the original discovery of the continent. It came earlier still, when America was only an image of the unknown, the unpredictable, "the other," in the minds of Europeans discontented with their own ways of life and yearning for a new world elsewhere. The idea of America was born during the early years of the Renaissance in the minds of explorers, philosophers, social critics, artists, and seers, and the quest for a New World metaphysics arose when this idea started to generate fresh speculation about the nature of the universe—or the nature of human experience—and the principles underlying it.

Once begun, this quest spread rapidly during the eras of discovery and colonization and in a variety of ways. Evidence of it can be found throughout the history of the American experience: in F. Scott Fitzgerald's creation of a new religion of wonder and awe from the meretricious symbols of American success no less than in William Bradford's history of God's direction and sustenance in the building of the Plymouth Colony; in Hart Crane's desire (stated in "Proem: To Brooklyn Bridge") to "Of the curveship lend a myth to God" no less than in Cotton Mather's celebration of the "mighty acts of God" in creating the American commonwealth; in Shakespeare's depiction of the New World in the colors of Arcadian enchantment and delight no less than in Walter Rauschenbusch's design for transforming the American social order into the Kingdom of God on earth. And this quest goes on even where there is no overt reference to America, but rather only a deeply felt response to possibilities and problems somehow characteristic of or native to America. It can be discerned, for example, in H. Richard Niebuhr's consideration of the relationship between (as he entitled one of his books) "radical monotheism and western culture" as well as in Montaigne's reflections on cannibals and cannibalism; in Wallace Stevens's thoughts about the nature of poetry as well as in William James's speculations about the nature of truth; in Mark Twain's cynicism about civic piety as well as in Charles W. Eliot's espousal of a kind of piety of civility. Far from remaining the special province of any one group or class of thinkers, the quest for a New World metaphysics is very nearly the most distinctive expression of spiritual experience in the New World.

Taking its earliest form in the Renaissance, the quest for a New World metaphysics passed through successive historical phases which have provided the organizing principle for this anthology. Commencing with the initial period of imagination and exploration ("Presentiments," 1492–1607), the quest for a New World metaphysics progressed from the period of early colonization and settlement ("Preparations, 1607–1740"), through the period of the consolidation of republican institutions ("Loomings, 1740–1830"), into the period of westward expansion and industrial development ("Realizations, 1830–1915"), then to a period of modern cultural change and radical experimentation ("Rejections and Revisions, 1915–1950"), and finally to the most recent period of cultural reformation and renewal ("Recoveries, 1950–1980"). None of these phases stands out sharply from its neighbors, but there are changes of emphasis and shifts in orientation of sufficient magnitude and significance to make it possible to perceive a kind of periodic development. It is important, however, to emphasize that what has developed is not a unified tradition but a concert of interests or configuration of concerns which, though various in kind and form, nonetheless all tend to excite fresh inquiry into the idea of order or metaphysic latent in the experience of America.

O strange New World, thet yit wast never young,
Whose youth from thee be gripin' need was wrung,
Brown foundlin' o' the woods, whose baby-bed
Was prowled roun' by the Injun's cracklin' tread,
An' who grew'st strong thru shifts an' wants an' pains,
Nussed by stern men with empires in their brains.

James Russell Lowell
The Biglow Papers

The land was ours before we were the land's.
She was our land more than a hundred years
Before we were her people. She was ours
In Massachusetts, in Virginia
But we were England's, still colonials,
Possessing what we still were unpossessed by,
Possessed by what we now no more possessed.
Something we were withholding made us weak
Until we found out that it was ourselves
We were withholding from our land of living,
And forthwith found salvation in surrender.
Such as we were we gave ourselves outright
(The deed of gift was many deeds of war)
To the land vaguely realizing westward,
But still unstoried, artless, unenhanced,
Such as she was, such as she would become.

Robert Frost
"The Gift Outright"

I
Presentiments
(1492–1607)

American history does not commence with the first landing at Jamestown in 1607 or even with the establishment of the ill-fated colony on Roanoke Island off the coast of North Carolina in 1584. The real history of America begins earlier still, in the great age of Renaissance exploration, with the intellectual anticipations that fueled those original voyages of discovery and the spirtual reactions that followed them. In short, American history begins with the history of the imagination of America and that history turns out to be a fascinating and complex record not only of how Europeans first imagined America but also of the way in which America eventually altered the imagination of Europeans. America existed as a powerful ideal, a compelling symbol, long before it became a discovered fact, and the symbol or ideal of America was inseparable from the hopes, dreams, and fears it inspired among Europeans.

In this sense America was invented before it was discovered, or was discovered, as Edmundo O'Gorman and others have shown, as a result of its invention. Whatever America was destined to become socially or politically, the course of its spiritual destiny was already in fair measure fixed. Idea and fact, image and actuality, would thereafter consort together, and the historical and material reality of America would emerge from their union.

This section begins before Christopher Columbus's famous discovery in 1492, with an account of Leif Ericson's legendary earlier American landing, and it concludes somewhat after the establishment of the Jamestown settlement in Virginia in 1607, with George Herbert's prediction, in "The Church Militant," of the role that Christianity would play in the New World. All of the included material was written (in the words of Robert Frost's "The Gift Outright") before "the land was ours" and "before we were the land's." Yet these writings foreshadow many of the ways in which we would possess the land and be possessed by it.

Anonymous

Eric the Red is celebrated in legend as the founder of the earliest Scandanavian settlement in Greenland in 985 and also as the father of the first presumed European discoverer of America, Leif Ericson, "Leif the Lucky." This portion of the *Saga* tells of Leif's accidental landing on the island of Newfoundland. It suggests a number of motifs that will echo in much of literature of discovery that follows and will gradually swell into dominant themes that combine to form the characteristic American melody: the sense of destiny attached to exploration and colonization; the high purpose of exploration and settlement associated with the missionary errand of Christianity; the image of the New World as a bountiful virgin paradise; the correlation between New World discovery and works of deliverance and charity; and the underlying conviction that the success of this daring adventure is assured by the resourcefulness and courage of man and also by a beneficent and favoring Providence.

From *Saga of Eric the Red* (*ca.* 1000)

Eric was married to a woman named Thorhild, and had two sons; one of these was named Thorstein, and the other Leif. They were both promising men. Thorstein lived at home with his father, and there was not at that time a man in Greenland who was accounted of so great promise as he. Leif had sailed to Norway, where he was at the court of King Olaf Tryggvason. . . . He was well received by the king, who felt that he could see that Leif was a man of great accomplishments. Upon one occasion the king came to speech with Leif, and asks him, "Is it thy purpose to sail to Greenland in the summer?" "It is my purpose," said Leif, "if it be your will." "I believe it will be well," answers the king, "and thither thou shalt go upon my errand, to proclaim Christianity there." Leif replied that the king should decide, but gave it as his belief that it would be difficult to carry this mission to a successful issue in Greenland. The king replied that he knew of no man who would be better fitted for this undertaking, "and in thy hands the cause will surely prosper." "This can only be," said Leif, "if I enjoy the grace of your protection." Leif put to sea when his ship was ready for the voyage. For a long time he was tossed about upon the ocean, and came upon lands of which he had previously had no knowledge. There were self-sown wheat fields and vines growing there. There were also those trees there which are called "mausur," and of all these they took specimens. Some of the timbers were so large they they were used in building. Leif found men upon a wreck, and took them home with him, and procured quarters for them all during the winter. In this wise he showed his nobleness and goodness, since he introduced Christianity into the country, and saved the men from the wreck; and he was called Leif the Lucky ever after.

Christopher Columbus (1451?–1506)

Christopher Columbus saw his discovery of the New World more as a matter of divine Providence than of navigational expertise or heroic courage. In 1502 he wrote to his patrons, King Ferdinand and Queen Isabella of Spain, "Neither reason nor mathematics nor maps were any use to me: fully accomplished were the works of Isaiah." (Isaiah 11:10–12 prophesies that God will gather the dispersed faithful remnant of his people into a new redeemed community.) This sense of divine election for his epic mission was perhaps natural for Columbus, who arrived in Portugal (he had been born in Genoa, Italy) after a miraculous escape from shipwreck that brought him ashore almost atop the rock of Sagres with its famous academy of seamanship, established by Prince Henry the Navigator.

Columbus made four voyages to the New World in hope of reaching the Indies. The idea of reaching the East by sailing West did not originate with Columbus but was first suggested by a Florentine cartographer, Paolo Toscanelli; it was Columbus, however, who persevered in putting the idea to the test, although he suffered repeated rejections of his proposals, first from the king of Portugal, and then from Ferdinand and Isabella, who at last came reluctantly to his aid. Columbus was persistent and bold, driven on the one hand by his sense of divine election and on the other by his desire for personal honor and wealth. This combination of motives would be duplicated in America twice again, first during the age of Spanish exploration and conquest, and then in the era of the great robber barons of the Gilded Age.

On his first voyage Columbus landed at San Salvador in the Bahamas and then made his way to Cuba. His report of that voyage is interesting from several points of view. It gave Europeans their first glimpse of the virgin beauty and plenitude of the New World and an initial, rather idealized, picture of its natives. The letter shows that Columbus was as interested in worldly prosperity as he was in eternal merit, and that, as a Christian, he had no compunction in allowing the natives to regard their visitors as heavenly messengers capable of "the performance of apparent impossibilities," a description which Columbus, with understandable pride, applies to his voyage of discovery itself.

From *Letter of Lord Raphael Sanchez, Treasurer to Ferdinand and Isabella, King and Queen of Spain, on his First Voyage* (1492)

Knowing that it will afford you pleasure to learn that I have brought my undertaking to a successful termination, I have decided upon writing you this letter to acquaint you with all the events which have occurred in my voyage, and the discoveries which have resulted from it. Thirty-three days after my departure from Cadiz I reached the Indian sea, where I discovered many islands, thickly peopled, of which I took possession without resistance in the name of our most illustrious Monarch, by public proclamation and with unfurled banners.

... All these islands are very beautiful and distinguished by a diversity of scenery; they are filled with a great variety of trees of immense height, and which I believe to retain their foliage in all seasons; for when I saw them they were as verdant and luxuriant as they usually are in Spain in the month of May,— some of them were blossoming, some bearing fruit, and all flourishing in the greatest perfection, according to their respective stages of growth, and the nature and quality of each: yet the islands are not so thickly wooded as to be impassable. The nightingale and various birds were singing in countless numbers, and that in November, the month in which I arrived there. There are besides ... seven or eight kinds of palm trees, which, like all the other trees, herbs, and fruits, considerably surpass ours in height and beauty. The pines also are very handsome, and there are very extensive fields and meadows, a variety of birds, different kinds of honey, and many sorts of metals, but no iron. ... There are mountains of very great size and beauty, vast plains, groves, and very fruitful fields, admirably adapted for tillage, pasture, and habitation. The convenience and excellence of the harbours in this island, and the abundance of the rivers, so indispensable to the health of man, surpass anything that would be believed by one who had not seen it.

... The inhabitants of both sexes ... go always naked as they were born, with the exception of some of the women, who use the covering of a leaf, or small bough, or an apron of cotton which they prepare for that purpose. None of them, as I have already said, are possessed of any iron, neither have they weapons, being unacquainted with, and indeed incompetent to use them, not from any deformity of body (for they are well-formed), but because they are timid and full of fear.... As soon however as they see that they are safe, and have laid aside all fear, they are very simple and honest, and exceedingly liberal with all they have; none of them refusing anything he may possess when he is asked for it, but on the contrary inviting us to ask them. They exhibit great love towards all others in preference to themselves: they also give objects of great value for trifles, and content themselves with very little or nothing in turn.

They practice no kind of idolatry, but have a firm belief that all strength and power, and indeed all good things, are in heaven, and that I had descended from thence with these ships and sailors, and under this impression was I received after they had thrown aside their fears.

✍

... On my arrival at that sea, I had taken some Indians by force from the first island that I came to, in order that they might learn our language, and communicate to us what they knew respecting the country; which plan succeeded excellently, and was a great advantage to us, for in a short time, either by gestures and signs, or by words, we were enabled to understand each other. These men are still traveling with me, and although they have been with us now a·long time, they continue to entertain the idea that I have descended from heaven; and on our arrival at any new place they published this, crying out immediately with a loud voice to the other Indians, "Come, come and look upon beings of a celestial race": upon which both women and men, children and adults, young men and old, when they got rid of the fear they at first entertained, would come out in throngs, crowding the roads to see us, some bringing food, others drink, with astonishing affection and kindness.

✍

... As far as I have learned, every man throughout these islands is united to but one wife, with exception of the kings and princes, who are allowed to have twenty: the women seem to work more than the men. I could not clearly understand whether the people possess any private property, for I observed that one man had the charge of distributing various things to the rest, but especially meat and provisions and the like. I did not find, as some of us had expected, any cannibals amongst them, but on the contrary men of great deference and kindness.

✍

... Although all I have related may appear to be wonderful and unheard of, yet the results of my voyage would have been more astonishing if I had had at my disposal such ships as I required. But these great and marvellous results are not to be attributed to any merit of mine, but to the holy Christian faith, and to the piety and religion of our Sovereigns; for that which the unaided intellect of man could not compass, the spirit of God has granted to human exertions, for God is wont to hear the prayers of his servants who love his precepts even to the performance of apparent impossibilities. Thus it has happened to me in the present instance, who have accomplished a task to which the powers of mortal men had never hitherto attained; for if there have been those who have anywhere written or spoken of these islands, they have done so with doubts and conjectures, and no one has ever asserted that he has seen them, on which account their writings have been looked upon as little else than fables. Therefore let the king and queen, our princes and their most happy kingdoms, and all the other provinces of Christendom, render thanks to our Lord and Saviour Jesus Christ, who has granted us so great a victory and such prosperity. Let processions be made, and sacred feasts be held, and the temples be adorned with festive boughs. Let Christ rejoice on earth, as he rejoices in heaven in the prospect of the salvation of the souls of so many nations hitherto lost. Let us also rejoice, as well on account of the exaltation of our faith, as on account of the increase of our temporal prosperity, of which not only Spain, but all Christendom will be partakers.

Amerigo Vespucci (1454–1512)

Amerigo Vespucci, the man from whom the New World took its name, was an Italian merchant and navigator who gained his experience as an explorer of the Western hemisphere in the service of Spain.

There is some question as to whether Vespucci actually made the voyage on which he claims, in the following letter to Lorenzo de' Medici, to have discovered the "New World." In *Quatro Americi Navigationis,* written in Lisbon in 1504 and printed in Florence the following year, Vespucci claimed to have made four voyages of discovery. On the other hand, three personal letters addressed to the Medici suggest that there were only two voyages. This discrepancy has raised doubts about Vespucci's veracity, and has led some scholars to repudiate his extraordinary achievements as a navigator. The consensus is, however, that even if Vespucci was not strictly honest in his reporting, he was in fact the navigator on a voyage which led him to conclude that the new-found lands were not part of Asia, as was then believed, but a "mundus novus"—a New World.

The association of Vespucci's name with the "New World" began when M. Waldseemüller, a Dutch humanist, reprinted *Quatro Americi Navigationis* with an accompanying pamphlet of his own composition in which he proposed that the "New World" be named after Vespucci. This proposal was given added impetus by Waldseemüller's subsequent publication of a map or planisphere on which the name "America" appeared for the first time. Waldeseemüller himself applied the name only to the southern hemisphere of the "New World"; not until later was it extended to the northern hemisphere as well.

Vespucci's letter has considerable cultural as well as historical interest. He perpetuates Columbus's idea of the New World as a virgin paradise with its people living in a state of nature, He does not, however, paint an altogether pastoral picture of native life. War is common, and cannibalism an accepted custom—and the way in which he dwells on the potentially exploitable qualities of the New World casts a shadow over the primitive paradise he describes.

From *Mundus Novus* (Letter on His Third Voyage to Lorenzo Pietro Francesco de' Medici, 1503)

In passed days I wrote very fully to you of my return from the new countries, which have been found and explored with the ships, at the cost, and by the command, of this Most Serene King of Portugal; and it is lawful to call it a new world, because none of these countries were known to our ancestors, and to all who hear about them they will be entirely new. For the opinion of the ancients was, that the greater part of the world beyond the equinoctial line to the south was not land, but only sea, which they have called the Atlantic; and if they have affirmed that any continent is there, they have given many reasons for denying that it is inhabited. But this their opinion is false, and entirely opposed to the truth. My last voyage has proved it, for I have found a continent in that southern part; more populous and more full of animals than our Europe, or Asia, or Africa, and even more temperate and pleasant than any other region known to us, as will be explained further on. I shall write succinctly of the principal things only, and the things most worthy of notice and of being remembered, which I either saw or heard of in this new world, as presently will become manifest.

∽·∽·∽

It was on the 7th of August 1501, that we reached those countries, thanking our Lord God with solemn prayers, and celebrating a choral Mass. We knew that land to be a continent, and not an island, from its long beaches extending without trending round, the infinite number of inhabitants, the numerous tribes and peoples, the numerous kinds of wild animals unknown in our country, and many others never seen before by us, touching which it would take long to make reference. The clemency of God was shown forth to us by being brought to these regions; for the ships were in a leaking state, and in a few days our lives might have been lost in the sea. To Him be the honour and glory, and the grace of the action.

∽·∽·∽

As regards the people: we have found such a multitude in those countries that no one could enumerate them, as we read in the Apocalypse. They are people gentle and tractable, and all of both sexes go naked, not covering any part of their bodies, just as they came from their mothers' wombs, and so they go until their deaths. They have large, square-built bodies, and well proportioned. Their colour reddish, which I think is caused by their going naked and exposed to the sun. Their hair is plentiful and black. They are agile in walking, and of quick sight. They are of a free and good-looking expression of countenance, whch they themselves destroy by boring the nostrils and lips, the nose and ears; nor must you believe that the borings are small, nor that they only have one, for I have seen those who had no less than seven borings in the face, each one the size of a plum. . . .

They have no cloth, either of wool, flax, or cotton, because they have no need of it; nor have they any private property, everything being in common. They live amongst themselves without a king or ruler, each man being his own master, and having as many wives as they please. The children cohabit with the mothers, the brothers with the sisters, the male cousins with the female, and each one with the first he meets. They have no temples and no laws, nor are they idolaters. What more can I say! They live according to nature, and are more inclined to be Epicurean than Stoic. They have no commerce among each other, and they wage war without art or order. The old men make the youths do what they please, and incite them to fights, in which they mutually kill with great cruelty. They slaughter those who are captured, and the victors eat the vanquished; for human flesh is an ordinary article of food among them. You may be the more certain of this, because I have seen a man eat his children and wife; and I knew a man who was popularly credited to have eaten 300 human bodies. I was once in a certain city for twenty-seven days, where human flesh was hung up near the houses, in the same way as we expose butcher's meat. I say further that they were surprised that we did not eat our enemies, and use their flesh as food, for they say it is excellent. Their arms are bows and arrows, and when they go to war they cover no part of their bodies, being in this like beasts. We did all we could to persuade them to desist from their evil habits, and they promised us to leave off. The women, as I have said, go naked, and are very libidinous, yet their bodies are comely; but they are as wild as can be imagined.

They live for 150 years, and are rarely sick. If they are attacked by a disease they cure themselves with roots of some herbs. These are the most noteworthy things I know about them.

The air in this country is temperate and good, as we were able to learn from their accounts that there are never any pestilences or epidemics caused by bad air. Unless they meet with violent deaths, their lives are long. I believe this is because a southerly wind is always blowing, a south wind to them being what a north wind is to us. They are expert fishermen, and the sea is full of all kinds of fish. They are not hunters; I think because here there are many kinds of wild animals, principally lions and bears, innumerable serpents, and other horrible creatures and deformed beasts; also because there are vast forests and trees of immense size. They have not the courage to face such dangers naked and without defence.

The land is very fertile, abounding in many hills and valleys, and in large rivers, and is irrigated by very refreshing springs. It is covered with extensive and dense forests, which are almost impenetrable, and full of every kind of wild beast. Great trees grow without cultivation, of which many yield fruits pleasant to the taste and nourishing to the human body; and a great many have an opposite effect. the fruits are unlike those in our country; and there are innumerable different kinds of fruits and herbs, of which they make bread and excellent food. They also have seeds unlike ours. No kind of metal has been found except gold, in which the country abounds, though we have brought none back in this our first navigation. The natives, however, assured us that there was an immense quantity of gold underground, and nothing was to be had from them for a price. Pearls abound, as I wrote to you.

If I was to attempt to write of all the species of animals, it would be a long and tedious task. I believe certainly that our Pliny did not touch upon a thousandth part of the animals and birds that exist in this region; nor could an artist such as Policletus, succeed in painting them. All the trees are odoriferous, and some of them emit gums, oils, or other liquors. If they were our property, I do not doubt but that they would be useful to man. If the terrestrial paradise is in some part of this land, it cannot be very far from the coast we visited. It is, as I have told you, in a climate where the air is temperate at noon, being neither cold in winter nor hot in summer.

The present selection is more interesting for the light it sheds on the European imagination of America than for any information it provides about New world inhabitants or conditions. Martyr, too, idealizes primitive life in America. For him it epitomizes the "golden age" of mankind's history. Excluded from the New World paradise area all the things believed to impede or corrupt European civilization. In their place, in addition to natural freedom and justice, Martyr foresees an environment so continuously regenerative and beneficent as to satisfy the most demanding imagination.

Peter Martyr (1455–1526)

Peter Martyr, the Italian cleric Pietro Martine D'Anghiera, took up residence in Spain and made the acquaintance of many of the great explorers—Christopher Columbus, Vasco Da Gama, Hernando Cortez, Ferdinand Magellan. Deeply moved by their tales of discovery, Peter Martyr decided to combine their information with official documents in order to compile a systematic account of what they had found. Martyr's letters in *De Orbe Novo* (1511), which came to be called the *Decades of Peter Martyr,* have earned for him the title "first historian of America."

From *De Orbe Novo* (1511)

The islanders of Hispaniola, in my opinion, may be esteemed more fortunate than were the Latins, above all should they become converted to true religion. They go naked, they know neither weights nor measures, nor that source of all misfortunes, money; living in a golden age, without laws, without lying judges, without books, satisfied with their life, and in no wise solicitous for the future. Nevetheless ambition and the desire to rule trouble even them, and they fight amongst themselves, so that even in the golden age there is never a moment without war. . . .

It is proven that amongst them the land belongs to everybody, just as does the sun or the water. They know no difference between *meum* and *tuum*, that source of all evils. It requires so little to satisfy them that in that vast region there is always more land to cultivate than is needed. It is indeed a golden age, neither ditches, nor hedges, nor walls enclose their domains; they live in gardens open to all, without laws and without judges; their conduct is naturally equitable, and whoever injures his neighbour is considered a criminal and an outlaw.

Every creature in the sublunary world . . . that gives birth to something, either immediately afterwards closes the womb or rests a period. The new continent, however, is not governed by this rule, for each day it creates without ceasing and brings forth new products, which continues to furnish men gifted with power and an enthusiasm for novelties, sufficient material to satisfy their curiosity.

François Rabelais (1495?–1533)

Monk, scientist, priest, physician, educator, juridical scholar, utopian reformer, metaphysician, and humanist, François Rabelais is variously known as the father of French letters, a literary buffoon, a comic Homer, and the epitome of Renaissance man. His supreme achievement was the epic *Gargantua and Pantagruel* (1534–1562) for writing which he was branded a heretic, forced into temporary exile, and perhaps imprisoned as well. Rabelais outlasted the stormwind of criticism that the ribald earthiness and irreverent comedy of his great book aroused, and in time became a figure of some importance in the royal court of Francis I.

The present selection is from Book I of *Gargantua and Pantagruel*, published in 1534. It displays a different aspect of the utopian thought of the Renaissance. The treatment is humourous, but the implied criticism of existing religious attitudes and conventions is serious indeed. The belief in man's inherent goodness and reasonable nature calls to mind similar themes in Thomas More's *Utopia* and anticipates convictions expressed by American heirs of the Renaissance such as Benjamin Franklin, Thomas Jefferson, and James Madison.

From *Gargantua and Pantagruel* (1534)

Chapter 52: How Gargantua had the Abbey of Thélème built for the Monk

There only remained the monk to be provided for, and Gargantua wanted to make him abbot of Seuilly, but he refused the post. He next proposed to give him the abbey of Bourgueil or of Saint-Florant, whichever would suit him better, or both, if he fancied them. But the monk answered categorically that he wanted neither charge nor government of monks.

"For how should I be able to govern others," he said, "when I don't know how to govern myself? If it seems to you that I have done you, and may in the future do you welcome service, give me leave to found an abbey after my own devices."

This request pleased Gargantua, and he offered him all his land of Thélème, beside the River Loire, to within six miles of the great forest of Port-Huault. The monk then requested Gargantua to institute his religious order in an exactly contrary way to all others.

"First of all, then," said Gargantua, "you mustn't build walls round it. For all other abbeys have lofty walls (murs)."

"Yes," said the monk, "and not without reason. Where ther's a *mur* before and a *mur* behind, there are plenty of murmurs, envy, and mutual conspiracy."

Moreover, seeing that in certain monasteries in this world it is the custom that if any woman enters—I speak of chaste and honest women—they wash the place where she trod, it was ordained that if any monk or nun happened to enter here, the spot where he or she had stood should be scrupulously washed likewise. And because in the religious foundations of this world everything is encompassed, limited, and regulated by hours, it was decreed that there should be no clock or dial at all, but that affairs should be conducted according to chance and opportunity. For Gargantua said that the greatest waste of time he knew was the counting of hours—what good does it do?—and the greatest nonsense in the world was to regulate one's life by the sound of a bell, instead of by the promptings of reason and good sense. Item, because at that time they put no women into religious houses unless they were one-eyed, lame, hunchbacked, ugly, malformed, lunatic, half-witted, bewitched, and blemished, or men that were not sickly, low-born, stupid, or a burden on their family. . . .

"By the way," said the monk, "if a woman is neither fair nor good, what can you do with her?"

"Make her a nun," said Gargantua.

"Yes," said the monk, "and a sempstress of shirts."

It was decreed that here no women should be admitted unless they were beautiful, well-built, and sweet-natured, nor any men who were not handsome, well-built, and of pleasant nature also.

Item, because men never entered nunneries except secretly and by stealth, it was decreed that here there should be no women when there were no men, and no men where there were no women.

Item, because both men and women, once accepted into a monastic order, after their novitiate year, were compelled and bound to remain for ever, so long as they lived, it was decreed that both men and women, once accepted, could depart from there whenever they pleased, without let or hindrance.

Item, because ordinarily monks and nuns made three vows, that is of chastity, poverty, and obedience, it was decreed that there anyone could be regularly married, could become rich, and could live at liberty.

With regard to the lawful age of entry, women were to be received at from ten to fifteen, and men at from twelve to eighteen.

ᔓᘁᕒ

Chapter 57: *The Rules according to which the Thélèmites lived*

All their life was regulated not by laws, statutes, or rules, but according to their free will and pleasure. They rose from bed when they pleased, and drank, ate, worked, and slept when the fancy seized them. Nobody woke them; nobody compelled them either to eat or to drink, or to do anything else whatever. So it was that Gargantua had established it. In their rules there was only one clause:

DO WHAT YOU WILL

because people who are free, well-born, well-bred, and easy in honest company have a natural spur and instinct which drives them to virtuous deeds and deflects them from vice; and this they called honour. When these same men are depressed and enslaved by vile constraint and subjection, they use this noble quality which once impelled them freely towards virtue, to throw off and break this yoke of slavery. For we always strive after things forbidden and covet what is denied us.

Making use of this liberty, they most laudably rivalled one another in all of them doing what they saw pleased one. If some man or woman said, "Let us drink," they all drank; if he or she said, "Let us play," they all played; if it was "Let us go and amuse ourselves in the fields," everyone went there. If it were for hawking or hunting, the ladies, mounted on fine mares, with their grand palfreys following, each carried on their daintily gloved wrists a sparrow-hawk, a lanneret, or a merlin, the men carrying the other birds.

So nobly were they instructed that there was not a man or woman among them who could not read, write, sing, play musical instruments, speak five or six languages, and compose in them both verse and prose. Never were seen such worthy knights, so valiant, so nimble both on foot and horse; knights more vigorous, more agile, handier with all weapons than they were. Never were seen ladies so good-looking, so dainty, less tiresome, more skilled with the fingers and the needle, and in every free and honest womanly pursuit than they were.

For that reason, when the time came that anyone in that abbey, either at his parents' request or for any other reason, wished to leave it, he took with him one of the ladies, the one who had accepted him as her admirer, and they were married to one another; and if at Thélème they had lived in devotion and friendship, they lived in still greater devotion and friendship when they were marrried. Indeed, they loved one another to the end of their days as much as they had done on their wedding day. . . .

ᔓᘁᕒᔓᘁᕒᔓᘁᕒᔓᘁᕒᔓᘁᕒᔓᘁᕒ

Thomas More
(1478–1535)

Sir Thomas More was a Christian humanist and a statesman. As Lord Chancellor of England, he was executed by Henry VIII for refusing to accept the Act of Supremacy which established the king as supreme head of the Church of England. In his last words on the scaffold More summed up the Renaissance Christian ideal—he "died the king's good servant, but God's first." More's *Utopia,* written in Latin in 1516 and not translated into English until 1551, was composed in two parts. Book II, from which the present selection is taken, was written in 1515 while More was on a diplomatic mission in Flanders. It describes an imaginary communistic society, governed entirely by reason.

Inspired by the descriptions of the New World provided by Amerigo Vespucci and Peter Martyr, as well as the social and political views of such classical writers as Plato, Tacitus, and Pliny, More delineates a mode of life which presents the sharpest possible contrast to conditions of English society. In *Utopia* More identifies egotism as the root of all social and moral evil, and suggests that a communistic society in which goods are shared and pleasure never pursued at the expense of others is the only reasonable alternative to the destructive and self-interested public and private life of Christian Europe.

From *Utopia* (1551)

In their moral philosophy, they argue much as we do. They consider what things are truly good, both for the body and the mind, and whether it is proper to call external things good or only the gifts of the mind. They inquire into the nature of virtue and pleasure. But their chief concern is about human happiness, whether it consists of one thing or of many. They seem much inclined to the view that all or most of human happiness lies in pleasure. And what may seem strange, they seek support for their pleasure philosophy from religion, which is serious and stern, somewhat severe and forbidding. For they never discuss happiness without combining the rational principles of philosophy with principles taken from religion. They think any inquiry concerning true happiness weak and defective unless it is based on religion.

The religious principles are these: that the soul of man is immortal and by divine beneficence has been ordained for happiness; and after this life there are rewards appointed for our virtues and good works and punishment for our sins. They think that although these beliefs belong to religion, it is in accordance with reason that they be held and acknowledged. They do not hesitate to assert that if these were rejected, no one would be so stupid as not to discern that he ought to seek pleasure regardless of right and wrong. A man would only need to take care not to let a lesser pleasure stand in the way of the greater, and not to pursue a pleasure which brings sorrow in its train. From this point of view, it is sheer madness to pursue virtue, which seems hard and harsh, and to give up the pleasures of life and endure pain willingly, and all for nothing. For what can one hope for after a life without pleasure, that is, after a miserable life, if there is no reward after death?

The Utopians do not believe that there is happiness in all pleasures, but only in good and honest pleasures. To such, they believe, our nature is drawn as to its highest good by virtue itself. The opposite point of view is that happiness consists of virtue alone.

They define virtue as living according to nature. We have been ordained, they say, by God to this end. To follow nature is to conform to the dictates of reason in what we seek and avoid. The first dictate of reason is ardently to love and revere the Divine Majesty, to whom we owe what we are and whatever happiness we can reach. Secondly, reason warns us and summons us to lead our lives as calmly and cheerfully as we can, and to help all others in nature's fellowship to attain this good.

They disagree with the grim and gloomy eulogist of virtue, who hates pleasure and exhorts us to toils and vigils and squalid self-denial, and at the same time commands us to relieve the poverty and lighten the burdens of others in accordance with our humanity. He proclaims that this is the glory of human nature, to mitigate the sufferings of others and restore the joys of living—that is, pleasure—by driving grief away. If this is true, the Utopians argue, does it not follow that nature incites us to do the same for ourselves? If a joyful life (that is, one of pleasure) is bad, then we ought not to help others to it; on the contrary we ought to keep them from it. But if a joyful life is good, and if we are supposed to help others to enjoy one, why should we not seek such a life for ourselves as much as for others? For nature does not teach us to be harsh and cruel to ourselves while being kind and helpful to each other.

So they conclude that nature herself prescribes a life of joy (that is, of pleasure) as the goal of life. This is what they mean by saying that virtue is living according to nature. And as nature bids us mutually to make our lives merry and delightful, so she also bids us again and again not to destroy or diminish other people's pleasure in seeking our own. And in this they think nature is quite right. No one is so much above the rest of mankind that he is nature's sole care. She cherishes all alike whom she embraces in the community of the same form.

Consequently they believe that men shoud keep their private agreements, and should obey those public laws which a good ruler has justly decreed or which the people, influenced neither by force nor fraud, have freely sanctioned. For such laws determine the distribution of goods, and goods are a prerequisite of pleasure.

They think it is prudent for a man to pursue his own advantage so far as the laws allow, but they account it as piety for him to prefer the public good to his own. It is wrong for a man to seek his own pleasure by thwarting another's; but to decrease his own to add to the pleasure of others they count a work of humanity and benevolence, and one, moreover, which benefits him as much as he benefits others. For in time of need he may be repaid for his kindness. Even if this never happens, his awareness that he did a good deed and the recollection of the gratitude of those whom he benefited will delight his mind more than the pleasure he gave up would have pleased his body. Finally they believe what religion easily persuades a well-disposed mind to believe, that God repays the loss of a short and transitory pleasure with great and endless joy.

Thus after weighing the matter carefully, they conclude that all our actions, and among these our virtues, ultimately look toward pleasure and happiness as their end. They call pleasure all the acts and states of body or mind in which man naturally delights. But they include in their concept of pleasure only those appetites to which nature leads us. And they maintain that nature leads us only to the delights approved by right reason as well as by the senses, that is, only those delights by which we neither injure others, nor lose a greater pleasure for a less, nor suffer for later. Those attractions which are inconsistent with nature and which men call delights only by the emptiest of fictions (as if men could change their nature by changing their name), these things they say diminish happiness rather than increase it. For men whose minds are filled up with a false idea of pleasure have no room left for true pleasures and genuine delight.

These are their ideas of virtue and pleasure, and they think that human reason can find none truer, unless some heavenly revelation should inspire more sublime ideas in men. I have no time now to consider whether they are right

in these views or not, nor do I think it necessary, as I only undertook to give an account of their customs, not to defend them. Whatever the validity of these principles, I am sure that nowhere is there a more excellent people or a happier commonwealth.

Richard Eden
(1521–1576)

Richard Eden's translation of Peter Martyr's *The Decades of the New World or West India,* of which *De Orbe Novo* (1516) was one part, was an important event in the history of New World discovery. It made available for the first time in English a systematic account of the voyages of Columbus and others. This translation of Martyr's account was augmented by Richard Hakluyt (1553–1616), an English clergyman who compiled a record of all the known English voyages of discovery and in 1589 published *Principal Navigations, Voyages and Discoveries of the English Nation* (considerably expanded into three volumes in 1598–1600). This in turn was further expanded by Samuel Purchas (1575–1626) into several books, including *Hakluytus Posthumus or Purchas His Pilgrims* (1625). Part of the interest of these accounts lies in the way in which they furnished material for subsequent writers (see the selections from Montaigne's "Of Cannibals" and Shakespeare's "The Tempest"). They show how faith mingled with fact in European ideas about this part of the world.

The present selection from Eden's translation of Peter Martyr is noteworthy for the approach it takes to its subject, the color of the New World's native inhabitants. According to its thesis, diversity of color among men is a sign of divine omnipotence and wisdom. The perception that the variety of color among New World peoples was (or should be) a source of religious wonder and gratitude would soon be lost, not to be recovered until American Indian and later black Americans would open the eyes of their white compatriots to the heritage of spiritual riches in racial diversity.

From *The Decades of the New World or West India* by Peter Martyr (1555)

One of the marvellous things that God useth in the composition of man is colour, which doubtless can not be considered without great admiration in beholding one to be white, and another black, being colours utterly contrary. Some likewise to be yellow, which is between black and white, and other of other colours, as it were of divers liveries. And as these colours are to be marvelled at, even so is it to be considered how they differ from another as it were by degrees, forasmuch as some men are white after divers sorts of whiteness, yellow after divers manners of yellow, and black after divers sorts of blackness; and how from white they go to yellow by discolouring to brown and red, and to black by ash colour, and murrey somewhat lighter than black; and tawny like unto the West Indians which are altogether in general either purple or tawny like unto sod quinces, or of the colour of chestnuts or olives—which colour is to them natural and not by their going naked, as many have thought, albeit their nakedness have somewhat helped them thereunto. Therefore in like manner and with such diversity as men are commonly white in Europe and black in Africa, even with like variety are they tawny in these Indies, with divers degrees diversely inclining more or less to black or white. No less marvel is it to consider that men are white in Seville, and black at the cape of Buena Speranza, and of chestnut colour at the river of Plata, being all in equal degrees from the equinoctial line. Likewise that the men of Africa and Asia that live under the burnt line (called *Zona Torida*) are black, and not they that live beneath or on this side the same line as in Mexico, Yucatan, Quauhtema, Lian, Nicaragua, Panama, Santo Domingo, Paria, Cape, Saint Augustine, Lima, Quito and the other lands of Peru which touch in the same equinoctial.... It may seem that such variety of colours proceedeth of man, and not of the earth, which may well be although we be all born of Adam and Eve, and know not the cause why God hath ordained it, otherwise than to consider that his divine majesty hath done this as infinite other to declare his omnipotence and wisdom in such diversity of colours as appear not only in the nature of man, but the like also in beasts, birds and flowers, where diverse and contrary colours are seen in one little feather, or the leaves growing out of one little stalk. Another thing is also to be noted as touching these Indians, and this is that their hair is not curled as is the Moors' and Ethiopians' that inhabit the same clime; neither are they bald except very seldom, and that but little. All which things may give further occasion to philosophers to search the secrets of nature and complexions of men with the novelties of the new world. . . .

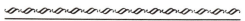

Michel de Montaigne (1533–1592)

Michel de Montaigne, French aristocrat and man of letters, is perhaps best remembered as the creator of a new literary form, the essay. *The Essays* were first published in 1580, and Montaigne continued to expand and revise them until his death. The work is one of the monuments of Renaissance culture.

Montaigne was remarkable for his breadth of perspective and general fair-mindedness. On the one hand, he had the classicist's respect for the past, its traditions and ideas. On the other, his clear and impartial intellect sometimes led him to espouse radical views and to question existing institutions. It could be said that Montaigne personified the humanistic ideal of Renaissance man. Free of bias and skeptical even of his own grounds of assurance, Montaigne's thinking is of greater importance almost because of the quality of his mind than because of the particular ideas with which he concerned himself.

In the following selection from "Of Cannibals," Montaigne considers some typical reports by New World discoverers and concludes that the European sense of spiritual superiority blurs and distorts a true perception of the facts. Comparing the qualities of "primitive" natives and "civilized" Europeans, Montaigne reverses the usual conclusions by finding civility in the place of barbarity, nobility in the place of savagery, and valor in the place of cunning and deceit. These perceptions gain authority from Montaigne's unwillingness to idealize or sentimentalize native life. Here as always, his intellectual realism justifies and supports the strength of his judgments.

From "Of Cannibals" (1580)

I had living with me for a long time a man who had lived for ten or twelve years in that other world which was discovered in our century, in that place where Villegaignon landed [Brazil, 1557], which he called *Antarctic France*. This discovery of an unbounded country seems to me worthy of consideration. . . .

... From what I have heard of that nation, I can see nothing barbarous or uncivilized about it, except that we all call barbarism that which does not fit in with our usages. And indeed we have no other level of truth and reason but the example and model of the opinions and usages of the country we live in. There we always see the perfect religion, the perfect government, the perfect and accomplished manner of doing all things. Those people are wild in the sense in which we call wild the fruits that Nature has produced by herself and in her ordinary progress; whereas in truth it is those we have altered artificially and diverted from the common order, that we should rather call wild. In the first we still see, in full life and vigour, the genuine and most natural and useful virtues and properties, which we have bastardized in the latter, and only adapted to please our corrupt taste. And yet in some of the uncultivated fruits of those countries there is a delicacy of flavour that is excellent even to our taste, and rivals even our own. It is not reasonable that art should gain the point of honour over our great and powerful mother Nature. We have so overburdened the beauty and richness of her works with our inventions, that we have quite smothered her. And yet, wherever she shines in her purity, she marvellously puts to shame our vain and trivial efforts,

Uncared, unmarked the ivy blossoms best;
Midst desert rocks the ilex clusters still;
And sweet the wild bird's untaught
   melody.   (Propertius)

With all our efforts we are unable to even to copy the nest of the smallest of little birds, its contexture, its beauty and convenience; not so much as the web of the poor spider.

All things, says Plato, are produced either by Nature, or by chance, or by art: the greatest and most beautiful by one or other of the two first; the least and most imperfect by the latter.

Those nations, then, appear to me so far barbarous in this sense, that their minds have been formed to a very slight degree, and that they are still very close to their original simplicity. They are still ruled by the laws of Nature, and very little corrupted by ours; but they are still in such a state of purity, that I am somtimes vexed that they were not known earlier, at a time when there were men who could have appreciated them better than we do.

I am sorry that Lycurgus and Plato had no knowledge of them, for it seems to me that what we have learned by contact with those nations surpasses not only all the beautiful colours in which the poets have depicted the golden age, and all their ingenuity in inventing a happy state of man, but also the conceptions and desires of Philosophy herself. They were incapable of imagining so pure and native a simplicity, as that which we see by experience; nor could they have believed that human society could have been maintained with so little human artifice and solder. This is a nation, I should say to Plato, which has no manner of traffic; no knowledge of letters; no science of numbers; no name of magistrate or statesman; no use for slaves; neither wealth nor poverty; no contracts; no successions; no partitions; no occupation but that of idleness; only a general respect of parents; no clothing; no agriculutre; no metals; no use of wine or corn. The very words denoting falsehood, treachery, dissimulation, avarice, envy, detraction, pardon, unheard of. How far removed from this perfection would he find the ideal republic he imagined! *Men newly come from the hands of the gods* (Seneca).

These manners first by nature taught.
(Virgil)

They have their wars with the nations beyond their mountains, further back on the mainland, to which they go quite naked, with no other weapons but bows or wooden swords pointed at one end, after the fashion of the tongues of our boar-spears. It is marvellous with what obstinacy they fight their battles, which never end but in massacre and bloodshed: for of routs and terrors they know not even the meaning. Each man brings back as a trophy the head of the enemy he has slain, and fixes it over the entrance to his dwelling. After treating his prisoner well for a considerable time, and giving him all that hospitality can devise, his captor convokes a great gathering of his acquaintance. He ties a cord to one of his prisoner's arms, holding him at some distance for fear of being hurt, and gives the other arm to be held in the same way by his best friend; and these two, in presence of the whole assembly, dispatch him with their swords. This done, they roast and eat him in common, and send bits of him to their absent friends. Not, as one might suppose for nourishment, as the ancient Scythians used to do, but to signify an extreme revenge.

I am not so much concerned that we should remark on the horrible barbarity of such acts, as that, whilst rightly judging their error, we should be so blind to our own. I think there is more barbarity in eating a live than a dead man, in tearing on the rack and torturing the body of a man still full of feeling, in roasting him piecemeal and giving him to be bitten and mangled by dogs and swine (as we have not only read, but seen within fresh memory, not between old enemies, but between neighbours and fellow citizens, and what is worse, under the cloak of piety and religion), than in roasting and eating him after he is dead.

We may therefore well call those people barbarians in respect to the rules of reason, but not in respect to ourselves, who surpass them in every kind of barbarity.

Their warfare is entirely noble and generous, and is as fair and excusable as can be expected in that human disease: their only motive being a zeal for valour. They do not strive to conquer new territory, for they still enjoy that luxuriance of nature which provides them, without labour and pains, with all necessary things in such abundance, that they have no need to enlarge their borders. They are still in that happy state of not desiring more than their natural needs demand: all that is over and above it is for them superfluity.

They generally call each other, if of the same age, brothers; if younger, children; and the old men are fathers to all the others. These latter leave to their heirs in common the full and undivided possession of their property, without any but that pure title that Nature gives to her creatures, by bringing them into the world. If their neighbours cross the mountains to attack them, and gain the victory over them, the acquisition of the victor is the glory and advantage of having proved himself the superior in valour and virtue, for otherwise they have no need for the spoils of the vanquished; and so they return to their own country, where they have no want of any necessaries, nor even of that great portion, which is to know how to enjoy happily their condition, and be content with it. These do the same in their turn. They ask of their prisonsers no other ransom but a confession and acknowledgement of being vanquished. But you will not find one in a whole century who would not rather die than yield, either by word or look, one tittle of an invincible greatness of courage; not one who would not rather be killed and eaten than even pray to be spared. They are very liberal in their treatment of their prisoners, in order to make life the more dear to them, and usually entertain them with threats of their impending death, the torments they will suffer, the preparations made to that end, the cutting up of their limbs, and the banquet that will be made at their expense. All this is done with the sole purpose of extorting from them a weak or spiritless word, or to give them a desire to escape, in order to gain the advantage of having terrified them and shaken their firmness. For indeed, if rightly taken, therein alone lies the real victory:

> The victor's wreath no triumphs more
>   attest
> Than when the foe's subjection is confest.
>   (Claudian)

✧✧✧

A man's value and estimation consists in heart and will: there lies his true honour. Valour is strength, not of legs and arms, but of heart and soul; it lies not in the goodness of our horse, or our weapons, but in our own. He who falls fighting with obstinate courage, *if his legs fail him, he fights on his knees* (Seneca). He who, in spite of being in danger of imminent death, abates nothing of his assurance, who, in yielding up his soul, still fixes on his enemy a firm and scornful glance, is vanquished, not by us, but by Fortune: he is slain but not conquered.

✧✧✧

To return to our narrative. Far from gibing in, in spite of all they suffer, these prisoners, on the contrary, during the two or three months that they are held in captivity, bear a cheerful countenance; they urge their captors to hasten to put them to the proof, defy them, insult them, reproach them with their cowardice and the number of battles lost against their own countrymen.

I have a song composed by a prisoner, which contains this outburst:

"Come boldly, every one of you, and assemble together to dine off me, for you shall at the same time eat your fathers and grandfathers, whose flesh has served to feed and nourish this body. These muscles, this flesh and these veins are yours, poor fools that you are! Can you not see that they still contain the substance of your ancestors' limbs? Relish them well, you will find that they have the flavour of your own flesh." A fiction that by no means savours of barbarity. In the pictures which represent these prisoners being executed or at the point of death, they are seen spitting in the face of their slayers or making mouths at them. Indeed they never cease to challenge and defy them by word and look until the breath is out of their body. Verily here we see men who are indeed savages if we compare them with ourselves: for either they must be so in good sooth, or we; there is a wonderful distance between their character and ours.

Three men of this nation, not knowing how dear, in tranquillity and happiness, it will one day cost them to know the corruptions of this side of the world, and that this intercourse will be the cause of their ruin, which indeed I imagine is already advanced (poor wretches, to be allured by the desire to see new things and to leave their own serene sky to come and see ours!), were at Rouen at a time when the late King Charles the Ninth was there. The King had a long talk with them. They were shown our ways, our pomp, the form of a fine city. After that somebody asked their opinion, desiring to know what they most wondered at. They mentioned three things, the third of which I am sorry to have forgotten, but I still remember two. They said that in the first place they thought it very strange that so many big men with beards, strong and armed, who were about the King (they were probably thinking of the Swiss who formed his guard) should submit to obey a child, and that they did not rather choose one of their own number to command them. Secondly (they have a way of speaking of men as if they were halves of another), that they had observed that there were men amongst us, full and gorged with all kinds of good things, and that their halves were begging at their doors, emaciated with hunger and poverty; and they thought it strange how these necessitous halves could suffer such injustice, and that they did not seize the others by the throat, or set fire to their houses.

I had a long talk with one of them; but I had an interpreter who followed my meaning so badly, and was at such a loss, in his stupidity, to take in my ideas, that I could get little satisfaction out of him. When I asked the native, "What he gained from his superior position among his people?" (for he was a captain, and our sailors called him a king), he said it was "to march foremost in war." How many men did he lead? He pointed to a piece of ground, to signify as many as that space could hold: it might be four of five thousand men. Did all his authority lapse with the war? He said "that this remained, that, when he visited the villages that were dependent on him, they made paths through their thickets, by which he might pass at his ease." All this does not sound too ill; but hold! they don't wear trousers.

⌇⌇⌇⌇⌇⌇⌇⌇⌇⌇⌇⌇⌇⌇⌇⌇⌇⌇⌇⌇⌇⌇⌇⌇⌇⌇⌇

Thomas Hariot (1560-1621)

In 1585-86 the English astronomer and mathematician Thomas Hariot served as scientific adviser for an expedition to Virginia organized by his friend Sir Walter Relegh. Hariot's *Brief and True Report* of that expedition was reprinted in the 1600 edition of Hakluyt's *Voyages*, from which the present selection is taken.

One of the earliest detailed reports on the religion of the American Indians, Hariot's work stands at the beginning of the continuing voluminous flow first of European and later of white American observations on the customs and beliefs of native Americans. His remarks provide a good example of the way in which the rites and beliefs of American primitives could be perceived and construed by the civilized European. They also reveal the way in which the Renaissance Christian imagined he was perceived by native Americans.

From *Brief and True Report of the New-found Land of Virginia* (1588)

In respect of us they are a people poor, and for want of skill and judgement in the knowledge and use of our things, do esteem our trifles before things of greater value. Notwithstanding, in their proper manner (considering the want of such means as we have), they seem very ingenious. For although they have no such tools, nor any such crafts, sciences, and arts as we, yet in those things they do, they show excellency of wit. And by how much they upon due consideration shall find our manner of knowledges and crafts to exceed theirs in perfection, and speed for doing or execution, by so much the more is it probable that they should desire our friendship and love, and have the greater respect for pleasing and obeying us. Whereby may be hoped, if means of good government be used, that they may in short time be brought to civility and the embracing of true religion.

Some religion they have already, which although it be far from the truth, yet being as it is, there is hope it may be the easier and sooner reformed.

They believe that there are many gods, which they call *Mantoac*, but of different sorts and degrees, one only chief and great god, which hath been from all eternity. Who, as they affirm, when he purposed to make the world, made first other gods of a principal order to be as means and instruments to be used in the creation and government to follow, and after the sun, moon, and stars as petty gods, and the instruments of the other order more principal. First, they say, were made waters, out of which by gods was made all diversity of creatures that are visible or invisible.

For mankind, they say a woman was made first which, by the working of one of the gods, conceived and brought forth children. And in such sort, they say, they had their beginning. But how many years or ages have passed since, they say they can make no relation, having no letters nor other such means as we to keep records of the particularities of times past, but only tradition from father to son.

They think that all the gods are of human shape, and therefore, they represent them by images in the forms of men, which they call *Kewasowok* (one alone is called *Kewas*). These they place in houses appropriate or temples, which they call *Machicomuck*, where they worship, pray, sing, and make many times offering unto them. In some *Machicomuck*, we have seen but one *Kewas*, in some two, and in other some three. The common sort think them to be also gods.

They believe also the immortality of the soul that, after this life as soon as the soul is departed from the body, according to the works it hath done, it is either carried to heaven, the habitat of gods, there to enjoy perpetual bliss and happiness, or else to a great pit or hole which they think to be in the furthest parts of their part of the world toward the sunset, there to burn continually. The place they call *Popogusso*.

For the confirmation of this opinion, they told me two stories of two men that had been lately dead and revived again. The one happened, but a few years before our coming into the country, of a wicked man, which having been dead and buried, the next day the earth of the grave being seen to move, was taken up again, who made declaration where his soul had been. That is to say, very near entering into *Popogusso*, had not one of the gods saved him, and gave him leave to return again and teach his friends what they should do to avoid that terrible place of torment. The other happened in the same year we were there, but in a town that was sixty miles from us, and it was told me for strange news, that one being dead, buried, and taken up again as the first, showed that although his body had lain dead in the grave, yet his soul was alive and had travelled far in a long broad way, on both sides whereof grew most delicate and pleasant trees. bearing more rare and excellent fruits than ever he had seen before or was able to express, and at length came to most brave and fair houses, near which he met his father that had been dead before, who gave him great charge to go back again and show his friends what good they were to do to enjoy the pleasures of that place, which when he had done he should after come again.

What subtlety soever be in the *Wiroances* and priests, this opinion worked so much in many of the common and simple sort of people, that it maketh them have great respect to their governors, and also great care what they do, to avoid torment after death, and to enjoy bliss, although notwithstanding there is punishment ordained for malefactors, as stealers, whoremongers, and other sort of wicked-doers, some punished with death, some with forfeitures, some with beating, according to the greatness of the facts.

And this is the sum of their religion, which I learned by having special familiarity with some of their priests. Wherein they were not so sure grounded, nor gave such credit to their traditions and stories, but through conversing with us they were brought into great doubts of their own, and no small admiration of ours, with earnest deisre in many, to learn more than we had means for want of perfect utterance in their language to express.

Most things they saw with us, as mathematical instruments, sea compasses, the virtue of the lodestone in drawing iron, a perspective glass whereby was showed many strange sights, burning glasses, wild fireworks, guns, hooks, writing and reading, spring-clocks that seem to go off themselves, and many other things that we had were so strange unto them, and so far exceeded their capacities to comprehend the reason and means how they should be made and done, that they thought they were rather the works of gods than of men, or at the leastwise, they had been given and taught by the gods. Which made many of them have such opinion of us, as that if they knew not the truth of God and religion already, it was rather to be had from us whom God so specially loved, than from a people that were so simple as they found themselves to be in comparison of us.

Whereupon greater credit was given unto that we spoke of, concerning such matters.

Many times and in every town where I came, according as I was able, I made declaration of the contents of the Bible, that therein was set forth the true and only God, and his mighty works, that therein was contained the true doctrine of salvation through christ, with many particulars of miracles and chief points of religion, as I was able then to utter, and thought fit for the time. And although I told them the book materially and of itself was not of any such virtue, as I thought they did conceive, but only the doctrine therein contained, yet would many be glad to touch it, to embrace it, to kiss it, to hold it to their breasts and heads, and stroke over all their body with it, to show their hungry desire of that knowledge which was spoken of.

$\backsim\backsim\backsim\backsim\backsim\backsim\backsim\backsim\backsim\backsim\backsim\backsim\backsim\backsim$

Sir Walter Relegh (1544-1618)

Sir Walter Ralegh was as poet, courtier, adventurer, explorer, soldier, and statesman in the time of Elixzabeth I. At the accession of James I he fell from favor, and was finally beheaded for treason. His unjust condemnastion, together with the memory of his exploits, made him a popular hero and an almost legendary figure.

In 1584 Ralegh organized the earliest English expedition to America in the hope of establishing a colony near Roanoke Island on what is now the coast of North Carolina. This ill-fated settlement eventually had to be abandoned, but not before Ralegh had named this new country "Virginia" in honor of his queen. In 1595 Ralegh organized and himself took part in an expedition to the Orinoco River, in South America. It was thus he came to write *The Discovery of Guiana.* The book largely failed to attract the support Ralegh wanted for a second attempt to establish an American colony, but it helped to fix the association of New World enterprises with the possibility of vast economic gain. Indeed, Ralegh's book is the best representation we have of what one scholar has described as "the shimmering mirage of gold and glory through which the sixteenth century saw the New World."

Ralegh was perhaps the first to introduce a motif which reappears often in writings concerned with "the American Dream," from Thomas Morton's *New English Canaan* to F. Scott Fitzgerald's *The Great Gatsby:* the association of images of sexual fulfillment with the satisfaction of the lust for material wealth. In the following selection Ralegh depicts the American continent as a virgin whose innocence remains intact but whose virtue may be assaulted without fear by whichever nation first lays claim to her beauties.

It is hardly surprising that this book helped to inspire the conquistadores and set in motion the plunder of the New World and its peoples.

From *The Discovery of Guiana* (1595)

The Empire of Guaiana is directly East from Peru towards the Sea, and lieth under the Equinoctial line, and it hath more abundance of gold than any part of Peru, and as many or more great Cities than ever Peru had when it flourished most; it is governed by the same laws, and the Emperor and people observe the same religion, and the same form and policies in government as were used in Peru, not differing in any part: and I have been assured by such of the Spaniards as have seen Manoa the Imperial City of Guiana, which the Spaniards call El Dorado, that for greatness, for the riches, and for the excellent seat, it far exceedeth any of the world, at least of so much of the world as is known to the Spanish nation. . . .

∽∾∾

This Martinez was he that Christened the city of Manoa by the name of El Dorado, and as Berreo informed me, upon this occasion: Those Guianians, and also the borderers, and all other in that tract which I have seen, are marvelous great drunkards; in which vice, I think no nation can compare with them: and at the time of their solemn feasts, when the emperor carowseth with his captains, tributaries, and governors, the manner is thus: All those that pledge him are first stripped naked, and their bodies annointed all over with a kind of white balsamum (by them called curca) of which there is great plenty, and yet very dear amongst them, and it is of all other the more precious, whereof we have had good experience: when they are annointed all over, certain servants of the emperor, having prepared gold made into fine powder, blow it through hollow canes upon their naked bodies, until they be all shining from the foot to the head: and this sort they sit drinking by twenties, and hundreds, and continue in drunkenness sometimes six or seven days together. The same is also confirmed by a letter written into Spain, which was intercepted, which M. Robert Duddeley told me he had seen. Upon this sight, and for the abundance of gold which he saw in the city, the images of gold in their temples, the plates, armors, and shields of gold which they use in the wars, he called it El Dorado.

❧❧❧

... I never saw a more beautiful country, nor more lively prospects, hills so raised here and there over the valleys, the river winding into divers branches, the plains adjoining without bush or stubble, all fair green grass, the ground of hard sand easy to march on, either for horse or foot, the deer crossing in every path, the birds toward the evening singing on every tree with a thousand several tunes, cranes and herons of white, crimson, and carnation perching in the river's side, the air fresh with a gentle Easterly wind, and every stone that we stooped to take up, promised either gold or silver by his complexion.

❧❧❧

... The common soldier shall here fight for gold, and pay himself instead of pence, with plates of half a foot broad, whereas he breaketh his bones in other wars for profit and penury. Those commanders and chieftains that shoot at honor and abundance, shall find there more rich and beautiful cities, more temples adorned with golden images, more sepulchers filled with treasure, then either Cortez found in Mexico, or Pizarro in Peru: and the shining glory of this conquest will eclipse all those so far extended beams of the Spanish nation. There is no country which yieldeth more pleasure to the inhabitants, either for those common delights of hunting, hawking, fishing, fowling, or the rest, than Guiana doth. It hath so many plains, clear rivers, abundance of Pheasants, Partridges, Quails, Rails, Cranes, Herons, and all other fowl: Deer of all sorts, Porks, Hares, Lions, Tigers, Leopards, and divers other sorts of beasts, either for chase, or food. . . .

❧❧❧

To conclude, Guiana is a country that hath yet her maidenhead, never sacked, turned, nor wrought, the face of the earth hath not been torn, nor the virtue and salt of the soil spent by manure, the graves have not been opened for gold, the mines not broken with sledges, nor their Images pulled down out of their temples. It hath never been entered by any army of strength, and never conquered or possessed by any christian prince. It is besides so defensible, that if two forts be built in one of the Provinces which I have seen, the flood setteth in so near the bank, where the channel also lies, that no ship can pass up but within

29

a Pike's length of the artillery, first of the one, and afterwards of the other: Which two Forts will be a sufficient guard both to the Empire of Inga, and to an hundred other several kingdoms, lying within the said river, even to the city of Quito in Peru.

Michael Drayton (1563–1631)

The minor English poet Michael Drayton was very conscious of England's former glories. In "To the Virginian Voyage," he shows himself concerned to protect and enhance the rich heritage of his nation. Sharing the typical Renaissance vision of the New World as "Earth's onely paradise," Drayton sees the colonization of America as an opportunity to revive England's diminished sense of national destiny and pride. The New World presents fresh challenges which should create a new generation of British heroes and New World poets to sing of their exploits.

"To the Virginian Voyage" (1606)

You brave heroique minds,
Worthy your countries name,
   That honour still pursue,
   Goe, and subdue,

Whilst loyt'ring hinds
Lurke here at home, with shame.

Britans, you stay too long,
Quickly aboord bestow you,
   And with a merry gale
   Swell your stretch'd sayle,
With vowes as strong,
As the winds that blow you.

Your course securely steere,
West and by south forth keepe,
   Rocks, lee-shores, nor sholes,
   When Eolus scowles,
You need not feare, So absolute the
     deepe.

And cheerefully at sea,
Successe you still intice,
   To get the pearle and gold,
   And ours to hold,
Virginia,
Earth's onely paradise.

Where nature hath in store,
Fowle, venison, and fish,
   And the fruitfull'st soyle,
   Without your toyle,
Three havests more,
All greater then you wish.

And the ambitious vine
Crownes with his purple masse,
   The Cedar reaching hie
   To kiss the sky,
The Cypresse, pine
And use-full Sassafras.

To whose, the golden age
Still natures lawes doth give,
   No other cares that tend,
But them to defend
From winters age,
That long there doth not live.

When as the lushious smell
Of that delicious land,
   Above the seas that flowes,
   The cleere wind throwes,
Your hearts to swell
Approching the deare strand.

In kenning of the shore
(Thanks to God first given,)
   O you the happy'st men,
   Be frolike then,
Let cannons roare,
Frighting the wide heaven.

And in regions farre
Such heroes bring yee foorth,
   As those from whom we came,
   And plant our name,
Under that starre
Not knowne unto our north.

And as there plenty growes
Of lawrell every where,
   Apollo's sacred tree,
   You it may see,
A poets browes
To crowne, that may sing there.

Thy voyages attend,
Industrious Hackluit,
   Whose reading shall inflame
   Men to seeke fame,
And much commend
To after-times thy wit.

William Shakespeare (1564–1616)

William Shakespeare, England's greatest playwright, was clearly aware of the symbolic importance of the New World. Shakespeare shared with so many of his Renaissance contemporaries a utopian perception of America as an idyllic place of spiritual regeneration and Arcadian enchantment. But he also saw a darker vision of this primitive and unknown land. In what has been called his American fable, "The Tempest," Shakespeare depicts America as a pastoral, Edenic landscape or garden. But he also glimpses another America: the "hideous wilderness" later to be perceived by William Bradford, Jonathan Edwards, Herman Melville, and others; the "anti-image," as one historian has put it, of America as a place of deception, treachery, and wickedness.

All of the following selections are taken from "The Tempest." The first is Prospero's speech reminding the spirit Ariel of what his life on the island had been like before Prospero came with his magic to rescue him from the clutches of "the foul witch Sycorax."

The second passage is spoken by Caliban, Sycorax's "freckled whelp hag-born," whose bestiality is a reflection in human form of the hideousness of the world without.

The third is Ferdinand's expression of wonder at hearing what seems to him to be the music of Nature itself.

And showing that the spell of this New World can enthrall even the dullest sensibilities, in the fourth selection the playwright demonstrates that Caliban, too, is vulnerable to the enchantments of "Earth's onely paradise."

The final selection is Miranda's exclamation of joyful amazement at her first sight of the court party.

From *The Tempest* (1611)

I. ii

Prospero: This blue-ey'd hag was hith-
er brought with child
And here was left by th' sailors. Thou,
my slave,
As thou report'st thyself, wast then her
servant;
And, for thou wast a spirit too delicate
To act her earthy and abhorr'd com-
mands,
Refusing her grand hests, she did con-
fine thee,
By help of her more potent ministers
And in her most unmitigable rage,
Into a cloven pine; within which rift
Imprison'd thou didst painfully remain
A dozen years; within which space she
died
And left thee there; where thou did'st
vent thy groans
As fast as mill-wheels strike. Then was
this island—
Save for the son that she did litter
here,
A freckled whelp hag-born—not hon-
our'd with
A human shape.

👌

Caliban: This island's mine, by
Sycorax my mother,
Which thou tak'st from me. When
thou cam'st first,
Thou strok'st me and made much of
me, wouldst give me
Water with berries in 't, and teach me
how
To name the bigger light, and how the
less,

That burn by day and night: and then
I lov'd thee
And show'd thee all the qualities o' th'
isle,
The fresh springs, brine-pits, barren
place and fertile:
Curs'd be I that did so! All the charms
Of Sycorax, toads, beetles, bats, light
on you!
For I am all the subjects that you have,
Which first was mine own king: and
here you sty me
In this hard rock, whiles you do keep
from me
The rest o' th' island.

👌

Ferdinand: Where should this music
be? i' th' air or th' earth?
It sounds no more: and, sure, it waits
upon
Some god o' th' island. Sitting on a
bank,
Weeping again the king my father's
wrack,
This music crept by me upon the
waters,
Allaying both their fury and my
passion
With its sweet air: thence I have
follow'd it,
Or it hath drawn me rather. But 'tis
gone.
No, it begins again.

👌

III.ii

Caliban: Be not afeard; the isle is full
of noises,
Sounds and sweet airs, that give
delight and hurt not.

Sometimes a thousand twangling
    instruments
Will hum about mine ears, and
    sometimes voices
That, if I then had wak'd after long
    sleep,
Will make me sleep again: and then, in
    dreaming,
The clouds methought would open
    and show riches
Ready to drop upon me, that, when I
    wak'd,
I cried to dream again.

V.i

Miranda: *O, wonder!*
How many goodly creatures are there
    here!
How beauteous mankind is! O brave
    new world,
That has such people in 't!

Francis Bacon
(1561–1626)

Few men have so clearly heralded a new
age as did Francis Bacon (1561–1626).
Philosopher, scientist, metaphysician,
man of letters, and statesman, Bacon
understood perhaps better than most of
his contemporaries that the middle ages
were over and that a new era had been
ushered in. Bacon gave expression to an
idea central to that new era, the modern
era, in *Novum organum* (1620). He wrote

that "Man, who is the servant and
interpreter of nature, can act and understand no further than he has observed, either in operation or in contemplation, of the method and order of
nature."

In *The New Atlantis,* Bacon describes a
utopian society where the scientific
spirit reigns supreme. In this society
there is a college of science, "Salomon's
House," dedicated to the empirical
study of "the works and creatures of
God." The following selection describes
that college—its purposes, instruments,
components and functions, and special
rites. The formal, stylized manner of
the speaker is well suited to the high
metaphysical calling of the college: to
seek "the knowledge of causes, and
secret motions of things; and the enlarging of the bounds of human empire, to
the effecting of all things possible."

From *The New Atlantis* (1627)

"God bless thee, my son; I will give thee
the greatest jewel I have. For I will impart unto thee, for the love of God and
men, a relation of the true state of Salomon's House . . . I will keep this order.
First, I will set forth unto you the end of
our foundation. Secondly, the preparations and instruments we have for our
works. Thirdly, the several employments and functions whereto our fellows are assigned. And fourthly, the ordinances and rites which we observe.

"The end of our foundation is the
knowledge of causes, and secret motions

of things; and the enlarging of the bounds of human empire, to the effecting of all things possible.

"The preparations and instruments are these. We have large and deep caves of several depths. . . . These caves we call the lower region, and we use them for all coagulations, indurations, refrigerations, and conservations of bodies. We use them likewise for the imitation of natural mines, and the producing also of new artificial metals. . . .

"We have burials in several earths, where we put divers cements, as the Chinese do their porcelain. But we have them in greater variety, and some of them more fine. . . .

"We have high towers, the highest about half a mile in height. . . . We use these towers, according to their several heights and situations, for insolation, refrigerations, conversation, and for the view of divers meteors. . . .

"We have great lakes, both salt and fresh, whereof we have use for the fish and fowl. We use them also for burials of some natural bodies, for we find a difference in things buried in earth, or in air below the earth, and things buried in water. . . .

"We have also a number of artificial wells and fountains. . . . And amongst them we have a water, which we call Water of Paradise, being by that we do to it made very sovereign for health and prolongation of life.

"We have also great and spacious houses, where we imitate and demonstrate meteors. . . .

"We have also certain chambers, which we call chamber of health, where we quality the air as we think good and

proper for the cure of divers diseases, and preservation of health.

"We have also fair and large baths, of several mixtures, for the cure of diseases, and the restoring of man's body from arefaction. . . .

"We have also large and various orchards and gardens, wherein we do not so much respect beauty as variety of ground and soil. . . .

"We have also means to make divers plants rise by mixtures of earths without seeds, and likewise to make divers new plants. . . .

"We have also parks, and enclosures of all sorts, of beasts and birds; which we use not only for view or rareness, but likewise for dissections and trials. . . .

"We have also particular pools where we make trials upon fishes. . . .

"I will not hold you long with recounting of our brewhouses, bake-houses, and kitchens, where are made divers drinks, breads, and meats, rare and of special effects. . . .

"We have dispensatories or shops of medicines. . . .

"We have also divers mechanical arts, which you have not. . . .

"We have also furnaces of great diversities, and that keep great diversities of heats: fierce and quick, strong and constant, soft and mild; blown, quiet, dry, moist, and the like. . . .

"We have also perspective houses, where we make demonstrations of all lights and radiations, and of all colours. . . .

"We have also precious stones of all kinds, many of them of great beauty and to you unknown. . . .

"We have also sound-houses, where

we practise and demonstrate all sounds and their generation. . . .

"We have also perfume-houses, wherewith we join also practices of taste. . . .

"We have also engine-houses, where are prepared engines and instruments for all sorts of motions. . . .

"We have also a mathematical-house, where are represented all instruments, as well as geometry as astronomy, exquisitely made.

"We have also houses of deceits of the senses, where we represent all manner of feats of juggling, false apparitions, impostures and illusions and their fallacies. And surely you will easily believe that we, that have so many things truly natural which induce admiration, could in a world of particulars deceive the senses if we would disguise those things, and labour to make them seem more miraculous. But we do hate all impostures and lies, insomuch as we have severely forbidden it to all our fellows, under pain of ignominy and fines, that they do not show any natural work or thing adorned or swelling, but only pure as it is, and without all affectation of strangeness.

"These are, my son, the riches of Salomon's House.

"For the several employments and offices of our fellows, we have twelve that sail into foreign countries . . . who bring us the books and abstracts, and patterns of experiments of all other parts. . . . These we call Merchants of Light.

"We have three that collect the experiments which are in all books. . . . These we call Depredators.

"We have three that collect the experiments of all mechanical arts, and also of liberal sciences, and also of practises which are not brought into arts. . . . These we call Mystery-men.

"We have three that try new experiments. . . . These we call Pioneers or Miners.

"We have three that draw the experiments of the former four into titles and tables. . . . These we call Compilers.

"We have three that bend themselves, looking into the experiments of their fellows, and cast about how to draw out of them things of use and practice for man's life and knowledge. . . . These we call dowry-men or Benefactors.

"Then after divers meetings and consults of our whole number, . . . we have three that take care out of them to direct new experiments, of a higher light, more penetrating into Nature than the former. . . . These we call Lamps.

∽∽∽

"For our ordinances and rites, we have two very long and fair galleries: in one of these we place patterns and samples of all manner of the more rare and excellent inventions; in the other we place the statues of all principal inventors. . . .

"We have certain hymns and services, which we say daily, of laud and thanks to God for His marvellous works. And forms of prayer, imploring His aid and blessing for the illumination of our labours, and the turning of them into good and holy uses.

"Lastly, we have circuits or visits, of divers principal cities of the kingdom; where, as it cometh to pass, we do publish such new profitable inventions as we think good. . . ."

And when he had said this he stood up; and I, as I had been taught, knelt down; and he laid his right hand on my head, and said, "God bless thee, my son, and God bless this relation which I have made. I give thee leave to publish it, for the good of other nations; for we here are in God's bosom, and land unknown." And so he left me; having assigned a value of about two thousand ducats for a bounty to me and my fellows. For they give great largesses, where they come, upon all occasions.

George Herbert (1593–1633)

George Herbert (1593–1633) was an English poet of the metaphysical school associated with John Donne. He wrote spiritual poetry characterised by unusual candor. As he confessed on his deathbed to his friend and editor, Nicholas Ferrar, Herbert desired to present in his poetry "a picture of the many spiritual conflicts that . . . passed between God and my soul, before I could subject mine to the will of Jesus my Master, in whose service I have now found perfect freedom." In *The Church Militant,* written in the year of his death, Herbert seems reconciled with his divine Master. In the following selection from that poem, Herbert portrays religion fleeing the corruption of the Old World to the unsullied purity of the New. But he knows that sin and darkness will inevitably follow the Church and stain the innocence of the West. He finds consolation in the idea that, as the Church moves west into the American wilderness, it also symbolically moves "east" to the time and place of promised final judgment.

Several themes emerge in this passage. Herbert foreshadows such Puritan fathers as William Bradford and John Winthrop in his belief that America will provide religion with a new beginning, or reformation. He also anticipates the view that America will provide a fresh and possibly decisive occasion for a new testing of religion, that America will indeed be, as John Winthrop forecast aboard the *Arabella,* a "City upon a Hill," a place where new reckonings will be made and new judgments delivered on the whole of the Western Christian inheritance.

From "The Church Militant" (1633)

Religion stands on tip-toe in our land,
Readie to passe to the *American* strand.
When height of malice, and prodigious
    lusts,
Impudent sinning, witchcrafts, and
    distrusts
(The marks of future bane) shall fill
    our cup
Unto the brimme, and make our
    measure up;

When *Sein* shall swallow *Tiber,* and the
    Thames
By letting in them both pollutes her
    streams:
When *Italie* of us shall have her will,
And all her calender of sinnes fulfill;
Whereby one may foretell, what sinnes
    next yeare
Shall both in *France* and *England*
    domineer:
Then shall Religion to *America* flee:
They have their times of Gospel, ev'n
    as we.
My God, thou dost prepare for them a
    way
By carrying first their gold from them
    away:
For gold and grace did never yet
    agree:
Religion alwaies sides with povertie.
We think we rob them, but we think
    amisse:
We are more poore, and they more
    rich by this.
Thou wilt revenge their quarrell,
    making grace
To pay our debts, and leave her
    ancient place
To go to them, while that which now
    their nation
But lends to us, shall be our
    desolation.
Yet as the Church shall thither
    westward flie,
So Sinne shall trace and dog her
    instantly:

They have their period also and set
    times
Both for their vertuous actions and
    their crimes.
And where of old the Empire and the
    Arts
Usher'd the Gospel ever in mens
    hearts,
Spain hath done one; when Arts
    perform the other,
The Church shall come, & Sinne the
    Church shall smother:
That when they have accomplished
    their round,
And met in th' east their first and
    ancient sound,
Judgement may meet them both &
    search them round.
Thus do both lights, as well in Church
    as Sunne,
Light one another, and together
    runne.
Thus also Sinne and Darknesse follow
    still
The Church and Sunne with all their
    power and skill.
But as the Sunne still goes both west
    and east;
So also did the Church by going west
Still eastward go; because it drew more
    neare
To time and place, where judgement
    shall appeare.
How deare to me, O God, thy counsels are!
    Who may with thee compare?

II
Preparations
(1607–1740)

The "invention of America" could not, needless to say, continue on a course independent of its historical exploration and settlement. When the colonization of the New World actually began, what had previously existed chiefly in the imagination as an object of desire began to come into clearer focus as a real place with specific outline and concrete conditions. But if the idea of America was now to be based on actual knowledge and experience, it was still to shape the spirituality of those who colonized it, and in ways sharply at variance with the theological expectations they brought with them.

The early colonists destined to have the greatest impact on an evolving American sensibility were notably religious, but their religion looked to the Old World rather than the New for its inspiration. As Samuel Danforth put it, in a sermon delivered in 1670, the original Puritan colonists had come to America for two reasons: to erect a new society organized as strictly as possible in accordance with principles laid down in the Hebrew and Christian scriptures, and to turn the example of this society into a source of regeneration for the religion of the Old World. But when Old World Christians failed to take any meaningful interest in this New World experiment, the American colonists were obliged to give up their idea of redeeming the rest of Western Christendom and concentrate on redeeming themselves. And from there it was only a short step for later colonists to translate the problem of redeeming themselves into a question of the redemptive possibilities of their New World environment. Hence in a comparatively short span of time, no more than several generations, changing conceptions of the symbolic meaning of America worked to transform Old World Puritans into fledgling New World metaphysicians. America was no longer just the symbolic frame of reference for their thinking, but one of its primary sources. Having originally been conceived merely as a suitable context for an exercise in religious regeneration, the New World was quickly converted into one of the agents in the regenerative process itself.

Alexander Whitaker (1585–1616?)

An Anglican clergyman who came to the newly established colony of Virginia in 1611, Alexander Whitaker served two parishes near Jamestown until his untimely death by drowning. This sermon, *Good Newes from Virginia,* is his only published work. Like many similar sermons designed for an English audience, it urges support of the American colony and gives a favorable description of the country.

Whitaker's sermon could be said to inaugurate what one historian has called the "celebrationist tradition" about America and its destiny. The following selection is notable for its attitude toward the Indians, whose conversion to Christianity it strongly urged. While believing the Indians to be "slaves of the divell," Whitaker admires their physical prowess, their dexterity at arms, their inventions, and their enlightened form of government. He argues passionately that the Indians are capable of receiving the Gospel; everything created bears the image of its Maker, Whitaker reasons, including these "sonnes of Adam," and Christians should show compassion toward the present miserable condition of these their brethren.

From *Good Newes from Virginia* (1613)

Let the miserable condition of these naked slaves of the divell move you to compassion toward them. They acknowledge that there is a great good God, but know him not, having the eyes of their understanding as yet blinded: wherefore they serve the divell for feare, after a most base manner, sacrificing sometimes (as I have heere heard) their owne Children to him. I have sent one Image of their god to the Counsell in England, which is painted upon one side of a toad-stoole, much like unto a deformed monster. Their Priests (whom they call Quiokosoughs) are no other but such as our English Witches are. They live naked in bodie, as if their shame of their sinne deserved no covering: Their names are as naked as their bodie: they esteeme it a vertue to lie, deceive and steale as their master the divell teacheth them. Much more might be said of their miserable condition, but I refer the particular narration of these things to some other season. If this bee their life, what thinke you shall become of them after death? but to be partakers with the divell and his angels in hell for evermore. Wherefore my brethren, put on the bowels of compassion, and let the lamentable estate of these miserable people enter in your consideration: One God created us, they have reasonable soules and intellectuall faculties as well as wee; we all have Adam for our common parent: yea, by nature the condition of us both is all one, the servants of sinne and slaves of the divell. Oh remember (I beseech you) what was the state of England before the Gospell was preached in our Countrey? How much better were we then, and concerning our soules health, then these now are? Let the word of the Lord sound out that it may be heard in these parts; and let your faith which is toward God spread it selfe abroad, and shew forth the charitable fruits of it in these barren parts of the world: And let him know that he which hath converted a sinner from going a stray out of his way, shall save a soule from death, and hide a multitude of sinnes.

But if any of us should misdoubt that this barbarous people is uncapable of such heavenly mysteries, let such men know that they are farre mistaken in the nature of these men, for besides the promise of God, which is without respect of persons, made as well to unwise men after the flesh, as to the wise &c. let us not thinke that these men are so simple as some have supposed them: for they are of bodie lustie, strong, and very nimble: they are a very understanding generation, quicke of apprehension, suddaine in their dispatches, subtile in their dealings, exquisite in their inventions, and industrious in their labour. I suppose the world hath no better markemen with their bow and arrowes then they be; they will kill birds flying, fishes swimming and beasts running; they shoote also with mervailous strength, they shot one of our men being unarmed quite through the bodie, and nailed both his armes to his bodie with one arrow: one of their Children also, about the age of 12. or 13. yeares, killed a bird with his arrow in my sight.

The service of their God is answerable to their life, being performed with great feare and attention, and many strange dumb shewes used in the same, stretching forth their limbes and straining their bodie, much like to the counterfeit women in England who faine themselves bewitched, or possessed of some evill spirit.

They stand in great awe of their Quiokosoughs or Priests, which are a generation of vipers even of Sathans owne brood. The manner of their life is much like to the popish Hermits of our age; for they live alone in the woods, in houses sequestred from the common course of men, neither may any man bee suffered to come into their house or to speake with them, but when this Priest doth call him. He taketh no care for his victuals, for all such kinde of things both bread and water, &c. are brought unto a place neere unto his cottage and there are left, which hee fetcheth for his proper neede. If they would have raine, or have lost any thing, they have their recourse to him, who conivreth for them, and many times prevaileth. If they be sicke, he is their Physition, if they bee wounded he sucketh them. At his command they make warre and peace, neither doe they any thing of moment without him. I will not bee teadious in these strange Narrations, when I have more perfectly entered into their secrets, you shall know all. Finally, there is a civill governement amongst them which they strictly observe, and shew thereby that the law of Nature dwelleth in them: for they have a rude kinde of Common-wealth, and rough government, wherein they both honour and obey their Kings, Parents, and Governours, both greater and lesse, they observe the limits of their owne possessions, and incroach not upon their neighbours dwellings. Murther is a capitall crime scarce heard of among them: adultery is the most severely punished, and so are their other offences. These unnurtured grounds of reason in them, may serve to incourage us: to instruct them in the knowledge of the true God, the rewarder of all righteousnesse, not doubting but that he that was powerfull to save us by his word, when we were nothing, will be mercifull also to these sonnes of Adam in his appointed time, in whom there bee remaining so many footsteps of Gods image. . . .

American settlement extend far beyond his adventures and misadventures in Jamestown. He later explored the coast as far north as Maine, and prepared maps and books to encourage further colonization. Captain John Smith, as he came to be called, appears to have been driven by a variety of motives including personal ambition, material gain, and even religious sentiment.

In the following selection, Smith argues for colonization, but whether discussing patriotic, religious, or economic considerations, he characteristically stresses the opportunity to take advantage of a good bargain. Subordinating theological to practical considerations, Smith seems the antithesis of his Puritan contemporaries,, but it may well be that Smith has had a greater number of spiritual descendants in America.

John Smith
(1580–1631)

John Smith bears one of the best known names in early American history, but he is generally little understood. Explorer, adventurer, administrator, cartographer, colonist, and author, Smith seems part hero and part rascal. A member of the Virginia Company's first expedition to Jamestown in 1607, Smith is best remembered for being captured by Indians and subsequently released as a result of the intercession of Chief Powhatan's daughter Pocahontas. But Smith's exploits and his service to the cause of

From *A Description of New England* (1616)

But it is not a work for everyone, to manage such an affair as makes a discovery and plants a colony. It requires all the best parts of art, judgement, courage, honesty, constancy, diligence, and industry to do but near well. Some are more proper for one thing than another, and therein are [they] to be employed, and nothing breeds more confusion than misplacing and misemploying men in their undertakings. Columbus, Cortes, Pizarro, De Soto, Magellan, and the rest served more than an apprenticeship to learn how to begin their most memorable attempts in the West Indies, which to the wonder of all ages successfully they effected, when many hundreds of others far above them in the world's opinion, being instructed but by relation, came to shame and confusion in actions of small moment, who doubtless in other matters were both wise, discreet, generous, and courageous. I say not this to detract anything from their incomparable merits but to answer those questionless questions that keep us back from imitating the worthiness of their brave spirits that advanced themselves from poor soldiers to great captains, their posterity to great lords, their king to be one of the greatest potentates on earth, and the fruits of their labors [to be] his greatest glory, power, and renown.

That part we call New England is betwixt the degrees of 41 and 45 [north latitude], but that part this discourse speaks of, stretches but from Penobscot to Cape Cod, some seventy-five leagues by a right line distant each from other, within which bounds I have seen at least forty several habitations upon the sea-coast and sounded about twenty-five excellent good harbors, in many whereof there is anchorage for 500 sail of ships of any burden, in some of them for 5,000. And more than 200 isles overgrown with good timber of divers sorts of wood, which do make so many harbors as requires a longer time than I had, to be well discovered.

∽◦∽

Who can desire more content, that has small means or but only his merit to advance his fortune, than to tread and plant that ground he has purchased by the hazard of his life? If he have but the taste of virtue and magnanimity, what to such a mind can be more pleasant than planting and building a foundation for his posterity, got from the rude earth by God's blessing and his own industry, without prejudice to any? If he have any grain of faith or zeal in religion, what can he do less hurtful to any or more agreeable to God than to seek to convert those poor savages to know Christ and humanity, whose labor with discretion will triple requite thy charge and pains? What so truly suits with honor and honesty as the discovering things unknown, erecting towns, peopling countries, informing the ignorant, reforming things unjust, teaching virtue, and gain to our native mother-country a kingdom to attend her, find employment for those that are idle because they know not what to do; [this is] so far from wronging any as to cause posterity to remember thee, and remembering thee, ever honor that remembrance with praise?

∽◦∽

I have not been so ill bred but I have tasted of plenty and pleasure as well as want and misery, nor does necessity yet or occasion of discontent force me to these endeavors, nor am I ignorant what small thanks I shall have for my pains or that many would have the world imagine them to be of great judgement that can but blemish these my designs by their witty objections and detractions, yet (I hope) my reasons with my deeds will so prevail with some that I shall not want employment in these affairs, to make the most blind see his own senselessness and incredulity, hoping that gain will make them effect that which religion, charity, and the common good cannot. It were but a poor device in me to deceive myself, much more the King, state, my friends, and country with these inducements which, seeing his Majesty has given permission, I wish all sorts of worthy, honest, industrious spirits would understand, and if they desire any further satisfaction, I will do my best to give it, not to persuade them to go only, but go with them, not leave them there, but live with them there.

I will not say, but by ill providing and undue managing, such courses may be taken [that] may make us miserable enough. But if I may have the execution of what I have projected, [then] if they want to eat, let them eat or never . . . [tolerate] me. If I perform what I say, I desire but that reward out of the gains [which] may suit my pains, quality, and condition. And if I abuse you with my tongue, take my head for satisfaction. If any dislike at the year's end, defraying their charge, by my consent they should freely return. I fear not want of company sufficient, were it but known what I know of those countries; and by the proof of that wealth I hope yearly to return, if God please to bless me from such accidents as are beyond my power in reason to prevent. For I am not so simple to think that every any other motive than wealth will ever erect there a commonwealth or draw company from their ease and humors at home to stay in New England to effect my purposes.

Mayflower Compact (1620)

A Relation or Journal of the beginning and proceedings of the English Plantation settled at Plimouth in New England, by certain English adventurers both merchants and others, with their difficult passage, their safe arrival, their joyful building of, and comfortable planting themselves in the now well defended town of New Plimouth, as also a relation of four several discoveries since made by some of the same English planters there resident, or *Mourt's Relation* as it is called, was the earliest printed record of the Pilgrims' landing in America. It was published in 1622 and is thought to be the work of either Edward Winslow or George Morton (G. Mourt). It was subsequently overshadowed by William Bradford's authoritative account of the Pilgrim settlement, *Of Plimouth Plantation. Mourt's Relation* is an unvarnished report of the first "errand into the wilderness" of New England, whereas Bradford's chronicle of the same events colors them in rich theological hues.

The "Mayflower Compact," composed in the ship's cabin on arrival from Holland, November 11, 1620, is the first American social contract. It was drawn up by leaders of the Plymouth expedition partly in response to the threat of sedition by Mayflower passengers not of their community, who were distraught over missing Virginia, the intended destination, and landing in what is now called New England instead. Although lacking the complex and subtle formulations furnished by John Winthrop ten years later in the sermon "A Modell of Christian Charity," the "Mayflower Compact" provides a concise summary of the Pilgrims' reasons for their expedition to the New World and the methods by which they proposed to accomplish their aims. The means were civil, but the end religious: to plant a colony united by covenant which would witness to God's glory and contribute to the advancement of the Christian religion.

nances, acts, constitutions, and offices from time to time, as shall be thought most meet and convenient for the general good of the colony; unto which we promise all due submission and obedience. In witness whereof we have hereto subscribed our names; Cape Cod, the 11th of November, in the year of the reign of our sovereign lord King James, of England, France and Ireland eighteenth and of Scotland fifty-fourth, Anno Domini 1620.

"Mayflower Compact" from *A Journal of the Pilgrims at Plymouth* (sometimes called *Mourt's Relation*, 1622)

In the name of God, Amen. We whose names are underwritten, the loyal subjects of our dread sovereign lord King James, by the grace of God, of Great Britain, France, and Ireland King, Defender of the Faith, etc.

Having undertaken, for the glory of God, and advancement of the Christian faith, and honor of our king and country, a voyage to plant the first colony in the northern parts of Virginia, do by these presents solemnly and mutually in the presence of God and one another, covenant, and combine ourselves together into a civil body politic, for our better ordering and preservation, and furtherance of the ends aforesaid; and by virtue hereof to enact, constitute, and frame such just and equal laws, ordi-

John Cotton
(1584–1652)

John Cotton, former Dean of Emmanuel College, Cambridge University, emigrated to America in 1633. He quickly became a prominent figure in the Massachusetts Bay Colony. Best known for his opposition to Anne Hutchinson and the Antinomians, who resisted his belief in the authority of the church and its offices as intermediary between God and man, and for his later clash with Roger Williams, who challenged his undemocratic views of civil and religious government in *The Bloudy Tenent of Persecution,* Cotton was an able but sometimes reactionary defender of New England Congregationalism.

Cotton wrote "God's Promise to His Plantations" while still in England. His central image of "planting" is interesting in several respects. This rich metaphor opens a treasury of apt scriptural references to describe God's work in the New World and to illuminate the meaning of the Puritan errand into the wilderness. It also anticipates the way in which later American writers would use images of Nature to describe the religious meaning and mission of what one cultural historian has called "Nature's nation."

From "Gods Promise to His Plantations" (1630)

Quest. What is it for God to plant a people?

Answr. It is a Metaphor taken from young Impes; I will plant them, that is, I will make them to take roote there; and that is, where they and their soyle agree well together, when they are well and sufficiently provided for, as a plant suckes nourishment from the soyle that fitteth it.

Secondly, When hee causeth them to grow as plants doe, in *Psal.* 80. 8, 9, 10, 11. When a man growes like a tree in tallnesse and strength, to more firmnesse and eminency, then hee may be said to be planted.

Thirdly, When God causeth them to *fructifie. Psal.* 1.5.

Fourthly, When he establisheth them there, then he plants, and rootes not up.

But here is something more especiall in this planting; for they were planted before in this land, and yet he promiseth here againe, that he will plant them

in their owne land; which doth imply first, That whatever former good estate they had already, he would prosper it, and increase it.

Secondly, God is said to plant a people more especially when they become *Trees of righteousnesse, Isay.* 61.3: That they may be called trees of righteousnesse, the planting of the Lord. So that there is implyed not onely a continuance of their former good estate, but that hee would make them a good people, a choice generation; which he did, first, by planting the Ordinances of God amongst them in a more glorious manner, as he did in *Salomons* time.

2. He would give his poeple a *a naile*, and *a place in his Tabernable, Isay.* 56.5. And that is to give us part in Christ; for so the Temple typified. So then hee plants us when hee gives us roote in Christ.

Thirdly, When he giveth us to *grow up in him as Calves in the stall. Mal.* 4.2, 3.

Fourthly, & to *bring forth much fruit,* Joh. 15.1, 2.

Fifthly, and to continue and abide in the state of grace. This is to plant us in his holy Sanctuary, he not rooting us up.

Reasons. This is taken from the kinde acceptance of *Davids* purpose to build God an house, because he saw it was done in the honesty of his heart, therefore he promiseth to give his people a place wherein they should abide forever as in a house of rest.

Secondly, it is taken from the office God takes upon him, when he is our planter, hee becomes our husbandman; and *if he plants us, who shall plucke us up? Isay.* 27.1, 2. *Job.* 34.29. When he giveth quiet, who can make trouble? If God be the Gardiner, who shall plucke up what he sets down? Every plantation that he hath not planted shall be plucked up, and what he hath planted shall surely be established.

Thirdly, from the nature of the blessing hee conferres upon us: When he promiseth to plant a people, their dayes shall be as the dayes of a Tree, *Isay.* 65.22: As the Oake is said to be an hundred yeares in growing, and an hundred yeares in decaying.

up in the sight of the entire world. He believed that the American Puritans had a special mission on behalf of Christendom, and was certain that these New World settlers had been divinely selected for this task and had made a covenant with their God. These assumptions, even though dissociated from their specific theological content, would decisively shape the religious imagination of subsequent generations of Americans.

John Winthrop (1587–1649)

John Winthrop was the first governor of the colony established at Massachusetts Bay in 1630. He was one of a small number of first-generation religious leaders whose beliefs and mode of life greatly influenced the formation of the American commonwealth and character. From Winthrop's *Journal,* begun as the small fleet of vessels was gathering off the Isle of Wight preparatory to the perilous Atlantic crossing, it is clear that he saw himself as a latter-day Moses leading his people to a New World Canaan.

The sermon "A Modell of Christian Charity" was delivered aboard the flagship Arabella; it expressed the social and theological ideal that the Puritans hoped to realize in the New World. Winthrop saw the American colony as an exemplary "City upon a Hill," raised

From "A Modell of Christian Charity" (1630)

God Almightie in his most holy and wise providence hath soe disposed of the Condicion of mankinde, as in all times some must be rich some poore, some highe and eminent in power and dignitie; others meane and in subieccion.

The Reason Hereof.

1. Reas: *First,* to hold conformity with the rest of his workes, being delighted to shewe for the glory of his wisdome in the variety and differance of the Creatures and the glory of his power, in ordering all these differences for the preservation and good of the whole, and the glory of his greatnes that as it is the glory of princes to have many officers, soe this great King will have many Stewards counting himselfe more honoured in dispenceing his guifts to man by man, then if hee did it by his owne immediate hand.

2. Reas: *Secondly,* That he might have the more occasion to manifest the worke of his Spirit: first, upon the wicked in moderateing and restraineing them: soe that the riche and mighty should not eate upp the poore, nor the poore, and dispised rise upp against theire superiours, and shake off theire yoake; 2ly in the regenerate in exercising his graces in them, as in the greate ones, theire love mercy, gentlenes, temperance etc., in the poore and inferiour sorte, theire faithe patience, obedience etc:

3. Reas: Thirdly, That every man might have need of other, and from hence they might be all knitt more nearly together in the Bond of brotherly affeccion: from hence it appeares plainely that noe man is made more honourable then another or more wealthy etc., out of any perticuler and singuler respect to himselfe but for the glory of his Creator and the Common good of the Creature, Man; Therefore God still reserves the propperty of these guifts to himselfe as Ezek: 16. 17. he there calls wealthe his gold and his silver etc. Prov: 3. 9. he claimes theire service as his due honour the Lord with thy riches etc. All men being thus (by divine providence) rancked into two sortes, riche and poore; under the first, are comprehended all such as are able to live comfortably by theire owne meanes duely improved; and all others are poore according to the former distribution. There are two rules whereby wee are to walke one towards another: JUSTICE and MERCY. These are allwayes distinguished in theire Act and in theire object, yet may they both concurre in the same Subject in eache respect; as sometimes there may be an occasion of shewing mercy to a rich man, in some sudden danger of distresse, and allsoe doeing of meere Justice to a poor man in regard of some perticuler contract etc. There is likewise a double Lawe by which wee are regulated in our conversacion one towardes another: in both the former respects, the lawe of nature and the lawe of grace, or the morrall lawe or the lawe of the gospell, to omitt the rule of Justice as not propperly belonging to this purpose otherwise then it may fall into consideracion in some perticuler Cases: By the first of these lawes man as he was enabled soe withall [is] commaunded to love his neighbour as himselfe upon this ground stands all the precepts of the morrall lawe, which concernes our dealings with men. To apply this to the works of mercy this lawe requires two things: First, that every man afford his help to another in every want or distresse; Secondly, That hee performe this out of the same affeccion, which makes him carefull of his owne good according to that of our Saviour Math: [7:12] Whatsoever ye woudl that men should doe to you. This was practised by Abraham and Lott in entertaineing the Angells and the old man of Gibea.

The Lawe of Grace or the Gospell hath some difference from the former as in these respectes first the lawe of nature was given to man in the estate of innocency; this of the gospell in the estate of regeneracy; 2ly, the former propounds one man to another, as the same fleshe and Image of god, this as a brother in Christ allsoe, and in the Communion of the same spirit and soe teacheth us to put a difference betweene Christians and others. Doe good to all especially to the household of faith; upon this ground the Israelites were to putt a difference betweene the brethren of such as were strangers though not of the Canaanites. 3ly. The Lawe of nature coule give noe rules for dealeing with enemies for all are to be considered as freinds in the estate of innocency, but the Gospell commaunds love to an enemy. proofe. If thine Enemie hunger feede him; Love your Enemies doe good to them that hate you Math: 5.44.

This Lawe of the Gospell propoundes likewise a difference of seasons and occasions. There is a time when a christian must sell all and give to the poore as they did in the Apostles times. There is a tyme allsoe when a christian (though they give not all yet) must give beyond theire ability, as they of Macedonia. Cor: 2. 6. Likewise community of perills calls for extraordinary liberallity and soe doth Community in some speciall service for the Churche. Lastly, when there is noe other meanes whereby our Christian brother may be releived in this distresse, wee must help him beyond our ability, rather then tempt God, in putting him upon help by miraculous or extraordinary meanes. . . .

It rests now to make some application of this discourse by the present designe which gave the occasion of writeing of it. Herein are 4 things to be propounded: first the persons, 2ly, the worke, 3ly, the end, 4ly the meanes.

1. For the persons, wee are a Company professing our selves fellow members of Christ, In which respect onely though wee were absent from eache other many miles, and had our imploy-

mentes as farre distant, yet wee ought to account our selves knitt together by this bond of love, and live in the excercise of it, if wee would have comforte of our being in Christ. . . .

2ly. for the worke wee have in hand, it is by a mutuall consent through a speciall overruleing providence, and a more then an ordinary approbation of the Churches of Christ to seeke out a place of Cohabitation and Consorteshipp under a due forme of Government both civill and ecclesiasticall. In such cases as this the care of the publique must oversway all private respects, by which not onely conscience, but meare Civill pollicy doth binde us; for it is a true rule that perticuler estates cannott subsist in the ruine of the publique.

3ly. The end is to improve our lives to doe more service to the Lord the comforte and encrease of the body of christe whereof wee are members that our selves and posterity may be the better preserved from the Common corrupcions of this evill world to serve the Lord and worke out our Salvacion under the power and purity of his holy Ordinances.

4ly. for the meanes whereby this must bee effected, they are 2fold, a Conformity with the worke and end wee aime at, these wee see are extraordinary, therefore wee must not content our selves with usuall ordinary meanes whatsoever wee did or ought to have done when wee lived in England, the same must wee doe and more allsoe wher wee goe: That which the most in theire Churches maineteine as a truthe in profession onely, wee must bring into familiar and constant practise, as in this duty of love wee must love brotherly without dissimulation, wee must love one another with a pure hearte fervently, wee must beare one anothers burthens, wee must not looke onely on our owne things, but allsoe on the things of our brethren, neither must wee think that the lord will beare with such faileings at our hands as hee dothe from these among whome wee have lived. . . . Thus stands the cause betweene God and us, wee are entered into Covenant with him for this worke, wee have taken out a Commission, the Lord hath given us leave to drawe our owne Articles wee have professed to enterprise these Accions upon these and these ends, wee have hereupon besought him of favour and blessing: Now if the Lord shall please to heare us, and bring us in peace to the place wee desire, then hath hee ratified this Covenant and sealed our Commission, [and] will expect a strickt performance of the Articles contained in it, but if wee shall neglect the observacion of these Articles which are the ends wee have propounded, and dissembling with our God, shall fall to embrace this present world and prosecute our carnall intencions, seekeing greate things for our selves and our posterity, the Lord will surely breake out in wrathe against us be revenged of such a periured people and make us knowe the price of the breache of such a Covenant.

Now the onely way to avoyde this shipwracke and to provide for our posterity is to followe the Counsell of Micha, to doe Justly, to love mercy, to walke humbly with our God, for this end, wee must be knitt together in this worke as one man, wee must entertaine each other in brotherly Affeccion, wee must be willing to abridge our selves of our superfluities, for the supply of others necessities, wee must uphold a familiar Commerce together in all meekenes, gentlenes, patience and liberallity, wee must delight in eache other, make others Condicions our owne reioyce together, mourne together, labour, and suffer together, allwayes haveing before our eyes our Commission and Community in the worke, our Community as members of the same body, soe shall wee keepe the unitie of the spirit in the bond of peace, the Lord will be our God and delight to dwell among us, as his owne people and will commaund a blessing upon us in all our wayes, soe that we shall see much more of his wisdome power goodnes and truthe then formerly wee have beene acquainted with, wee shall finde that the God of Israell is among us, when tenn of us shall be able to resist a thousand of our enemies, when hee shall make us a prayse and glory, that men shall say of succeeding plantacions: the lord make it like that of New England: for wee must Consider that wee shall be as a Citty upon a Hill, the eies of all people are uppon us; soe that if wee shall deale falsely with our god in this worke wee have undertaken and soe cause him to withdrawe his present help from us, wee shall be made a story and a by-word through the world, wee shall open the mouthes of enemies to speake evill of the wayes of god and all professours for Gods sake; we shall shame the faces of many of gods worthy servants, and cause theire prayers to be turned into Cursses upon' us till wee be consumed out of the good land whether wee are goeing: And to shutt upp this discourse with that exhortacion of Moses that faithfull servant of the Lord in his last farewell to Israell Deut. 30. Beloved there is now sett before us life, and good, deathe and evill in that wee are Commaunded this day to love the Lord our God, and to love one another to walke in his wayes and to keepe his Commaundements and his Ordinance, and his lawes, and the Articles of our Covenant with him that wee may live and be multiplyed, and that the Lord our God may blesse us in the land whether wee goe to possesse it: But if our heartes shall turne away soe that wee will not obey, but shall be seduced and worshipp other Gods, our pleasures, and proffitts, and serve them; it is propounded unto us this day, wee shall surely perishe out of the good Land whether wee passe over this vast Sea to possesse it:

> Therefore lett us choose life,
>   that wee, and our Seede,
>   may live; by obeying his
>   voyce, and cleaveing to him,
>   for hee is our life, and
>   our prosperity.

Thomas Morton
(1590?–1647)

Thomas Morton (1590?–1647), reputed (the record is unclear) to have been an English "petiefogger" or lawyer, came to Massachusetts as a trader in 1622. He was a gentleman of decidedly loose moral principles who attracted a disreputable band of rowdies to his home at Merry Mount. The Anglican Morton quickly aroused the suspicion and ire of his Puritan neighbors, partly by selling liquor and arms to the Indians. He was eventually imprisoned and twice sent back to England. During one period of exile, Morton set down his somewhat idiosyncratic views of America in *New English Canann.* Despite the Biblical title, Morton describes the New World experiment in terms considerably at variance with Puritan orthodoxy. The following selection is a song composed for Morton's notorious "Maypole" revels. It invokes a deity not recognized by his Christian neighbors.

From *New English Canaan* (1637)

Drinke and be merry, merry, merry
  boyes;
Let all your delight be in the Hymens
  ioyes;
Iô [Hail] to Hymen, now the day is
  come,
About the merry Maypole take a
  Roome.
  Make greene garlonds, bring bottles
    out
  And fill sweet Nectar, freely about.
  Uncover thy head and feare no
    harme,
  For hers good liquor to keep it
    warme.

Then drinke and be merry, &c.
Iô to Hymen, &c.
 Nectar is a thing assign'd
 by the Deities owne minde
 To cure the hart opprest with greife,
 And of good liquors is the cheife.
Then drinke, &c.
Iô to Hymen, &c.
 Give to the Mellancolly man
 A cup or two of 't now and than;
 This physick will soone revive his
  bloud,
 And made him be of a merrier
  mode.
Then drinke, &c.
Iô to Hymen, &c.
 Give to the Nymphe thats free from
  scorne
 No Irish stuff nor Scotch over
  worne.
 Lasses in beaver coats come away,
 Yee shall be welcome to us night
  and day.
To drinke and be merry, &c.
Iô to Hymen, &c.

Roger Williams
(1613–1683)

Often described as the father of religious tolerance in America, Roger Williams emigrated to New England in 1631. He was soon banished from the Massachusetts Bay Colony for his democratic views of church government. He eventually made his way to present-day Rhode Island where he established the first settlement at Providence in 1636. He finally succeeded in obtaining a charter for the new colony in 1644. Famous for his work among the Indians, in 1643 Williams published the first book on their language, *A Key into the Language of America.* Williams continued to move toward the theological Left, from Separatist to Baptist and finally to "Seeker"—repudiating all orthodox creeds without abandoning his basic allegiance to the Christian faith.

The first selection is taken from William's most celebrated work, *The Bloudy Tenent of Persecution,* which was written in protest against the doctrine that God requires uniformity in religious belief and practice. Williams insisted that all religious groups and individuals were entitled to religious liberty as a natural right. He thus anticipated such Enlightenment thinkers as Benjamin Franklin and Thomas Jefferson, who would call for the separation of church and state and insist on the state's civil responsibility to protect religious freedom.

In the second selection, from *The Hireling Ministry None of Christs,* Williams contends that freedom of belief will in fact assist rather than impede the spread of Christianity in America.

From *The Bloudy Tenent of Persecution* (1644)

First, That the blood of so many hundred thousand soules of Protestants and Papists, spilt in the Wars of present and former Ages, for their respective Consciences, is not required nor accepted by Jesus Christ the Prince of Peace.

Secondly, Pregnant Scriptures and Arguments are throughout the Worke proposed against the Doctrine of persecution for cause of Conscience.

Thirdly, Satisfactorie Answers are given to Scriptures, and objections produced by Mr. Calvin, Beza, Mr. Cotton, and the Ministers of the New English Churches and others former and later, tending to prove the Doctrine of persecution for cause of Conscience.

Fourthly, The Doctrine of persecution for cause of Conscience, is proved guilty of all the blood of the Soules crying for vengeance under the Altar.

Fifthly, All Civill States with their Officers of justice in their respective constitutions and administrations are proved essentially Civill, and therefore not Judges, Governours or Defendours of the Spirituall or Christian state and Worship.

Sixthly, It is the will and command of God, that (since the comming of his Sonne the Lord Jesus) a permission of the most Paganish, Jewish, Turkish, or Antichristian consciences and worships, bee granted to all men in all Nations and Countries: and they are onely to bee fought against with that Sword which is only (in Soule matters) able to conquer, to wit, the Swords of Gods Spirit, the Word of God.

Seventhly, The State of the Land of Israel, the Kings and people thereof in Peace & War, is proved figurative and ceremoniall, and no patterne nor president for any Kingdome or civill state in the world to follow.

Eighthly, God requireth not an uniformity of Religion to be inacted and inforced in any civill state; which inforced uniformity (sooner or later) is the greatest occasion of civill Warre, ravishing of conscience, persecution of Christ Jesus in his servants, and of the hypocrisie and destruction of millions of souls.

Ninthly, In holding an inforced uniformity of Religion in a civill state, we must necessarily disclaime our desires and hopes of the Jewes conversion to Christ.

Tenthly, An inforced uniformity of Religion throughout a Nation or civill state, confounds the Civill and Religious, denies the principles of Christianity and civility, and that Jesus Christ is come in the Flesh.

Eleventhly, The permission of other consciences and worships then a state professeth, only can (according to God) procure a firme and lasting peace (good assurance being taken according to the wisdome of the civill state for uniformity of civill obedience from all sorts.)

Twelfthly, lastly, true civility and Christianity may both flourish in a state or Kingdome, notwithstanding the permission of divers and contrary consciences, either of Jew or Gentile. . . .

From *The Hireling Ministry None of Christs* (1652)

What is then the express duty of the Civill Magistrate, as to Christ Jesus his Gospell and Kingdome?

I answer, I know how wofully that Scripture, Kings shall be they nursing Fathers, &c, hath been abused, and elsewhere I have at large discussed that, and other such Objections: At present, I humbly conceive, that the great Duty of the Magistrate as to spirituals, will turne upon these two Hinges.

First, In removing the Civill Bars, Obstructions, Hinderances, in taking of those Yoaks, that pinch the very Soules and consciences of men, such as yet are the payments of Tithes, and the Maintenance of Ministers, they have not faith in: Such are the inforced Oaths, and some ceremonies therein, in all the Courts of Justice, such are the holy Marryings, holy buryings, &c.

Secondly, In a free and absolute permission of the consciences of all men, in what is meerly spirituall, not the very consciences of the Jews, nor the consciences of the Turkes or Papists, or Pagans themselves excepted.

But how will this Propagate the Gospell of Christ Jesus?

I answer thus, The first grand Design of Christ Jesus is, to destroy and consume his Mortal enemy Antichrist. This must be done by the breath of his Mouth in his Prophets and Witnesses: Now the Nations of the World, have impiously stopt this heavenly breath, and stifled the Lord Jesus in his Servants: Now if it shall please the civill State to remove the state bars, set up to resist the holy Spirit of God in his servants (whom yet finally to resist, is not in all the powers of the world) I humbly conceive that the civill state hath made a fair progresse in promoting the Gospel of Jesus Christ.

This Mercy and freedome is due to the (meerly) religious consciences of all men in the world. Is there no more due from the Magistrate to Christ Jesus his saints and Kingdome?

I answer, While I plead the Conscience of All men to be at Liberty, doubtlesse I must plead the Liberty of the Magistrates conscience also, and therefore were his bounties and donations to his Bishops and Ministers, as large as those of Constantine; who, but the holy Spirit of God in the mouths of his Prophets can restrain him? Onely let not Caesar, (as Constantine in his setled prosperity did) rob the God of Heaven of his Rights and Liberties.

. . . It is the duty of all that are in Authority, and of all that are able, to countenance, incourage, and supply such true Voluntiers as give and devote themselves to the service and Ministry of Christ Jesus in any kind: although it be also the duty, and will be the practice of all such whom the Spirit of God sends upon any work of Christs, rather to work as Paul did, among the Corinthians and Thessalonians, then the work and service of their Lord and Master, should be neglected.

Such true Christian worthies (whether endowed with humane Learning, or without it) will alone be found that despised modell which the God of Heaven will onely blesse; that poor handfull and three hundred out of Israels thirty two thousand by whom the work of the God of Israel must be effected.[38] And if this course be effected in the three Nations, the bodies and soules of the three Nations will be more and more at peace, and in a fairer way than ever, to that peace which is Eternall when this world is gone.

William Bradford (1590–1657)

William Bradford was among the first group of Pilgrims who arrived in America aboard the *Mayflower* in 1620. He was the undisputed leader of the Plymouth colony during its early period, and served for almost thirty years as its governor. Bradford began to write his history of the Plymouth plantation about 1630, but did not complete it until 1651.

Of Plymouth Plantation is a theological history of the first New England settlement. To Bradford the destiny of the Plymouth colony was guided by divine Providence, and he believed that the history of the colony would arouse in the minds and hearts of his readers that sense of inspiration and thanksgiving which the experience had brought to the hearts and minds of those who had lived it. His narrative includes many striking and representative images: the plight of the Pilgrims waiting in Holland for an opportunity to sail, as circumstances became more and more difficult and time began to grow short for the older members of the community; the mixture of hope and dread with which the Pilgrims faced the prospect of the dangerous crossing to an unknown land; the courageous realism of the

Pilgrims in assessing their chances of survival and success; the unwelcoming aspect of their new home when they first reached the shores of America; the heavy toll in suffering and death endured during the earliest months in the New World; and the quiet heroism and devotion of the few unstricken Pilgrims who nursed the colony through its first winter of sickness and despair. With his vivid and moving account of the Pilgrims' arrival in America, Bradford planted some of the most durable images which subsequent generations of Americans would use to define themselves religiously—of America as a kind of last chance for mankind; of the American adventure as a voyage into the unknown and the untried; of the American people as a community knit together by suffering and upheld by realistic hope; and of the American experience as representative of triumph over adversity and victory over death.

From *Of Plymouth Plantation* (1630–1651)

Chapter IV. *Showing the Reasons and Causes of Their Removal*

After they had lived in this city [Leyden, Holland] about some eleven or twelve years . . . and sundry of them were taken away by death and many others began to be well stricken in years (the grave mistress of Experience having taught them many things), those prudent governors with sundry of the sagest members began both deeply to apprehend their present dangers and wisely to foresee the future and think of timely remedy. In the agitation of their thoughts, and much discourse of things hereabout, at length they began to incline to this conclusion: of removal to some other place. Not out of any newfangledness or other such like giddy humor by which men are oftentimes transported to their great hurt and danger, but for sundry weighty and solid reasons, some of the chief of which I will here briefly touch.

And first, they saw and found by experience the hardness of the place and country to be such as few in comparison would come to them, and fewer that would bide it out and continue with them. For many that came to them, and many more that desired to be with them, could not endure that great labour and hard fare, with other inconveniences which they underwent and were contented with. . . . Yea, some preferred and chose the prisons in England rather than this liberty in Holland with these afflictions. But it was thought that if a better and easier place of living could be had, it would draw many and take away these discouragements. . . .

Secondly. They say that though the people generally bore all these difficulties very cheerfully and with a resolute courage, being in the best and strength of their years, yet old age began to steal on many of them; and their great and continual labours, with other crosses and sorrows, hastened it before the time. So as it was not only probably thought, but apparently seen, that within a few years more they would be in danger to scatter, by necessities pressing them, or sink under their burdens, or both. . . .

Thirdly. As necessity was a taskmaster over them so they were forced to be such, not only to their servants but in a sort to their dearest children, the which as it did not a little wound the tender hearts of many a loving father and mother, so it produced likewise sundry sad and sorrowful effects. For many of their children that were of best dispositions and gracious inclinations, having learned to bear the yoke in their youth and willing to bear part of their parents' burden, were oftentimes so oppressed with their heavy labours that though their minds were free and willing, yet their bodies bowed under the weight of the same, and became decrepit in their early youth, the vigour of nature being consumed in the very bud as it were. But that which was more lamentable, and of all sorrows most heavy to be borne, was that many of their children, by these occasions and the great licentiousness of youth in that country, and the manifold temptations of the place, were drawn away by evil examples into extravagant and dangerous courses, getting the reins off their necks and departing from their parents. . . .

Lastly (and which was not least), a great hope and inward zeal they had of laying some good foundation, or at least to make some way thereunto, for the propagating and advancing the gospel of the kingdom of Christ in those remote parts of the world; yea, though they should be but even as steppingstones unto others for the performing of so great a work.

These and some other like reasons moved them to undertake this resolution of their removal; the which they afterward prosecuted with so great difficulties, as by the sequel will appear.

The place they had thoughts on was some of those vast and unpeopled countries of America, which are fruitful and fit for habitation, being devoid of all civil inhabitants, where there are only savage and brutish men which range up and down, little otherwise than the wild beasts of the same. This proposition being made public and coming to the scanning of all, it raised many variable opinions amongst men and caused many fears and doubts amongst themselves. Some, from their reasons and hopes conceived, laboured to stir up and encourage the rest to undertake and prosecute the same; others again, out of their fears, objected against it and sought to divert from it; alleging many things, and those neither unreasonable nor unprobable; as that it was a great design and subject to many unconceivable perils and dangers; as, besides the casualties of the sea (which none can be freed from), the length of the voyage was such as the weak bodies of women and other persons worn out with age and travail (as many of them were) could never be able to endure. And yet if they should, the miseries of the land which they should be exposed unto would be too hard to be borne and likely, some or all of them together, to consume and utterly to ruinate them. For there they should be liable to famine and nakedness and the want, in a manner, of all things. The change of air, diet and drinking of water would infect their bodies with sore sicknesses and grievous diseases. And also those which should escape or overcome these difficulties should yet be in continual danger of the savage people, who are cruel, barbarous and most treacherous, being most furious in their rage and merciless where they overcome; not being content only to kill and take away life, but delight to torment men in the most bloody manner that may be; flaying some alive with the shells of fishes, cutting off the members and joints of others by piecemeal and broiling on the coals, eat the collops of their flesh in their sight whilst they live, with other cruelties horrible to be related.

And surely it could not be thought but the very hearing of these things could not but move the very bowels of men to grate within them and make the weak to quake and tremble. It was further objected that it would require greater sums of money to furnish such a voyage and to fit them with necessaries, than their consumed estates would amount to; and yet they must as well look to be seconded with supplies as presently to be transported. Also many precedents of ill success and lamentable miseries befallen others in the like designs were easy to be found, and not forgotten to be alleged; besides their own experience, in their former troubles and hardship in their removal into Holland, and how hard a thing it was for them to live in that strange place, though it was a neighbor country and a civil and rich commonwealth.

It was answered, that all great and honorable actions are accompanied with great difficulties and must be both enterprised and overcome with answerable courages. It was granted the dangers were great, but not desperate. The difficulties were many, but not invincible. For though there were many of them likely, yet they were not certain. It might be sundry of the things feared might never befall; others by provident care and the use of good means might in a great measure be prevented; and all of them, through the help of God, by fortitude and patience, might either be borne or overcome. True it was that such attempts were not to be made and undertaken without good ground and reason, not rashly or lightly as many have done for curiosity or hope of gain, etc. But their condition was not ordinary, their ends were good and honorable, their calling lawful and urgent; and therefore they might expect the blessing of God in their preceeding. Yea, though they should lose their lives in this action, yet might they have comfort in the same and their endeavors would be honorable. . . .

Chapter IX. *Of their Voyage, and how they Passed the Sea; and of their Safe Arrival at Cape Cod*

These troubles being blown over, and now all being compact together in one ship, they put to sea again with a prosperous wind, which continued divers days together, which was some encouragement unto them; yet, according to the usual manner, many were afflicted with seasickness. . . .

After they had enjoyed fair winds and weather for a season, they were encountered many times with cross winds and met with many fierce storms with which the ship was shrewdly shaken, and her upper works made very leaky; and one of the main beams in the midships was bowed and cracked, which put them in some fear that the ship could not be able to perform the voyage. . . .

In sundry of these storms the winds were so fierce and the seas so high, as they could not bear a knot of sail, but were forced to hull for divers days together. . . .

But to omit the other things (that I may be brief), after long beating at sea they fell with that land which is called Cape Cod; that which being made and certainly known to be it, they were not a little joyful. . . .

Being thus arrived in a good harbor, and brought safe to land, they fell upon their knees and blessed the God of heaven who had brought them over the vast and furious ocean, and delivered them from all the perils and miseries thereof, again to set their feet on the firm and stable earth, their proper element. And no marvel if they were thus joyful, seeing wise Seneca was so affected with sailing a few miles on the coast of his own Italy, as he affirmed, that he had rather remain twenty years on his way by land than pass by sea to any place in a short time, so tedious and dreadful was the same unto him.

But here I cannot but stay and make a pause, and stand half amazed at this poor people's present condition; and so I think will the reader, too, when he well considers the same. Being thus passed the vast ocean, and a sea of troubles before in their preparation (as may be remembered by that which went before), they had now no friends to welcome them nor inns to entertain or refresh their weatherbeaten bodies; no houses or much less towns to repair to, to seek for succour. It is recorded in Scripture, as a mercy to the Apostle and his shipwrecked company, that the barbarians showed them no small kindness in refreshing them, but these savage barbarians, when they met with them (as after will appear), were readier to fill their sides full of arrows than otherwise. And for the season it was winter, and they that know the winters of that country know them to be sharp and violent, and subject to cruel and fierce storms, dangerous to travel to known places, much more to search an unknown coast. Besides, what could they see but a hideous and desolate wilderness, full of wild beasts and wild men— and what multitudes there might be of them they knew not. Neither could they, as it were, go up to the top of Pisgah to view from this wilderness a more goodly country to feed their hopes; for which way soever they turned their eyes (save upward to the heavens) they could have little solace or content in respect of any outward objects. For summer being done, all things stand upon them with a weatherbeaten face, and the whole country, full of woods and thickets, represented a wild and savage hue. If they looked behind them, there was the mighty ocean which they had passed and was now as a main bar and gulf to separate them from all the civil parts of the world. If it be said they had a ship to

succour them, it is true; but what heard they daily from the master and company? But that with speed they should look out a place (with their shallop) where they would be, at some near distance; for the season was such as he would not stir from thence till a safe harbor was discovered by them, where they would be, and he might go without danger; and that victuals consumed apace but he must and would keep sufficient for themselves and their return. Yea, it was uttered by some that if they got not a place in time, they would turn them and their goods ashore and leave them. Let it also be considered what weak hopes of supply and succour they left behind them, that might bear up their minds in this sad condition and trials they were under; and they would not but be very small. It is true, indeed, the affections and love of their brethren at Leyden was cordial and entire towards them, but they had little power to help them or themselves. . . .

What could now sustain them but the spirit of God and His grace? May not and ought not the children of these fathers rightly say: "Our fathers were Englishmen which came over this great ocean, and were ready to perish in this wilderness; but they cried unto the Lord, and He heard their voice and looked on their adversity" (Deut. 26:5,7), "Let them therefore praise the Lord, because He is good: and His mercies endure forever. Yea, let them which have been redeemed of the Lord, shew how He hath delivered them from the hand of the oppressor. When they wandered in the desert wilderness out of the way, and found no city to dwell in, both hungry and thirsty, their soul was overwhelmed in them. Let them confess before the Lord His loving kindness and His wonderful works before the sons of men" (Psal. 107:1–5, 8). . . .

❧❧❧

Chapter XI. *The Remainder of Anno 1620*

. . . In these hard and difficult beginnings they found some discontents and murmurings arise amongst some, and mutinous speeches and carriages in others; but they were soon quelled and overcome by the wisdom, patience, and just equal carriage of things, by the governor and better part, which clave faithfully together in the main.

But that which was most sad and lamentable was, that in two or three months' time half of their company died, especially in January and February, being the depth of winter, and wanting houses and other comforts; being infected with the scurvy and other diseases which this long voyage and their inaccommodate condition had brought upon them. So as there died sometimes two or three of a day in the foresaid time, that of one hundred and odd persons, scarce fifty remained. And of these in the time of most distress, there was but six or seven sound persons who to their great commendations, be it spoken, spared no pains night nor day, but with abundance of toil and hazard of their own health, fetched them wood, made them fires, dressed them meat, made their beds, washed their loathsome clothes, clothed and unclothed them. In a word, did all the homely and necessary offices for them which dainty and queasy stomachs cannot endure to hear named; and all this willingly and cheerfully, without any grudging in the least, showing herein their true love unto their friends and brethren; a rare example and worthy to be remembered. Two of these seven were Mr. William Brewster, their reverend Elder, and Myles Standish, their Captain and military commander, unto whom myself and many others were much beholden in our low and sick condition. And yet the Lord so upheld these persons as in this general calamity they were not at all infected either with sickness or lameness. And what I have said of these I may say of many others who died in this general visitation, and others yet living; that whilst they had heath, yea, or any strength continuing, they were not wanting to any that had need of them. And I doubt not but their recompense is with the Lord.

❧❧❧❧❧❧❧❧❧❧❧❧❧❧

Anne Bradstreet (1612?–1672)

Anne Bradstreet (1612?–1672) came to America aboard the *Arabella* in 1630. She must have heard John Winthrop's sermon proclaiming the great work to which the Massachusetts Bay colonists were called, but she was at first unenthusiastic about Winthrop's "City upon a Hill." In her sixtieth year she wrote to her children (in the letter here reproduced) that on her arrival she had "found a new world and new manners" against which her "heart rose" in rebellion.

Anne Bradstreet was able to overcome her early apprehensions and her initial resistance to the American wilderness, but the candor of her response to the often harsh realities of her experience continued to be an outstanding characteristic of her writing. As each of the three poems included here makes clear, her sensitivity of feeling colored her Puritan orthodoxy in subtle and unexpected ways. She knew religion as an affair of the heart as well as of the intellect, and felt the necessity to bring these two aspects of religious experience into harmony. In this respect, Anne Bradstreet anticipated later American thinkers as diverse as Jonathan Edwards, Walt Whitman, and F. Scott Fitzgerald, who would see in the image of America itself a spiritual force with the power to clarify and intensify the responses of the human heart.

"To My Dear Children" (1672)

This Book by Any yet unread
I leave for you when I am dead,
That, being gone, here you may find
What was your living mother's mind.
Make use of what I leave in Love
And God shall bless you from above.

A.B.

My Dear Children,

I, knowing by experience that the exhortations of parents take most effect when the speakers leave to speak, and those especially sink deepest which are spoke latest—and being ignorant whether on my death bed I shall have opportunity to speak to any of you, much less to All—thought it best, whilst I was able to compose some short matters, (for what else to call them I know not) and bequeath to you, that when I am no more with you, yet I may be daily in your remembrance, (Although that is the least in my aim in what I now do) but that you may gain some spiritual Advantage by my experience. I have not studied in this you read to show my skill, but to declare the Truth—not to set forth myself, but the Glory of God. If I had minded the former, it had been perhaps better pleasing to you,—but seeing that last is the best, let it be best pleasing to you.

The method I will observe shall be this—I will begin with God's dealing with me from my childhood to this Day. In my young years, about 6 or 7 as I take it, I began to make conscience of my ways, and what I knew was sinful, as lying, disobedience to Parents, etc. I avoided it. If at any time I was overtaken with the like evils, it was a great Trouble. I could not be at rest 'til by prayer I had confest it unto God. I was also troubled at the neglect of Private Duties, though: too often tardy that way. I also found much comfort in reading the Scriptures, especially those places I thought most concerned my Condition, and as I grew to have more understanding, so the more solace I took in them.

In a long fit of sickness which I had on my bed I often communed with my heart, and made my supplication to the most High who set me free from that affliction.

But as I grew up to be about 14 or 15 I found my heart more carnal, and sitting loose from God, vanity and the follies of youth take hold of me.

About 16, the Lord laid his hand sore upon me and smote me with the small-pox. When I was in my affliction, I besought the Lord, and confessed my Pride and Vanity and he was entreated of me, and again restored me. But I rendered not to him according to the benefit received.

After a short time I changed my condition and was married, and came into this Country, where I found a new world and new manners, at which my heart rose. But after I was convinced it was the way of God, I submitted to it and joined to the church at Boston.

After some time I fell into a lingering sickness like a consumption, together with a lameness, which correction I saw the Lord sent to humble and try me and do me Good: and it was not altogether ineffectual.

It pleased God to keep me a long time without a child, which was a great grief to me, and cost me many prayers and tears before I obtained one, and after him gave me many more, of whom I now take the care, that as I have brought you into the world, and with great pains, weakness, cares, and fears brought you to this, I now travail in birth again of you till Christ be formed in you.

Among all my experiences of God's gracious Dealings with me I have constantly observed this, that he hath never suffered me long to sit loose from him, but by one affliction or other hath made me look home, and search what was amiss—so usually thus it hath been with me that I have no sooner felt my heart out of order, but I have expected correction for it, which most commonly hath been upon my own person, in sickness, weakness, pains, sometimes on my soul, in Doubts and fears of God's displeasure, and my sincerity towards him, sometimes he hath smote a child with sickness, sometimes chastened by losses in estate,—and these Times (through: his great mercy) have been times of my greatest Getting and Advantage, yea I have found them the Times when the Lord hath manifested the most Love to me. Then have I gone to searching, and have said with David, Lord search me and try me, see what ways of wickedness are in me, and lead me in the way everlasting: and seldom or never but I have found either some sin I lay under which God would have reformed, or some duty neglected which he would have performed. And by his help I have laid Vows and Bonds upon my Soul to perform his righteous commands.

If at any time you are chastened of God, take it as thankfully and joyfully as in greatest mercies, for if you be his you shall reap the greatest benefit by it. It hath been no small support to me in times of Darkness when the Almighty hath hid his face from me, that yet I have had abundance of sweetness and refreshment after affliction, and more circumspection in my walking after I have been afflicted. I have been with God like an untoward child, that no longer then the rod has been on my back (or at least in fight) but I have been apt to forget him and myself too. Before I was afflicted I went astray, but now I keep thy statutes.

I have had great experience of God's hearing my Prayers, and returning comfortable Answers to me, either in granting the Thing I prayed for, or else in satisfying my mind without it; and I have been confident it hath been from him, because I have found my heart through his goodness enlarged in thankfulness to him.

I have often been perplexed that I have not found that constant joy in my pilgrimage and refreshing which I supposed most of the servants of God have; although he hath not left me altogether without the witness of his holy spirit, who hath oft given me his word and set to his Seal that it shall be well with me. I have sometimes tasted of that hidden Manna that the world knows not, and have set up my Ebenezer, and have resolved with myself that against such a promise, such tastes of sweetness, the Gates of Hell shall never prevail. Yet have I many times sinkings and droopings, and not enjoyed that felicity that sometimes I have done. But when I have been in darkness and seen no light, yet have I desired to stay myself upon the Lord.

And, when I have been in sickness and pain, I have thought if the Lord would but lift up the light of his Countenance upon me, although: he ground me to powder, it would be but light to me; yea, oft have I thought were it hell itself, and could there find the Love of God toward me, it would be a Heaven. And, could I have been in Heaven without the Love of God, it would have been a Hell to me; for, in Truth, it is the absence and presence of God that make Heaven or Hell.

Many times hath Satan troubled me concerning the verity of the scriptures, many times by Atheism how I could know whether there was a God; I never saw any miracles to confirm me, and those which I read of how did I know but they were feigned. That there is a God my Reason would soon tell me by the wondrous works that I see, the vast frame of the Heaven and the Earth, the order of all things, night and day, Summer and Winter, Spring and Autumn, the daily providing for this great household upon the Earth, the preserving and directing of all to its proper end. The consideration of these things would with amazement certainly resolve me that there is an Eternal Being.

But how should I know he is such a God as I worship in Trinity, and such a Saviour as I rely upon? though: this hath thousands of times been suggested to me, yet God hath helped me over. I have argued this with myself. That there is a God I see. If ever this God hath revealed himself, it must be in his word, and this must be it or none. Have I not found that operation by it that no humane Invention can work upon the Soul? hath not Judgments befallen Divers who have scorned and contemned it? hath it not been preserved through: All Ages maugre all the heathen Tyrants and all of the enemies who have opposed it? Is there any story but that which shows the beginnings of Times, and how the world came to be as we see? Do we not know the prophecies in it fulfilled which could not have been so long foretold by any but God himself?

When I have got over this Block, then have I another put in my way, That admit this be the true God whom we worship, and that be his word, yet why may not the Popish Religion be the right? They have the same God, the same Christ, the same word: they only interpret it one way, we another.

This hath sometimes struck with me, and more it would, but the vain fooleries that are in their Religion, together with their lying miracles and cruel persecutions of the Saints, which admit were they as they term them, yet not so to be dealt withal.

The consideration of these things and many the like would soon turn me to my own Religion again.

But some new Troubles I have had since the world has been filled with Blasphemy, and Sectaries, and some who have been accounted sincere Christians have been carried away with them, that sometimes I have said, Is there faith upon the earth? and I have not known what to think. But then I have remembered the words of Christ that so it must be, and that, if it were possible, the very elect should be deceived. Behold, saith our Saviour, I have told you before. That hath stayed my heart, and I can now say, Return, O my Soul, to thy Rest,

upon this Rock Christ Jesus will I build my faith; and, if I perish, I perish. But I know all the Powers of Hell shall never prevail against it. I know whom I have trusted, and whom I have believed, and that he is able to keep that I have committed to his charge.

Now to the King, Immortal, Eternal, and invisible, the only wise God, be Honour and Glory for ever and ever! Amen.

This was written in much sickness and weakness, and is very weakly and imperfectly done; but, if you can pick any Benefit out of it, it is the mark which I aimed at.

"A Letter to Her Husband, Absent upon Public Employment" (1678)

My head, my heart, mine Eyes, my
    life, nay more,
My joy, my Magazine of earthly store,
If two be one, as surely thou and I,
How stayest thou there, whilst I at
    Ipswich lie?
So many steps, head from the heart to
    sever
If but a neck, soon should we be
    together:
I like the earth this season, mourn in
    black,
My Sun is gone so far in's Zodiac,
Whom whilst I 'joy'd, nor storms, nor
    frosts I felt,
His warmth such frigid colds did cause
    to melt.

My chilled limbs now numbed lie
    forlorn;
Return, return sweet Sol from
    Capricorn;
In this dead time, alas, what can I
    more
Than view those fruits which through
    thy heat I bore?
Which sweet contentment yield me for
    a space,
True living Pictures of their Father's
    face.
O strange effect! now thou art
    Southward gone,
I weary grow, the tedious day so long;
But when thou Northward to me shalt
    return,
I wish my Sun may never set, but burn
Within the Cancer of my glowing
    breast,
The welcome house of him my dearest
    guest.
Where ever, ever stay, and go not
    thence,
Till nature's sad decree shall call thee
    hence;
Flesh of thy flesh, bone of thy bone,
I here, thou there, yet both but one.

"To My Dear and Loving Husband" (1678)

If ever two were one, then surely we.
If ever man were lov'd by wife, then
    thee;
If ever wife was happy in a man,
Compare with me ye women if you
    can.

I prize thy love more than whole
    Mines of gold,
Or all the riches that the East doth
    hold.
My love is such that Rivers cannot
    quench,
Nor ought but love from thee, give
    recompence.
Thy love is such I can no way repay,
The heavens reward thee manifold I
    pray.
Then while we live, in love lets so
    persevere,
That when we live no more, we may
    live ever.

"Here Follows Some Verses upon the Burning of Our House July 10th, 1666" (1678)

In silent night when rest I took,
For sorrow near I did not look,
I waken'd was with thundering noise
And piteous shrieks of dreadful voice.
That fearful sound of fire and fire,
Let no man know is my desire.

I, staring up, the light did spy,
And to my God my heart did cry
To strengthen me in my Distress
And not to leave me succorless.
Then coming out beheld apace,
The flame consume my dwelling place.

And, when I could no longer look,
I blest his Name that gave and took,
That laid my goods now in the dust:
Yea so it was, and so 'twas just.

It was his own: it was not mine;
far be it that I should repine.

He might of All justly bereft,
But yet sufficient for us left.
When by the ruins oft I passed,
My sorrowing eyes aside did cast,
And here and there the places spy
Where oft I sat, and long did lie.

Here stood that trunk, and there that
    chest;
There lay that store I counted best:
My pleasant things in ashes lie,
And them behold no more shall I.
Under thy roof no guest shall sit,
Nor at thy table eat a bit.

No pleasant tale shall e're be told,
Nor things recounted done of old.
No candle e're shall shine in Thee,
Nor bridegroom's voice ere heard shall
    be.
In silence ever shalt thou lie;
Adieu, Adieu; All's vanity.

Then straight I 'gan my heart to chide,
And did thy wealth on earth abide?
Didst fix thy hope on mouldering
    dust,
The arm of flesh didst make thy trust?
Raise up thy thoughts above the sky,
That dunghill mists away may fly.

Thou has an house on high erect
Fram'd by that mighty Architect,
With Glory richly furnished,
Stands permanent though this be fled.
It's purchased, and paid for too
By him who hath enough to do.

A Price so vast as is unknown,
Yet, by his Gift, is made thine own.
There's wealth enough, I need no
    more;

Farewell my Pelf, farewell my Store.
The world no longer let me Love,
My hope and treasure lies Above.

Edward Taylor
(1644?–1729)

Although his *Poetical Works* remained
unpublished until 1939, Edward Taylor
is now regarded as America's finest
colonial poet, belonging to the tradition
of such English metaphysical and devo-
tional poets as John Donne, George
Herbert, Richard Crashaw, and Henry
Vaughan.

Taylor, a Harvard graduate and Congregational minister, spent his forma-
tive years in England, and his poetry
reveals no particular interest in the New
World as such. The style in which it is
written can hardly be said to conform to
Puritan ideals of directness and plain
speaking. Taylor excelled, however, as
can be seen in "Huswifery," in expressing his profound religious feelings
through the use of homely images
drawn from the daily life of Puritan
New England. Moreover, his religious
raptures, for a Puritan somewhat striking, are balanced by the deep sense of
personal unworthiness characteristic of
Puritan devotion.

"Huswifery"

Make me, O Lord, thy Spining Wheele
    compleate.
    Thy Holy Worde my Distaff make
    for mee.
Make mine Affections thy Swift Flyers
    neate
    And make my Soule thy holy Spoole
    to bee.
    My Conversation make to be thy
    Reele
    And reele the yarn thereon spun of
    thy Wheele.

Make me thy Loome then, knit therein
    this Twine:
    And make thy Holy Spirit, Lord,
    winde quills:
Then weave the Web thyselfe. The
    yarn is fine.
    Thine Ordinances make my Fulling
    Mills.
    Then dy the same in Heavenly
    Colours Choice,
    All pinkt with Varnisht Flowers of
    Paradise.

Then cloath therewith mine
    Understanding, Will,
    Affections, Judgment, Conscience,
    Memory
My Words, and Actions, that their
    shine may fill
    My wayes with glory and thee
    glorify.
    Then mine apparell shall display
    before yee
    That I am Cloathd in Holy robes for
    glory.

"Meditation One" (1682)

What Love is this of thine, that Cannot
    bee
    In thine Infinity, O Lord, Confinde,
Unless it in thy very Person see,
    Infinity, and Finity Conjoyn'd?
    What hath thy Godhead, as not
    satisfide
    Marri'de our Manhood, making it its
    Bride?

Oh, Matchless Love! filling Heaven to
    the brim!
    O're running it: all running o're
    beside
This World! Nay Overflowing Hell;
    wherein
    For thine Elect, there rose a mighty
    Tide!
    That there our Veans might
    through thy Person bleed,
    To quench those flames, that else
    would on us feed.

Oh! that thy Love might overflow my
    Heart!
    To fire the same with Love: for
    Love I would.
But oh! my streight'ned Breast! my
    Lifeless Sparke!
    My Fireless Flame! What Chilly
    Love, and Cold?
    In measure small! In Manner Chilly!
    See.
    Lord blow the Coal: Thy Love
    Enflame in mee.

Mary Rowlandson (1635?–1678?)

Mary Rowlandson was the wife of a Congregational minister in Lancaster, Massachusetts. On February 1, 1675, during the Narragansett Indian uprising known as King Philip's War, Lancaster was attacked and burned. Mrs. Rowlandson and three of her children were taken captive. She was a prisoner for nearly three months before she and her two surviving children were ransomed and freed. Not only did Mrs. Rowlandson suffer captivity among hostile and unpredictable enemies, but she was forced to endure the rigors of the ordinary life of an Indian woman. Her "captivity narrative," the first of many accounts of similar experiences, was published after her death and became one of the most widely read books in late seventeenth-century America.

Mrs. Rowlandson wrote her account in gratitude for God's merciful deliverance and to testify to her belief in the providential origin and meaning of her trials, but her narrative also provides one of the earliest detailed pictures of Indian life. In addition, it shows us the resources a devout Puritan could muster against "demonic" forces and almost unspeakable suffering. Mrs. Rowlandson's captivity narrative also suggests, perhaps unintentionally, what the "Americanization" of the Christian, or submission to what she calls "this Wilderness-condition," could conceivably cost. It helped to establish in the minds of many the harrowing confrontation of the civilized with the primitive as the archetypal pattern of that process of acculturation.

Narrative of the Captivity and Restauration of Mrs. Mary Rowlandson (1682)

On the tenth of February 1675, Came the Indians with great numbers upon Lancaster: Their first coming was about Sun-rising; hearing the noise of some Guns, we looked out; several Houses were burning, and the Smoke ascending to Heaven. There were five persons taken in one house, the Father, and the Mother and a sucking Child, they knockt on the head; the other two they took and carried away alive. Their were two others, who being out of their Garison upon some occasion were set upon; one was knockt on the head, the other escaped: Another their was who running along was shot and wounded, and fell down; he begged of them his life, promising them Money (as they told me) but they would not hearken to him but knockt him in head, and stript him naked, and split open his Bowels. Another seeing many of the Indians about his Barn, ventured and went out, but was quickly shot down. There were three others belonging to the same Garison who were killed; the Indians getting up upon the roof of the Barn, had advantage to shoot down upon them over their Fortification. Thus these murtherous wretches went on, burning, and destroying before them.

At length they came and beset our own house, and quickly it was the dolefullest day that ever mine eyes saw. The House stood upon the edg of a hill; some of the Indians got behind the hill, others into the Barn, and others behind any thing that could shelter them; from all which places they shot against the House, so that the Bullets seemed to fly like hail; and quickly they wounded one man among us, then another, and then a third, About two hours (according to my observation, in that amazing time) they had been about the house before they prevailed to fire it (which they did with Flax and Hemp, which they brought out of the Barn, and there being no defence about the House, only two Flankers at two opposite corners and one of them not finished) they fired it once and one ventured out and quenched it, but they quickly fired it again, and that took. Now is the dreadfull hour come, that I have often heard of (in time of War, as it was the case of others) but now mine eyes see it. Some in our house were fighting for their lives, others wallowing in their blood, the House on fire over our heads, and the bloody Heathen ready to knock us on the head, if we stirred out. Now might we hear Mothers and Children crying out for themselves, and one another, Lord, What shall we do? Then I took my Children (and one of my sisters, hers) to go forth and leave the house: but as soon as we came to the door and appeared, the Indians shot so thick that the bulletts rattled against the House, as if one had taken an handfull of stones and threw them, so that we were fain to give back. We had six stout Dogs belonging to our Garrison, but none of them would stir, though another time, if any Indian had come to the door, they were ready to fly upon him and tear him down. The Lord hereby would make us the more to acknowledge his hand, and to see that our help is always in him. But out we must go, the fire increasing, and coming along behind us, roaring, and the Indians gaping before us with their Guns, Spears and Hatchets to devour us. No sooner were we out of the House, but my Brother in Law (being before wounded, in defending the house, in or near the throat) fell down dead, wherat the Indians scornfully shouted, and hallowed, and were presently upon him, stripping off his cloaths, the bulletts flying thick, one went through my side, and the same (as would seem) through the bowels and hand of my dear Child in my arms. One of my elder Sisters Children, named William, had then his Leg broken, which the Indians perceiving, they knockt him on head. Thus were we butchered by those merciless Heathen, standing amazed, with the blood running down to our heels. My eldest Sister being yet in the House, and seeing those wofull sights, the Infidels haling Mothers one way, and Children another, and some wallowing in their blood: and her elder Son telling her that her Son William was dead, and my self was wounded, she said, And, Lord, let me dy with them; which was no sooner said, but she was struck with a Bullet, and fell down dead over the threshold. I hope she is reaping the fruit of her good labours, being faithfull to the service of God in her place. In her younger years she lay under much trouble upon spiritual accounts, till it pleased God to make that precious Scripture take hold of her heart, 2 Cor. 12. 9. *And he said unto me, my Grace is sufficient for thee.* More then twenty years after I have heard her tell how sweet and comfortable that place was to her. But to return: The Indians laid hold of us, pulling me one way, and the Children another, and said, Come go along with us; I told them they would kill me: they answered, If I were willing to go along with them, they would not hurt me.

Oh the dolefull sight that now was to behold at this House! *Come, behold the works of the Lord, what dissolations he has made in the Earth.* Of thirty seven persons who were in this one House, none escaped either present death, or a bitter captivity, save only one, who might say as he, Job 1. 15, *And I only am escaped alone to tell the News.* There were twelve killed, some shot, some stab'd with their Spears, some knock'd down with their Hatchets. When we are in prosperity, Oh the little that we think of such dreadfull sights, and to see our dear Friends, and Relations ly bleeding out their heart-blood upon the ground. There was one who was chopt into the head with a Hatchet, and stript naked, and yet was crawling up and down. It is a solemn sight to see so many Christians lying in their blood, some here, and some there, like a company of Sheep torn by Wolves, All of them stript naked by a company of hell-hounds, roaring, singing, ranting and insulting, as if they would have torn our very hearts out; yet the Lord by his Almighty power preserved a number of us from death, for there were twenty-four of us taken alive and carried Captive.

I had often before this said, that if the Indians should come, I should chuse rather to be killed by them then taken alive but when it came to the tryal my mind changed; their glittering weapons so daunted my spirit, that I chose rather to go along with those (as I may say) ravenous Beasts, then that moment to end my dayes; and that I may the better declare what happened to me during that grievous Captivity, I shall particularly speak of the severall Removes we had up and down the Wilderness.

The first Remove

Now away we must go with those Barbarous Creatures, with our bodies wounded and bleeding, and our hearts no less than our bodies. About a mile we went that night, up upon a hill within sight of the Town, where they intended to lodge. There was hard by a vacant house (deserted by the English before, for fear of the Indians). I asked them whither I might not lodge in the house that night to which they answered, what will you love English men still? this was the dolefullest night that ever my eyes saw. Oh the roaring, and singing and danceing, and yelling of those black creatures in the night, which made the place a lively resemblance of hell. And as miserable was the wast that was there made, of Horses, Cattle, Sheep, Swine, Calves, Lambs, Roasting Pigs, and Fowl (which they had plundered in the Town) some roasting, some lying and burning, and some boyling to feed our merciless Enemies; who were joyful enough though we were disconsolate. To add to the dolefulness of the former day, and the dismalness of the present night: my thoughts ran upon my losses and sad bereaved condition. All was gone, my Husband gone (at least separated from me, he being in the Bay; and to add to my grief, the Indians told me they would kill him as he came homeward) my Children gone, my Relations and Friends gone, our House and home and all our comforts within door, and without, all was gone, (except my life) and I knew not but the next moment that might go too. There remained nothing to me but one poor wounded Babe, and it seemed at present worse than death that it was in such a pitiful condition, bespeaking Compassion, and I had no refreshing for it, nor suitable things to revive it. Little do many think what is the savageness and bruitishness of this barbarous Enemy, I even those that seem to profess more than others among them, when the English have fallen into their hands.

Those seven that were killed at Lancaster the summer before upon a Sabbath day, and the one that was afterward killed upon a week day, were slain and mangled in a barbarous manner, by one-ey'd John, and Marlborough's Praying Indians, which Capt. Mosely brought to Boston, as the Indians told me.

The second Remove

But now, the next morning, I must turn my back upon the Town, and travel with them into the vast and desolate Wilderness, I knew not whither. It is not my tongue, or pen can express the sorrows of my heart, and bitterness of my spirit, that I had at this departure: but God was with me, in a wonderfull manner, carrying me along, and bearing up my spirit, that it did not quite fail. One of the Indians carried my poor wounded Babe upon a horse, it went moaning all along, I shall dy, I shall dy. I went on foot after it, with sorrow that cannot be exprest. At length I took it off the horse, and carried it in my armes till my strength failed, and I fell down with it: Then they set me upon a horse with my wounded Child in my lap, and there being no furniture upon the horse back, as we were going down a steep hill, we both fell over the horses head, at which they like inhumane creatures laught, and rejoyced to see it, though I thought we should there have ended our dayes, as overcome with so many difficulties. But the Lord renewed my strength still, and carried me along, that I might see more of his Power; yea, so much that I could never have thought of, had I not experienced it.

After this it quickly began to snow, and when night came on, they stopt: and now down I must sit in the snow, by a little fire, and a few boughs behind me, with my sick Child in my lap; and calling much for water, being now (through the wound) fallen into a violent Fever. My own wound also growing so stiff, that I could scarce sit down or rise up; yet so it must be, that I must sit all this cold winter night upon the cold snowy ground, with my sick Child in my armes, looking that every hour would be the last of its life; and having no

Christian friend near me, either to comfort or help me. Oh, I may see the wonderfull power of God, that my Spirit did not utterly sink under my affliction: still the Lord upheld me with his gracious and mercifull Spirit, and we were both alive to see the light of the next morning.

The third Remove

The morning being come, they prepared to go on their way. One of the Indians got up upon a horse, and they set me up behind him, with my poor sick Babe in my lap. A very wearisome and tedious day I had of it; what with my own wound, and my Childs being so exceeding sick, and in a lamentable condition with her wound. It may be easily judged what a poor feeble condition we were in, there being not the least crumb of refreshing that came within either of our mouths, from Wednesday night to Saturday night, except only a little cold water. This day in the afternoon, about an hour by Sun, we came to the place where they intended, *viz.* an Indian Town, called Wenimesset, Norward of Quabaug. When we were come, Oh the number of Pagans (now merciless enemies) that there came about me, that I may say as David, Psal. 27. 13, *I had fainted, unless I had believed,* etc. The next day was the Sabbath: I then remembered how careless I had been of Gods holy time, how many Sabbaths I had lost and misspent, and how evily I had walked in Gods sight; which lay so close unto my spirit, that it was easie for me to see how righteous it was with God to cut off the thread of my life, and cast me out of his presence for ever. Yet the Lord still shewed mercy to me, and upheld me; and as he wounded me with one hand, so he healed me with the other. This day there came to me one Robbert Pepper (a man belonging to Roxbury) who was taken in Captain Beers his Fight, and had been now a considerable time with the Indians; and up with them almost as far as Albany, to see king Philip, as he told me, and was now very lately come into these parts. Hearing, I say, that I was in this Indian Town, he obtained leave to come and see me. He told me, he himself was wounded in the leg at Captain Beers his Fight; and was not able some time to go, but as they carried him, and as he took Oaken leaves and laid to his wound, and through the blessing of God he was able to travel again. Then I took Oaken leaves and laid to my side, and with the blessing of God it cured me also; yet before the cure was wrought, I may say, as it is in Psal. 38, 5, 6. *My wounds stink and are corrupt, I am troubled, I am bowed down greatly, I go mourning all the day long.* I sat much alone with a poor wounded Child in my lap, which moaned night and day, having nothing to revive the body, or cheer the spirits of her, but in stead of that, sometimes one Indian would come and tell me one hour, that your Master will knock your Child in the head, and then a second, and then a third, your Master will quickly knock your Child in the head.

This was the comfort I had from them, miserable comforters are ye all, as he said. Thus nine dayes I sat upon my knees, with my Babe in my lap, till my flesh was raw again; my Child being even ready to depart this sorrowfull world, they bade me carry it out to another Wigwam (I suppose because they would not be troubled with such spectacles) Whither I went with a very heavy heart, and down I sat with the picture of death in my lap. About two houres in the night, my sweet Babe like a Lambe departed this life, on Feb. 18, 1675. It being about six yeares, and five months old. It was nine dayes from the first wounding, in this miserable condition, without any refreshing of one nature or other, except a little cold water. I cannot, but take notice, how at another time I could not bear to be in the room where any dead person was, but now the case is changed; I must and could ly down by my dead Babe, side by side all the night after. I have thought since of the wonderfull goodness of God to me, in preserving me in the use of my reason and senses, in that distressed time, that I did not use wicked and violent means to end my own miserable life. In the morning, when they understood that my child was dead they sent for me home to my Masters Wigwam: (by my Master in this writing, must be understood Quanopin, who was a Saggamore, and married King Phillips wives Sister; not that he first took me, but I was sold to him by another Narrhaganset Indian, who took me when first I came out of the Garison). I went to take up my dead child in my arms to carry it with me, but they bid me let it alone: there was no resisting, but goe I must and leave it. When I had been at my masters wigwam, I took the first opportunity I could get, to go look after my dead child: when I came I askt them what they had done with it? then they told me it was upon the hill: then they went and shewed me where it was, where I saw the ground was newly digged, and there they told me they had buried it: There I left that Child in the Wilderness, and must commit it, and my self also in this Wilderness-condition, to him who is above all. . . .

୧୦୨

I can remember the time, when I used to sleep quietly without workings in my thoughts, whole nights together, but now it is other wayes with me. When all are fast about me, and no eye open, but his who ever waketh, my thoughts are upon things past, upon the awfull dispensation of the Lord towards us; upon his wonderfull power and might, in carrying of us through so many difficulties, in returning us in safety, and suffering none to hurt us. I remember in the night season, how the other day I was in the midst of thousands of enemies, and nothing but death before me: It is then hard work to perswade my self, that ever I should be satisfied with bread again. But now we are fed with the finest of the Wheat, and, as I may say, With honey out of the rock: In stead of the Husk, we have the fatted Calf: The thoughts of these things in the particulars of them, and of the love and goodness of God towards us, make it true of me, what David said of himself, Psal. 6. 5. *I watered my Couch with my tears.* Oh! the wonderfull power of God that mine eyes have seen, affording matter enough for my thoughts to run in, that when others are sleeping mine eyes are weeping.

I have seen the extreme vanity of this

World: One hour I have been in health, and wealth, wanting nothing: But the next hour in sickness and wounds, and death, having nothing but sorrow and affliction.

Before I knew what affliction meant, I was ready sometimes to wish for it. When I lived in prosperity, having the comforts of the World about me, my relations by me, my Heart chearfull, and taking little care for any thing; and yet seeing many, whom I preferred before my self, under many tryals and afflictions, in sickness, weakness, poverty, losses, crosses, and cares of the World, I should be sometimes jealous least I should have my portion in this life, and that Scripture would come to my mind, Heb. 12. 6. *For whom the Lord loveth he chasteneth, and scourgeth every Son whom he receiveth.* But now I see the Lord had his time to scourge and chasten me. The portion of some is to have their afflictions by drops, now one drop and then another; but the dregs of the Cup, the Wine of astonishment, like a sweeping rain that leaveth no food, did the Lord prepare to be my portion. Affliction I wanted, and affliction I had, full measure (I thought) pressed down and running over; yet I see, when God calls a Person to any thing, and through never so many difficulties, yet he is fully able to carry them through and make them see, and say they have been gainers thereby. And I hope I can say in some measure, As David did, *It is good for me that I have been afflicted.* The Lord hath shewed me the vanity of these outward things. That they are the Vanity of vanities, and vexation of spirit; that they are but a shadow, a blast, a bubble, and things of no continuance. That we must rely on God himself, and our whole dependance must be upon him. If trouble from smaller matters begin to arise in me, I have something at hand to check my self with, and say, why am I troubled? It was but the other day that if I had had the world, I would have given it for my freedom, or to have been a Servant to a Christian. I have learned to look beyond present and smaller troubles, and to be quieted under them, as Moses said, Exod. 14. 13. *Stand still and see the salvation of the Lord.*

William Penn
(1644–1718)

William Penn (1644–1718), the Quaker founder of Pennsylvania, shared with Puritan colonists such as John Winthrop and John Cotton the belief that America should be a holy commonwealth, "a thing sacred in its institution and end." With nonconformist Roger Williams, however, Penn believed that the government of that commonwealth should serve rather than coerce its people. Penn's "Preface to the [Pennsylvania] Frame of Government" is thus reminiscent of, yet significantly different from, earlier charters of the New England colonies. The second selection, "Primitive Christianity Revived," provides a concise statement of the metaphysics on which Penn's political theory is based.

"Preface to the [Pennsylvania] Frame of Government" (1682)

When the great and wise God had made the world, of all his creatures, it pleased him to chuse man his Deputy to rule it: and to fit him for so great a charge and trust, he did not only qualify him with skill and power, but with integrity to use them justly. This native goodness was equally his honour and his happiness; and whilst he stood here, all went well; there was no need of coercive or compulsive means; the precept of divine love and truth, in his bosom, was the guide and keeper of his innocency. But lust prevailing against duty, made a lamentable breach upon it; and the law, that before had no power over him, took place upon him, and his disobedient posterity, that such as would not live conformable to the holy law within, should fall under the reproof and correction of the just law without, in a judicial administration.

This the Apostle teaches in divers of his epistles: "The law (says he) was added because of transgression:" In another place, "Knowing that the law was not made for the righteous man; but for the disobedient and ungodly, for sinners, for unholy and prophane, for murderers, for whoremongers, for them that defile themselves with mankind, and for man-stealers, for lyers, for perjured persons," &c., but this is not all, he opens and carries the matter of government a little further: "Let every soul be subject to the higher powers; for there is no power but of God. The powers that be are ordained of God: whosoever therefore resisteth the power, resisteth the ordinance of God. For rulers are not a terror to good works, but to evil: wilt thou then not be afraid of the power? do that which is good, and thou shalt have praise of the same." "He is the minister of God to thee for good." "Wherefore ye must needs be subject, not only for wrath, but for conscience sake."

This settles the divine right of government beyond exception, and that for two ends: first, to terrify evil doers: secondly, to cherish those that do well; which gives government a life beyond corruption, and makes it as durable in the world, as good men shall be. So that government seems to me a part of religion itself, a thing sacred in its institution and end. For, if it does not directly remove the cause, it crushes the effects of evil, and is as such, (though a lower, yet) an emanation of the same Divine Power, that is both author and object of pure religion; the difference lying here, that the one is more free and mental, the other more corporal and compulsive in its operations: but that is only to evil doers; government itself being otherwise as capable of kindness, goodness and charity, as a more private society. They weakly err, that think there is no other use of government, than correction, which is the coarsest part of it: daily experience tells us, that the care and regulation of many other affairs, more soft, and daily necessary, make up much of the greatest part of government; and which must have followed the peopling of the world, had Adam never fell, and will continue among men, on earth, under the highest attainments they may arrive at, by the coming of the blessed Second Adam, the Lord from heaven. Thus much of government in general, as to its rise and end.

For particular frames and models, it will become me to say little; and comparatively I will say nothing. My reasons are:

First. That the age is too nice and difficult for it; there being nothing the wits of men are more busy and divided upon. It is true, they seem to agree to the end, to wit, happiness; but, in the means, they differ, as to divine, so to this human felicity; and the cause is much the same, not always want of light and knowledge, but want of using them rightly. Men side with their passions against their reason, and their sinister interests have so strong a bias upon their minds, that they lean to them against the good of the things they know.

Secondly. I do not find a model in the world, that time, place, and some singular emergences have not necessarily altered; nor is it easy to frame a civil government, that shall serve all places alike.

Thirdly. I know what is said by the several admirers of monarchy, aristocracy, and democracy, which are the rule of one, a few, and many, and are the three common ideas of government, when men discourse on the subject. But I chuse to solve the controversy with this small distinction, and it belongs to all three: Any government is free to the people under it (whatever be the frame) where the laws rule, and the people are a party to those laws, and more than this is tyranny, oligarchy, or confusion.

But, lastly, when all is said, there is hardly one frame of government in the world so ill designed by its first founders, that, in good hands, would not do well enough; and story tells us, the best, in ill ones, can do nothing that is great or good; witness the Jewish and Roman states. Governments, like clocks, go from the motion men give them; and as governments are made and moved by men, so by them they are ruined too. Wherefore governments rather depend upon men, than men upon governments. Let men be good, and the government cannot be bad; if it be ill, they will cure it. But, if men be bad, let the government be never so good, they will endeavor to warp and spoil it to their turn.

I know some say, let us have good laws, and no matter for the men that execute them: but let them consider, that though good laws do well, good men do better: for good laws may want good men, and be abolished or evaded [invaded in Franklin's print] by ill men; but good men will never want good laws, nor suffer ill ones. It is true, good laws have some awe upon ill ministers, but that is where they have not power to escape or abolish them, and the people are generally wise and good: but a loose and depraved people (which is the question) love laws and an administration like themselves. That, therefore, which makes a good constitution, must keep it, viz: men of wisdom and virtue, qualities, that because they descend not with worldly inheritances, must be carefully propagated by a virtuous education of youth; for which after ages will owe more to the care and prudence of founders, and the successive magistracy, than to their parents, for their private patrimonies.

These considerations of the weight of government, and the nice and various opinions about it, made it uneasy to me to think of publishing the ensuing frame and conditional laws, forseeing both the censures, they will meet with, from men of differing humours and engagements, and the occasion they may give of discourse beyond my design.

But, next to the power of necessity, (which is a solicitor, that will take no denial) this induced me to a compliance, that we have (with reverence to God, and good conscience to men) to the best of our skill, contrived and composed the frame and laws of this government, to the great end of all government, viz: To support power in reverence with the people, and to secure the people from the abuse of power; that they may be free by their just obedience, and the magistrates honourable, for their just administration: for liberty without obedience is confusion, and obedience without liberty is slavery. To carry this evenness is partly owing to the constitution, and partly to the magistracy: where either of these fail, government will be subject to convulsions; but where both are wanting, it must be totally subverted; then where both meet, the government is like to endure. Which I humbly pray and hope God will please to make the lot of this of Pensilvania. Amen.

From *Primitive Christianity Revived* (1696)

C h a p. I. §. 1. Their [i.e., Quakers'] Fundamental Principle. §. 2. The Nature of it. §. 3. Called by several Names. §. 4. They refer all to this, as to Faith and Practice, Ministry and Worship.

§. 1. THAT which the People call'd Quakers lay down, as a Main Fundamental in Religion, is this, That God, through Christ, hath placed a Principle in every Man, to inform him of his Duty, and to enable him to do it; and that those that Live up to this Principle, are the People of God, and those that Live in Disobedience to it, are not God's People, whatever Name they may bear, or Profession they may make of Religion. This is their Ancient, First, and Standing Testimony: With this they began, and this they bore, and do bear to the World.

§. 2. By this Principle they understand something that is Divine; and though in Man, yet not of Man, but of God; and that it came from Him, and leads to Him all those that will be led by it.

§. 3. There are divers Ways of Speaking that have been led to use, by which they declare and express what this Principle is, about which I think fit to Precaution the Reader, viz. They call it, The Light of Christ within Man, or, Light Within, which is their Ancient, and most General and Familiar Phrase, also the (a) Manifestation (b) or Appearance of Christ (c), the (d) Witness of God, the (e) Seed of God, the (f) Seed of the Kingdom, (g) Wisdom, the (h) Word in the Heart, the Grace (i) that appears to all Men, the (k) Spirit given to every Man to profit with, the (l) Truth in the Inward Parts, the (m) Spiritual Leaven, that Leavens the whole Lump of Man: Which are many of them Figurative Expressions, but all of them such as the Holy Ghost hath used, and which will be used in this Treatise, as they are most frequently in the Writings and Ministry of this People. But that this Variety and Manner of Expression may not occasion any Misapprehension or Confusion in the Understanding of the Reader, I would have him know, that they always mean by these Terms, or Denominations, not another, but the same Principle, before mentioned: Which, as I said, though it be in Man, is not of Man, but of God, and therefore Divine: And One in it self, tho' diversly expressed by the Holy Men, according to the Various Manifestations and Operations thereof.

§. 4. It is to this Principle of Light, Life and Grace, that this People refer all: For they say it is the Great Agent in Religion; That, without which, there is no Conviction, so no Conversion, or Regeneration; and consequently no entring into the Kingdom of God. That is to say, there can be no True Sight of Sin, nor Sorrow for it, and therefore no forsaking or overcoming of it, or Remission or Justification from it. A Necessary and Powerful Principle indeed, when neither Sanctification, nor Justification can be had without it. In short, there is no becoming Virtuous, Holy and Good, without this Principle; no Acceptance with God, nor Peace of Soul, but through it. But on the con-trary, that the Reason of so much Irreligion among Christians, so much Superstition, instead of Devotion, and so much Profession without Enjoyment, and so little Heart-Reformation, is, because People in Relgion, Overlook this Principle, and leave it behind them. . . .

Germantown Quakers

As early as 1657, George Fox, the English founder of the Quaker sect, preached that all men are equal in the sight of God, and urged his fellow Quakers to show mercy toward slaves. By 1671, Fox was proposing that all slaves be freed after an initial period of bondage, and by 1676 Quaker William Edmundson was prepared to ask why Negroes should be enslaved at all. In 1688 four American Quakers in Germantown, Pennsylvania, signed a resolution, here reproduced, denouncing the institution of slavery. Holding it "a terrour or fairfull thing that men should be handeld so," these Germantown Quakers appealed to the reason and conscience of their Quaker co-religionists. The resolution yielded no immediate results, and indeed was lost for almost two centuries, but it was a sign of things to come. The first antislavery tract appeared in America in 1693, and in 1758 the Philadelphia Yearly Meeting finally took action against slavetrading and slaveholding among Quakers.

Quaker Resolution Against Slavery (1688)

This is to the Monthly Meeting held at Rigert Worrells.

These are the reasons why we are against the traffick of mens-body as followeth: Is there any that would be done or handled at this manner? viz. to be sold or made a slave for all the time of his life? How fearfull & fainthearted are many on sea when they see a strange vassel being afraid it should be a Turck, and they should be tacken and sold for Slaves in Turckey. Now what is this better done as Turcks doe? yea rather is it worse for them, wch say they are Christians for we hear, that the most part of such Negers are brought heither against their will & consent, and that many of them are stollen. Now tho' they are black, we cannot conceive there is more liberty to have them slaves, as it is to have other white ones. There is a saying, that we shall doe to all men, licke as we will be done our selves: macking no difference of what generation, descent, or Colour they are. And those who steal or robb men, and those who buy or purchase them, are they not all alicke? Here is liberty of Conscience, wch is right & reasonable, here ought to be lickewise liberty of the body, except of evildoers, wch is an other case. But to bring men hither, or to robb and sell them against their will, we stand against. In Europe there are many oppressed for Conscience sacke; and here there are those oppressed wch are of a black Colour. And we, who know that men must not comitt adultery, some doe comitt adultery in others, separating wifes from their housbands, and giving them to others and some sell the children of those poor Creatures to other men. Oh! doe consider well this things, you who doe it, if you would be done at this manner? and if it is done according Christianity? you surpass Holland & Germany in this thing. This mackes an ill report in all those Countries of Europe, where they hear off, that the Quackers doe here handel men, Licke they handel there the Cattel; and for that reason some have no mind or inclination to come hither. And who shall maintaine this your cause or plaid for it? Truely we can not do so except you shall inform us better hereoff, viz. that christians have liberty to practise this things. Pray! What thing in the world can be done worse towarts us then if men should robb or steal us away & sell us for slaves to strange Countries, separating housband from their wife & children. Being now this is not done at that manner we will be done at, therefore we contradict & are against this traffick of men body. And we who profess that it is not lawfull to steal, must lickewise avoid to purchase such things as are stolen, but rather help to stop this robbing and stealing if possibel and such men ought to be delivred out of the hands of the Robbers and set free as well as in Europe. Then is Pensilvania to have a good report, in stead it hath now a bad one for this sacke in other Countries. Especially whereas the Europeans are desirous to know in what manner the Quackers doe rule in their Province & most of them doe loock upon us with an envious eye. But if this is done well, what shall we say, is don evil?

If once these slaves (wch they say are so wicked and stubbern men) should joint themselves, fight for their freedom and handel their masters & mastrisses, as they did handel them before; will these masters and mastrisses tacke the sword at hand & warr against these poor slaves, licke we are able to belive, some will not refuse to doe? Or have these negers not as much right to fight for their freedom, as you have to keep them slaves?

Now consider well this thing, if it is good or bad? and in case you find it to be good to handel these blacks at that manner, we desire & require you hereby lovingly that you may informe us herein, which at this time never was done, viz. that Christians have Liberty to do so, to the end we shall be satisfied in this point, & satisfie lickewise our good friends & acquaintances in our natif Country, to whose it is a terrour or fairfull thing that men should be handeld so in Pensilvania.

This was is from our monthly meeting at Germantown hold the 18 of the 2 month 1688 to be delivred to the monthly meeting at Richard Warrels.

Cotton Mather
(1633–1728)

Cotton Mather was the last of a family of famous New England divines. A man of inexhaustible energy and prodigious learning, Cotton Mather produced over 450 works in the course of an active life fraught with controversy. He is perhaps most often thought of in connection with the Salem witch trials, of which he approved, although he thought that the demon-possessed should be treated by prayer and fasting rather than hanged. Mather was perhaps the last embattled defender of the old Puritan ideal in a time of rapid social, political, and religious change. His crowning achievement was an ecclesiastical history of New England, *Magnalia Christi Americana,* which chronicles the mighty acts of God in the New World from the time of the Plymouth landing to the end of the seventeenth century.

From *Magnalia Christi Americana* (1702)

1. I WRITE the WONDERS of the CHRISTIAN RELIGION, flying from the depravations of Europe, to the American Strand; and, assisted by the Holy Author of that Religion, I do with all conscience of Truth, required therein by Him, who is the Truth itself, report the wonderful displays of His infinite Power, Wisdom, Goodness, and Faithfulness, wherewith His Divine Providence hath irradiated an Indian Wilderness.

I relate the Considerable Matters, that produced and attended the First Settlement of COLONIES, which have been renowned for the degree of REFORMA-

TION, professed and attained by Evangelical Churches, erected in those ends of the earth; and a Field being thus prepared, I proceed unto a relation of the Considerable Matters which have been acted thereupon.

I first introduce the Actors, that have in a more exemplary manner served those Colonies; and give Remarkable Occurrences, in the exemplary Lives of many Magistrates, and of more Ministers, who so lived as to leave unto Posterity examples worthy of everlasting remembrance.

I add hereunto, the Notables of the only Protestant University that ever shone in that hemisphere of the New World; with particular instances of Criolians, in our Biography, provoking the whole world with vertuous objects of emulation.

I introduce then, the Actions of a more eminent importance, that have signalized those Colonies: whether the Establishments, directed by their Synods; with a rich variety of Synodical and Ecclesiastical Determinations; or, the Disturbances, with which they have been from all sorts of temptations and enemies tempestuated; and the Methods by which they have still weathered out each horrible tempest.

And into the midst of these Actions, I interpose an entire Book, wherein there is, with all possible veracity, a Collection made of Memorable Occurrences, and amazing Judgments and Mercies befalling many particular persons among the people of New-England.

Let my readers expect all that I have promised them, in this Bill of Fare; and it may be they will find themselves entertained with yet many other passages, above and beyond their expectation, deserving likewise a room in History: in all which, there will be nothing but the Author's too mean way of preparing so great entertainments, to reproach the Invitation.

2. . . . The sum of the matter is, that from the very beginning of the REFORMATION in the English Nation, there hath always been a generation of Godly Men, desirous to pursue the Reformation of Religion, according to the Word of God, and the Example of the best Reformed Churches; and answering the character of Good Men, given by Josephus, in his Paraphrase on the words of Samuel to Saul [Mather here gives the Greek], "They think they do nothing right in the service of God, but what they do according to the command of God." And there hath been another generation of men, who have still employed the power which they have generally still had in their hands, not only to stop the progress of the desired Reformation, but also, with innumerable vexations, to persecute those that most heartily wishes well unto it. . . . 'Tis very certain, that the first Reformers never intended that what they did should be the absolute boundary of Reformation, so that it should be a sin to proceed any further; as, by their own going beyond Wickliff, and changing and growing in their own Models also, and the confessions of Cranmer, with the *Scripta Anglicana* of Bucer, and a thousand other things, was abundantly demonstrated. But after a fruitless expectation, wherein the truest friends of the Reformation long waited for to have that which

Heylin himself owns to have been the design of the first Reformers, followed as it should have been, a party very unjustly arrogating to themselves the venerable name of *The Church of England,* by numberless oppressions, grievously smote those their Fellow-Servants. Then 'twas that, as our great OWEN hath expressed it, "Multitudes of pious, peaceable Protestants, were driven, by their severities, to leave their native country, and seek a refuge for their lives and liberties, with freedom for the worship of God, in a wilderness, in the ends of the earth."

3. It is the History of these PROTESTANTS that is here attempted: PROTESTANTS that highly honoured and affected the Church of England, and humbly petition to be a part of it: but by the mistakes of a few powerful brethren, driven to seek a place for the exercise of the Protestant Religion, according to the light of their consciences, in the desarts of America. And in this attempt I have proposed, not only to preserve and secure the interest of Religion in the Churches of that little country NEW-ENGLAND, so far as the Lord Jesus Christ may please to bless it for that end, but also to offer unto the Churches of the Reformation, abroad in the world, some small Memorials, that may be serviceable unto the designs of Reformation, whereto, I believe, they are quickly to be awakened. . . . It may be, 'tis not possible for me to do a greater service unto the Churches on the best Island of the universe, than to give a distinct relation of those great examples which have been occurring among Churches of exiles, that were driven out of that Island, into an horrible wilderness, meerly for their being well-willers unto the Reformation. . . . I do not say, that the Churches of New-England are the most regular that can be; yet do I say, and am sure, that they are very like unto those that were in the first ages of Christianity. And if I assert that, in the Reformation of the Church, the state of it in those first Ages is to be not a little considered, the great Peter Ramus, among others, has emboldened me. For when the Cardinal of Lorrain, the Maecenas of that great man, was offended at him, for turning Protestant, he replied [here Mather gives the Latin]: "Among the many favours with which your bounty has enriched me, I shall keep one in everlasting remembrance—I mean the lesson I have learned through your reply to the Poissy Conference, that of fifteen centuries since Christ, the first was the truly golden era of the Church, and that the rest have been successive periods of degeneracy; when therefore I had the power of choosing between them, I preferred the golden age." In short, the first Age was the golden age: to return unto that, will make a man a Protestant, and, I may add, a Puritan. 'Tis possible that our Lord Jesus Christ carried some thousands of Reformers into the retirements of an American desart, on purpose that, with an opportunity granted unto many of his faithful servants, to enjoy the precious liberty of their Ministry, though in the midst of many temptations all their days, He might there, to them first, and then by them, give a specimen of many good things, which He would have His Churches elsewhere

aspire and arise unto; and this being done, he knows not whether there be not all done, that New-England was planted for; and whether the Plantation may not, soon after this, come to nothing. Upon that expression in the sacred Scripture, "Cast the unprofitable servant into outer darkness," it hath been imagined by some, that the *Regiones exterae* [remote regions] of America, are the *Tenebrae exteriores* [outer darkness] which the unprofitable are there condemned unto. No doubt, the authors of those Ecclesiastical impositions and severities, which drove the English Christians into the dark regions of America, esteemed those Christians to be a very unprofitable sort of creatures. But behold, ye European Churches, there are golden Candlesticks in the midst of this "outer darkness": unto the upright children of Abraham, here hath arisen light in darkness. And, let us humbly speak it, it shall be profitable for you to consider the light which from the midst of this "outer darkness," is now to be darted over unto the other side of the Atlantick Ocean. But we must therewithal ask your Prayers, that these "golden Candlesticks" may not quickly be "removed out of their place!"

4. But whether New-England may live any where else or no, it must live in our History! . . .

III
Loomings
(1740–1830)

The century or so between the disintegration of the old theocratic dream of building a Christian society in the wilderness and its replacement by the newer republican ambition of carving a democratic nation out of the great American forest was momentous in America's cultural and spiritual history. The explicitly religious worldview of the Puritans was displaced by the ostensibly secular worldview of the Enlightenment, but the course of American empire charted by the framers of the Declaration of Independence and the Constitution was no less sacred in orientation than that projected by the fathers for Plymouth Plantation and Massachusetts Bay. Whereas the Puritans envisioned America as a Holy Commonwealth, their Revolutionary successors defined her as Nature's Nation. Both groups, however, saw the American people as embarked on a mission of more than merely temporal significance that could best be described in relation to the symbolic properties of the landscape which held their destiny. Puritan and Republican alike were searching for an intellectual formulation that would satisfactorily define their sense of mission and at the same time prove adaptable to the ever-changing, unpredictable, and strangely compelling facts of New World experience. If neither group quite found this formulation, their common quest nonetheless became the chief metaphysical preoccupation of their respective historical descendants who would divide between them virtually the whole of the American religious heritage.

Jonathan Edwards
(1703–1758)

Jonathan Edwards is widely regarded as America's greatest native-born theologian. This estimation is based not only on the range, subtlety, and consistency of his thinking, but also on its passion, power, and originality. Virtually alone among his contemporaries, Edwards saw clearly the cancerous growth of self-regard that lay beneath the religious platitudes and theological formulas by which men and women in his age justified themselves to their God. Edwards did not content himself with merely exposing this spiritual cancer, for he believed that the critique of faith must be followed by its renewal—a renewal not only in the head, but also in the heart. Edwards thus undertook to reform the whole edifice of Puritan spirtuality by awakening a fresh understanding of religion's seat in the affections.

Though Edwards's life was comparatively short, his literary output was prodigious, especially in view of his active and frequently controversial ministry. He helped to touch the match to the religious conflagration of the 1730s and 1740s, which became known as the Great Awakening. Later, he became embroiled in the bitter controversy that would eventually cost him his parish in Northhampton, Massachusetts. He refused to compromise on standards for church membership and was finally sent packing into the New England wilderness to serve as a missionary to the Indians. Despite these distractions, Edward's pen was ceaselessly active, producing everything from spiritual biography and autobiography to narratives of the religious awakening; from treatises on morality and the will to his great works on original sin and the purpose of Creation; from miscellaneous journals and notebooks to sermons like his famous "Sinners in the Hands of an Angry God" and "A Divine and Supernatural Light."

The following selections reflect some of the diversity of Edwards's writing as well as its underlying unity. A number of recurring themes demonstrate his continuity with earlier currents of American religious thought even as they look toward other currents that would grow much stronger in the future: the reaffirmation of the centrality of the feelings to religious understanding, the necessity of distinguishing true religion from false, the priority of experience as a theological category, and the conviction that the universe has no other purpose than to display, in its own natural beauty, the reflected glory of its Maker.

From *A Faithful Narrative of the Surprising Word of God* (1737)

At the latter end of the year 1733, there appeared a very unusual flexibleness, and yielding to advice, in our young people. It had been too long their manner to make the evening after the sabbath, and after our public lecture, to be especially the times of their mirth, and company-keeping. But a sermon was now preached on the sabbath before the lecture, to shew the evil tendency of the practice, and to persuade them to reform it; and it was urged on heads of families that it should be a thing agreed upon among them, to govern their families, and keep their children at home, at these times. It was also more privately moved, that they should meet together the next day, in their several neighbourhoods, to know each other's minds; which was accordingly done, and the motion complied with throughout the town. But parents found little or no occasion for the exercise of government in the case. The young people declared themselves convinced by what they had heard from the pulpit, and were willing of themselves to comply with the counsel that had been given: and it was immediately, and, I suppose, almost universally complied with; and there was a thorough reformation of these disorders thenceforward, which has continued ever since.

Presently after this, there began to appear a remarkable religious concern at a little village belonging to the congregation, called Pascommuck, where a few families were settled, at about three miles distance from the main body of the town. At this place a number of persons seemed to be savingly wrought upon. In the April following, anno 1734, there happened a very sudden and awful death of a young man in the bloom of his youth; who being violently seized with the pleurisy, and taken immediately very delirious, died in about two days; which (together with what was preached publicly on that occasion) much affected many young people. This was followed with another death of a young married woman, who had been considerable exercised in mind about the salvation of her soul, before she was ill, and was in great distress, in the beginning of her illness: but seemed to have satisfying evidences of God's saving mercy to her, before her death: so that she died very full of comfort, in a most earnest and moving manner, warning and counselling others. This served to contribute to render solemn the spirits of many young persons; and there began evidently to appear more of a religious concern on people's minds.

In the fall of the year I proposed it to the young people, that they should agree among themselves to spend the evenings after lectures in social religion, and to that end divide themselves into several companies to meet in various parts of the town; which was accordingly done, and those meetings have been since continued, and the example imitated by elder people. This was followed with the death of an elderly person, which was attended with many unusual circumstances, by which many were much moved and affected.

About this time began the great noise, in this part of the country, about Arminianism, which seemed to appear with a very threatening aspect upon the interest of religion here. The friends of vital piety trembled for fear of the issue; but it seemed, contrary to their fear, strongly to be over-ruled for the promoting of religion. Many who looked on themselves as in a Christless condition, seemed to be awakened by it, with fear that God was about to withdraw from the land, and that we should be given up to heterodoxy and corrupt principles; and that then their opportunity for obtaining salvation would be past. Many who were brought a little to doubt about the truth of the doctrines they had hitherto been taught, seemed to have a kind of trembling fear with their doubts, lest they should be led into by-paths, to their eternal undoing; and they seemed, with much concern and engagedness of mind, to enquire what was indeed the way in which they must come to be accepted with God. There were some things said publicly on that occasion, concerning justification by faith alone.

Although great fault was found with meddling with the controversy in the pulpit, by such a person, and at that time—and though it was ridiculed by many elsewhere—yet it proved a word spoken in season here; and was most evidently attended with a very remarkable blessing of heaven to the souls of the people in this town. They received thence a general satisfaction, with respect to the main thing in question, which they had been in trembling doubts and concern about; and their minds were engaged the more earnestly to seek that they might come to be accepted of God, and saved in the way of the gospel, which had been made evident to them to be the true and only way. And then it was, in the latter part of December, that the spirit of God

began extraordinarily to set in, and wonderfully to work amongst us; and there were, very suddenly, one after another, five or six persons, who were to all appearance savingly converted, and some of them wrought upon in a very remarkable manner.

Particularly, I was surprised with the relation of a young woman, who had been one of the greatest company-keepers in the whole town. When she came to me, I had never heard that she was become in any wise serious, but by the conversation I then had with her, it appeared to me, that what she gave an account of, was a glorious work of God's infinite power and sovereign grace; and that God had given her a new heart, truly broken and sanctified. I could not then doubt of it, and have seen much in my acquaintance with her since to confirm it.

Though the work was glorious, yet I was filled with concern about the effect it might have upon others. I was ready to conclude, (though too rashly) that some would be hardened by it, in carelessness and looseness of life; and would take occasion from it to open their mouths in reproaches of religion. But the event was the reverse, to a wonderful degree. God made it, I suppose, the greatest occasion of awakening to others, of any thing that ever came to pass in the town. I have had abundant opportunity to know the effect it had, by my private conversation with many. The news of it seemed to be almost like a flash of lightning, upon the hearts of young people, all over the town, and upon many others. Those persons amongst us, who used to be farthest from seriousness, and that I most feared would make an ill improvement of it, seemed greatly to be awakened with it. Many went to talk with her, concerning what she had met with; and what appeared in her seemed to be to the satisfaction of all that did so.

Presently upon this, a great and earnest concern about the great things of religion, and the eternal world, became universal in all parts of the town, and among persons of all degrees, and all ages. The noise amongst the dry bones waxed louder and louder; all other talk but about spiritual and eternal things was soon thrown by; all the conversation, in all companies and upon all occasions, was upon these things only, unless so much as was necessary for people carrying on their ordinary secular business. Other discourse than of the things of religion, would scarcely be tolerated in any company. The minds of people were wonderfully taken off from the world, it was treated amongst us as a thing of very little consequence. They seemed to follow their worldly business, more as a part of their duty, than from any disposition they had to it; the temptation now seemed to lie on that hand, to neglect worldly affairs too much, and to spend too much time in the immediate exercise of religion. This was exceedingly misrepresented by reports that were spread in distant parts of the land, as though the people here had wholly thrown by all worldly business, and betook themselves entirely to reading and praying, and such like religious exercises.

But although people did not ordinarily neglect their worldly business; yet Religion was with all sorts the great concern, and the world was a thing only by the bye. The only thing in their view was to get the kingdom of heaven, and every one appeared pressing into it. The engagedness of their hearts in this great concern could not be hid, it appeared in their very countenances. It then was a dreadful thing amongst us to lie out of Christ, in danger every day of dropping into hell; and what persons minds were intent upon, was to escape for their lives, and to fly from the wrath to come. All would eagerly lay hold of opportunities for their souls; and were wont very often to meet together in private houses, for religious purposes: and such meetings when appointed were greatly thronged.

There was scarcely a single person in the town, old or young, left unconcerned about the great things of the eternal world. Those who were wont to be the vainest, and loosest; and those who had been most disposed to think, and speak slightly of vital and experimental religion, were now generally subject to great awakenings. And the work of conversion was carried on in a most astonishing manner, and increased more and more; souls did as it were come by flocks to Jesus Christ. From day to day, for many months together, might be seen evident instances of sinners brought out of darkness into marvellous light, and delivered out of a horrible pit, and from the miry clay, and set upon a rock with a new song of praise to God in their mouths.

This work of God, as it was carried on,

and the number of true saints multiplied, soon made a glorious alteration in the town; so that in the spring and summer following, anno 1735, the town seemed to be full of the presence of God: it never was so full of love, nor of joy, and yet so full of distress, as it was then. There were remarkable tokens of God's presence in almost every house. It was a time of joy in families on account of salvation being brought unto them; parents rejoicing over their children as new born, and husbands over their wives, and wives over their husbands. The goings of God were then seen in his sanctuary, God's day was a delight, and his tabernacles were amiable. Our public assemblies were then beautiful; the congregation was alive in God's service, every one earnestly intent on the public worship, every hearer eager to drink in the words of the minister as they came from his mouth; the assembly in general were, from time to time, in tears while the word was preached; some weeping with sorrow and distress, others with joy and love, others with pity and concern for the souls of their neighbours.

Our public praises were then greatly enlivened; God was then served in our psalmody, in some measure in the beauty of holiness. It has been observable, that there has been scarce any part of divine worship, wherein good men amongst us have had grace so drawn forth, and their hearts so lifted up in the ways of God, as in singing his praises. Our congregation excelled all that ever I knew in the external part of the duty before, the men generally carrying regularly, and well, three parts of music,

and the women a part by themselves; but now they were evidently wont to sing with unusual elevation of heart and voice, which made the duty pleasant indeed.

In all companies, on other days, on whatever occasions persons met together, Christ was to be heard of and seen in the midst of them. Our young people when they met, were wont to spend the time in talking of the excellency and dying love of Jesus Christ, the glory of the way of salvation, the wonderful, free, and sovereign grace of God, his glorious work in the conversion of a soul, the truth and certainty of the great things of God's word, the sweetness of the views of his perfections, &c. And even at weddings, which formerly were mere occasions of mirth and jollity, there was now no discourse of any thing but religion, and no appearance of any but spiritual mirth. Those amongst us who had been formerly converted, were greatly enlivened, and renewed with fresh and extraordinary incomes of the spirit of God; though some much more than others, according to the measure of the gift of Christ. Many who before had laboured under difficulties about their own state, had now their doubts removed by more satisfying experience, and more clear discoveries of God's love.

When this work first appeared, and was so extraordinarily carried on amongst us in the winter, others round about us seemed not to know what to make of it. Many scoffed at and ridiculed it; and some compared what we called conversion, to certain distempers.

But it was very observable of many, who occasionally came amongst us from abroad with disregardful hearts, that what they saw here cured them of such a temper of mind. Strangers were generally surprised to find things so much beyond what they had heard, and were wont to tell others that the state of the town could not be conceived of by those who had not seen it. The notice that was taken of it by the people who came to town on occasion of the court that sat here in the beginning of March, was very observable. And those who came from the neighbourhood to our public lectures, were for the most part remarkably affected. Many who came to town, on one occasion or other, had their consciences smitten, and awakened; and went home with wounded hearts, and with those impressions that never wore off till they had hopefully a saving issue; and those who before had serious thoughts, had their awakenings and convictions greatly increased. There were many instances of persons who came from abroad on visits, or on business, who had not been long here before, to all appearance, they were savingly wrought upon; and partook of that shower of divine blessing which God rained down here, and went home rejoicing; till at length the same work began evidently to appear and prevail in several other towns in the county.

This work seemed to be at its greatest height in this town in the former part of the spring, in March and April. At that time, God's work in the conversion of souls was carried on amongst us in so wonderful a manner, that, so far as I can judge, it appears to have been at the rate, at least, of four persons in a day; or near thirty in a week, take one with another, for five or six weeks together. When God in so remarkable a manner took the work into his own hands, there was as much done in a day or two as at ordinary times, with all endeavours that men can use, and with such a blessing as we commonly have, is done in a year.

I am very sensible how apt many would be, if they should see the account I have here given, presently to think with themselves that I am very fond of making a great many converts, and of magnifying the matter; and to think that, for want of judgment, I take every religious pang and enthusiastic conceit for saving conversion. I do not much wonder, if they should be apt to think so; and, for this reason, I have forborne to publish an account of this great work of God, though I have often been solicited. But having now a special call to give an account of it, upon mature consideration I thought it might not be beside my duty to declare this amazing work, as it appeared to me to be indeed divine, and to conceal no part of the glory of it; leaving it with God to take care of the credit of his own work, and running the venture of any censorious thoughts which might be entertained of me to my disadvantage. That distant persons may be under as great advantage as may be, to judge for themselves of this matter, I would be a little more large and particular.

From *Personal Narrative* (1740)

I had a variety of concerns and exercises about my soul, from my childhood; but I had two more remarkable seasons of awakening, before I met with that change, by which I was brought to those new dispostions, and that new sense of things, that I have since had. The first time was when I was a boy, some years before I went to college, at a time of remarkable awakening in my father's congregation. I was then very much affected for many months, and concerned about the things of religion, and my soul's salvation; and was abundant in religious duties. I used to pray five times a day in secret, and to spend much time in religious conversation with other boys; and used to meet with them to pray together. I experienced I know not what kind of delight in religion. My mind was much engaged in it, and had much self-righteous pleasure; and it was my delight to abound in religious duties. I, with some of my school-mates, joined together, and built a booth in a swamp, in a very retired spot, for a place of prayer.—And besides, I had particular secret places of my own in the woods, where I used to retire by myself; and was from time to time much affected. My affections seemed to be lively and easily moved, and I seemed to be in my element, when engaged in religious duties. And I am ready to think, many are deceived with such affections, and such a kind of delight as I then had in religion, and mistake it for grace.

But, in process of time, my convictions and affections wore off; and I entirely lost all those affections and delights, and left off secret prayer, at least as to any constant preference of it; and returned like a dog to his vomit, and went on in the ways of sin. Indeed, I was at times very uneasy, especially towards the latter part of my time at college; when it pleased God, to seize me with a pleurisy; in which he brought me nigh to the grave, and shook me over the pit of hell. And yet, it was not long after my recovery, before I fell again into my old ways of sin. But God would not suffer me to go on with any quietness; I had great and violent inward struggles, till, after many conflicts with wicked inclinations, repeated resolutions, and bonds that I laid myself under by a kind of vows to God, I was brought wholly to break off all former wicked ways, and all ways of known outward sin; and to apply myself to seek salvation, and practise many religious duties; but without that kind of affection and delight which I had formerly experienced. My concern now wrought more, by inward struggles, and conflicts, and self-reflections. I made seeking my salvation, the main business of my life. But yet, it seems to me, I sought it after a miserable manner; which has made me sometimes since to question, whether ever it issued in that which was saving; being ready to doubt, whether such miserable seeking ever succeeded. I was indeed brought to seek salvation, in a manner that I never was before; I felt a spirit to part with all things in the world, for an interest in Christ. My concern continued and prevailed, with many exercising thoughts and inward struggles; but yet it never seemed to be proper, to express that concern by the name of terror.

From my childhood up, my mind had been full of objections against the doctrine of God's sovereignty, in choosing whom he would to eternal life, and rejecting whom he pleased; leaving them eternally to perish, and be everlastingly tormented in hell. It used to appear like a horrible doctrine to me. But I remember the time very well, when I seemed to be convinced, and fully satisfied, as to this sovereignty of God, and his justice in thus eternally disposing of men, according to his sovereign pleasure. But never could give an account, how, or by what means, I was thus convinced, not in the least imagining at the time, nor a long time after, that there was any extraordinary influence of God's Spirit in it; but only that now I saw further, and my reason apprehended the justice and reasonableness of it. However, my mind rested in it; and it put an end to all those cavils and objections. And there has been a wonderful alteration in my mind, with respect to the doctrine of God's sovereignty, from that day to this; so that I scarce ever have found so much as the rising of an objection against it, in the most absolute sense, in God shewing mercy to whom he will shew mercy, and hardening whom he will. God's absolute sovereignty and justice, with respect to salvation and damnation, is what my mind seems to rest assured of, as much as of any thing that I see with my eyes; at least it is so at times. But I have often, since the first conviction, had quite another kind of sense of God's sovereignty than I had then. I have often since had not only a conviction, but a *delightful* conviction. The doctrine has very often appeared exceedingly pleasant, bright, and sweet. Absolute sovereignty is what I love to ascribe to God. But my first conviction was not so.

The first instance, that I remember, of that sort of inward, sweet delight in God and divine things, that I have lived much in since, was on reading those words, 1 Tim. i. 17. *Now unto the King eternal, immortal, invisible, the only wise God, be honour and glory for ever and ever, Amen.* As I read the words, there came into my soul, and was as it were diffused through it, a sense of the glory of the Divine Being; a new sense, quite different from any thing I ever experienced before. Never any words of Scripture seemed to me as these words did. I thought with myself, how excellent a Being that was, and how happy I should be, if I might enjoy that God, and be rapt up to him in heaven, and be as it were swallowed up in him for ever! I kept saying, and as it were singing, over these words of scripture to myself; and went to pray to God that I might enjoy him, and prayed in a manner quite different from what I used to do; with a new sort of affection. But it never came into my thought, that there was any thing spiritual, or of a saving nature in this.

From about that time, I began to have a new kind of apprehensions and ideas of Christ, and the work of redemption, and the glorious way of salvation by him. An inward, sweet sense of these things, at times, came into my heart; and my soul was led away in pleasant views and contemplations of them. And my mind was greatly engaged to spend my time in reading and meditating on Christ, on the beauty and excellency of his person, and the lovely way of salvation by free grace in him. I found no books so delightful to me, as those that treated of these subjects. Those words Cant. ii. 1. used to abundantly with me, *I am the Rose of Sharon, and the Lily of the valleys.* The words seemed to me, sweetly to represent the loveliness and beauty of Jesus Christ. The whole book of Canticles used to be pleasant to me, and I used to be much in reading it, about that time; and found, from time to time, an inward sweetness, that would carry me away, in my contemplations. This I know not how to express otherwise, than by a calm, sweet abstraction of soul from all the concerns of this world; and sometimes a kind of vision, or fixed ideas and imaginations, of being alone in the mountains, or some solitary wilderness, far from all mankind, sweetly conversing with Christ, and wrapt and swallowed up in God. The sense I had of divine things, would often of a sudden kindle up, as it were, a sweet burning in my heart; an ardour of soul, that I know not how to express.

Not long after I first began to experience these things, I gave an account to my father of some things that had passed in my mind. I was pretty much affected by the discourse we had together; and when the discourse was ended, I walked abroad alone, in a solitary place in my father's pasture, for contemplation. And as I was walking there, and looking upon the sky and clouds, there came into my mind so sweet a sense of the glorious *majesty* and *grace* of God, as I know not how to express.—I seemed to see them both in a sweet conjunction; majesty and meekness joined together: it was a sweet, and gentle, and holy majesty; and also a majestic meekness; an awful sweetness, a high, and great, and holy gentleness.

After this my sense of divine things gradually increased, and became more and more lively, and had more of that inward sweetness. The appearance of every thing was altered; there seemed to be, as it were, a calm, sweet, cast, or appearance of divine glory, in almost every thing. God's excellency, his wisdom, his purity and love, seemed to appear in every thing; in the sun, moon and stars; in the clouds and blue sky; in the grass, flowers, trees; in the water and all nature; which used greatly to fix my mind. I often used to sit and view the moon for a long time; and in the day, spent much time in viewing the clouds and sky, to behold the sweet glory of God in these things: in the meantime, singing forth, with a low voice, my contemplations of the Creator and Redeemer. And scarce any thing, among all the works of nature, was so sweet to me as thunder and lightning; formerly nothing had been so terrible to me. Before, I used to be uncommonly terrified with thunder, and to be struck with terror when I saw a thunder-storm rising; but now, on the contrary, it rejoiced me. I felt God, if I may so speak, at the first appearance of a thunder storm; and used to take the opportunity, at such times, to fix myself in order to view the clouds, and see the lightnings play, and hear the majestic and awful voice of God's thunder, which oftentimes was exceedingly entertaining, leading me to sweet contemplations of my great and glorious God. While thus engaged, it always seemed natural for me to sing, or chant forth my meditations; or, to speak my thoughts in soliloquies with a singing voice.

I felt then great satisfaction, as to my good estate; but that did not content me. I had vehement longings of soul after God and Christ, and after more holiness, wherwith my heart seemed to be full, and ready to break; which often brought to my mind the words of the Psalmist, Psal. cxix. 28. *My soul breaketh for the longing it hath.* I often felt a mourning and lamenting in my heart, that I had not turned to God sooner, that I might have had more time to grow in grace. My mind was greatly fixed on divine things; almost perpetually in the contemplation of them. I spent most of my time in thinking of divine things, year after year; often walking alone in the woods, and solitary places, for meditation, soliloquy, and prayer, and converse with God; and it was always my manner, at such times, to sing forth my contemplations. I was almost constantly in ejaculatory prayer, wherever I was. Prayer seemed to be natural to me, as the breath by which the inward burnings of my heart had vent. The delights which I now felt in the things of religion, were of an exceedingly different kind from those before-mentioned, that I had when a boy; and what then I had no more notion of, that one born blind has of pleasant and beautiful colours. They were of a more inward, pure, soul-animating and refreshing nature.

Those former delights never reached the heart; and did not arise from any sight of the divine excellency of the things or God; of any taste of the soul-satisfying and life-giving good there is in them.

Since I came to Northampton, I have often had sweet complacency in God, in views of his glorious perfections, and of the excellency of Jesus Christ. God has appeared to me a glorious and lovely Being, chiefly on account of his holiness. The holiness of God has always appeared to me the most lovely of all his attributes. The doctrines of God's absolute sovereignty, and free grace, in shewing mercy to whom he would shew mercy; and man's absolute dependence on the operations of God's Holy Spirit, have very often appeared to me as sweet and glorious doctrines. These doctrines have been much my delight. God's sovereignty has ever appeared to me, a great part of his glory. It has often been my delight to approach God, and adore him as a sovereign God, and ask sovereign mercy of him.

I have loved the doctrines of the gospel; they have been to my soul like green pastures. The gospel has seemed to me the richest treasure; the treasure that I have most desired, and longed that it might dwell richly in me. The way of salvation by Christ, has appeared, in a general way, glorious and excellent, most pleasant and most beautiful. It has often seemed to me, that it would, in a great measure, spoil heaven, to receive it in any other way. That text has often been affecting and delightful to me, Isa.

xxxii, 2, *A man shall be an hiding place from the wind, and a covert from the tempest, &c.*

It has often appeared to me delightful, to be united to Christ; to have him for my head, and to be a member of his body; also to have Christ for my teacher and prophet. I very often think with sweetness, and longings, and pantings of soul, of being a little child, taking hold of Christ, to be led by him through the wilderness of this world. That text, Matt. xviii. 3, has often been sweet to me, *Except ye be converted and become as little children, &c.* I love to think of coming to Christ, to receive salvation of him, poor in spirit, and quite empty of self, humbly exalting him alone; cut off entirely from my own root, in order to grow into, and out of Christ: to have god in Christ to be all in all; and to live by faith on the Son of God, a life of humble, unfeigned confidence in him. That Scripture has often been sweet to me, Psal. cxv. 1, *Not unto us, O Lord, not unto us, but unto thy name give glory, for thy mercy, and for thy truth's sake.* And those words of Christ, Luke x. 21, *In that hour Jesus rejoiced in spirit, and said, I thank thee, O Father, Lord of heaven and earth, that thou hast hid these things from the wise and prudent, and hast revealed them unto babes: even so, Father, for so it seemed good in thy sight.* That sovereignty of God, which Christ rejoiced in, seemed to me worthy of such joy; and that rejoicing seemed to show the excellency of Christ, and of what spirit he was.

Sometimes, only mentioning a single word, caused my heart to burn within me; or only seeing the name of Christ, or the name of some attribute of God.

And God has appeared glorious to me, on account of the Trinity. It has made me have exalting thoughts of God, that he subsists in three persons: Father, Son, and Holy Ghost. The sweetest joys and delights I have experienced, have not been those that have arisen from a hope of my own good estate; but in a direct view of the glorious things of the gospel. When I enjoy this sweetness, it seems to carry me above the thoughts of my own estate; it seems, at such times, a loss that I cannot bear, to take off my eye from the glorious, pleasant object I behold without me, to turn my eye in upon myself, and my own good estate.

My heart has been much on the advancement of Christ's kingdom in the world. The histories of the past advancement of Christ's kingdom have been sweet to me. When I have read histories of past ages, the pleasantest thing, in all my reading, has been, to read of the kingdom of Christ being promoted. And when I have expected, in my reading, to come to any such thing, I have rejoiced in the prospect, all the way as I read. And my mind has been much entertained and delighted with the scripture promises and prophecies, which relate to the future glorious advancement of Christ's kingdom upon earth.

I have sometimes had a sense of the excellent fulness of Christ, and his meetness and suitableness as a Saviour; whereby he has appeared to me, far above all, the chief of ten thousands. His blood and atonement have appeared sweet, and his righteousness sweet; which was always accompanied with ardency of spirit; and inward strugglings and breathings, and groanings that cannot be uttered, to be emptied of myself, and swallowed up in Christ.

Once, as I rode out into the woods for my health, in 1737, having alighted from my horse in a retired place, as my manner commonly has been, to walk for divine contemplation and prayer, I had a view, that for me was extraordinary, of the glory of the Son of God, as Mediator between God and man, and his wonderful, great, full, pure and sweet grace and love, and meek and gentle condescension. This grace that appeared so calm and sweet, appeared also great above the heavens. The person of Christ appeared ineffably excellent, with an excellency great enough to swallow up all thought and conception—which continued, as near as I can judge, about an hour; which kept me the greater part of the time, in a flood of tears, and weeping aloud. I felt an ardency of soul to be, what I know not otherwise how to express, emptied and annihilated; to lie in the dust, and to be full of Christ alone; to love him with a holy and pure love; to trust in him; to live upon him; to serve and follow him; and to be perfectly sanctified and made pure, with a divine and heavenly purity. I have, several other times, had views very much of the same nature, and which have had the same effects.

I have, many times, had a sense of the glory of the Third Person in the Trinity, in his office of Sanctifier; in his holy operations, communicating divine light and life to the soul. God in the communications of his holy spirit, has appeared as an infinite fountain of divine glory and sweetness; being full and sufficient to fill and satisfy the soul; pouring forth itself in sweet communications; like the sun in its glory, sweetly and pleasantly diffusing light and life. And I have sometimes had an affecting sense of the excellency of the word of God as a word of life; as the light of life; a sweet, excellent, life-giving word; accompanied with a thirsting after that word, that it might dwell richly in my heart.

Often, since I lived in this town, I have had very affecting views of my own sinfulness and vileness; very frequently to such a degree, as to hold me in a kind of loud weeping, sometimes for a considerable time together; so that I have often been forced to shut myself up. I have had a vastly greater sense of my own wickedness, and the badness of my heart, than ever I had before my conversion. It has often appeared to me, that if God should mark iniquity against me, I should appear the very worst of all mankind; of all that have been, since the beginning of the world, to this time: and that I should have by far the lowest place in hell. When others, that have come to talk with me about their soul-concerns, have expressed the sense they have had of their own wickedness, by saying, that it seemed to them, that they were as bad as the devil himself; I thought their expressions seemed exceeding faint and feeble, to represent my wickedness.

My wickedness, as I am in myself, has long appeared to me perfectly ineffable, and swallowing up all thought and imagination; like an infinite deluge, or mountains over my head. I know not how to express better what my sins appear to me to be, than by heaping infinite upon infinite, and multiplying infinite by infinite. Very often, for these many years, these expressions are in my mind, and in my mouth, "Infinite upon infinite—Infinite upon infinite!" When I look into my heart, and take a view of my wickedness, it looks like an abyss, infinitely deeper than hell. And it appears to me, that were it not for free grace, exalted and raised up to the infinite height of all the fulness and glory of the great Jehovah, and the arm of his power and grace stretched forth in all the majesty of his power, and in all the glory of his sovereignty, I should appear sunk down in my sins below hell itself; far beyond the sight of every thing, but the eye of sovereign grace, that can pierce even down to such a depth. And yet, it seems to me that my conviction of sin is exceedingly small, and faint; it is enough to amaze me, that I have no more sense of my sin. I know certainly, that I have very little sense of my sinfulness. When I have had turns of weeping and crying for my sins, I thought I knew at the time, that my repentance was nothing to my sin.

I have greatly longed of late, for a broken heart, and to lie low before God; and, when I ask for humility, I cannot bear the thoughts of being no more humble than other christians. It seems to me, that though their degrees of humility may be suitable for them, yet it would be a vile self-exaltation in me, not to be the lowest in humility of all mankind. Others speak of their longing to be "humbled to the dust;" that may be a proper expression for them, but I always think of myself, that I ought, and it is an expression that has long been natural for me to use in prayer, "to lie infinitely low before God." And it is affecting to think, how ignorant I was, when a young christian, of the bottomless, infinite depths of wickedness, pride, hypocrisy and deceit, left in my heart.

I have a much greater sense of my universal, exceeding dependance on God's grace and strength, and mere good pleasure, of late, than I used formerly to have; and have experienced more of an abhorrence of my own righteousness. The very thought of any joy arising in me, on any consideration of my own amiableness, performances, or experiences, or any goodness of heart, or life, is nauseous and detestable to me. And yet, I am greatly afflicted with a proud and self-righteous spirit, much more sensibly than I used to be formerly. I see that serpent rising and putting forth its head continually, every where, all around me.

Though it seems to me, that in some respects, I was a far better christian, for two or three years after my first conversion, than I am now; and lived in a more constant delight and pleasure; yet of late years, I have had a more full and constant sense of the absolute sovereignty of God, and a delight in that sovereignty; and have had more of a sense of the glory of Christ, as a Mediator revealed in the gospel. On one Saturday night, in particular, I had such a discovery of the excellency of the gospel above all other doctrines, that I could not but say to myself, "This is my chosen light, my chosen doctrine": and of Christ, "This is my chosen Prophet." It appeared sweet, beyond all expression, to follow Christ, and to be taught, and enlightened, and instructed by him; to learn of him, and live to him. Another Saturday night, (*Jan.* 1739) I had such a sense, how sweet and blessed a thing it was to walk in the way of duty; to do that which was right and meet to be done, and agreeable to the holy mind of God; that it caused me to break forth into a kind of loud weeping, which held me some time, so that I was forced to shut myself up, and fasten the doors. I could not but, as it were, cry out, "How happy are they, who do that which is right in the sight of God! They are blessed indeed, *they* are the happy ones!" I had, at the same time, a very affecting sense, how meet and suitable it was that God should govern the world, and order all things according to his own pleasure; and I rejoiced in it, that God reigned, and that his will was done.

From *A Treatise Concerning Religious Affections* (1746)

1 PETER i. 8
Whom having not seen, ye love; in whom though now ye see him not, yet believing, ye rejoice with joy unspeakable and full of glory.

Sect. I

Introductory Remarks respecting the Affections

In these words, the apostle represents the state of the Christians to whom he wrote, under persecutions. To these persecutions he has respect, in the two preceding verses, when he speaks of *the trial of their faith,* and of *their being in heaviness through manifold temptations.*

Such *trials* are of threefold benefit to true religion. Hereby the *truth* of it is manifested, it appears to be indeed *true religion.* Trials, above all other things, have a tendency to distinguish true religion and false, and to cause the difference between them evidently to appear. Hence they are called by the name of *trials,* in the verse preceding the text, and innumerable other places.— They try the faith and religion of professors, of what sort it is, as apparent gold is tried in the fire, and manifested, whether it be true gold or not. And the faith of true Christians, being thus tried and proved to be true, is *found to praise, and honour, and glory.*

And then, these trials not only manifest the *truth* of true religion, but they make its genuine *beauty* and *amiableness* remarkably to appear. True virtue never appears so lovely, as when it is most oppressed: and the divine excellency of real Christianity, is never exhibited with such advantage, as when under the greatest trials. Then it is that true faith appears much more precious than gold; and upon this account, is *found to praise, and honour, and glory.*

Again, another benefit of such trials to true religion, is that they *purify* and *increase* it. They not only manifest it to be *true,* but also tend to *refine* it, and deliver it from those mixtures of what is false, which encumber and impede it; that nothing may be left but that which is true. They not only shew the amiableness of true religion to the best advantage, but they tend to increase its beauty by establishing and confirming it; making it more lively and vigourous, and purifying it from those things that obscured its lustre and glory. As gold that is tried in the fire is purged from its alloy, and all remainders of dross, and comes forth more beautiful; so true faith being tried as gold is tried in the fire, becomes more precious; and thus also is *found unto praise, and honour, and glory.* The apostle seems to have respect to each of these benefits in the verse preceding the text.

And, in the text, the apostle observes how true religion *operated* in these Christians under their persecutions, whereby these benefits appeared in them; or what manner of operation it was, whereby their religion, under persecution, was manifested to be *true* religion in its genuine *beauty* and *amiableness,* and also appeared to be *increased* and *purified,* and so was like to be *found unto praise, and honour, and glory, at the appearing of Jesus Christ.* And there were two kinds of operation, or exercise of true religion, in them, under their sufferings, that the apostle takes notice of in the text, wherein these benefits appeared.

1. *Love to Christ. Whom having not seen, ye love.* The world was ready to wonder, what strange principle it was, that influenced them to expose themselves to so great sufferings, to forsake the things that were seen, and renounce all that was dear and pleasant, which was the object of sense. They seemed to the men of the world as if they were beside themselves, and to act as though they hated themselves; there was nothing in *their* view, that could induce them thus to suffer, or to support them under, and carry them through such trials. But although there was nothing that the world saw, or that the Christians themselves ever saw with their bodily eyes, that thus influenced and supported them, yet they had a supernatural principle of love to something *unseen;* they loved Jesus Christ, for they saw him spiritually, whom the world saw not, and whom they themselves had never seen with bodily eyes.

2. *Joy in Christ.* Though their outward sufferings were very grievous, yet their inward spiritual joys were greater than their sufferings; and these supported them, and enabled them to suffer with cheerfulness.

There are two things which the apostle takes notice of in the text concerning this joy. 1. The manner in which it rises, the way in which Christ, though unseen, is the foundation of it, *viz.* by *faith;* which is the evidence of things not seen; *In whom, though now ye see him not, yet* BELIEVING, *ye rejoice.* 2. The *nature* of this joy; *unspeakable, and full of glory. Unspeakable* in the *kind* of it; very different from worldy joys, and carnal delights; of a vastly more pure, sublime, and heavenly nature, being something supernatural, and truly divine, and so ineffably excellent! the sublimity and exquisite sweetness of which, there were no words to set forth. *Unspeakable* also in *degree;* it having pleased God to give them this holy joy with a liberal hand, in their state of persecution.

Their joy was *full of glory.* Although the joy was unspeakable, and no words were sufficient to describe it; yet something might be said of it, and no words more fit to represent its excellency than these, that it was *full of glory;* or, as it is in the original, *glorified joy.* In rejoicing with this joy, their minds were filled, as it were, with a glorious brightness, and their natures exalted and perfected. It was a most worthy, noble rejoicing, that did not corrupt and debase the mind, as many carnal joys do; but did greatly beautify and dignify it. It was a prelibation of the joy of heaven, that raised their minds to a degree of heavenly blessedness; it filled their minds with the light of God's glory, and made themselves to shine with some communication of that glory.

Hence the proposition or doctrine, that I would raise from these words is this, TRUE RELIGION, IN GREAT PART, CONSISTS IN HOLY AFFECTIONS.

We see that the apostle, in remarking the operations and exercises of religion in these Christians, when it had its greatest trial by persecution, as gold is tried in the fire—and when it not only proved true, but was most pure from dross and mixtures—and when it appeared in them most in its genuine excellency and native beauty, and was found to praise, and honour, and glory—he singles out the religious affections of *love* and *joy,* as those exercises, wherein their religion did thus appear *true, pure* and *glorious.*

Here it may be inquired, what the *affections* of the mind are?—I answer, The affections are no other than the more vigorous and *sensible exercises of the inclination and will* of the soul.

God has endued the soul with two principal faculties: The one, that by which it is capable of *perception* and speculation, or by which it discerns, and judges of things; which is called the *understanding.* The other, that by which the soul is some way *inclined* with respect to the things it views or considers: or it is the faculty by which the soul beholds things—not as an indifferent unaffected spectator, but—either as liking or disliking, pleased or displeased, approving or rejecting. This faculty is called by various names: it is sometimes called the *inclination;* and, as it respects the actions determined and governed by it, the *will:* and the *mind,* with regard to the exercises of this faculty, is often called the *heart.*

The *exercises* of this last faculty are of two sorts; either those by which the soul is carried out towards the things in view in *approving* them, being pleased with, and inclined to them; or, those in which the soul opposes the things in view, in *disapproving* them; and in being displeased with, averse from, and rejecting them. And as the exercises of the inclination are various in their *kinds,* so they are much more various in their *degrees.* There are some exercises of pleasedness or displeasedness, inclination or disinclination, wherein the soul is carried but a little beyond a state of perfect indifference. And there are other degrees, wherein the approbation or dislike, pleasedness or aversion, are stronger; wherein we may rise higher and higher, till the soul comes to act vigorously and sensibly, and its actings are with that strength, that (through the laws of union which the Creator has fixed between soul and body) the motion of the blood and animal spirits begins to be sensibly altered: whence oftentimes arises some bodily sensation, especially about the *heart* and vitals, which are the fountain of the fluids of the body. Whence it comes to pass, that the *mind*, with regard to the exercises of this faculty, perhaps in all nations and ages, is called *the heart*. And it is to be noted, that they are these more vigorous and sensible exercises of this faculty, which are called the *affections*.

The *will*, and the *affections* of the soul, are not two faculties; the affections are not essentially distinct from the will, nor do they differ from the mere *actings* of the will and inclination, but only in the liveliness and sensibility of exercise.—It must be confessed, that language is here somewhat imperfect, the meaning of words in a considerable measure loose and unfixed, and not precisely limited by custom which governs the use of language. In some sense, the affection of the soul differs nothing at all from the will and inclination, and the will never is in any exercise further than it is *affected;* it is not moved out of a state of perfect indifference, any otherwise than as it is *affected* one way or another. But yet there are many actings of the will and inclination, that are not so commonly called *affections.* In every thing we do, wherein we act voluntarily, there is an exercise of the will and inclination. It is our inclination that governs us in our actions; but *all the actings* of the inclination and will, are not ordinarily called affections. Yet, what are commonly called affections are not essentially different from them, but only in the *degree* and *manner* of exercise. In every act of

the will whatsoever, the soul either likes or dislikes, is either inclined or disinclined to what is in view. These are not *essentially* different from the affections of *love* and *hatred.* A liking or inclination of the soul to a thing, if it be in a high degree vigorous and lively, is the very same thing with the affection of *love:* and a disliking and disinclining, if in a great degree, is the very same with *hatred.* In every act of the will *for,* or *towards* something not present, the soul is in some degree *inclined* to that thing; and that inclination, if in a considerable degree, is the very same with the affection of *desire.* And in every degree of an act of the will, wherein the soul approves of something present, there is a degree of pleasedness; and that pleasedness, if it be in a considerable degree, is the very same with the affection of *joy* or *delight.* And if the will disapproves of what is present, the soul is in some degree displeased, and if that displeasedness be great, it is the very same with the affection of *grief* or *sorrow.*

Such seems to be our nature, and such the laws of the union of soul and body, that there never is in any case whatsoever, any lively and vigorous exercise of the inclination, without some effect upon the body, in some alteration of the motion of its fluids, and especially of the animal spirits. And, on the other hand, from the same laws of union, over the consitution of the body, and the motion of its fluids, may promote the exercise of the affections. But yet, it is not the body, but the mind only, that is the proper seat of the affections. The body of man is no more capable of being really the subject of love or hatred, joy or sorrow, fear or hope, than the body of a tree, or than the same body of man is capable of thinking and understanding. As it is the soul only that has ideas, so it is the soul only that is pleased or displeased with its ideas. As it is the soul only that thinks, so it is the soul only that loves or hates, rejoices or is grieved at what it thinks of. Nor are these motions of the animal spirits, and fluids of the body, any thing properly belonging to the *nature* of the affections; though they always *accompany* them in the present state; but are only effects or concomitants of the affections, which are entirely distinct from the affections themselves, and no way essential to them; so that an unbodied spirit may be as capable of love and hatred, joy or sorrow, hope or fear, or other affections, as one that is united to a body.

The *affections* and *passions* are frequently spoken of as the same; and yet, in the more common use of speech, there is in some respect a difference. *Affection* is a word, that in its ordinary signification, seems to be something more extensive than *passion*, being used for all vigorous lively actings of the will or inclination; but *passion* is used for those that are more sudden, and whose effects on the animal spirits are more violent, the mind being more overpowered, and less in its own command.

As all the exercises of inclination and will are concerned either in approving and liking, or disapproving and rejecting; so the affections are of two sorts; they are those by which the soul is carried out to what is in view, cleaving *to* it, or *seeking* it; or those by which it is averse *from* it, and *opposes* it. Of the former sort are *love, desire, hope, joy, gratitude, complacence.* Of the latter kind, are *hatred, fear, anger, grief,* and such like; which it is needless now to stand particularly to define.

And there are some affections wherein there is a *composition* of each of the aforementioned kinds of actings of the will; as in the affection of *pity,* there is something of the *former kind,* towards the person suffering, and something of the *latter,* towards what he suffers. And so in *zeal,* there is in it high *approbation* of some person or thing, together with vigorous *opposition* to what is conceived to be contrary to it.

Sect. II

True Religion, in great part, consists in the Affections

1. What has been said of the *nature* of the affections makes this evident; and may be sufficient, without adding any thing further, to put this matter out of doubt; for who will deny that true religion consists, in a great measure, in vigorous and lively actings of the *inclination* and *will* of the soul, or the fervent exercises of the *heart?* That religion which God requires, and will accept, does not consist in weak, dull, and lifeless wishes, raising us but a little above a state of indifference. God, in his word, greatly insists upon it, that we be in good earnest, *fervent in spirit,* and our hearts vigorously engaged in religion: Rom. xii. 11. *Be ye fervent in spirit, serving the Lord.* Deut. x. 12. *And now Israel, what doth the Lord thy God require of thee, but to fear the Lord the God, to walk in all his ways,*

and to love him, and to serve the Lord thy God with all thy heart, and with all thy soul? And chap. vi. 4, 5. Hear, O Israel, the Lord our God is one Lord; and thou shalt love the Lord thy God with all thy heart, and with all thy soul, and with all thy might. It is such a fervent, vigorous engagedness of the heart in religion, that is the fruit of a real circumcision of the heart, or true regeneration, and that has the promises of life; Deut. xxx. 6. *And the Lord thy God will circumcise thine heart, and the heart of thy seed, to love the Lord thy God with all thy heart, and with all thy soul, that thou mayest live.*

If we be not in good earnest in religion, and our wills and inclinations be not strongly exercised, we are nothing. The things of religion are so great, that there can be no suitableness in the exercises of our hearts, to their nature and importance, unless they be lively and powerful. In nothing is vigour in the actings of our inclinations so requisite, as in religion; and in nothing is lukewarmness so odious. True religion is evermore a powerful thing; and the power of it appears, in the first place, in its exercises in the heart, its principal and original seat. Hence true religion is called the *power of godliness,* in distinction from external appearances, which are *the form* of it, 2 Tim. iii. 5. *Having a form of godliness, but denying the power of it.* The Spirit of God, in those who have sound and solid religion, is a spirit of powerful holy affection; and, therefore, God is said *to have given them the Spirit of power, and of love, and of a sound mind,* (2 Tim. i. 7.) And such, when they receive the Spirit of God in his sanctifying and saving influences, are said to be *baptized* *with the Holy Ghost, and with fire;* by reason of the power and fervour of those exercises which the Spirit of God excites in them, and whereby *their hearts,* when grace is in exercise, may be said to *burn within them.* (Luke xxiv. 32.)

The business of *religion* is, from time to time, compared to those *exercises,* wherein men are wont to have their hearts and strength greatly exercised and engaged; such as running, wrestling or agonizing for a great prize or crown, and fighting with strong enemies that seek our lives, and warring as those that by violence take a city or kingdom. Though true grace has various degrees, and there are some who are but babes in Christ, in whom the exercise of the inclination and will towards divine and heavenly things, is compartively weak; yet every one that has the power of godliness, has his inclinations and heart exercised towards God and divine things with such strength and vigour, that these holy exercises prevail in him above all carnal or natural affections, and are effectual to overcome them; for every true disciple of Christ, *loves him above father or mother, wife and children, brethren and sisters, houses and lands, yea more than his own life.* Hence it follows, that wherever true religion is, there are vigorous exercises of the inclination and will towards divine objects: but by what was said before, the vigorous, lively, and sensible exercises of the will, are no other than the *affections* of the soul.

2. The Author of our nature has not only given us affections, but has made them very much the spring of actions. As the *affections* not only necessarily belong to the *human nature,* but are a

very *great part* of it; so (inasmuch as by regeneration persons are renewed in the whole man) *holy affections* not only necessarily belong to *true religion,* but are a very great part of such religion. And as true religion is practical, and God hath so constituted the human nature, that the affections are very much the spring of men's actions, this also shews, that true religion must consist very much in the affections.

Such is man's nature, that he is very inactive, any otherwise than he is influenced by either *love* or *hatred, desire, hope, fear,* or some other affection. These affections we see to be the moving springs in all the affairs of life, which engage men in all their pursuits; and especially in all affairs wherein they are earnestly engaged, and which they pursue with vigour. We see the world of mankind exceedingly busy and active; and their affections are the springs of motion; take away all *love* and *hatred,* all *hope* and *fear,* all *anger, zeal,* and affectionate *desire,* and the world would be, in a great measure, motionless and dead: there would be no such thing as activity amongst mankind, or any earnest pursuit whatsoever. It is affection that engages the covetous man, and him that is greedy of worldly profits; it is by the affections that the ambitious man is put forward in his pursuit of worldly glory; and the affections also actuate the voluptuous man, in his pleasure and sensual delights. The world continues, from age to age, in a continual commotion and agitation, in pursuit of these things; but take away affection, and the *spring* of all this motion would be gone; the motion itself would cease. And as in worldly things, worldly affections are very much the spring of men's motion and action; so in religious matters, the spring of their actions are very much religious affections: he that has doctrinal knowledge and speculation only, without affection, never is *engaged* in the business of religion.

3. Nothing is more manifest *in fact,* than that the things of religion take hold of men's souls no further than they *affect* them. There are multitudes who often hear the word of God, things infinitely great and important, and which most nearly concern them, yet all seems to be wholly ineffectual upon them, and to make no alteration in their dispostion or behaviour; the reason is, they are not *affected* with what they hear. There are many who often hear of the glorious perfections of God, his almighty power, boundless wisdom, infinite majesty, and that holiness by which he is of purer eyes than to behold evil, and cannot look on iniquity; together with his infinite goodness and mercy. They hear of the great works of God's wisdom, power, and goodness, wherein there appear the admirable manifestations of these perfections. They hear particularly of the unspeakable love of God and Christ, and what Christ has done and suffered. They hear of the great things of another world, of eternal misery, in bearing the fierceness and wrath of almighty God; and of endless blessedness and glory in the presence of God, and the enjoyment of his love. They also hear the peremptory commands of God, his gracious counsels and warnings, and the sweet invitations of the gospel. Yet they remain as before,

with no sensible alteration, either in heart or practice, because they are not affected with what they hear. I am bold to assert, that there never was any considerable change wrought in the mind or conversation of any person, by any thing of a religious nature that ever he read, heard or saw, who had not his affections moved. Never was a natural man engaged earnestly to seek his salvation; never were any such brought to cry after wisdom, and lift up their voice for understanding, and to wrestle with God in prayer for mercy; and never was one humbled, and brought to the foot of God, from any thing that ever he heard or imagined of his own unworthiness and deservings of God's displeasure: nor was ever one induced to fly for refuge unto Christ, while his heart remained *unaffected.* Nor was there ever a saint awakened out of a cold, lifeless frame, or recovered from a declining state in religion, and brought back from a lamentable departure from God, without having his heart *affected.* And, in a word, there never was any thing *considerable* brought to pass in the heart or life of any man living, by the things of religion, that had not his heart *deeply affected* by those things.

4. The holy scriptures every where place religion very much in the affections; such as fear, hope, love, hatred, desire, joy, sorrow, gratitude, compassion, and zeal.

The scriptures place much of religion in godly *fear;* insomuch that an experience of it is often spoken of as the character of those who are truly religious persons. *They tremble at God's word, they fear before him, their flesh trembles for*

fear of him, they are afraid of his judgments, his excellency makes them afraid, and his dread falls upon them, &c. An appellation commonly given the saints in scripture, is, *fearers of God,* or *they that fear the Lord.* And because this is a great part of true godliness, hence true godliness in general is very commonly called *the fear of God.*

So *hope* in God, and in the promises of his word, is often spoken of in the scripture, as a very considerable *part of true religion.* It is mentioned as one of the three great things of which religion consists, 1 Cor. xiii. 13. Hope in the Lord is also frequently mentioned as the *character of the saints:* Psal. cxlvi. 5. *Happy is he that hath the God of Jacob for his help, whose* HOPE *is in the Lord his God.* Jer. xvii. 7. *Blessed is the man that trusteth in the Lord, and whose* HOPE *the Lord is.* Psal. xxxi 24. *Be of good courage, and he shall strengthen your heart, all ye that* HOPE *in the Lord.* And the like in many other places. Religious fear and hope are, once and again, joined together, as jointly constituting the character of the true saints; Psal. xxxiii. 18. *Behold, the eye of the Lord is upon them that* FEAR *him, upon them that* HOPE *in his mercy.* Psal. cxlvii. 11. *The Lord taketh pleasure in them that* FEAR *him, in those that* HOPE *in his mercy.* Hope is so great a part of true religion, that the apostle says *we are saved by* HOPE, Rom. viii. 24. And this is spoken of as *the helmet* of the Christian soldier, 1 Thess. v. 8. *And for an helmet the* HOPE *of salvation;* and the sure and stedfast *anchor* of the soul, which preserves it from being cast away by the storms of this evil world, Heb. vi. 19. *Which* HOPE *we have as an anchor of the soul, both sure and stedfast, and which entereth into that within the veil.* It is spoken of as a great benefit which true saints receive by Christ's resurrection, 1 Pet. i. 3. *Blessed by the God and Father of our Lord Jesus Christ, which, according to his abundant mercy, hath begotten us again unto a lively* HOPE, *by the resurrection of Jesus Christ from the dead.*

The scriptures place religion very much in the affection of *love;* love to God, and the Lord Jesus Christ; love to the people of God, and to mankind. The texts in which this is manifest, both in the Old Testament and New, are innumerable. But of this more afterwards. . . .

From *Dissertation Concerning the End for Which God Created the World* (1765)

SHEWING, THAT THE ULTIMATE END
OF THE CREATION
OF THE WORLD IS BUT ONE,
AND WHAT THAT ONE END IS.

From what has been observed in the last section, it appears, if the whole of what is said relating to this affair be duly weighed, and one part compared with another, we shall have reason to think that the design of the Spirit of God is not to represent God's ultimate end as *manifold,* but as ONE. For though it be signified by various names, yet they appear not to be names of *different* things, but various names involving

each other in their meaning; either different names of the *same thing,* or names of several parts of *one whole;* or of the same whole viewed in *various lights,* or in its *different respects* and relations. For it appears, that all that is ever spoken of in the scripture as an ultimate end of God's works, is included in that one phrase, *the glory of God;* which is the name by which the ultimate end of God's works is most commonly called in scripture; and seems most aptly to signify the thing.

The thing signified by that name, *the glory of God,* when spoken of as the supreme and ultimate end of all God's works, is the emanation and true external expression of God's internal glory and fulness; meaning by his *fulness,* what has already been explained; or, in other words, God's internal glory, in a true and just exhibition, or external existence of it. It is confessed, that there is a degree of obscurity in these definitions; but perhaps an obscurity which is unavoidable, through the imperfection of language to express things of so sublime a nature. And therefore the thing may possibly be better understood, by using a variety of expressions, by a particular consideration of it, as it were, by parts, than by any short definition.

It includes the *exercise* of God's perfections to produce a proper *effect,* in opposition to their lying eternally dormant and ineffectual: as his power being eternally without any act or fruit of that power; his wisdom eternally ineffectual in any wise production, or prudent disposal of any thing, &c. The *manifestation* of his internal glory to created understandings. The *communication* of the infinite fulness of God to the creature. The creature's high *esteem* of God, love to him, and complacence and joy in him; and the proper *exercises* and *expressions* of these.

These at first view may appear to be entirely distinct things: but if we more closely consider the matter, they will all appear to be ONE thing, in a variety of views and relations. They are all but the *emanation of God's glory;* or the excellent brightness and fulness of the divinity *diffused, overflowing,* and as it were *enlarged;* or in one word, *existing and extra.* God *exercising* his perfection to produce a proper *effect,* is not distinct from the emanation or *communication* of his *fulness:* for this is the effect, viz. his *fullness communicated,* and the producing of this effect is the communication of his fulness; and there is nothing in this effectual exerting of God's perfection, but the emanation of God's internal glory.

Now God's *internal* glory is either in his understanding or will. The glory or fulness of his *understanding* is his knowledge. The internal glory and fulness of God, having its special seat in his *will,* is his holiness and happiness. The *whole* of God's *internal* good or glory is in these three things, viz. his infinite *knowledge;* his infinite virtue or *holiness,* and his infinite joy and *happiness.* Indeed there are a great many attributes in God, according to our way of conceiving them: but all may be reduced to these; or to their degree, circumstances and relations. We have no conception of God's *power,* different from the degree of these things, with a certain relation of them to effects. God's *infinity* is not properly a distinct *kind* of good, but only expresses the *degree* of good there is in him. So God's *eternity* is not a distinct good; but is the duration of good. His *immutability* is still the same good, with a negation of change. So that, as I said, the *fulness* of the Godhead is the fulness of his *understanding,* consisting in his knowledge; and the fulness of his *will,* consisting in his virtue and happiness.

And therefore, the *external* glory of God consists in the *communication* of these. The communication of his knowledge is chiefly in giving the *knowledge of himself:* for this is the knowledge in which the fulness of God's understanding chiefly consists. And thus we see how the manifestation of God's glory to created understandings, and their seeing and knowing it, is not distinct from an emanation or communication of God's fulness, but clearly implied in it. Again, the communication of God's virtue or holiness is principally in communicating the *love of himself.* And thus we see how, not only the creature's seeing and knowing God's excellence, but also supremely esteeming and loving him, belongs to the communication of *God's fulness.* And the communication of God's joy and happiness consists chiefly in communicating to the creature that happiness and joy which consists in *rejoicing in God,* and in his glorious excellency; for in such joy God's own happiness does principally consist. And in these things, *knowing* God's excellency, *loving* God for it, and *rejoicing* in it; and in the *exercise* and *expression* of these, consists God's honour and praise; so that these are clearly implied in that glory of God, which consists in the *emanation* of his internal glory.

And though all these things, which seem to be so various, are signified by that glory which the scripture speaks of as the ultimate end of all God's works; yet it is manifest there is no greater, and no other variety in it, than in the internal and essential glory of God itself. God's internal glory is partly in his understanding, and partly in his will. And this internal glory, as seated in the will of God, implies both his holiness and his happiness: both are evidently God's glory, according to the use of the phrase. So that as God's external glory is only the emanation of his internal, this variety necessarily follows. And again, it hence appears that here is no other variety or distinction, but what necessarily arises from the distinct faculties of the creature to which the communication is made, as created in the image of God: even as having these two faculties of understanding and will. God communicates himself to the *understanding* of the creature, in giving him the *knowledge* of his glory; and to the *will* of the creature, in giving him *holiness*, consisting primarily in the love of God: and in giving the creature *happiness* chiefly consisting in *joy* in God. These are the sum of that emanation of divine fulness called in scripture, *the glory of God.* The first part of this glory is call *truth,* the latter *grace,* John i. 14. "We beheld his *glory,* the glory of the only begotten of the Father, full of *grace* and *truth.*"

Thus we see that the great end of God's works, which is so variously expressed in scripture, is indeed but ONE; and this *one* end is most properly and comprehensively called, THE GLORY OF GOD; by which name it is most commonly called in scripture; and is fitly compared to an effulgence or emanation of light from a luminary. Light is the external expression, exhibition, and manifestation of the excellency of the luminary, of the sun for instance: It is the abundant, extensive emanation and communication of the fulness of the sun to innumerable beings that partake of it. It is by this that the sun itself is seen, and his glory beheld, and all other things are discovered: it is by a participation of this communication from the sun, that surrounding objects receive all their lustre, beauty, and brightness. It is by this that all nature receives life, comfort, and joy. Light is abundantly used in scripture to represent and signify these three things knowledge, holiness, and happiness.

Jonathan Mayhew (1720–1766)

Jonathan Mayhew, for almost twenty years pastor of Boston's West Church, was a religious thinker whose ideas were somewhat ahead of his time. A liberal Christian who repudiated the doctrine of the Trinity, affirmed the existence of free will, and defended the right of private judgment, Mayhew's views involved him in numerous controversies. The following selection, in which Mayhew establishes the religious grounds on which he saw civil disobedience as both legitimate and necessary, allies him with a later generation of thinkers who were to frame the argument, at once civil, moral, and, religious, for America's declaration of independence from English tyranny.

From *A Discourse Concerning Unlimited Submission and Non-Resistance to the Higher Powers* (1750)

Thus it appears, that the common argument, grounded upon this passage [Romans 13:1–3], in favor of universal, and passive obedience, really overthrows itself, by proving too much, if it proves any thing at all; namely, that no civil officer is, in any case whatever, to be resisted, though acting in express contradiction to the design of his office; which no man, in his senses, ever did, or can assert.

If we calmly consider the nature of the thing itself, nothing can well be imagined more directly contrary to common sense, than to suppose that millions of people should be subjected to the arbitrary, precarious pleasure of one single man; (who has naturally no superiority over them in point of authority) so that their estates, and every thing that is valuable in life, and even their lives also, shall be absolutely at his disposal, if he happens to be wanton and capricious enough to demand them. What unprejudiced man can

think, that God made ALL to be thus subservient to the lawless pleasure and phrenzy of ONE, so that it shall always be a sin to resist him! Nothing but the most plain and express revelation from heaven could make a sober impartial man believe such a monstrous, unaccountable doctrine, and, indeed, the thing itself, appears so shocking—so out of all proportion, that it may be questioned, whether all the miracles that ever were wrought, could make it credible, that this doctrine really came from God. At present, there is not the least syllable in scripture which gives any countenance to it. The hereditary, indefeasible, divine right of kings, and the doctrine of non-resistance, which is built upon the supposition of such a right, are altogether as fabulous and chimerical, as transubstantiation; or any of the most absurd reveries of ancient or modern visionaries. These notions are fetched neither from divine revelation, nor human reason; and if they are derived from neither of those sources, it is not much matter from whence they come, or whither they go. Only it is a pity that such doctrines should be propagated in society, to raise factions and rebellions, as we see they have in fact, been both in the last, and in the present, REIGN.

But then, if unlimited submission and passive obedience to the higher powers, in all possible cases, be not a duty, it will be asked, "How far are we obliged to submit? If we may innocently disobey and resist in some cases, why not in all? Where shall we stop? What is the measure of our duty? This doctrine tends to the total dissolution of civil government;

and to introduce such scenes of wild anarchy and confusion, as are more fatal to society than the worst tyranny."

After this manner, some men object; and, indeed, this is the most plausible thing that can be said in favor of such an absolute submission as they plead for. But the worst (or rather the best) of it, is, that there is very little strength or solidity in it. For similar difficulties may be raised with respect to almost every duty of natural and revealed religion.—To instance only in two, both of which are near akin, and indeed exactly parallel, to the case before us. It is unquestionably the duty of children to submit to their parents; and of servants, to their masters. But no one asserts, that it is their duty to obey, and submit to them, in all supposeable cases; or universally a sin to resist them. Now does this tend to subvert the just authority of parents and masters? Or to introduce confusion and anarchy into private families? No. How then does the same principle tend to unhinge the government of that larger family, the body politic? We know, in general, that children and servants are obliged to obey their parents and masters respectively. We know also, with equal certainty, that they are not obliged to submit to them in all things, without exception; but may, in some cases, reasonably, and therefore innocently, resist them. These principles are acknowledged upon all hands, whatever difficulty there may be in fixing the exact limits of submission. Now there is at least as much difficulty in stating the measure of duty in these two cases, as in the case of rulers and subjects. So that this is really no objection, at least no

reasonable one, against resistance to the higher powers: Or, if it is one, it will hold equally against resistance in the other cases mentioned.—It is indeed true, that turbulent, vicious-minded men, may take occasion from this principle, that their rulers may, in some cases, be lawfully resisted, to raise factions and disturbances in the state; and to make resistance where resistance is needless, and therefore, sinful. But is it not equally true, that children and servants of turbulent, vicious minds, may take occasion from this principle, that parents and masters may, in some cases be lawfully resisted, to resist when resistance is unnecessary, and therefore, criminal? Is the principal in either case false in itself, merely because it may be abused; and applied to legitimate disobedience and resistance in those instances, to which it ought not to be applied? According to this way of arguing, their will be no true principles in the world; for there are none but what may be wrested and perverted to serve bad purposes, either through the weakness or wickedness of men.

A PEOPLE, really oppressed to a great degree by their sovereign, cannot well be insensible when they are so oppressed. And such a people (if I may allude to an ancient fable) have like the hesperian fruit, a *dragon* for their protector and guardian: Nor would they have any reason to mourn, if some *hercules* should appear to dispatch him—For a nation thus abused to arise unanimously, and to resist their prince, even to the dethroning him, is not criminal; but a reasonable way of vindicating their liberties and just rights; it is making use of the means, and the only means, which God has put into their power, for mutual and self-defence. And it would be highly criminal in them, not to make use of this means. It would be stupid tameness, and unaccountable folly, for whole nations to suffer one unreasonable, ambitious and cruel man, to wanton and riot in their misery. And in such a case it would, of the two, be more rational to suppose, that they that did NOT resist, than that they who did, would receive to themselves damnation.

of taxes as a carefully considered act of civil disobedience; and he was the first prominent American religious figure to work out a serious and compelling case against the institution of slavery.

"Some Considerations on the Keeping of Negroes" challenges the moral and religious grounds on which others defended their right to own slaves. The quiet dignity and compassion with which he states his argument, as well as the premises and conclusions of that argument, show Woolman as the poet Samuel Taylor Coleridge saw him—a model of Christian charity.

John Woolman
(1720–1772)

John Wooman (1720–1772) has been overshadowed by such eighteenth-century theologians as Johnathan Edwards and Charles Chauncy, and he has never achieved the fame of his fellow Quaker and mystic, John Greenleaf Whittier. Yet Charles Lamb confessed that Woolman's autobiographical *Journal* was the only American book he ever read twice, and Ralph Waldo Emerson declared that he found more wisdom in its pages than in "any other book written since the days of the apostles."

Woolman was among the first of his countrymen to confront the issue of poverty in America and to point out its degrading effect on rich and poor alike; he anticipated Henry David Thoreau by almost a century in using non-payment

From "Some Considerations on the Keeping of Negroes" (1754)

As many times there are different motives to the same actions; and one does that from a generous heart, which another does for selfish ends.—The like may be said in this case.

There are various circumstances amongst them that keep negroes, and different ways by which they fall under their care; and, I doubt not, there are many well-disposed persons amongst them, who desire rather to manage wisely and justly in this difficult matter, than to make gain of it.

But the general disadvantage which these poor Africans lie under in an enlightened christian country, having often filled me with real sadness, and been like undigested matter on my mind, I now think it my duty, through Divine aid, to offer some thoughts thereon to the consideration of others.

When we remember that all nations are of one blood, Gen. iii. 20. that in this world we are but sojourners; that we are subject to the like afflictions and infirmities of body, the like disorders and frailties in mind, the like temptations, the same death, and the same judgment; and, that the all-wise Being is judge and Lord over us all, it seems to raise an idea of a general brotherhood, and a disposition easy to be touched with a feeling of each other's afflictions: but when we forget those things, and look chiefly at our outward circumstances, in this and some ages past, constantly retaining in our minds the distinction betwixt us and them, with respect to our knowledge and improvement in things divine, natural and artificial, our breasts being apt to be filled with fond notions of superiority, there is danger of erring in our conduct toward them.

We allow them to be of the same species with ourselves; the odds is, we are a higher station, and enjoy greater favours than they. And when it is thus, that our heavenly Father endoweth some of his children with distinguished gifts, they are intended for good ends; but if those thus gifted are thereby lifted up above their brethren, not considering themselves as debtors to the weak, nor behaving themselves as faithful stewards, none who judge impartially can suppose them free from ingratitude.

When a people dwell under the liberal distribution of favours from heaven, it behoves them carefully to inspect their ways, and consider the purposes for which those favours were bestowed; lest, through forgetfulness of God, and misusing his gifts, they incur his heavy displeasure, whose judgments are just and equal, who exalteth and humbleth to the dust as he seeth meet.

It appears by Holy Record, that men under high favours have been apt to err in their opinions concerning others. Thus Israel, according to the description of the prophet, Isa. lxv. 5. when exceedingly corrupted and degenerated, yet remembered they were the chosen people of God: and could say, "stand by thyself, come not near me, for I am holier than thou." That this was no chance language, but their common opinion of other people, more fully appears, by considering the circumstances which attended when God was beginning to fulfil his precious promises concerning the gathering of the Gentiles.

The Most-High, in a vision, undeceived Peter, first prepared his heart to believe; and, at the house of Cornelius, shewed him of a certainty that God was no respecter of persons.

The effusion of the Holy Ghost upon a people, with whom they, the Jewish christians, would not so much as eat, was strange to them. All they of the circumcision were astonished to see it; and the apostles and brethren of Judea contended with Peter about it, till he, having rehearsed the whole matter, and fully shewn that the Father's love was unlimited, they are thereat struck with admiration, and cry out, "Then hath God also to the Gentiles granted repentance unto life!"

The opinion of peculiar favours being confined to them, was deeply rooted, or else the above instance had been less strange to them for these reasons:—First, They were generally acquainted with the writings of the prophets, by whom this time was repeatedly spoken of, and pointed at. Secondly, Our blessed Lord shortly before expressly said, "I have other sheep, not of this fold, them also must I bring," &c. Lastly, His words to them after his resurrection, at the very time of his ascension, "Ye shall be witnesses unto me, not only in Jerusalem, Judea, and Samaria, but to the uttermost parts of the earth."

Those concurring circumstances, one would think, might have raised a strong expectation of seeing such a time; yet, when it came, it proved matter of offense and astonishment.

To consider mankind otherwise than brethren, to think favours are peculiar to one nation, and exclude others, plainly supposes a darkness in the understanding: for as God's love is universal, so, where the mind is sufficiently influenced by it, it begets a likeness of itself, and the heart is enlarged towards all men. Again, to conclude a people froward, perverse, and worse, by nature, than others, (who ungratefully receive favours, and apply them to bad ends) this will excite a behaviour toward them unbecoming the excellence of true religion.

To prevent such error, let us calmly consider their circumstance; and, the better to do it, make their case ours. Suppose, then, that our ancestors and we had been exposed to constant servitude, in the more servile and inferior employments of life; that we had been destitute of the help of reading and good company; that amongst ourselves we had few wise and pious instructors; that the religious amongst our superiors seldom took notice of us; that while others, in ease, have plentifully heaped up the fruit of our labour, we had received barely enough to relieve nature; and, being wholly at the command of others, had generally been treated as a contemptible, ignorant part of mankind: should we, in that case, be less abject than they now are? Again, if oppression be so hard to bear, that a wise man is made mad by it, Eccl. vii. 7. then a series of those things altering the behaviour and manners of a people, is what may reasonably be expected.

When our property is taken contrary to our mind, by means, appearing to us unjust, it is only through Divine influence, and the enlargement of heart from thence proceeding, that we can love our reputed oppressors: if the negroes fall short in this, an uneasy, if not a disconsolate disposition, will be awakened, and remain like seeds in their minds, producing sloth and many other habits appearing odious to us; with which, being free men, they, perhaps, had not been chargeable. These, and other circumstances, rightly considered, will lessen that too great disparity which some make between us and them.

Integrity of heart hath appeared in some of them; so that, if we continue in the word of Christ (previous to discipleship, John, viii. 31.) and our conduct toward them be seasoned with his love, we may hope to see the good effect of it:

the which, in a good degree, is the case with some into whose hands they have fallen: but that too many treat them otherwise, not seeming conscious of any neglect, is, alas! too evident.

When self-love presides in our minds, our opinions are biased in our own favour; in this condition, being concerned with a people so situated that they have no voice to plead their own cause, there is danger of using ourselves to an undisturbed partiality; till, by long custom, the mind becomes reconciled with it, and the judgment itself infected.

To humbly apply to God for wisdom, that we may thereby be enabled to see things as they are, and ought to be, is very needful; hereby the hidden things of darkness may be brought to light, and the judgment made clear: we shall then consider mankind as brethren. Though different degrees and a variety of qualifications and abilities, one dependant on another, be admitted, yet high thoughts will be laid aside, and all men treated as becometh the sons of one father, agreeable to the doctrine of Christ Jesus.

He hath laid down the best criterion, by which mankind ought to judge of their own conduct, and others judge for them of their's, one towards another, viz. "Whatsoever ye would that men should do unto you, do ye even so to them." I take it, that all men, by nature, are equally entitled to the equity of this rule, and under the indispensable obligations of it. One man ought not to look upon another man, or society of men, as so far beneath him, but that he should put himself in their place, in all his actions towards them, and bring all to this test, viz. "How should I approve of this conduct, were I in their circumstances, and they in mine?" A. Arscot's Considerations, p. III. fol. 107.

This doctrine being of a moral, unchangeable nature, hath been likewise inculcated in the former dispensation; "If a stranger sojourn with thee in your land, ye shall not vex him; but the stranger that dwelleth with you shall be as one born amongst you, and thou shalt love him as thyself." Lev. xix. 33, 34. Had these people come voluntarily and dwelt amongst us, to have called them strangers would be proper; and their being brought by force, with regret and a languishing mind, may well raise compassion in a heart rightly disposed: but there is nothing in such treatment, which, upon a wise and judicious consideration, will any ways lessen their right of being treated as strangers. If the treatment which many of them meet with be rightly examined, and compared with those precepts, "Thou shalt not vex him, nor oppress him; he shall be as one born amongst you, and thou shalt love him as thyself," Lev. xix. 33. Deut. xxvii. 19. there will appear an important difference betwixt them.

It may be objected, there is cost of purchase, and risque of their lives to them who possess them, and therefore needful that they make the best use of their time. In a practice just and reasonable, such objections may have weight; but if the work be wrong from the beginning, there is little or no force in them. If I purchase a man who hath never forfeited his liberty, the natural right of freedom is in him; and shall I keep him and his posterity in servitude and ignorance? "How should I approve of this conduct, were I in his circumstances, and he in mine?" It may be thought, that to treat them as we would willingly be treated, our gain by them would be inconsiderable: and it were, in divers respects, better than there were none in our country.

We may further consider, that they are now amongst us, and those of our nation the cause of their being here; that whatsoever difficulty accrues thereon, we are justly chargeable with; and to bear all inconveniences attending it, with a serious and weighty concern of mind to do our duty by them, is the best we can do. To seek a remedy by continuing the oppression, because we have power to do it, and see others do it, will, I apprehend, not be doing as we would be done by.

How deeply soever men are involved in the most exquisite difficulties, sincerity of heart, and upright walking before God, freely submitting to his providence, is the most sure remedy: he only is able to relieve, not only persons, but nations, in their greatest calamities.

As some in most religious societies, amongst the English, are concerned in importing or purchasing the inhabitants of Africa as slaves; and as the professors of christianity of several other nations do the like; these circumstances tend to make people less apt to examine the practice so closely as they would, if such a thing had not been, but was now proposed to be entered upon. It is however, our duty, and what concerns us individually, as creatures accountable to our Creator, to employ rightly the understanding which he hath given us, in humbly endeavouring to be acquainted with his will concerning us, and with the nature and tendency of those things which we practise: for as justice remains to be justice, so many people, of reputation in the world, joining with wrong things, do not excuse others in joining with them, nor make the consequence of their proceedings less dreadful in the final issue, than it would be otherwise.

Where unrighteousness is justified from one age to another, it is like dark matter gathering into clouds over us. We may know that this gloom will remain till the cause be removed by a reformation, or change of times; and may feel a desire, from a love of equity, to speak on the occasion; yet, where error is so strong, that it may not be spoken against; without some prospect of inconvenience to the speaker, this difficulty is likely to operate on our weakness, and quench the good desires in us; except we dwell so steadily under the weight of it, as to be made willing to "endure hardness" on that account.

Where men exert their talents against vices generally accounted such, the ill effects whereof are presently perceived in a government, all men who regard their own temporal good, are likely to approve the work. But when that which is inconsistent with perfect equity hath the law, or countenance of the great in its favour, though the tendency thereof be quite contrary to the true happiness of mankind, in an equal, if not greater degree, than many things accounted reproachful to christians; yet, as these ill effects are not generally perceived, they who labour to dissuade from such things, which people believe accord with their interest, have many difficulties to encounter.

The repeated charges which God gave to his prophets, imply the danger they were in of erring on this hand. "Be not afraid of their faces; for I am with thee, to deliver thee, saith the Lord." Jer. i. 8. "Speak all the words that I command thee to speak to them, diminish not a word." Jer. xxvi. 2. "And thou, son of man, be not afraid of them, nor dismayed at their looks. Speak my words to them, whether they will hear or forbear." Ezek. ii. 6, 7.

Under an apprehension of duty, I offer some further considerations on this subject, having endeavoured some years to consider it candidly. I have observed people of our own colour, whose abilities have been inferior to the affairs which relate to their convenient subsistence, who have been taken care of by others, and the profit of such work as they could do, applied toward their support.—I believe there are such amongst negroes; and that some people in whose hands they are, keep them with no view of outward profit; do not consider them as black men, who, as such, ought to serve white men; but account them persons who have need of guardians, and, as such, take care of them; yet, where equal care is taken in all parts of education, I do not apprehend cases of this kind are likely to occur more frequently amongst one sort of people than another.

It looks to me that the slave-trade was founded and hath generally been carried on, in a wrong spirit; that the effects of it are detrimental to the real prosperity of our country; and will be more so, except we cease from the common motives of keeping them, and treat them in future agreeable to Truth and pure justice.

Negroes may be imported, who, for their cruelty to their countrymen, and the evil disposition of their minds, may be unfit to be at liberty; and if we, as lovers of righteousness, undertake the management of them, we should have a full and clear knowledge of their crimes, and of those circumstances which might operate in their favour; but the difficulty of obtaining this is so great, that we have great reason to be cautious therein. But, should it plainly appear that absolute subjection was a condition the most proper for the person who is purchased, yet the innocent children ought not to be made slaves, because their parents sinned.

We have account in holy scripture of some families suffering, where mention is only made of the heads of the family committing wickedness; and it is likely that the degenerate Jews, misunderstanding some occurrences of this kind, took occasion to charge God with being unequal; so that a saying became common. "The fathers have eaten sour grapes, and the children's teeth are set on edge." Jeremiah and Ezekiel, two of the inspired prophets, who lived near the same time, were concerned to correct this error. Ezekiel is large on the subject. First, he reproves them for their error. "What mean ye, that ye do so," chap. xviii. verse 2. "As I live, saith the Lord God, ye shall not have occasion any more to use this proverb in Israel." The words, "any more," have reference to time past;

intimating, that though they had not rightly understood some things they had heard or seen, and thence supposed the proverb to be well grounded; yet, henceforth, they might know of a certainty, that the ways of God are all equal; that as sure as the Most High liveth, so sure men are only answerable for their own sins.— He thus sums up the matter, ver. 20. "The soul that sinneth, it shall die. The son shall not bear the iniquity of the father; neither shall the father bear the iniquity of the son. The righteousness of the righteous shall be upon him; and the wickedness of the wicked shall be upon him."

Where men are wicked, they commonly are a means of corrupting the succeeding age; and thereby hasten those outward calamities, which fall on nations when their iniquities are full.

Men may pursue means which are not agreeable to perfect purity, with a view to increase the wealth and happiness of their offspring, and thereby make the way of virtue more difficult to them. And though the ill example of a parent, or a multitude, does not excuse a man in doing evil, yet the mind being early impressed with vicious notions and practices, and nurtured up in ways of getting treasure which are not the ways of Truth; this wrong spirit getting first possession, and being thus strengthened, frequently prevents due attention to the true spirit of wisdom, so that they exceed in wickedness those who lived before them. And, in this channel, though parents labour, as they think, to forward the happiness of their children, it proves a means of forwarding their calamity. This being the case in the age next before the grievous calamity in the seige of Jerusalem, and carrying Judah captive to Babylon, they might say with propriety, This came upon us because our fathers forsook God, and because we did worse than our fathers. See Jer. vii. 26.

As the generation next before them inwardly turned away from God, who yet awaited to be gracious; and as they, in that age, continued in those things which necessarily separated from perfect goodness, growing more stubborn, till the judgments of God were poured out upon them, they might properly say, "Our fathers have sinned, and we have borne their inequities:" Lam. v. 7. And yet, wicked as their fathers were, had they not succeeded them in their wickedness, they had not borne their iniquities.

To suppose it right, that an innocent man shall at this day be excluded from the common rules of justice; be deprived of that liberty, which is the natural right of human creatures; and be a slave to others during life, on account of a sin committed by his immediate parents, or a sin committed by Ham, the son of Noah, is a supposition too gross to be admitted into the mind of any person, who sincerely desires to be governed by solid principles.

~~~~~~~~~~~~~~~~~~~~~~~~~~~

Thomas Jefferson (1734–1826)

The third President of the United States and chief author of the Declaration of Independence, Thomas Jefferson, was one of the most gifted statesmen in American history. In addition to his achievements in public life, Jefferson was an imaginative scientist, a brilliant architect, an able naturalist, a skilled political theorist, and a capable student of religion and ethics. Surely no document in our national history has been more important than the Declaration of Independence, nor has any set out more clearly the ethical, religious, and social views of the Founding Fathers. In its defense of the idea that a sovereign people may overthrow any government that systematically deprives them of their inalienable rights as human beings, the Declaration bases its argument upon an escalating series of offenses that reaches its peak (at least in the original version authored by Jefferson) with the outrage against humanity committed by England in promoting and participating in the traffic in slaves.

Two other selections illustrate the civil and theological grounds for Jefferson's defense of freedom of religion. The first comes from Jefferson's only book, which was written in response to questions put to him by the secretary of the French legation in Philadelphia with respect to conditions in the State of Virginia. The second is the act Jefferson drafted for the establishment of religious freedom in Virginia. In Jefferson's argument that reason is the best arbiter of religious disputes and truth its own worthiest defense, we see the basic tenets of what one scholar has called "the Enlightenment *as* religion."

From *Autobiography*

The Framing of the Declaration of Independence, 1776

It appearing in the course of these debates, that the colonies of New York, New Jersey, Pennsylvania, Delaware, Maryland, and South Carolina were not yet matured for falling from the parent stem, but that they were fast advancing to that state, it was thought most prudent to wait a while for them, and to postpone the final decision to July 1st; but, that this might occasion as little delay as possible, a committee was appointed to prepare a Declaration of Independence. The committee were John Adams, Dr. Franklin, Roger Sherman, Robert R. Livingston, and myself. Committees were also appointed, at the same time, to prepare a plan of confederation for the colonies, and to state the terms proper to be proposed for foreign alliance. The committee for drawing the Declaration of Independence, desired me to do it. It was accordingly done, and being approved by them, I reported it to the House on Friday, the 28th of June, when it was read, and ordered to lie on the table. On Monday, the 1st of July, the House resolved itself into a committee of the whole, and resumed the consideration of the original motion made by the delegates of Virginia, which, being again debated through the day, was carried in the affirmative by the votes of New Hampshire, Connecticut, Massachusetts, Rhode Island, New Jersey, Maryland, Virginia, North Carolina and Georgia. South Carolina and Pennsylvania voted against it. Delaware had but two members present, and they were divided. The delegates from New York declared they were for it themselves, and were assured their constituents were for it; but that their instructions having been drawn near a twelve-month before, when reconciliation was still the general object, they were enjoined by them to do nothing which should impede that object. They, therefore, thought themselves not justifiable in voting on either side, and asked leave to withdraw from the question; which was given them. The committee rose and reported their resolution to the House. Mr. Edward Rutledge, of South Carolina, then requested the determination might be put off to the next day, as he believed his colleagues, though they disapproved of the resolution, would then join in it for the sake of unanimity. The ultimate question, whether the House would agree to the resolution of the committee, was accordingly postponed to the next day, when it was again moved, and South Carolina concurred in voting for it. In the meantime, a third member had come post from the Delaware counties, and turned the vote of that colony in favor of the resolution. Members of a different sentiment attending that morning from Pennsylvania also, her vote was changed, so that the whole twelve colonies who were authorized to vote at all, gave their voices for it; and, within a few days, the convention of New York approved of it, and thus supplied the void occasioned by the withdrawing of her delegates from the vote.

Congress proceeded the same day to consider the Declaration of Independence, which had been reported and lain on the table the Friday preceding, and on Monday referred to a committee of the whole. The pusillanimous idea that we had friends in England worth keeping terms with, still haunted the minds of many. For this reason, those passages which conveyed censures on the people of England were struck out, lest they should give them offence. The clause too, reprobating the enslaving the inhabitants of Africa, was struck out in complaisance to South Carolina and Georgia, who had never attempted to restrain the importation of slaves, and who, on the contrary, still wished to continue it. Our northern brethren also, I believe, felt a little tender under those censures; for though their people had very few slaves themselves, yet they had been pretty considerable carriers of them to others. The debates, having taken up the greater parts of the 2d, 3d, and 4th days of July, were, on the evening of the last, closed; the Declaration was reported by the committee, agreed to by the House, and signed by every member present, except Mr. Dickinson. As the sentiments of men are known not only by what they receive, but what they reject also, I will state the form of the Declaration as originally reported.[1]

A Declaration by the Representatives of the United States of America, in General Congress Assembled

When, in the course of human events, it becomes necessary for one people to

[1]The parts deleted by Congress are printed in italics and enclosed in brackets; those inserted by Congress are printed in capitals.

dissolve the political bands which have connected them with another, and to assume among the powers of the earth the separate and equal station to which the laws of nature and of nature's God entitle them, a decent respect to the opinions of mankind requires that they should declare the causes which impel them to the separation.

We hold these truths to be self evident: that all men are created equal; that they are endowed by their Creator with CERTAIN [*inherent and*] inalienable rights; that among these are life, liberty, and the pursuit of happiness; that to secure these rights, governments are instituted among men, deriving their just powers from the consent of the governed; that whenever any form of government becomes destructive of these ends, it is the right of the people to alter or to abolish it, and to institute new government, laying its foundation on such principles, and organizing its powers in such form, as to them shall seem most likely to effect their safety and happiness. Prudence, indeed, will dictate that governments long established should not be changed for light and transient causes; and accordingly all experience hath shown that mankind are more disposed to suffer while evils are sufferable, than to right themselves by abolishing the forms to which they are accustomed. But when a long train of abuses and usurpations, [*begun at a distinguished period and*] pursuing invariably the same object, evinces a design to reduce them under absolute despotism, it is their right, it is their duty to throw off such government, and to provide such sufferance new guards for their

future security. Such has been the patient sufferance of these colonies; and such is now the necessity which constrains them to ALTER [*expunge*] their former systems of government. The history of the present king of Great Britain is a history of REPEATED [*unremitting*] injuries and usurpations, ALL HAVING [*among which appears no solitary fact to contradict the uniform tenor of the rest, but all have*] in direct object the establishment of an absolute tyranny over these states. To prove this, let facts be submitted to a candid world [*for the truth of which we pledge a faith yet unsullied by falsehood*].

He has refused his assent to laws the most wholesome and necessary for the public good.

He has forbidden his governors to pass laws of immediate and pressing importance, unless suspended in their operation till his assent should be obtained; and, when so suspended, he has utterly neglected to attend to them.

He has refused to pass other laws for the accommodation of large districts of people, unless those people would relinquish the right of representation in the legislature, a right inestimable to them, and formidable to tyrants only.

He has called together legislative bodies at places unusual, uncomfortable, and distant from the depository of their public records, for the sole purpose of fatiguing them into compliance with his measures.

He has dissolved representative houses repeatedly [*and continually*] for opposing with manly firmness his invasions on the rights of the people.

He has refused for a long time after

such dissolutions to cause others to be elected, whereby the legislative powers, incapable of annihilation, have returned to the people at large for their exercise, the state remaining, in the meantime, exposed to all the dangers of invasion from without and convulsions within.

He has endeavored to prevent the population of these states; for that purpose obstructing the laws for naturalization of foreigners, refusing to pass others to encourage their migrations hither, and raising the conditions of new appropriations of lands.

He has OBSTRUCTED [*suffered*] the administration of justice BY [*totally to cease in some of these states*] refusing his assent to laws for establishing judiciary powers.

He has made [*our*] judges dependent on his will alone for the tenure of their offices, and the amount and payment of their salaries.

He has erected a multitude of new offices [*by a self-assumed power*], and sent hither swarms of new officers to harass our people and eat out their substance.

He has kept among us in times of peace standing armies [*and ships of war*] without the consent of our legislatures.

He has affected to render the military independent of, and superior to, the civil power.

He has combined with others to subject us to a jurisdiction foreign to our constitutions and unacknowledged by our laws, giving his assent to their acts of pretended legislation for quartering large bodies of armed troops among us; for protecting them by a mock trial from punishment for any murders which they should commit on the inhabitants of these states; for cutting off

our trade with all parts of the world; for imposing taxes on us without consent; for depriving us IN MANY CASES of the benefits of trial by jury; for transporting us beyond seas to be tried for pretended offences; for abolishing the free system of English laws in a neighboring province, establishing therein an arbitrary government, and enlarging its boundaries, so as to render it at once an example and fit instrument for introducing the same absolute rule into these COLONIES [*states*]; for taking away our charters, abolishing our most valuable laws, and altering fundamentally the forms of our governments; for suspending our own legislatures, and declaring themselves invested with power to legislate for us in all cases whatsoever.

He has abdicated government here BY DECLARING US OUT OF HIS PROTECTION, AND WAGING WAR AGAINST US [*withdrawing his governors, and declaring us out of his allegiance and protection*].

He has plundered our seas, ravaged our coasts, burnt our towns, and destroyed the lives of our people.

He is at this time transporting large armies of foreign mercenaries to complete the works of death, desolation and tyranny already begun with circumstances of cruelty and perfidy SCARCELY PARALLELED IN THE MOST BARBAROUS AGES, AND TOTALLY unworthy the head of a civilized nation.

He has constrained our fellow citizens taken captive on the high seas, to bear arms against their country, to become the executioners of their friends and brethren, or to fall themselves by their hands.

He has EXCITED DOMESTIC INSURREC-

TION AMONG US, AND HAS endeavored to bring on the inhabitants of our frontiers, the merciless Indian savages, whose known rule of warfare is an undistinguished destruction of all ages, sexes and conditions [*of existence*].

[*He has incited treasonable insurrections of our fellow citizens, with the allurements of forfeiture and confiscation of our property.*

He has waged cruel war against human nature itself, violating its most sacred rights of life and liberty in the persons of a distant people who never offended him, captivating and carrying them into slavery in another hemisphere, or to incur miserable death in their transportation hither. This piratical warfare, the opprobrium of INFIDEL *powers, is the warfare of the* CHRISTIAN *king of Great Britain. Determined to keep open a market where* MEN *should be bought and sold, he has prostituted his negative for suppressing every legislative attempt to prohibit or to restrain this execrable commerce. And that this assemblage of horrors might want no fact of distinguished die, he is now exciting those very people to rise in arms among us, and to purchase that liberty of which he has deprived them, by murding the people on whom he also obtruded them: thus paying off former crimes committed against the* LIBERTIES *of one people, with crimes which he urges them to commit against the* LIVES *of another.*]

In every stage of these oppressions we have petitioned for redress in the most humble terms: our repeated petitions have been answered only by repeated injuries.

A prince whose character is thus marked by every act which may define a tyrant is unfit to be the ruler of a FREE people [*who mean to be free. Future ages will scarcely believe that the hardiness of one*

man adventured, within the short compass of twelve years only, to lay a foundation so broad and so undisguised for tyranny over a people fostered and fixed in principles of freedom.]

Nor have we been wanting in attentions to our British brethren. We have warned them from time to time of attempts by their legislature to extend AN UNWARRANTABLE [*a*] juridsiction over US [*these our states*]. We have reminded them of the circumstances of our emigration and settlement here [*no one of which could warrant so strange a pretension: that these were effected at the expense of our own blood and treasure, unassisted by the wealth or the strength of Great Britain: that in constituting indeed our several forms of government, we had adopted one common king, thereby laying a foundation for perpetual league and amity with them: but that submission to their parliament was no part of our constitution, nor ever in idea, if history may be credited: and,*], we HAVE appealed to their native justice and magnanimity AND WE HAVE CONJURED THEM BY [*as well as to*] the ties of our common kindred to disavow these usurpations which WOULD INEVITABLY [*were likely to*] interrupt our connection and correspondence. They too have been deaf to the voice of justice and of consanguinity. WE MUST THERE-FORE [*and when occasions have been given them, by the regular course of their laws, of removing from their councils the disturbers of our harmony, they have, by their free election, re-established them in power. At this very time too, they are permitting their chief magistrate to send over not only soldiers of our common blood, but Scotch and foreign mercenaries to invade and destroy us. These facts have given the last stab to agonizing affection, and manly spirit bids us to renounce forever these unfeeling brethren. We must endeavor to forget our former love for them, and hold them as we hold the rest of mankind, enemies in war, in peace friends. We might have a free and a great people together; but a communication of grandeur and of freedom, it seems, is below their dignity. Be it so, since they will have it. The road to happiness and to glory is open to us, too. We will tred it apart from them, and]* acquiesce in the necessity which denounces our [*eternal*] separation AND HOLD THEM AS WE HOLD THE REST OF MANKIND, ENEMIES IN WAR, IN PEACE FRIENDS.

We therefore the representatives of the United States of America in General Congress assembled, do in the name, and by the authority of the good people of these [*states reject and renounce all allegiance and subjection to the kings of Great Britain and all others who may hereafter claim by, through or under them; we utterly dissolve all political connection which may heretofore have substituted between us and the people or parliament of Great Britain: and finally we do assert and declare these colonies to be free and independent states,*] and that as free and independent states, they have full power to levy war, conclude peace, contract alliances, establish commerce, and to do all other acts and things which independent states may of right do.

And for the support of this declaration, we mutually pledge to each other our lives, our fortunes, and our sacred honor.[2]

We, therefore, the representatives of the United States of America in General

[2]This is Jefferson's version of the conclusion; the following paragraph is the version finally adopted by congress.

Congress assembled, appealing to the supreme judge of the world for the rectitude of our intentions, do in the name, and by the authority of the good people of these colonies, solemnly publish and declare, that these united colonies are, and of right ought to be free and independent states; that they are absolved from all allegiance to the British crown, and that all political connection between them and the state of Great Britain is, and ought to be, totally dissolved; and that as free and independent states, they have full power to levy war, conclude peace, contract alliances, establish commerce, and to do all other acts and things which independent states may of right do.

And for the support of this declaration, with a firm reliance on the protection of divine providence, we mutually pledge to each other our lives, our fortunes, and our sacred honor.

The Declaration thus signed on the 4th, on paper, was engrossed on parchment, and signed again on the 2d of August.

From *Notes on the State of Virginia* (1785)

The error seems not sufficiently eradicated, that the operations of the mind, as well as the acts of the body, are subject to the coercion of the laws. But our rulers can have no authority over such natural rights, only as we have submitted to them. The rights of conscience we never submitted, we could not submit. We are answerable for them to our God. The legitimate powers of government extend to such acts only as are injurious to others. But it does me no injury for my neighbor to say there are twenty gods, or no God. It neither picks my pocket nor breaks my leg. If it be said, his testimony in a court of justice cannot be relied on, reject it then, and be the stigma on him. Constraint may make him worse by making him a hypocrite, but it will never make him a truer man. It may fix him obstinately in his errors, but will not cure them. Reason and free inquiry are the only effectual agents against error. Give a loose to them, they will support the true religion by bringing every false one to their tribunal, to the test of their investigation. They are the natural enemies of error, and of error only. Had not the Roman government permitted free inquiry, Christianity could never have been introduced. Had not free inquiry been indulged at the era of the reformation, the corruptions of Christianity could not have been purged away. If it be restrained now, the present corruptions will be protected, and new ones encouraged. Was the government to prescribe to us our medicine and diet, our bodies would be in such keeping as our souls are now. Thus in France the emetic was once forbidden as a medicine, and the potato as an article of food. Government is just as infallible, too, when it fixes systems in physics. Galileo was sent to the Inquisition for affirming that the earth was a sphere; the government had declared it to be as flat as a trencher, and Galileo was obliged to abjure his error. This error, however, at length prevailed, the earth became a globe, and Descartes declared it was whirled round its axis by a vortex. The government in which he lived was wise enough to see that this was no question of civil jurisdiction, or we should all have been involved by authority in vortices. In fact, the vortices have been exploded, and the Newtonian principle of gravitation is now more firmly established, on the basis of reason, than it would be were the government to step in, and to make it an article of necessary faith. Reason and experiment have been indulged, and error has fled before them. It is error alone which needs the support of government. Truth can stand by itself. Subject opinion to coercion: whom will you make your inquisitors? Fallible men; men governed by bad passions, by private as well as public reasons. And why subject it to coercion? To produce uniformity. But is uniformity of opinion desirable? No more than of face and stature. Introduce the bed of Procrustes then, and as there is danger that the large men may beat the small, make us all of a size, by lopping the former and stretching the latter. Difference of opinion is advantageous in religion. The several sects perform the office of a *censor morum* over such other. Is uniformity attainable? Millons of innocent men, women, and children, since the introduction of Christianity, have been burnt, tortured, fined, imprisoned; yet we have not advanced one inch towards uniformity. What has been the effect of coercion? To make one half the world fools, and the other half hypocrites. To support roguery and error all over the earth. Let us reflect that it is inhabited by a thousand millions of people. That these profess probably a thousand different systems of religion. That ours is but one of that thousand. That if there be but one right, and ours that one, we should wish to see the nine hundred and ninety-nine wandering sects gathered into the fold of truth. But against such a majority we cannot effect this by force. Reason and persuasion are the only practicable instruments. To make way for these, free inquiry must be indulged; and how can we wish others to indulge it while we refuse it ourselves.

"An Act for Establishing Religious Freedom" (1786)

I. Whereas Almighty God hath created the mind free; that all attempts to influence it by temporal punishments or burthens, or by civil incapacitations, tend only to beget habits of hypocrisy and meanness, and are a departure from the plan of the Holy author of our religion, who being Lord both of body and mind, yet chose not to propagate it by coercions on either, as was in his Almighty power to do; that the impious presumption of legislators and rulers, civil as well as ecclesiastical, who being themselves but fallible and uninspired men, have assumed dominion over the faith of others, setting up their own opinions and modes of thinking as the only true and infallible, and as such endeavouring to impose them on others, hath established and maintained false religions over the greatest part of the world, and through all time; that to compel a man to furnish contributions of money for the propagation of opinions which he disbelieves, is sinful and tyrannical; that even the forcing him to support this or that teacher of his own religious persuasion, is depriving him of the comfortable liberty of giving his contributions to the particular pastor, whose morals he would make his pattern, and whose powers he feels most persuasive to righteousness, and is withdrawing from the ministry those temporary rewards, which proceeding from an approbation of their personal conduct, are an additional incitement to earnest and unremitting labours for the instruction of mankind; that our civil rights have no dependence on our religious opinions, any more than our opinions in physics or geometry; that therefore the proscribing any citizen as unworthy the public confidence by laying upon him an incapacity of being called to offices of trust and emolument, unless he profess or renounce this or that religious opinion, is depriving him injuriously of those privileges and advantages to which in common with his fellow-citizens he has a natural right; that it tends only to corrupt the principles of that religion it is meant to encourage, by bribing with a monopoly of worldly honours and emoluments, those who will externally profess and conform to it; that though indeed these are criminal who do not withstand such temptation, yet neither are those innocent who lay the bait in their way; that to suffer the civil magistrate to intrude his powers into the field of opinion, and to restrain the profession or propagation of principles on suppostion of their ill tendency, is a dangerous fallacy, which at once destroys all religious liberty, because he being of course judge of that tendency will make his opinions the rule of judgment, and approve or condemn the sentiments of others only as they shall square with or differ from his own; that it is time enough for the rightful purposes of civil government, for its officers to interfere when principles break out into overt acts against peace and good order; and finally, that truth is great and will prevail if left to herself, that she is the proper and sufficient antagonist to error, and has nothing to fear from the conflict, unless by human interpostion disarmed of her natural weapons, free argument and debate, errors ceasing to be dangerous when it is permitted freely to contradict them:

II. *Be it enacted by the General Assembly,* That no man shall be compelled to frequent or support any religious worship, place, or ministry whatsoever, nor shall be enforced, restrained, molested, or burthened in his body or goods, nor shall otherwise suffer on account of his religious opinions or belief; but that all men shall be free to profess, and by argument to maintain, their opinion in matters of religion, and that the same shall in no wise diminish, enlarge, or affect their civil capacities.

III. And though we well know that this assembly elected by the people for the ordinary purposes of legislation only, have no power to restrain the acts of succeeding assemblies, constituted with powers equal to our own, and that therefore to declare this act to be irrevocable would be of no effect in law; yet we are free to declare, and do declare, that the rights hereby asserted are of the natural rights of mankind, and that if any act shall be hereafter passed to repeal the present, or to narrow its operation, such act will be an infringement of natural right.

J. Hector St. Jean de Crèvecoeur (1735–1818)

Frenchman Michel-Guillaume Jean de Crèvecoeur emigrated to Canada and served under Montcalm in the last of the French and Indian Wars. After the war, Crèvecoeur, a trained cartographer, explored the vast wilderness of the Great Lakes region and eventually settled in New York State. In 1765 he became an American citizen under the assumed name of J. Hector St. John de Crèvecoeur, took up farming, and began writing his celebrated *Letters.* Despite his idealization of the self-reliant American husbandman, whom he pictured as continually regenerated by the land from which he wrests his living, Crèvecoeur apparently found his loyalties divided on the eve of the Revolution and during the War of Independence was forced to return to France. When he came back to America at the war's end, he found his farm destroyed, his wife dead, and his children separated, but he eventually managed to put the remaining pieces of his life together again and before his permanent return to France in 1790 even served for a time with distinction as the French consul in New York.

Crèvecoeur's famous question "What then is the American, this new man?" has been asked from the earliest years of Renaissance discovery to the present. Crèvecoeur's own answer—that the American is one who derives new manners, morals, and metaphysics from the new mode of life he has been obliged to adopt in the New World—has also had its echo down through the years among all those who conceive of the American environment as somehow decisive in the development of American character and consciousness.

From *Letters from an American Farmer* (1782)

What Is an American?

I wish I could be acquainted with the feelings and thoughts which must agitate the heart and present themselves to the mind of an enlightened Englishman, when he first lands on this continent. He must greatly rejoice that he lived at a time to see this fair country discovered and settled; he must necessarily feel a share of national pride, when he views the chain of settlements which embellishes these extended shores. When he says to himself, this is the work of my countrymen, who, when convulsed by factions, afflicted by a variety of miseries and wants, restless and impatient, took refuge here. They brought along with them their national genius, to which they principally owe what liberty they enjoy, and what substance they possess. Here he sees the industry of his native country displayed in a new manner, and traces in their works the embryos of all the arts, sciences, and ingenuity which flourish in Europe. Here he beholds fair cities, substantial villages, extensive fields, an immense country filled with decent houses, good roads, orchards, meadows, and bridges, where an hundred years ago all was wild, woody, and uncultivated! What a train of pleasing ideas this fair spectacle must suggest; it is a prospect which must inspire a good citizen with the most heartfelt pleasure. The diffuclty consists in the manner of viewing so extensive a scene. He is arrived on a new continent; a modern society offers itself to his contemplation, different from what he had hitherto seen. It is not composed, as in Europe, of great lords who possess everything, and a herd of people who have nothing. Here are no aristocratical families, no courts, no kings, no bishops, no ecclesiastical dominion, no invisible power giving to a few a very visible one; no great manufacturers employing thousands, no great refinements of luxury. The rich and the poor are not so far removed from each other as they are in Europe. Some few towns excepted, we are all tillers of the earth, from Nova Scotia to West Florida.

We are a people of cultivators, scattered over an immense territory, communicating with each other by means of good roads and navigable rivers, united by the silken bands of mild government, all respecting the laws, without dreading their power, because they are equitable. We are all animated with the spirit of an industry which is unfettered and unrestrained, because each person works for himself. If he travels through our rural districts he views not the hostile castle, and the haughty mansion, contrasted with the clay-built hut and miserable cabin, where cattle and men help to keep each other warm, and dwell in meanness, smoke, and indigence. A pleasing uniformity of decent competence appears throughout our habitations. The meanest of our log-houses is a dry and comfortable habitation. Lawyer or merchant are the fairest titles our towns afford; that of a farmer is the only appellation of the rural inhabitants of our country. It must take some time ere he can reconcile himself to our dictionary, which is but short in words of dignity, and names of honour. There, on a Sunday, he sees a congregation of respectable farmers and their wives, all clad in neat homespun, well mounted, or riding in their own humble waggons. There is not among them an esquire, saving the unlettered magistrate. There he sees a parson as simple as his flock, a farmer who does not riot on the labour of others. We have no princes, for whom we toil, starve, and bleed: we are the most perfect society now existing in the world. Here man is free as he ought to be; nor is this pleasing equality so transitory as many others are. Many ages will not see the shores of our great lakes replenished with inland nations, nor the unknown bounds of North America entirely peopled. Who can tell how far it extends? Who can tell the millions of men whom it will feed and contain? for no European foot has as yet travelled half the extent of this might continent!

The next wish of this traveller will be to know whence came all these people? they are a mixture of English, Scotch, Irish, French, Dutch, Germans, and Swedes. From this promiscuous breed, that race now called Americans have arisen. The eastern provinces must indeed be expected, as being the unmixed descendants of Englishmen. I have heard many wish that they had been more intermixed also: for my part, I am no wisher, and think it much better as it has happened. They exhibit a most conspicuous figure in this great and variegated picture; they too enter for a great share in the pleasing perspective displayed in these thirteen provinces. I know it is fashionable to reflect on them, but I respect them for what they have done; for the accuracy and wisdom with which they have settled their territory; for the decency of their manners; for their early love of letters; their ancient college, the first in this hemisphere; for their industry; which to me who am but a farmer, is the criterion of everything. There never was a people, situated as they are, who with so ungrateful a soil have done more in so short a time. Do you think that the monarchical ingredients which are more prevalent in other governments, have purged them from all foul stains? Their histories assert the contrary.

In this great American asylum, the poor of Europe have by some means met together, and in consequence of various causes; to what purpose should they ask one another what countrymen they are? Alas, two thirds of them had no country. Can a wretch who wanders about, who works and starves, whose life is a continual scene of sore affliction or pinching penury; can that man call England or any other kingdom his country? A country that had no bread for him, whose fields procured him no harvest, who met with nothing but the frowns of the rich, the severity of the laws, with jails and punishments; who owned not a single foot of the extensive surface of this planet? No! urged by a variety of motives, here they came. Every thing has tended to regenerate them; new laws, a new mode of living, a new social system; here they are become men: in Europe they were as so many useless plants, wanting vegetative mould, and refreshing showers; they withered, and were mowed down by want, hunger, and war; but now by the power of transplantation, like all other plants they have taken root and flourished! Formerly they were not numbered in any civil lists of their country, except in those of the poor; here they rank as citizens. By what invisible power has this surprising metamorphosis been performed? By that of the laws and that of their industry. The laws, the indulgent laws, protect them as they arrive, stamping on them the symbol of adoption; they receive ample rewards for their labours; these accumulated rewards procure them lands; those lands confer on them the title of freemen, and to that title every benefit is affixed which men can possibly require. This is the great operation daily performed by our laws. From whence proceed these laws? From our government. Whence the government? It is derived from the original genius and strong desire of the people ratified and confirmed by the crown. This is the great chain which links us all, this is the picture which every province exhibits, Nova Scotia excepted. There the crown has done all; either there were no people who had genius, or it was not much attended to: the consequence is, that the province is very thinly inhabited indeed; the power of the crown in conjunction with the musketos has prevented men from settling there. Yet some parts of it flourished once, and it contained a mild harmless set of people. But for the fault of a few leaders, the whole were banished. The greatest political error the crown ever committed in America, was to cut off men from a country which wanted nothing but men!

What attachment can a poor European emigrant have for a country where he had nothing? The knowledge of the language, the love of a few kindred as poor as himself, were the only cords that tied him: his country is now that which gives him land, bread, protection, and consequence: *Ubi panis ibi patria,* is the motto of all emigrants. What then is the American, this new man? He is either an European, or the descendant of an European, hence that strange mixture of blood, which you will find in no other country. I could point out to you a family whose grandfather was an Englishman, whose wife was Dutch, whose son married a French woman, and whose present four sons have now four wives of different nations. *He* is an American, who, leaving behind him all his ancient prejudices and manners, receives new ones from the new mode of life he has embraced, the new government he obeys, and the new rank he holds. He becomes an American by being received in the broad lap of our great *Alma Mater*. Here individuals of all nations are melted into a new race of men, whose labours and posterity will one day cause great changes in the world. Americans are the western pilgrims, who are carrying along with them that great mass of arts, sciences, vigour, and industry which began long since in the east; they will finish the great circle. The Americans were once scattered all over Europe; here they are incorporated into one of the finest systems of population which has ever appeared, and which will hereafter become distinct by the power of the different climates they inhabit. The American ought therefore to love this country much better than that wherein either he or his forefathers were born. Here the rewards of his industry follow with equal steps the progress of his labour; his labour is founded on the basis of nature, *self-interest;* can it want a stronger allurement? Wives and children, who before in vain demanded of him a morsel of bread, now, fat and frolicsome, gladly help their father to clear those fields whence exuberant crops are to arise to feed and to clothe them all; without any part being claimed, either by a despotic prince, a rich abbot, or a mighty lord. Here

religion demands but little of him; a small voluntary salary to the minister, and gratitude to God; can he refuse these? The American is a new man, who acts upon new principles; he must therefore entertain new ideas, and form new opinions. From involuntary idleness, servile dependence, penury, and useless labour, he has passed to toils of a very different nature, rewarded by ample subsistence.—This is an American.

He who would wish to see America in its proper light, and have a true idea of its feeble beginnings and barbarous rudiments, must visit our extended line of frontiers where the last settlers dwell, and where he may see the first labours of settlement, the mode of clearing the earth, in all their different appearances; where men are wholly left dependent on their native tempers, and on the spur of uncertain industry, which often fails when not sanctified by the efficacy of a few moral rules. There, remote from the power of example and check of shame, many families exhibit the most hideous parts of our society. They are a kind of forlorn hope, preceding by ten or twelve years the most respectable army of veterans which come after them. In that space, prosperity will polish some, vice and the law will drive off the rest, who uniting again with others like themselves will recede still farther; making room for more industrious people, who will finish their improvements, convert the loghouse into a convenient habitation, and rejoicing that the first heavy labours are finished, will change in a few years that hitherto barbarous country into a fine fertile, well regulated district. Such is our progress, such is the march of the Europeans toward the interior parts of this continent. In all societies there are off-casts; this impure part serves as our precursors or pioneers; my father himself was one of that class, but he came upon honest principles, and was therefore one of the few who held fast; by good conduct and temperance, he transmitted to me his fair inheritance, when not above one in fourteen of his contemporaries had the same good fortune.

Forty years ago this smiling country was thus inhabited; it is now purged, a general decency of manners prevails throughout, and such has been the fate of our best countries.

Exclusive of those general characteristics, each province has its own, founded on the government, climate, mode of husbandry, customs, and peculiarity of circumstances. Europeans submit insensibly to these great powers, and become, in the course of a few generations, not only Americans in general, but either Pennsylvanians, Virginians, or provincials under some other name. Whoever traverses the continent must easily observe those strong differences, which will grow more evident in time. The inhabitants of Canada, Massachusetts, the middle provinces, the southern ones will be as different as their climates; their only points of unity will be those of religion and language.

ᕐᕐᕐ

But to return to our back settlers. I must tell you, that there is something in the proximity of the woods, which is very singular. It is with men as it is with the plants and animals that grow and live in the forests; they are entirely different from those that live in the plains. I will candidly tell you all my thoughts but you are not to expect that I shall advance any reasons. By living in or near the woods, their actions are regulated by the wildness of the neighbourhood. The deer often come to eat their grain, the wolves to destroy their sheep, the bears to keel their hogs, the foxes to catch their poultry. This surrounding hostility immediately puts the gun into their hands; they watch these animals, they kill some; and thus by defending their property, they soon become professed hunters; this is the progress; once hunters, farewell to the plough. The chase renders them ferocious, gloomy, and unsociable; a hunter wants no neighbour, he rather hates them, because he dreads the competition. In a little time their success in the woods makes them neglect their tillage. They trust to the natural fecundity of the earth, and therefore do little; carelessness in fencing often exposes what little they sow to destruction; they are not at home to watch; in order therefore to make up the deficiency, they go oftener to the woods. That new mode of life brings along with it a new set of manners, which I cannot easily describe. These new manners being grafted on the old stock, produce a strange sort of lawless profligacy, the impressions of which are indelible. The manners of the Indian natives are respectable, compared with this European medley. Their wives and children live in sloth and inactivity; and having no proper pursuits, you may judge what education the latter receive. Their tender minds have nothing else to contemplate but the example of their parents; like them they grow up a mongrel breed, half civilised, half savage, except nature stamps on them some constitutional propensities. That rich, that voluptuous sentiment is gone that struck them so forcibly; the possession of their freeholds no longer conveys to their minds the same pleasure and pride. To all these reasons you must add, their lonely situation, and you cannot imagine what an effect on manners the great distances they live from each other has! Consider one of the last settlements in its first view: of what is it composed? Europeans who have not that sufficient share of knowledge they ought to have, in order to prosper; people who have suddenly passed from oppression, dread of government, and fear of laws, into the unlimited freedom of the woods. This sudden change must have a very great effect on most men, and on that class particularly. Eating of wild meat, whatever you may think, tends to alter their temper: though all the proof I can adduce, is, that I have seen it: and having no place of worship to resort to, what little society this might afford is denied them. The Sunday meetings, exclusive of religious benefits, were the only social bonds that might have inspired them with some degree of emulation in neatness. Is it then surprising to see men thus situated, immersed in great and heavy labours, degenerate a little? It is rather a wonder the effect is not more diffusive. The Moravians and the Quakers are the only instances in

exception to what I have advanced. The first never settle singly, it is a colony of the society which emigrates; they carry with them their forms, worship, rules, and decency: the others never begin so hard, they are always about to buy improvements, in which there is a great advantage, for by that time the country is recovered from its first barbarity. Thus our bad people are those who are half cultivators and half hunters; and the worst of them are those who have degenerated altogether into the hunting state. As old ploughmen and new men of the woods, as Europeans and new made Indians, they contract the vices of both; they adopt the moroseness and ferocity of a native, without his mildness, or even his industry at home. If manners are not refined, at least they are rendered simple and inoffensive by tilling the earth; all our wants are supplied by it, our time is divided between labour and rest, and leaves none for the commission of great misdeeds. As hunters it is divided between the toil of the chase, the idleness of repose, or the indulgence of inebriation. Hunting is but a licentious idle life, and if it does not always pervert good dispositions; yet, when it is united with bad luck, it leads to want: want stimulates that propensity to rapacity and injustice, too natural to needy men, which is the fatal gradation. After this explanation of the effects which follow by living in the woods, shall we yet vainly flatter ourselves with the hope of converting the Indians? We should rather begin with converting our back-settlers; and now if I dare mention the name of religion, its sweet accents would be lost in the immensity of these woods. Men thus placed are not fit either to receive or remember its mild instructions; they want temples and ministers, but as soon as men cease to remain at home, and begin to lead an erratic life, let them be either tawny or white, they cease to be its disciples.

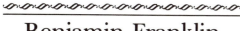

Benjamin Franklin (1706–1790)

No figure from our past seems quite so thoroughly American as Benjamin Franklin (1707–1790). An apostle of the Protestant work-ethic and a prototype of Emerson's image of the self-reliant individual, Franklin seems the very epitome of the self-made man and thus one of our classic American types. But this printer turned businessman, inventor, humorist, maxim-maker, and philosopher, whose spectacular financial success permitted him to retire at the age of forty and devote the rest of his life to public service and private scientific pursuits, was far more various and complex than he is usually credited with being. Yankee entrepreneur, Puritan workaholic, experimental scientist, free-thinking Deist, and Enlightenment moralist: Franklin has been called them all but may well remain most American precisely by eluding definition as any one of them. Melville probably said it best when in his novel *Israel Potter* he de-

scribes Franklin simply as "Jack of all trades, master of each and mastered by none—the type and genius of this land."

Franklin's *Autobiography* was written in several installments beginning in 1771 and was left unfinished at his death. The following selections are concerned with Franklin's religious background, his plan for arriving at moral perfection, his never-completed larger project to found a national society for the spread of virtue, and the nonsectarian creed he intended to base it on, which contained, as he thought, "the essentials of every known religion." What is perhaps most revolutionary or modern about Franklin's creed is the "doctrine," to use his own word, that lay at its heart: "vicious actions are not hurtful because they are forbidden, but forbidden because they are hurtful. . . ."

From *The Autobiography* (1784, 1788)

I had been religiously educated as a Presbyterian; and tho' some of the dogmas of that persuasion, such as *the eternal decrees of God, election, reprobation, etc.,* appeared to me unintelligible, others doubtful, and I early absented myself from the public assemblies of the sect, Sunday being my studying day, I never was without some religious principles. I never doubted, for instance, the existence of the Deity; that he made the world, and govern'd it by his Providence; that the most acceptable service of God was the doing good to man; that our souls are immortal; and that all crime will be punished, and virtue rewarded, either here or hereafter. These I esteem'd the essentials of every religion; and, being to be found in all the religions we had in our country, I respected them all, tho' with different degrees of respect, as I found them more or less mix'd with other articles, which, without any tendency to inspire, promote, or confirm morality, serv'd principally to divide us, and make us unfriendly to one another. This respect to all, with an opinion that the worst had some good effects, induc'd me to avoid all discourse that might tend to lessen the good opinion another might have of his own religion; and as our province increas'd in people, and new places of worship were continually wanted, and generally erected by voluntary contribution, my mite for such purpose, whatever might be the sect, was never refused.

Tho' I seldom attended any public worship, I had still an opinion of its propriety, and of its utility when rightly conducted, and I regularly paid my annual subscription for the support of the only Presbyterian minister or meeting we had in Philadelphia. He us'd to visit me sometimes as a friend, and admonish me to attend his administrations, and I was now and then prevail'd on to do so, once for five Sundays successively. Had he been in my opinion a good preacher, perhaps I might have continued, notwithstanding the occasion I had for the Sunday's leisure in my course of study; but his discourses were chiefly either polemic arguments, or explications of the peculiar doctrines of our sect, and were all to me very dry, uninteresting, and unedifying, since not a single moral principle was inculcated or enforc'd, their aim seeming to be rather to make us Presbyterians than good citizens.

At length he took for his text that verse of the fourth chapter of Philippians, *"Finally, brethren, whatsoever things are true, honest, just, pure, lovely, or of good report, if there be any virtue, or any praise, think on these things."* And I imagin'd, in a sermon on such a text, we could not miss of having some morality. But he confin'd himself to five points only, as meant by the apostle, viz.: 1. Keeping holy the Sabbath day. 2. Being diligent in reading the holy Scriptures. 3. Attending duly the publick worship. 4. Partaking of the Sacrament. 5. Paying a due respect to God's ministers. These might be all good things; but, as they were not the kind of good things that I expected from that text, I despaired of ever meeting with them from any other, was disgusted, and attended his preaching no more. I had some years before compos'd a little Liturgy, of form of prayer, for my own private use (viz., in 1728), entitled, *Articles of Belief and Acts of Religion.* I return'd to the use of this, and went no more to the public assemblies. My conduct might be blameable, but I leave it, without attempting further to excuse it; my present purpose being to relate facts, and not to make apologies for them.

It was about this time I conceiv'd the bold and arduous project of arriving at moral perfection. I wish'd to live without committing any fault at any time; I would conquer all that either natural inclination, custom, or company might lead me into. As I knew, or thought I knew, what was right and wrong, I did not see why I might not always do the one and avoid the other. But I soon found I had undertaken a task of more difficulty than I had imagined. While my care was employ'd in guarding against one fault, I was often surprised by another; habit took the advantage of inattention; inclination was sometimes too strong for reason. I concluded, at length, that the mere speculative conviction that it was our interest to be completely virtuous, was not sufficient to prevent our slipping; and that the contrary habits must be broken, and good ones acquired and established, before we can have any dependence on a steady, uniform rectitude of conduct. For this purpose I therefore contrived the following method.

In the various enumerations of the moral virtues I had met with in my reading, I found the catalogue more or less numerous, as different writers included more or fewer ideas under the same name. Temperance, for example, was by some confined to eating and drinking, while by others it was extended to mean the moderating every other pleasure, appetite, inclination, or passion, bodily or mental, even to our avarice and ambition. I propos'd to myself, for the sake of clearness, to use rather more names, with fewer ideas annex'd to each, than a few names with more ideas; and I included under thirteen names of virtues all that at that time occurr'd to me as necessary or desirable, and annexed to each a short precept, which fully express'd the extent I gave to its meaning.

These names of virtues, with their precepts, were:

1. Temperance

Eat not to dullness; drink not to elevation.

2. Silence

Speak not but what may benefit others or yourself; avoid trifling conversation.

3. Order

Let all your things have their places; let each part of your business have its time.

4. Resolution

Resolve to perform what you ought; perform without fail what you resolve.

5. Frugality

Make no expense but to do good to others or yourself; i.e., waste nothing.

6. Industry

Lose no time; be always employ'd in something useful; cut off all unnecessary actions.

7. Sincerity

Use no hurtful deceit; think innocently and justly, and, if you speak, speak accordingly.

8. Justice

Wrong none by doing injuries, or omitting the benefits that are your duty.

9. Moderation

Avoid extreams; forbear resenting injuries so much as you think they deserve.

10. Cleanliness

Tolerate no uncleanliness in body, cloaths, or habitation.

11. Tranquillity

Be not disturbed at trifles, or at accidents common or unavoidable.

12. Chastity

Rarely use venery but for health or offspring, never to dulness, weakness, or the injury of your own or another's peace or reputation.

13. Humility

Imitate Jesus and Socrates.

My intention being to acquire the *habitude* of all these virtues, I judg'd it would be well not to distract my attention by attempting the whole at once, but to fix it on one of them at a time; and, when I should be master of that, then to proceed to another, and so on, till I should have gone thro' the thirteen; and, as the previous acquisition of some might facilitate the acquisition of certain others, I arrang'd them with that view, as they stand above. Temperance first, as it tends to procure that coolness and clearness of head, which is so necessary where constant vigilance was to be kept up, and guard maintained against the unremitting attraction of ancient habits, and the force of perpetual temptations. This being acquir'd and establish'd, Silence would be more easy; and my desire being to gain knowledge at the same time that I improv'd in virtue, and considering that in conversation it was obtain'd rather by the use of ears than of the tongue, and therefore wishing to break a habit I was getting into of prattling, punning, and joking, which only made me acceptable to trifling company, I gave *Silence* the second place. This and the next, *Order,* I expected would allow me more time for attending to my project and my studies. *Resolution,* once become habitual, would keep me firm in my endeavours to obtain all the subsequent virtues; *Frugality* and *Industry* freeing me from my remaining debt, and producing affluence and independence, would make more easy the practice of Sincerity and Justice, etc., etc. Conceiving then, that, agreeably to the advice of Pythagoras in his Golden Verses, daily examination would be necessary, I contrived the following method for conducting that examination.

I made a little book, in which I allotted a page for each of the virtues. I rul'd each page with red ink, so as to have seven columns, one for each day of the week, marking each column with a letter for the day. I cross'd these columns with thirteen red lines, marking the beginning of each line with the first letter of one of the virtues, on which line, and in its proper column, I might mark, by a little black spot, every fault I found upon examination to have been committed respecting that virtue upon that day.

In truth, I found myself incorrigible with respect to Order; and now I am grown old, and my memory bad, I feel very sensibly the want of it. But, on the whole, tho' I never arrived at the perfection I had been so ambitious of obtaining, but fell far short of it, yet I was, by the endeavour, a better and a happier man than I otherwise should have been if I had not attempted it; as those who aim at perfect writing by imitating the engraved copies, tho' they never reach the wish'd-for excellence of those copies, their hand is mended by the endeavour, and is tolerable while it continues fair and legible.

It may be well my posterity should be informed that to this little artifice, with the blessing of God, their ancestor ow'd the constant felicity of his life, down to his 79th year in which this is written. What reverses may attend the remainder is the hand of Providence; but, if they arrive, the reflection on past happiness enjoy'd ought to help his bearing them with more resignation. To Temperance he ascribes his long-continued health, and what is still left to him of a good constitution; to Industry and Frugality, the early easiness of his circumstances and acquisition of his fortune, with all that knowledge that enabled him to be a useful citizen, and obtained for him some degree of reputation among the learned; to Sincerity and Justice, the confidence of his country, and the honorable employs it conferred upon him; and to the joint influence of the whole mass of the virtues, even in the imperfect state he was able to acquire them, all that evenness of temper, and

that cheerfulness in conversation, which makes his company still sought for, and agreeable even to his younger acquaintance. I hope, therefore, that some of my descendants may follow the example and reap the benefit.

It will be remark'd that, tho' my scheme was not wholly without religion, there was in it no mark of any of the distinguishing tenets of any particular sect. I had purposely avoided them; for, being fully persuaded of the utility and excellency of my method, and that it might be serviceable to people in all religions, and intending some time or other to publish it, I would not have any thing in it that should prejudice any one, of any sect, against it. I purposed writing a little comment on each virtue, in which I would have shown the advantages of possessing it, and the mischiefs attending its opposite vice: and I should have called my book THE ART OF VIRTUE, because it would have shown the means and manner of obtaining virtue, which would have distinguished it from the mere exhortation to be good, that does not instruct and indicate the means, but is like the apostle's man of verbal charity, who only without showing to the naked and hungry how or where they might get clothes or victuals, exhorted them to be fed and clothed.— James ii. 15, 16.

But it so happened that my intention of writing and publishing this comment was never fulfilled. I did, indeed, from time to time, put down short hints of the sentiments, reasonings, etc., to be made use of in it, some of which I have still by me; but the necessary close attention to private business in the earlier part of my life, and public business since, had occasioned my postponing it; for, it being connected in my mind with *a great and extensive project,* that required the whole man to execute, and which an unforeseen succession of employs prevented my attending to, it has hitherto remain'd unfinish'd.

In this piece it was my design to explain and enforce this doctrine, that vicious actions are not hurtful because they are forbidden, but forbidden because they are hurtful, the nature of man alone considered; that it was, therefore, every one's interest to be virtuous who wish'd to be happy even in this world; and I should, from this circumstance (there being always in the world a number of rich merchants, nobility, states, and princes, who have need of honest instruments for the management of their affairs, and such being so rare), have endeavoured to convince young persons that no qualities were so likely to make a poor man's fortune as those of probity and integrity.

Having mentioned *a great and extensive project* which I had conceiv'd, it seems proper that some account should be here given of that project and its object. Its first rise in my mind appears in the following little paper, accidentally preserv'd, viz.:

Observations on my reading history, In Library, May 19th, 1731.

"That the great affairs of the world, the wars, revolutions, etc., are carried on and affected by parties.

"That the view of these parties is their present general interest, or what they take to be such.

"That the different views of these different parties occasion all confusion.

"That while a party is carrying on a general design, each man has his particular private interest in view.

"That as soon as a party has gain'd its general point, each member becomes intent upon his particular interest; which, thwarting others, breaks that party into divisions, and occasions more confusion.

"That few in public affairs act from a meer view of the good of their country, whatever they may pretend; and, tho' their actings bring real good to their country, yet men primarily considered that their own and their country's interest was united, and did not act from a principle of benevolence.

"That fewer still, in public affairs, act with a view to the good of mankind.

"There seems to me at present to be great occasion for raising a United Party for Virtue, by forming the virtuous and good men of all nations into a regular body, to be govern'd by suitable good and wise rules, which good and wise men may probably be more unanimous in their obedience to, than common people are to common laws.

"I at present think that whoever attempts this aright, and is well qualified, can not fail of pleasing God, and of meeting with success. B.F."

Revolving this project in my mind, as to be undertaken herafter, when my circumstances should afford me the necessary leisure, I put down from time to time, on pieces of paper, such thoughts as occurr'd to me respecting it. Most of these are lost; but I find one purporting to be the substance of an intended creed, containing, as I thought, the essentials of every known religion, and being free of every thing that might shock the professors of any religion. It is express'd in these words, viz.:

"That there is one God, who made all things.

"That he governs the world by his providence.

"That he ought to be worshiped by adoration, prayer, and thanksgiving.

"But that the most acceptable service of God is doing good to man.

"That the soul is immortal.

"And that God will certainly reward virtue and punish vice, either here or hereafter."

My ideas at that time were, that the sect should be begun and spread at first among young and single men only; that each person to be initiated should not only declare his assent to such creed, but should have exercised himself with the thirteen weeks' examination and practice of the virtues, as in the before-mention'd model; that the existence of such a society should be kept a secret, till it was become more considerable, to prevent solicitations for the admission of improper persons, but that the members should each of them search among his acquaintance for ingenuous, well-disposed youths, to whom, with prudent caution, the scheme should be gradually communicated; that the members should engage to afford their advice, assistance, and support to each other in promoting one another's interests, business, and advancement in life; that, for distinction, we should be call'd *The Society of the Free and Easy:* free, as being, by the general practice and habit of the virtues, free from the dominion of vice; and particularly by the practice of industry and frugality, free from debt, which exposes a man to confinement, and a species of slavery to his creditors.

This is as much as I can now recollect of the project, except that I communicated it in part to two young men, who adopted it with some enthusiasm; but my then narrow circumstances, and the necessity I was under of sticking close to my business, occasion'd my postponing the further prosecution of it at that time; and my multifarious occupations, public and private, induc'd me to continue postponing, so that it has been omitted till I have no longer strength or activity left sufficient for such an enterprise; tho' I am still of opinion that it was a practicable scheme, and might have been very useful, by forming a great number of good citizens; and I was not discourag'd by the seeming magnitude of the undertaking, as I have always thought that one man of tolerable abilities may work great changes, and accomplish great affairs among mankind, if he first forms a good plan, and cutting off all amusements or other employments that would divert his attention, makes the execution of that same plan his sole study and business.

James O'Kelly
(1735?–1826)

James O'Kelly was an Irish immigrant who fought with the patriots during the American Revolution and later converted to Methodism and became an itinerant minister in southern Virginia and North Carolina. O'Kelly gained a certain prominence both because of his opposition to the spread of ecclesiastical authority (which eventually led him to help form a new Protestant sect called "The Christian Church" which lasted until 1931) and because of his objection to the institution of Negro slavery. In an age still struggling to understand the meaning of such things, O'Kelly was a courageous religious advocate of freedom and equality among all men.

From *Essay on Negro-Slavery* (1789)

Section I

. . . Their situation (generally) is as follows:——The [slave] families are miserably crowded together in dirty pens, without any real family-comfort, even where the husband and wife dwell together under one master: their conception and birth (too commonly) are not as private as that of brutes in the forest! A slave hath not power to do those duties incumbent on him towards his family; nor the satisfaction of being with them in sickness and distress. They are deprived of the liberty of seeking GOD and their souls' salvation in many instances. In a word, slavery is insufferable in its nature. A slave is looked upon as the property of the master, who is his own legislator (as touching the slave) to curse, abuse, drive rigorously, sell, change, give, &c. Yea, beat without restriction; mark, brand, and castrate him: and even when life itself is taken away, it is but very little regarded. Perhaps there may be a small stir if one is murdered, but it is nothing but a sham-inquisition! His wife and children (if slaves) are all saleable property; so that the slave cannot say that even his life is his own. They see their wives and children in suffering circumstances, but have no way to relieve them! They see their bleeding backs, but dare not say, "Why this abuse?" They are torn from each other to satisfy debts, and to be parted among the favoured legatees. This is tolerated by the sons of liberty, who risked their lives to deliver themselves from political bondage. . . .

Sect. II

O my brethren, these poor afflicted people do not deserve this treatment at our hands. Whatever has been done among Jews or barbarious nations, such doings do not become Christians. From the beginning it was not so. Man's authority over beasts is a donation from GOD, but man's absolute authority over man is no donation from GOD. Indeed the authority man hath over birds and beasts is under certain restrictions: the ox may plough and tread out the grain, but must not be muzzled. Creatures may be used, and every creature is good, but nothing must be abused. . . .

Sect. IV

The Son of GOD did not come to destroy lives, but to save. Neither did he come to enslave men's persons, but to preach the great jubilee. Involuntary slavery directly opposes the benevolent purposes of the Christian religion. The Christian religion is the pure undefiled religion, gathering proselytes from every nation into one fold. The Christian, who through the Spirit hath received a divine nature, even the mind of Christ, hath learned of his great master to be meek to his countrymen, neighbours and brethren, and the inhabitants of the remotest regions as well as of the nearest. He calls no man common or unclean. He is like his Father and his Master, whose sun shines upon the evil and the good, and who sends rain on the just and the unjust.

Remember, that "of one blood GOD made all nations," Africa not excepted. Where the gospel-light and religion take root, the dark places of the earth cease from their cruelty. The Father hath given all flesh to his Son: His bounds are from sea to sea, and from the rivers to the ends of the earth; and by the gospel is now calling his sons from far, and his daughters from the ends of the earth.

Therefore be wise, O kings of nations; and you rulers of America, be instructed, and break the jaws of the wicked, and take the spoils out of his teeth. Will a man rob GOD? Ye have robbed him, even this whole nation, in seizing and enslaving the purchase of Christ's blood. We read in the Revelation, ch. xviii. of selling the souls of men, but it is not left as an example for Christians. Is not America in this respect a sister to Babylon and Rome there spoken of? When shall our church be purified from spiritual whoredom, and this species of antichrist?

The primitive Christians did not support their ministers upon the hire of slaves procured for that purpose. May my fellow-labourers of different churches feel what I write, be convicted, by no means offended; and no longer support the gracious general gospel by the sweat and blood of the objects of GOD's mercy and subjects of gospel-grace! This hath more the appearance of wolves than shepherds. Yet I humbly pray, that I may not be looked upon as an enemy to any man, because I tell the truth. I will allow as much as possible for the prejudice of education and former ignorance of blind guides. But now light is come, let us put off the works of darkness. . . .

Sect. V

As a servant of the Church, many of you have known me several years, and my manner of behaving amongst you, especially in my native country, Virginia. I stand at your bar: testify against me. Have not I laboured among you, crying against all sin, night and day with many tears? Have I not taught you the same thing in private, both by precept and example, as well as in public—holiness to the Lord? Say, brethren, have I not gone through perils concerning this thing? Twice the clubs have been raised to beat me; once the pointed dagger was presented against me, but GOD protected me by a life-guard of the daughters of my people. Now my life is threatened; yet I must defend this truth, and hope that my testimony will be received among you, my brethren. . . .

There are many mouths open against me, as if I were the only person who ever cried out against the evil practice of slavery. The British constitution abhors it: slavery cannot be introduced into England by any foreign law, no, nor have an existence there. The gentlemen who formed our bill of rights call slavery *an inhuman negative.* Our revolution can be justified on no other principles. Our government stands on the basis of natural liberty, as the birthright of all human beings.

Our worthy gentlemen in the North begin to abhor it with hatred. I trust some of our Virginians do in their hearts disapprove of it. Several begin to declare against it. Some (a few) worthy men in our state have liberated their slaves. Several of our worthy members (in our church) have unloosed the heavy burdens. The Lord spare the people in Carolina, who refuse to give the honest Quakers liberty of conscience.

I could produce many more weighty testimonies, but I decline; only I must call upon that secret friend of mine in my reader's own breast. What need is there of any further witness to prove a matter so glaring to every man of sentiment?

Thomas Paine
(1737–1809)

Thomas Paine emigrated to America from England in 1774 with the help of Benjamin Franklin, who had been impressed by Paine's knowledge and interests. He was best known as a political pamphleteer, and his broadsides against tyranny and oppression encouraged the American rebellion. Paine's polemics and his outspoken, freethinking religious views frequently got him into trouble with authorities in England and France as well as America, and eventually left him forsaken, poor and broken in health.

Though *The Age of Reason* (1797) is Paine's great work in defense of Deism—his other important books are *Common Sense* (1776) and *The Rights of Man* (1792)—his religious views were most succinctly expressed in the following essay, published in Elihu Palmer's *Prospect* near the end of Paine's life. Regarded by many of his contemporaries, in the words of one of them, as "a loathsome reptile," Paine has continued to suffer from the general opinion voiced by Theodore Roosevelt that he was "a filthy little athiest." However, nothing could be further from the whole truth. As Paine stated in *The Age of Reason* in language that would have won assent from most of the Founding Fathers, he found the most compelling argument for the existence of God "in the immensity of the creation" and "the unchangeable order by which the incomprehensible whole is governed."

From "Of the Religion of Deism Compared with the Christian Religion, and the Superiority of the Former over the Latter" (1804)

Every person, of whatever religious denomination he may be, is a DEIST in the first article of his Creed. Deism, from the Latin word *Deus,* God, is the belief of a God, and this belief is the first article of every man's creed.

It is on this article, universally consented to by all mankind, that the Deist builds his church, and here he rests. Whenever we step aside from this article, by mixing it with articles of human invention, we wander into a labyrinth of uncertainty and fable, and become exposed to every kind of imposition by pretenders to revelation.

The Persian shows the Zend-Avesta of Zoroaster, the lawgiver of Persia, and calls it the divine law; the Bramin shows the *Shaster,* revealed, he says, by God to Brama, and given to him out of a cloud; the Jew shows what he calls the Law of Moses, given, he says, by God, on the Mount Sinai; the Christian shows a collection of books and epistles, written by nobody knows who, and called the New Testament; and the Mahometan shows the Koran, given, he says, by God to Mahomet: each of these calls itself *revealed religion,* and the *only* true Word of God, and this the followers of each profess to believe from the habit of education, and each believes the others are imposed upon.

But when the divine gift of reason begins to expand itself in the mind and calls man to reflection, he then reads and contemplates God and His works, and not in the books pretending to be revelation. The creation is the Bible of the true believer in God. Everything in this vast volume inspires him with sublime ideas of the Creator. The little and paltry, and often obscene, tales of the Bible sink into wretchedness when put in comparison with this mighty work.

The Deist needs none of those tricks and shows called miracles to confirm his faith, for what can be a greater miracle than the creation itself and his own existence?

There is a happiness in Deism, when rightly understood, that is not to be found in any other system of religion. All other systems have something in them that either shock our reason, or are repugnant to it, and man, if he thinks at all, must stifle his reason in order to force himself to believe them.

But in Deism our reason and our belief become happily united. The wonderful structure of the universe, and everything we behold in the system of the creation, prove to us, far better than books can do, the existence of a God, and at the same time proclaim His attributes.

It is by the exercise of our reason that we are enabled to contemplate God in His works, and imitate Him in His way. When we see His care and goodness extended over all His creatures, it teaches us our duty toward each other, while it calls forth our gratitude to Him. It is by forgetting God in His works, and running after the books of pretended revelation, that man has wandered from the straight path of duty and happiness, and become by turns the victim of doubt and the dupe of delusion.

Except in the first article in the Christian creed, that of believing in God, there is not an article in it but fills the mind with doubt as to the truth of it, the instant man begins to think. Now every article in a creed that is necessary to the happiness and salvation of man ought to be as evident to the reason and comprehension of man as the first article is, for God has not given us reason for the purpose of confounding us, but that we should use it for our own happiness and His glory.

The truth of the first article is proved by God Himself, and is universal; for *the creation is of itself demonstration of the existence of a Creator.* But the second article, that of God's begetting a son, is not proved in like manner, and stands on no other authority than that of a tale.

Certain books in what is called the New Testament tell us that Joseph dreamed that the angel told him so (Matthew i. 20): "And behold the angel of the Lord appeared to Joseph, in a dream, saying, Joseph, thou son of David, fear not to take unto thee Mary thy wife, for that which is conceived in her is of the Holy Ghost."

The evidence upon this article bears no comparison with the evidence upon the first article, and therefore is not entitled to the same credit, and ought not to be made an article in a creed, because the evidence of it is defective, and what evidence there is is doubtful and suspicious. We do not believe the first article on the authority of books, whether called Bibles or Korans, nor yet on the visionary authority of dreams, but on the authority of God's own visible works in the creation.

The nations who never heard of such books, nor of such people as Jews, Christians or Mahometans, believe the existence of God as fully as we do, because it is self-evident. The work of man's hands is a proof of the existence of man as fully as his personal appearance would be.

When we see a watch, we have as positive evidence of the existence of a watchmaker, as if we saw him; and in like manner the creation is evidence to our reason and our senses of the existence of a Creator. But there is nothing in the works of God that is evidence that He begat a son, nor anything in the system of creation that corroborates such an idea, and, therefore, we are not authorized in believing it. . . .

The four books called the Evangelists, Matthew, Mark, Luke and John, which give, or pretend to give, the birth, sayings, life, preaching, and death of Jesus Christ, make no mention of what is called the fall of man; nor is the name of Adam to be found in any of those books, which it certainly would be if the writers of them believed that Jesus was begotten, born and died for the purpose of redeeming mankind from the sin which Adam had brought into the world. Jesus never speaks of Adam himself, of the Garden of Eden, nor of what is called the fall of man.

But the Church of Rome having set up its new religion, which it called Christianity, invented the creed which it named the Apostles's Creed, in which it calls Jesus the *only son of God, conceived by the Holy Ghost, and born of the Virgin Mary;* things of which it is impossible that man or woman can have any idea, and consequently no belief but in words; and for which there is no authority but the idle story of Joseph's dream in the first chapter of Matthew, which any designing impostor or foolish fanatic might make.

It then manufactured the allegories in the book of Genesis into fact, and the allegorical tree of life and the tree of knowledge into real trees, contrary to the belief of the first Christians, and for which there is not the least authority in any of the books of the New Testament; for in none of them is there any mention made of such place as the Garden of Eden, nor of anything that is said to have happened there.,

But the Church of Rome could not erect the person called Jesus into a Savior of the world without making the allegories in the book of Genesis into fact, though the New Testament, as before observed, gives no authority for it. All at once the allegorical tree of knowledge became, according to the Chruch, a real tree, the fruit of it real fruit, and the eating of it sinful.

As priestcraft was always the enemy of knowledge, because priestcraft supports itself by keeping people in delusion and ignorance, it was consistent with its policy to make the acquisition of knowledge a real sin.

The Church of Rome having done this, it then brings forward Jesus the son of Mary as suffering death to redeem mankind from sin, which Adam, it says, had brought into the world by eating the fruit of the tree of knowledge. But as it is impossible for reason to believe such a story, because it can see no reason for it, nor have any evidence of it, the Church then tells us we must not regard our reason, but must *believe,* as it were, and that through thick and thin, as if God had given man reason like a plaything, or a rattle, on purpose to make fun of him. . . .

The dogma of the redemption is the fable of priestcraft invented since the time the New Testament was compiled, and the agreeable delusion of it suited with the depravity of immoral livers. When men are taught to ascribe all their own crimes and vices to the temptations of the devil, and to believe that Jesus, by his death, rubs all off, and pays their passage to heaven gratis, they become as careless in morals as a spendthrift would be of money were he told that his father had engaged to pay off all his scores.

It is a doctrine not only dangerous to morals in this world, but to our happiness in the next world, because it holds out such a cheap, easy, and lazy way of getting to heaven, as has a tendency to induce men to hug the delusion of it to their own injury.

But there are times when men have serious thoughts, and it is at such times, when they begin to think, that they begin to doubt the truth of the Christian religion; and well they may, for it is too fanciful and too full of conjecture, inconsistency, improbability and irrationality to afford consolation to the thoughful man. His reason revolts against his creed. He sees that none of its articles are proved, or can be proved.

He may believe that such a person as is called Jesus (for Christ was not his name) was born and grew to be a man, because it is no more than a natural and probable case. But who is to prove he is the son of God, that he was begotten by the Holy Ghost? Of these things there can be no proof; and that which admits not of proof, and is against the laws of probability and the order of nature, which God Himself has established, is not an object for belief. God has not given man reason to embarrass him, but to prevent his being imposed upon.

He may believe that Jesus was crucified, because many others were crucified, but who is to prove he was crucified *for the sins of the world*? This article has no evidence, not even in the New Testament; and if it had, where is the proof that the New Testament, in relating things neither probable nor probable, is to be believed as true?

When an article in a creed does not admit of proof nor of probability, the salvo is to call it revelation; but this is only putting one difficulty in the place of another, for it is as impossible to prove a thing to be revelation as it is to prove that Mary was gotten with child by the Holy Ghost.

Here it is that the religion of Deism is superior to the Christian religion. It is free from all those invented and torturing articles that shock our reason or injure our humanity, and with which the Christian religion abounds. Its creeds is pure, and sublimely simple. It believes in God, and there it rests.

It honors reason as the choicest gift of God to man, and the faculty by which he is enabled to contemplate the power, wisdom and goodness of the Creator displayed in the creation; and reposing itself on His protection, both here and hereafter, it avoids all presumptuous beliefs, and rejects, as the fabulous inventions of men, all books pretending to relevation.

James Fenimore Cooper (1789–1851)

James Fenimore Cooper was the first major American writer of fiction consciously to use his art to comment on and criticize America itself. He wrote the Leatherstocking Tales over a period of nearly twenty years, beginning with *The Pioneers* (1823) and concluding with *The Deerslayer* (1841). The hunter and trapper Natty Bumppo personifies Cooper's ideal of the native integrity of the American wilderness.

Cooper reversed normal chronological order in writing the Leatherstocking Tales, which commence toward the end of Natty's life when he is shunned by the people of the communities encroaching on his forest domain, and culminate with Natty's youthful initiation into a world of Nature as yet unspoiled by the advance of civilization. D.H. Lawrence felt that Cooper, in tracing his protagonist's career back from old age to golden youth, had delineated the outline of the true American myth. In Lawrence's view, America begins old and withered, and develops through a two-stage process, sloughing off the exhausted European consciousness and revealing the newly formed consciousness and identity underneath.

The Prairie (1826), from which the following selection is taken, is the third novel in the series, and concerns Natty's last adventures and his death.

From *The Prairie* (1827)

[The death of Natty Bumppo]

When they entered the town, its inhabitants were seen collected in an open space, where they were arranged with the customary deference to age and rank. The whole formed a large circle, in the centre of which were perhaps a dozen of the principal chiefs. Hard-Heart waved his hand as he approached, and, as the mass of bodies opened he rode through, followed by his companions. Here they dismounted; and as the beasts were led apart, the strangers found themselves environed by a thousand grave, composed, but solicitous faces.

Middleton gazed about him in growing concern, for no cry, no song, no shout welcomed him among a people, from whom he had so lately parted with regret. His uneasiness, not to say apprehensions, was shared by all his followers. Determination and stern resolution began to assume the place of anxiety in every eye, as each man silently felt for his arms, and assured himself that his several weapons were in a state for service. But there was no answering symptom of hostility on the part of their hosts. Hard-Heart beckoned for Middleton and Paul to follow, leading the way towards the cluster of forms that occupied the centre of the circle. Here the visitors found a solution of all the movements which had given them so much reason for apprehension.

The trapper was placed on a rude seat, which had been made, with studied care, to support his frame in an upright and easy attitude. The first glance of the eye told his former friends, that the old man was at length called upon to pay the last tribute of nature. His eye was glazed, and apparently as devoid of sight as of expression. his features were a little more sunken and strongly marked than formerly; but there, all change, so far as exterior was concerned, might be said to have ceased. His approaching end was not to be ascribed to any positive disease, but had been a gradual and mild decay of the physical powers. Life, it is true, still lingered in his system; but it was as if at times entirely ready to depart, and then it would appear to re-animate the sinking form, reluctant to give up the possession of a tenement that had never been corrupted by vice or undermined by disease. It would have been no violent fancy to have imagined that the spirit fluttered about the placid lips of the old woodsman, reluctant to depart from a shell that had so long given it an honest and honorable shelter.

His body was placed so as to let the light of the setting sun fall upon the solemn features. His head was bare, the long thin locks of grey fluttering lightly in the evening breeze. His rifle lay upon his knee, and the other accoutrements of the chase were placed at his side, within reach of his hand. Between his feet lay the figure of a hound, with its head crouching to the earth, as if it slumbered; and so perfectly easy and natural was its position, that a second glance was necessary to tell Middleton he saw only the skin of Hector, stuffed, by Indian tenderness and ingenuity, in a manner to represent the living animal. His own dog was playing at a distance with the child of Tachechana and Mah-toree. The mother herself stood at hand, holding in her arms a second offspring, that might boast of a percentage no less honorable than that which belonged to the son of Hard-Heart. Le Balafré was seated nigh the dying trapper, with every mark about his person that the hour of his own departure was not far distant. The rest of those immediately in the centre were aged men, who had apparently drawn near in order to observe the manner in which a just and fearless warrior would depart on the greatest of his journeys.

The old man was reaping the rewards of a life remarkable for temperance and activity, in a tranquil and placid death. His vigor in a manner endured to the very last. Decay, when it did occur, was rapid, but free from pain. He had hunted with the tribe in the spring, and even throughout most of the summer; when his limbs suddenly refused to perform their customary offices. A sympathizing weakness took possession of all his faculties; and the Pawnees believed that they were going to lose, in this unexpected manner, a sage and counsellor whom they had begun both to love and respect. But, as we have already said, the immortal occupant seemed unwilling to desert its tenement. The lamp of life flickered, without becoming extinguished. On the morning of the day on which Middleton arrived, there was a general reviving of the powers of the whole man. His tongue was again heard in wholesome maxims, and his eye from time to time recognised the persons of his friends. It merely proved to be a brief and final intercourse with the world, on the part of one who had already been considered, as to mental communion, to have taken his leave of it for ever.

When he had placed his guests in front of the dying man, Hard-Heart, after a pause, that proceeded as much from sorrow as decorum, leaned a little forward, and demanded—

"Does my father hear the words of his son?"

"Speak," returned the trapper, in tones that issued from his chest, but which were rendered awfully distinct by the stillness that reigned in the place. "I am about to depart from the village of the Loups, and shortly shall be beyond the reach of your voice."

"Let the wise chief have no cares for

his journey," continued Hard-Heart, with an earnest solicitude that led him to forget, for the moment, that others were waiting to address his adopted parent; "a hundred Loups shall clear his path from briars."

"Pawnee, I die, as I have lived, a Christian man!" resumed the trapper, with a force of voice that had the same startling effect on his hearers as is produced by the trumpet, when its blast rises suddenly and freely on the air, after its obstructed sounds have been heard struggling in the distance: "as I came into life so will I leave it. Horses and arms are not needed to stand in the presence of the Great Spirit of my people. He knows my color, and according to my gifts will he judge my deeds."

"My father will tell my young men how many Mingoes he has struck, and what acts of valor and justice he has done, that they may know how to imitate him."

"A boastful tongue is not heard in the heaven of a white man!" solemnly returned the old man. "What I have done He has seen. His eyes are always open. That which has been well done will he remember; wherein I have been wrong will he not forget to chastise, though he will do the same in mercy. No, my son; a Pale-face may not sing his own praises, and hope to have them acceptable before his God!"

A little disappointed, the young partisan stepped modestly back, making way for the recent comers to approach. Middleton took one of the meagre hands of the trapper, and struggling to command his voice, he succeeded in announcing his presence.

The old man listened like one whose thoughts were dwelling on a very different subject; but when the other had succeeded in making him understand that he was present, an expression of joyful recognition passed over his faded features.

"I hope you have not so soon forgotten those whom you so materially served!" Middleton concluded. "It would pain me to think my hold on your memory was so light."

"Little that I have ever seen is forgotten," returned the trapper: "I am at the close of many weary days, but there is not one among them all that I could wish to overlook. I remember you, with the whole of your company; ay, and your gran'ther, that went before you. I am glad that you have come back upon these plains, for I had need of one who speaks the English, since little faith can be put in the traders of these regions. Will you do a favor to an old and dying man?"

"Name it," said Middleton, "it shall be done."

"It is a far journey to send such trifles," resumed the old man, who spoke at short intervals, as strength and breath permitted; "a far and weary journey is the same; but kindesses and friendships are things not to be forgotten. There is a settlement among the Otsego hills—"

"I know the place," interrupted Middleton, observing that he spoke with increasing difficulty; "proceed to tell me what you would have done."

"Take this rifle, and pouch, and horn, and send them to the person whose name is graven on the plates of the stock—a trader cut the letters with his knife,—for it is long that I have intended to send him such a token of my love!"

"It shall be so. Is there more that you could wish?"

"Little else have I to bestow. My traps I give to my Indian son; for honestly and kindly has he kept his faith. Let him stand before me."

Middleton explained to the chief what the trapper had said, and relinquished his own place to the other.

"Pawnee," continued the old man, always changing his language to suit the person he addressed, and not unfrequently according to the ideas he expressed, "it is a custom of my people for the father to leave his blessing with the son before he shuts his eyes for ever. This blessing I give to you; take it; for the prayers of a Christian man will never make the path of a just warrior to the blessed prairies either longer or more tangled. May the God of a white man look on your deeds with friendly eyes, and may you never commit an act that shall cause him to darken his face. I know not whether we shall ever meet again. There are many traditions concerning the place of Good Spirits. It is not for one like me, old and experienced though I am, to set up my opinions against a nation's. You believe in the blessed prairies, and I have faith in the sayings of my fathers. If both are true our parting will be final; but if it should prove that the same meaning is hid under different words, we shall yet stand together, Pawnee, before the face of your Wahcondah, who will then be no other than my God. There is much to

be said in favor of both religions, for each seems suited to its own people, and no doubt it was so intended. I fear I have not altogether followed the gifts of my color, inasmuch as I find it a little painful to give up for ever the use of the rifle, and the comforts of the chase. But then the fault has been my own, seeing that it could not have been His. Ay, Hector," he continued, leaning forward a little, and feeling for the ears of the hound, "our parting has come at last, dog, and it will be a long hunt. You have been an honest, and a bold, and a faithful hound. Pawnee, you cannot slay the pup on my grave, for where a Christian dog falls there he lies for ever; but you can be kind to him after I am gone, for the love you bear his master."

"The words of my father are in my ears," returned the young partisan, making a grave and respectful gesture of assent.

"Do you hear what the chief has promised, dog!" demanded the trapper, making an effort to attract the notice of the insensible effigy of his hound. Receiving no answering look, nor hearing any friendly whine, the old man felt for the mouth, and endeavored to force his hand between the cold lips. The truth then flashed upon him, although he was far from perceiving the whole extent of the deception. Falling back in his seat, he hung his head, like one who felt a severe and unexpected shock. Profiting by this momentary forgetfulness, two young Indians removed the skin with the same delicacy of feeling that had induced them to attempt the pious fraud.

"The dog is dead!" muttered the trapper, after a pause of many minutes; "a hound has his time as well as a man; and well has he filled his days! Captain," he added, making an effort to wave his hand for Middleton, "I am glad you have come; for though kind, and well meaning according to the gifts of their color, these Indians are not the men to lay the head of a white man in his grave. I have been thinking, too, of this dog at my feet; it will not do to set forth the opinion that a Christian can expect to meet his hound again; still there can be little harm in placing what is left of so faithful a servant nigh the bones of his master."

"It shall be as you desire."

"I'm glad you think with me in this matter. In order, then, to save labor, lay the pup at my feet; or for that matter, put him side by side. A hunter need never be ashamed to be found in company with his dog!"

"I charge myself with your wish."

The old man made a long, and apparently a musing pause. At times he raised his eyes wistfully, as if he would again address Middleton, but some innate feeling appeared always to suppress his words. The other, who observed his hesitation, inquired in a way most likely to encourge him to proceed whether there was aught else that he could wish to have done.

"I am without kith or kin in the wide world!" the trapper answered: "when I am gone there will be an end of my race. We have never been chiefs; but honest, and useful in our way. I hope it cannot be denied we have always proved ourselves. My father lies buried near the sea, and the bones of his son will whiten on the prairies—"

"Name the spot, and your remains shall be placed by the side of your father," interrupted Middleton.

"Not so, not so, Captain. Let me sleep where I have lived—beyond the din of the settlements! Still I see no need why the grave of an honest man should be hid, like a Red-skin in his ambushment. I paid a man in the settlements to make and put a graven stone at the head of my father's resting-place. It was of the value of twelve beaver-skins, and cunningly and curiously was it carved! Then it told to all comers that the body of such a Christian lay beneath; and it spoke of his manner of life, of his years, and of his honesty. When we had done with the Frenchers in the old war I made a journey to the spot, in order to see that all was rightly performed, and glad I am to say, the workman had not forgotten his faith."

"And such a stone you would have at your grave!"

"I! no, no, I have no son but Hard-Heart, and it is little that an Indian knows of white fashions and usages. Besides, I am his debtor already, seeing it is so little I have done since I have lived in his tribe. The rifle might bring the value of such a thing—but then I know it will give the boy pleasure to hang the piece in his hall, for many is the deer and the bird that he has seen it destroy. No, no, the gun must be sent to him whose name is graven on the lock!"

"But there is one who would gladly prove his affection in the way you wish; he who owes you not only his own deliverance from so many dangers, but who inherits a heavy debt of gratitude from his ancestors. The stone shall be put at the head of your grave."

The old man extended his emaciated hand, and gave the other a squeeze of thanks.

"I thought you might be willing to do it, but I was backward in asking the favor," he said, "seeing that you are not of my kin. Put no boastful words on the same, but just the name, the age, and the time of the death, with something from the holy book; no more, no more. My name will then not be altogether lost on 'arth; I need no more."

Middleton intimated his assent, and then followed a pause that was only broken by distant and broken sentences from the dying man. He appeared now to have closed his accounts with the world, and to await merely for the final summons to quit it. Middleton and Hard-Heart placed themselves on opposite sides of his seat, and watched with melancholy solicitude, the variations of his countenance. For two hours there was no very sensible alteration. The expression of his faded and time-worn features was that of a calm and dignified repose. From time to time he spoke, uttering some brief sentence in the way of advice, or asking some simple questions concerning those in whose fortunes he took a friendly interest. During the whole of that solemn and anxious period each individual of the tribe kept his place, in the most self-restrained patience. When the old man spoke, all bent their heads to listen; and when his words were uttered, they seemed to ponder on their wisdom and usefulness.

As the flame drew nigher to the socket his voice was hushed, and there were moments when his attendants doubted whether he still belonged to the living.

Middleton, who watched each wavering expression of his weather-beaten visage, with the interest of a keen observer of human nature, softened by the tenderness of personal regard, fancied he could read the workings of the old man's soul in the strong lineaments of his countenance. Perhaps what the enlightened soldier took for the delusion of mistaken opinion did actually occur—for who has returned from that unknown world to explain by what forms, and in what manner, he was introduced into its awful precincts? Without pretending to explain what must ever be a mystery to the quick, we shall simply relate facts as they occurred.

The trapper had remained nearly motionless for an hour. His eyes alone had occasionally opened and shut. When opened, his gaze seemed fastened on the clouds which hung around the western horizon, reflecting the bright colors, and giving form and loveliness to the glorious tints of an American sunset. The hour—the calm beauty of the season—the occasion, all conspired to fill the spectators with solemn awe. Suddenly, while musing on the remakable position in which he was placed, Middleton felt the hand which he held grasp his own with incredible power, and the old man, supported on either side by his friends, rose upright to his feet. For a moment he looked about him, as if to invite all in presence to listen (the lingering remnant of human frailty), and then, with a fine military elevation of the head, and with a voice that might be heard in every part of that numerous assembly, he pronounced the word—

"Here!"

A movement so entirely unexpected, and the air of grandeur and humility which were so remarkably united in the mien of the trapper, together with the clear and uncommon force of his utterance, produced a short period of confusion in the faculties of all present. When Middleton and Hard-Heart, each of whom had involuntarily extended a hand to support the form of the old man, turned to him again, they found that the subject of their interest was removed for ever beyond the necessity of their care. They mournfully placed the body in its seat, and Le Balafré arose to announce the termination of the scene to the tribe. The voice of the old Indian seemed a sort of echo from that invisible world to which the meek spirit of the trapper had just departed.

"A valiant, a just, and a wise warrior, has gone on the path which will lead him to the blessed grounds of his people!" he said. "When the voice of the Wahcondah called him, he was ready to answer. Go, my children; remember the just chief of the Pale-faces, and clear your own tracks from briars."

The grave was made beneath the shade of some noble oaks. It has been carefully watched to the present hour by the Pawnees of the Loup, and is often shown to the traveller and the trader as a spot where a just Whiteman sleeps. In due time the stone was placed at its head, with the simple inscription, which the trapper had himself requested. The only liberty, taken by Middleton, was to add—*"May no wanton hand ever disturb his remains!"*

William Ellery Channing (1780–1842)

William Ellery Channing was one of the fathers of religious liberalism in America. Pastor of the Federal Street Congregational Church in Boston from 1803 until his death, Channing delivered his most famous sermon at the ordination of Jared Sparks in Baltimore in 1819. In this sermon he set forth his argument against Calvinism in unequivocal terms and outlined what would become the basic tenets of American Unitarianism. Channing is an important transitional figure between the Old Light rationalism of such orthodox Christians as Charles Chauncy and the philosophical idealism of such Transcendentalists as Ralph Waldo Emerson and Theodore Parker.

From "Unitarian Christianity" (1830)

There are two natural divisions under which my thoughts will be arranged. I shall endeavour to unfold, 1st, The principles which we adopt in interpreting the Scriptures. And 2dly, Some of the doctrines, which the Scriptures, so interpreted, seem to us clearly to express.

I. We regard the Scriptures as the records of God's successive revelations to mankind, and particularly of the last and most perfect revelation of his will by Jesus Christ. Whatever doctrines seem to us to be clearly taught in the Scriptures, we receive without reserve or exception. We do not, however, attach equal importance to all the books in this collection. Our religion, we believe, lies chiefly in the New Testament. The dispensation of Moses, compared with that of Jesus, we consider as adapted to the childhood of the human race, a preparation for a nobler system, and chiefly useful now as serving to confirm and illustrate the Christian Scriptures. Jesus Christ is the only master of Christians, and whatever he taught, either during his personal ministry, or by his inspired apostles, we regard as of divine authority, and profess to make the rule of our lives. . . .

Our leading principle in interpreting Scripture is this, that the Bible is a book written for men, in the language of men, and that its meaning is to be sought in the same manner, as that of other books. We believe that God, when he speaks to the human race, conforms, if we may so say, to the established rules of speaking and writing. How else would the Scriptures avail us more, than if communicated in an unknown tongue?

Now all books, and all conversation, require in the reader or hearer the constant exercise of reason; or their true import is only to be obtained by continual comparison and inference. Human language, you well know, admits various interpretations; and every word and every sentence must be modified and explained according to the subject which is discussed, according to the purposes, feelings, circumstances and principles of the writer, and according to the genius and idioms of the language which he uses. These are acknowledged principles in the interpretation of human writings; and a man, whose words we should explain without reference to these principles, would reproach us justly with a criminal want of candor, and an intention of obscuring or distorting his meaning. . . .

Enough has been said to show, in what sense we make use of reason in interpreting Scripture. From a variety of possible interpretations, we select that, which accords with the nature of the subject and the state of the writer, with the connexion of the passage, with the general strain of Scripture, with the known character and will of God, and with the obvious and acknowledged laws of nature. In other words, we believe that God never contradicts, in one part of Scripture, what he teaches in another; and never contradicts, in revelation, what he teaches in his works and providence. And we, therefore, distrust every interpretation, which, after deliberate attention, seems repugnant to any established truth. We reason about the Bible precisely as civilians do about the constitution under which we live; who, you know, are accustomed to limit one provision of that venerable instrument by others, and to fix the precise import of its parts, by inquiring into its general spirit, into the intentions of its authors, and into the prevalent feelings, impressions, and circumstances of the time when it was framed. Without these principles of interpretation, we frankly acknowledge, that we cannot defend the divine authority of the Scriptures. Deny us this latitude, and we must abandon this book to its enemies.

II. Having thus stated the principles according to which we interpret Scripture, I now proceed to the second great head of this discourse, which is, to state some of the views, which we derive from that sacred book, particularly those which distinguish us from other Christians.

1. In the first place, we believe in the doctrine of GOD'S UNITY, or that there is one God, and one only. To this truth we give infinite importance, and we feel ourselves bound to take heed, lest any man spoil us of it by vain philosophy. The proposition, that there is one God, seems to us exceedingly plain. We understand by it, that there is one being, one mind, one person, one intelligent agent, and one only, to whom underived and infinite perfection and dominion belong. We conceive, that these words could have conveyed no other meaning to the simple and uncultivated people, who were set apart to be depositaries of this great truth, and who were utterly incapable of understanding those hair-breadth distinctions between being and person, which the sagacity of latter ages has discovered. We find no intimation, that this language was to be taken in an unusual sense, or that God's unity was a quite different thing from the oneness of other intelligent beings.

We object to the doctrine of the trinity, that whilst acknowledging in words, it subverts in effect, the unity of God. According to this doctrine, there are three infinite and equal persons, possessing supreme divinity, called the Father, Son, and Holy Ghost. Each of these persons, as described by theologians, has his own particular consciousness, will, and perceptions. They love each other, converse with each other, and delight in each other's society. They perform different parts in man's redemption, each having his appropriate office, and neither doing the work of the other. The Son is mediator and not the Father. The Father sends the Son, and is not himself sent; nor is he conscious, like the Son, of taking flesh. Here then, we have three intelligent agents, possessed of different consciousnesses, different wills, and different perceptions, performing different acts, and sustaining different relations; and if these things do not imply and constitute three minds or beings, we are utterly at a loss to know how three minds or beings are to be formed. It is difference of properties, and acts, and consciousness, which leads us to the belief of different intelligent beings, and if this mark fails us, our whole knowledge falls; we have no proof, that all the agents and persons in the universe are not one and the same mind. When we attempt to conceive of three Gods, we can do nothing more, than represent to ourselves three agents, distinguished from each other by similar marks and peculiarities to those, which separate the persons of the trinity; and when common Christians hear these persons spoken of as conversing with each other, loving each other, and performing different acts, how can they help regarding them as different beings, different minds? . . .

⟋⟍⟋⟍⟋⟍

2. Having thus given our views of the unity of God, I proceed in the second place to observe, that we believe in the unity of Jesus Christ. We believe that Jesus is one mind, one soul, one being, as truly as we are, and equally distinct from the one God. We complain of the doctrine of the trinity, that not satisfied with making God three beings, it makes Jesus two beings, and thus introduces infinite confusion into our conceptions of his character. This corruption of Christianity, alike repugnant to common sense, and to the general strain of scripture, is a remarkable proof of the power of a false philosophy in disfiguring the simple truth of Jesus.

According to this doctrine, Jesus Christ, instead of being one mind, one conscious intelligent principle, whom we can understand, consists of two souls, two minds; the one divine, the other human; the one weak, the other almighty; the one ignorant, the one omniscient. Now we maintain, that this is to make Christ two beings. To denominate him one person, one being, and yet to suppose him made up of two minds, infinitely different from each other, is to abuse and confound language, and to throw darkness over all our conceptions of intelligent natures. According to the common doctrine, each of these two minds in Christ has its own consciousness, its own will, its own perceptions. They have in fact no common properties. The divine mind feels none of the wants and sorrows of the human, and the human is infinitely removed from the perfection and happiness of the divine. Can you conceive of two beings in the universe more distinct? We have always thought that one person was constituted and distinguished by one consciousness. The doctrine, that one and the same person should have two consciousnesses, two wills, two souls, infinitely different from each other, this we think an enormous tax on human credulity. . . .

⟋⟍⟋⟍⟋⟍

3. Having thus given our belief on two great points, namely, that there is one God, and that Jesus Christ is a being distinct from, and inferior to God, I now proceed to another point on which we lay still greater stress. We believe in the *moral perfection of God*. We consider no part of theology so important as that which treats of God's moral character; and we value our views of Christianity chiefly, as they assert his amiable and venerable attributes. . . .

We believe that God is infinitely good, kind, benevolent, in the proper sense of these words; good in disposition, as well as in act; good, not to a few, but to all; good to every individual, as well as to the general system.

We believe, too, that God is just; but we never forget, that his justice is the justice of a good being, dwelling in the same mind, and acting in harmony, with perfect benevolence. . . .

To give our views of God, in one word, we believe in his Parental character. We ascribe to him, not only the name, but the dispositions and principles of a father. We believe that he has a father's concern for his creatures, a father's desire for their improvement, a father's equity in proportioning his commands to their powers, a father's joy in their progress, a father's readiness to receive the penitent, and a father's justice for the incorrigible. We look upon this world as a place of education, in which he is training men by prosperity and adversity, by aids and obstructions, by conflicts of reason and passion, by motives to duty and temptations to sin, by a various discipline suited to free and moral beings, for union with himself, and for a sublime and ever growing virtue in heaven.

Now we object to the systems of religion, which prevail among us, that they are adverse, in a greater or less degree, to these purifying, comforting, and honorable views of God, that they take from us our Father in heaven, and substitute for him a being, whom we cannot love if we would, and whom we ought not to love if we could. We object, particularly on this ground, to that system, which arrogates to itself the name of Orthodoxy, and which is now industriously propagated through our country. This system indeed takes various shapes, but in all it casts dishonor on the Creator. According to its old and genuine form, it teaches, that God brings us into life wholly depraved, so that under the innocent features of our childhood, is hidden a nature averse to all good and propense to all evil, a nature, which exposes us to God's displeasure and wrath, even before we have acquired power to understand our duties, or to reflect upon our actions. According to a more modern exposi-

tion, it teaches, that we came from the hands of our Maker with such a constitution and are placed under such influences and circumstances, as to render certain and infallible the total depravity of every human being, from the first moment of his moral agency; and it also teaches, that the offence of the child, who brings into life this ceaseless tendency to unmingled crime, exposes him to the sentence of everlasting damnation. Now, according to the plainest principles of morality, we maintain, that a natural constitution of the mind, unfailingly disposing it to evil and to evil alone, would absolve it from guilt; that to give existence under this condition would argue unspeakable cruelty, and that to punish the sin of this unhappily constituted child with endless ruin, would be a wrong unparalleled by the most merciless despotism.

This system also teaches, that God selects from this corrupt mass a number to be saved, and plucks them, by a special influence, from the common ruin; that the rest of mankind, though left without that special grace which their conversion requires, are commanded to repent under penalty of aggravated woe; and that forgiveness is promised them on terms, which their very constitution infallibly disposes them to reject, and in rejecting which they awfully enhance the punishments of hell. These proffers of forgiveness and exhortations of amendment, to beings born under a blighting curse, fill our minds with horror, which we want words to express. . . .

◦∙◦∙◦

4. Having thus spoken of the unity of God; of the unity of Jesus, and his inferiority to God; and of the perfections of the divine character; I now proceed to give our views of the mediation of Christ and of the purposes of his mission. With regard to the great object, which Jesus came to accomplish, there seem to be no possibility of mistake. We believe, that he was sent by the Father to effect a moral, or spiritual deliverance of mankind; that is, to rescue men from sin and its consequences, and to bring them to a state of everlasting purity and happiness. We believe, too, that he accomplishes this sublime purpose by a variety of methods; by his instructions respecting God's unity, parental character, and moral government, which are admirably fitted to reclaim the world from idolatry and impiety, to the knowledge, love, and obedience of the Creator; by his promises of pardon to the penitent, and of divine assistance to those, who labor for progress in moral excellence; by the light which he has thrown on the path of duty; by his own spotless example, in which the loveliness and sublimity of virtue shine forth to warm and quicken, as well as guide us to perfection; by his threatenings against incorrigible guilt; by his glorious discoveries of immortality; by his sufferings and death; by that signal event, the resurrection, which powerfully bore witness to his divine mission, and brought down to men's senses a future life; by his continual intercession, which obtains for us spiritual aid and blessings; and by the power with which he is invested of raising the dead, judging the world, and conferring the everlasting rewards, promised to the faithful.

◊◊◊

5. Having thus stated our views of the highest object of Christ's mission, that it is the recovery of men to virtue, or holiness, I shall now, in the last place, give our views of the nature of christian virtue, or true holiness. We believe that all virtue has its foundation in the moral nature of man, that is, in conscience, or his sense of duty, and in the power of forming his temper and life according to conscience. We believe that these moral faculties are the grounds of responsibility, and the highest distinctions of human nature, and that no act is praiseworthy, any farther than it springs from their exertion. We believe, that no dispositions infused into us without our own moral activity, are of the nature of virtue, and therefore, we reject the doctrine of irresistible divine influence on the human mind, moulding it into goodness, as marble is hewn into a statue. Such goodness, if this word may be used, would not be the object of moral approbation, any more than the instinctive affections of inferior animals, or the constitutional amiableness of human beings. . . .

Among the virtues, we give the first place to the love of God. We believe, that this principle is the true end and happiness of our being, that we were made for union with our Creator, that his infinite perfection is the only sufficient object and true resting place for the insatiable desires and unlimited capacities of the human mind, and that without him, our noblest sentiments, admiration, veneration, hope, and love, would wither and decay. . . .

Another important branch of virtue, we believe to be love to Christ. The greatness of the work of Jesus, the spirit with which he executed it, and the sufferings which he bore for our salvation, we feel to be strong claims on our gratitude and veneration. We see in nature no beauty to be compared with the loveliness of his character, nor do we find on earth a benefactor, to whom we owe an equal debt. We read his history with delight, and learn from it the perfection of our nature.

IV
Realizations
(1830–1915)

Americans in this period were more acutely conscious than in any other of the need to formulate a definition of the meaning of America in terms of changes in outlook America made necessary and the form of life it made possible. But this struggle for self-definition was to result in many metaphysics rather than one. The reasons for the great diversity of belief in this period were several: fundamental changes in the conditions of life as the nation shifted from an agrarian to an industrial economy and the population became less rural and more urban; the rise of modern science with its attendant series of new and often challenging assumptions about the nature of the physical universe; the massive influx of immigrants whose different customs and ideas often resisted assimilation; rapid development of new sections of the country which contributed to a sense of regional diversity and local distinctiveness; and the terrible conflict of the Civil War which dramatized the emergent pluralism of morals and manners associated with these years.

During this era, Walt Whitman gave perhaps the most explicit expression to this need for a new American "idea of order" to capture and express the meaning of the American experiment. And those who heard Whitman's call tended to follow his lead by supplying not one interpretation for the meaning of "these States," as Whitman described them, but a multitude of often conflicting and sometimes contradictory interpretations, their sense and significance frequently residing in the oppositions among them.

Ralph Waldo Emerson set the tone for the discussion of New World metaphysics in this period by subsuming what the Puritans meant by God and the men of the Enlightenment meant by Nature under the designation of Experience. Emerson's intention, like that of other individuals of the period, from Herman Melville to Henry Adams, from Henry David Thoreau to George Santayana, was neither to describe experience nor simply to develop a philosophy of it. Although expressing themselves in different terms, they all sought to restore man's right relationship to experience. The problem, as they conceived it, was less to understand experience than to have it—to experience life fully and truly. As Thoreau put it, "Be it life or death, we crave only reality. If we are really dying, let us hear the rattle in our throats and feel cold in the extremities; if we are alive, let us go about our business."

Ralph Waldo Emerson (1803–1882)

In this ringing challenge to his age, Ralph Waldo Emerson, essayist, poet, and philospher, produced the central manifesto of the American Transcendentalist movement and set forth the terms in which virtually all subsequent American thinkers and writers would attempt to define the meaning of America's nature and destiny. Complaining that his own era was too retrospective, that it looked at life through other men's eyes, Emerson asked, "Why should not we also enjoy an original relation to the universe?" and his fellow countrymen seemed to reply, "Why not, indeed!" For stating so radically the questions with which later generations of Americans would be compelled to wrestle, and never fully resolve, Emerson is justly regarded as the spiritual father of modern American literature and his book *Nature* as our literary and metaphysical "Declaration of Independence." *Nature* recalls the belief of the earliest New England theocrats in the cosmic significance of their errand into the wilderness. It echoes the hope which had survived from Peter Martyr and Jonathan Edwards to Hector St. John de Crevecoeur that humanity could be reborn in the natural environment of the New World. And it anticipates the conviction later expressed by W. E. B. DuBois and William Faulkner, no less than by Walt Whitman and Hart Crane, that the restoration of man's correct relation to the divinity that shapes his ends demands his willing submission to the materials of the American experience.

From *Nature* (1836)

"Nature is but an image or imitation of
    wisdom, the last
  thing of the soul; nature being a thing
    which doth only
  do, but not know."—Plotinus
                              (epigraph of 1836)

A subtle chain of countless rings
The next unto the farthest brings;
The eye reads omens where it goes;
And speaks all languages the rose;
And, striving to be man, the worm
    Mounts through all the spires of form.
                              (epigraph of 1849)

Introduction

Our age is retrospective. It builds the sepulchres of the fathers. It writes biographies, histories, and criticism. The foregoing generations beheld God and nature face to face; we, through their eyes. Why should not we also enjoy an original relation to the universe? Why should not we have a poetry and philosphy of insight and not of tradition, and a religion by revelation to us, and not the history of theirs? Embosomed for a season in nature, whose floods of life stream around and through us, and invite us, by the powers they supply, to action proportioned to nature, why should we grope among the dry bones of the past, or put the living generation into masquerade out of its faded wardrobe? The sun shines today also. There is more wool and flax in the fields. There are new lands, new men, new thoughts. Let us demand our own works and laws and worship.

Undoubtedly, we have no questions to ask which are unanswerable. We must trust the perfection of the creation so far as to believe that whatever curiosity the order of things has awakened in our minds, the order of things can satisfy. Every man's condition is a solution in hieroglyphic to those inquiries he would put. He acts it as life, before he apprehends it as truth. In like manner, nature is already, in its forms and tendencies, describing its own design. Let us interrogate the great apparition that shines so peacefully around us. Let us inquire, to what end is nature?

All science has one aim, namely, to find a theory of nature. We have theories of races and of functions, but scarcely yet a remote approach to an idea of creation. We are now so far from the road to truth, that religious teachers dispute and hate each other, and speculative men are esteemed unsound and frivolous. But to a sound judgment, the most abstract truth is the most practical. Whenever a true theory appears, it will be its own evidence. Its test is, that it will explain all phenomena. Now many are thought not only unexplained but inexplicable; as language, sleep, madness, dreams, beasts, sex.

Philosophically considered, the universe is composed of Nature and the Soul. Strictly speaking, therefore, all that is separate from us, all which Philosophy distinguishes as the NOT ME, that is, both nature and art, all other men and my own body, must be ranked under this name, NATURE. In enumerating the values of nature and casting up their sum, I shall use the word in both senses;—in its common and in its philosophical import. In inquiries so general as our present one, the inaccuracy is not material; no confusion of thought will occur. *Nature,* in the common sense, refers to essences unchanged by man; space, the air, the river, the leaf. *Art* is applied to the mixture of his will with the same things, as in a house, a canal, a statue, a picture. But his operations taken together are so insignificant, a little chipping, baking, patching, and washing, that in an impression so grand as that of the world on the human mind, they do not vary the result.

1. Nature

To go into solitude, a man needs to retire as much from his chamber as from society. I am not solitary whilst I read and write, though nobody is with me. But if a man would be alone, let him look at the stars. The rays that come from those heavenly worlds will separate between him and what he touches. One might think the atmosphere was made transparent with this design, to give man, in the heavenly bodies, the perpetual presence of the sublime. Seen in the streets of cities, how great they are! If the stars should appear one night in a thousand years, how would men believe and adore; and preserve for many generations the remembrance of the city of God which had been shown. But every night come out these envoys of beauty, and light the universe with their admonsihing smile.

The stars awaken a certain reverence, because though always present, they are inaccessible; but all natural objects make a kindred impression, when the mind is open to their influence. Nature never wears a mean appearance. Neither does the wisest man extort her secret, and lose his curiosity by finding out all her perfection. Nature never became a toy to a wise spirit. The flowers, the animals, the mountains, reflected the wisdom of his best hour, as much as they had delighted the simplicity of his childhood.

When we speak of nature in this manner, we have a distinct but most poetical sense in the mind. We mean the integrity of impression made by manifold natural objects. It is this which distinguishes the stick of timber of the wood-cutter from the tree of the poet. The charming landscape which I saw this morning is indubitably made up of some twenty or thirty farms. Miller owns this field. Locke that, and Manning the woodland beyond. But none of them owns the landscape. There is a property in the horizon which no man has but he whose eye can integrate all the parts, that is, the poet. This is the best part of these men's farms, yet to this their warranty-deeds give no title.

To speak truly, few adult persons can see nature. Most persons do not see the sun. At least they have a very superficial seeing. The sun illuminates only the eye of the man, but shines into the eye and the heart of the child. The lover of nature is he whose inward and outward senses are still truly adjusted to each other; who has retained the spirit of infancy even into the era of manhood. His intercourse with heaven and earth becomes part of his daily food. In the presence of nature a wild delight runs through the man, in spite of real sorrows. Nature says,—he is my creature, and maugre all his impertinent griefs, he shall be glad with me. Not the sun or the summer alone, but every hour and season yields its tribute of delight; for every hour and change corresponds to and authorizes a different state of the mind, from breathless noon to grimmest midnight. Nature is a setting that fits equally well a comic or a mourning piece. In good health, the air is a cordial of incredible virtue. Crossing a bare common, in snow puddles, at twilight, under a clouded sky, without having in my thoughts any occurrence of special good fortune, I have enjoyed a perfect exhilaration. I am glad to the brink of fear. In the woods, too, a man casts off his years, as the snake his slough, and at what period soever of life is always a child. In the woods is perpetual youth. Within these plantations of God, a decorum and sanctity reign, a perennial festival is dressed, and the guest sees not how he should tire of them in a thousand years. In the woods, we return to reason and faith. There I feel that nothing can befall me in life,—no disgrace, no calamity (leaving me my eyes), which nature cannot repair. Standing on the bare ground,—my head bathed by the blithe air and uplifted into infinite space,—all mean egotism vanishes. I become a transparent eyeball; I am nothing; I see all; the currents of the Universal Being circulate through me; I am part or parcel of God. The name of the nearest friend sounds then foreign and accidental: to be brothers, to be acquaintances, master or servant, is then a trifle and a disturbance. I am the lover of uncontained and immortal beauty. In the wilderness, I find something more dear and connate than in streets or villages. In the tranquil landscape, and especially in the distant line of the horizon, man beholds somewhat as beautiful as his own nature.

The greatest delight which the fields and woods minister is the suggestion of an occult relation between man and the vegetable. I am not alone and unacknowledged. They nod to me, and I to them. The waving of the boughs in the storm is new to me and old. It takes me by surprise, and yet is not unknown. Its effect is like that of a higher thought or a better emotion coming over me, when I deemed I was thinking justly or doing right.

Yet it is certain that the power to produce this delight does not reside in nature, but in man, or in a harmony of both. It is necessary to use these pleasures with great temperance. For nature is not always tricked in holiday attire, but the same scene which yesterday breathed perfume and glittered as for the frolic of the nymphs is overspread with melancholy today. Nature always wears the colors of the spirit. To a man laboring under calamity, the heat of his own fire hath sadness in it. Then there is a kind of contempt of the landscape felt by him who has just lost by death a dear friend. The sky is less grand as it shuts down over less worth in the population.

2. Commodity

Whoever considers the final cause of the world will discern a multitude of uses that enter as parts into that result. They all admit of being thrown into one of the following classes: Commodity; Beauty; Language; and Discipline.

Under the general name of commodity, I rank all those advantages which our senses owe to nature. This, of course, is a benefit which is temporary and mediate, not ultimate, like its service to the soul. Yet although low, it is perfect in its kind, and is the only use of nature which all men apprehend. The misery of man appears like childish petulance, when we explore the steady and prodigal provision that has been made for his support and delight on this green ball which floats him through the heavens. What angels invented these splended ornaments, these rich conveniences, this ocean of air above, this ocean of water beneath, this firmament of earth between? this zodiac of lights, this tent of dropping clouds, this striped coat of climates, this four-fold year? Beasts, fire, water, stones, and corn serve him. The field is at once his floor, his work-yard, his play-ground, his garden, and his bed.

"More servants wait on man
Than he'll take notice of."

Nature, in its ministry to man, is not only the material, but is also the process and the result. All the parts incessantly work into each other's hands for the profit of man. The wind sows the seed; the sun evaporates the sea; the wind blows the vapor to the field; the ice, on the other side of the planet, condenses rain on this; the rain feeds the plant; the plant feeds the animal; and thus the endless circulations of the divine charity nourish man.

The useful arts are reproductions or new combinations by the wit of man, of the same natural benefactors. He no longer waits for favoring gales, but by means of steam, he realizes the fable of Acolus's bag, and carries the two and thirty winds in the boiler of his boat. To diminish friction, he paves the road with iron bars, and mounting a coach with a ship-load of men, animals, and merchandise behind him, he darts through the country, from town to town, like an eagle or a swallow through the air. By the aggregate of these aids, how is the face of the world changed, from the era of Noah to that of Napoleon! The private poor man hath cities, ships, canals, bridges, built for him. He goes to the post-office, and the human race run on his errands; to the book-shop, and the human race read and write of all that happens, for him; to the court-house, and nations repair his wrongs. He sets his house upon the road, and the human race go forth every morning, and shovel out the snow, and cut a path for him.

But there is no need of specifying particulars in this class of uses. The catalogue is endless, and the examples so obvious, that I shall leave them to the reader's reflection with the general re-mark, that this mercenary benefit is one which has respect to a farther good. A man is fed, not that he may be fed, but that he may work.

3. Beauty

A nobler want of man is served by nature, namely, the love of Beauty.

The ancient Greeks called the world Κόσμος [order], beauty. Such is the constitution of all things, or such the plastic power of the human eye, that the primary forms, as the sky, the mountain, the tree, the animal, give us a delight *in and for themselves;* a pleasure arising from outline, color, motion, and grouping. This seems partly owing to the eye itself. The eye is the best of artists. By the mutual action of its structure and of the laws of light, perspective is produced, which integrates every mass of objects, of what character soever, into a well colored and shaded globe, so that where the particular objects are mean and unaffecting, the landscape which they compose is round and symmetrical. And as the eye is the best composer, so light is the first of painters. There is no object so foul that intense light will not make beautiful. And the stimulus it affords to the sense, and a sort of infinitude which it hath, like space and time, make all matter gay. Even the corpse has its own beauty. But besides this general grace diffused over nature, almost all the individual forms are agreeable to the eye, as is proved by our endless imitations of some of them, as the acorn, the grape, the pine-cone, the wheat-ear, the egg, the wings and forms of most birds, the lion's claw, the serpent, the butterfly, sea-shells, flames, clouds, buds, leaves, and the forms of many trees, as the palm.

For better consideration, we may distribute the aspects of Beauty in a three fold manner.

1. First, the simple perception of natural forms is a delight. The influence of the forms and actions in nature is so needful to man, that, in its lowest functions, it seems to lie on the confines of commodity and beauty. To the body and mind which have been cramped by noxious work or company, nature is medicinal and restores their tone. The tradesman, the attorney comes out of the din and craft of the street and sees the sky and the woods, and is a man again. In their eternal calm he finds himself. The health of the eye seems to demand a horizon. We are never tired, so long as we can see far enough.

But in other hours, Nature satisfies by its loveliness, and without any mixture of corporeal benefit. I see the spectacle of morning from the hilltop over against my house, from daybreak to sunrise, with emotions which an angel might share. The long slender bars of cloud float like fishes in the sea of crimson light. From the earth, as a shore, I look out into that silent sea. I seem to partake its rapid transformations; the active enchantment reaches my dust, and I dilate and conspire with the morning wind. How does Nature deify us with a few and cheap elements! Give me health and a day, and I will make the pomp of emperors ridiculous. The dawn is my Assyria; the sunset and moonrise my Paphos, and unimaginable realms of faerie; broad noon shall be my England of the senses and the understanding; the night shall be my Germany of mystic philosophy and dreams.

Not less excellent, except for our less susceptibility in the afternoon, was the charm, last evening, of a January sunset. The western clouds divided and subdivided themselves into pink flakes modulated with tints of unspeakable softness, and the air had so much life and sweetness that it was a pain to come within doors. What was it that nature would say? Was there no meaning in the live repose of the valley behind the mill, and which Homer or Shakespeare could not re-form for me in words? The leafless trees become spires of flame in the sunset, with the blue cast for their background, and the stars of the dead calices of flowers, and every withered stem and stubble rimed with frost, contribute something to the mute music.

The inhabitants of cities suppose that the country landscape is pleasant only half the year. I please myself with the graces of the winter scenery, and believe that we are as much touched by it as by the genial influences of summer. To the attentive eye, each moment of the year has its own beauty, and in the same field, it beholds, every hour, a picture which was never seen before, and which shall never be seen again. The heavens change every moment, and reflect their glory or gloom on the plains beneath. The state of the crop in the surrounding farms alters the expression of the earth from week to week. The succession of native plants in the pastures and roadsides, which makes the silent clock by which time tells the summer hours, will make even the divisions of the day sensible to a keen observer. The tribes of birds and insects, like the plants punctual to their time, follow each other, and the year has room for it all. By water-courses, the variety is greater. In July, the blue pontederia or pickerel-weed blooms in large beds in the shallow parts of our pleasant river, and swarms with yellow butterflies in continual motion. Art cannot rival this pomp of purple and gold. Indeed the river is a perpetual gala, and boasts each month a new ornament.

But this beauty of Nature which is seen and felt as beauty, is the least part. The shows of day, the dewy morning, the rainbow, mountains, orchards in blossom, stars, moonlight, shadows in still water, and the like, if too eagerly hunted, become shows merely, and mock us with their unreality. Go out of the house to see the moon, and 'tis mere tinsel; it will not please as when its light shines upon your necessary journey. The beauty that shimmers in the yellow afternoons of October, who ever could clutch it? Go forth to find it, and it is gone; 'tis only a mirage as you look from the windows of diligence.

2. The presence of a higher, namely, of the spiritual element is essential to its perfection. The high and divine beauty which can be loved without effeminacy, is that which is found in combination with the human will. Beauty is the mark God sets upon virtue. Every natural action is graceful. Every heroic act is also decent, and causes the place and the bystanders to shine. We are taught by great actions that the universe is the property of every individual in it. Every rational creature has all nature for his dowry and estate. It is his, if he will. He may divest himself of it; he may creep into a corner, and abdicate his kindgom, as most men do, but he is entitled to the world by his constitution. In proportion to the energy of his thought and will, he takes up the world into himself. "All those things for which men plough, build, or sail, obey virtue," said Sallust. "The winds and waves," said Gibbon, "are always on the side of the ablest navigators." So are the sun and moon and all the stars of heaven. When a noble act is done,—perchance in a scene of great natural beauty; when Leonidas and his three hundred martyrs consume one day in dying, and the sun and moon come each and look at them once in the steep defile of Thermopylae; when Arnold Winkelried, in the high Alps, under the shadow of the avalanche, gathers in his side a sheaf of Austrian spears to break the line for his comrades; are not these heroes entitled to add the beauty of the scene to the beauty of the deed? When the bark of Columbus nears the shore of America;—before it the beach lined with savages, fleeing out of all their huts of cane; the sea behind; and the purple mountains of the Indian Archipelago around, can we separate the man from the living picture? Does not the New World clothe his form with her palm-groves and savannahs as fit drapery? Ever does natural beauty steal in like air, and envelope great actions. When Sir Harry Vane was dragged up the Tower-hill, sitting on a sled, to suffer death as the champion of the English laws, one of the multitude cried out to him, "You never sate on so glorious a seat!" Charles

II, to intimidate the citizens of London, caused the patriot Lord Russell to be drawn in an open coach through the principal streets of the city on his way to the scaffold. "But," his biographer says, "the multitude imagined they saw liberty and virtue sitting by his side." In private places, among sordid objects, an act of truth or heroism seems at once to draw to itself the sky as its temple, the sun as its candle. Nature stretches out her arms to embrace man, only let his thoughts be of equal greatness. Willingly does she follow his steps with the rose and the violet, and bend her lines of grandeur and grace to the decoration of her darling child. Only let his thoughts be of equal scope, and the frame will suit the picture. A virtuous man is in unison with her works, and makes the central figure of the visible sphere. Homer, Pindar, Socrates, Phocion, associate themselves fitly in our memory with the geography and climate of Greece. The visible heavens and earth sympathize with Jesus. And in common life whosoever has seen a person of powerful character and happy genius, will have remarked how easily he took all things along with him,—the persons, the opinions, and the day, and nature become ancillary to a man.

3. There is still another aspect under which the beauty of the world may be viewed, namely, as it becomes an object of the intellect. Beside the relation of things to virtue, they have a relation to thought. The intellect searches out the absolute order of things as they stand in the mind of God, and without the colors of affection. The intellectual and the active powers seem to succeed each other, and the exclusive activity of the one generates the exclusive activity of the other. There is something unfriendly in each to the other, but they are like the alternate periods of feeding and working in animals; each prepares and will be followed by the other. Therefore does beauty, which, in relation to actions, as we have seen, comes unsought, and comes because it is unsought, remain for the apprehension and pursuit of the intellect; and then again, in its turn, of the active power. Nothing divine dies. All good is eternally reproductive. The beauty of nature re-forms itself in the mind, and not for barren contemplation, but for new creation.

All men are in some degree impressed by the face of the world; some men even to delight. This love of beauty is Taste. Others have the same love in such excess, that, not content with admiring, they seek to embody it in new forms. The creation of beauty is Art.

The production of a work of art throws a light upon the mystery of humanity. A work of art is an abstract or epitome of the world. It is the result or expression of nature, in miniature. For although the works of nature are innumerable and all different, the result or the expression of them all is similar and single. Nature is a sea of forms radically alike and even unique. A leaf, a sunbeam, a landscape, the ocean, make an analogous impression on the mind. What is common to them all,—that perfectness and harmony, is beauty. The standard of beauty is the entire circuit of natural forms,—the totality of nature; which the Italians expressed by defining beauty "il più nell' uno" [the man in one]. Nothing is quite beautiful alone; nothing but is beautiful in the whole. A single object is only so far beautiful as it suggests this universal grace. The poet, the painter, the sculptor, the musician, the architect, seek each to concentrate this radiance of the world on one point, and each in his several work to satisfy the love of beauty which stimulates him to produce. Thus is Art a nature passed through the alembic of man. Thus in art does Nature work through the will of a man filled with the beauty of her first works.

The world thus exists to the soul to satisfy the desire of beauty. This element I call an ultimate end. No reason can be asked or given why the soul seeks beauty. Beauty, in its largest and profoundest sense, is one expression for the universe. God is the all-fair. Truth, and goodness, and beauty, are but different faces of the same All. But beauty in nature is not ultimate. It is the herald of inward and eternal beauty, and is not alone a solid and satisfactory good. It must stand as a part, and not as yet the last or highest expression of the final cause of Nature.

4. Language

Language is a third use which Nature subserves to man. Nature is the vehicle of thought, and in a simple, double, and threefold degree.

1. Words are signs of natural facts.
2. Particular natural facts are symbols of particular spiritual facts.
3. Nature is the symbol of spirit.

1. Words are signs of natural facts. The use of natural history is to give us aid in supernatural history; the use of the outer creation, to give us language for the beings and changes of the inward creation. Every word which is used to express a moral or intellectual fact, if traced to its root, is found to be borrowed from some material appearance. *Right* means *straight; wrong* means *twisted. Spirit* primarily means *wind; transgression,* the *crossing of a line; supercilious,* the *raising of the eyebrow.* We say the *heart* to express emotion, the *head* to denote thought; and *thought* and *emotion* are words borrowed from sensible things, and now appropriated to spiritual nature. Most of the process by which this transformation is made, is hidden from us in the remote time when language was framed; but the same tendency may be daily observed in children. Children and savages use only nouns or names of things, which they convert into verbs, and apply to analogous mental acts.

2. But this origin of all words that convey a spiritual import,—so conspicuous a fact in the history of language,—is our least debt to nature. It is not words only that are emblematic; it is things which are emblematic. Every natural fact is a symbol of some spiritual fact. Every appearance in nature corresponds to some state of the mind, and that state of mind can only be described by presenting that natural appearance as its picture. An enraged man is a lion, a cunning man is a fox, a firm man is a rock, a learned man is a torch. A lamb is innocence; a snake is subtle spite; flowers express to us the

delicate affections. Light and darkness are our familiar expression for knowledge and ignorance; and heat for love. Visible distance behind and before us, is respectively our image of memory and hope.

Who looks upon a river in a meditative hour and is not reminded of the flux of all things? Throw a stone into the stream, and the circles that propagate themselves are the beautiful type of all influence. Man is conscious of a universal soul within or behind his individual life, wherein, as in a firmament, the natures of Justice, Truth, Love, Freedom, arise and shine. This universal soul he calls Reason: it is not mine, or thine, or his, but we are its; we are its property and men. And the blue sky in which the private earth is buried, the sky with its eternal calm, and full of everlasting orbs, is the type of Reason. That which intellectually considered we call Reason, considered in relation to nature, we call Spirit. Spirit is the Creator. Spirit hath life in itself. And man in all ages and countries embodies it in his language as the FATHER.

It is easily seen that there is nothing lucky or capricious in these analogies, but that they are constant, and pervade nature. There are not the dreams of a few poets, here and there, but man is an analogist, and studies relations in all objects. He is placed in the center of beings, and a ray of relation passes from every other being to him. And neither can man be understood without these objects, nor these objects without man. All the facts in natural history taken by themselves, have no value, but are barren, like a single sex. But marry it to human history, and it is full of life. Whole floras, all Linnaeus' and Buffon's volumes, are dry catalogues of facts; but the most trivial of these facts, the habit of a plant, the organs, or work, or noise of an insect, applied to the illustration of a fact in intellectual philosophy, or in any way associated to human nature, affects us in the most lively and agreeable manner. The seed of a plant,—to what affecting analogies in the nature of man is that little fruit made use of, in all discourse, up to the voice of Paul, who calls the human corpse a seed,—"It is sown a natural body; it is raised a spiritual body." The motion of the earth round its axis and round the sun, makes the day and the year. These are certain amounts of brute light and heat. But is there no intent of an analogy between man's life and the seasons? And do the seasons gain no grandeur or pathos from that analogy? The instincts of the ant are very unimportant considered as the ant's; but the moment a ray of relation is seen to extend from it to man, and the little drudge is seen to be a monitor, a little body with a mighty heart, then all its habits, even that said to be recently observed, that it never sleeps, become sublime.

Because of this radical correspondence between visible things and human thoughts, savages, who have only what is necessary, converse in figures. As we go back in history, language becomes more picturesque, until its infancy, when it is all poetry; or all spiritual facts are represented by natural symbols. The same symbols are found to make the original elements of all languages. It has moreover been observed, that the idioms of all languages approach each other in passages of the greatest eloquence and power. And as this is the first language, so is it the last. This immediate dependence of language upon nature, this conversion of an outward phenomenon into a type of somewhat in human life, never loses its power to affect us. It is this which gives that piquancy to the conversation of a strong-natured farmer or back-woodsman, which all men relish.

A man's power to connect his thought with its proper symbol, and so to utter it, depends on the simplicity of his character, that is, upon his love of truth and his desire to communicate it without loss. The corruption of man is followed by the corruption of language. When simplicity of character and the sovereignty of ideas is broken up by the prevalence of secondary desires,—the desire of riches, of pleasure, of power, and of praise,—and duplicity and falsehood take place of simplicity and truth, the power over nature as an interpreter of the will is in a degree lost; new imagery ceases to be created, and old words are perverted to stand for things which are not; a paper currency is employed, when there is no bullion in the vaults. In due time the fraud is manifest, and words lose all power to stimulate the understanding or the affections. Hundreds of writers may be found in every long-civilized nation who for a short time believe and make others believe that they see and utter truths, who do not of themselves clothe one thought in its natural garment, but who feed unconsciously on the language created by the primary writers of the country, those, namely, who hold primarily on nature.

But wise men pierce this rotten diction and fasten words again to visible things; so that picturesque language is at once a commanding certificate that he who employs it is a man in alliance with truth and God. The moment our discourse rises above the ground line of familiar facts and is inflamed with passion or exalted by thought, it clothes itself in images. A man conversing in earnest, if he watch his intellectual processes, will find that a material image more or less luminous arises in his mind, contemporaneous with every thought, which furnishes the vestment of the thought. Hence, good writing and brilliant discourse are perpetual allegories. This imagery is spontaneous. It is the blending of experience with the present action of the mind. It is proper creation. It is the working of the Original Cause through the instruments he has already made.

These facts may suggest the advantage which the country-life possesses, for a powerful mind, over the artificial and curtailed life of cities. We know more from nature than we can at will communicate. Its light flows into the mind evermore, and we forget its presence. The poet, the orator, bred in the woods, whose senses have been nourished by their fair and appeasing changes, year after year, without design and without heed,—shall not lose their lesson altogether, in the roar of cities or the broil of politics. Long hereafter, amidst agitation and terror in national coucils,—in the hour of revolution,—these solemn images shall reappear in their morning lustre, as fit symbols and words of the thoughts which the passing events shall awaken. At the call of a noble sentiment, again the woods wave, the pines murmur, the river rolls and shines, and the cattle low upon the mountains, as he saw and heard them in his infancy. And with these forms, the spells of persuasion, the keys of power are put into his hands.

3. We are thus assisted by natural objects in the expression of particular meanings. But how great a language to convey such pepper-corn informations! Did it need such noble races of creatures, this profusion of forms, this host of orbs in heaven, to furnish man with the dictionary and grammar of his municipal speech? Whilst we use this grand cipher to expedite the affairs of our pot and kettle, we feel that we have not yet put it to its use, neither are able. We are like travelers using the cinders of a volcano to roast their eggs. Whilst we see that it always stands ready to clothe what we would say, we cannot avoid the question whether the characters are not significant of themselves. Have mountains, and waves, and skies, no significance but what we consciously give them when we employ them as emblems of our thoughts? The world is emblematic. Parts of speech are metaphors, because the whole of nature is a metaphor of the human mind. The laws of moral nature answer to those of matter as face to face in a glass. "The visible world and the relation of its parts, is the dial plate of the invisible." The axioms of physics translate the laws of ethics. Thus, "the whole is greater than its part"; "reaction is equal to action"; " the smallest weight may be made to lift the greatest, the difference of weight being compensated by time"; and many the like propositions, which have an ethical as well as physical sense. These propositions have a much more extensive and universal sense when applied to human life, than when confined to technical use.

In like manner, the memorable words of history and the proverbs of nations consist usually of a natural fact, selected as a picture or parable of a moral truth. Thus; A rolling stone gathers no moss; A bird in the hand is worth two in the bush; A cripple in the right way will beat a racer in the wrong; Make hay while the sun shines; 'Tis hard to carry a full cup even; Vinegar is the son of wine; The last ounce broke the camel's back; Long-lived trees make roots first;—and the like. In their primary sense these are trivial facts, but we repeat them for the value of their analogical import. What is true of proverbs, is true of all fables, parables, and allegories.

This relation between the mind and matter is not fancied by some poet, but stands in the will of God, and so is free to be known by all men. It appears to men, or it does not appear. When in fortunate hours we ponder this miracle, the wise man doubts if at all other times he is not blind and deaf;

> "Can such things be,
> And overcome us like a summer's cloud,
> Without our special wonder?"

for the universe becomes transparent, and the light of higher laws than its own shines through it. It is the standing problem which has exercised the wonder and the study of every fine genius since the world began; from the era of the Egyptians and the Brahmins to that of Pythagoras, of Plato, of Bacon, of Leibnitz, of Swedenborg. There sits the Sphinx at the road-side, and from age to age, as each prophet comes by, he tries his fortune at reading her riddle. There seems to be a necessity in spirit to manifest itself in material forms; and day and night, river and storm, beast and bird, acid and alkali, preëxist in necessary Ideas in the mind of God, and are what they are by virtue of preceding affections in the world of spirit. A Fact is the end or last issue of spirit. The visible creation is the terminus or the circumference of the invisible world. "Material objects," said a French philosopher, "are necessarily kinds of *scoriae* [dross] of the substantial thoughts of the Creator, which must always preserve an exact relation to their first origin; in other words, visible nature must have a spiritual and moral side."

This doctrine is abstruse, and though the images of "garment," "scoriae," "mirror," etc., may stimulate the fancy, we must summon the aid of subtler and more vital expositors to make it plain. "Every scripture is to be interpreted by the same spirit which gave it forth,"—is the fundamental law of criticism. A life in harmony with Nature, the love of truth and of virtue, will purge the eyes to understand her text. By degrees we may come to know the primitive sense of the permanent objects of nature, so that the world shall be to us an open book, and every form significant of its hidden life and final cause.

A new interest surprises us, whilst, under the view now suggested, we contemplate the fearful extent and multitude of objects; since "every object rightly seen, unlocks a new faculty of the soul." That which was unconscious truth, becomes, when interpreted and defined in an object, a part of the domain of knowledge,—a new weapon in the magazine of power.

6. Idealism

Thus is the unspeakable but intelligible and practicable meaning of the world conveyed to man, the immortal pupil, in every object of sense. To this one end of Discipline, all parts of nature conspire.

A noble doubt perpetually suggests itself,—whether this end be not the Final Cause of the Universe; and whether nature outwardly exists. It is a sufficient account of that Appearance we call the World, that God will teach a human mind, and so makes it the receiver of a certain number of congruent sensations, which we call sun and moon, man and woman, house and trade. In my utter impotence to test the authenticity of the report of my senses, to know whether the impressions they make on me correspond with outlying objects, what difference does it make, whether Orion is up there in heaven, or some god paints the image in the firmament of the soul? The relations of parts and the end of the whole remaining the same, what is the difference, whether land and sea interact, and worlds revolve and intermingle without number or end,—deep yawning under deep, and galaxy balancing galaxy, throughout absolute space,—or whether, without relations of time and space, the same appearances are inscribed in the constant faith of man? Whether nature enjoy a substantial existence without, or is only in the apocalypse of the mind, it is alike useful and alike venerable to me. Be it what it may, it is ideal to me so long as I cannot try the accuracy of my senses.

The frivolous make themselves merry with the Ideal theory, as if its consequences were burlesque; as if it affected the stability of nature. It surely does not. God never jests with us, and will not compromise the end of nature by permitting any inconsequence in its procession. Any distrust of the permanence of laws would paralyze the faculties of man. Their permanence is sacredly respected, and his faith therein is perfect. The wheels and springs of man are all set to the hypothesis of the permanence of nature. We are not built like a ship to be tossed, but like a house to stand. It is a natural consequence of this structure, that so long as the active powers predominate over the reflective, we resist with indignation any hint that nature is more short-lived or mutable than spirit. The broker, the wheelwright, the carpenter, the tollman, are much displeased at the intimation.

But whilst we acquiesce entirely in the permanence of natural laws, the question of the absolute existence of nature still remains open. It is the uniform effect of culture on the human mind, not to shake our faith in the stability of particular phenomena, as of heat, water, azote; but to lead us to regard nature as a phenomenon, not a substance; to attribute necessary existence to spirit; to esteem nature as an accident and an effect.

To the senses and the unrenewed understanding, belongs a sort of instinctive belief in the absolute existence of nature. In their view man and nature are indissolubly joined. Things are ultimates, and they never look beyond their sphere. The presence of Reason mars this faith. The first effort of thought tends to relax this despotism of the senses which binds us to nature as if we were a part of it, and shows us nature aloof, and, as it were, afloat. Until this higher agency intervened, the animal eye sees, with wonderful accuracy, sharp outlines and colored surfaces. When the eye of Reason opens, to outline and surface are at once added grace and expression. These proceed from imagination and affection, and abate somewhat of the angular distinctness of objects. If the Reason be stimulated to more earnest vision, outlines and surfaces become transparent, and are no longer seen; causes and spirits are seen through them. The best moments of life are these delicious awakenings of the higher powers, and the reverential withdrawing of nature before its God.

Let us proceed to indicate the effects of culture.

1. Our first institution [instruction] in the Ideal philosophy is a hint from Nature herself.

Nature is made to conspire with spirit to emancipate us. Certain mechanical changes, a small alteration in our local position, apprizes us of a dualism. We are strangely affected by seeing the shore from a moving ship, from a balloon, or through the tints of an unusual sky. The least change in our point of view gives the whole world a pictorial air. A man who seldom rides, needs only to get into a coach and traverse his own town, to turn the street into a puppet-show. The men, the women,—talking, running, bartering, fighting,—the earnest mechanic, the lounger, the beggar, the boys, the dogs are unrealized at once, or, at least, wholly detached from all relation to the observer, and seen as apparent, not substantial beings. What new thoughts are suggested by seeing a face of country quite familiar, in the rapid movement of the railroad car! Nay, the most wonted objects, (make a very slight change in the point of vision), please us most.

... But I own there is something ungrateful in expanding too curiously the particulars of the general proposition, that all culture tends to imbue us with idealism. I have no hostility to nature, but a child's love to it. I expand and live in the warm day like corn and melons. Let us speak her fair. I do not wish to fling stones at my beautiful mother, nor soil my gentle nest. I only wish to indicate the true position of nature in regard to man, wherein to establish man all right education tends; as the ground which to attain is the object of human life, that is, of man's connection with nature. Culture inverts the vulgar views of nature, and brings the mind to call that apparent which it uses to call real, and that real which it uses to call visionary. Children, it is true, believe in the external world. The belief that it appears only, is an after-thought, but with culture this faith will as surely arise on the mind as did the first.

The advantage of the ideal theory over the popular faith is this, that it presents the world in precisely that view which is most desirable to the mind. It is, in fact, the view which Reason, both speculative and practical, that is, philosophy and virtue take. For seen in the light of thought, the world always is phenomenal; and virtue subordinates it to the mind. Idealism sees the world in God. It beholds the whole circle of persons and things, of actions and events, of country and religion, not as painfully accumulated, atom after atom, act after act, in an aged creeping Past, but as one vast picture which God paints on the instant eternity for the contemplation of the soul. Therefore the soul holds itself off from a too trivial and microscopic study of the universal tablet. It respects the end too much to immerse itself in the means. It sees something more important in Christianity than the scandals of ecclesiastical history or the niceties of criticism; and, very incurious concerning persons or miracles, and not at all disturbed by chasms of historical evidence, it accepts from God the phenomenon, as it finds it, as the pure and awful form of religion in the world. It is not hot and passionate at the appearance of what it calls its own good or bad fortune, at the union or opposition of other persons. No man is its enemy. It accepts whatsoever befalls, as part of its lesson. It is a watcher more than a doer, and it is a doer, only that it may the better watch.

7. Spirit

It is essential to a true theory of nature and of man, that it should contain somewhat progressive. Uses that are exhausted or that may be, and facts that end in the statement, cannot be all that is true of the brave lodging wherein man is harbored, and wherein all his faculties find appropriate and endless exercise. And all the uses of nature admit of being summed in one, which yields the activity of an an infinite scope. Through all its kingdoms, to the suburbs and outskirts of things, it is faithful to the cause whence it had its origin. It always speaks of Spirit. It suggests the absolute. It is a perpetual effect. It is a great shadow pointing always to the sun behind us.

The aspect of Nature is devout. Like the figure of Jesus, she stands with bended head, and hands folded upon the breast. The happiest man is he who learns from nature the lessons of worship.

Of that ineffable essence which we call Spirit, he that thinks most, will say least. We can foresee God in the coarse, and, as it were, distant phenomena of matter; but when we try to define and describe himself, both language and thought desert us, and we are as helpless as fools and savages. That essence refuses to be recorded in propositions, but when man has worshipped him intellectually, the noblest ministry of nature is to stand as the apparition of God. It is the organ through which the universal spirit speaks to the individual, and strives to lead back the individual to it.

When we consider Spirit, we see that the views already presented do not include the whole circumference of man. We must add some related thoughts.

Three problems are put by nature to the mind: What is matter? Whence is it? and Whereto? The first of these questions only, the ideal theory answers. Idealism saith: matter is a phenomenon, not a substance. Idealism acquaints us with the total disparity between the evidence of our own being and the evidence of the world's being. The one is perfect; the other, incapable of any assurance; the mind is a part of the nature of things; the world is a divine dream, from which we may presently awake to the glories and certainties of day. Idealism is a hypothesis to account for nature by other principles than those of carpentry and chemistry. Yet, if it only deny the existence of matter, it does not satisfy the demands of the spirit. It leaves God out of me. It leaves me in the splendid labyrinth of my perceptions, to wander without end. Then the heart resists it, because it balks the affections in denying substantive being to men and women. Nature is so pervaded with human life that there is something of humanity in all and in every particular. But this theory makes nature foreign to me, and does not account for that consanguinity which we acknowledge to it.

Let it stand then, in the present state of our knowledge, merely as a useful introductory hypothesis, serving to apprize us of the eternal distinction between the soul and the world.

But when, following the invisible steps of thought, we come to inquire, Whence is matter? and Whereto? many truths arise to us out of the recesses of consciousness. We learn that the highest is present to the soul of man; that the dread universal essence, which is not wisdom, or love, or beauty, or power, but all in one, and each entirely, is that for which all things exist, and that by which they are; that spirit creates; that behind nature, throughout nature, spirit is present; one and not compound it does not act upon us from without, that is, in space and time, but spiritually, or through ourselves: therefore, that spirit, that is, the Supreme Being, does not build up nature around us, but puts it forth through us, as the life of the tree puts forth new branches and leaves through the pores of the old. As a plant upon the earth, so a man rests upon the bosom of God; he is nourished by unfailing fountains, and draws at his need inexhaustible power. Who can set bounds to the possibilities of man? Once inhale the upper air, being admitted to behold the absolute natures of justice and truth, and we learn that man has access to the entire mind of the Creator, is himself the creator in the finite. This view, which admonishes me where the sources of wisdom and power lie, and points to virtue as to

> "The golden key
> Which opes the palace of eternity,"

carries upon its face the highest certificate of truth, because it animates me to create my own world through the purification of my soul.

The world proceeds from the same spirit as the body of man. It is a remoter and inferior incarnation of God, a projection of God in the unconscious. But it differs from the body in one important respect. It is not, like that, now subjected to the human will. Its serene order is inviolable by us. It is, therefore, to us, the present expositor of the divine mind. It is a fixed point whereby we may measure our departure. As we degenerate, the contrast between us and our house is more evident. We are as much strangers in nature as we are aliens from God. We do not understand the notes of birds. The fox and the deer run away from us; the bear and tiger rend us. We do not know the uses of more than a few plants, as corn and the apple, the potato and the vine. Is not the landscape, every glimpse of which hath a grandeur, a face of him? Yet this may show us what discord is between man and nature, for you cannot freely admire a noble landscape if laborers are digging in the field hard by. The poet finds something ridiculous in his delight until he is out of the sight of men.

8. Prospects

In inquiries respecting the laws of the world and the frame of things, the highest reason is always the truest. That which seems faintly possible, it is so refined, is often faint and dim because it is deepest seated in the mind among the eternal verities. Empirical science is apt to cloud the sight, and by the very knowledge of functions and processes to bereave the student of the manly contemplation of the whole. The savant becomes unpoetic. But the best read naturalist who lends an entire and devout attention to truth, will see that there remains much to learn of his relation to the world, and that it is not to be learned by any addition or subtraction or other comparison of known quantities, but is arrived at by untaught sallies of the spirit, by a continual self-recovery, and by entire humility. He will perceive that there are far more excellent qualities in the student than preciseness and infallibility; that a guess is often more fruitful than an indisputable affirmation, and that a dream may let us deeper into the secret of nature than a hundred concerted experiments.

For the problems to be solved are precisely those which the physiologist and the naturalist omit to state. It is not so pertinent to man to know all the individuals of the animal kingdom, as it is to know whence and whereto is this tyrannizing unity in his constitution, which evermore separates and classifies things, endeavoring to reduce the most diverse to one form. When I behold a rich landscape, it is less to my purpose to recite correctly the order and superposition of the strata, than to know why all thought of multitude is lost in a tranquil sense of unity. I cannot greatly honor minuteness in details, so long as there is no hint to explain the relation between things and thoughts; no ray upon the *metaphysics* of conchology, of botany, of the arts, to show the relation of the forms of flowers, shells, animals, architecture, to the mind, and build science upon ideas. In a cabinet of natural history, we become sensible of a certain occult recognition and sympathy in regard to the most unwieldly and eccentric forms of beast, fish, and insect. The American who has been confined, in his own country, to the sight of buildings designed after foreign models, is surprised on entering York Minster or St. Peter's at Rome, by the feeling that these structures are imitations also,— faint copies of an invisible archetype. Nor has science sufficient humanity, so long as the naturalist overlooks that wonderful congruity which subsists between man and the world; of which he is lord, not because he is the most subtile inhabitant, but because he is its head and heart, and finds something of himself in every great and small thing, in every mountain stratum, in every new law of color, fact of astronomy, or atmospheric influence which observation or analysis lays open. A perception of this mystery inspires the muse of George Herbert, the beautiful psalmist of the seventeenth century. The following lines are part of his little poem on Man.

"Man is all symmetry,
Full of proportions, one limb to another,
  And all to all the world besides.
  Each part may call the farthest, brother;
For head with foot hath private amity,
  And both with moons and tides.

"Nothing hath got so far
But man hath caught and kept it as his
    prey;
  His eyes dismount the highest star:
  He is in little all the sphere.
Herbs gladly cure our flesh, because that
    they
  Find their acquaintance there.

"For us, the winds do blow,
The earth doth rest, heaven move, and
    fountains flow;

Nothing we see, but means our good,
  As our delight, or as our treasure;
The whole is either our cupboard of food,
  Or cabinet of pleasure.

"The stars have us to bed:
Night draws the curtain; which the sun
    withdraws.
  Music and light attend our head.
  All things unto our flesh are kind,
In their descent and being; to our mind,
  In their ascent and cause.

"More servants wait on man
Than he'll take notice of. In every path,
  He treads down that which doth
    befriend him
  When sickness makes him pale and wan.
Oh mighty love! Man is one world, and
  hath
  Another to attend him."

The perception of this class of truths makes the attraction which draws men to science, but the end is lost sight of in attention to the means. In view of this half-sight of science, we accept the sentence of Plato, that "poetry comes nearer to vital truth than history." Every surmise and vaticination of the mind is entitled to a certain respect, and we learn to prefer imperfect theories, and sentences which contain glimpses of truth, to digested systems which have no one valuable suggestion. A wise writer will feel that the ends of study and composition are best answered by announcing undiscovered regions of thought, and so communicating, through hope, new activity to the torpid spirit.

I shall therefore conclude this essay with some traditions of man and nature, which a certain poet sang to me; and which, as they have always been in the world, and perhaps reappear to every bard, may be both history and prophecy.

"The foundations of man are not in matter, but in spirit. But the element of spirit is eternity. To it, therefore, the longest series of events, the oldest chronologies are young and recent. In the cycle of the universal man, from whom the known individuals proceed, centuries are points, and all history is but the epoch of one degradation.

"We distrust and deny inwardly our sympathy with nature. We own and disown our relation to it, by turns. We are like Nebuchadnezzar, dethroned, bereft of reason, and eating grass like an ox. But who can set limits to the remedial force of spirit?

"A man is a god in ruins. When men are innocent, life shall be longer, and shall pass into the immortal as gently as we awake from dreams. Now, the world would be insane and rabid, if these disorganizations should last for hundreds of years. It is kept in check by death and infancy. Infancy is the perpetual Messiah, which comes into the arms of fallen men, and pleads with them to return to paradise.

"Man is the dwarf of himself. Once he was permeated and dissolved by spirit. He filled nature with his overflowing currents. Out from him sprang the sun and moon; from man the sun, from woman the moon. The laws of his mind, the periods of his actions externized themselves into day and night, into the year and the seasons. But, having made for himself this huge shell, his waters retired; he no longer fills the veins and

189

veinlets; he is shrunk to a drop. He sees that the structure still fits him, but fits him colossally. Say, rather, once it fitted him, now it corresponds to him from far and on high. He adores timidly his own work. Now is man the follower of the sun, and woman the follower of the moon. Yet sometimes he starts in his slumber, and wonders at himself and his house, and muses strangely at the resemblance betwixt him and it. He perceives that if his law is still paramount, if still he have elemental power, if his word is sterling yet in nature, it is not conscious power, it is not inferior but superior to his will. It is instinct." Thus my Orphic poet sang.

At present, man applies to nature but half his force. He works on the world with his understanding alone. He lives in it and masters it by a penny-wisdom; and he that works most in it is but a half-man, and whilst his arms are strong and his digestion good, his mind is imbruted, and he is a selfish savage. His relation to nature, his power over it, is through the understanding, as by manure; the economic use of fire, wind, water, and the mariner's needle; steam, coal, chemical agriculture; the repairs of the human body by the dentist and the surgeon. This is such a resumption of power as if a banished king should buy his territories inch by inch, instead of vaulting at once into his throne. Meantime, in the thick darkness, there are not wanting gleams of a better light—occasional examples of the action of man upon nature with his entire force,—with reason as well as understanding. Such examples are, the traditions of miracles in the earliest antiquity of all nations;

the history of Jesus Christ; the achievements of a principle, as in religious and political revolutions, and in the abolition of the slave-trade; the miracles of enthusiasm, as those reported of Swedenborg, Hohenlohe, and the Shakers; many obscure and yet contested facts, now arranged under the name of Animal Magnetism; prayer; eloquence; self-healing; and the wisdom of children. These are examples of Reason's momentary grasp of the scepter; the exertions of a power which exists not in time or space, but an instantaneous instreaming causing power. The difference between the actual and the ideal force of man is happily figured by the schoolmen, in saying, that the knowledge of man is an evening knowledge, *vespertina cognitio*, but that of God is a morning knowledge, *matutina cognitio*.

The problem of restoring to the world original and eternal beauty is solved by the redemption of the soul. The ruin or the blank that we see when we look at nature, is in our own eye. The axis of vision is not coincident with the axis of things, and so they appear not transparent but opaque. The reason why the world lacks unity, and lies broken and in heaps, is because man is disunited with himself. He cannot be a naturalist until he satisfies all the demands of the spirit. Love is as much its demand as perception. Indeed, neither can be perfect without the other. In the uttermost meaning of the words, thought is devout, and devotion is thought. Deep calls unto deep. But in actual life, the marriage is not celebrated. There are innocent men who worship God after the tradition of their fathers, but their sense of duty has not yet extended to the use of all their faculties. And there are patient naturalists, but they freeze their subject under the wintry light of the understanding. Is not prayer also a study of truth,—a sally of the soul into the unfound infinite? No man ever prayed heartily without learning something. But when a faithful thinker, resolute to detach every object from personal relations and see it in the light of thought, shall, at the same time, kindle science with the fire of the holiest affections, then will God go forth anew into the creation.

It will not need, when the mind is prepared for study, to search for objects. The invariable mark of wisdom is to see the miraculous in the common. What is a day? What is a year? What is summer? What is woman? What is a child? What is sleep? To our blindness, these things seem unaffecting. We make fables to hide the baldness of the fact and conform it, as we say, to the higher law of the mind. But when the fact is seen under the light of an idea, the gaudy fable fades and shrivels. We behold the real higher law. To the wise, therefore, a fact is true poetry, and the most beautiful of fables. These wonders are brought to our own door. You also are a man. Man and woman and their social life, poverty, labor, sleep, fear, fortune, are known to you. Learn that none of these things is superficial, but that each phenomenon has its roots in the faculties and affections of the mind. Whilst the abstract question occupies your intellect, nature brings it in the concrete to be solved by your hands. It

were a wise inquiry for the closet, to compare, point by point, especially at remarkable crises in life, our daily history with the rise and progress of ideas in the mind.

So shall we come to look at the world with new eyes. It shall answer the endless inquiry of the intellect,—What is truth? and of the affections,—What is good? by yielding itself passive to the educated Will. Then shall come to pass what my poet said: "Nature is not fixed but fluid. Spirit alters, molds, makes it. The immobility or bruteness of nature is the absence of the spirit; to pure spirit it is fluid, it is volatile, it is obedient. Every spirit builds itself a house, and beyond its house a world, and beyond its world a heaven. Know then that the world exists for you. For you is the phenomenon perfect. What we are, that only can we see. All that Adam had, all that Caesar could, you have and can do. Adam called his house, heaven and earth; Caesar called his house, Rome; you perhaps call yours, a cobbler's trade; a hundred acres of ploughed land; or a scholar's garret. Yet line for line and point for point your dominion is as great as theirs, though without fine names. Build therefore your own world. As fast as you conform your life to the pure idea in your mind, that will unfold its great proportions. A correspondent revolution in things will attend the influx of the spirit. So fast will disagreeable appearances, swine, spiders, snakes, pests, mad-houses, prisons, enemies, vanish; they are temporary and shall be no more seen. The sordor and filths of nature, the sun shall dry up and the wind exhale. As when the summer comes from the south the snow-banks melt and the face of the earth becomes green before it, so shall the advancing spirit create its ornaments along its path, and carry with it the beauty it visits and the song which enchants it; it shall draw beautiful faces, warm hearts, wise discourse, and heroic acts, around its way, until evil is no more seen. The kingdom of man over nature, which cometh not with observations,—a dominion such as now is beyond his dream of God,—he shall enter without more wonder than the blind man feels who is gradually restored to perfect sight."

Frederick Douglass (1817–1895)

Frederick Douglass was born a slave. He escaped to freedom in 1838 and soon after became popular as a lecturer for the anti-slavery societies. Because of his native gifts and an education unusually good for a slave, Douglass's oratory was so impressive that some of his auditors began to question his claims about his background. Douglass wrote his *Narrative,* from which the following selection is taken, in part to silence their doubts. The disparity between the professed beliefs of the Christian religion and the actual religious practice of most Christians had scarcely gone unnoticed during the antebellum era. Douglass's indictment, however, is particularly damning both because of his eloquent insight into the time's iniquity and because he had experienced at first hand "the slaveholding religion of the land."

From *Narrative of the Life of Frederick Douglass* (1845)

I find, since reading over the foregoing Narrative, that I have, in several instances, spoken in such a tone and manner, respecting religion, as may possibly lead those unacquainted with my religious views to suppose me an opponent of all religion. To remove the liability of such misapprehension, I deem it proper to append the following brief explanation. What I have said respecting and against religion, I mean strictly to apply to the *slaveholding religion* of this land, and with no possible reference to Christianity proper; for, between the Christianity of this land, and the Christianity of Christ, I recognize the widest possible difference—so wide, that to receive the one as good, pure, and holy, is of necessity to reject the other as bad, corrupt, and wicked. To be the friend of the one, is of necessity to be the enemy of the other. I love the pure, peaceable, and impartial Christianity of Christ: I therefore hate the corrupt, slaveholding, women-whipping, cradle-plundering, partial and hypocritical Christianity of this land. Indeed, I can see no reason, but the most deceitful one, for calling the religion of this land Christianity. I look upon it as the climax of all misnomers, the boldest of all frauds, and the grossest of all libels. Never was there a clearer case of "stealing the livery of the court of heaven to serve the devil in." I am filled with unutterable loathing when I contemplate the religious pomp and show, together with the horrible inconsistencies, which every where surround me. We have men-stealers for ministers, women-whippers for missionaries, and cradle-plunderers for church members. The man who wields the blood-clotted cowskin during the week fills the pulpit on Sunday, and claims to be a minister of the meek and lowly Jesus. The man who robs me of my earnings at the end of each week meets me as a class-leader on Sunday morning, to show me the way of life, and the path of salvation. He who sells my sister, for purposes of prostitution, stands forth as the pious advocate of purity. He who proclaims it a religious duty to read the Bible denies me the right of learning to read the name of the God who made me. He who is the religious advocate of marriage robs whole millions of its sacred influence, and leaves them to the ravages of wholesale pollution. The warm defender of the sacredness of the family relation is the same that scatters whole families,—sundering husbands and wives, parents and children, sisters and brothers,—leaving the hut vacant, and the hearth desolate. We see the thief preaching against theft, and the adulterer against adultery. We have men sold to build churches, women sold to support the gospel, and babes sold to purchase Bibles for the *poor heathen! all for the glory of God and the good of souls!*

The slave auctioneer's bell and the church-going bell chime in with each other, and the bitter cries of the heart-broken slave are drowned in the religious shouts of his pious master. Revivals of religion and revivals in the slave-trade go hand in hand together. The slave prison and the church stand near each other. The clanking of fetters and the rattling of chains in the prison, and the pious psalm and solemn prayer in the church, may be heard at the same time. The dealers in the bodies and souls of men erect their stand in the presence of the pulpit, and they mutually help each other. The dealer gives his blood-stained gold to support the pulpit, and the pulpit, in return, covers his infernal business with the garb of Christianity. Here we have religion and robbery the allies of each other—devils dressed in angels' robes, and hell presenting the semblance of paradise.

"Just God! and these are they
   Who minister at thine altar, God of
      right!
Men who their hands, with prayer and
      blessing, lay
   On Israel's ark of light.

"What! preach, and kidnap men?
   Give thanks, and rob thy own afflicted
      poor?
Talk of thy glorious liberty, and then
   Bolt hard the captive's door?

"What! servants of thy own
   Merciful Son, who came to seek and
     save
The homeless and the outcast, fettering
     down
   The tasked and plundered slave!

"Pilate and Herod friends!
　　Chief priests and rulers, as of old,
　　　combine!
Just God and holy! is that church which
　　lends
　　Strength to the spoiler thine?"

The Christianity of America is a Christianity, of whose votaries it may be as truly said, as it was of the ancient scribes and Pharisees, "They bind heavy burdens, and grievous to be borne, and lay them on men's shoulders, but they themselves will not move them with one of their fingers. All their works they do for to be seen of men.—They love the upper-most rooms at feasts, and the chief seats in the synagogues, ... and to be called of men, Rabbi, Rabbi.— But woe unto you scribes and Pharisees, hypocrites! for ye shut up the kingdom of heaven against men; for ye neither go in yourselves, neither suffer ye them that are entering to go in. Ye devour widows' houses, and for a pretence make long prayers; therefore ye shall receive the greater damnation. Ye compass sea and land to make one proselyte, and when he is made, ye make him twofold more the child of hell than yourselves.—Woe unto you, scribes and Pharisees, hypocrites! for ye pay tithe of mint, and anise, and cumin, and have omitted the weightier matters of the law, judgment, mercy, and faith; these ought ye to have done, and not to leave the other undone. Ye blind guides! which strain at a gnat, and swallow a camel. Woe unto you, scribes and Pharisees, hypocrites! for ye make clean the outside of the cup and of the platter; but within, they are full of extortion and excess.—Woe unto you, scribes and Pharisees, hypocrites! for ye are like unto whited sepulchres, which indeed appear beautiful outward, but are within full of dead men's bones, and of all uncleanness. Even so ye also outwardly appear righteous unto men, but within ye are full of hypocrisy and iniquity."

Dark and terrible as is this picture, I hold it to be strictly true of the overwhelming mass of professed Christians in America. They strain at a gnat, and swallow a camel. Could any thing be more true of our churches? They would be shocked at the proposition of fellowshipping a *sheep*-stealer; and at the same time they hug to their communion a *man*-stealer, and brand me with being an infidel, if I find fault with them for it. They attend with Pharisaical strictness to the outward forms of religion, and at the same time neglect the weightier matters of the law, judgment, mercy, and faith. They are always ready to sacrifice, but seldom to show mercy. They are they who are represented as professing to love God whom they have not seen, whilst they hate their brother whom they have seen. They love the heathen on the other side of the globe. They can pray for him, pay money to have the Bible put into his hand, and missionaries to instruct him; while they despise and totally neglect the heathen at their own doors.

Such is, very briefly, my view of the religion of this land; and to avoid any misunderstanding, growing out of the use of general terms, I mean, by the religion of this land, that which is revealed in the words, deeds, and actions, of those bodies, north and south, calling themselves Christian churches, and yet in union with slaveholders. It is against religion, as presented by these bodies, that I have felt it my duty to testify. . . .

Nathaniel Hawthorne (1804–1864)

Nathaniel Hawthorne was considered by Herman Melville to be virtually alone among his generation in combining what Melville described as "a boundless sympathy with all forms of being," with a "blackness, ten times black." Speculating on the source of this sense of blackness in Hawthorne, which complements his "Indian summer sunlight," Melville wondered

> Whether Hawthorne has simply availed himself of this mystical blackness as a means of the wondrous effects he makes it produce in his lights and shades; or whether there really lurks in him, perhaps unknown to himself, a touch of Puritanic gloom:—this, I cannot altogether tell. Certain it is, however, that this great power of blackness in him derives its force from its appeals to that Calvinistic sense of Innate Depravity and Original Sin, from whose visitations, in some shape or other, no deeply thinking mind is always and wholly free. For in certain moods, no man can weigh this world, without throwing in something, somehow like

Original Sin, to strike the uneven balance. ("Hawthorne and His Mosses," 1850)

In "Young Goodman Brown," Hawthorne explores the consequences of one man's refusal to accept certain things on faith. Goodman Brown risks the loss of his soul in order to enquire beyond the rightful limits of human curiosity into the true moral characters of his ancestors, his neighbors, and even his wife.

"Young Goodman Brown" (1835)

Young Goodman Brown came forth at sunset into the street at Salem village; but put his head back, after crossing the threshold, to exchange a parting kiss with his young wife. And Faith, as the wife was aptly named, thrust her own pretty head into the street, letting the wind play with the pink ribbons of her cap while she called to Goodman Brown.

"Dearest heart," whispered she, softly and rather sadly, when her lips were close to his ear, "prithee put off your journey until sunrise and sleep in your own bed to-night. A lone woman is troubled with such dreams and such thoughts that she's afeard of herself sometimes. Pray tarry with me this night, dear husband, of all nights in the year."

"My love and my Faith," replied young Goodman Brown, "of all nights in the year, this one night must I tarry away from thee. My journey, as thou callest it, forth and back again, must needs be done 'twixt now and sunrise. What, my sweet, pretty wife, dost thou doubt me already, and we but three months married?"

"Then God bless you!" said Faith, with the pink ribbons; "and may you find all well when you come back."

"Amen!" cried Goodman Brown. "Say thy prayers, dear Faith, and go to bed at dusk, and no harm will come to thee."

So they parted; and the young man pursued his way until, being about to turn the corner by the meeting-house, he looked back and saw the head of Faith still peeping after him with a melancholy air, in spite of her pink ribbons.

"Poor little Faith!" thought he, for his heart smote him. "What a wretch am I to leave her on such an errand! She talks of dreams, too. Methought as she spoke there was trouble in her face, as if a dream had warned her what work is to be done to-night. But no, no; 't would kill her to think it. Well, she's a blessed angel on earth; and after this one night I'll cling to her skirts and follow her to heaven."

With this excellent resolve for the future, Goodman Brown felt himself justified in making more haste on his present evil purpose. He had taken a dreary road, darkened by all the gloomiest trees of the forest, which barely stood aside to let the narrow path creep through, and closed immediately behind. It was all as lonely as could be; and there is this peculiarity in such a solitude, that the traveler knows not who may be concealed by the innumerable trunks and the thick boughs overhead; so that with lonely footsteps he may yet be passing through an unseen multitude.

"There may be a devilish Indian behind every tree," said Goodman Brown to himself; and he glanced fearfully behind him as he added, "What if the devil himself should be at my very elbow!"

His head being turned back, he passed a crook of the road, and, looking forward again, beheld the figure of a man, in grave and decent attire, seated at the foot of an old tree. He arose at Goodman Brown's approach and walked onward side by side with him.

"You are late, Goodman Brown," said he. "The clock of the Old South was striking as I came through Boston, and that is full fifteen minutes agone."

"Faith kept me back a while," replied the young man, with a tremor in his voice, caused by the sudden appearance of his companion, though not wholly unexpected.

It was now deep dusk in the forest, and deepest in that part of it where these two were journeying. As nearly as could be discerned, the second traveller was about fifty years old, apparently in the same rank of life as Goodman Brown, and bearing a considerable resemblance to him, though perhaps more in expression than features. Still they might have been taken for father and son. And yet, though the elder person was as simply clad as the younger, and as simple in manner too, he had an indescribable air of one who knew the world, and who would not have felt abashed at the governor's dinner table or in King William's court, were it possible that his affairs should call him thither. But the only thing about him that could be fixed upon as remarkable was his staff, which bore the likeness of a great black snake, so curiously wrought that it might almost be seen to twist and wriggle itself like a living serpent. This, of course, must have been an ocular deception, assisted by the uncertain light.

"Come, Goodman Brown," cried his fellow-traveller, "this is a dull pace for the beginning of a journey. Take my staff, if you are so soon weary."

"Friend," said the other, exchanging his slow pace for a full stop, "having kept covenant by meeting thee here, it is my purpose now to return whence I came. I have scruples touching the matter thou wot'st of.'

"Sayest thou so?" replied he of the serpent, smiling apart. "Let us walk on, nevertheless, reasoning as we go; and if I convince thee not thou shalt turn back. We are but a little way in the forest yet."

"Too far! too far!" exlaimed the goodman, unconsciously resuming his walk. "My father never went into the woods on such an errand, nor his father before him. We have been a race of honest men and good Christians since the days of the martyrs; and shall I be the first of the name of Brown that ever took this path and kept"—

"Such company, thou wouldst say," observed the elder person, interpreting his pause. "Well said, Goodman Brown! I have been as well acquainted with your family as with ever a one among the Puritans; and that's no trifle to say. I

helped your grandfather, the constable, when he lashed the Quaker woman so smartly through the streets of Salem; and it was I that brought your father a pitch-pine knot, kindled at my own hearth, to set fire to an Indian village, in King Philip's war. They were my good friends, both; and many a pleasant walk have we had along this path, and returned merrily after midnight. I would fain be friends with you for their sake."

"If it be as thou sayest," relied Goodman Brown, "I marvel they never spoke of these matters; or, verily, I marvel not, seeing that the least rumor of the sort would have driven them from New England. We are a people of prayer, and good works to boot, and abide no such wickedness."

"Wickedness or not," said the traveller with the twisted staff, "I have a very general acquaintance here in New England. The deacons of many a church have drunk the communion wine with me; the select-men of divers towns make me their chairman; and a majority of the Great and General Court are firm supporters of my interest. The governor and I, too—But these are state secrets."

"Can this be so?" cried Goodman Brown, with a stare of amazement at his undisturbed companion. "Howbeit, I have nothing to do with the governor and council; they have their own ways, and are no rule for a simple husbandman like me. But, were I to go on with thee, how should I meet the eye of that good old man, our minister, at Salem village? Oh, his voice would make me tremble both Sabbath day and lecture day."

Thus far the elder traveller had listened wtih due gravity; but now burst into a fit of irrepressible mirth, shaking himself so violently that his snake-like staff actually seemed to wriggle in sympathy.

"Ha! ha! ha!" shouted he again and again; then composing himself, "Well, go on, Goodman Brown, go on; but, prithee, don't kill me with laughing."

"Well, then, to end the matter at once," said Goodman Brown, considerably nettled, "there is my wife, Faith. It would break her dear little heart; and I'd rather break my own."

"Nay, if that be the case," answered the other, "e'en go thy ways, Goodman Brown. I would not for twenty old women like the one hobbling before us that Faith should come to any harm.

As he spoke he pointed his staff at a female figure on the path, in whom Goodman Brown recognized a very pious and exemplary dame, who had taught him his catechism in youth, and was still his moral and spiritual adviser, jointly with the minister and Deacon Gookin.

"A marvel, truly, that Goody Cloyse should be so far in the wilderness at nightfall," said he. "But with your leave, friend, I shall take a cut through the woods until we have left this Christian woman behind. Being a stranger to you, she might ask whom I was consorting with and whither I was going."

"Be it so," said his fellow-traveller. "Betake you to the woods, and let me keep the path."

Accordingly the young man turned aside, but took care to watch his companion, who advanced softly along the road until he had come within a staff's length of the old dame. She, meanwhile, was making the best of her way, with singular speed for so aged a woman, and mumbling some indistinct words—a prayer, doubtless—as she went. The traveller put forth his staff and touched her withered neck with what seemed the serpent's tail.

"The devil!" screamed the pious old lady.

"Then Goody CLoyse knows her old friend?" observed the traveller, confronting her and leaning on his writhing stick.

"Ah, forsooth, and is it your worship indeed?" cried the good dame. "Yea, truly is it, and in the very image of my old gossip, Goodman Brown, the grandfather of the silly fellow that now is. But—would your worship believe it?— my broomstick hath strangely disappeared, stolen, as I suspect, by that unhanged witch, Good Cory, and that, too, when I was all anointed with the juice of smallage, and cinquefoil, and wolf's bane"—

"Mingled with fine wheat and the fat of a new-born babe," said the shape of old Goodman Brown.

"Ah, your worship knows the recipe," cried the old lady, cackling aloud. "So, as I was saying, being all ready for the meeting, and no horse to ride on, I made up my mind to foot it; for they tell me there is a nice young man to be taken into communion to-night. But now your good worship will lend me your arm, and we shall be there in a twinkling.

"That can hardly be," answered her friend. "I may not spare you my arm,

Goody Cloyse; but here is my staff, if you will."

So saying, he threw it down at her feet, where, perhaps, it assumed life, being one of the rods which its owner had formerly lent to the Egyptian magi. Of this fact, however, Goodman Brown could not take cognizance. He had cast up his eyes in astonishment, and, looking down again, beheld neither Goody Cloyse nor the serpentine staff, but his fellow-traveller alone, who waited for him as calmly as if nothing had happened.

"That old woman taught me my catechism," said the young man; and there was a world of meaning in this simple comment.

They continued to walk onward, while the elder traveller exhorted his companion to make good speed and persevere in the path, discoursing so aptly that his arguments seemed rather to spring up in the bosom of his auditor than to be suggested by himself. As they went, he plucked a branch of maple to serve for a walking stick, and began to strip it of the twigs and little boughs, which were wet with evening dew. The moment his fingers touched them they became strangely withered and dried up as with a week's sunshine. Thus the pair proceeded, at a good free pace, until suddenly, in a gloomy hollow of the road, Goodman Brown sat himself down on the stump of a tree and refused to go any farther.

"Friend," said he, stubbornly, "my mind is made up. Not another step will I budge on this errand. What if a wretched old woman do choose to go to the devil when I thought she was going to heaven: is that any reason why I should quit my dear Faith and go after her?"

"You will think better of this by and by," said his acquaintance, composedly. "Sit here and rest yourself a while; and when you feel like moving again, there is my staff to help you along."

Without more words, he threw his companion the maple stick, and was as speedily out of sight, as if he had vanished into the deepening gloom. The young man sat a few moments by the roadside, applauding himself greatly, and thinking with how clear a conscience he should meet the minister in his morning walk, nor shrink from the eye of good old Deacon Gookin. And what calm sleep would be his that very night, which was to have been spent so wickedly, but so purely and sweetly now, in the arms of Faith! Amidst these pleasant and praiseworthy meditations, Goodman Brown heard the tramp of horses along the road, and deemed it advisable to conceal himself within the verge of the forest, conscious of the guilty purpose that had brought him thither, though now so happily turned from it.

On came the hoof tramps and the voices of the riders, two grave old voices, conversing soberly as they drew near. These mingled sounds appeared to pass along the road, within a few yards of the young man's hiding-place; but, owing doubtless to the depth of the gloom at that particular spot, neither the travellers nor their steeds were visible. Though their figures brushed the small boughs by the wayside, it could not be seen that they intercepted, even for a moment, the faint gleam from the strip of bright sky athwart which they must have passed. Goodman Brown alternately crouched and stood on tiptoe, pulling aside the branches and thrusting forth his head as far as he durst without discerning so much as a shadow. It vexed him the more, because he could have sworn, were such a thing possible, that he recognized the voices of the minister and Deacon Gookin, jogging along quietly, as they were wont to do, when bound to some ordination or ecclesiastical council. While yet within hearing, one of the riders stopped to pluck a switch.

"Of the two, reverend sir," said the voice like the deacon's, "I had rather miss an ordination dinner than to-night's meeting. They tell me that some of our community are to be here from Falmouth and beyond, and others from Connecticut and Rhode Island, besides several of the Indian powwows, who, after their fashion, know almost as much deviltry as the best of us. Moreover, there is a goodly young woman to be taken into communion."

"Mighty well, Deacon Gookin!" replied the solemn old tones of the minister. "Spur up, or we shall be late. Nothing can be done, you know, until I get on the ground."

The hoofs clattered again; and the voices, talking so strangely in the empty air; passed on through the forest, where no church had ever been gathered or solitary Christian prayed. Whither, then, could these holy men be journeying so deep into the heathen wilderness? Young Goodman Brown caught hold of a tree for support, being ready to sink down on the ground, faint and overburdened with the heavy sickness of his heart. He looked up to the sky, doubting whether there really was a heaven above him. Yet there was the blue arch, and the stars brightening in it.

"With heaven above and Faith below, I will yet stand firm against the devil!" cried Goodman Brown.

While he still gazed upward into the deep arch of the firmament and had lifted his hands to pray, a cloud, though no wind was stirring, hurried across the zenith and hid the brightening stars. The blue sky was still visible, except directly overhead, where this black mass of cloud was sweeping swiftly northward. Aloft in the air, as if from the depths of the cloud, came a confused and doubtful sound of voices. Once the listener fancied that he could distinguish the accents of towns-people of his own, men and women, both pious and ungodly, many of whom he had met at the communion table, and had seen others rioting at the tavern. The next moment, so indistinct were the sounds, he doubted whether he had heard aught but the murmur of the old forest, whispering without a wind. Then came a stronger swell of those familiar tones, heard daily in the sunshine at Salem village, but never until now from a cloud of night. There was one voice, of a young woman, uttering lamentations, yet with an uncertain sorrow, and entreating for some favor, which, perhaps, it would grieve her to obtain; and all the unseen multitude, both saints and sinners, seemed to encourage her onward.

"Faith!" shouted Goodman Brown, in a voice of agony and desperation; and the echoes of the forest mocked him, crying, "Faith! Faith!" as if bewildered wretches were seeking her all through the wilderness.

The cry of grief, rage, and terror was yet piercing the night, when the unhappy husband held his breath for a response. There was a scream, drowned immediately in a louder murmur of voices, fading into far-off laughter, as the dark cloud swept away, leaving the clear and silent sky above Goodman Brown. But something fluttered lightly down through the air and caught on the branch of a tree. The young man seized it, and beheld a pink ribbon.

"My Faith is gone!" cried he, after one stupefied moment. "There is no good on earth; and sin is but a name. Come, devil; for to thee is this world given."

And, maddened with despair, so that he laughed loud and long, did Goodman Brown grasp his staff and set forth again, at such a rate that he seemed to fly along the forest path rather than to walk or run. The road grew wilder and drearier and more faintly traced, and vanished at length, leaving him in the heart of the dark wilderness, still rushing onward with the instinct that guides mortal man to evil. The whole forest was peopled with frightful sounds—the creaking of the trees, the howling of wild beasts, and the yell of Indians; while sometimes the wind tolled like a distant church bell, and sometimes gave a broad roar around the traveller, as if all Nature were laughing him to scorn. But he was himself the chief horror of the scene, and shrank not from its other horrors.

"Ha! ha! ha!" roared Goodman Brown when the wind laughed at him. "Let us hear which will laugh loudest. Think not to frighten me with your deviltry. Come witch, come wizard, come Indian powwow, come devil himself, and here comes Goodman Brown. You may as well fear him as he fear you."

In truth, all through the haunted forest there could be nothing more frightful than the figure of Goodman Brown. On he flew among the black pines, brandishing his staff with frenzied-gestures, now giving vent to an inspiration of horrid blasphemy, and now shouting forth such laughter as set all the echoes of the forest laughing like demons around him. The fiend in his own shape is less hideous than when he rages in the breast of man. Thus sped the demoniac on his course, until, quivering among the trees, he saw a red light before him, as when the felled trunks and branches of a clearing have been set on fire, and throw up their lurid blaze against the sky, at the hour of midnight. He paused, in a lull of the tempest that had driven him onward, and heard the swell of what seemed a hymn, rolling solemnly from a distance with the weight of many voices. He knew the tune; it was a familiar one in the choir of the village meeting-house. The verse died heavily away, and was lengthened by a chorus, not of human voices, but of all the sounds of the benighted wilderness pealing in awful harmony together. Goodman Brown cried out, and his cry was lost to his own ear by its unison with the cry of the desert.

In the interval of silence he stole forward until the light glared full upon his eyes. At one extremity of an open space, hemmed in by the dark wall of the forest, arose a rock, bearing some rude, natural resemblance either to an altar, or a pulpit, and surrounded by four blazing pines, their tops aflame, their stems untouched, like candles at an evening meeting. The mass of foliage that had overgrown the summit of the rock was all on fire, blazing high into the night and fitfully illuminating the whole field. Each pendent twig and leafy festoon was in a blaze. As the red light arose and fell, a numerous congregation alternately shone forth, then disappeared in shadow, and again grew, as it were, out of the darkness, peopling the heart of the solitary woods at once.

"A grave and dark-clad company," quoth Goodman Brown.

In truth they were such. Among them, quivering to and fro between gloom and splendor, appeared faces that would be seen next day at the council board of the province, and others which, Sabbath after Sabbath, looked devoutly heavenward, and benignantly over the crowded pews, from the holiest pulpits in the land. Some affirm that the lady of the governor was there. At least there were high dames well known to her; and wives of honored husbands, and widows, a great multitude, and ancient maidens, all of excellent repute, and fair young girls, who trembled lest their mothers should espy them. Either the sudden gleams of light flashing over the obscure field bedazzled Goodman Brown, or he recognized a score of the church members of Salem village famous for their especial sanctity. Good old Deacon Gookin

had arrived, and waited at the skirts of that venerable saint, his revered pastor. But, irreverently consorting with these grave, reputable, and pious people, these elders of the church, these chaste dames and dewy virgins, there were men of dissolute lives and women of spotted fame, wretches given over to all mean and filthy vice, and suspected even of horrid crimes. It was strange to see that the good shrank not from the wicked, nor were the sinners abashed by the saints. Scattered also among their pale-faced enemies were the Indian priests, or powwows, who had often scared their native forest with more hideous incantations than any known to English witchcraft.

"But where is Faith?" thought Goodman Brown; and, as hope came into his heart, he trembled.

Another verse of the hymn arose, a slow and mournful strain, such as the pious love, but joined to words which expressed all that our nature can conceive of sin, and darkly hinted at far more. Unfathomable to mere mortals is the lore of fiends. Verse after verse was sung; and still the chorus of the desert swelled between like the deepest tone of a mighty organ; and with the final peal of that dreadful anthem there came a sound, as if the roaring wind, the rushing streams, the howling beasts, and every other voice of the unconcerted wilderness were mingling and according with the voice of guilty man in homage to the prince of all. The four blazing pines threw up a loftier flame, and obscurely discovered shapes and visages of horron on the smoke wreaths above the impious assembly. At the same moment the fire on the rock shot redly forth and formed a glowing arch above its base, where now appeared a figure. With reverence be it spoken, the figure bore no slight similitude, both in garb and manner, to some grave divine of the New England churches.

"Bring forth the converts!" cried a voice that echoed through the field and rolled into the forest.

At the word, Goodman Brown stepped forth from the shadow of the trees and approached the congregation, with whom he felt a loathful brotherhood by the sympathy of all that was wicked in his heart. He could have well-nigh sworn that the shape of his own dead father beckoned him to advance, looking downward from a smoke wreath, while a woman, with dim features of despair, threw out her hand to warn him back. Was it his mother? But he had no power to retreat one step, nor to resist, even in thought, when the minister and good old Deacon Gookin seized his arms and led him to the blazing rock. Thither came also the slender form of a veiled female, led between Goody Cloyse, that pious teacher of the catechism, and Martha Carrier, who had received the devil's promise to be queen of hell. A rampant hag was she. And there stood the proselytes beneath the canopy of fire.

"Welcome, my children," said the dark figure, "to the communion of your race. You have found thus young your nature and your destiny. My children, look behind you!"

They turned; and flashing forth, as it were, in a sheet of flame, the fiend worshippers were seen; the smile of welcome gleamed darkly on every visage.

"There," resumed the sable form, "are all whom ye have reverenced from youth. Ye deemed them holier than yourselves, and shrank from your own sin, contrasting it with their lives of righteousness and prayerful aspirations heavenward. Yet here are they all in my worshipping assembly. This night it shall be granted you to know their secret deeds: how hoary-bearded elders of the church have whispered wanton words to the young maids of their households; how many a woman, eager for widows' weeds, has given her husband a drink at bedtime and let him sleep his last sleep in her bosom; how beardless youths have made haste to inherit their fathers' wealth; and how fair damsels—blush not, sweet ones—have dug little graves in the garden, and bidden me, the sole guest, to an infant's funeral. By the sympathy of your human hearts for sin ye shall scent out all the places—whether in church, bed-chamber, street, field, or forest—where crime has been committed, and shall exult to behold the whole earth one stain of guilt, one mighty blood spot. Far more than this. It shall be yours to penetrate, in every bosom, the deep mystery of sin, the fountain of all wicked arts, and which inexhaustibly supplies more evil impulses than human power— than my power at its utmost—can make manifest in deeds. And now, my children, look upon each other."

They did so; and, by the blaze of the hell-kindled torches, the wretched man beheld his Faith, and the wife her husband, trembling before that unhallowed altar.

"Lo, there ye stand, my children," said the figure, in a deep and solemn tone, almost sad with its despairing awfulness, as if his once angelic nature could yet mourn for our miserable race. "Depending upon one another's hearts, ye had still hoped that virtue were not all a dream. Now are ye undeceived. Evil is the nature of mankind. Evil must be your only happiness. Welcome again, my children, to the communion of your race."

"Welcome," repeated the fiend worshippers, in one cry of despair and triumph.

And there they stood, the only pair, as it seemed, who were yet hesitating on the verge of wickedness in this dark world. A basin was hollowed, naturally, in the rock. Did it contain water, reddened by the lurid light? or was it blood? or, perchance, a liquid flame? Herein did the shape of evil dip his hand and prepare to lay the mark of baptism upon their foreheads, that they might be partakers of the mystery of sin, more conscious of the secret guilt of others, both in deed and thought, than they could now be of their own. The husband cast one look at his pale wife, and Faith at him. What polluted wretches would the next glance show them to each other, shuddering alike at what they disclosed and what they saw!

"Faith! Faith!" cried the husband, "look up to heaven, and resist the wicked one."

Whether Faith obeyed he knew not. Hardly had he spoken when he found himself amid calm night and solitude, listening to a roar of the wind which died heavily away through the forest.

He staggered against the rock, and felt it chill and damp; while a hanging twig, that had been all on fire, besprinkled his cheek with the coldest dew.

The next morning young Goodman Brown came slowly into the street of Salem village, staring around him like a bewildered man. The good old minister was taking a walk along the graveyard to get an appetite for breakfast and meditate his sermon, and bestowed a blessing, as he passed, on Goodman Brown. He shrank from the venerable saint as if to avoid an anathema. Old Deacon Gookin was at domestic worship, and the holy words of his prayer were heard through the open window. "What God doth the wizard pray to?" quoth Goodman Brown. Goody Cloyse, that excellent old Christian, stood in the early sunshine at her own lattice, catechizing a little girl who had brought her a pint of morning's milk. Goodman Brown snatched away the child as from the grasp of the fiend himself. Turning the corner by the meeting-house, he spied the head of Faith, with the pink ribbons, gazing anxiously forth, and bursting into such joy at sight of him that she skipped along the street and almost kissed her husband before the whole village. But Goodman Brown looked sternly and sadly into her face, and passed on without a greeting.

Had Goodman Brown fallen asleep in the forest and only dreamed a wild dream of a witch-meeting?

Be it so if you will; but, alas! it was a dream of evil omen for young Goodman Brown. A stern, a sad, a darkly meditative, a distrustful, if not a desperate man did he become from the night of that fearful dream. On the Sabbath day, when the congregaton were singing a holy psalm, he could not listen because an anthem of sin rushed loudly upon his ear and drowned all the blessed strain. When the minister spoke from the pulpit with power and fervid eloquence, and, with his hand on the open Bible, of the sacred truths of our religion, and of saint-like lives and triumphant deaths, and of future bliss or misery unutterable, then did Goodman Brown turn pale, dreading lest the roof should thunder down upon the gray blasphemer and his hearers. Often, awaking suddenly at midnight, he shrank from the bosom of Faith;and at morning or eventide, when the family knelt down at prayer, he scowled and muttered to himself, and gazed sternly at his wife, and turned away. And when he had lived long, and was borne to his grave a hoary corpse, followed by Faith, an aged woman, and children and grandchildren, a goodly procession, besides neighbors not a few, they carved no hopeful verse upon his tombstone, for his dying hour was gloom.

Herman Melville (1819–1891)

Herman Melville came close to defining himself in "Hawthorne and His Mosses" when he spoke of the things "that make Shakespeare Shakespeare"—"those deep far-away things in him; those occasional flashings-forth of the intuitive Truth in him; those short, quick probings at the very axis of reality." Melville provided further insight into these qualities when, in a letter to Hawthorne, he noted his older friend's embodiment of "the tragicalness of human thought in its own unbiassed, native, and profounder workings" and commented on its significance:

> We think that into no recorded mind has the intense feeling of the visible truth ever entered more deeply than into this man's. By visible truth, we mean the apprehension of the absolute condition of present things as they strike the eye of the man who fears them not, though they do their worst to him,—the man who, like Russia or the British Empire, declares himself a sovereign nature (in himself) amid the powers of heaven, hell, and earth. He may perish; but so long as he exists he insists upon treating with all Powers upon an equal basis. If any of those other Powers choose to withhold certain secrets, let them; that does not impair my sovereignty in myself; that does not make me tributary. And perhaps, after all, there is *no* secret.

As to whether there is or isn't a secret, whether there is or isn't more to reality than what can be seen, Melville remained of a divided mind. In the first selection, the sermon by Father Mapple that Ishmael hears in the whaleman's chapel in New Bedford before he boards the Pequod to embark on the search for Moby Dick, Melville writes as if there *were* a secret and man must cast off from the safe moorings of home and hearth into the dangerous seas of experience to find it. In the second selection, the pamphlet by Plotinus Plinlimmon that the young hero of Melville's novel *Pierre* finds in the course of his frantic attempt to overcome spiritual despair, Melville gives way to the other side of his mind and writes as if there *were not* a secret and man must accommodate himself to a world lacking any deeper metaphysical meaning than that which resides in "the absolute condition of present things." If Melville never fully resolves this issue, his inner confict about it nonetheless makes him more culturally respresentative. For like so many other thinkers and writers in the American tradition, Melville's meaning and power is to be found in his contradictions rather than elsewhere.

From *Moby-Dick* (1851)

The Sermon

Father Mapple rose, and in a mild voice of unassuming authority ordered the scattered people to condense. "Starboard gangway, there! side away to larboard—larboard gangway, to starboard! Midships! midships!"

There was a low rumbling of heavy sea-boots among the benches, and a still slighter shuffling of women's shoes, and all was quiet again, and every eye on the preacher.

He paused a little; then kneeling in the pulpit's bows, folded his large brown hands across his chest, uplifted his closed eyes, and offered a prayer so deeply devout that he seemed kneeling and praying at the bottom of the sea.

This ended, in prolonged solemn tones, like a continual tolling of a bell in a ship that is foundering at sea in a fog—in such tones he commenced reading the following hymn; but changing his manner towards the concluding stanzas, burst forth with a pealing exultation and joy—

"The ribs and terrors in the whale,
    Arched over me a dismal gloom,
While all God's sun-lit waves rolled by,
    And lift me deepening down to doom.

"I saw the opening maw of hell,
    With endless pains and sorrows there;
Which none but they that feel can tell—
    Oh, I was plunging to despair.

"In black distress, I called my God,
    When I could scarce believe him mine,
He bowed his ear to my complaints—
    No more the whale did me confine.

"With speed he flew to my relief,
    As on a radiant dolphin borne;
Awful, yet bright, as lightning shone
    The face of my Deliverer God.

"My song for ever shall record
    That terrible, that joyful hour;
I give the glory to my God,
    His all the mercy and the power."

Nearly all joined in singing this hymn, which swelled high above the howling of the storm. A brief pause ensued; the preacher slowly turned over the leaves of the Bible, and at last, folding his hand down upon the proper page, said: "Beloved shipmates, clinch the last verse of the first chapter of Jonah—'And God had prepared a great fish to swallow up Jonah.'

"Shipmates, this book, containing only four chapters—four yarns—is one of the smallest strands in the mighty cable of the Scriptures. Yet what depths of the soul does Jonah's deep sea-line sound! what a pregnant lesson to us is this prophet! What a noble thing is that canticle in the fish's belly! How billow-like and boisterously grand! We feel the floods surging over us; we sound with him to the kelpy bottom of the waters; sea-weed and all the slime of the sea is about us! But *what* is this lesson that the book of Jonah teaches? Shipmates, it is a two-stranded lesson; a lesson to us all as sinful men, and a lesson to me as a pilot of the living God. As sinful men, it is a lesson to us all, because it is a story of the sin, hard-heartedness, suddenly awakened fears, the swift punishment, repentance, prayers, and finally the deliverance and joy of Jonah. As with all sinners among men, the sin of this son of Amittai was in his wilful disobedience of the command of God—never mind now what that command was, or how conveyed—which he found a hard command. But all the things that God would have us do are hard for us to do—remember that—and hence, he oftener commands us than endeavors to persuade. And if we obey God, we must disobey ourselves; and it is in this disobeying ourselves, wherein the hardness of obeying God consists.

"With this sin of disobedience in him, Jonah still further flouts at God, by seeking to flee from Him. He thinks that a ship made by men, will carry him into countries where God does not reign, but only the Captains of this earth. He skulks about the wharves of Joppa, and seeks a ship that's bound for Tarshish. There lurks, perhaps, a hith-erto unheeded meaning here. By all accounts Tarshish could have been no other city than the modern Cadiz. That's the opinion of learned men. And where is Cadiz, shipmates? Cadiz is in Spain; as far by water, from Joppa, as Jonah could possibly have sailed in those ancient days, when the Atlantic was an almost unknown sea. Because Joppa, the modern Jaffa, shipmates, is on the most easterly coast of the Medit-erranean, the Syrian; and Tarshish or Cadiz more than two thousand miles to the westward from that, just outside the Straits of Gibraltar. See ye not then, shipmates, that Jonah sought to fee world-wide from God? Miserable man! Oh! most contemptible and worthy of all scorn; with slouched hat and guilty eye, skulking from his God; prowling among the shipping like a vile burglar hastening to cross the seas. So dis-ordered, self-condemning is his look, that had there been policemen in those days, Jonah, on the mere suspicion of something wrong, had been arrested ere he touched a deck. How plainly he's a fugitive! no baggage, not a hat-box, valise, or carpet-bag,—no friends ac-company him to the wharf with their adieux. At last, after much dodging search, he finds the Tarshish ship re-ceiving the last items of her cargo; and as he steps on board to see its Captain in the cabin, all the sailors for the moment desist from hoisting in the goods, to mark the stranger's evil eye. Jonah sees this; but in vain he tries to look all ease and confidence; in vain essays his wretched smile. Strong intuitions of the man assure the mariners he can be no innocent. In their gamesome but still serious way, one whispers to the other—'Jack, he's robbed a widow;' or, 'Joe, do you mark him; he's a bigamist;' or, 'Harry lad, I guess he's the adulterer that broke jail in old Gomorrah, or belike, one of the missing murderers from Sodom.' Another runs to read the bill that's stuck against the spile upon the wharf to which the ship is moored, offering five hundred gold coins for the apprehension of a parricide, and containing a description of his person. He reads, and looks from Jonah to the bill; while all his sympathetic shipmates now crowd around Jonah, prepared to lay their hands upon him. Frighted Jonah trembles, and summoning all his boldness to his face, only looks so much more a coward. He will not confess himself suspected; but that itself is strong suspicion. So he makes the best of it; and when the sailors find him not to be the man that is advertised, they let him pass, and he descends into the cabin.

" 'Who's there?' cries the Captain at his busy desk, hurriedly making out his papers for the Customs—'Who's there?' Oh! how that harmless question mangles Jonah! For the instant he almost turns to flee again. But he rallies. 'I seek a passage in this ship to Tarshish; how soon sail ye, sir?' Thus far the busy Captain had not looked up to Jonah, though the man now stands before him; but no sooner does he hear that hollow voice, than he darts a scrutinizing glance. 'We sail with the next coming tide,' at last he slowly answered, still intently eyeing him. 'No sooner, sir?'—

'Soon enough for any honest man that goes a passenger.' Ha! Jonah, that's another stab. But he swiftly calls away the Captain from that scent. 'I'll sail with ye,'—he says,—'the passage money, how much is that?—I'll pay now.' For it is particularly written, shipmates, as if it were a thing not to be overlooked in this history, 'that he paid the fare thereof' ere the craft did sail. And taken with the context, this is full of meaning.

"Now Jonah's Captain, shipmates, was one whose discernment detects crime in any, but whose cupidity exposes it only in the penniless. In this world, shipmates, sin that pays its way can travel freely, and without a passport; whereas Virtue, if a pauper, is stopped at all frontiers. So Jonah's Captain prepares to test the length of Jonah's purse, ere he judge him openly. He charges him thrice the usual sum; and it's assented to. Then the Captain knows that Jonah is a fugitive; but at the same time resolves to help a flight that paves its rear with gold. Yet when Jonah fairly takes out his purse, prudent suspicions still molest the Captain. He rings every coin to find a counterfeit. Not a forger, any way, he mutters; and Jonah is put down for his passage. 'Point out my state-room, Sir,' says Jonah now, 'I'm travel-weary; I need sleep.' 'Thou look'st like it,' says the Captain, 'there's thy room.' Jonah enters, and would lock the door, but the lock contains no key. Hearing him foolishly fumbling there, the Captain laughs lowly to himself, and mutters something about the doors of convicts' cells being never allowed to be locked within. All dressed and dusty as he is, Jonah throws himself into his berth, and finds the little state-room ceiling almost resting on his forehead. The air is close, and Jonah gasps. Then, in that contracted hole, sunk, too, beneath the ship's water-line, Jonah feels the heralding presentiment of that stifling hour, when the whale shall hold him in the smallest of his bowel's wards.

"Screwed at its axis against the side, a swinging lamp slightly oscillates in Jonah's room; and the ship, heeling over towards the wharf with the weight of the last bales received, the lamp, flame and all, though in slight motion, still maintains a permanent obliquity with reference to the room; though, in truth, infallibly straight itself, it but made obvious the false, lying levels among which it hung. The lamp alarms and frightens Jonah; as lying in his berth his tormented eyes roll round the place, and this thus far successful fugitive finds no refuge for his restless glance. But that contradiction in the lamp more and more appals him. The floor, the ceiling, and the side, are all awry. 'Oh! so my conscience hangs in me!' he groans, 'straight upward, so it burns; but the chambers of my soul are all in crookedness!'

"Like one who after a night of drunken revelry hies to his bed, still reeling, but with conscience yet pricking him, as the plungings of the Roman race-horse but so much the more strike his steel tags into him; as one who in that miserable plight still turns and turns in giddy anguish, praying God for annihilation until the fit be passed and at last amid the whirl of woe he feels, a deep stupor steals over him, as over the man who bleeds to death, for conscience is the wound, and there's naught to staunch it; so, after sore wrestlings in his berth, Jonah's prodigy of ponderous misery drags him drowning down to sleep.

"And now the time of tide has come; the ship casts off her cables; and from the deserted wharf the uncheered ship for Tarshish, all careening, glides to sea. That ship, my friends, was the first of recorded smugglers! the contraband was Jonah. But the sea rebels; he will not bear the wicked burden. A dreadful storm comes on, the ship is like to break. But now when the boatswain calls all hands to lighten her; when boxes, bales, and jars are clattering overboard; when the wind is shrieking, and the men are yelling, and every plank thunders with trampling feet right over Jonah's head; in all this raging tumult, Jonah sleeps his hideous sleep. He sees no black sky and raging sea, feels not the reeling timbers, and little hears he or heeds he the far rush of the mighty whale, which even now with open mouth is cleaving the seas after him. Aye, shipmates, Jonah as gone down into the sides of the ship—a berth in the cabin as I have taken it, and was fast asleep. But the frightened master comes to him, and shrieks in his dead ear, 'What meanest thou, O sleeper! arise!' Startled from his lethargy by that direful cry, Jonah staggers to his feet, and stumbling to the deck, grasps a shroud, to look out upon the sea. But at that moment he is sprung upon by a panther billow leaping over the bulwarks. Wave after wave thus leaps into the ship, and finding no speedy vent runs roaring fore and aft, till the mariners come nigh to drowning while yet afloat. And ever, as the white moon shows her affrighted face from the steep gullies in the blackness overhead, aghast Jonah sees the rearing bowsprit pointing high upward, but soon beat downward again towards the tormented deep.

"Terrors upon terrors run shouting through his soul. In all his cringing attitudes, the God-fugitive is now too plainly known. The sailors mark him; more and more certain grow their suspicions of him, and at last, fully to test the truth, by referring the whole matter to high Heaven, they fall to casting lots, to see for whose cause this great tempest was upon them. The lot is Jonah's; that discovered, then how furiously they mob him with their questions. 'What is thine occupation? Whence comest thou? Thy country? What people?' But mark now, my shipmates, the behavior of poor Jonah. The eager mariners but ask him who he is, and where from; whereas, they not only receive an answer to those questions, but likewise another answer to a question not put by them, but the unsolicited answer is forced from Jonah by the hard hand of God that is upon him.

" 'I am a Hebrew,' he cries—and then—'I fear the Lord the God of Heaven who hath made the sea and dry land!' Fear him, O Jonah? Aye, well mightest thou fear the Lord God *then!* Straightway, he now goes on to make a full confession; whereupon the mariners became more and more appalled, but still are pitiful. For when Jonah, not yet supplicating God for mercy, since he but too well knew the darkness of his deserts,—when wretched Jonah cries out

to them to take him and cast him forth into the sea, for he knew that for *his* sake this great tempest was upon them; they mercifully turn from him, and seek by other means to save the ship. But all in vain; the indignant gale howls louder; then, with one hand raised invokingly to God, with the other they not unreluctantly lay hold of Jonah.

"And now behold Jonah taken up as an anchor and dropped into the sea; when instantly an oily calmness floats out from the east, and the sea is still, as Jonah carries down the gale with him, leaving smooth water behind. He goes down in the whirling heart of such a masterless commotion that he scarce heeds the moment when he drops seething into the yawning jaws awaiting him; and the whale shoots-to all his ivory teeth, like so many white bolts, upon his prison. Then Jonah prayed unto the Lord out of the fish's belly. But observe his prayer, and learn a weighty lesson. For sinful as he is, Jonah does not weep and wail for direct deliverance. He feels that his dreadful punishment is just. He leaves all his deliverance to God, contenting himself with this, that spite of all his pains and pangs, he will still look towards His holy temple. And here, shipmates, is true and faithful repentance; not clamorous for pardon, but grateful for punishment. And how pleasing to God was this conduct in Jonah, is shown in the eventual deliverance of him from the sea and the whale. Shipmates, I do not place Jonah before you to be copied for his sin but I do place him before you as a model for repentance. Sin not; but if you do, take heed to repent of it like Jonah."

While he was speaking these words, the howling of the shrieking, slanting storm without seemed to add new power to the preacher, who, when describing Jonah's sea-storm, seemed tossed by a storm himself. His deep chest heaved as with a ground-swell; his tossed arms seemed the warring elements at work; and the thunders that rolled away from off his swarthy brow, and the light leaping from his eye, made all his simple hearers look on him with a quick fear that was strange to them.

There now came a lull in his look, as he silently turned over the leaves of the Book once more; and, at last, standing motionless, with closed eyes, for the moment, seemed communing with God and himself.

But again he leaned over towards the people, and bowing his head lowly, with an aspect of the deepest yet manliest humility, he spake these words:

"Shipmates, God has laid but one hand upon you; both his hands press upon me. I have read ye by what murky light may be mine the lesson that Jonah teaches to all sinners; and therefore to ye, and still more to me, for I am a greater sinner than ye. And now how gladly would I come down from this mast-head and sit on the hatches there where you sit, and listen as you listen, while some one of you reads *me* that other and more awful lesson which Jonah teaches to *me,* as a pilot of the living God. How being an anointed pilot-prophet, or speaker of true things, and bidden by the Lord to sound those unwelcome truths in the ears of a wicked Nineveh, Jonah, appalled at the hostility he should raise, fled from his mission, and sought to escape his duty and his God by taking ship at Joppa. But God is everywhere; Tarshish he never reached. As we have seen, God came upon him in the whale, and swallowed him down to living gulfs of doom, and with swift slantings tore him along 'into the midst of the seas,' where the eddying depths sucked him ten thousand fathoms down, and 'the weeds were wrapped about his head,' and all the watery world of woe bowled over him. Yet even then beyond the reach of any plummet—'out of the belly of hell'— when the whale grounded upon the ocean's utmost bones, even then, God heard and engulphed, repenting prophet when he cried. Then God spake unto the fish; and from the shuddering cold and blackness of the sea, the whale came breeching up towards the warm and pleasant sun, and all the delights of air and earth; and 'vomited out Jonah upon the dry land;' when the word of the Lord came a second time; and Jonah, bruised and beaten—his ears, like two sea-shells, still multitudinously murmuring of the ocean—Jonah did the Almighty's bidding. And what was that, shipmates? To preach the Truth to the face of Falsehood! That was it!

"This, shipmates, this is that other lesson; and woe to that pilot of the living God who slights it. Woe to him whom this world charms from Gospel duty! Woe to him who seeks to pour oil upon the waters when God has brewed them into a gale! Woe to him who seeks to please rather than to appal! Woe to him whose good name is more to him than goodness! Woe to him who, in this world, courts not dishonor!

Woe to him who would not be true, even though to be false were salvation! Yea, woe to him who, as the great Pilot Paul has it, while preaching to others is himself a castaway!"

He drooped and fell away from himself for a moment; then lifting his face to them again, showed a deep joy in his eyes, as he cried out with a heavenly enthusiasm,—"But oh! shipmates! on the starboard hand of every woe, there is a sure delight; and higher the top of that delight, than the bottom of the woe is deep. Is not the main-truck higher than the kelson is low? Delight is to him—a far, far upward, and inward delight— who against the proud gods and commodores of this earth, ever stands forth his own inexorable self. Delight is to him whose strong arms yet support him, when the ship of this base treacherous world has gone down beneath him. Delight is to him, who gives no quarter in the truth, and kills, burns, and destroys all sin though he pluck it out from under the robes of Senators and Judges. Delight,—top-gallant delight is to him, who acknowledges no law or lord, but the Lord his God, and is only a patriot to heaven. Delight is to him, whom all the waves of the billows of the seas of the boisterous mob can never shake from this sure Keel of the Ages. And eternal delight and deliciousness will be his, who coming to lay him down, can say with his final breath—O Father!—chiefly known to me by Thy rod—mortal or immortal, here I die. I have striven to be Thine, more than to be this world's, or mine own. Yet this is nothing; I leave eternity to Thee; for what is man that he should live out the lifetime of his God?"

He said no more, but slowly waving a benediction, covered his face with his hands, and so remained kneeling, till all the people had departed, and he was left alone in the place.

From *Pierre* (1852)

"EI"*

BY

PLOTINUS PLINLIMMON,

(In Three Hundred and Thirty-Three Lectures).

LECTURE FIRST.

CHRONOMETRICALS AND HOROLOGICALS,

(Being not so much the Portal, as part of the temporary Scaffold to the Portal of this New Philosophy).

"Few of us doubt, gentlemen, that human life on this earth is but a state of probation; which among other things implies, that here below, we mortals have only to do with things provisional. Accordingly, I hold that all our so-called wisdom is likewise but provisional.

"This preamble laid down, I begin.

"It seems to me, in my visions, that there is a certain most rare order of human souls, which if carefully carried in the body will almost always and everywhere give Heaven's own Truth, with some small grains of variance. For peculiarly coming from God, the sole source of that heavenly truth, and the great Greenwich hill and tower from which the universal meridians are far

*"Ei" is the Greek word for "if" (editor's note).

212

out into infinity reckoned; such souls seem as London sea-chronometers (*Greek,* time-namers) which as the London ship floats past Greenwich down the Thames, are accurately adjusted by Greenwich time, and if heedfully kept, will still give that same time, even though carried to the Azores. True, in nearly all cases of long, remote voyages—to China, say—chronometers of the best make, and the most carefully treated, will gradually more or less vary from Greenwich time, without the possibility of the error being corrected by direct comparison with their great standard; but skilful and devout observations of the stars by the sextant will serve materially to lessen such errors. And besides, there is such a thing as *rating* a chronometer; that is, having ascertained its degree of organic inaccuracy, however small, then in all subsequent chronometrical calculations, that ascertained loss or gain can be readily added or deducted, as the case may be. Then again, on these long voyages, the chronometer may be corrected by comparing it with the chronometer of some other ship at sea, more recently from home.

"No in an artificial world like ours, the soul of man is further removed from its God and the Heavenly Truth, than the chronometer carried to China, is from Greenwich. And, as that chronometer, if at all accurate, will pronounce it to be 12 o'clock high-noon, when the China local watches say, perhaps, it is 12 o'clock midnight; so the chronometric soul, if in this world true to its great Greenwich in the other, will always, in its so-called intuitions of right and wrong, be contradicting the mere local standards and watchmaker's brains of this earth.

"Bacon's brains were mere watchmaker's brains; but Christ was a chronometer; and the most exquisitely adjusted and exact one, and the least affected by all terrestrial jarrings, of any that have ever come to us. And the reason why his teachings seemed to folly to the Jews, was because he carried that Heaven's time in Jerusalem, while the Jews carried Jerusalem time there. Did he not expressly say—My wisdom (time) is not of this world? But whatever is really peculiar in the wisdom of Christ seems precisely the same folly to-day as it did 1850 years ago. Because, in all that interval his bequeathed chronometer has still preserved its original Heaven's time, and the general Jerusalem of this world has likewise carefully preserved its own.

"But though the chronometer carried from Greenwich to China, should truly exhibit in China what the time may be at Greenwich at any moment; yet, though thereby it must necessarily contradict China time, it does by no means thence follow, that with respect to China, the China watches are at all out of the way, Precisely the reverse. For the fact of that variance is a presumption that, with respect to China, the Chinese watches must be all right; and consequently as the China watches are right as to China, so the Greenwich chronometers must be wrong as to China. Besides, of what use to the Chinaman would a Greenwich chronometer, keeping Greenwich time, be? Were he thereby to regulate his daily actions, he would be guilty of all manner of absurdities:—going to bed at noon, say, when his neighbours would be sitting down to dinner. And thus, though the earthly wisdom of man be heavenly folly to God; so also, conversely, is the heavenly wisdom of God an earthly folly to man. Literally speaking, this is so. Nor does the God at the heavenly Greenwich expect common men to keep Greenwich wisdom in this remote Chinese world of ours; because such a thing were unprofitable for them here, and, indeed, a falsification of Himself, inasmuch as in that case, China time would be identical with Greenwich time, which would make Greenwich time wrong.

"But why then does God now and then send a heavenly chronometer (as a meteoric stone) into the world, uselessly as it would seem, to give the lie to all the world's time-keepers? Because He is unwilling to leave man without some occasional testimony to this:—that though man's Chinese notions of things may answer well enough here, they are by no means universally applicable, and that the central Greenwich in which he dwells goes by a somewhat different method from this world. And yet it follows not from this, that God's truth is one thing and man's truth another; but—as above hinted, and as will be further elucidated in subsequent lectures—by their very contradictions they are made to correspond.

"By inference it follows, also, that he who finding in himself a chronometrical soul, seeks practically to force that heavenly time upon the earth; in such an attempt he can never succeed, with an absolute and essential success. And as

for himself, if he seek to regulate his own daily conduct by it, he will but array all men's earthly time-keepers against him, and thereby work himself woe and death. Both these things are plainly evinced in the character and fate of Christ, and the past and present condition of the religion he taught. But here one thing is to be especially observed. Though Christ encountered woe in both the precept and the practice of his chronometricals, yet did he remain throughout entirely without folly or sin. Whereas, almost invariably, with inferior beings, the absolute effort to live in this world according to the strict letter of the chronometricals is, somehow, apt to involve those inferior beings eventually in strange, *unique* follies and sins, unimagined before. It is the story of the Ephesian matron, allegorised.

"To any earnest man of insight, a faithful contemplation of these ideas concerning Chronometricals and Horologicals, will serve to render provisionally far less dark some few of the otherwise obscurest things which have hitherto tormented the honest-thinking men of all ages. What man who carries a heavenly soul in him, has not groaned to perceive, that unless he committed a sort of suicide as to the practical things of this world, he never can hope to regulate his earthly conduct by the same heavenly soul? And yet by an infallible instinct he knows, that that monitor cannot be wrong in itself.

"And where is the earnest and righteous philosopher, gentlemen, who looking right and left, and up and down, through all the ages of the world, the present included; where is there such an one who has not a thousand times been struck with a sort of infidel idea, that whatever other worlds God may be Lord of, he is not the Lord of this; for else this world would seem to give the lie to Him; so utterly repugnant seem its ways to the instinctively known ways of Heaven. But it is not, and cannot be so; nor will he who regards this chronometrical conceit aright, ever more be conscious of that horrible idea. For he will then see, or seem to see, that this world's seeming incompatibility with God, absolutely results from its meridional correspondence with Him.

"This chronometrical conceit does by no means involve the justification of all the acts which wicked men may perform. For in their wickedness downright wicked men sin as much against their own horologes, as against the heavenly chronometer. That this is so, their spontaneous liability to remorse does plainly evince. No, this conceit merely goes to show, that for the mass of men; the highest abstract heavenly righteousness is not only impossible, but would be entirely out of place, and positively wrong in a world like this. To turn the left cheek if the right be smitten, is chronometrical; hence, no average son of man ever did such a thing. To give *all* that thou hast to the poor, this too is chronometrical; hence no average son of man ever did such a thing. Nevertheless, if a man gives with a certain self-considerate generosity to the poor; abstains from doing downright ill to any man; does his convenient best in a general way to do

good to his whole race; takes watchful loving care of his wife and children, relatives, and friends; is perfectly tolerant to all other men's opinions, whatever they may be; is an honest dealer, an honest citizen, and all that; and more especially if he believe that there is a God for infidels, as well as for believers, and acts upon that belief; then, though such a man falls infinitely short of the chronometrical standard, though all his actions are entirely horologic;—yet such a man need never lastingly despond, because he is sometimes guilty of some minor offence:—hasty words, impulsively returning a blow, fits of domestic petulance, selfish enjoyment of a glass of wine while he knows there are those around him who lack a loaf of bread. I say he need never lastingly despond on account of his perpetual liability to these things; because *not* to do them, and their like, would be to be an angel, a chronometer; whereas, he is a man and a horologe.

"Yet does the horologe itself teach, that all liabilities to these things should be checked as much as possible, though it is certain they can never be utterly eradicated. They are only to be checked, then, because, if entirely unrestrained, they would finally run into utter selfishness and human demonism, which, as before hinted, are not by any means justified by the horologe.

"In short, this chronometrical and horological conceit, in sum, seems to teach this:—That in things terrestrial (horological) a man must not be governed by ideas celestial (chronometrical); that certain minor self-renunciations in this life his own mere instinct for his own everyday general well-being will teach him to make, but he must by no means make a complete unconditional sacrifice of himself in behalf of any other being, or any cause, or any conceit. (For, does aught else completely and unconditionally sacrifice itself for him? God's own sun does not abate one title of its heat in July, however you swoon with that heat in the sun. And if it *did* abate its heat on your behalf, then the wheat and the rye would not ripen; and so, for the incidental benefit of one, a whole population would suffer.)

"A virtuous expediency, then, seems the highest desirable or attainable earthly excellence for the mass of men, and is the only earthly excellence that their Creator intended for them. When they go to heaven, it will be quite another thing. There, they can freely turn the left cheek, because there the right cheek will never be smitten. There they can freely give all to the poor, for *there* will be no poor to give to. A due appreciation of this matter will do good to man. For, hitherto, being authoritatively taught by his dogmatical teachers that he must, while on earth, aim at heaven, and attain it, too, in all his earthly acts, on pain of eternal wrath; and finding by experience that this is utterly impossible; in his despair, he is too apt to run clean away into all manner of moral abandonment, self-deceit, and hypocrisy (cloaked, however, mostly under an aspect of the most respectable devotion); or else he openly runs, like a mad dog, into atheism. Whereas, let men be taught those Chronometricals and Horologicals, and while still retaining every common-sense incentive to whatever of virtue be practicable and desirable, and having these incentives strengthened, too, by the consciousness of powers to attain their mark; then there would be an end to that fatal despair of becoming at all good, which has too often proved the vice-producing result in many minds of the undiluted chronometrical doctrines hitherto taught to mankind. But if any man say, that such a doctrine as this I lay down is false, is impious; I would charitably refer that man to the history of Christendom for the last 1800 years; and ask him, whether, in spite of all the maxims of Christ, that history is not just as full of blood, violence, wrong, and iniquity of every kind, as any previous portion of the world's story? Therefore, it follows, that so far as practical results are concerned—regarded in a purely earthly light—the only great original moral doctrine of Christianity (*i.e.* the chronometrical gratuitous return of good for evil, as distinguished from the horological forgiveness of injuries taught by some of the Pagan philosophers), has been found (horologically) a false one; because after 1800 years' inculcation from tens of thousands of pulpits, it has proved entirely impracticable.

"I but lay down, then, what the best mortal men do daily practise; and what all really wicked men are very far removed from. I present consolation to the earnest man, who, among all his human frailties, is still agonisingly conscious of the beauty of chronometrical excellence. I hold up a practicable virtue to the vicious; and interfere not with the enternal truth, that, sooner or later, in all cases, downright vice is downright woe.

"Moreover: if——"

But here the pamphlet was torn, and came to a most untidy termination.

Harriet Beecher Stowe (1811–1896)

On meeting of Harriet Beecher Stowe Abraham Lincoln was heard to remark, "So this is the little lady who made this big war." Lincoln's statement was not a complete exaggeration. *Uncle Tom's Cabin* (1852) created a surge of anti-slavery feeling in the North and throughout the world. Its extraordinary impact exceeded the fondest hopes of the author. In its first year, Mrs. Stowe's novel sold more than three hundred thousand copies nationally, two and a half million worldwide.

In the "Concluding Remarks" of *Uncle Tom's Cabin,* here reproduced, Mrs. Stowe addresses the reader directly (as indeed she does throughout the novel in numerous asides and preachments), and suggests specific approaches to the resolution of the problem of slavery.

From *Uncle Tom's Cabin* (1852)

Concluding Remarks

For many years of her life, the author avoided all reading upon or allusion to the subject of slavery, considering it as too painful to be inquired into, and one which advancing light and civilization would certainly live down. But, since the legislative act of 1850, when she heard, with perfect surprise and consternation, Christian and humane people actually recommending the remanding escaped fugitives into slavery, as duty binding on good citizens—when she heard, on all hands, from kind, compassionate and estimable people, in the free states of the North, deliberations and discussions as to what Christian duty could be on this head,—she could only think, These men and Christians cannot know what slavery is; if they did, such a question could never be open for discussion. And from this arose a desire to exhibit it in a *living dramatic reality.* She had endeavored to show it fairly, in its best and its worst phases. In its *best* aspect, she has, perhaps, been successful; but, oh! who shall say what yet remains untold in that valley and shadow of death, that lies the other side?

To you, generous, noble-minded men and women, of the South,—you, whose virtue, and magnanimity and purity of character, are the greater for the severer trial it has encountered,—to you is her appeal. Have you not, in your own secret souls, in your own private conversings, felt that there are woes and evils, in this accursed system, far beyond what are here shadowed, or can be shadowed? Can it be otherwise? Is *man* ever a creature to be trusted with wholly irresponsible power? And does not the slave system, by denying the slave all legal right of testimony, make every individual owner an irresponsible despot? Can anybody fail to make the inference what the practical result will be? If there is, as we admit, a public sentiment among you, men of honor, justice and humanity, is there not also another kind of public sentiment among the ruffian, the brutal and debased? And cannot the ruffian, the brutal, the debased, by slave law, own just as many slaves as the best and purest? Are the honorable, the just, the high-minded and compassionate, the majority anywhere in this world?

The slave-trade is now, by American law, considered as piracy. But a slave-trade, as systematic as ever was carried on on the coast of Africa, is an inevitable attendant and result of American slavery. And its heart-break and its horrors, *can* they be told?

The writer has given only a faint shadow, a dim picture, of the anguish and despair that are, at this very moment, riving thousands of hearts, shattering thousands of families, and driving a helpless and sensitive race to frenzy and despair. There are those living who know the mothers whom this accursed traffic has driven to the murder of their children; and themselves seeking in death a shelter from woes more dreaded than death. Nothing of tragedy can be written, can be spoken, can be conceived, that equals the frightful reality of scenes daily and hourly acting on our shores, beneath the shadow of American law, and the shadow of the cross of Christ.

And now, men and women of America, is this a thing to be trifled with, apologized for, and passed over in silence? Farmers of Massachusetts, of New Hampshire, of Vermont, of Connecticut, who read this book by the blaze of your winter-evening fire,—strong-hearted, generous sailors and ship-owners of Maine,—is this a thing for you to countenance and encourage? Brave and generous men of New York, farmers of rich and joyous Ohio, and ye of the wide prairie states,—answer, is this a thing for you to protect and countenance? And you, mothers of America,—you who have learned, by the cradles of your own children, to love and feel for all mankind—by the sacred love you bear your child; by your joy in his beautiful, spotless infancy; by the motherly pity and tenderness with which you guide his growing years; by the anxieties of his education; by the prayers you breathe for his soul's eternal good;—I beseech you, pity the mother who has all your affections, and not one legal right to protect, guide, or educate, the child of her bosom! By the sick hour of your child; by those dying eyes, which you can never forget; by those last cries, that wrung your heart when you could neither help nor save; by the desolation of that empty cradle, that silent nursery,—I beseech you, pity those mothers that are constantly made childless by the American slave-trade! And say mothers of America, is this a thing to be defended, sympathized with, passed over in silence?

Do you say that the people of the free states have nothing to do with it, and can do nothing? Would to God this were true! But it is not true. The people of the free states have defended, encouraged, and participated; and are more guilty for it, before God, than the South, in that they have *not* the apology of education or custom.

If the mothers of the free states had all felt as they should, in times past, the sons of the free states would not have been the holders, and, proverbially, the hardest masters of slaves; the sons of the free states would not have connived at the extension of slavery, in our national body; the sons of the free states would not, as they do, trade the souls and bodies of men as an equivalent to money, in their mercantile dealings. There are multitudes of slaves temporarily owned, and sold again, by merchants in northern cities; and shall the whole guilt or obloquy of slavery fall only on the South?

Northern men, northern mothers, northern Christians, have something more to do than denounce their brethren at the South; they have to look to the evil among themselves.

But, what can any individual do? Of that, every individual can judge. There is one thing that every individual can do,—they can see to it they *they feel right.* An atmosphere of sympathetic influence encircles every human being; and the man or woman who *feels* strongly, healthily and justly, on the great interests of humanity, is a constant benefactor to the human race. See, then, to your sympathies in this matter! Are they in harmony with the sympathies of Christ? or are they swayed and perverted by the sophistries of worldly policy?

Christian men and women of the North! still further,—you have another power; you can *pray!* Do you believe in prayer? or has it become an indistinct apostolic tradition? You pray for the heathen abroad; pray also for the heathen at home. And pray for those distressed Christians whose whole chance of religious improvement is an accident of trade and sale; from whom any adherence to the morals of Christianity is, in many cases, an impossibility, unless they have given them, from above, the courage and grace of martyrdom.

But, still more. On the shores of our free states are emerging the poor, shattered, broken remnants of families,—men and women, escaped, by miraculous providences from the surges of slavery,—feeble in knowledge, and, in many cases, infirm in moral constitution, from a system which confounds and confuses every principle of Christianity and morality. They come to seek a refuge among you; they come to seek education, knowledge, Christianity.

What do you owe to these poor unfortunates, oh Christians? Does not every American Christian owe to the African race some effort at reparation for the wrongs that the American nation has brought upon them? Shall the doors of churches and school-houses be shut upon them? Shall states arise and shake them out? Shall the church of Christ hear in silence the taunt that is thrown at them, and shrink away from the helpless hand that they stretch out; and, by her silence, encourage the cruelty that would chase them from our borders? If it must be so, it will be a mournful spectacle. If it must be so, the country will have reason to tremble, when it remembers that the fate of nations is in the hands of One who is very pitiful, and of tender compassion.

～～～

This is an age of the world when nations are trembling and convulsed. A mighty influence is abroad, surging and heaving the world, as with an earthquake. And is America safe? Every nation that carries in its bosom great and unredressed injustice has in it the elements of this last convulsion.

For what is this mighty influence thus rousing in all nations and languages those groanings that cannot be uttered, for man's freedom and equality?

O, Church of Christ, read the signs of the times! Is not this power the spirit of HIM whose kingdom is yet to come, and whose will to be done on earth as it is in heaven?

But who may abide the day of his appearing? "for that day shall burn as an oven: and he shall appear as a swift witness against those that oppress the hireling in his wages, the widow and the fatherless, and that *turn aside the stranger in his right:* and he shall break in pieces the oppressor."

Are not these dread words for a nation bearing in her bosom so mighty an injustice? Christians! every time that you pray that the kingdom of Christ may come can you forget that prophecy associates, in dread fellowship, the *day of vengeance* with the year of his redeemed?

A day of grace is yet held out to us. Both North and South have been guilty before God; and the *Christian church* has a heavy account to answer. Not by combining together, to protect injustice and cruelty, and making a common capital of sin, is this Union to be saved,—but by repentance, justice and mercy; for, not surer is the eternal law by which the millstone sinks in the ocean, than that stronger law, by which injustice and cruelty shall bring on nations the wrath of Almighty God!

～～～～～～～～～～～～～～～
Black American Folksongs

The folk songs of the black South are a part of the heritage of all Americans. The origins and significance of this music are much disputed. Some scholars say that verbal, rhythmic, and musical indications point to a primarily African origin, while others believe that parallels with the spirituals and folk music of white Americans reflect the adaptation of indigenous as well as imported forms. Some insist that the songs were inspired primarily by religious feelings, and others see them as protest songs, or at least, in the words of W. E. B. DuBois, "sorrow songs."

There is equal disagreement about the manner in which they were composed. They may have come out of churches led in worship by a singing preacher who would supply lines of song to which the congregation responded. They may have been created and transmitted (especially after the Emancipation) by itinerant black musicians. In any case, it is clear that many of these songs were widely known in slave quarters throughout the South. When they passed from the slaves to their white masters and finally to the American people as a whole, they carried the stamp of the poetic, religious, and musical genius of black America. The selections which follow speak eloquently of courage and humor in a time of sorrow, and of joyous faith in the midst of tribulations.

Dere's No Hidin' Place Down Dere

Dere's no hidin' place down dere,
Dere's no hidin' place down dere.
Oh I went to de rock to hide my face,
De rock cried out. "No hidin' place,
Dere's no hidin' place down dere."

Oh de rock cried, "I'm burnin' too."
Oh de rock cried, "I'm burnin' too."
Oh de rock cried, "I'm burnin' too,
I want to go to hebben as well as you,
Dere's no hidin' place down dere."

Oh de sinner man he gambled an' fell,
Oh de sinner man he gambled an' fell,
Oh de sinner man gambled, he
    gambled an' fell,
He wanted to go to hebben, but he
    had to go to hell,
Dere's no hidin' place down dere.

Joshua Fit de Battle ob Jerico

Joshua fit de battle ob Jerico,
Jerico, Jerico,
Joshua fit de battle ob Jerico,
An' de walls come tumblin' down.

You may talk about yo' king ob
    Gideon,
You may talk about yo' man ob Saul,
Dere's none like good ole Joshua!
At de battle ob Jerico.

Up to de walls ob Jerico
He marched with spear in han'.
"Go blow dem ram horns," Joshua
    cried,
"Kase de battle am in my han'."

Den de lam' ram sheep horns begin
    to blow,
Trumpets begin to soun'
Joshua commanded de chillen to
    shout,
An' de walls come tumblin' down.

Dat mornin', Joshua fit de battle ob
    Jerico,
Jerico, Jerico,
Joshua fit de battle ob Jerico,
An' de walls come tumblin' down.

Swing Low, Sweet Chariot

Swing low, sweet chariot, comin' fer to
    carry me home.
Swing low, sweet chariot, comin' fer to
    carry me home.

I looked over Jordan, an' what did I
    see,

Comin' fer to carry me home?
A band of angels comin' after me,
Comin' fer to carry me home.
Swing low, etc.

If you get-a dere befo' I do,
Comin' fer to carry me home,
Tell all my friends I'm comin' too,
Comin' fer to carry me home.

Swing low, etc.

Go Down, Moses

Go down, Moses, way down in Egypt
    land,
Tell ole Pharaoh, to let my people go.

When Israel was in Egypt's land:
Let my people go.
Oppressed so hard they could not
    stand,
Let my people go.

Go down, Moses, etc.

"Thus spoke the Lord," bold Moses
    said;
Let my people go.
If not I'll smite your first-born dead.
Let my people go.

Go down, Moses, etc.

I Know Moonrise

I know moonrise, I know starrise,
Lay dis body down.

I walk in de moonlight, I walk in de
    starlight,
To lay dis body down.

I walk in de graveyard, I walk through
    de graveyard,
To lay dis body down.
I'll lie in de grave and stretch out my
    arms;
Lay dis body down.

I go to de judgment in de evenin' of
    de day,
When I lay dis body down;
And my soul and yore soul will meet
    in de day
When I lay dis body down.

Run, Nigger, Run

Do, please, marster, don't ketch me,
Ketch dat nigger behin' dat tree;
He stole money en I stole none,
Put him in the calaboose des for fun!
Chorus:
    Oh, run nigger, run! de patter-roller
        ketch you.
    Run, nigger, run! hit's almos' day!
    Oh, run, nigger, run! de patter-roller
        ketch you.
    Run, nigger, run! hit's almos' day!

Some folks say dat a nigger won't steal,
But I kotch one in my corn-fiel';
He run ter de eas', he run ter de wes',
He run he head in a hornet nes'!

De sun am set, dis nigger am free;
De yaller gals he goes to see;
I heard a man cry, "Run, doggone
    you,"

Run, nigger, run, patter-roller ketch
    you.

Wid eyes wide open and head hangin'
    down,
Like de rabbit before de houn',
Dis nigger streak it for de pasture;
Nigger run fast, white man run faster.

And ober de fence as slick as a eel
Dis nigger jumped all but his heel;
De white man ketch dat fast, you see,
And tied it tight around' de tree.

Dis nigger heard dat old whip crack,ko
But nebber stopped fur to look back;
I started home as straight as a bee
And left my heel tied aroun' de tree.

My ol' Miss, he prommus me
Dat when she died, she set me free;
But she done dead dis many year ago,
en yer I'm hoein' de same ol' row!

I'm a-hoein' across, I'm a-hoein' aroun',
I'm a'clean' up some mo' new groun'.
Whar I lif' so hard, I lif' so free,
Dat my sins rise up in front er me!

But some er dese days my time will
    come,
I'll year dat bugle, I'll year dat drum,
I'll see dem armies a-marchin' along,
I'll lif' my head en jine der song—
I'll dine no mo' behin' dat tree,
W'en de angels flock fer to wait on
    me!

Jump, Jim Crow

Come listen all you gals and boys,
Ise just from Tuckyhoe,

I'm goin' to sing a little song,
My name's Jim Crow.

Chorus:
    Wheel about and turn about
    And do jis' so
    Ebry time I wheel about
    I jump Jim Crow.

I went down to de river,
I didn't mean to stay,
But dere I saw so many gals
I couldn't get away.

And arter I been dere awhile
I t'ought I push my boat;
But I tumbled in de river
An' I find myself afloat.
I git upon a flat boat
I cotch de Uncle Sam;
Den I went to see de place where
Dey killed de Packenham.

An' den I go to Orleans
An' feel so full of fight
Dey put me in de calaboose
An' keep me dere all night.

When I got out I hit a man.
His name I now forgot:
But dere was noting left of him
'Cept a little grease spot.

Henry David Thoreau
(1817–1862)

Few Americans have been so receptive
to the spiritual possibilities of the
American environment or so convinced

of man's need for regeneration as Henry David Thoreau. Although he used the imagery and language of Nature rather than of orthodox Christianity, Thoreau was no less certain than the Puritans before him that man must be reborn in order to become whole and that man's rebirth depends on recovering a true relation with the source and energies of life itself. But Thoreau differed from the Puritans in his belief that the source and energies of life are not transcendent *above,* but wholly immanent *within* the natural order, and that every individual, and not just the elect, can lay claim to them.

These two chapters from *Walden* describe the moral and religious project that Thoreau set for himself in withdrawing temporarily from the society of Concord and exploring the solitude of life in the woods beside Walden Pond. In "Where I Lived, and What I Lived For," Thoreau describes the nature of his quest as a kind of inverted spiritual odyssey which attempts to negotiate a transcendence downward "through the mud and slush of opinion, and prejudice, and tradition, . . . till we come to a hard bottom and rocks in place, which we can call *reality,* and say, This is, and no mistake." In the "Conclusion," he looks back on his religious experiment in "home cosmography" and tries to extrapolate from the lessons he has learned along the way.

From *Walden; or, Life in the Woods* (1854)

Where I Lived, and What I Lived For

. . . The present was my next experiment of this kind, which I purpose to describe more at length; for convenience, putting the experience of two years into one. As I have said, I do not propose to write an ode to dejection, but to brag as lustily as chanticleer in the morning, standing on this roost, if only to wake my neighbors up.

When first I took up my abode in the woods, that is, began to spend my nights as well as my days there, which, by accident, was on Independence day, or the fourth of July, 1845, my house was not finished for winter, but was merely a defence against the rain, without plastering or chimney, the walls being of rough weather-stained boards, with wide chinks, which made it cool at night. The upright white hewn studs and freshly planed door and window casings gave it a clean and airy look, especially in the morning, when its timbers were saturated with dew, so that I fancied that by noon some sweet gum would exude from them. To my imagination it retained throughout the day more or less of this auroral character, reminding me of a certain house on a mountain which I had visited the year before. This was an airy and unplastered cabin, fit to entertain a travelling god, and where a goddess might trail her garments. The winds which passed over my dwelling were such as sweep over the ridges of mountains, bearing the broken strains, or celestial parts only, of terrestrial music. The morning wind forever blows, the poem of creation is uninterrupted; but few are the ears that hear it. Olympus is but the outside of the earth every where.

The only house I had been the owner of before, if I except a boat, was a tent, which I used occasionally when making excursions in the summer, and this is still rolled up in my garret; but the boat, after passing from hand to hand, has gone down the stream of time. With this more substantial shelter about me, I had made some progress toward settling in the world. This frame, so slightly clad, was a sort of crystallization around me, and reacted on the builder. It was suggestive somewhat as a picture in outlines. I did not need to go out doors to take the air, for the atmosphere within had lost none of its freshness. It was not so much within doors as behind a door where I sat, even in the rainiest weather. The Harivansa says, "An abode without birds is like a meat without seasoning." Such was not my abode, for I found myself suddenly neighbor to the birds; not by having imprisoned one, but having caged myself near them. I was not only nearer to some of those which commonly frequent the garden and the orchard, but to those wilder and more thrilling songsters of the forest which never, or rarely, serenade a villager,—the woodthrush, the veery, the scarlet tanager, the field-sparrow, the whippoorwill, and many others.

I was seated by the shore of a small pond, about a mile and a half south of the village of Concord and somewhat higher than it, in the midst of an extensive wood between that town and Lincoln, and about two miles south of that our only field known to fame, Concord Battle Ground; but I was so low in the woods that the opposite shore, half a mile off, like the rest, covered with wood, was my most distant horizon. For the first week, whenever I looked out on the pond it impressed me like a tarn high up on the side of a mountain, its bottom far above the surface of other lakes, and, as the sun arose, I saw it throwing off its nightly clothing of mist, and here and there, by degrees, its soft ripples or its smooth reflecting surface was revealed, while the mists, like ghosts, were stealthily withdrawing in every direction into the woods, as at the breaking up of some nocturnal conventicle. The very dew seemed to hang upon the trees later into the day than usual, as on the sides of mountains.

This small lake was of most value as a neighbor in the intervals of a gentle rain storm in August, when, both air and water being perfectly still, but the sky overcast, mid-afternoon had all the serenity of evening, and the wood-thrush sang around, and was heard from shore to shore. A lake like this is never smoother than at such a time; and the clear portion of the air above it being shallow and darkened by clouds, the water, full of light and reflections, becomes a lower heaven itself so much the more important. From a hill top near by, where the wood had been recently cut off, there was a pleasing vista southward across the pond, through a wide indentation in the hills which form the shore there, where their opposite sides sloping toward each other suggested a stream flowing out in that direction through a wooded valley, but stream there was none. That way I looked between and over the near green hills to some distant and higher ones in the horizon, tinged with blue. Indeed, by standing on tiptoe I could catch a glimpse of some of the peaks of the still bluer and more distant mountain ranges in the north-west, those true-blue coins from heaven's own mint, and also of some portion of the village. But in other directions, even from this point, I could not see over or beyond the woods which surrounded me. It is well to have some water in your neighborhood, to give buoyancy to and float the earth. One value even of the smallest well is, that when you look into it you see that earth is not continent but insular. This is important as that it keeps butter cool. When I looked across the pond from this peak toward the Sudbury meadows, which in time of flood I distinguished elevated perhaps by a mirage in their seething valley, like a coin in a basin, all the earth beyond the pond appeared like a thin crust insulated and floated even by this small sheet of intervening water, and I was reminded that this on which I dwelt was but *dry land.*

Though the view from my door was still more contracted, I did not feel crowded or confined in the least. There was pasture enough for my imagination. The low shrub-oak plateau to which the opposite shore arose, stretched away toward the prairies of the West and the steppes of Tartary, affording ample room for all the roving families of men. "There are none happy in the world but beings who enjoy freely a vast horizon,"—said Damodara, when his herds required new and larger pastures.

Both place and time were changed, and I dwelt nearer to those parts of the universe and to those eras in history which had most attracted me. Where I lived was as far off as many a region viewed nightly by astronomers. We are wont to imagine rare and delectable places in some remote and more celestial corner of the system, behind the constellation of Cassiopeia's Chair, far from noise and disturbance. I discovered that my house actually had its site in such a withdrawn, but forever new and unprofaned, part of the universe. If it were worth the while to settle in those parts near to the Pleiades or the Hyades, to Aldebaran or Altair, then I was really there, or at an equal remoteness from the life which I had left behind, dwindled and twinkling with as fine a ray to my nearest neighbor, and to be seen only in the moonless nights by him. Such was that part of creation where I had squatted;—

> "There was a shepherd that did live,
> And held his thoughts as high
> As were the mounts whereon his flocks
> Did hourly feed him by."

What should we think of the shepherd's life if his flocks always wandered to higher pastures than his thoughts?

Every morning was a cheerful invitation to make my life of equal simplicity, and I may say innocence, with Nature herself. I have been as sincere a worshipper of Aurora as the Greeks. I got up early and bathed in the pond; that was a religious exercise, and one of the best things which I did. They say that characters were engraven on the bathing tub of king Tching-thang to this effect: "Renew thyself completely each day; do it again, and again, and forever again." I can understand that. Morning brings back the heroic ages. I was as much affected by the faint hum of a mosquito making its invisible and unimaginable tour through my apartment at earliest dawn, when I was sitting with door and windows open, as I could be by any trumpet that ever sang of fame. It was Homer's requiem; itself an Iliad and Odyssey in the air, singing its own wrath and wanderings. There was something cosmical about it; a standing advertisement, till forbidden, of the everlasting vigor and fertility of the world. The morning, which is the most memorable season of the day, is the awakening hour. Then there is least somnolence in us; and for an hour, at least, some part of us awakes which slumbers all the rest of the day and night. Little is to be expected of that day, if it can be called a day, to which we are not awakened by our Genius, but by the mechanical nudgings of some servitor, are not awakened by our own newly-acquired force and aspirations from within, accompanied by the undulations of celestial music, instead of factory bells, and a fragrance filling the air—to a higher life than we fell asleep from; and thus the darkness bear its fruit, and prove itself to be good, no less than the light. That man who does not

believe that each day contains an earlier, more sacred, and auroral hour than he has yet profaned, has despaired of life, and is pursuing a descending and darkening way. After a partial cessation of his sensuous life, the soul of man or its organs rather, are reinvigorated each day, and his Genius tries again what noble life it can make. All memorable events, I should say, transpire in morning time and in a morning atomsphere. The Vedas say, "All intelligences awake with the morning." Poetry and art, and the fairest and most memorable of the actions of men, date from such an hour. All poets and heroes, like Memnon, are the children of Aurora, and emit their music at sunrise. To him whose elastic and vigorous thought keeps pace with the sun, the day is a perpetual morning. It matters not what the clocks say or the attitudes and labors of men. Morning is when I am awake and there is a dawn in me. Moral reform is the effort to throw off sleep. Why is it that men give so poor an account of their day if they have not been slumbering? They are not such poor calculators. If they had not been overcome with drowsiness they would have performed something. The millions are awake enough for physical labor; but only one in a million is awake enough for effective intellectual exertion, only one in a hundred millions to a poetic or divine life. To be awake is to be alive. I have never yet met a man who was quite awake. How could I have looked him in the face?

We must learn to reawaken and keep ourselves awake, not by mechanical aids, but by an infinite expectation of the dawn, which does not forsake us in our soundest sleep. I know of no more encouraging fact than the unquestionable ability of man to elevate his life by a conscious endeavor. It is something to be able to paint a particular picture, or to carve a statue, and so to make a few objects beautiful; but it is far more glorious to carve and paint the very atmosphere and medium through which we look, which morally we can do. To affect the quality of the day, that is the highest of arts. Every man is tasked to make his life, even in its details, worthy of the contemplation of his most elevated and critical hour. If we refused, or rather used up, such paltry information as we get, the oracles would distinctly inform us how this might be done.

I went to the woods because I wished to live deliberately, to front only the essential facts of life, and see if I could not learn what it had to teach, and not, when I came to die, discover that I had not lived. I did not wish to live what was not life, living is so dear; nor did I wish to practise resignation, unless it was quite necessary. I wanted to live deep and suck out all the marrow of life, to live so sturdily and Spartan-like as to put to rout all that was not life, to cut a broad swath and shave close, to drive life into a corner, and reduce it to its lowest terms, and, if it proved to be mean, why then to get the whole and genuine meanness of it, and publish its meanness to the world; or if it were sublime, to know it by experience, and be able to give a true account of it in my next excursion. For most men, it appears to me, are in a strange uncertainty about it, whether it is of the devil or of God, and have *somewhat hastily* concluded that it is the chief end of man here to "glorify God and enjoy him forever."

Still we live meanly, like ants; though the fable tells us that we were long ago changed into men; like pygmies we fight with cranes; it is error upon error, and clout upon clout, and our best virtue has for its occasion a superfluous and evitable wretchedness. Our life is frittered away by detail. An honest man has hardly need to count more than his ten fingers, or in extreme cases he may add his ten toes, and lump the rest. Simplicity, simplicity, simplicity! I say, let your affairs be as two or three, and not a hundred or a thousand; instead of a million count half a dozen, and keep your accounts on your thumb nail. In the midst of this chopping sea of civilized life, such are the clouds and storms and quicksands and thousand-and-one items to be allowed for, that a man has to live, if he would not founder and go to the bottom and not make his port at all, by dead reckoning, and he must be a great calculator indeed who succeeds. Simplify, simplify. Instead of three meals a day, if it be necessary eat but one; instead of a hundred dishes, five; and reduce other things in proportion. Our life is like a German Confederacy, made up of petty states, with its boundary forever fluctuating, so that even a German cannot tell you how it is bounded at any moment. The nation itself, with all its so called internal improvements, which, by the way, are all external and superficial, is just such an unwieldy and overgrown establishment, cluttered with furniture and tripped up by its own traps, ruined by luxury and heedless expense, by want of calculation and a worthy aim, as the million households in the land; and the only cure for it as for them is in a rigid economy, a stern and more than Spartan simplicity of life and elevation of purpose. It lives too fast. Men think that it is essential that the *Nation* have commerce, and export ice, and talk through a telegraph, and ride thirty miles an hour, without a doubt, whether *they* do or not; but whether we should live like baboons or like men, is a little uncertain. If we do not get out sleepers, and forge rails, and devote days and nights to the work, but go to tinkering upon our *lives* to improve *them,* who will build railroads? And if railroads are not built, how shall we get to heaven in season? But if we stay at home and mind our business, who will want railroads? We do not ride on the railroad; it rides upon us. Did you ever think what those sleepers are that underlie the railroad? Each one is a man, an Irishman, or a Yankee man. The rails are laid on them, and they are covered with sand, and the cars run smoothly over them. They are sound sleepers, I assure you. And every few years a new lot is laid down and run over; so that, if some have the pleasure of riding on a rail, others have the misfortune to be ridden upon. And when they run over a man that is walking in his sleep, a supernumerary sleeper in the wrong position, and wake him up, they suddenly stop the cars, and make a hue and cry about it, as if this were an exception. I am glad to know that it takes a gang of men for every five miles to keep the sleepers down and level in their beds as it is, for this is a sign that they may sometime get up again.

Why should we live with such hurry and waste of life? We are determined to be starved before we are hungry. Men say that a stitch in time saves nine, and so they take a thousand stitches to-day to save nine to-morrow. As for *work,* we haven't any of any consequence. We have the Saint Vitus' dance, and cannot possibly keep our heads still. If I should only give a few pulls at the parish bell-rope, as for a fire, that is, without setting the bell, there is hardly a man on his farm in the outskirts of Concord, notwithstanding that press of engagements which was his excuse so many times this morning, nor a boy, nor a woman, I might almost say, but would forsake all and follow that sound, not mainly to save property from the flames, but, if we will confess the truth, much more to see it burn, since burn it must, and we, be it known, did not set it on fire,—or to see it put out, and have a hand in it, if that is done as handsomely; yes, even if it were the parish church itself. Hardly a man takes a half hour's nap after dinner, but when he wakes he holds up his head and asks, "What's the news?" as if the rest of mankind had stood his sentinels. Some give directions to be waked every half hour, doubtless for no other purpose; and then, to pay for it, they tell what they have dreamed. After a night's sleep the news is as indispensable as the breakfast. "Pray tell me any thing new that has happened to a man any where on this globe,"—and he reads it over his coffee and rolls, that a man has had his eyes gouged out this morning on the Wachito River; never dreaming the while that he lives in the dark unfathomed mammoth cave of this world, and has but the rudiment of an eye himself.

For my part, I could easily do without the post-office. I think that there are very few important communications made through it. To speak critically, I never received more than one or two letters in my life—I wrote this some years ago—that were worth the postage. The penny-post is, commonly, an institution through which you seriously offer a man that penny for his thoughts which is so often safely offered in jest. And I am sure that I never read any memorable news in a newspaper. If we read of one man robbed, or murdered, or killed by accident, or one house burned, or one vessel wrecked, or one steamboat blown up, or one cow run over on the Western Railroad, or one mad dog killed, or one lot of grasshoppers in the winter,—we never need read of another. One is enough. If you are acquainted with the principle, what do you care for a myriad instances and applications? To a philosopher all *news,* as it is called, is gossip, and they who edit and read it are old women over their tea. Yet not a few are greedy after this gossip. There was such a rush, as I hear, the other day at one of the offices to learn the foreign news by the last arrival, that several large squares of plate glass belonging to the establishment were broken by the pressure,— news which I seriously think a ready wit might write a twelvemonth or twelve years beforehand with sufficient accuracy. As for Spain, for instance, if you

know how to throw in Don Carlos and the Infanta, and Don Pedro and Seville and Granada, from time to time in the right proportions,—they may have changed the names a little since I saw the papers,—and serve up a bull-fight when other entertainments fail, it will be true to the letter, and give us as good an idea of the exact state or ruin of things in Spain as the most succinct and lucid ·reports under this head in the newspapers; and as for England, almost the last significant scrap of news from that quarter was the revolution of 1649; and if you have learned the history of her crops for an average year, you never need attend to that thing again, unless your speculations are of a merely pecuniary character. If one may judge who rarely looks into the newspapers, nothing new does ever happen in foreign parts, a French revolution not excepted.

What news! how much more important to know what that is which was never old! "Kieou-he-yu (great dignitary of the state of Wei) sent a man to Khoung-tseu to know his news. Khoung-tseu caused the messenger to be seated near him, and questioned him in these terms: What is your master doing? The messenger answered with respect: My master desires to diminish the number of his faults, but he cannot come to the end of them. The messenger being gone, the philosopher remarked: What a worthy messenger! What a worthy messenger!" The preacher, instead of vexing the ears of drowsy farmers on their day of rest at the end of the week,—for Sunday is the fit conclusion of an ill spent week, and not the fresh and brave beginning of a new one,—with this one other draggle-tail of a sermon, should shout with thundering voice,—"Pause! Avast! Why so seeming fast, but deadly slow?"

Shams and delusions are esteemed for soundest truths, while reality is fabulous. If men would steadily observe realities only, and not allow themselves to be deluded, life, to compare it with such things as we know, would be like a fairy tale and the Arabian Nights' Entertainments. If we respected only what is inevitable and has a right to be, music and poetry would resound along the streets. When we are unhurried and wise, we perceive that only great and worthy things have any permanent and absolute existence,—that petty fears and petty pleasures are but the shadow of the reality. This is always exhilarating and sublime. By closing the eyes and slumbering, and consenting to be deceived by shows, men establish and confirm their daily life of routine and habit every where, which still is built on purely illusory foundations. Children, who play life, discern its true law and relations more clearly than men, who fail to live it worthily, but who think they are wiser by experience, that is, by failure. I have read in a Hindoo book, that "there was a king's son, who, being expelled in infancy from his native city, was brought up by a forester, and, growing up to maturity in that state, imagined himself to belong to the barbarous race with which he lived. One of his father's ministers having discovered him, revealed to him what he was, and the misconception of his character was removed, and he knew himself to be a prince. So soul," continues the Hindoo philosopher, "from the circumstances in which it is placed, mistakes its own character, until the truth is revealed to it by some holy teacher, and then it knows itself to be *Brahme*." I perceive that we inhabitants of New England live this mean life that we do because our vision does not penetrate the surface of things. We think that that *is* which *appears* to be. If a man should walk through this town and see only the reality, where, think you, would the "Mill-dam" go to? If he should give us an account of the realities he beheld there, we should not recognize the place in his description. Look at a meeting-house, or a court-house, or a jail, or a shop, or a dwelling-house, and say what that thing really is before a true gaze, and they would all go to pieces in your account of them. Men esteem truth remote, in the outskirts of the system, behind the farthest star, before Adam and after the last man. In eternity there is indeed something true and sublime. But all these times and places and occasions are now and here. God himself culminates in the present moment, and will never be more divine in the lapse of all the ages. And we are enabled to apprehend at all what is sublime and noble only by the perpetual instilling and drenching of the reality that surrounds us. The universe constantly and obediently answers to our conceptions; whether we travel fast or slow, the track is laid for us. Let us spend our lives in conceiving then. The poet or the artist never yet had so fair and noble a design but some of his posterity at least could accomplish it.

Let us spend one day as deliberately as Nature, and not be thrown off the track by every nutshell and mosquito's wing that falls on the rails. Let us rise early and fast, or break fast, gently and without perturbation; let company come and let company go, let the bells ring and the children cry,—determined to make a day of it. Why should we knock under and go with the stream? Let us not be upset and overwhelmed in that terrible rapid and whirlpool called a dinner, situated in the meridian shallows. Weather this danger and you are safe, for the rest of the way is down hill. With unrelaxed nerves, with morning vigor, sail by it, looking another way, tied to the mast like Ulysses. If the engine whistles, let it whistle till it is hoarse for its pains. If the bell rings, why should we run? We will consider what kind of music they are like. Let us settle ourselves, and work and wedge our feet downward through the mud and slush of opinion, and prejudice, and tradition, and delusion, and appearance, that alluvion which covers the globe, through Paris and London, through New York and Boston and Concord, through church and state, through poetry and philosophy and religion, till we come to a hard bottom and rocks in place, which we can call *reality,* and say, This is, and no mistake; and then begin, having a *point d'appui,* below freshet and frost and fire, a place where you might found a wall or a state, or set a lamp-post safely, or perhaps a gauge, not a Nilometer, but a realometer, that future ages might know how deep a freshet of shams and appearances had gathered from time to time. If you stand right fronting and face to face to a fact, you will see the sun glimmer on both its surfaces, as if it were a cimeter, and feel its sweet edge dividing you through the heart and marrow, and so you will happily conclude your mortal career. Be it life or death, we crave only reality. If we are really dying, let us hear the rattle in our throats and feel cold in the extremities; if we are alive, let us go about our business.

Time is but the stream I go a-fishing in. I drink at it; but while I drink I see the sandy bottom and detect how shallow it is. Its thin current slides away, but eternity remains. I would drink deeper; fish in the sky, whose bottom is pebbly with stars. I cannot count one. I know not the first letter of the alphabet. I have always been regretting that I was not as wise as the day I was born. The intellect is a cleaver; it discerns and rifts its way into the secret of things. I do not wish to be any more busy with my hands than is necessary. My head is hands and feet. I feel all my best faculties concentrated in it. My instinct tells me that my head is an organ for burrowing, as some creatures use their snout and fore-paws, and with it I would mine and burrow my way through these hills. I think that the richest vein is somewhere hereabouts; so by the divining rod and thin rising vapors I judge; and here I will begin to mine.

Conclusion

To the sick the doctors wisely recommend a change of air and scenery. Thank Heaven, here is not all the world. The buck-eye does not grow in New England, and the mocking-bird is rarely heard here. The wild-goose is more of a cosmopolite than we; he breaks his fast in Canada, takes a luncheon in the Ohio, and plumes himself for the night in a southern bayou. Even the bison, to some extent, keeps pace with the seasons, cropping the pastures of the Colorado only till a greener and sweeter grass awaits him by the Yellowstone. Yet we think that if rail-fences are pulled down, and stone-walls piled up on our farms, bounds are henceforth set to our lives and our fates decided. If you are chosen town-clerk, forsooth, you cannot go to Tierra del Fuego this summer: but you may go to the land of infernal fire nevertheless. The universe is wider than our views of it.

Yet we should oftener look over the tafferel of our craft, like curious passengers, and not make the voyage like stupid sailors picking oakum. The other side of the globe is but the home of our correspondent. Our voyageing is only great-circle sailing, and the doctors prescribe for diseases of the skin merely. One hastens to Southern Africa to chase the giraffe; but surely that is not the game he would be after. How long, pray, would a man hunt giraffes if he could? Snipes and woodcocks also may afford rare sport; but I trust it would be nobler game to shoot one's self.—

"Direct your eye right inward, and you'll
    find
A thousand regions in your mind
Yet undiscovered. Travel them, and be
Expert in home-cosmography."

What does Africa,—what does the West stand for? Is not our own interior white on the chart? black though it may prove, like the coast, when discovered. Is it the source of the Nile, or the Niger, or the Mississippi, or a North-West Passage around this continent, that we would find? Are these the problems which most concern mankind? Is Franklin the only man who is lost, that his wife should be so earnest to find him? Does Mr. Grinnell know where he himself is? Be rather the Mungo Park, the Lewis and Clarke and Frobisher, of your own streams and oceans; explore your own higher latitudes,—with shiploads of preserved meats to support you, if they be necessary; and pile the empty cans sky-high for a sign. Were preserved meats invented to preserve meat merely? Nay, be a Columbus to whole new continents and worlds within you, opening new channels, not of trade, but of thought. Every man is the lord of a realm beside which the earthly empire of the Czar is but a petty state, a hummock left by the ice. Yet some can be patriotic who have no *self*-respect, and sacrifice the greater to the less. They love the soil which makes their graves, but have no sympathy with the spirit which may still animate their clay. Patriotism is a maggot in their heads. What was the meaning of that South-Sea Exploring Expedition, with all its parade and expense, but an indirect recognition of the fact, that there are continents and seas in the moral world, to which every man is an isthmus or an inlet, yet unexplored by him, but that it is easier to sail many thousand miles through cold and storm and cannibals, in a government ship, with five hundred men and boys to assist one, than it is to explore the private sea, the Atlantic and Pacific Ocean of one's being alone.—

"Erret, et extremos alter scrutetur Iberos.
Plus habet hic vitae, plus habet ille viae."

Let them wander and scrutinize the
     outlandish Australians.
I have more of God, they more of the
     road.

It is not worth the while to go round the world to count the cats in Zanzibar. Yet do this even till you can do better, and you may perhaps find some "Symmes' Hole" by which to get at the inside at last. England and France, Spain and Portugal, Gold Coast and Slave Coast, all front on this private sea; but no bark from them has ventured out of sight of land, though it is without doubt the direct way to India. If you would learn to speak all tongues and conform to the customs of all nations, if you would travel farther than all travellers, be naturalized in all climes, and cause the Sphinx to dash her head against a stone, even obey the precept of the old philosopher, and Explore thyself. Herein are demanded the eye and the nerve. Only the defeated and deserters go to the wars, cowards that run away and enlist. Start now on that farthest western way, which does not pause at the Mississippi or the Pacific, nor conduct toward a worn-out China or Japan, but leads on direct a tangent to this sphere, summer and winter, day and night, sun down, moon down, and at last earth down too.

It is said that Mirabeau took to highway robbery "to ascertain what degree of resolution was necessary in order to place one's self in formal opposition to the most sacred laws of society." He declared that "a soldier who fights in the ranks does not require half so much courage as a foot-pad,"—"that honor and religion have never stood in the way of a well-considered and a firm resolve." This was manly, as the world goes; and yet it was idle, if not desperate. A saner man would have found himself often enough "in formal opposition" to what are deemed "the most sacred laws of society," through obedience to yet more sacred laws, and so have tested his resolution without going out of his way. It is not for a man to put himself in such an attitude to society, but to maintain himself in whatever attitude he find himself through obedience to the laws of his being, which will never be one of opposition to a just government, if he should chance to meet with such.

I left the woods for as good a reason as I went there. Perhaps it seemed to me that I had several more lives to live, and could not spare any more time for that one. It is remarkable how easily and insensibly we fall into a particular route, and make a beaten track for ourselves. I had not lived there a week before my feet wore a path from my door to the pond-side; and though it is five or six years since I trod it, it is still quite distinct. It is true, I fear that others may have fallen into it, and so helped to keep it open. The surface of the earth is soft and impressible by the feet of men: and so with the paths which the mind travels. How worn and dusty, then, must be the highways of the world, how deep the ruts of tradition and conformity! I did not wish to take a cabin passage, but rather to go before the mast and on the deck of the world, for there I could best see the moonlight amid the mountains. I do not wish to go below now.

I learned this, at least, by my experiment; that if one advances confidently in the direction of his dreams, and endeavors to live the life which he has imagined, he will meet with a success unexpected in common hours. He will put some things behind, will pass an invisible boundary; new, universal, and more liberal laws will begin to establish themselves around and within him; or the old laws be expanded, and interpreted in his favor in a more liberal sense, and he will live with the license of a higher order of beings. In proportion as he simplifies his life, the laws of the universe will appear less complex, and solitude will not be solitude, nor poverty poverty, nor weakness weakness. If you have built castles in the air, your work need not be lost; that is where they should be. Now put the foundations under them.

It is a ridiculous demand which England and America make, that you shall speak so that they can understand you. Neither men nor toad-stools grow so. As if that were important, and there were not enough to understand you without them. As if Nature could support but one order of understandings, could not sustain birds as well as quadrupeds, flying as well as creeping things, and *hush* and *who*, which Bright can understand, were the best English. As if there were safety in stupidity alone. I fear chiefly lest my expression may not be *extra-vagant* enough, may not wander far enough beyond the narrow limits of my daily experience, so as to be ade-

quate to the truth of which I have been convinced. *Extra vagance!* it depends on how you are yarded. The migrating buffalo, which seeks new pastures in another latitude, is not extravagant like the cow which kicks over the pail, leaps the cow-yard fence, and runs after her calf, in milking time. I desire to speak somewhere *without* bounds; like a man in a waking moment, to men in their waking moments; for I am convinced that I cannot exaggerate enough even to lay the foundation of a true expression. Who that has heard a strain of music feared then lest he should speak extravagantly any more forever? In view of the future or possible, we should live quite laxly and undefined in front, our outlines dim and misty on that side; as our shadows reveal an insensible perspiration toward the sun. The volatile truth of our words should continually betray the inadequacy of the residual statement. Their truth is instantly *translated;* its literal monument alone remains. The words which express our faith and piety are not definite; yet they are significant and fragrant like frankincense to superior natures.

Why level downward to our dullest perception always, and praise that as common sense? The commonest sense is the sense of men asleep, which they express by snoring. Sometimes we are inclined to class those who are once-and-a-half witted with the half-witted, because we appreciate only a third part of their wit. Some would find fault with the morning-red, if they ever got up early enough. "They pretend," as I hear, "that the verses of Kabir have four different senses; illusion, spirit, intellect, and the exoteric doctrine of the Vedas;" but in this part of the world it is considered a ground for complaint if a man's writings admit of more than one interpretation. While England endeavors to cure the potato-rot, will not any endeavor to cure the brain-rot, which prevails so much more widely and fatally?

I do not suppose that I have attained to obscurity, but I should be proud if no more fatal fault were found with my pages on this score than was found with the Walden ice. Southern customers objected to its blue color, which is the evidence of its purity, as if it were muddy, and preferred the Cambridge ice, which is white, but tastes of weeds. The purity men love is like the mists which envelop the earth, and not like the azure ether beyond.

Some are dinning in our ears that we Americans, and moderns generally, are intellectual dwarfs compared with the ancients, or even the Elizabethan men. But what is that to the purpose? A living dog is better than a dead lion. Shall a man go and hang himself because he belongs to the race of pygmies, and not be the biggest pygmy that he can? Let every one mind his own business, and endeavor to be what he was made.

Why should we be in such desperate haste to succeed, and in such desperate enterprises? If a man does not keep pace with his companions, perhaps it is because he hears a different drummer. Let him step to the music which he hears, however measured or far away. It is not important that he should mature as soon as an apple-tree or an oak. Shall he turn his spring into summer? If the condition of things which we were made for is not yet, what were any reality which we can substitute? We will not be shipwrecked on a vain reality. Shall we with pains erect a heaven of blue glass over ourselves, though when it is done we shall be sure to gaze still at the true ethereal heaven far above, as if the former were not?

There was an artist in the city of Kouroo who was disposed to strive after perfection. One day it came into his mind to make a staff. Having considered that in an imperfect work time is an ingredient, but into a perfect work time does not enter, he said to himself, It shall be perfect in all respects, though I should do nothing else in my life. He proceeded instantly to the forest for wood, being resolved that it should not be made of unsuitable material; and as he searched for and rejected stick after stick, his friends gradually deserted him, for they grew old in their works and died, but he grew not older by a moment. His singleness of purpose and resolution, and his elevated piety, endowed him, without his knowledge, with perennial youth. As he made no compromise with Time, Time kept out of his way, and only sighed at a distance because he could not overcome him. Before he had found a stock in all respects suitable the city of Kouroo was a hoary ruin, and he sat on one of its mounds to peel the stick. Before he had given it the proper shape the dynasty of the Candahars was at an end, and with the point of the stick he wrote the name of the last of that race in the sand, and then resumed his work. By the time he had smoothed and polished the staff Kalpa was no longer the pole-star; and ere he had put on the ferule and the head adorned with precious stones, Brahma had awoke and slumbered many times. But why do I stay to mention these things? When the finishing stroke was put to his work, it suddenly expanded before the eyes of the astonished artist into the fairest of all the creations of Brahma. He had made a new system in making a staff, a world with full and fair proportions; in which, though the old cities and dynasties had passed away, fairer and more glorious ones had taken their places. And now he saw by the heap of shavings still fresh at his feet, that, for him and his work, the former lapse of time had been an illusion, and that no more time had elapsed than is required for a single scintillation from the brain of Brahma to fall on and inflame the tinder of a mortal brain. The material was pure, and his art was pure; how could the result be other than wonderful?

No face which we can give to a matter will stead us so well at last as the truth. This alone wears well. For the most part, we are not where we are, but in a false position. Through an infirmity of our natures, we suppose a case, and put ourselves into it, and hence are in two cases at the same time, and it is doubly difficult to get out. In sane moments we regard only the facts, the case that is. Say what you have to say, not what you ought. Any truth is better than make-believe. Tom Hyde, the tinker, standing on the gallows, was asked if he had anything to say. "Tell the tailors," said he, "to remember to make a knot in their thread before they take the first stitch." His companion's prayer is forgotten.

However mean your life is, meet it and live it; do not shun it and call it hard names. It is not so bad as you are. It looks poorest when you are richest. The fault-finder will find faults even in paradise. Love your life, poor as it is. You may perhaps have some pleasant, thrilling, glorious hours, even in a poor-house. The setting sun is reflected from the windows of the alms-house as brightly as from the rich man's abode; the snow melts before its door as early in the spring. I do not see but a quiet mind may live as contentedly there, and have as cheering thoughts, as in a palace. The town's poor seem to me often to live the most independent lives of any. May be they are simply great enough to receive without misgiving. Most think that they are above being supported by the town; but it oftener happens that they are not above supporting themselves by dishonest means, which should be more disreputable. Cultivate poverty like a garden herb, like sage. Do not trouble yourself much to get new things, whether clothes or friends. Turn the old; return to them. Things do not change, we change. Sell your clothes and keep your thoughts. God will see that you do not want society. If I were confined to a corner of a garret all my days, like a spider, the world would be just as large to me while I had my thoughts about me. The philosopher said: "From an army of three divisions one can take away its general, and put it in disorder; from the man the most abject and vulgar one cannot take away his thought." Do not seek so anxiously to be developed, to subject yourself to many influences to be played on; it is all dissipation. Humility like darkness reveals the heavenly lights. The shadows of poverty and meanness gather around us, "and lo! creation widens to our view." We are often reminded that if there were bestowed on us the wealth of Crœsus, our aims must still be the same, and our means essentially the same. Moreover, if you are restricted in your range by poverty, if you cannot buy books and newspapers, for instance, you are but confined to the most significant and vital experiences; you are compelled to deal with the material which yields the most sugar and the most starch. It is life near the bone where it is sweetest. You are defended from being a trifler. No man loses ever on a lower level by magnanimity on a higher. Superfluous wealth can buy superfluities only. Money is not required to buy one necessary of the soul.

I live in the angle of a leaden wall, into whose composition was poured a little alloy of bell metal. Often, in the repose of mid-day, there reaches my ears a confused *tintinnabulum* from without. It is the noise of my contemporaries. My neighbors tell me of their adventures with famous gentlemen and ladies, what notabilities they met at the dinner-table; but I am no more interested in such things than in the contents of the Daily Times. The interest and the conversation are about costume and manners chiefly; but a goose is a goose still, dress it as you will. They tell me of California and Texas, of England and the Indies, of the Hon. Mr. —— of Georgia or Massachusetts, all transient and fleeting phenomena, till I am ready to leap from their court-yard like the Mameluke bey. I delight to come to my bearings,—not walk in procession with pomp and parade, in a conspicuous place, but to walk even with the Builder of the universe, if I may,—not to live in this restless, nervous, bustling, trivial Nineteenth Century, but stand or sit thoughtfully while it goes by. What are men celebrating? They are all on a committee of arrangements, and hourly expect a speech from somebody. God is only the president of the day, and Webster is his orator. I love to weigh, to settle, to gravitate toward that which most strongly and rightfully attracts me;— not hang by the beam of the scale and try to weigh less,—not suppose a case, but take the case that is; to travel the only path I can, and that on which no power can resist me. It affords me no satisfaction to commence to spring an arch before I have got a solid foundation. Let us not play at kittlybenders. There is a solid bottom every where. We read that the traveller asked the boy if the swamp before him had a hard bottom. The boy replied that it had. But presently the traveller's horse sank in up to the girths, and he observed to the boy, "I thought you said that this bog had a hard bottom." "So it has," answered the latter, "but you have not got half way to it yet." So it is with the bogs and quicksands of society; but he is an old boy that knows it. Only what is thought said or done at a certain rare coincidence is good. I would not be one of those who will foolishly drive a nail into mere lath and plastering; such a deed would keep me awake nights. Give me a hammer, and let me feel for the furrowing. Do not depend on the putty. Drive a nail home and clinch it so faithfully that you can wake up in the night and think of your work with satisfaction,—a work at which you would not be ashamed to invoke the Muse. So will help you God, and so only. Every nail driven should be as another rivet in the machine of the universe, you carrying on the work.

Rather than love, than money, than fame, give me truth. I sat at a table where were rich food and wine in abundance, and obsequious attendance, but sincerity and truth were not; and I went away hungry from the inhospitable board. The hospitality was as cold as the ices. I thought that there was no need of ice to freeze them. They talked to me of the age of the wine and the fame of the vintage; but I thought of an older, a newer, and purer wine, of a more glorious vintage, which they had not got, and could not buy. The style, the house and grounds and "entertainment" pass for nothing with me. I called on the king, but he made me wait in his hall, and conducted like a man incapacitated for hospitality. There was a man in my neighborhood who lived in a hollow tree. His manners were truly regal. I should have done better had I called on him.

How long shall we sit in our porticoes practising idle and musty virtues, which any work would make impertinent? As if one were to begin the day with long-suffering, and hire a man to hoe his potatoes; and in the afternoon go forth to practise Christian meekness and charity with goodness aforethought! Consider the China pride and stagnant self-complacency of mankind. This generation reclines a little to congratulate itself on being the last of an illustrious line; and in Boston and London and Paris and Rome, thinking of its long descent, it speaks of its progress in art and science and literature with satisfaction. There are the Records of the Philosophical Societies, and the public Eulogies of *Great Men!* It is the good Adam contemplating his own virtue. "Yes, we have done great deeds, and sung divine songs, which shall never die,"—that is, as long as *we* can remember them. The learned societies and great men of Assyria,—where are they? What youthful philosophers and experimentalists we are! There is not one of my readers who has yet lived a whole human life. These may be but the spring months in the life of the race. If we have had the seven-years' itch, we have not seen the seventeen-year locust yet in Concord. We are acquainted with a mere pellicle of the globe on which we live. Most have not delved six feet beneath the surface, nor leaped as many above it. We know not where we are. Beside, we are sound asleep nearly half our time. Yet we esteem ourselves wise, and have an established order on the surface. Truly, we are deep thinkers, we are ambitious spirits! As I stand over the insect crawling amid the pine needles on the forest floor, and endeavoring to conceal itself from my sight, and ask myself why it will cherish those humble thoughts, and hide its head from me who might, perhaps, be its benefactor, and impart to its race some cheering information, I am reminded of the greater Benefactor and Intelligence that stands over me the human insect.

There is an incessant influx of novelty into the world, and yet we tolerate incredible dulness. I need only suggest what kind of sermons are still listened to in the most enlightened countries. There are such words as joy and sorrow, but they are only the burden of a psalm, sung with a nasal twang, while we believe in the ordinary and mean. We think that we can change our clothes only. It is said that the British Empire is very large and respectable, and that the United States are a first-rate power. We do not believe that a tide rises and falls behind every man which can float the British Empire like a chip, if he should ever harbor it in his mind. Who knows what sort of seventeen-year locust will next come out of the ground? The government of the world I live in was not framed, like that of Britain, in after-dinner conversations over the wine.

The life in us is like the water in the river. It may rise this year higher than man has ever known it, and flood the parched uplands; even this may be the eventful year, which will drown out all our muskrats. It was not always dry land where we dwell. I see far inland the banks which the stream anciently washed, before science began to record its freshets. Every one has heard the story which has gone the rounds of New England, of a strong and beautiful bug which came out of the dry leaf of an old table of apple-tree wood, which had stood in a farmer's kitchen for sixty years, first in Connecticut, and afterward in Massachusetts,—from an egg deposited in the lving tree many years earlier still, as appeared by counting the annual layers beyond it; which was heard gnawing out for several weeks, hatched perchance by the heat of an urn. Who does not feel his faith in a resurrection and immortality strengthened by hearing of this? Who knows what beautiful and winged life, whose egg has been buried for ages under many concentric layers of woodenness in the dead dry life of society, deposited at first in the alburnum of the green and living tree, which has been gradually converted into the semblance of its well-seasoned tomb,—heard perchance gnawing out now for years by the astonished family of man, as they sat round the festive board,—may unexpectedly come forth from amidst society's most trivial and handselled furniture, to enjoy its perfect summer life at last!

I do not say that John or Jonathan will realize all this; but such is the character of that morrow which mere lapse of time can never make to dawn. The light which puts out our eyes is darkness to us. Only that day dawns to which we are awake. There is more day to dawn. The sun is but a morning star.

Walt Whitman
(1819–1892)

Do I contradict myself?
Very well then I contradict myself,
(I am large, I contain multitudes.)
"Song of Myself"

Walt Whitman responded so directly to Emerson's challenge in *Nature* and "The American Scholar" that he almost seems to have stepped out of Emerson's pages. Here was a poet who wanted to cultivate the prospective rather than the retrospective eye, who was determined to make the relation between the self and the not-self, the Me and the not-Me, his great theme, and who would seek to absorb and embrace all the dense particulars of America in his poems.

The following selections, organized chronologically, reveal the development of Whitman's ideas and the changing personae he adopted to express them. They begin with his translation of Emerson's "infinity of the private man" into the divinity of the poet as the most representative man in the Preface to the 1855 edition of *Leaves of Grass*. Then in successive poems from the bouyant "Song of the Open Road" to the meditative and nearly despondent "A Noiseless, Patient Spider," Whitman tries to realize his dream of spiritual affluence by becoming a man who "confronts all the shows he sees by equivalents out of the stronger wealth of himself." Of the possible inconsistencies within himself as poet and his great diversity of feeling and belief, Whitman wrote,

From *Leaves of Grass* (1855)

Preface

The Americans of all nations at any time upon the earth have probably the fullest poetical nature. The United States themselves are essentially the greatest poem. In the history of the earth hitherto the largest and most stirring appear tame and orderly to their ampler largeness and stir. Here at last is something in the doings of man that corresponds with the broadcast doings of the day and night. Here is not merely a nation but a teeming nation of nations. Here is action untied from strings necessarily blind to particulars and details magnificently moving in vast masses. Here is the hospitality which forever indicates heroes. . . . Here are the roughs and beards and space and ruggedness and nonchalance that the soul loves. Here the performance disdaining the trivial unapproached in the tremendous audacity of its crowds and groupings and the push of its perspective spreads with crampless and flowing breadth and showers its prolific and splendid extravagance. One sees it must indeed own the riches of the summer and winter, and need never be bankrupt while corn grows from the ground or the orchards drop apples or the bays contain fish or men beget children upon women.

❧❧❧

Of all nations the United States with veins full of poetical stuff most need poets and will doubtless have the greatest and use them the greatest. Their Presidents shall not be their common referee so much as their poets shall. Of all mankind the great poet is the equable man. Not in him but off from him things are grotesque or eccentric or fail of their sanity. Nothing out of its place is good and nothing in its place is bad. He bestows on every object or quality its fit proportions neither more nor less. He is the arbiter of the diverse and he is the key. He is the equalizer of his age and land. . . .

The greatest poet hardly knows pettiness or triviality. If he breathes into any thing that was before thought small it dilates with the grandeur and life of the universe. He is a seer . . . he is individual . . . he is complete in himself . . . the others are as good as he, only he sees it and they do not. He is not one of the chorus . . . he does not stop for any regulations . . . he is the president of regulation. What the eyesight does to the rest he does to the rest. Who knows the curious mystery of the eyesight? The other senses corroborate themselves, but this is removed from any proof but its own and foreruns the identities of the spiritual world. A single glance of it mocks all the investigations of man and all the instruments and books of the earth and all reasoning. What is marvellous? what is unlikely? what is impossible or baseless or vague?

after you have once just opened the space of a peach-pit and given audience to far and near and to the sunset and had all things enter with electric swiftness softly and duly without confusion or jostling or jam.

❧❧❧

The American bards shall be marked for generosity and affection and for encouraging competitors. . . . They shall be kosmos . . . without monopoly or secrecy . . . glad to pass any thing to any one . . . hungry for equals night and day. They shall not be careful of riches and privilege . . . they shall be riches and privilege . . . they shall perceive who the most affluent man is. The most affluent man is he that confronts all the shows he sees by equivalents out of the stronger wealth of himself. The American bard shall delineate no class of persons nor one or two out of the strata of interests nor love most nor truth most nor the soul most nor the body most . . . and not be for the eastern states more than the western or the northern states more than the southern.

❧❧❧

There will soon be no more priests. Their work is done. They may wait awhile . . . perhaps a generation or two . . . dropping off by degrees. A superior breed shall take their place . . . the gangs of kosmos and prophets en masse shall take their place. A new order shall arise and they shall be the priests of man, and every man shall be his own priest. The churches built under their umbrage shall be the churches of men and women. Through the divinity of themselves shall the kosmos and the new breed of poets be interpreters of men and women and of all events and things. They shall find their inspiration in real objects today, symptoms of the past and future. . . . They shall not deign to defend immortality or God or the perfection of things or liberty or the exquisite beauty and reality of the soul. They shall arise in America and be responded to from the remainder of the earth.

From *Song of the Open Road*

Afoot and light-hearted, I take to the
   open road,
Healthy, free, the world before me,
The long, brown path before me,
   leading wherever I choose.

Henceforth I ask not good fortune—I
   myself am good fortune;
Henceforth I whimper no more,
   postpone no more, need nothing,
Strong and content, I travel the open
   road.

The earth—that is sufficient;
I do not want the constellations any
   nearer:
I know they are very well where they
   are;
I know they suffice for those who
   belong to them.

(Still here I carry my old delicious
   burdens;
I carry them, men and women—I
   carry them with me wherever I
   go;

I swear it is impossible for me to get
   rid of them;
I am fill'd with them, and I will fill
   them in return.)

2

You road I enter upon and look
   around! I believe you are not all
   that is here;
I believe that much unseen is also
   here.

Here the profound lesson of
   reception, neither preference or
   denial;
The black with his woolly head, the
   felon, the diseas'd, the illiterate
   person, are not denied;
The birth, the hasting after the
   physician, the beggar's tramp, the
   drunkard's stagger, the laughing
   party of mechanics,
The escaped youth, the rich person's
   carriage, the fop, the eloping
   couple,
The early market-man, the hearse, the
   moving of furniture into the town,
   the return back from the town,
They pass—I also pass—anything
   passes—none can be interdicted;
None but are accepted—none but are
   dear to me.

3

You air that serves me with breath to
   speak!
You objects that call from diffusion my
   meanings, and give them shape!
You light that wraps me and all things
   in delicate equable showers!

You paths worn in the irregular
    hollows by the roadsides!
I think you are latent with unseen
    existences—you are so dear to me.

You flagg'd walks of the cities! you
    strong curbs at the edges!
You ferries! you planks and posts of
    wharves! you timber-lined sides!
    you distant ships!
You rows of houses! you
    window-pierced façades! you
    roofs!
You porches and entrances! you
    copings and iron guards!
You windows whose transparent shells
    might expose so much!
You doors and ascending steps! you
    arches!
You gray stones of interminable
    pavements! you trodden crossings!
From all that has been near you, I
    believe you have imparted to
    yourselves, and now would impart
    the same secretly to me;
From the living and the dead I think
    you have peopled your impassive
    surfaces, and the spirits thereof
    would be evident and amicable
    with me.

4

The earth expanding right hand and
    left hand,
The picture alive, every part in its best
    light,
The music falling in where it is
    wanted, and stopping where it is
    not wanted,
The cheerful voice of the public
  . road—the gay fresh sentiment of
    the road.

O highway I travel! O public road! do
    you say to me, *Do not leave me?*
Do you say, *Venture not? If you leave me,*
    you are lost?
Do you say, *I am already prepared—I am*
    well-eaten and undenied—adhere to
    me?

O public road! I say back, I am not
    afraid to leave you—yet I love
    you;
You express me better than I can
    express myself;
You shall be more to me than my
    poem.

I think heroic deeds were all conceiv'd
    in the open air, and all great
    poems also;
I think I could stop here myself, and
    do miracles;
(My judgments, thoughts, I henceforth
    try by the open air, the road;)
I think whatever I shall meet on the
    road I shall like, and whoever
    beholds me shall like me;
I think whoever I see must be happy.

5

From this hour, freedom!
From this hour I ordain myself loos'd
    of limits and imaginary lines,
Going where I list, my own master,
    total and absolute,
Listening to others, and considering
    well what they say,
Pausing, searching, receiving,
    contemplating,
Gently, but with undeniable will,
    divesting myself of the holds that
    would hold me.

I inhale great draughts of space;
The east and the west are mine, and
    the north and the south are mine.
I am larger, better than I thought;
I did not know I held so much
    goodness.
All seems beautiful to me;
I can repeat over to men and women,
    You have done such good to me, I
    would do the same to you.

I will recruit for myself and you as I
    go;
I will scatter myself among men and
    women as I go;
I will toss the new gladness and
    roughness among them;
Whoever denies me, it shall not
    trouble me;
Whoever accepts me, he or she shall
    be blessed, and shall bless me.

"As Adam, Early in the Morning"

As Adam, early in the morning,
Walking forth from the bower,
    refresh'd with sleep;
Behold me where I pass—hear my
    voice—approach,
Touch me—touch the palm of your
    hand to my Body as I pass;
Be not afraid of my Body.

"Facing West from California's Shores"

Facing west, from California's shores,
Inquiring, tireless, seeking what is yet
    unfound,
I, a child, very old, over waves,
    towards the house of maternity,
    the land of migrations, look afar,
Look off the shores of my Western
    Sea—the circle almost circled;
For, starting westward from
    Hindustan, from the vales of
    Kashmere,
From Asia—from the north—from the
    God, the sage, and the hero,
From the south—from the flowery
    peninsulas, and the spice islands;
Long having wander'd since—round
    the earth having wander'd.
Now I face home again—very pleas'd
    and joyous;
(But where is what I started for, so
    long ago?
And why is it yet unfound?)

"Pioneers! O Pioneers!"

1

Come, my tan-faced children,
Follow well in order, get your weapons
    ready;
Have you your pistols? have you your
    sharp edged axes?
    Pioneers! O pioneers!

2

For we cannot tarry here,
We must march my darlings, we must
bear the brunt of danger,
We, the youthful sinewy races, all the
rest on us depend,
Pioneers! O pioneers!

3

O you youths, western youths,
So impatient, full of action, full of
manly pride and friendship,
Plain I see you, western youths, see
you tramping with the foremost,
Pioneers! O pioneers!

4

Have the elder races halted?
Do they droop and end their lesson,
wearied, over there beyond the
seas?
We take up the task eternal, and the
burden, and the lesson,
Pioneers! O pioneers!

5

All the past we leave behind;
We debouch upon a newer, mightier
world, varied world,
Fresh and strong the world we seize,
world of labor and the march.
Pioneers! O pioneers!

6

We detachments steady throwing,
Down the edges, through the passes,
up the mountains steep,

Conquering, holding, daring,
venturing, as we go, the unknown
ways,
Pioneers! O pioneers!

7

We primeval forests felling,
We the rivers stemming, vexing we,
and piercing deep the mines
within;
We the surface broad surveying, we
the virgin soil upheaving,
Pioneers! O pioneers!

8

Colorado men are we,
From the peaks gigantic, from the
great sierras and the high
plateaus,
From the mine and from the gully,
from the hunting trail we come,
Pioneers! O pioneers!

9

From Nebraska, from Arkansas,
Central inland race are we, from
Missouri, with the continental
blood intervein'd;
All the hands of comrades clasping, all
the Southern, all the Northern,
Pioneers! O pioneers!

10

O resistless, restless race!
O beloved race in all! O my breast
aches with tender love for all!
O I mourn and yet exult—I am rapt
with love for all,
Pioneers! O pioneers!

11

Rise the mighty mother mistress,
Waving high the delicate mistress, over
    all the starry mistress, (bend your
    heads all,)
Raise the fang'd and warlike mistress,
    stern, impassive, weapon'd
    mistress,
        Pioneers! O pioneers!

12

See, my children, resolute children,
By those swarms upon our rear, we
    must never yield or falter,
Ages back in ghostly millions,
    frowning there behind us urging,
        Pioneers! O pioneers!

13

On and on, the compact ranks,
With accessions ever waiting, with the
    places of the dead quickly fill'd,
Through the battle, through defeat,
    moving yet and never stopping,
        Pioneers! O pioneers!

14

O to die advancing on!
Are there some of us to droop and
    die? has the hour come?
Then upon the march we fittest die,
    soon and sure the gap is fill'd,
        Pioneers! O pioneers!

15

All the pulses of the world,
Falling in, they beat for us, with the
    western movement beat;

Holding single or together, steady
    moving, to the front, all for us,
        Pioneers! O pioneers!

16

Life's involv'd and varied pageants,
All the forms and shows, all the
    workmen at their work,
All the seamen and the landsmen, all
    the masters with their slaves,
        Pioneers! O pioneers!

17

All the hapless silent lovers,
All the prisoners in the prisons, all the
    righteous and the wicked,
All the joyous, all the sorrowing, all
    the living, all the dying,
        Pioneers! O pioneers!

18

I too with my soul and body,
We, a curious trio, picking, wandering
    on our way,
Through these shores, amid the
    shadows, with the apparitions
    pressing,
        Pioneers! O pioneers!

19

Lo! the darting bowling orb!
Lo! the brother orbs around! all the
    clustering suns and planets;
All the dazzling days, all the mystic
    nights with dreams,
        Pioneers! O pioneers!

20

These are of us, they are with us,
All for primal needed work, while the
followers there in embryo wait
behind,
We to-day's procession heading, we the
route for travel clearing,
    Pioneers! O pioneers!

21

O you daughters of the west!
O you young and elder daughters! O
you mothers and you wives!
Never must you be divided, in our
ranks you move united,
    Pioneers! O pioneers!

22

Minstrels latent on the prairies!
(Shrouded bards of other lands! you
may sleep—you have done your
work;)
Soon I hear you coming warbling,
soon you rise and tramp amid us,
    Pioneers! O pioneers!

23

Not for delectations sweet,
Not the cushion and the slipper, not
the peaceful and the studious;
Not the riches safe and palling, not for
us the tame enjoyment,
    Pioneers! O pioneers!

24

Do the feasters gluttonous feast?
Do the corpulent sleepers sleep? have
they lock'd and bolted doors?

Still be ours the diet hard, and the
blanket on the ground,
    Pioneers! O pioneers!

25

Has the night descended?
Was the road of late so toilsome? did
we stop discouraged, nodding on
our way?
Yet a passing hour I yield you, in your
tracks to pause oblivious,
    Pioneers! O pioneers!

26

Till with sound of trumpet,
Far, far off the day-break call—hark!
how loud and clear I hear it wind;
Swift! to the head of the army!—swift!
spring to your places,
    Pioneers! O pioneers!

"Years of the Modern"

Years of the modern! years of the
unperform'd!
Your horizon rises—I see it parting
away for more august dramas;
I see not America only—I see not only
Liberty's nation, but other nations
preparing;
I see tremendous entrances and
exits—I see new combinations—I
see the solidarity of races;
I see that force advancing with
irresistible power on the world's
stage;

(Have the old forces, the old wars,
    played their parts? are the acts
    suitable to them closed?)
I see Freedom, completely arm'd, and
    victorious, and very haughty, with
    Law on one side, and Peace on the
    other,
A stupendous Trio, all issuing forth
    against the idea of caste;
—What historic denouements are these
    we so rapidly approach?
I see men marching and
    countermarching by swift millions;
I see the frontiers and boundaries of
    the old aristocracies broken;
I see the landmarks of European kings
    removed;
I see this day the People beginning
    their landmarks, (all others give
    way;)
—Never were such sharp questions
    ask'd as this day;
Never was average man, his soul, more
    energetic, more like a God;
Lo! how he urges and urges, leaving
    the masses no rest;
His daring foot is on the land and sea
    everywhere—he colonizes the
    Pacific, the archipelagoes;
With the steam-ship, the electric
    telegraph, the newspaper, the
    wholesale engines of war,
With these, and the world-spreading
    factories, he interlinks all
    geography, all lands;
—What whispers are these, O lands,
    running ahead of you, passing
    under the seas?
Are all nations communing? is there
    going to be but one heart to the
    globe?
Is humanity forming, en-masse?—for

lo! tyrants tremble, crowns grow
    dim;
The earth, restive, confronts a new
    era, perhaps a general divine war;
No one knows what will happen
    next—such portents fill the days
    and nights;
Years prophetical! the space ahead as I
    walk, as I vainly try to pierce it, is
    full of phantoms;
Unborn deeds, things soon to be,
    project their shapes around me;
This incredible rush and heat—this
    strange extatic fever of dreams, O
    years!
Your dreams, O years, how they
    penetrate through me! (I know
    not whether I sleep or wake!)
The perform'd America and Europe
    grow dim, retiring in shadow
    behind me,
The unperform'd, more gigantic than
    ever, advance, advance upon me.

"A Noiseless, Patient Spider"

A noiseless, patient spider,
I mark'd, where, on a little
    promontory, it stood, isolated;
Mark'd how, to explore the vacant,
    vast surrounding,
It launch'd forth filament, filament,
    filament, out of itself;
Ever unreeling them—ever tirelessly
    speeding them.

And you, O my Soul, where you stand,
Surrounded, surrounded, in
    measureless oceans of space,

Ceaselessly musing, venturing,
    throwing,—seeking the spheres,
    to connect them;
Till the bridge you will need, be
    form'd—till the ductile anchor
    hold;
Till the gossamer thread you fling,
    catch somewhere, O my Soul.

From *Democratic Vistas* (1871)

Present literature, while magnificently fulfilling certain popular demands, with plenteous knowledge and verbal smartness, is profoundly sophisticated, insane, and its very joy is morbid. It needs tally and express Nature, and the spirit of Nature, and to know and obey the standards. I say the question of Nature, largely considered, involves the questions of the aesthetic, the emotional, and the religious—and involves happiness. A fitly born and bred race, growing up in right conditions of outdoor as much as indoor harmony, activity and development, would probably, from and in those conditions, find it enough merely *to live*—and would, in their relations to the sky, air, water, trees, etc., and to the countless common shows and in the fact of life itself, discover and achieve happiness—with Being suffused night and day by wholesome extasy, surpassing all the pleasures that wealth, amusement, and even gratified intellect, erudition, or the sense of art, can give.

In the prophetic literature of these States (the reader of my speculations will miss their principal stress unless he allows well for the point that a new Literature, perhaps a new Metaphysics, certainly a new Poetry, are to be, in my opinion, the only sure and worthy supports and expressions of the American Democracy), Nature, true Nature, and the true idea of Nature, long absent, must, above all, become fully restored, enlarged, and must furnish the pervading atmosphere to poems, and the test of all high literary and aesthetic compositions. I do not mean the smooth walks, trimm'd hedges, poseys and nightingales of the English poets, but the whole orb, with its geologic history, the kosmos, carrying fire and snow, that rolls through the illimitable areas, light as a feather, though weighing billions of tons. Furthermore, as by what we now partially call Nature is intended, at most, only what is entertainable by the physical conscience, the sense of matter, and of good animal health—on these it must be distinctly accumulated, incorporated, that man, comprehending these, has, in towering superaddition, the moral and spiritual consciences, indicating his destination beyond the ostensible, the mortal.

To the heights of such estimate of Nature indeed ascending, we proceed to make observations for our Vistas, breathing rarest air. What is I believe called Idealism seems to me to suggest (guarding against extravagance, and ever modified even by its opposite) the course of inquiry and desert of favor for our New World metaphysics, their foundation of and in literature, giving hue to all.

The elevating and etherealizing ideas of the unknown and of unreality must be brought forward with authority, as they are the legitimate heirs of the known, and of reality, and at least as great as their parents. Fearless of scoffing, and of the ostent, let us take our stand, our ground, and never desert it, to confront the growing excess and arrogance of realism. To the cry, now victorious—the cry of sense, science, flesh, incomes, farms, merchandise, logic, intellect, demonstrations, solid perpetuities, buildings of brick and iron, or even the facts of the shows of trees, earth, rocks, etc., fear not, my brethren, my sisters, to sound out with equally determin'd voice, that conviction brooding within the recesses of every envision'd soul—illusions! apparitions! figments all! True, we must not condemn the show, neither absolutely deny it, for the indispensability of its meanings; but how clearly we see that, migrate in soul to what we can already conceive of superior and spiritual points of view, and palpable as it seems under present relations, it all and several might, nay certainly would, fall apart and vanish.

I hail with joy the oceanic, variegated, intense practical energy, the demand for facts, even the business materialism of the current age, our States. But woe to the age and land in which these things, movements, stopping at themselves, do not tend to ideas. As fuel to flame, and flame to the heavens, so must wealth, science, materialism—even this democracy of which we make so much—unerringly feed the highest mind, the soul. Infinitude the flight: fathomless the mystery. Man, so diminutive, dilates beyond the sensible universe, competes with, outcopes space and time, meditating even one great idea. Thus, and thus only, does a human being, his spirit, ascend above, and justify objective Nature, which, probably nothing in itself, is incredibly and divinely serviceable, indispensable, real, here. And as the purport of objective Nature is doubtless folded, hidden, somewhere here—as somewhere here is what this globe and its manifold forms, and the light of day, and night's darkness, and life itself, with all its experiences, are for—it is here the great literature, especially verse, must get its inspiration and throbbing blood. Then may we attain to a poetry worthy the immortal soul of man, and which, while absorbing materials, and, in their own sense, the shows of Nature, will, above all, have, both directly and indirectly, a freeing, fluidizing, expanding, religious character, exulting with science, fructifying the moral elements, and stimulating aspirations, and meditations on the unknown.

Emily Dickinson (1830–1886)

Emily Dickinson produced the extraordinary poetry for which she is remembered while a recluse in her Amherst, Massachusetts, home. Although she never doubted the existence of God, she was frequently oppressed by consciousness of his distance—even his absence—and by the accompanying feelings of abandonment, isolation, and impotence. While other believers could find at least mimimal consolation in the near proximity of a stern Father, a severe Judge, or a fearful Protector, Emily Dickinson often felt only the negative presence of a dreadful Emptiness, an aweful Vastness, a threatening Infinitude.

As various critics have noted, however, her doubt and even her despair were movements within the framework of a kind of faith. Her skepticism was nourished by her apprehension of "the missing All" which, as she remarked, "prevented Me/From missing minor Things." Her faith, such as it was, fed on unbidden and almost miraculous moments of ecstacy, of transport, usually evoked by Nature. Sometimes the radiance of these moments served only to accentuate the surrounding darkness. At other times they confirmed the lesson taught in "Success is counted sweetest," where only those who have lost "the Flag . . . Can tell the definition/So clear of Victory." In either case, as she reasoned in another poem, "Better an ignis fatuus"—false hope or misleading revelation—"than no illumine at all."

"There's a certain Slant of light" (*ca.* 1861)

There's a certain Slant of light,
Winter Afternoons—
That oppresses, like the Heft
Of Cathedral Tunes—

Heavenly Hurt, it gives us—
We can find no scar,
But internal difference,
Where the Meanings, are—

None may teach it—Any—
'Tis the Seal Despair—
An imperial affliction
Sent us of the Air—

When it comes, the Landscape listens—
Shadows—hold their breath—
When it goes, 'tis like the Distance
On the look of Death—

"I felt a Funeral, in my Brain" (*ca.* 1861)

I felt a Funeral, in my Brain,
And Mourners to and fro
Kept treading—treading—till it seemed
That Sense was breaking through—

And when they all were seated,
A Service, like a Drum—
Kept beating—beating—till I thought
My Mind was going numb—

And then I heard them lift a Box
And creak across my Soul
With those same Boots of Lead, again,
Then Space—began to toll,

As all the Heavens were a Bell,
And Being, but an Ear,
And I, and Silence, some strange Race
Wrecked, solitary, here—

And then a Plank in Reason, broke,
And I dropped down, and down—
And hit a World, at every plunge,
And Finished knowing—then—

"I heard a Fly buzz—when I died—" (*ca.* 1862)

I heard a Fly buzz—when I died—
The Stillness in the Room
Was like the Stillness in the Air—
Between the Heaves of Storm—

The Eyes around—had wrung them
dry—
And Breaths were gathering firm
For that last Onset—when the King
Be witnessed—in the Room—

I willed my Keepsakes—Signed away
What portion of me be
Assignable—and then it was
There interposed a Fly—

With Blue—uncertain stumbling
Buzz—
Between the light—and me—
And then the Windows failed—and
then
I could not 'see to see—

"It was not Death, for I stood up" (*ca.* 1862)

It was not Death, for I stood up,
And all the Dead, lie down—
It was not Night, for all the Bells
Put out their Tongues, for Noon.

It was not Frost, for on my Flesh
I felt Siroccos—crawl—
Nor Fire—for just my Marble feet
Could keep a Chancel, cool—

And yet, it tasted, like them all,
The Figures I have seen
Set orderly, for Burial,
Reminded me, of mine—

As if my life were shaven,
And fitted to a frame,
And could not breathe without a key,
And 'twas like Midnight, some—

When everything that ticked—has
stopped—
And Space stares all around—
Or Grisly frosts—first Autumn morns,
Repeal the Beating Ground—

But, most, like Chaos—Stopless—
cool—
Without a Chance, or Spar—
Or even a Report of Land—
To justify—Despair.

"My period had come for Prayer—" (*ca.* 1862)

My period had come for Prayer—
No other Art—would do—

My Tactics missed a rudiment—
Creator—Was it you?

God grows above—so those who pray
Horizons—must ascend—
And so I stepped upon the North
To see this Curious Friend—

His House was not—no sign had He—
By Chimney—nor by Door
Could I infer his Residence—
Vast Prairies of Air

Unbroken by a Settler—
Were all that I could see—
Infinitude—Had'st Thou no Face
That I might look on Thee?

The Silence condescended—
Creation stopped—for Me—
But awed beyond my errand—
I worshipped—did not "pray"—

"Presentiment—is that long Shadow—on the Lawn—" (ca. 1863)

Presentiment—is that long Shadow—
    on the Lawn—
Indicative that Suns go down—

The Notice to the startled Grass
That Darkness—is about to pass—

"Finding is the first Act" (ca. 1864)

Finding is the first Act
The second, loss,
Third, Expedition for
The "Golden Fleece"

Fourth, no Discovery—
Fifth, no Crew—
Finally, no Golden Fleece—
Jason—sham—too.

"The Missing All—prevented Me" (ca. 1865)

The Missing All—prevented Me
From missing minor Things.
If nothing larger than a World's
Departure from a Hinge—
Or Sun's extinction, be observed—
'Twas not so large that I
Could lift my Forehead from my work
For Curiosity.

"Tell all the Truth but tell it slant—" (ca. 1868)

Tell all the Truth but tell it slant—
Success in Circuit lies
Too bright for our infirm Delight
The Truth's superb surprise

As Lightning to the Children eased
With explanation kind
The Truth must dazzle gradually
Or every man be blind—

Abraham Lincoln
(1809–1865)

Sixteenth President of the United States, Abraham Lincoln has perhaps generated more controversy and elicited more extreme reactions than any other figure in our national history. He was reviled as a tyrant by Southern secessionists, accepted as a realist by Northern moderates, embraced as an idealist by white Abolitionists and black freedmen after the Emancipation Proclamation, transformed by his assassination into a quasi-religious martyr for national unity, and ultimately apotheosized into a tragic, even epic, hero whose saga would be played out on the national stage by succeeding generations of bards and chroniclers. Lincoln doubtless possessed qualities lending themselves to each of these interpretations and many more besides.

Some saw his early reactions to slavery, as recorded in the "Letter to Horace Greeley," as the result of an underlying pragmatism, in this case concerned with the preservation of the Union. Others perceived the political religion to which he elevated his mystique of the Union, evident in his "Meditation on the Divine Will," to be far more determinative for him than any theological beliefs of a more conventional sort. To still others, looking at the "Gettysburg Address," Lincoln's religious convictions seem to have centered on the mystery of life and

death and the tragic paradox that the freedom of some must inevitably be purchased by the sacrifice of others. Yet again, judging from his "Second Inaugural," Lincoln's confidence that history is in the hands of a sovereign God whose will no individual, group, or sector may presume to know appears to override the tragedy of loss and give to suffering a providential meaning of the sort it held for America's earliest Puritan settlers. Whatever the case, there is no gainsaying the fact that Lincoln's nonsectarian religious views have held a deep and lasting appeal for many Americans.

"Letter to Horace Greeley"
(1862)

Hon. Horace Greely:

ExECUTIVE MANSION,

Dear Sir: Washington, August 22, 1862.

I have just read yours of the 19th. addressed to myself through the New-York Tribune. If there be in it any statements, or assumptions of fact, which I may know to be erroneous, I do not, now and here, controvert them. If there be in it any inferences which I may believe to be falsely drawn, I do not now and here, argue against them. If there be perceptible in it an impatient and dictatorial tone, I waive it in deference to an old friend, whose heart I have always supposed to be right:

As to the policy I "seem to be pursuing" as you say, I have not meant to leave any one in doubt.

I would save the Union. I would save it the shortest way under the Constitution. The sooner the national authority can be restored; the nearer the Union will be "the Union as it was." If there be those who would not save the Union, unless they could at the same time *save* slavery, I do not agree with them. If there be those who would not save the Union unless they could at the same time *destroy* slavery, I do not agree with them. My paramount object in this struggle *is* to save the Union, and is *not* either to save or to destroy slavery. If I could save the Union without freeing *any* slave I would do it, and if I could save it by freeing *all* the slaves I would do it; and if I could save it by freeing some and leaving others alone I would also do that. What I do about slavery, and the colored race, I do because I believe it helps to save the Union; and what I forbear, I forbear because I do *not* believe it would help to save the Union. I shall do *less* whenever I shall believe what I am doing hurts the cause, and I shall do *more* whenever I shall believe doing more will help the cause. I shall try to correct errors when shown to be errors; and I shall adopt new views so fast as they shall appear to be true views.

I have here stated my purpose according to my view of *official* duty; and I intend no modification of my oft-expressed *personal* wish that all men every where could be free.

Yours,
A. Lincoln

"Meditation on the Divine Will" (1862)

The will of God prevails. In great contests each party claims to act in accordance with the will of God. Both *may* be, and one *must* be wrong. God can not be *for*, and *against* the same thing at the same time. In the present civil war it is quite possible that God's purpose is something different from the purpose of either party—and yet the human instrumentalities, working just as they do, are of the best adaptation to effect His purpose. I am almost ready to say this is probably true—that God wills this contest, and wills that it shall not end yet. By his mere quiet power, on the minds of the now contestants, He could have either *saved* or *destroyed* the Union without a human contest. Yet the contest began. And having begun He could give the final victory to either side any day. Yet the contest proceeds.

"Gettysburg Address" (1863)

Four score and seven years ago our fathers brought forth on this continent, a new nation, conceived in liberty, and dedicated to the proposition that all men are created equal.

Now we are engaged in a great civil war, testing whether that nation, or any nation so conceived and so dedicated, can long endure. We are met on a great battlefield of that war. We have come to dedicate a portion of that field, as a final resting place for those who here gave their lives that that nation might live. It is altogether fitting and proper that we should do this.

But, in a larger sense, we cannot dedicate—we cannot consecrate—we cannot hallow—this ground. The brave men, living and dead, who struggled here, have consecrated it, far above our poor power to add or detract. The world will little note, nor long remember what we say here, but it can never forget what they did here. It is for us the living, rather, to be dedicated here to the unfinished work which they who fought here have thus far so nobly advanced. It is rather for us to be here dedicated to the great task remaining before us—that from these honored dead we take increased devotion to that cause for which they gave the last full measure of devotion—that we here highly resolved that these dead shall not have died in vain—that this nation, under God, shall have a new birth of freedom—and that government of the people, by the people, for the people, shall not perish from the earth.

"Second Inaugural Address" (1865)

At this second appearing to take the oath of the presidential office, there is less occasion for an extended address than there was at the first. Then a statement, somewhat in detail, of a course to be pursued, seemed fitting and proper. Now, at the expiration of four years, during which public declarations have been constantly called forth on every point and phase of the great contest which still absorbs the attention, and engrosses the energies of the nation, little that is new could be presented. The progress of our arms, upon which all else chiefly depends, is as well known to the public as to myself; and it is, I trust, reasonably satisfactory and encouraging to all. With high hope for the future, no prediction in regard to it is ventured.

On the occasion corresponding to this four years ago, all thoughts were anxiously directed to an impending civil war. All dreaded it—all sought to avert it. While the inaugural address was being delivered from this place, devoted altogether to *saving* the Union without war, insurgent agents were in the city seeking to *destroy* it without war—seeking to dissolve the Union, and divide effects, by negotiation. Both parties deprecated war; but one of them would *make* war rather than let the nation survive; and the other would *accept* war rather than let it perish. And the war came.

One eighth of the whole population were colored slaves, not distributed generally over the Union, but localized in the Southern part of it. These slaves constituted a peculiar and powerful interest. All knew that this interest was, somehow, the cause of the war. To strengthen, perpetuate, and extend this interest was the object for which the insurgents would rend the Union, even by war; while the government claimed no right to do more than to restrict the territorial enlargement of it. Neither party expected for the war, the magnitude, or the duration, which it has already attained. Neither anticipated that the *cause* of the conflict might cease with, or even before, the conflict itself should cease. Each looked for an easier triumph, and a result less fundamental and astounding. Both read the same Bible, and pray to the same God; and each invokes His aid against the other. It may seem strange that any men should dare to ask a just God's assistance in wringing their bread from the sweat of other men's faces; but let us judge not that we be not judged. The prayers of both could not be answered; that of neither has been answered fully. The Almighty has His own purposes. "Woe unto the world because of offenses! for it must needs be that offenses come; but woe to that man by whom the offense cometh!" If we shall suppose that American slavery is one of those offenses which, in the providence of God, must needs come, but which, having continued through His appointed time, He now wills to remove, and that He gives to both North and South, this terrible war, as the woe due to those by whom the offense came, shall we discern therein any departure from those divine attributes which the believers in a Living God always ascribe to Him? Fondly do we hope—fervently do we pray—that this mighty scourge of war may speedily pass away. Yet, if God wills that it continue, until all the wealth piled by the bondman's two hundred and fifty years of unrequited toil shall be sunk, and until every drop of blood drawn

with the lash, shall be paid by another drawn with the sword, as was said three thousand years ago, so still it must be said "the judgments of the Lord, are true and righteous altogether."

With malice toward none; with charity for all; with firmness in the right, as God gives us to see the right, let us strive on to finish the work we are in; to bind up the nation's wounds; to care for him who shall have borne the battle, and for his widow, and his orphan—to do all which may achieve and cherish a just, and lasting peace, among ourselves, and with all nations.

Henry James, Senior (1811-1882)

Henry James, Senior, father of philosopher William James and novelist Henry James, was a religious thinker and man of letters who was frequently at odds with the conservative Protestant theologians of his day as well as with their Unitarian and Transcendentalist critics. More adept at criticizing the systems of others than at constructing his own, a task at which he nonetheless labored the whole of his life, James brought to his work a vigorous commitment to what he perceived to be the divine potential of man's natural humanity and a discerning eye for all forms of intellectual as well as religious pretension.

James's call for a weekday rather

than a Sunday divinity, "grimy with the dust and sweat of our most carnal appetites and passions," is of a piece with his good-natured jibe at Emerson for seeming, as it were, too "divinely begotten," too "virgin-born." Religion for James was not an affair of moral rectitude or theological orthodoxy but of spiritual regeneration which could only be achieved through a recovery of man's sense of oneness with his fellows. In this he was aided by the work of the seventeenth-century mystic Emmanuel Swedenborg, which furnished James with the germ of his central ideas about our "Divine Natural Humanity" and society as the redeemed form of man.

From *The Secret of Swedenborg* (1869)

While deism as an intellectual tradition continues doubtless to survive, it seems at the same time to be losing all hold upon the living thought of men, being trampled under foot by the advance of a scientific naturalism. Paganism and science are indeed plainly incompatible terms. The conception of a private or unemployed divine force in the world—the conception of a deity unimplicated in the nature, the progress, and the destiny of man—is utterly repugnant to human thought; and if such a conception were the true logical alternative of atheism, science would erelong everwhere, as she is now doing in Germany,

confess herself atheistic. But the true battle-field is not nearly so narrow as this. The rational alternative of atheism is not deism, but christianity, and science accordingly would be atheistic at a very cheap if not wholly gratuitous rate, should it become so only to avoid the deistic hypothesis of creation. The deistic hypothesis then is effectually dead and buried for scientific purposes. That it is rapidly becoming so even for the needs of the religious instinct also, we have a lively augury furnished us in the current popularity of two very naive and amiable religious books, which unconsciously put a new face upon the atheistic controversy by attempting to give revelation itself a strictly rational aspect, and so bring it within the legitimate domain of science. One of these books is named *Ecce Homo,* the other *Ecce Deus.* They are both of them interesting in themselves, but much more so, I think, as indicating a certain progress in religious thought, which tends to the disowning of any deity out of strictly human proportions, out of the proportions of our own nature; or, what is the same thing, tends to disallow all personal and admit only a spiritual infinitude, which is the infinitude of character. I for my own part rejoice extremely in this brightening of our intellectual skies. I hope the day is now no longer so distant as once it seemed, when the idle, pampered, and mischievous force which men have everywhere superstitiously worshipped as divine, and sought to placate by all manner of cruel, slavish, and mercenary observances, may be utterly effaced in the resurrection lineaments of that spotless unfriended youth, who in the world's darkest hour allied his own godward hopes with the fortunes only of the most defiled, the most diseased, the most disowned of human kind, and so for the first and only time on earth avouched a breadth in the meanest human bosom every way fit to house and domesticate the infinite divine love. Long before Christ, the lover had freely bled for his mistress, the friend for his friend, the parent for his child, the patriot for his country. History shows no record however of any but him steadfastly choosing death at the hands of fanatical self-seeking men, lest *by simply consenting to live* he should become the object of their filthy and fulsome devotion. In other words, many a man had previously illustrated the creative benignity in every form of *passionate* self-surrender and self-sacrifice. He alone, in the teeth of every passionate impulse known to the human heart—that is to say, in sheer despite of every tie of familiarity, of friendship, of coutry, of religion, that ordinarily makes life sweet and sacred—surrendered himself to death in clear, unforced, spontaneous homage to universal love.

But then it must be frankly admitted on the other hand that a certain adverse omen declares itself in the religious arena; not however among the positive or doctrinal orthodox sort, so much as among those of a negative or sentimental unitarian hue. It is fast growing a fashion, for example, among our so-called "radical" religious contemporaries, vehemently to patronize Christ's humanity, by way of more effectually discountenancing his conventional divine repute. I too dislike the altogether musty and incoherent divinity ascribed to Christ by the church—a divinity which is intensely accidental and no way incidental to his ineffably tempted, suffering, and yet victorious spiritual manhood. But it is notoriously bad policy to confirm one's self in a mere negative attitude of mind, especially on questions of such intellectual pith and moment as this, and I therefore caution the movers of the new crusade to bethink themselves in time, whether, after all, the only divinity which is capable of permanent recognition at men's hands must not necessarily wear their own form? I find myself incapable, for my own part, of honoring the pretension of any diety to my allegiance, who insists upon standing eternally aloof from my own nature, and by that fact confesses himself personally incommensurate and unsympathetic with my basest, most sensuous, and controlling personal necessities. It is an easy enough thing to find a holiday God who is all too selfish to be touched with the infirmities of his own creatures—a God, for example, who has naught to do but receive assiduous court for a work of creation done myriads of ages ago, and which is reputed to have cost him in the doing neither pains nor patience, neither affection nor thought, but simply the utterance of a dramatic work; and who is willing, accordingly, to accept our decorous sunday homage in ample quittance of obligations so unconsciously incurred on our part, so lightly rendered and so penuriously sanctioned on his. Every sect, every nation, every family almost, offers some pet idol of this description to your worship. But I am free to confess that I have long outgrown this loutish conception of deity. I can no longer bring myself to adore a charactersitic activity in the God of my worship, which falls below the secular average of human character. In fact, what I crave with all my heart and understanding—what my very flesh and bones cry out for—is no longer a sunday but a week-day divinity, a working God, grimy with the dust and sweat of our most carnal appetites and passions, and bent, not for an instant upon inflating our worthless pietistic righteousness, but upon the patient, toilsome, thorough cleansing of our physical and moral existence from the odious defilement it has contracted, until we each and all present at last in body and mind the deathless effigy of his own uncreated loveliness. And no clear revelation do I get of such a God outside the personality of Jesus Christ. It would be gross affectation then in me at least to doubt that he, whom all men in the exact measure of their own veracious manhood acknowledge and adore *as supreme among men,* will always continue to smile at the simulated homage—at the purely voluntary or calculated deference—which is paid to any unknown or unrevealed and transcendental deus, who is yet too superb to subside into the dimensions of his sacred human worth.

Mr. Emerson (1884)

At all events, if we are still to go on cherishing any such luxury as a private conscience towards God, I greatly prefer for my own part that it should be an evil conscience. Conscience was always intended as a rebuke and never as an exhilaration to the private citizen; and so let it flourish till the end of our wearisome civilization. There are many signs, however, that this end is near. My recently deceased friend Mr. Emerson, for example, was all his days an arch traitor to our existing civilized regimen, inasmuch as he unconsciously managed to set aside its fundamental principle in doing without conscience, which was the entire secret of his very exceptional interest to men's speculation. He betrayed it to be sure without being at all aware of what he was doing; but this was really all that he distinctively did to my observation. His nature had always been so innocent, so unaffectedly innocent, that when in later life he began to cultivate a club consciousness, and to sip a glass of wine or smoke a cigar, I felt very much outraged by it. I felt very much as if some renowned Boston belle had suddenly collapsed and undertaken to sell newspapers at a street corner. "Why, Emerson, is this *you* doing such things?" I exclaimed. "What profanation! Do throw the unclean things behind your back!" But, no; he was actually proud of his accomplishments! This came from his never knowing (intellectually) what he stood for in the evolution of New England life. He was lineally descended to begin with, from a half-score of comatose New England clergymen, in whose behalf probably the religious instinct had been used up. Or, what to their experience had been religion, became in that of their descendant *life*. The actual truth, at any rate, was that he never felt a movement of the life of conscience from the day of his birth till that of his death. I could never see any signs of such a life in him. I remember, to be sure, that he had a great gift of friendship, and that he was very plucky in behalf of his friends whenever they felt themselves assailed—as plucky as a woman. For instance, whenever Wendell Phillips ventilated his not untimely wit at the expense of our club-house politicians, Emerson, hearing his friends among these latter complain, grew indignant, and for several days you would hear nothing from his lips but excessive eulogies of Mr. Garrison, which sounded like nothing else in the world but revilings of Mr. Phillips. But bless our heart! there was not a bit of conscience in a bushel of such experiences, but only wounded friendship, which is a totally different and much lower thing.

The infallible mark of conscience is that it is always a subjective judgment couched in some such language as this: "God be merciful to *me* a sinner!" and never an objective judgment such as this: *God damn Wendell Phillips, or some other of my friends!* This latter judgment is always an outbreak of ungovernable temper on our part, and was never known to reach the ear of God save in this guise: *God* BLESS *W. P. or any other friend implicated!* Now Emerson was seriously incapable of a subjective judgment upon himself; he did not know the inward difference between good and evil, so far as he was himself concerned. No doubt he perfectly comprehended the outward or moral difference be-

tween these things; but I insist upon it that he never so much as dreamed of any inward or spiritual difference between them. For this difference is vitally seen only when oneself seems unchangeably evil to his own sight, and one's neighbor unchangeably good in the comparison. How could Emerson ever have known this difference? I am satisfied that he never in his life had felt a temptation *to bear false-witness* against his neighbor, *to steal, to commit adultery, or to murder;* how then should he have ever experienced what is technically called a conviction of sin?—that is, a conviction of himself as *evil* before God, and all other men as *good.* One gets a conviction of the evil that attaches to the natural selfhood in man in no other way than— as I can myself attest—by this growing acquaintance with his own moral infirmity, and the consequent gradual decline of his self-respect. For I myself had known all these temptations—in forms of course more or less modified—by the time I was fourteen or fifteen years old; so that by the time I had got to be twenty-five or thirty (which was the date of my first acquaintance with Emerson) I was saturated with a sense of spiritual evil—no man ever more so possibly, since I felt thoroughly *self*-condemned before God. Good heavens! how soothed and comforted I was by the innocent lovely look of my new acquaintance, by his tender courtesy, his generous laudatory appreciation of my crude literary ventures! and how I used to lock myself up with him in his bed-room, swearing that before the door was opened I would arrive at the secret of his immense superiority to the common herd of literary men! I might just as well have locked myself up with a handful of diamonds, so far as any capacity of self-cognizance existed in him. I found in fact, before I had been with him a week, that the immense superiority I ascribed to him was altogether personal or practical—by no means intellectual; that it came to him by birth or genius like a woman's beauty or charm of manners; that no other account was to be given of it in truth than that Emerson himself was an unsexed woman, a veritable fruit of almighty power in the sphere of our *nature*.

This after a while grew to be a great discovery to me; but I was always more or less provoked to think that Emerson himself should take no intellecutal stock in it. On the whole I may say that at first I was greatly disappointed in him, because his intellect never kept the promise which his lovely face and manners held out to me. He was to my senses a literal divine presence in the house with me; and we cannot recognize literal divine presences in our houses without feeling sure that they will be able to say something of critical importance to one's intellect. It turned out that any average old dame in a horse-car would have satisfied my intellectual rapacity just as well as Emerson. My standing intellectual embarrassment for years had been to get at the bottom of the difference between law and gospel in humanity—between the head and the heart of things—between the great God almighty, in short, and the intensely wooden and ridiculous gods of the nations. Emerson, I discovered immediately, had never been the least of an expert in this sort of knowledge; and though his immense personal fascination always kept up, he at once lost all intellectual prestige to my regard. I even thought that I had never seen a man more profoundly devoid of spiritual understanding. This prejudice grew, of course, out of my having inherited an altogether narrow ecclesiastical notion of what spiritual understanding was. I supposed it consisted unmistakably in some doctrinal lore concerning man's regeneration, to which, however, my new friend was plainly and signally incompetent. Emerson, in fact, derided this doctrine, smiling benignly whenever it was mentioned. I could make neither head nor tail of him according to men's ordinary standards—the only thing that I was sure of being that he, like Christ, was somehow divinely begotten. He seemed to me unmistakably virgin-born whenever I looked at him, and reminded me of nothing so much as of those persons dear to Christ's heart who should come after him professing no allegiance to him—having never heard his name pronounced, and yet perfectly fulfilling his will. He never seemed for a moment to antagonize the church of his own consent, but only out of condescension to his interlocutor's weakness. In fact he was to all appearance entirely ignorant of the church's existence until you recalled it to his imagination; and even then I never knew anything so implacably and uniformly mild as his judgments of it were. He had apparently lived all his life in a world where it was only subterraneously known; and, try as you would, you could never persuade him that any the least living power attached to it. The same profound incredulity characterized him in regard to the State; and it was only in his enfeebled later years that he ever lent himself to the idea of society as its destined divine form. I am not sure indeed that the lending was ever very serious. But he was always greedy, with all a Yankee's greediness, after facts, and would at least appear to listen to you with earnest respect and sympathy whenever you plead for society as the redeemed form of our nature.

In short he was, as I have said before, fundamentally treacherous to civilization, without being at all aware himself of the fact. He himself, I venture to say, was peculiarly unaware of the fact. He appeared to me utterly unconscious of himself as either good or evil. He had no conscience, in fact, and lived by perception, which is an altogether lower or less spiritual faculty. The more universalized a man is by genius or natural birth, the less is he spiritually individualized, making up in breadth of endowment what he lacks in depth. This was remarkably the case with Emerson. In his books or public capacity he was constantly electrifying you by sayings full of divine inspiration. In his talk or private capacity he was one of the least remunerative men I have ever encountered. No man could look at him speaking (or when he was silent either, for that matter) without having a vision of the divinest beauty. But when you went to him to hold discourse about the wondrous phenomenon, you found him absolutely destitute of reflective power. He had apparently no private personal-ity; and if any visitor thought he discerned traces of such a thing, you may take for granted that the visitor himself was a man of large imaginative resources. He was nothing else than a show-figure of almighty power in our nature; and that he was destitute of all the apparatus of humbuggery that goes to eke out more or less the private pretension in humanity, only completed and confirmed the extraordinary fascination that belonged to him. He was full of living inspiration to me whenever I saw him; and yet I could find in him no trivial sign of the selfhood which I found in other men. He was like a vestal virgin, indeed, always in ministry upon the altar; but the vestal virgin had doubtless a prosaic side also, which related her to commonplace people. Now Emerson was so far *unlike* the virgin: he had no prosaic side relating him to ordinary people. Judge Hoar and Mr. John Forbes constituted his spontaneous political conscience; and his domestic one (equally spontaneous) was supplied by loving members of his own family—so that he only connected with the race at secondhand, and found all the material business of life such as voting and the payment of taxes transacted for *him* with marvellous lack of friction.

Incontestably the main thing about him, however, as I have already said, was that he unconsciously brought you face to face with the infinite in humanity. When I looked upon myself, or upon the ordinary rabble of ecclesiastics and politicians, everything in us seemed ridiculously undivine. When I looked upon Emerson, these same undivine things were what gave *him* his manifest divine charm. The reason was that in him everything seemed innocent by the transparent absence of selfhood, and in us everything seemed foul and false by its preternatural activity. The difference between us was made by innocence altogether. I never thought it was a real or spiritual difference, but only a natural or apparent one. But such as it was, it gave me my first living impression of the great God almighty who alone is at work in human affairs, avouching his awful and adorable spiritual infinitude only through the death and hell wrapped up in our finite experience. This was Emerson's incontestable virtue to every one who appreciated him, that he recognized no God outside of himself and his interlocutor, and recognized him there only as the *liason* between the two, taking care that all their intercourse should be holy with a holiness undreamed of before by man or angel. For it is not a holiness taught by books or the example of tiresome, diseased, self-conscious saints, but simply by one's redeemed flesh and blood. In short, the only holiness which Emerson recognized, and for which he consistently lived, was innocence. And innocence—glory be to God's spiritual incarnation in our nature!—has no other root in us than our unconscious flesh and bones. That is to say, it attaches only to what is definitively universal or natural in our experience, and hence appropriates itself to individuals only in so far as they learn to denude themselves of personality or self-consciousness; which reminds one of Christ's mystical saying: *He that findeth his life (in himself) shall lose it, and he that loseth his life for my sake shall find it.*

Horace Bushnell (1802-1876)

Horace Bushnell was a major exponent of theological liberalism in the mid-nineteenth century. Best known for his eloquent defense of Christian nurture against the revivalists' claim of "instant" salvation through conversion, Bushnell also made an important contribution to the theory of religious language. He argued that ideas cannot be dissociated from the words in which they are expressed——that the images and symbols by which we apprehend reality themselves delimit whatever part of reality we can apprehend. Bushnell's theories, though quite lost on most of his contemporaries, had far-reaching consequences for the understanding of creeds and doctrines as well as the interpretation of Scripture that have only recently come to be appreciated.

In the following sermon, Bushnell summarizes ideas he developed at greater length and subtlety in his "Preliminary Dissertation on the Nature of Language as Related to Thought and Spirit" in *God in Christ* (1849), and "Language and Doctrine" in *Christ in Theology* (1851).

From *Our Gospel a Gift to the Imagination* (1869)

I shall endeavor to exhibit, as far as I can in the restricted limits of this article, the fact that our Christian Gospel is a Gift more especially to the Human Imagination. It offers itself first of all and principally to the interpretative imaginings and discernings of faith, never, save in that manner, to the constructive processes of logic and speculative opinion. It is, in one sense, pictorial; its every line or lineament is traced in some image or metaphor, and by no possible ingenuity can it be gotten away from metaphor; for as certainly as one metaphoric image is escaped by a definition, another will be taken up, and must be, to fill its place in the definition itself. Mathematical language is a scheme of exact notation. All words that are names of mere physical acts and objects are literal, and even animals can, so far, learn their own names and the meaning of many acts done or commanded. But no animal ever understood a metaphor: that belongs to intelligence, and to man as a creature of intelligence; being a power to see, in all images, the faces of truth, and take their sense, or read their meaning, when thrown up in language before the imagination.

Holding now this view of truth as presenting itself always by images metaphorically significant, never by any other possible means or media, it is very clear that all our modes of use and processes of interpretation must be powerfully affected by such a discovery.

First of all it must follow, as a principal consequence, that truth is to be gotten by a right beholding of the forms or images by which it is expressed. Ingenuity will miss it by overdoing; mere industry will do scarcely more than muddle it; only candor, a graciously open, clean candor will find it. We can take the sense of its images, only by offering a perfectly receptive imagination to them, a plate to fall upon that is flavored by no partisanship, corrugated by no bigotry, blotched by no prejudice or passion, warped by no self-will. There is nothing we cannot make out of them, by a very little abuse, or perversity. They are innocent people who can never vindicate themselves when wronged, further than to simply stand and wait for a more ingenuous beholding. And it is to be a very great part of our honor and advantage in the truth, that we have it by the clean docility and noble reverence that make us capable of it. We shall not be afraid of worshiping its images; for they are not graven images, but faces that express the truth because they are faces of God. We want, in fact, as a first condition, a mind so given to truth that our love and reverence shall open all our sympathies to it and quite indispose us to any violent practice on its terms.

All mere logically constructive practice on them, twisting meanings into them, or out of them, that are only deducible from their forms and are no part of their real significance, must be jealously restrained. Nicodemus was falling straightway into this kind of mischief, when the words "born again" put him on asking, whether a man can be born of his mother a second time? It was in the form of the words, but how far off from their meaning! So, when it is declared that God is a rock and that God is a river, what follows, since things that are equal to the same things are, in strict logic, equal to one another, but that a rock is a river? Meantime God was not declared to be either rock or river, except in a very partial, metaphoric way. In the same way Christ is called a priest, and a sacrifice, and it follows in good logic that a priest is a sacrifice. Nobody happens, it is true, to have reasoned in just this manner, but how many do reason that, being called a priest and a sacrifice, he must be exactly both in the sense of the ritual; when, in fact, he is neither priest nor sacrifice, save in such a sense as these words, taken as metaphors, are able to convey. Nothing is to be gotten ever, by spinning conclusions out of the mere forms or images of truth, but mischief and delusion. And the record of religion is full of just this kind of delusion. All mere logical handlings are vicious, unless they are so far qualified by insight that insight gives the truth, and then, of course, they are not wanted. Indeed, there is nothing in which the world is so miserably cheated, as in the admiration it yields to what is most logically deductive concerning moral and religious questions. It is even the worst kind of fault, unless it be only meant, as it often is when we say it, that they are written with true intellectual insight, which is a very different matter.

But we must have science, some will remember; is there any hope for theologic science left? None at all, I answer most unequivocally. Human language is a gift to the imagination so essentially metaphoric, warp and woof, that it has no exact blocks and meaning to build a science of. Who would ever think of building up a science of Homer, Shakespeare, Milton? And the Bible is not a whit less poetic, or a whit less metaphoric, or a particle less difficult to be propositionized in the terms of the understanding. Shall we then have nothing to answer, when the sweeping question is put, why philosophy and every other study should make advances, and theology be only spinning its old circles and revising and re-revising its old problems? It must be enough to answer that philosophy, metaphysical philosophy, having only metaphor to work in, is under exactly the same limitation; that it is always backing and filling, and turning and returning, in the same manner; that nobody can name a single question that has ever been settled by all the systems it has built and the newly contrived nomenclatures it has invented. Working always in metaphors and fooling itself, how commonly, by metaphor, it gets a valuable gynmastic in words, and prepares to a more full and many-sided conception of words. So far it is fruitful and good, and just so far also is the scientific labor of theology. After all it is simple insight in both, and not speculation, that has the true discernment. Words give up their deepest, truest meaning, only when they are read as images of the same.

But we must have definitions, it will

be urged, else we cannot be sure what we mean by our words, and when we have the definitions, why can we not have science? But if we mean by definitions an exact literal measurement of ideas, no such thing is possible. In what we call our definitions, whether in theology, or moral philosophy, we only put one set of metaphors in place of another, and, if we understand ourselves, there may be a certain use in doing it, even as there is in shifting our weight upon the other leg; perhaps we make ourselves more intelligible by doing it. And yet there is a very great imposture lurking almost always in these definitions. Thus if I may define a definition, the very word shows it to be a bounding off; where it happens, not unlikely, that a whole heaven's breadth of meaning is bounded out and lost; where again, secondly, it results that the narrow part bounded in and cleared of all grand overplus of meaning, is just as much diminished as it is made more clear and certain; and thirdly, that what one has bounded out another will have bounded in, either in whole or in part; whereupon debates begin, and schools, and sects arise, clinging to their several half-truths and doing fierce battle for them. And probably another and still worse result will appear; for the generous broad natures that were going to be captivated by truth's free images, having them now defined and set in propositional statements, will, how often, be offended by their narrow theologic look and reject them utterly. Nothing makes infidels more surely than the spinning, splitting, nerveless refinements of theology. This endeavor, always going on, to

get the truths of religion away from the imagination, into propositions of the speculative understanding, makes a most dreary and sad history,—a history of divisions, recriminations, famishings, vanishings and general uncharitableness. Lively, full, fresh, free as they were, the definitions commonly cut off their wings and reduce them to mere pebbles of significance. Before they were plants alive and in flower, now the flavors are gone, the juices dried and the skeleton parts packed away and classified in the dry herbarium called theology.

We deplore, how often, with how great concern, and with prayers to God in which we wrestle heavily, our manifold sects and divisions. We turn the matter every way, contriving new platforms and better articles of dogma, and commonly find that, instead of gathering ourselves into a new and more complete unity, we have only raised new sects and aggravated the previous distractions. And yet many cannot conceive that the gospel is a faith, only in that way to be received, and so the bond of unity. They are going still to think out a gospel, assuming that the Church has no other hope as regards this matter but in the completing of a scientific theology; which will probably be accomplished about the same time that words are substituted by algebraic notations, and poetry reduced to the methods of the calculus or the logarithmmic tables. There was never a hope wider of reason. The solar system will die before either that or the hope of a complete philosophy is accomplished. No, we must go back to words, and compose our differences in them as they are, exploring them more by our faith and less by our speculative thinking. Having them as a gift to the imagination, we must stay in them as such, and feel out our agreement there in a common trust, and love, and worship.

Here then is the point on which all sects and divisions may be gravitating and coming into settled unity. What is wanted, above all things, for this end is not that we carefully compose our scientific theology, but that we properly observe, and are principally concerned to know God in his own appointed images and symbols. We must get our light by perusing the faces of his truth; we must behold him with reverent desire in the mirrors that reveal him, caring more to have our insight purged than to spin deductions and frame propositions that are in the modes of science or of system. We shall of course have opinions concerning it. A considerable activity in opinions is even desirable, because it will sharpen our perceptiveness of the symbols and draw us on, in that manner, towards a more general and perfect aggreement. Only our opinions must be opinions, not laws, either to us or to anybody; perhaps they will change color somewhat even by tomorrow. We must also understand that our opinions or propositional statements are just as truly in metaphor as the scripture itself, only metaphor probably which is a good deal more covert and often as much more ambiguous. We may draw as many creeds as we please, the more the better, if we duly understand that they are standards only as being in

metaphor, and not in terms of exact notation. None the less properly standard is the Nicene Creed, that it is given visibly to the imagination, and has even its highest merit at the point where it takes on figure up to the degree of paradox: "God of God, Light of Light, Very God of Very God." Visibly absurd, impossible, false to mere speculation, it is even the more sublimely solidly true. There has never, in fact, been a dissent from it which did not take it away first from the imagination and give it to the notional understanding.

And yet there will be many who can see no possibility, taking this view of the Christian truth, of any thing solid left. We set every thing afloat, they will say; nothing definite and fixed remains to be the base-work of a firm-set, stanchly effective gospel. What is the Christian truth but a dissolving view of something to be known only by its shadows? But we are easily imposed upon here by what has no such value as we think. We commence our thinking process at some point, we analyze, we deduce, we define, we construct, and when we have gotten the given truth out of its scripture images into our own, and made an opinion or definited thing of it, we think we have touched bottom in it and feel a certain confidence of having so much now established. But the reason is, not that we have made the truth more true, but that we have entered our own self-assertion into it in making an opinion or dogma of it, and have so far given a positivity to it that is from ourselves. And yet, the real fact is exactly contrary; viz. , that there is just as much less of solidity in it as there is more that is from ourselves. We take up, for example, the doctrine so-called of repentance, and we find a certain word representing it which means thinking over, changing the mind, and then we lay it down as the positive doctrine that repentance is forming a new governing purpose. That sounds very definite, quite scientific; something we have now found that is clear and determinate. But it turns out, after a few years of preaching in this strain, that the truth we thought so solid is so inadequately true after all as not to have the value we supposed. As a merely one-figure doctrine it is of the lean-kine order, and we get no sense of breadth and body in the change defined, till we bring in all the other figures, the "godly sorrow," the "carefulness," the "self-clearing," the "indignation," the "fear," the "vehement desire," the "zeal," the "revenge," conceiving all these fruits to be from God's inward cogency working thus in us to will and to do. Now we take broad hold; these are the solidities of a completely, roundly adequate conception.

We never so utterly mistake as when we attempt to build up in terms of opinion something more solid and decisively controlling, than what comes to us in the terms of the imagination; that is, by metaphor. The Scriptures, we repeat how often, commend us to "sound doctrine," and assuming this to be the same as doctrine well speculated, we begin to magnify and breed sound doctrine after that fashion; whereas, they only mean sound-making, health-restoring doctrine; which is sure enough indeed to keep good, because it is sure to be wanted, having always in it the spirit of

power, and of a love, and of sound mind. The most food-full doctrine is, in this view, the soundest. Is there any theologic article or church confession more solid and fixedly standard-like in its ideas than the Psalms and the Prophets? The parables of Christ,—what are they but images and figures visible given to the imagination? We turn them a thousand ways in our interpretations, it may be, but we revere them none the less and hold them none the less firmly, that they are rich enough to justify this liberty. A particular one of them in fact, the parable of the prodigal son, is even a kind of pole-star in the sky of the gospel, about which formulas, and creeds, and confessions, are always revolving in ephemeral changes, while that abides and shines. Again there is nothing, as we are wont to feel, that is more solid than our heavenly state, and we call it, in that view, the city that hath foundations. And yet we have no formula that defines it, and no single word of description for it that is not confessedly a figure. It is a garden, a tabernacle, a bosom of Abraham, a new Jerusalem, a city of God cubically built on stones that are gems. If then, nothing is solid, as some will be ready to judge, that is representable only in terms of the imagination, our hopes are all afloat in the sky, or on the air, and our heaven is but a phantom-state which, determinately speaking, is just nowhere and nothing. And yet we do not think so. No Christian man or woman has any such misgiving. Again, why is it that no dogmatic solution of the cross, solid enough to hold the faith of the world, has ever yet been made, while the gospel figures of it are accepted always, rested in and regarded as the pillar of all comfort and hope?

Glancing for just a moment at one or two more strictly human illustrations, what utterance of mortal mind, in what scheme of theology or church confession, has ever proved its adamantine property as fixedly as the Apostles' Creed? And yet there is not a single word of opinion or speculated wisdom in it. It stands wholly in figure, or what is no wise different, in facts that were given to be figure. But if there is any realm of central, astronomic order, it has been this fact-form, truly Copernican confession, about which all the orbits of all the saints, have, in all ages, been revolving.

Summon again for comparison two such masters of doctrine as Turretin and Bunyan; one a great expounder in the school of dogma, and the other a teacher by and before the imagination. Which of these shall we say is the more solid and immovably fixed in authority? The venerable dogmatizer is already far gone by, and will ere long be rather a milestone of history than a living part of it. His carefully squared blocks of opinion and the theologic temple he built of them for all ages to come are already time-worn, crumbling visibly away, like the stones of Tyre, and as if the burden of Tyre were upon them. But the glorious Bunyan fire still burns, because it is fire, kindles the world's imagination more and more, and claims a right to live till the sun itself dies out in the sky. His Pilgrim holds on his way still fresh and strong as ever, nay, fresher and stronger than ever, never to be put off the road till the last traveler heavenward

is conducted in. And yet he saw beforehand that he was likely to be considered a very light kind of teacher, and bespoke more patience than some could think he deserved.

"But must I needs want solidness, because
  By metaphors I speak? Were not God's
    laws,
His gospel laws, in olden time, set forth,
  By Shadows, Types, and Metaphors? Yet
    loth
Will any sober man be to find fault
With them, lest he be found for to assault
The highest Wisdom! No, he rather
    stoops,
And seeks to find out, by what 'Pins,' and
    'Loops,'
By 'Calves,' and 'Sheep,' by 'Heifers,' and
    by 'Rams,'
By 'Birds,' and 'Herbs,' and by the blood
    of 'Lambs,'
God speaketh to him; and happy is he
THAT FINDS THE LIGHT AND GRACE THAT
    IN THEM BE."

Francis Parkman
(1823–1893)

Francis Parkman has been called the "Melville" of nineteenth-century American historians and, like Melville, he was a mass of contradictions. A Boston Brahmin who made his chief subject the life and death of the American forest; a man so weakened in health and beset by nervous disorders affecting his concentration and eyesight that he had to employ a special instrument which permitted him to write without looking at his manuscript, yet still managed to produce twelve large volumes, at a pace sometimes as slow as six lines per day—Parkman found his heroes far from the precincts of New England, among those Indians and whites who could survive in a natural world filled with adversity and violence. Parkman saw in the American wilderness a world still challenging and treacherous enough to test the greatness of the human spirit; and in René-Robert Cavelier, Sieur de la Salle, Parkman discovered someone who met that test.

La Salle explored the Great Lakes region and eventually succeeded in presenting France with the whole territory he named "Louisiana," a territory that stretched "from the Alleghenies to the Rocky Mountains; from the Rio Grande and the Gulf to the farthest springs of the Missouri." In the end, however, this man who personified to Parkman the virtues of physical courage, moral fortitude, practical resourcefulness, and heroic purpose was murdered by one of his own men. La Salle's triumph was thus also his tragedy: the uncompromising standards against which he measured himself were to prove unacceptable and intolerable to those who followed him.

From *LaSalle and the Discovery of the Great West* (1869)

The travellers were crossing a marshy prairie towards a distant belt of woods, that followed the course of a little river. They led with them their five horses, laden with their scanty baggage, and, with what was of no less importance, their stock of presents for Indians. Some wore the remains of the clothing they had worn from France, eked out with deer-skins, dressed in the Indian manner; and some had coats of old sail-cloth. Here was La Salle, in whom one would have known, at a glance, the chief of the party; and the priest, Cavelier, who seems to have shared not one of the high traits of his younger brother. Here, too, were their nephews, Moranget and the boy Cavelier, now about seventeen years old; the trusty soldier Joutel; and the friar Anastase Douay. Duhaut followed, a man of respectable birth and education; and Liotot, the surgeon of the party. At home, they might perhaps have lived and died with a fair repute; but the wilderness is a rude touchstone, which often reveals traits that would have lain buried and unsuspected in civilized life. The German Hiens, the ex-buccaneer, was also of the number. He had probably sailed with an English crew; for he was sometimes knows as *Gemme Anglais,* or "English Jem." The Sieur de Marle; Teissier, a pilot; L'Archevêque, a servant of Duhaut; and others, to the number in all of seventeen,—made up the party; to which is to be added Nika, La Salle's Shawnee hunter, who, as well as another Indian, had twice crossed the ocean with him, and still followed his fortunes with an admiring though undemonstrative fidelity.

They passed the prairie, and neared the forest. Here they saw buffalo; the hunters approached, and killed several of them. Then they traversed the woods; found and forded the shallow and rushy stream, and pushed through the forest beyond, till they again reached the open prairie. Heavy clouds gathered over them, and it rained all night; but they sheltered themselves under the fresh hides of the buffalo they had killed.

Holding a northerly course, the travellers crossed the Brazos, and reached the waters of the Trinity. The weather was unfavorable, and on one occasion they encamped in the rain during four or five days together. It was not an harmonious company. La Salle's cold and haughty reserve had returned, at least for those of his followers to whom he was not partial. Duhaut and the surgeon Liotot, both of whom were men of some property, had a large pecuniary stake in the enterprise, and were disappointed and incensed at its ruinous result. They had a quarrel with young Moranget, whose hot and hasty temper was as little fitted to conciliate as was the harsh reserve of his uncle. Already at Fort St. Louis, Duhaut had intrigued among the men; and the mild admonition of Joutel had not, it seems, sufficed to divert him from his sinister purposes. Liotot, it is said, had secretly sworn vengeance against La Salle, whom he charged with having caused the death of his brother, or, as some will have it, his nephew. On one of the former journeys this young man's strength had failed; and, La Salle having ordered him to return to the fort, he had been killed by Indians on the way.

The party moved again as the weather improved, and on the 15th of March encamped within a few miles of a spot which La Salle had passed on his preceding journey, and where he had left a quantity of Indian corn and beans in *cache;* that is to say, hidden in the ground or in a hollow tree. As provisions were falling short, he sent a party from the camp to find it. These men were Duhaut, Liotot, Hiens the buccaneer, Teissier, L'Archevêque, Nika the hunter, and La Salle's servant Saget. They opened the *cache,* and found the contents spoiled; but as they returned from their bootless errand they saw buffalo, and Nika shot two of them. They now encamped on the spot, and set the servant to inform La Salle, in order that he might send horses to bring in the meat. Accordingly, on the next day, he directed Moranget and De Marle, with the necessary horses, to go with Saget to the hunters' camp. When they arrived, they found that Duhaut and his companions had already cut up the meat, and laid it upon scaffolds for smoking, though it was not yet so dry as, it seems, this process required. Duhaut and the others had also put by, for themselves, the marrow-bones and certain portions of the meat, to which, by woodland custom, they had a perfect right. Moranget, whose rashness and violence had once before caused a fatal catastrophe, fell into a more unreasonable fit of rage, berated and menaced Duhaut and his party, and ended by seizing upon the whole of the meat, including the reserved portions. This added fuel to the fire of Duhaut's old grudge against Moranget and his uncle.

273

There is reason to think that he had harbored deadly designs, the execution of which was only hastened by the present outbreak. The surgeon also bore hatred against Moranget, whom he had nursed with constant attention when wounded by an Indian arrow, and who had since repaid him with abuse. These two now took counsel apart with Hiens, Teissier, and L'Archevêque; and it was resolved to kill Moranget that night. Nika, La Salle's devoted follower, and Saget, his faithful servant, must die with him. All of the five were of one mind except the pilot Teissier, who neither aided nor opposed he plot.

Night came, the woods grew dark; the evening meal was finished, and the evening pipes were smoked. The order of the guard was arranged; and, doubtless by design, the first hour of the night was assigned to Moranget, the second to Saget, and the third to Nika. Gun in hand, each stood watch in turn over the silent but not sleeping forms around him, till, his time expiring, he called the man who was to relieve him, wrapped himself in his blanket, and was soon buried in a slumber that was to be his last. Now the assassins rose. Duhaut and Hiens stood with their guns cocked, ready to shoot down any one of the destined victims who should resist or fly. The surgeon, with an axe, stole towards the three sleepers, and struck a rapid blow at each in turn. Saget and Nika died with little movement; but Moranget started spasmodically into a sitting posture, gasping and unable to speak; and the murderers compelled De Marle, who was not in their plot, to compromise himself by despatching him.

The flood gates of murder were open, and the torrent must have its way. Vengeance and safety alike demanded the death of La Salle. Hiens, or "English Jem," alone seems to have hesitated; for he was one of those to whom that stern commander had always been partial. Meanwhile, the intended victim was still at his camp, about six miles distant. It is easy to picture, with sufficient accuracy, the features of the scene,—the sheds of bark and branches, beneath which, among blankets and buffalo-robes, camp-utensils, pack-saddles, rude harness, guns, powder-horns, and bullet-pouches, the men lounged away the hour, sleeping or smoking, or talking among themselves; the blackened kettles that hung from tripods of poles over the fires; the Indians strolling about the place or lying, like dogs in the sun, with eyes half-shut, yet all observant; and, in the neighboring meadow, the horses grazing under the eye of the watchman.

It was the 18th of March. Moranget and his companions had been expected to return the night before; but the whole day passed, and they did not appear. La Salle became very anxious. He resolved to go and look for them; but not well knowing the way, he told the Indians who were about the camp that he would give them a hatchet if they would guide him. One of them accepted the offer; and La Salle prepared to set out in the morning, at the same time directing Joutel to be ready to go with him. Joutel says: "That evening, while we were talking about what could have happened to the absent men, he seemed to have a presentiment of what was to take place. He asked me if I had

274

heard of any machinations against them, or if I had noticed any bad design on the part of Duhaut and the rest. I answered that I had heard nothing, except that they sometimes complained of being found fault with so often; and that this was all I knew; besides which, as they were persuaded that I was in his interest, they would not have told me of any bad design they might have. We were very uneasy all the rest of the evening."

In the morning, La Salle set out with his Indian guide. He had changed his mind with regard to Joutel, whom he now directed to remain in charge of the camp and to keep a careful watch. He told the friar Anastase Douay to come with him instead of Joutel, whose gun, which was the best in the party, he borrowed for the occasion, as well as his pistol. The three proceeded on their way,—La Salle, the friar, and the Indian. "All the way," writes the friar, "he spoke to me of nothing but matters of piety, grace, and predestation; enlarging on the debt he owed to God, who had saved him from so many perils during more than twenty years of travel in America. Suddenly, I saw him overwhelmed with a profound sadness, for which he himself could not account. He was so much moved that I scarcely knew him." He soon recovered his usual calmness; and they walked on till they approached the camp of Duhaut, which was on the farther side of a small river. Looking about him with the eye of a woodsman, La Salle saw two eagles circling in the air nearly over him, as if attracted by carcasses of beasts or men. He fired his gun and his pistol, as a

summons to any of his followers who might be within hearing. The shots reached the ears of the conspirators. Rightly conjecturing by whom they were fired, several of them, led by Duhaut, crossed the river at a little distance above, where trees or other intervening objects hid them from sight. Duhaut and the surgeon crouched like Indians in the long, dry, reed-like grass of the last summer's growth, while L'Archevêque stood in sight near the bank. La Salle, continuing to advance, soon saw him, and, calling to him, demanded where was Moranget. The man, without lifting his hat, or any show of respect, replied in an agitated and broken voice, but with a tone of studied insolence, that Moranget was strolling about somewhere. La Salle rebuked and menaced him. He rejoined with increased insolence, drawing back, as he spoke, towards the ambuscade, while the incensed commander advanced to chastise him. At that moment a shot was fired from the grass, instantly followed by another; and, pierced through the brain, La Salle dropped dead.

The friar at his side stood terrorstricken, unable to advance or to fly; when Duhaut, rising from the ambuscade, called out to him to take courage, for he had nothing to fear. The murderers now came forward, and with wild looks gathered about their victim. "There thou liest, great Bashaw! There thou liest!" exclaimed the surgeon Liotot, in base exultation over the unconscious corpse. With mockery and insult, they stripped it naked, dragged it into the bushes, and left it there, a prey to the buzzards and the wolves.

Thus the vigor of his manhood, at the age of forty-three, died Robert Cavelier de la Salle, "one of the greatest men," writes Tonty, "of this age"; without question one of the most remarkable explorers whose names live in history. His faithful officer Joutel thus sketches his portrait: "His firmness, his courage, his great knowledge of the arts and sciences, which made him equal to every undertaking, and his untiring energy, which enabled him to surmount every obstacle, would have won at last a glorious success for his grand enterprise, had not all his fine qualities been counterbalanced by a haughtiness of manner which often made him insupportable, and by a harshness towards those under his command which drew upon him an implacable hatred, and was at last the cause of this death."

The enthusiasm of the disinterested and chivalrous Champlain was not the enthusiasm of La Salle; nor had he any part in the self-devoted zeal of the early Jesuit explorers. He belonged not to the age of the knight-errant and the saint, but to the modern world of practical study and practical action. He was the hero not of a principle nor of a faith, but simply of a fixed idea and a determined purpose. As often happens with concentred and energetic natures, his purpose was to him a passion and an inspiration; and he clung to it with a certain fanaticism of devotion. It was the offspring of an ambition vast and comprehensive, yet acting in the interest both of France and of civilization.

Serious in all things, incapable of the lighter pleasures, incapable of repose, finding no joy but in the pursuit of great designs, too shy for society and too reserved for popularity, often unsympathetic and always seeming so, smothering emotions which he could not utter, schooled to universal distrust, stern to his followers and pitiless to himself, bearing the brunt of every hardship and every danger, demanding of others an equal constancy joined to an implicit deference, heeding no counsel but his own, attempting the impossible and grasping at what was too vast to hold— he contained in his own complex and painful nature the chief springs of his triumphs, his failures, and his death.

It is easy to reckon up his defects, but it is not easy to hide from sight the Roman virtues that redeemed them. Beset by a throng of enemies, he stands, like the King of Israel, head and shoulders above them all. He was a tower of adamant, against whose impregnable front hardship and danger, the rage of man and of the elements, the southern sun, the northern blast, fatigue, famine, disease, delay, disappointment, and deferred hope emptied their quivers in vain. That very pride which, Coriolanus-like, declared itself most sternly in the thickest press of foes, has in it something to challenge admiration. Never, under the impenetrable mail of paladin or crusader, beat a heart of more intrepid mettle than within the stoic panoply that armed the breast of La Salle. To estimate aright the marvels of his patient fortitude, one must follow on his track through the vast scene of his interminable journeyings,—those thousands of weary miles of forest, marsh, and river, where, again and again, in the bitterness of baffled striving, the untiring pilgrim pushed onward towards the goal which he was never to attain. America owes him an enduring memory; for in this masculine figure she sees the pioneer who guided her to the possession of her richest heritage.

North American Indian Oratory

The art of oratory was highly cultivated and refined by the North American Indians. In many tribes it was essential to leadership. Decisions in the tribal council usually had to be unanimous, and the authority of the leader was often as dependent upon his powers of persuasion as upon his prowess as a warrior.

Since nearly all the surviving early Indian oratory was transcribed by whites, it is not surprising that the bulk of it is concerned with Indian-white relations. What is surprising, given the history of those relations, is that so much of it is not only dignified and restrained, but often magnanimous. Even when Indian orators are protesting the monstrous injustices, deceptions, and betrayals committed against their people, their tone is never shrill, accusatory, or self-pitying. Their case is based on humane as well as religious grounds, and their appeal is always to the nobler side of their antagonists.

It has sometimes been countered that the eloquence of Indian oratory is attributable to the fact that it was transcribed by sympathetic whites who wanted to put the Indian cause in its most attractive light. Fortunately, there are enough reliable translations of Indian oratory to leave little doubt as to the skill of its practitioners.

The following selections begin in the first years of American colonization and continue almost to the end of the nineteenth century. They are presented together here in order to preserve the integrity of the story they tell, a story of special importance to the religious meaning of the American experience. It is a story both of the moral and religious corruptions to which the white version of the American experience was susceptible and of the spiritual resources on which American Indians could draw, and which they transmitted, to give new meaning to the experience of the land.

Chief Powhatan (1609)

Chief Powhatan presided over a confederacy of Algonquin tribes that roamed the territory of Virginia and Maryland at the time of the first English settlement at Jamestown in 1607. The generally amicable nature of early relations between Indians and whites appears to have been attributable to Powhatan's influence. His daughter Pocahontas actually married one of the settlers, John Rolfe. After Powhatan's death hostilities broke out, and the Indians began a fourteen-year war in which they attempted to exterminate the whites.

The following speech was given by Powhatan in 1609 at Werowcomico (Gloucester County) and reported by John Smith.

Why will you take by force what you may obtain by love? Why will you destroy us who supply you with food? What can you get by war? . . . We are unarmed, and willing to give you what you ask, if you come in a friendly manner. . . .

I am not so simple as not to know it is better to eat good meat, sleep comfortably, live quietly with my women and children, laugh and be merry with the English, and being their friend, trade for their copper and hatchets, than to run away from them. . . .

Take away your guns and swords, the cause of all our jealousy, or you may die in the same manner.

Chief Logan (1774)

In 1774 the colonial governor called a council in an attempt to end the Indian war of revenge provoked by white atrocities against the "Mingos," a band of friendly Iroquois in the upper Ohio River valley. Chief Logan's address to that council won him the admiration of Thomas Jefferson. Logan reminded his white brothers that the senseless slaughter of all his living relations had created his need to balance the scales of justice. Having accomplished his revenge, Chief Logan once again embraced peace as enthusiastically as he had sought retribution.

I appeal to any white man to say, if ever he entered Logan's cabin hungry, and he gave him not meat; if ever he came cold and naked, and he clothed him not. During the course of the last long and bloody war, Logan remained idle in his cabin, an advocate for peace. Such was my love for the whites that my countrymen pointed as they passed, and said, "Logan is the friend of the white man." I had even thought to have lived with you, but for the injuries of one man, Colonel Cressap, who last spring, in cold blood and unprovoked, murdered all the relations of Logan, not even sparing my women and children. There runs not a drop of my blood in the veins of any living creature. This called on me for revenge. I have sought it; I have killed many; I have fully glutted my vengeance. For my countrymen I rejoice at the beams of peace. But do not harbor a thought that mine is the joy of fear. Logan never felt fear! He will not turn on his heel to save his life. Who is there to mourn for Logan? Not one.

Chief Pachgantschilias (1787)

In 1787 Chief Pachgantschilias of the Delawares delivered this warning to a group of Christianized Indians at Gnadenhütten, Pennsylvania. It was taken down by a Moravian missionary who was among the listeners. The bitterness and cynicism of these words hold up a mirror to the double-dealing and betrayal that whites so often inflicted on

Indians. These stark phrases are eloquent of suffering and despair.

I admit that there are good white men, but they bear no proportion to the bad; the bad must be the strongest, for they rule. They do what they please. They enslave those who are not of their color, although created by the same Great Spirit who created them. They would make slaves of us if they could; but as they cannot do it, they kill us. There is no faith to be placed in their words. They are not like the Indians, who are only enemies while at war, and are friends in peace. They will say to an Indian, "My friend; my brother!" They will take him by the hand, and, at the same moment, destroy him. And so you will also be treated by them before long. Remember that this day I have warned you to beware of such friends as these. I know the Long-knives. They are not to be trusted.

Chief Tecumseh (1810)

The Shawnee Chief Tecumseh was outraged by the sale of Indian lands to whites. In this particular case, he believed that there was special cause for resentment, as the Indians involved were inebriated and thus easily manipulated by their white brothers. Characteristically, his protest is not restricted to the specific offense, but involves the larger issue raised by the Indians' feeling for the land: "Sell a country! Why not sell the air, the

great sea, as well as the earth? Did not the Great Spirit make them all for the use of his children?"

Houses are built for you to hold councils in; Indians hold theirs in the open air. I am a Shawnee. My forefathers were warriors. Their son is a warrior. From them I take my only existence. From my tribe I take nothing. I have made myself what I am. And I would that I could make the red people as great as the conceptions of my own mind, when I think of the Great Spirit that rules over us all. . . . I would not then come to Governor Harrison to ask him to tear up the treaty. But I would say to him, "Brother, you have the liberty to return to your own country."

You wish to prevent the Indians from doing as we wish them, to unite and let them consider their lands as the common property of the whole. You take the tribes aside and advise them not to come into this measure. . . . You want by your distinctions of Indian tribes, in allotting to each a particular, to make them war with each other. You never see an Indian endeavor to make the white people do this. You are continually driving the red people, when at last you will drive them onto the great lake, where they can neither stand nor work.

Since my residence at Tippecanoe, we have endeavored to level all distinctions, to destroy village chiefs, by whom all mischiefs are done. It is they who sell the land to the Americans. Brother, this land that was sold, and the goods that was given for it, was only done by a few. . . . In the future we are prepared to punish those who propose to sell land to the Americans. If you continue to purchase them, it will make war among the different tribes, and, at last I do not know what will be the consequences among the white people. Brother, I wish you would take pity on the red people and do as I have requested. If you will not give up the land and do cross the boundary of our present settlement, it will be very hard, and produce great trouble between us.

The way, the only way to stop this evil is for the red men to unite in claiming a common and equal right in the land, as it was at first, and should be now—for it was never divided, but belongs to all. No tribe has the right to sell, even to each other, much less to strangers. . . . *Sell a country! Why not sell the air, the great sea, as well as the earth? Did not the Great Spirit make them all for the use of his children?*

How can we have confidence in the white people!

When Jesus Christ came upon the earth you killed Him and nailed Him to the cross. You thought He was dead, and you were mistaken. You have Shakers among you and you laugh and make light of their worship.

Everything I have told you is the truth. The Great Spirit has inspired me.

Chief Sharitarish (1822)

Chief Sharitarish was a Pawnee. He delivered this speech to President James Monroe and John C. Calhoun, the Secretary of War, *in Washington, D.C. on February 4, 1822, having traveled to the capitol under the protection of Major James O'Fallon to plead the case of his people.*

My Great Father: I have traveled a great distance to see you—I have seen you and my heart rejoices. I have heard your words—they have entered one ear and shall not escape the other, and I will carry them to my people as pure as they came from your mouth.

My Great Father: . . . If I am here now and have seen your people, your houses, your vessels on the big lake, and a great many wonderful things far beyond my comprehension, which appear to have been made by the Great Spirit and placed in your hands, I am indebted to my Father [Major Benjamin O'Fallon] here, who invited me from home, under whose wings I have been protected. . . . but there is still another Great Father to whom I am much indebted—it is the Father of us all. . . . The Great Spirit made us all—he made my skin red, and yours white; he placed us on this earth, and intended that we should live differently from each other.

He made the whites to cultivate the earth, and feed on domestic animals; but he made us, red skins, to rove through the uncultivated woods and plains; to feed on wild animals; and to dress with their skins. He also intended that we should go to war—to take scalps—steal horses from and triumph over our enemies—cultivate peace at home, and promote the happiness of each other.

My Great Father: Some of your good chiefs, as they called [missionaries], have proposed to send some of their good people among us to change our habits, to make us work and live like the white people. . . . You love your country—you love your people—you love the manner in which they live, and you think your people brave. I am like you, my Great Father, I love my country—I love my people—I love the manner in which we live, and think myself and warriors brave. Spare me then, my Father; let me enjoy me country, and I will trade skins with your people. I have grown up, and lived thus long without work—I am in hopes you will suffer me to die without it. We have plenty of buffalo, beaver, deer, and other wild animals—we have an abundance of horses—we have everything we want—we have plenty of land, if you will keep your people off of it. . . .

There was a time when we did not know the whites—our wants were then fewer than they are now. They were always within our control—we had then seen nothing which we could not get. Before our intercourse with the whites, who have caused such a destruction in our game, we could lie down to sleep, and when we awoke we would find the buffalo feeding around our camp—but now we are killing them for their skins, and feeding the wolves with their flesh, to make our children cry over their bones.

Here, my Great Father, is a pipe which I present you as I am accustomed to present pipes to all the red skins in peace with us. It is filled with such tobacco as we were accustomed to smoke before we knew the white people. It is pleasant, and the spontaneous growth of the most remote parts of our country. I know that the robes, leggings, moccasins, bear claws, etc., are of little value to you, but we wish you to have them deposited and preserved in some conspicuous part of your lodge, so that when we are gone and the sod turned over our bones, if our children should visit this place, as we do now, they may see and recognize with pleasure the deposits of their fathers; and reflect on the times that are past.

Chief Cobb (1843)

The Treaty of Dancing Rabbit Creek, 1830, was just one of many infamous episodes in the history of Indian-white relations. It compelled the Choctaws of Mississippi to move to Oklahoma. A small number of the Choctaws had been exempted from the Treaty, and told that they could retain their ancestral lands. When this promise was broken in 1843 and the remaining Choctaws were ordered to follow their brethren westward, Chief Cobb delivered the following speech to the Indian agent.

BROTHER: We have heard your words as from the lips of our father, the great white chief at Washington, and my people have asked me to reply. The red man has no books, and when he wants to say what he thinks, he speaks from the mouth, like his fathers before him. He is afraid of *writing*. When he *speaks,* he knows what he says. The Great Spirit hears him. *Writing* is the invention of the palefaces. It gives birth to trouble and fighting. The Great Spirit *talks*. We hear him in the thunder, in the sound of the wind, and in the water. He never *writes*.

BROTHER: When you were young, we were strong. We fought at your side. But now our arms are broken. You have grown big. My people have grown little.

BROTHER: My voice is weak. You can scarcely hear me. It is not the shout of a warrior, but the cry of a baby. I have lost my voice mourning the sufferings of my people. These are their graves, and in those old pines you hear the ghosts of our dead. Their ashes are here, and we have been left behind to guard them. Our warriors have nearly all gone to the far country in the west. But our dead are *here*. Shall we go too and leave their bones to the wolves?

BROTHER: Two sleeps have passed since we heard you talk. We have thought about what you said. You ask us to leave our country, and you say it is our father's wish. We do not want to offend our father. We respect him and we respect you, his son. But the Choctaw always thinks. We want time to answer.

BROTHER: Our hearts are full. Twelve winters ago our chiefs sold our country. Every warrior you see here was opposed to that treaty. If the dead could have been counted, the treaty would never have been made. They were here, but they were not seen or heard. Their tears were in the rain, their voices were in the wind. But the palefaces did not know it, and our land was taken away.

BROTHER: We do not complain now. The Choctaw suffers, but he does not weep. You have the strong arm, we cannot resist. But the white man worships the Great Spirit. The red man worships him too. The Great Spirit loves truth. When you took our country, you promised us land. There is your promise in the book. Twelve times the trees have dropped their leaves, but we have received no land. Our lodges have been taken from us. The white man's plough turns up the bones of our fathers. We dare not kindle our fires. And yet you told us we could stay here and you would give us land.

BROTHER: Is this *truth?* But we believe, now that our great father knows our condition, that he will hear us. We are like mourning orphans in our own country. But our father will take us by the hand. When he fulfills his promise, we will answer his talk. He means well. We know it. But we cannot think now. Suffering has made children of us. When our business is settled, we will be men again. Then we will talk to our great father about what he has proposed.

BROTHER: You stand in the moccasins of a great chief. You speak the words of a great nation, and your talk was long. My people are small. Their shadow barely reaches to your knee. They are scattered and gone. When I shout, I hear my own voice in the forest, but no shout answers back. This is why my words are few. I have nothing more to say, but to tell what I have said to the tall chief of the palefaces, whose brother stands by your side.

Chief Seattle (1854)

Chief Seattle was a Dwamish Indian who presided over all the tribes inhabiting the region of Puget Sound. He made this speech to the Governor of the Washington territory in connection with the Port Elliot Treaty of 1855, which he eventually signed. Chief Seattle realized that resistance was futile and that the Indian must resign himself to his fate. In one of the most moving of all passages of Indian oratory, Chief Seattle looks beyond the inevitable extinction of the Indian, and foresees his survival in the American imagination as part of the legacy of the wilderness.

Yonder sky that has wept tears of compassion upon my people for centuries untold, and which to us appears changeless and eternal, may change. Today is fair. Tomorrow it may be overcast with clouds. My words are like the stars that never change. Whatever Seattle says the great chief at Washington can rely upon with as much certainty as he can upon the return of the sun or the seasons. The White Chief says that Big Chief at Washington sends us greetings of friendship and goodwill. That is kind of him for we know he has little need of our friendship in return. His people are many. They are like that grass that covers vast prairies. My people are few. They resemble the scattering trees of a storm-swept plain. . . . I will not dwell on, nor mourn over, our untimely decay, nor reproach our paleface brothers with hastening it, as we too may have been somewhat to blame. . . .

Your God is not our God. Your God loves your people and hates mine. He folds his strong and protecting arms lovingly about the paleface and leads him by the hand as a father leads his infant son—but He has forsaken His red children—if they really are His. Our God, the Great Spirit, seems also to have forsaken us. Your God makes your people strong every day. Soon they will fill the land. Our people are ebbing away like a rapidly receding tide that will never return. The white man's God cannot love our people or He would protect them. They seem to be orphans who can look nowhere for help. How then can we be brothers? . . . We are two distinct races with separate origins and separate destinies. There is little in common between us.

To us the ashes of our ancestors are sacred and their resting place is hallowed ground. You wander far from the graves of your ancestors and seemingly without regret. Your religion was written upon tables of stone by the iron finger of your God so that you could not forget. The Red Man could never comprehend nor remember it. Our religion is the traditions of our ancestors—the dreams of our old men, given them in solemn hours of night by the Great Spirit; and the visions of our sachems; and it is written in the hearts of our people.

Your dead cease to love you and the land of their nativity as soon as they pass the portals of the tomb and wander way beyond the stars. They are soon forgotten and never return. Our dead never forget the beautiful world that gave them being.

Day and night cannot dwell together.

The Red Man has ever fled the approach of the White Man, as the morning mist flees before the morning sun. However, your proposition seems fair and I think that my people will accept it and will retire to the reservation you offer them. Then we will dwell apart in peace. . . . It matters little where we pass the remnant of our days. They will not be many. A few more moons; a few more winters—and not one of the descendants of the mighty hosts that once moved over this broad land or lived in happy homes, protected by the Great Spirit, will remain to mourn over the graves of a people once more powerful and hopeful than yours. But why should I mourn at the untimely fate of my people? Tribe follows tribe, and nation follows nation, like the waves of the sea. It is the order of nature, and regret is useless. Your time of decay may be distant, but it will surely come, for even the White Man whose God walked and talked with him as friend with friend, cannot be exempt from the common destiny. We may be brothers after all. We will see. . . .

Every part of this soil is sacred in the estimation of my people. Every hillside, every valley, every plain and grove, has been hallowed by some sad or happy event in days long vanished. The very dust upon which you now stand responds more lovingly to their footsteps than to yours, because it is rich with the blood of our ancestors and our bare feet are conscious of the sympathetic touch. Even the little children who lived here and rejoiced here for a brief season will love these somber solitudes and at eventide they greet shadowy returning spir-

its. And when the last Red Man shall have perished, and the memory of my tribe shall have become a myth among the White Men, these shores will swarm with the invisible dead of my tribe, and when your children's children think themselves alone in the field, the store, the shop, upon the highway, or in the silence of the pathless woods, they will not be alone. At night when the street of your cities and villages are silent and you think them deserted, they will throng with the returning hosts that once filled and still love this beautiful land. The White Man will never be alone.

Let him be just and deal kindly with my people, for the dead are not powerless. Dead, did I say? There is no death, only a change of worlds.

Chief Joseph (1879)

The long and tragic saga of the Nez Perce tribe began at the dawn of the nineteenth century and ended in the first years of the twentieth. The Nez Perce provided shelter, supplies, and comfort to the Lewis and Clark expedition after its harrowing crossing of the Rockies. For fifty years thereafter the tribe remained in the Wallowa Valley of the Oregon territory and prided itself on its amicable relations with whites. In time, however, the progress of Western settlement put increasing pressure on the Nez Perce to relinquish their lands and retire to a reservation. Some complied but others, led by Chief Joseph, refused. When new pressure was applied, the old chief's son, young Chief Joseph, appealed to President Grant for protection and for a time received it. Before long, however, the order restricting white settlement of Nez Perce lands was revoked and in 1877 a military force was dispatched to remove the Indians to a reservation. Chief Joseph was compelled to submit, but the conditions for removal imposed by the army proved impossible to meet, and a small group of angry and desperate braves killed some whites. Then the war between the United States and the Nez Perce began in earnest.

Chief Joseph attempted to escape to Canada with the remainder of his tribe, but with over four hundred women, children, and old people in addition to his two hundred fifty warriors, it was impossible, and Chief Joseph was forced to surrender. The terms of surrender were broken by the U.S., and instead of being returned to their reservation in the West the tribe was shipped to Fort Leavenworth in Kansas. Many had died in flight and now many more would die in captivity.

Chief Joseph was finally granted permission to travel to Washington, D.C. to plead the cause of his people. He met with many government officials and even managed to publish an account of his people's odyssey and sufferings in the prestigious North American Review. All this was to no avail. Chief Joseph returned to Kansas, and his people, after prolonged suffering, were returned to the reservation set aside for them. But he and one hundred braves judged to be dangerous were sent to another reservation hundreds of miles distant and separated from the tribe forever. It was there, in 1904, that Chief Joseph finally died of what the post physician diagnosed as "a broken heart."

I believe General Miles would have kept his word if he could have done so. I do not blame him for what we have suf-

fered since the surrender. I do not know who is to blame. We gave up all our horses—over eleven hundred—and all our saddles—over one hundred—and we have not heard from them since. Somebody has got our horses.

General Miles turned my people over to another soldier, and we were taken to Bismarck. Captain Johnson, who now had charge of us, received an order to take us to Fort Leavenworth. At Leavenworth we were placed on a low river bottom, with no water except river-water to drink and cook with. We had always lived in a healthy country, where the mountains were high and the water was cold and clear. Many of my people sickened and died, and we buried them in this strange land. I can not tell how much my heart suffered for my people while at Leavenworth. The Great Spirit Chief who rules above seemed to be looking some other way, and did not see what was being done to my people.

During the hot days we received notice that we were to be moved farther away from our own country. We were not asked if we were willing to go. We were ordered to get into the railroad-cars. Three of my people died on the way to Baxter Springs. It was worse to die there than to die fighting in the mountains.

We were moved from Baxter Springs to the Indian Territory, and set down without our lodges. We had but little medicine, and we were nearly all sick. Seventy of my people have died since we moved there.

We have had a great many visitors who have talked many ways. Some of the chiefs from Washington came to see us, and selected land for us to live upon. We have not moved to that land, for it is not a good place to live.

The Commissioner Chief came to see us. I told him, as I told every one, that I expected General Miles's word would be carried out. He said it "could not be done; that white men now lived in my country and all the land was taken up; that, if I returned to Wallowa, I could not live in peace; that law-papers were out against young men who began the war, and that the Government could not protect my people." This talk fell like a heavy stone upon my heart. I saw that I could not gain anything by talking to him. Other law chiefs [the congressional committee] came to see me and said they would help me to get a healthy country. I did not know who to believe. The white people have too many chiefs. They do not understand each other. They do not talk alike.

The Commissioner Chief invited me to go wtih him and hunt for a better home than we have how. I like the land we found (west of the Osage reservation) better than any place I have seen in that country; but it is not a healthy land. There are no mountains and rivers. The water is warm. It is not a good country for stock. I do not believe my peple can live there. I am afraid they will all die. The Indians who occupy that country are dying off. I promised Chief Hayt to go there, and do the best I could until the Government got ready to make good General Miles's word. I was not satisfied, but I could not help myself.

Then the Inspector Chief came to my camp and we had a long talk. He said I ought to have a home in the mountain country north, and that he would write a letter to the Great Chief at Washington. Again the hope of seeing the mountains of Idaho and Oregon grew up in my heart.

At last I was granted permission to come to Washington and bring my friend Yellow Bull and our interpreter with me. I am glad we came. I have shaken hands with a great many friends, but there are some things I want to know which no one seems able to explain. I can not understand how the Government sends a man out to fight us, as it did General Miles, and then breaks his word. Such a Government has something wrong about it. I can not understand why so many chiefs are allowed to talk so many different ways, and promise so many different things. I have seen the Great Father Chief [the President], the next Great Chief [the Secretary of the Interior], the Commissioner Chief, and the Law Chief [General Butler], and many other law chiefs [Congressman], and they all say they are my friends, and that I shall have justice, but while their mouths all talk right I do not understand why nothing is done for my people. I have heard talk and talk, but nothing is done. Good words do not last long unless they amount to something. Words do not pay for my dead people. They do not pay for my country now overrun by white men. They do not protect my father's grave. They do not pay for all my horses and cattle. Good words will not give me back my children. Good words will not make good the promise of your War Chief General Miles. Good words will not give my people good health and stop them from dying. Good words will not get my people a home where they can live in peace and take care of themselves. I am tried of talk that comes to nothing. It makes my heart sick when I remember all the good words and all the broken promises. There has been too much talking by men who had no right to talk. Too many misrepresentations have been made, too many misunderstandings have come up between the white men about the Indians. If the white man wants to live in peace with the Indian he can live in peace. There need be no trouble. Treat all men alike. Give them all the same law. Give them all an even chance to live and grow. All men were made by the same Great Spirit Chief. They are all brothers. The earth is the mother of all people, and all people should have equal rights upon it. You might as well expect the rivers to run backward as that any man who was born a free man should be contented when penned up and denied liberty to go where he pleases. If you tie a horse to a stake, do you expect he will grow fat? If you pen an Indian up on a small spot of earth, and compel him to stay there, he will not be contented, nor will he grow and prosper. I have asked some of the great white chiefs where they get their authority to say to the Indian that he shall stay in one place, while he sees the white men going where they please. They can not tell me.

I only ask of the Government to be treated as all other men are treated. If I can not go to my own home, let me have a home in some country where my people will not die so fast. I would like to go to Bitter Root Valley. There my people would be healthy; where they are now they are dying. Three have died since I left my camp to come to Washington.

When I think of our condition my heart is heavy. I see men of my race trated as outlaws and driven from country to country, or shot down like animals.

I know that my race must change. We can not hold our own with the white men as we are. We only ask an even chance to live as other men live. We ask to be recognized as men. We ask that the same law shall work alike on all men. If the Indian breaks the law, punish him by the law. If the white man breaks the law, punish him also.

Let me be a free man—free to travel, free to stop, free to work, free to trade where I choose, free to choose my own teachers, free to follow the religion of my fathers, free to think and talk and act for myself—and I will obey every law, or submit to the penalty.

Whenever the white man treats the Indian as they treat each other, then we will have no more wars. We shall all be alike—brothers of one father and one mother, with one sky above us and one country around us, and one government for all. Then the Great Spirit Chief who rules above will smile upon this land, and send rain to wash out the bloody spots made by brothers' hands from the face of the earth. For this time the Indian race are waiting and praying. I hope that no more groans of wounded men and women will ever go to the ear of the Great Spirit Chief above, and that all people may be one people.

In-mut-too-yah-lat-lat has spoken for his people.

W. E. B. DuBois (1868–1963)

W. E. B. (William Edward Burghardt) DuBois, black educator, author, and intellectual leader, taught economics and history at Atlanta University from 1897 to 1910. In 1909, DuBois helped to found the National Association for the Advancement of Colored People. As the editor of *Crisis,* the magazine of the N.A.A.C.P., he made significant contributions to American cultural sociology. An opponent of the conciliatory racial politics of Booker T. Washington, DuBois was a fearless and resourceful champion of full equality for black people in America, and was an articulate exponent of the integrity and worth of black American culture.

From *The Souls of Black Folk*

Of Our Spiritual Strivings

O water, voice of my heart, crying in the
    sand,
  All night long crying with a mournful
    cry,
As I lie and listen, and cannot understand
    The voice of my heart in my side or
    the voice of the sea,
  O water, crying for rest, is it I, is it I?
    All night long the water is crying to
    me.

Unresting water, there shall never be rest
  Till the last moon droop and the last tide
    fail,
And the fire of the end begin to burn in
    the west;
    And the heart shall be weary and won-
    der and cry like the sea,
  All life long crying without avail,
    As the water all night long is crying to
    me.

                   Arthur Symons

Between me and the other world there is ever an unasked question: unasked by some through feelings of delicacy; by others through the difficulty of rightly framing it. All, nevertheless, flutter round it. They approach me in a half-hesitant sort of way, eye me curiously or compassionately, and then, instead of saying directly, How does it feel to be a problem? they say, I know an excellent colored man in my town; or, I fought at Mechanicsville; or, Do not these Southern outrages make your blood boil? At these I smile, or am interested, or reduce the boiling to a simmer, as the occasion may require. To the real question, How does it feel to be a problem? I answer seldom a word.

And yet, being a problem is a strange experience,—peculiar even for one who has never been anything else, save perhaps in babyhood and in Europe. It is in the early days of rollicking boyhood that the revelation first bursts upon one, all in a day, as it were. I remember well when the shadow swept across me. I was a little thing, away up in the hills of New England, where the dark Housatonic winds between Hoosac and Taghkanic to the sea. In a wee wooden schoolhouse, something put it into the boys' and girls' heads to buy gorgeous visiting-cards—ten cents a package—and exchange. The exchange was merry, till one girl, a tall newcomer, refused my card,—refused it peremptorily, with a glance. Then it dawned upon me with a certain suddenness that I was different from the others; or like, mayhap, in heart and life and longing, but shut out from their world by a vast veil. I had thereafter no desire to tear down that veil, to creep through; I held all beyond it in common contempt, and lived above it in a region of blue sky and great wandering shadows. That sky was bluest when I could beat my mates at examination-time, or beat them at a foot-race, or even beat their stringy heads. Alas, with the years all this fine contempt began to fade; for the worlds I longed for, and all their dazzling opportunities, were theirs, not mine. But they should not keep these prizes, I said; some, all, I would wrest from them. Just how I would do it I could never decide: by reading law, by healing the sick, by telling the wonderful tales that swam in my head,—some way. With other black boys the strife was not so fiercely sunny: their youth shrunk into tasteless sycophancy, or into silent hatred of the pale world about them and mocking distrust of everything white; or wasted itself in a bitter cry, Why did God make me an outcast and a stranger in mine own house? The shades of the prison-house closed round about us all: walls strait and stubborn to the whitest, but relentlessly narrow, tall, and unscalable to sons of night who must plod darkly on in resignation, or beat unavailing palms against the stone, or steadily, half hopelessly, watch the streak of blue above.

After the Egyptian and Indian, the Greek and Roman, the Teuton and Mongolian, the Negro is a sort of seventh son, born with a veil, and gifted with second-sight in this American world,—a world which yields him no true self-consciousness, but only lets him see himself through the revelation of the other world. It is a peculiar sensation, this double-consciousness, this sense of always looking at one's self through the eyes of others, of measuring one's soul by the tape of a world that looks on in amused contempt and pity. One ever feels his two-ness,—an American, a Negro; two souls, two thoughts, two unreconciled strivings; two warring ideals in one dark body, whose dogged strength alone keeps it from being torn asunder.

The history of the American Negro is the history of this strife,—this longing to attain self-conscious manhood, to merge his double self into a better and truer self. In this merging he wishes neither of the older selves to be lost. He would not Africanize America, for America has too much to teach the world and Africa. He would not bleach his Negro soul in a flood of white Americanism, for he knows that Negro blood has a message for the world. He simply wishes to make it possible for a man to be both a Negro and an American, without being cursed and spit upon by his fellows, without having the doors of Opportunity closed roughly in his face.

This, then, is the end of his striving: to be a co-worker in the kingdom of culture, to escape both death and isolation, to husband and use his best powers and his latent genius. These powers of body and mind have in the past been strangely wasted, dispersed, or forgotten. The shadow of a mighty Negro past flits through the tale of Ethiopia the Shadowy and of Egypt the Sphinx. Throughout history, the powers of single black men flash here and there like falling stars, and die sometimes before the world has rightly gauged their brightness. Here in America, in the few days since Emancipation, the black man's turning hither and thither in hesitant and doubtful striving has often made his very strength to lose effectiveness, to seem like absence of power, like weakness. And yet it is not weakness,—it is the contradiction of double aims. The double-aimed struggle of the black artisan—on the one hand to escape white contempt for a nation of mere hewers of wood and drawers of water, and on the other hand to plough and nail and dig for a poverty-stricken horde—could only result in making him a poor craftsman, for he had but half a heart in either cause. By the poverty and ignorance of his people, the Negro minister or doctor was tempted toward quackery and demagogy; and by the criticism of the other world, toward ideals that made him ashamed of his lowly tasks. The would-be black *savant* was confronted by the paradox that the knowledge his people needed was a twice-told tale to his white neighbors, while the knowledge which would teach the white world was Greek to his own flesh and blood. The innate love of harmony and beauty that set the ruder souls of his people a-dancing and a-singing raised but confusion and doubt in the soul of the black artist; for the beauty revealed to him was the soul-beauty of a race which his larger audience despised, and he could not articulate the message of another people. This waste of double aims, this seeking to satisfy two unreconciled ideals, has wrought sad havoc with the courage and faith and deeds of ten thousand thousand people,—has sent them often wooing false gods and invoking false means of salvation, and at times has even semed about to make them ashamed of themselves.

Away back in the days of bondage they thought to see in one divine event the end of all doubt and disappointment; few men ever worshipped Freedom with half such unquestioning faith as did the American Negro for two centuries. To him, so far as he thought and dreamed, slavery was indeed the sum of all villainies, the cause of all sorrow, the root of all prejudice; Emancipation was the key to a promised land of sweeter beauty than ever stretched before the eyes of wearied Israelites. In song and exhortation swelled one refrain—Liberty; in his tears and curses the God he implored had Freedom in his right hand. At last it came,—suddenly, fearfully, like a dream. With one wild carnival of blood and passion came the message in his own plaintive cadences:—

> "Shout, O children!
>   Shout, you're free!
>   For God has bought your liberty!"

Years have passed away since then,— ten, twenty, forty; forty years of national life, forty years of renewal and development, and yet the swarthy spectre sits in its accustomed seat at the Nation's feast. In vain do we cry to this our vastest social problem:—

"Take any shape but that, and my firm nerves
  Shall never tremble!"

The Nation has not yet found peace from its sins; the freedman has not yet found in freedom his promised land. Whatever of good may have come in these years of change, the shadow of a deep disappointment rests upon the Negro people,—a disappointment all the more bitter because the unattained ideal was unbounded save by the simple ignorance of a lowly people.

The first decade was merely a prolongation of the vain search for freedom, the boon that seemed ever barely to elude their grasp,—like a tantalizing will-o'-the-wisp, maddening and misleading the headless host. The holocaust of war, the terrors of the Ku-Klux Klan, the lies of carpet-baggers, the disorganization of industry, and the contradictory advice of friends and foes, left the bewildered serf with no new watchword beyond the old cry for freedom. As the time flew, however, he began to grasp a new idea. The ideal of liberty demanded for its attainment powerful means, and these the Fifteenth Amendment gave him. The ballot, which before he had looked upon as a visible sign of freedom, he now regarded as the chief means of gaining and perfecting the liberty with which war had partially endowed him. And why not? Had not votes made war and emancipated millions? Had not votes enfranchised the freedmen? Was anything impossible to a power that had done all this? A million black men started with renewed zeal to vote themselves into the kingdom. So the decade flew away, the revolution of 1876 came, and left the half-free serf weary, wondering, but still inspired. Slowly but steadily, in the following years, a new vision began gradually to replace the dream of political power,—a powerful movement, the rise of another ideal to guide the unguided, another pillar of fire by night after a clouded day. It was the ideal of "book-learning"; the curiosity, born of compulsory ignorance, to know and test the power of the cabalistic letters of the white man, the longing to know. Here at last seemed to have been discovered the mountain path to Canaan; longer than the highway of Emancipation and law, steep and rugged, but straight, leading to heights high enough to overlook life.

Up the new path the advance guard toiled, slowly heavily, doggedly; only those who have watched and guided the faltering feet, the misty minds, the dull understandings, of the dark pupils of these schools know how faithfully, how piteously, this people strove to learn. It was weary work. The cold statistician wrote down the inches of progress here and there, noted also where here and there a foot had slipped or some one had fallen. To the tired climbers, the horizon was ever dark, the mists were often cold, the Canaan was always dim and far away. If, however, the vistas disclosed as yet no goal, no resting-place, little but flattery and criticism, the journey at least gave leisure for reflection and self-examination; it changed the child of Emancipation to the youth with dawning self-consciousness, self-realization, self-respect. In those sombre forests of his striving his own soul rose before him, and he saw himself,—darkly as through a veil; and yet he saw in himself some faint revelation of his power, of his mission. He began to have a dim feeling that, to attain his place in the world, he must be himself, and not another. For the first time he sought to analyze the burden he bore upon his back, that dead-weight of social degradation partially masked behind a half-named Negro problem. He felt his poverty; without a cent, without a home, without land, tools, or savings, he had entered into competition with rich, landed, skilled neighbors. To be a poor man is hard, but to be a poor race in a land of dollars is the very bottom of hardships. He felt the weight of his ignorance,—not simply of letters, but of life, of business, of the humanities; the accumulated sloth and shirking and awkwardness of decades and centuries shackled his hands and feet. Nor was his burden all poverty and ignorance. The red stain of bastardy, which two centuries of systematic legal defilement of Negro women had stamped upon his race, meant not only the loss of ancient African chastity, but also the hereditary weight of a mass of corruption from white adulterers, threatening almost the obliteration of the Negro home.

A people thus handicapped ought not to be asked to race with the world, but rather allowed to give all its time and thought to its own social problems. But alas! while sociologists gleefully count his bastards and his prostitutes, the very soul of the toiling, sweating black man is darkened by the shadow of a vast despair. Men call the shadow prejudice, and learnedly explain it as the natural defence of culture against barbarism, learning against ignorance, purity against crime, the "higher" against the "lower" races. To which the Negro cries Amen! and swears that to so much of this strange prejudice as is founded on just homage to civilization, culture, righteousness, and progress, he humbly bows and meekly does obeisance. But before that nameless prejudice that leaps beyond all this he stands helpless, dismayed, and well-nigh speechless; before that personal disrespect and mockery, the ridicule and systematic humiliation, the distortion of fact and wanton license of fancy, the cynical ignoring of the better and the boisterous welcoming of the worse, the all-pervading desire to inculcate disdain for everything black, from Toussaint to the devil,—before this there rises a sickening despair that would disarm and discourage any nation save that black host to whom "discouragement" is an unwritten word.

But the facing of so vast a prejudice could not but bring the inevitable self-questioning, self-disparagement, and lowering of ideals which ever accompany repression and breed in an atmosphere of contempt and hate. Whisperings and portents came borne upon the four winds: Lo! we are diseased and dying, cried the dark hosts; we cannot write, our voting is vain; what need of education, since we must always cook and serve? And the Nation echoed and enforced this self-criticism, saying: Be content to be servants, and nothing more; what need of higher culture for half-men? Away with the black man's ballot, by force or fraud,—and behold the suicide of a race! Nevertheless, out of the evil came something of good,—the more careful adjustment of education to real life, the clearer perception of the Negroes' social responsibilities, and the sobering realization of the meaning of progress.

So dawned the time of *Sturm und Drang:* storm and stress to-day rocks our little boat on the mad waters of the world-sea; there is within and without the sound of conflict, the burning of body and rending of soul; inspiration strives with doubt, and faith with vain questionings. The bright ideals of the past,—physical freedom, political power, the training of brains and the training of hands,—all these in turn have waxed and waned, until even the last grows dim and overcast. Are they all wrong,—all false? No, not that, but each alone was over-simple and incomplete,—the dreams of a credulous race-childhood, or the fond imaginings of the other world which does not know and does not want to know our power. To be really true, all these ideals must be melted and welded into one. The training of the schools we need to-day more than ever,—the training of deft hands, quick eyes and ears, and above all the broader, deeper, higher culture of gifted minds and pure hearts. The power of the ballot we need in sheer self-defence,—else what shall save us from a second slavery? Freedom, too, the long-sought, we still seek,—the free-dom of life and limb, the freedom to work and think, the freedom to love and aspire. Work, culture, liberty,—all these we need, not singly but together, not successively but together, each growing and aiding each, and all striving toward that vaster ideal that swims before the Negro people, the ideal of human brotherhood, gained through the unifying ideal of Race; the ideal of fostering and developing the traits and talents of the Negro, not in opposition to or contempt for other races, but rather in large conformity to the greater ideals of the American Republic, in order that some day on American soil two world-races may give each to each those characteristics both so sadly lack. We the darker ones come even now not altogether empty-handed: there are to-day no truer exponents of the pure human spirit of the Declaration of Independence than the American Negroes; there is no true American music but the wild sweet melodies of the Negro slave; the American fairy tales and folk-lore are Indian and African; and, all in all, we black men seem the sole oasis of simple faith and reverence in a dusty desert of dollars and smartness. Will America be poorer if she replace her brutal dyspeptic blundering with light-hearted but determined Negro humility? or her coarse and cruel wit with loving jovial good-humor? or her vulgar music with the soul of the Sorrow Songs?

Merely a concrete test of the underlying principles of the great republic is the Negro Problem, and the spiritual striving of the freedmen's sons is the travail of souls whose burden is almost beyond the measure of their strength, but who bear it in the name of an historic race, in the name of this the land of their fathers' fathers, and in the name of human opportunity.

And now what I have briefly sketched in large outline let me on coming pages tell again in many ways, with loving emphasis and deeper detail, that men may listen to the striving in the souls of black folk. . . .

Mark Twain (1835–1910)

The development of New World metaphysics has frequently been attended by irreverent attacks on prevailing dogma and morality. No one was better at satirizing outworn and inhumane religious forms and ideas than Samuel Langhorne Clemens (1835–1910), better known as Mark Twain. Beginning his career as a writer of journalistic humor, Mark Twain created an authentic American idiom that he used deftly in works such as *The Innocents Abroad* (1869), *The Gilded Age* (1873), *The Adventures of Huckleberry Finn* (1884), and *The Tragedy of Pudd'nhead Wilson* (1894), to expose the spiritual pretensions and moral blindness of the time. In later years, there was an undercurrent of pessimism in much of Twain's humor, and in such books as *The Man That*

Corrupted Hadleyburg (1900), *What Is Man?* (1906), and *The Mysterious Stranger* (1916) he gave full expression to his sardonic and despairing vision. "The War Prayer" shows us this darker side of Mark Twain.

"The War Prayer" (1904)

It was a time of great and exalting excitement. The country was up in arms, the war was on, in every breast burned the holy fire of patriotism; the drums were beating, the bands playing, the toy pistols popping, the bunched firecrackers hissing and spluttering; on every hand and far down the receding and fading spread of roofs and balconies a fluttering wilderness of flags flashed in the sun; daily the young volunteers marched down the wide avenue gay and fine in their new uniforms, the proud fathers and mothers and sisters and sweethearts cheering them with voices choked with happy emotion as they swung by; nightly the packed mass meetings listened, panting, to patriot oratory which stirred the deepest deeps of their hearts, and which they interrupted at briefest intervals with cyclones of applause, the tears running down their cheeks the while; in the churches the pastors preached devotion to flag and country, and invoked the God of Battles, beseeching His aid in our good cause in outpouring of fervid eloquence which moved every listener. It was indeed a glad and gracious time, and the half dozen rash spirits that ventured to disapprove of the war and cast a doubt upon its righteousness straightway got such a stern and angry warning that for their personal safety's sake they quickly shrank out of sight and offended no more in that way.

Sunday morning came—next day the battalions would leave for the front; the church was filled; the volunteers were there, their young faces alight with martial dreams—visions of the stern advance, the gathering momentum, the rushing charge, the flashing sabers, the flight of the foe, the tumult, the enveloping smoke, the fierce pursuit, the surrender!—then home from the war, bronzed heroes, welcomed, adored, submerged in golden seas of glory! With the volunteers sat their dear ones, proud, happy, and envied by the neighbors and friends who had no sons and brothers to send forth to the field of honor, there to win for the flag, or, failing, die the noblest of noble deaths. The service proceeded; a war chapter from the Old Testament was read; the first prayer was said; it was followed by an organ burst that shook the building, and with one impulse the house rose, with glowing eyes and beating hearts, and poured out that tremendous invocation—

"God the all-terrible! Thou who ordainest,
  Thunder thy clarion and lightning thy
    sword!"

Then came the "long" prayer. None could remember the like of it for passionate pleading and moving and beautiful language. The burden of its supplication was, that an ever-merciful and benignant Father of us all would watch over our noble young soldiers, and aid, comfort, and encourage them in their patriotic work; bless them, shield them in the day of battle and the hour of peril, bear them in His mighty hand, make them strong and confident, invincible in the bloody onset; help them to crush the foe, grant to them and to their flag and country imperishable honor and glory—

An aged stranger entered and moved with slow and noiseless step up the main aisle, his eyes fixed upon the minister, his long body clothes in a robe that reached to his feet, his head bare, his white hair descending in a frothy cataract to his shoulders, his seamy face unnaturally pale, pale even to ghastliness. With all eyes following him and wondering, he made his silent way; without pausing, he ascended to the preacher's side and stood there, waiting. With shut lids the preacher, unconscious of his presence, continued his moving prayer, and at last finished it with the words, uttered in fervent appeal, "Bless our arms, grant us the victory, O Lord our God, Father and Protector of our land and flag!"

The stranger touched his arm, motioned him to step aside—which the startled minister did—and took his place. During some moments he surveyed the spellbound audience with solemn eyes, in which burned an uncanny light; then in a deep voice he said:

"I come from the Throne—bearing a message from Almighty God!" The words smote the house with shock; if the stranger perceived it he gave no attention. "He has heard the prayer of His servant and shepherd, and will grant it if such shall be your desire after I, His messenger, shall have explained to you its import—that is to say, its full import. For it is like unto many of the prayers of men, in that it asks for more than he who utters it is aware of—except he pause and think.

"God's servant and yours has prayed his prayer. Has he paused and taken thought? Is it one prayer? No, it is two—one uttered, the other not. Both have reached the ear of Him Who heareth all supplications, the spoken and the unspoken. Ponder this—keep it in mind. If you would beseech a blessing upon yourself, beware! lest without intent you invoke a curse upon a neighbor at the same time. If you pray for the blessing of rain upon your crop which needs it, by that act you are possibly praying for a curse upon some neighbor's crop which may not need rain and can be injured by it.

"You have heard your servant's prayer—the uttered part of it. I am commissioned of God to put into words the other part of it—that part which the pastor—and also you in your hearts—fervently prayed silently. And ignorantly and unthinkingly? God grant that it was so! You heard these words: 'Grant us the victory, O Lord our God!' That is sufficient. The *whole* of the uttered prayer is compact into those pregnant words. Elaborations were not necessary. When you have prayed for victory you have prayed for many unmentioned results which follow victory—*must* follow it, cannot help but follow it. Upon the listening spirit of God the Father fell also the unspoken part of the prayer.

He commandeth me to put it into words. Listen!

O Lord our Father, our young patriots, idols of our hearts, go forth to battle—be Thou near them! With them—in spirit—we also go forth from the sweet peace of our beloved firesides to smite the foe. O Lord our God, help us to tear their soldiers to bloody shreds with our shells; help us to cover their smiling fields with the pale forms of their patriot dead; help us to drown the thunder of the guns with the shrieks of their wounded, writhing in pain; help us lay waste their humble homes with a hurricane of fire; help us wring the hearts of their unoffending widows with unavailing grief; help us to turn them out roofless with their little children to wander unfriended the wastes of their desolated land in rags and hunger and thirst, sports of the sun flames of summer and the icy winds of winter, broken in spirit, worn with travail, imploring thee for the refuge of the grave and denied it—for our sakes who adore Thee, Lord, blast their hopes, blight their lives, protract their bitter pilgrimage, make heavy their steps, water their way with their tears, stain the white snow with the blood of their wounded feet! We ask it, in the spirit of love, of Him Who is the Source of Love, and Who is the ever-faithful refuge and friend of all that are sore beset and seek His aid with humble and contrite hearts. Amen."

(After a pause.) "Ye have prayed it; if ye still desire it, speak! the messenger of the Most High waits."

It was believed afterward that the man was a lunatic, because there was no sense in what he said.

Henry Adams
(1838–1918)

Henry Adams was the last representative of a most distinguished Boston family. His grandfather, John Quincy Adams, was the second President of the United States. His father, Charles Francis Adams, was American Ambassador to England during the Civil War.

Adams abandoned his early plans to pursue a career as a statesman, and devoted himself to a life of contemplation and scholarship. Adam's monumental study of diplomacy and politics in the early years of the American republic, *A History of the United States During the Administrations of Jefferson and Madison* (9 vols., 1889–1891), and his history of medieval spirituality entitled *Mont-Saint-Michel and Chartres* (1904) are surpassed by his greatest work, *The Autobiography of Henry Adams* (1907). In this selection from the most famous chapter of the *Autobiography*, Adams contrasts what he considered the primary image of thirteenth-century spiritual energy, the Virgin, with what he thought was the dominant image of twentieth-century force, the Dynamo.

From *The Education of Henry Adams* (1907)

The Dynamo and the Virgin

Until the Great Exposition of 1900 closed its doors in November, Adams haunted it, aching to absorb knowledge, and helpless to find it. He would have liked to know how much of it could have been grasped by the best-informed man in the world. While he was thus meditating chaos, Langley came by, and showed it to him. At Langley's behest, the Exhibition dropped its superfluous rags and stripped itself to the skin, for Langley knew what to study, and why, and how; while Adams might as well have stood outside in the night, staring at the Milky Way. Yet Langley said nothing new, and taught nothing that one might not have learned from Lord Bacon, three hundred years before; but though one should have known the "Advancement of Science" as well as one knew the "Comedy of Errors," the literary knowledge counted for nothing until some teacher should show how to apply it. Bacon took a vast deal of trouble in teaching King James I and his subjects, American or other, towards the year 1620, that true science was the development or economy of forces; yet an elderly American in 1900 knew neither the formula nor the forces; or even so much as to say to himself that his historical business in the Exposition concerned only the economies or developments of force since 1893, when he began the study at Chicago.

Nothing in education is so astonishing

as the amount of ignorance it accumulates in the form of inert facts. Adams had looked at most of the accumulations of art in the storehouses called Art Museums; yet he did not know how to look at the art exhibits of 1900. He had studied Karl Marx and his doctrines of history with profound attention, yet he could not apply them at Paris. Langley, with the ease of a great master of experiment, threw out of the field every exhibit that did not reveal a new application of force, and naturally threw out, to begin with, almost the whole art exhibit. Equally, he ignored almost the whole industrial exhibit. He led his pupil directly to the forces. His chief interest was in new motors to make his airship feasible, and he taught Adams the astonishing complexities of the new Daimler motor, and of the automobile, which, since 1893, had become a nightmare at a hundred kilometres an hour, almost as destructive as the electric tram which was only ten years older; and threatening to become as terrible as the locomotive steam-engine itself, which was almost exactly Adam's own age.

Then he showed his scholar the great hall of dynamos, and explained how little he knew about electricity or force of any kind, even of his own special sun, which spouted heat in inconceivable volume, but which, as far as he knew, might spout less or more, at any time, for all the certainty he felt in it. To him, the dynamo itself was but an ingenious channel for conveying somewhere the heat latent in a few tons of poor coal hidden in a dirty engine-house carefully kept out of sight; but to Adams the dynamo became a symbol of infinity. As he grew accustomed to the great gallery of machines, he began to feel the forty-foot dynamos as a moral force, much as the early Christians felt the Cross. The planet itself seemed less impressive, in its old-fashioned, deliberate, annual or daily revolution, than this huge wheel, revolving within arm's-length at some vertiginous speed, and barely murmuring—scarcely humming an audible warning to stand a hair's-breadth further for respect of power—while it would not wake the baby lying close against its frame. Before the end, one began to pray to it; inherited instinct taught the natural expression of man before silent and infinite force. Among the thousand symbols of ultimate energy, the dynamo was not so human as some, but it was the most expressive.

Yet the dynamo, next to the steam-engine, was the most familiar of exhibits. For Adams's objects its value lay chiefly in its occult mechanism. Between the dynamo in the gallery of machines and the engine-house outside, the break of continuity amounted to abysmal fracture for a historian's objects. No more relation could he discover between the steam and the electric current than between the Cross and the cathedral. The forces were interchangeable if not reversible, but he could see only an absolute *fiat* in electricity as in faith. Langley could not help him. Indeed, Langley seemed to be worried by the same trouble, for he constantly repeated that the new forces were anarchical, and specially that he was not responsible for the new rays, that were little short of parricidal in their wicked spirit towards science. His own rays, with which he had doubled the solar spectrum, were altogether harmless and beneficent; but Radium denied its God—or, what was to Langley the same thing, denied the truths of his Science. The force was wholly new.

A historian who asked only to learn enough to be as futile as Langley or Kelvin, made rapid progress under this teaching, and mixed himself up in the tangle of ideas until he achieved a sort of Paradise of ignorance vastly consoling to his fatigued senses. He wrapped himself in vibrations and rays which were new, and he would have hugged Marconi and Branly had he met them, as he hugged the dynamo; while he lost his arithmetic in trying to figure out the equation between the discoveries and the economies of force. The economies, like the discoveries, were absolute, super-sensual, occult; incapable of expression in horsepower. What mathematical equivalent could he suggest as the value of a Branly coherer? Frozen air, or the electric furnace, had some scale of measurement, no doubt, if somebody could invent a thermometer adequate to the purpose; but X-rays had played no part whatever in man's consciousness, and the atom itself had figured only as a fiction of thought. In these seven years man had translated himself into a new universe which had no common scale of measurement with the old. He had entered a supersensual world, in which he could measure nothing except by chance collisions of movements imperceptible to his senses, perhaps even imperceptible to his instruments, but perceptible to each other, and so to some known ray at the end of the scale. Langley seemed prepared for anything, even for an indeterminable number of universes interfused—physics stark mad in metaphysics.

Historians undertake to arrange sequences,—called stories, or histories—assuming in silence a relation of cause and effect. These assumptions, hidden in the depths of dusty libraries, have been astounding, but commonly unconscious and childlike; so much so, that if any captious critic were to drag them to light, historians would probably reply, with one voice, that they had never supposed themselves required to know what they were talking about. Adams, for one, had toiled in vain to find out what he meant. He had even published a dozen volumes of American history for no other purpose than to satisfy himself whether, by the severest process of stating, with the least possible comment, such facts as seemed sure, in such order as seemed rigorously consequent, he could fix for a familiar moment a necessary sequence of human movement. The result had satisfied him as little as at Harvard College. Where he saw sequence, other men saw something quite different, and no one saw the same unit of measure. He cared little about his experiments and less about his statesmen, who seemed to him quite as ignorant as himself and, as a rule, no more honest; but he insisted on a relation of sequence, and if he could not reach it by one method, he would try as many methods as science knew. Satisfied that the sequence of men led to nothing and that the sequence of their society could lead no further, while the mere sequence of time was artificial, and the sequence of thought was chaos, he turned at last to the sequence of force; and thus it happened that, after ten years' pursuit, he found himself lying in the Gallery of Machines at the Great Exposition of 1900, his historical neck broken by the sudden irruption of forces totally new.

Since no one else showed much concern, an elderly person without other cares had no need to betray alarm. The year 1900 was not the first to upset schoolmasters. Copernicus and Galileo had broken many professional necks about 1600; Columbus had stood the world on its head towards 1500; but the nearest approach to the revolution of 1900 was that of 310, when Constantine set up the Cross. The rays that Langley disowned, as well as those which he fathered, were occult, supersensual, irrational; they were a revelation of mysterious energy like that of the Cross; they were what, in terms of mediæval science, were called immediate modes of the divine substance.

The historian was thus reduced to his last resources. Clearly if he was bound to reduce all these forces to a common value, this common value could have no measure but that of their attraction on his own mind. He must treat them as they had been felt; as convertible, reversible, interchangeable attractions on thought. He made up his mind to venture it; he would risk translating rays into faith. Such a reversible process would vastly amuse a chemist, but the chemist could not deny that he, or some of his fellow physicists, could feel the force of both. When Adams was a boy in Boston, the best chemist in the place had probably never heard of Venus except by way of scandal, or of the Virgin except as idolatry; neither had he heard of dynamos or automobiles or radium; yet his mind was ready to feel the force of all, though the rays were unborn and the women were dead.

Here opened another totally new education, which promised to be by far the most hazardous of all. The knife-edge along which he must crawl, like Sir Lancelot in the twelfth century, divided two kingdoms of force which had nothing in common but attraction. They were as different as a magnet is from gravitation, supposing one knew what a magnet was, or gravitation, or love. The force of the Virgin was still felt at Lourdes, and seemed to be as potent as X-rays; but in America neither Venus nor Virgin ever had value as force—at most as sentiment. No American had ever been truly afraid of either.

This problem in dynamics gravely perplexed an American historian. The Woman had once been supreme; in France she still seemed potent, not merely as a sentiment, but as a force. Why was she unknown in America? For evidently America was ashamed of her, and she was ashamed of herself, otherwise they would not have strewn fig-leaves so profusely all over her. When she was a true force, she was ignorant of fig-leaves, but the monthly-magazine-made American female had not a feature that would have been recognized by Adam. The trait was notorious, and often humorous, but any one brought up among Puritans knew that sex was sin. In any previous age, sex was strength. Neither art nor beauty was needed. Every one, even among Puritans, knew that neither Diana of the

Ephesians nor any of the Oriental god-desses was worshipped for her beauty. She was goddess because of her force; she was the animated dynamo; she was reproduction—the greatest and most mysterious of all energies; all she needed was to be fecund. Singularly enough, not one of Adams's many schools of education had ever drawn his attention to the opening lines of Lucre-tius, though they were perhaps the finest in all Latin literature, where the poet invoked Venus exactly as Dante invoked the Virgin:—

> "Quae quoniam rerum naturam *sola*
>   gubernas."
> [Since therefore you alone govern the
>   nature of things.]

The Venus of Epicurean philosophy survived in the Virgin of the Schools:—

> "Donna, sei tanto grande, e tanto vali,
>   Che qual vuol grazia, e a te non ricorre,
>   Sua disianza vuol volar senz' ali."
>
> [Lady, you are so great and so prevailing
>   That whoever wishes grace and does not
>   turn to you,
>   His desire wishes to fly without wings.]

All this was to American thought as though it had never existed. The true American knew something of the facts, but nothing of the feelings; he read the letter, but he never felt the law. Before this historical chasm, a mind like that of Adams felt itself helpless; he turned from the Virgin to the Dynamo as though he were a Branly coherer. On one side, at the Louvre and at Chartres, as he knew by the record of work

actually done and still before his eyes, was the highest energy ever known to man, the creator of four-fifths of his noblest art, exercising vastly more at-traction over the human mind than all the steam-engines and dynamos ever dreamed of; and yet this energy was unknown to the American mind. An American Virgin would never dare command; an American Venus would never dare exist.

The question, which to any plain American of the nineteenth century seemed as remote as it did to Adams, drew him almost violently to study, once it was posed; and on this point Langleys were as useless as though they were Herbert Spencers or dynamos. The idea survived only as art. There one turned as naturally as though the artist were himself a woman. Adams began to ponder, asking himself whether he knew of any American artist who had ever insisted on the power of sex, as every classic had always done; but he could think only of Walt Whitman; Bret Harte, as far as the magazines would let him venture; and one or two painters, for the flesh-tones. All the rest had used sex for sentiment, never for force; to them, Eve was a tender flower, and Herodias an unfeminine horror. Ameri-can art, like the American language and American education, was as far as possi-ble sexless. Society regarded this victory over sex as its greatest triumph, and the historian readily admitted it, since the moral issue, for the moment, did not concern one who was studying the rela-tions of unmoral force. He cared noth-ing for the sex of the dynamo until he could measure its energy.

William James
(1842–1910)

William James is often considered the most culturally representative of America's philosophers because of his distinctive optimism, because of his emphasis on choice and action, and because he believed that ideas can only be understood in terms of their practical consequences. These attitudes are frequently associated with the philosophical outlook known as pragmatism. A philosophy purportedly this-wordly in orientation and grounded in experience, pragmatism seems peculiarly well suited to a secular world of commercial enterprise and materialistic expansion. Actually, however, James viewed pragmatism as a philosophical method and theory of truth which neither denies nor discounts the reality of religious experience, but furnishes powerful arguments for its importance.

The following selection, published in *The Will To Believe and Other Essays in Popular Philosophy* (1898), addresses a question James spent much of his life trying to resolve: why should we not commit suicide? Characteristically, his answer revealed his acceptance of an element of spiritual risk and his faith in a sense of "maybes." Only in the following century would a philosopher and theologian supply a metaphysical definition of the religious belief inherent in James's attitudes, when Paul Tillich coined the phrase "the courage to be."

From "Is Life Worth Living?"
(1895)

To come immediately to the heart of my theme, then, what I propose is to imagine ourselves reasoning with a fellow-mortal who is on such terms with life that the only comfort left him is to brood on the assurance, "You may end it when you will." What reasons can we plead that may render such a brother (or sister) willing to take up the burden again? Ordinary Christians, reasoning with would-be suicides, have little to offer them beyond the usual negative, "Thou shalt not." God alone is master of life and death, they say, and it is a blasphemous act to anticipate his absolving hand. But can *we* find nothing richer or more positive than this, no reflections to urge whereby the suicide may actually see, and in all sad seriousness feel, that in spite of adverse appearances even for him life is still worth living? There are suicides and suicides (in the United States about three thousand of them every year), and I must frankly confess that with perhaps the majority of these my suggestions are impotent to deal. Where suicide is the result of insanity or sudden frenzied impulse, reflection is impotent to arrest its headway; and cases like these belong to the ultimate mystery of evil, concerning which I can only offer considerations tending toward religious patience at the end of this hour. My task, let me say now, is practically narrow, and my words are to deal only with that metaphysical *tedium vitae* which is peculiar to reflecting men. Most of you are devoted, for good or ill, to the reflective life. Many of you are students of philosophy, and have already felt in your own persons the scepticism and unreality that too much grubbing in the abstract roots of things will breed. This is, indeed, one of the regular fruits of the over-studious career. Too much questioning and too little active responsibility lead, almost as often as too much sensualism does, to the edge of the slope, at the bottom of which lie pessimism and the nightmare or suicidal view of life. But to the diseases which reflection breeds, still further reflection can oppose effective remedies; and it is of the melancholy and *Weltschmerz* bred of reflection that I now proceed to speak.

Let me say, immediately, that my final appeal is to nothing more recondite than religious faith. So far as my argument is to be destructive, it will consist in nothing more than the sweeping away of certain views that often keep the springs of religious faith compressed; and so far as it is to be constructive, it will consist in holding up to the light of day certain considerations calculated to let loose these springs in a normal, natural way. Pessimism is essentially a religious disease. In the form of it to which you are most liable, it consists in nothing but a religious demand to which there comes no normal religious reply.

Now, there are two stages of recovery from this disease, two different levels upon which one may emerge from the midnight view to the daylight view of things, and I must treat of them in turn. The second stage is the more complete and joyous, and it corresponds to the freer exercise of religious trust and fancy. There are, as is well known, persons who are naturally very free in this regard, others who are not at all so. There are persons, for instance, whom we find indulging to their heart's content in prospects of immortality; and there are others who experience the greatest difficulty in making such a notion seem real to themselves at all. These latter persons are tied to their senses, restricted to their natural experience; and many of them, moreover, feel a sort of intellectual loyalty to what they call "hard facts," which is positively shocked by the easy excursions into the unseen that other people make at the bare call of sentiment. Minds of either class may, however, be intensely religious. They may equally desire atonement and reconciliation, and crave acquiecence and communion with the total soul of things. But the craving, when the mind is pent in to the hard facts, especially as science now reveals them, can breed pessimism, quite as easily as it breeds optimism when it inspires religious trust and fancy to wing their way to another and a better world.

That is why I call pessimism an essentially religious disease. The nightmare view of life has plenty of organic sources; but its great reflective source has at all times been the contradiction between the phenomena of nature and the craving of the heart to believe that behind nature there is a spirit whose expression nature is. What philosophers call "natural theology" has been one way of appeasing this craving; that poetry of nature in which our English literature is so rich has been another way. Now, suppose a mind of the latter of our two classes, whose imagination is pent in consequently, and who takes its facts "hard"; suppose it, moreover, to feel strongly the craving for communion, and yet to realize how desperately difficult it is to construe the scientific order of nature either theologically or poetically,—and what result *can* there be but inner discord and contradiction? Now, this inner discord (merely as discord) can be relieved in either of two ways: The longing to read the facts religiously may cease, and leave the bare facts by themselves; or, supplementary facts may be discovered or believed-in, which permit the religious reading to go on. These two ways of relief are the two stages of recovery, the two levels of escape from pessimism, to which I made allusion a moment ago, and which the sequel will, I trust, make more clear.

And now, in turning to what religion may have to say to the question, I come to what is the soul of my discourse. Religion has meant many things in human history; but when from now onward I use the word I mean to use it in the supernaturalist sense, as declaring that the so-called order of nature, which constitutes this world's experience, is only one portion of the total universe, and that there stretches beyond this visible world an unseen world of which we now know nothing positive, but in its relation to which the true significance of our present mundane life consists. A man's religious faith (whatever more special items of doctrine it may involve) means for me essentially his faith in the existence of an unseen order of some kind in which the riddles of the natural order may be found explained. In the more developed religions the natural world has always been regarded as the mere scaffolding or vestibule of a truer, more eternal world, and affirmed to be a sphere of education, trial, or redemption. In these religions, one must in some fashion die to the natural life before one can enter into life eternal. The notion that this physical world of wind and water, where the sun rises and the moon sets, is absolutely and ultimately the divinely aimed-at and established thing, is one which we find only in very early religions, such as that of the most primitive Jews. It is this natural religion (primitive still, in spite of the fact that poets and men of science whose good-will exceeds their perspicacity keep publishing it in new editions tuned to our contemporary ears) that, as I said a while ago, has suffered definitive bankruptcy in the opinion of a circle of persons, among whom I must count myself, and who are growing more numerous every day. For such persons the physical order of nature, taken simply as science knows it, cannot be held to reveal any one harmonious spiritual intent. It is mere *weather,* as Chauncey Wright called it, doing and undoing without end.

Now, I wish to make you feel, if I can in the short remainder of this hour, that we have a right to believe the physical order to be only a partial order; that we have a right to supplement it by an unseen spiritual order which we assume on trust, if only thereby life may seem to us better worth living again. But as such a trust will seem to some of you sadly mystical and execrably unscientific, I must first say a word or two to weaken the veto which you may consider that science opposes to our act.

There is included in human nature an ingrained naturalism and materialism of mind which can only admit facts that are actually tangible. Of this sort of mind the entity called "science" is the idol. Fondness for the word "scientist" is one of the notes by which you may know its votaries; and its short way of killing any opinion that it disbelieves in is to call it "unscientific." It must be granted that there is no slight excuse for this. Science has made such glorious leaps in the last three hundred years, and extended our knowledge of nature so enormously both in general and in detail; men of science, moreover, have as a class displayed such admirable virtues,—that it is no wonder if the worshippers of science lose their head. In this very University, accordingly, I have heard more than one teacher say that all the fundamental conceptions of truth have already been found by science, and that the future has only the details of the picture to fill in. But the slightest reflection on the real conditions will suffice to show how barbaric such notions are. They show such a lack of scientific imagination, that it is hard to see how one who is actively advancing any part of science can make a mistake so crude. Think how many absolutely new scientific conceptions have arisen in our own generation, how many new problems have been formulated that were never thought of before, and then cast an eye upon the brevity of science's career. It began with Galileo, not three hundred years ago. Four thinkers since Galileo, each informing his successor of what discoveries his own lifetime had seen achieved, might have passed the torch of science into our hands as we sit here in this room. Indeed, for the matter of that, an audience much smaller than the present one, an audience of some five or six score people, if each person in it could speak for his own generation, would carry us away to the black unknown of the human species, to days without a document or monument to tell their tale. Is it credible that such a mushroom knowledge, such a growth overnight as this, *can* represent more than the minutest glimpse of what the universe will really prove to be when adequately understood? No! our science is a drop, our ignorance a sea. Whatever else be certain, this at least is certain,—that the world of our present natural knowledge *is* enveloped in a larger world of *some* sort of whose residual properties we at present can frame no positive idea.

Agnostic positivism, of course, admits this principle theoretically in the most cordial terms, but insists that we must not turn it to any practical use. We have no right, this doctrine tells us, to dream dreams, or suppose anything about the unseen part of the universe, merely because to do so may be for what we are pleased to call our highest interests. We must always wait for sensible evidence for our beliefs; and where such evidence is inaccessible we must frame no hypotheses whatever. Of course this is a safe enough position *in abstracto*. If a thinker had no stake in the unknown, no vital needs, to live or languish according to what the unseen world contained, a philosophic neutrality and refusal to believe either one way or the other would be his wisest cue. But, unfortunately, neutrality is not only inwardly difficult, it is also outwardly unrealizable, where our relations to an alternative are practical and vital. This is because, as the psychologists tell us, belief and doubt are living attitudes, and involve conduct on our part. Our only way, for example, of doubting, or refusing to believe, that a certain thing *is,* is continuing to act as if it were *not.* If, for instance, I refuse to believe that the room is getting cold, I leave the windows open and light no fire just as if it still were warm. If I doubt that you are worthy of my confidence, I keep you uninformed of all my secrets just as if you were *un*worthy of the same. If I doubt the need of insuring my house, I leave it uninsured as much as if I believed there were no need. And so if I must not believe that the world is divine, I can only express that refusal by declining ever to act distinctively as if it were so, which can only mean acting on certain critical occasions as if it were *not* so, or in an irreligious way. There are, you see, inevitable occasions in life when inaction is a kind of action, and must count as action, and when not to be for it is to be practically against; and in all such cases strict and consistent neutrality is an unattainable thing.

And, after all, is not this duty of neutrality where only our inner interests would lead us to believe, the most ridiculous of commands? Is it not sheer dogmatic folly to say that our inner interests can have no real connection with the forces that the hidden world may contain? In other cases divinations based on inner interests have proved prophetic enough. Take science itself! Without an imperious inner demand on our part for ideal logical and mathematical harmonies, we should never have attained to proving that such harmonies lie hidden between all the chinks and interstices of the crude natural world. Hardly a law has been established in science, hardly a fact ascertained, which was not first sought after, often with sweat and blood, to gratify an inner need. Whence such needs come from we do not know: we find them in us, and biological psychology so far only classes them with Darwin's accidental variations. But the inner need of believing that this world of nature is a sign of something more spiritual and eternal than itself is just as strong and authoritative in those who feel it, as the inner need of uniform laws of causation ever can be in a professionally scientific head. The toil of many generations has proved the latter need prophetic. Why *may* not the former one be prophetic, too? And if needs of ours outrun the visible universe, why *may* not that be a sign that an invisible universe is there? What, in short, has authority to debar us from trusting our religious demands? Science as such assuredly has no authority, for she can only say what is, not what is not; and the agnostic "thou shalt not believe without coercive sensible evidence" is simply an expression (free to any one to make) of private personal appetite for evidence of a certain peculiar kind.

Now, when I speak of trusting our religious demands, just what do I mean by "trusting"? Is the word to carry with it license to define in detail an invisible world, and to anathematize and excommunicate those whose trust is different? Certainly not! Our faculties of belief were not primarily given us to make orthodoxies and heresies withal; they were given us to live by. And to trust our religious demands means first of all to live in the light of them, and to act as if the invisible world which they suggest were real. It is a fact of human nature, that men can live and die by the help of a sort of faith that goes without a single dogma or definition. The bare assurance that this natural order is not ultimate but a mere sign or vision, the external staging of a many-storied universe, in which spiritual forces have the last word and are eternal,—this bare assurance is to such men enough to make life seem worth living in spite of every contrary presumption suggested by its circumstances on the natural plane. Destroy this inner assurance, however, vague as it is, and all the light and radiance of existence is extinguished for these persons at a stroke. Often enough the wild-eyed look at life—the suicidal mood—will then set in.

And now the application comes directly home to you and me. Probably to almost every one of us here the most adverse life would seem well worth living, if we only could be *certain* that our bravery and patience with it were terminating and eventuating and bear-

ing fruit somewhere in an unseen spiritual world. But granting we are not certain, does it then follow that a bare trust in such a world is a fool's paradise and lubberland, or rather that it is a living attitude in which we are free to indulge? Well, we are free to trust at our own risks anything that is not impossible, and that can bring analogies to bear in its behalf. That the world of physics is probably not absolute, all the converging multitude of arguments that make in favor of idealism tend to prove; and that our whole physical life may lie soaking in a spiritual atmosphere, a dimension of being that we at present have no organ for apprehending, is vividly suggested to us by the analogy of the life of our domestic animals. Our dogs, for example, are in our human life but not of it. They witness hourly the outward body of events whose inner meaning cannot, by any possible operation, be revealed to their intelligence,— events in which they themselves often play the cardinal part. My terrier bites a teasing boy, for example, and the father demands damages. The dog may be present at every step of the negotiations, and see the money paid, without an inkling of what it all means, without a suspicion that it has anything to do with *him;* and he never *can* know in his natural dog's life. Or take another case which used greatly to impress me in my medical-student days. Consider a poor dog whom they are vivisecting in a laboratory. He lies strapped on a board and shrieking at his executioners, and to his own dark consciousness is literally in a sort of hell. He cannot see a single redeeming ray in the whole business;

and yet all these diabolical-seeming events are often controlled by human intentions with which, if his poor benighted mind could only be made to catch a glimpse of them, all that is heroic in him would religiously acquiesce. Healing truth, relief to future sufferings of beast and man, are to be bought by them. It may be genuinely a process of redemption. Lying on his back on the board there he may be performing a function incalculably higher than any that prosperous canine life admits of; and yet, of the whole performance, this function is the one portion that must remain absolutely beyond his ken.

Now turn from this to the life of man. In the dog's life we see the world invisible to him because we live in both worlds. In human life, although we only see our world, and his within it, yet encompassing both these worlds a still wider world may be there, as unseen by us as our world is by him; and to believe in that world *may* be the most essential function that our lives in this world have to perform. But "*may* be! *may* be!" one now hears the positivist contemptuously exclaim; "what use can a scientific life have for maybes?" Well, I reply, the "scientific" life itself has much to do with maybes, and human life at large has everything to do with them. So far as man stands for anything, and is productive or originative at all, his entire vital function may be said to have to deal with maybes. Not a victory is gained, not a deed of faithfulness or courage is done, except upon a maybe; not a service, not a sally of generosity, not a scientific exploration or experiment or textbook, that may not be a mistake. It is only by risking our persons from one hour to another that we live at all. And often enough our faith beforehand in an uncertified result *is the only thing that makes the result come true.* Suppose, for instance, that you are climbing a mountain, and have worked yourself into a position from which the only escape is by a terrible leap. Have faith that you can successfully make it, and your feet are nerved to its accomplishment. But mistrust yourself, and think of all the sweet things you have heard the scientists say of *maybes,* and you will hesitate so long that, at last, all unstrung and trembling, and launching yourself in a moment of despair, you roll in the abyss. In such a case (and it belongs to an enormous class), the part of wisdom as well as of courage is to *believe what is in the line of your needs,* for only by such belief is the need fulfilled. Refuse to believe, and you shall indeed be right, for you shall irretrievably perish. But believe, and again you shall be right, for you shall save yourself. You make one or the other of two possible universes true by your trust or mistrust,—both universes having been only *maybes,* in this particular, before you contributed your act.

Now, it appears to me that the question whether life is worth living is subject to conditions logically much like these. It does, indeed, depend on you *the liver.* If you surrender to the nightmare view and crown the evil edifice by your own suicide, you have indeed made a picture totally black. Pessimism, completed by your act, is true beyond a doubt, so far as your world goes. Your mistrust of life has removed whatever worth your own enduring existence might have given to it; and now, throughout the whole sphere of possible influence of that existence, the mistrust has proved itself to have had divining power. But suppose, on the other hand, that instead of giving way to the nightmare view you cling to it that this world is not the *ultimatum.* Suppose you find yourself a very well-spring, as Wordsworth says, of—

"Zeal, and the virtue to exist by faith
  As soldiers live by courage; as, by strength
  Of heart, the sailor fights with roaring
    seas."

Suppose, however thickly evils crowd upon you, that your unconquerable subjectivity proves to be their match, and that you find a more wonderful joy than any passive pleasure can bring in trusting ever in the larger whole. Have you not now made life worth living on these terms? What sort of a thing would life really be, with your qualities ready for a tussle with it, if it only brought fair weather and gave these higher faculties of yours no scope? Please remember that optimism and pessimism are definitions of the world, and that our own reactions on the world, small as they are in bulk, are integral parts of the whole thing, and necessarily help to determine the definition. They may even be the decisive elements in determining the definition. A large mass can have its unstable equilibrium overturned by the addition of a feather's weight; a long phrase may have its sense reversed by the addition of the three letters *n-o-t.* This life *is* worth living, we can say, *since it is what we make it, from the moral point of view;* and we are determined to make it from that point of view, so far as we have anything to do with it, a success.

Now, in this description of faiths that verify themselves I have assumed that our faith in an invisible order is what inspires those efforts and that patience which make this visible order good for moral men. Our faith in the seen world's goodness (goodness now meaning fitness for successful moral and religious life) has verified itself by leaning on our faith in the unseen world. But will our faith in the unseen world similarly verify itself? Who knows?

Once more it is a case of *maybe;* and once more *maybes* are the essence of the situation. I confess that I do not see why the very existence of an invisible world may not in part depend on the personal response which any one of us may make to the religious appeal. God himself, in short, may draw vital strength and increase of very being from our fidelity. For my own part, I do not know what the sweat and blood and tragedy of this life mean, if they mean anything short of this. If this life be not a real fight, in which something is eternally gained for the universe by success, it is no better than a game of private theatricals from which one may withdraw at will. But it *feels* like a real fight,—as if there were something really wild in the universe which we, with all our idealities and faithfulnesses, are needed to redeem; and first of all to redeem our own hearts from atheisms and fears. For such a half-wild, half-saved universe our nature is adapted. The deepest thing in our nature is this *Binnenleben* (as a

German doctor lately has called it), this dumb region of the heart in which we dwell alone with our willingnesses and unwillingnesses, our faiths and fears. As through the cracks and crannies of caverns those waters exude from the earth's bosom which then form the fountain-heads of springs, so in these crepuscular depths of personality the sources of all our outer deeds and decisions take their rise. Here is our deepest organ of communication with the nature of things; and compared with these concrete movements of our soul all abstract statements and scientific arguments—the veto, for example, which the strict positivist pronounces upon our faith—sound to us like mere chatterings of the teeth. For here possibilities, not finished facts, are the realities with which we have actively to deal; and to quote my friend William Salter, of the Philadelphia Ethical Society, "as the essence of courage is to stake one's life on a possibility, so the essence of faith is to believe that the possibility exists."

These, then, are my last words to you: Be not afraid of life. Believe that life *is* worth living, and your belief will help create the fact. The 'scientific proof' that you are right may not be clear before the day of judgment (or some stage of being which that expression may serve to symbolize) is reached. But the faithful fighters of this hour, or the beings that then and there will represent them, may then turn to the faint-hearted, who here decline to go on, with words like those with which Henry IV. greeted the tardy Crillon after a great

victory had been gained: "Hang your-self, brave Crillon! we fought at Arques, and you were not there."

Charles William Eliot (1834–1926)

Charles William Eliot was president of Harvard University for forty years and edited *The Harvard Classics,* a fifty-volume selection of the world's greatest literature. His thought exemplifies the intellectual and religious sensibility of the educated elite in the Genteel Era. Hopeful, enlightened, and reasonable, Eliot and his followers played a central role in the evolution of the nascent civil religion of America into an American religion of civility. In *The Religion of the Future,* from which the present selection is drawn, Eliot carries the secularization of Christianity about as far as it can conceivably go.

From *The Religion of the Future* (1909)

I shall attempt to state without reserve and in simplest terms free from technicalities, first, what the religion of the future seems likely not to be, and secondly, what it may reasonably be expected to be. My point of view is that of an American layman, whose observing and thinking life has covered the extraordinary period since the *Voyage of the Beagle* was published, anaesthesia and the telegraph came into use, Herbert Spencer issued his first series of papers on evolution, Kuenen, Robertson Smith, and Wellhausen developed and vindicated Biblical criticism, J.S. Mill's *Principles of Political Economy* appeared, and the United States by going to war with Mexico set in operation the forces which abolished slavery on the American continent—the period within which mechanical power came to be widely distributed through the explosive engine and the applications of electricity, and all the great fundamental industries of civilized mankind were reconstructed.

I. The religion of the future will not be based on authority, either spiritual or temporal. The decline of reliance upon absolute authority is one of the most significant phenomena of the modern world. . . .

2. It is hardly necessary to say that in the religion of the future there will be no personifications of the primitive forces of nature, such as light, fire, frost, wind, storm, and earthquake. . . .

3. There will be in the religion of the future no worship, express or implied, of dead ancestors, teachers, or rulers; no more tribal, racial, or tutelary gods; no identification of any human being, however majestic in character, with the Eternal Deity. . . .

4. In the religious life of the future the primary object will not be the personal welfare or safety of the individual in this world or any other. That safety, that welfare or salvation, may be incidentally secured, but it will not be the prime object in view. The religious person will not think of his own welfare or security, but of service to others, and of contributions to the common good. . . .

5. The religion of the future will not be propitiatory, sacrificial, or expiatory. . . .

6. The religion of the future will not perpetuate the Hebrew anthropomorphic representations of God, conceptions which were carried in large measure into institutional Christianity. It will not think of God as an enlarged and glorified man. . . .

7. The religion of the future will not be gloomy, ascetic, or maledictory. It will not deal chiefly with sorrow and death, but with joy and life. It will not care so much to account for the evil and the ugly in the world as to interpret the good and the beautiful. . . .

Josiah Royce
(1855–1916)

Josiah Royce was for most of his professional life a professor of philosophy at Harvard. He is typically seen as the intellectual opposite of his colleague William James. James was a pluralist; Royce was a monist. James was empirical; Royce was an idealist. James was tough-minded; Royce was tender-minded. But such contrasts can be misleading. The following chapter from *The Sources of Religious Insight* (1912), perhaps the best introduction to Royce's philosophy, is essentially an explication and expansion of an idea frequently expressed by William James. James believed that our experience of any particular object, event, other person, etc. is attended by a sense of the "More," a superfluity of meaning which as a datum of consciousness is just as real as the person, event, or object itself, and just as deserving of philosophical scrutiny. Starting from this idea, Royce goes on to posit the existence of a "superhuman" or, in the strict sense, "supernatural" consciousness in man. Royce argues that it is this superhuman consciousness which enables us to grasp things in a unity transcending the fragments of connectedness which at any moment we directly perceive.

The Sources of Religious Insight (1912)

The Superhuman and the Supernatural

In my general sketch of the characteristics of human nature which awaken in us the sense of our need for salvation, I laid stress . . . upon our narrowness of outlook as one principal and pervasive defect of man as he naturally is constituted. . . . Now man's narrowness of natural outlook upon life is first of all due to something which I have to call the "form" of human consciousness. . . .

But technical clearness as to such topics is hard to attain. Allow me, then, to insist with some care upon matters which are as influential in moulding our whole destiny as they are commonly neglected in our discussions of the problems of life and of reality.

Man can attend to but a very narrow range of facts at any one instant. Commonsense observation shows you this. Psychological experiment emphasises it in manifold ways. Listen to a rhythmic series of beats—drum beats—or the strokes of an engine, or the feet of horses passing by in the street. You cannot directly grasp with entire clearness more than a very brief sequence of these beats, or other sounds, or of rhythmic phrases of any kind. If the rhythm of a regularly repeated set of sounds is too long, or too complex, it becomes confused for you. You cannot make out by your direct attention what it is at least until it has by repetition grown familiar. Let several objects be brought before you at once. You can attend to one and then to another at pleasure if only they stay there to be attended to. But only a very few distinct objects can be suddenly seen at once, and at a single glance, and recognised, through that one instantaneous presentation, for what they are. If the objects are revealed to you in the darkness by an electric spark, or are seen through a single slit in a screen that rapidly moves before your eyes—so that the objects are exposed to your observation only during the extremely brief time when the slit passes directly between them and your eyes—this limit of your power to grasp between them and your eyes—this limit of your power to grasp several distinct objects at once, upon a single inspection, can be experimentally tested. The results of such experiments concern us here only in the most general way. Enough—as such tests show—what one may call the *span* of our consciousness, its power to grasp many facts in any one individual moment of our lives, is extremely limited. It is limited as to the number of simultaneously presented facts that we can grasp at one view, can distinguish, and recognise, and hold clearly before us. It is also limited with regard to the number and the duration of the successive facts that we can so face as directly to grasp the character of their succession, rhythmic or otherwise.

Now this limitation of the span of our consciousness is, I repeat, an ever-present defect of our human type of conscious life. That is why I call it a defect in the "form" of our conscious life. It is not a defect limited to the use of any one of our senses. It is not a failure of eyes or of ears to furnish to us a sufficient variety of facts to observe. On the contrary, both our eyes and our ears almost constantly rain in upon us, especially during our more desultory waking life, an over-wealth of impressions. If we want to know facts, and to attain clearness, we have to pick out a few of these impressions, from instant to instant, for more careful direct inspection. In any case, then, this limitation is not due to the defects of our senses. It is our whole conscious make-up, our characteristic way of becoming aware of things, which is expressed by this limitation of our conscious span. On this plan our human consciousness is formed. Thus our type of awareness is constituted. In this way we are all doomed to live. It is our human fate to grasp clearly only a few facts or ideas at any one instant. And so, being what we are, we have to make the best of our human nature.

Meanwhile, it is our very essence as reasonable beings that we are always contending with the consequences of this our natural narrowness of span. We are always actively rebelling at our own form of consciousness, so long as we are trying to know or to do anything significant. We want to grasp many things at once, not merely a few. We want to survey life in long stretches, not merely in instantaneous glimpses. We are always like beings who have to see our universe through the cracks that our successive instants open before us, and as quickly close again. And we want to see things, *not* through these instantaneous cracks, but without intervening walls, with wide outlook, and in all their true variety and unity. Nor is this rebellion of ours against the mere form of consciousness any merely idle curiosity or peevish seeking for a barren wealth of varieties. Salvation itself is at stake in this struggle for a wider clearness of outlook. The wisest souls, as we have throughout seen, agree with common-sense prudence in the desire to see at any one instant greater varieties of ideas and of objects than our form of consciousness permits us to grasp. To escape from the limitations imposed upon us by the natural narrowness of our span of consciousness—by the form of consciousness in which we live—this is the common interest of science and of religion, of the more contemplative and of the more active aspects of our higher nature. *Our form of consciousness is one of our chief human sorrows.*

By devices such as the rhythmic presentation of facts to our attention we can do something—not very much—to enlarge our span of consciousness. But for most purposes we can make only an *indirect,* not a *direct,* escape from our limitations of span. Our salvation depends upon the winning of such indirect successes. Indirectly we escape, in so far as we use our powers of habit-forming, of memory, and of abstraction, to prepare for us objects of momentary experience such as have come to acquire for us a wide range of meaning, so that, when we get before our momentary attention but a few of these objects at once, we still are able to comprehend, after our human fashion, ranges and connections and unities of fact which the narrow form of our span of consciousness forbids us to grasp with directness. Thus, the repetition of similar experiences form habits such that each element of some new instant of passing experience comes to us saturated with the meaning that, as we look back upon our past life, we suppose to have resulted from the whole course of what has happened. And through such endlessly varied processes of habit-forming, we come to reach stages of insight in which the instantaneous presentation of a few facts gets for us, at a given moment, the value of an indirect appreciation of what we never directly grasp—that is, the value of a wide survey of life. All that we usually call knowledge is due to such indirect grasping of what the instant can only hint to us, although we usually feel as if this indirect presentation were itself a direct insight. Let me exemplify: The odour of a flower may come to us burdened with a meaning that we regard as the total result of a whole summer of our life. The wrinkled face of an old man reveals to us, in its momentarily presented traces, the signs of what we take to have been his lifetime's experience and slowly won personal character. And, in very much the same way, almost any passing experience may seem to us to speak with the voice of years, or even of ages, of human life. To take yet another instance: a single musical chord epitomises the result of all our former hearings of the musical composition which it introduces.

In this way we live, despite our narrowness, *as if* we saw widely; and we constantly view *as if it were* our actual experience, a sense and connection of things which actually never gets fully translated in any moment of our lives, but is always simply presupposed as the interpretation which a wider view of life *would* verify. Thus bounded in the nutshell of the passing instant, we count ourselves (in one way or another, and whatever our opinions), kings of the infinite realm of experience, or would do so were it not that, like Hamlet, we have so many "bad dreams," which make us doubt the correctness of our interpretations, and feel our need of an escape from this stubborn natural prison of our own form of consciousness. We therefore appeal, in all our truth-seeking, to a wider view than our own present view.

Our most systematic mode of indirect escape from the consequences of our narrow span of consciousness, is the mode which our thinking processes, that is, our dealings with abstract and general ideas exemplify.

Such abstract and general ideas, as we earlier saw, are means to ends—never ends in themselves. By means of generalisation or abstraction we can gradually come to choose signs which we can more or less successfully substitute for long series of presented objects of experience; and we can also train ourselves into active ways of estimating or of describing things—ways such, that by reminding ourselves of these our active attitudes toward the business of life, we can seem to ourselves to epitomise in an instant the sense of years or even of ages of human experience. Such signs and symbols and attitudes constitute our store of general and abstract ideas. Our more or less systematic and voluntary thinking is a process of observing, at one or another instant, the connections and the meanings of a very few of these our signs and attitudes at once. We actively put together these ideas of ours, and watch, at the instant, the little connections that then and there are able to appear, despite the narrowness of our span of consciousness. That, for instance, is what happens when we add up columns of figures, or think out a problem, or plan our practical lives. But because each of the ideas used, each of these signs or symbols or attitudes, can be more or less safely substituted for some vast body of facts of experience, what we observe only in and through our narrow span can indirectly help us

to appreciate something whose real meaning only a very wide range of experience, a consciousness whose span is enormously vaster than ours, could possibly present directly.

Thus, confined to our own form and span of consciousness as we are, we spend our lives in acquiring or devising ways to accomplish indirectly what we are forbidden directly to attain, namely, the discovery of truth and of meaning such as only a consciousness of another form than ours can realise. Now, as I maintained in our third and fourth lectures, *the whole validity and value of this indirect procedure of ours depends upon the principle that such a wider view of things, such a larger unity of consciousness, such a direct grasp of the meanings at which we indirectly but ceaselessly aim is a reality in the universe.* As I there maintained, *the whole reality of the universe itself must be defined, in terms of the reality of such an inclusive and direct grasp of the whole sense of things.* I can here only repeat my opinion that this thesis is one which nobody can deny without self-contradiction.

Now the difference between the narrow form of consciousness that we human beings possess and the wider and widest forms of consciousness whose reality every common-sense effort to give sense to life, and every scientific effort to discover the total verdict of experience presupposes—the difference, I say, between these two forms of consciousness is *literally* expressed by calling the one form (the form that we all possess) *human,* and by calling the other form (the form of a wider consciousness which views experience as it is) *superhuman.* The wider conscious

315

view of things that we share only indirectly, through the devices just pointed out, is certainly not human; for no mortal man ever directly possesses it. It is real; for, as we saw in our study of the reason, if you deny this assertion in one shape, you reaffirm it in another. For you can define the truth and falsity of your opinions only by presupposing a wider view that sees as a whole what you see in fragments. That unity of consciousness which we presuppose in all our indirect efforts to get into touch with its direct view of truth is above our level. It includes what we actually get before us in our form of consciousness. It also includes all that we are trying to grasp indirectly. Now what is not human, and is above our level, and includes all of our insight, but transcends and corrects our indirect efforts by its direct grasp of facts as they are, can best be called superhuman. *The thesis that such a superhuman consciousness is a reality is a thesis precisely equivalent to the assertion that our experience has any real sense or connection whatever* beyond the mere fragment of connectedness that, at any one instant, we directly grasp.

Furthermore, to call such a larger consciousness—inclusive of our own, but differing from ours, in form, by the vastness of its span and the variety and completeness of the connections that it surveys—to call it, I say, a *supernatural* consciousness is to use a phraseology that can be very deliberately and, if you choose, technically defended. By "natural" we mean simply: Subject to the laws which hold for the sorts of beings whose character and behaviour our empirical sciences can study. If you suddenly found that you could personally and individually and clearly grasp, by an act of direct attention, the sense and connection of thousands of experiences at once, instead of the three or four presented facts of experience whose relations you can now directly observe in any one of your moments of consciousness, you would indeed say that you had been miraculously transformed into another type of being whose insight had acquired an angelic sort of wealth and clearness. But whenever you assert (as every scientific theory, and every common-sense opinion, regarding the real connections of the facts of human experience requires you to assert), that not only thousands, but a countless collection of data of human experience actually possess a perfectly coherent total sense and meaning, such as no individual man ever directly observes, this your assertion, which undertakes to be a report of facts, and which explicitly relates to facts of experience, implies the assertion that there exists such a superhuman survey of the real nature and connection of our own natural realm of conscious life. We ourselves are strictly limited by the natural conditions that determine our own form of consciousness. And no conditions can be regarded by us as more characteristically natural than are these. For us human beings to transcend those conditions, by surveying countless data at once, would require an uttermost exception to the natural laws which are found to govern our human type of consciousness. To believe that any man ever had accomplished the direct survey of the whole range of the physical connections of the solar and stellar systems at once—in other words, had grasped the whole range of astronomical experience in a single act of attention—would be to believe that a most incredible miracle had at some time taken place—an incredible miracle so far as any knowledge that we now possess enables us to foresee what the natural conditions under which man lives, and is, in human form, conscious, permit. But, on the other hand, to accept, as we all do, the validity of that scientific interpretation of the data of human experience which astronomy reports is to acknowledge that such an interpretation more or less completely records a system of facts which are nothing if they are not in some definite sense empirical, although, in their wholeness, they are experienced by no man. That is, the acceptance of the substantial truth of astronomy involves the acknowledgment that some such, to us simply superhuman, consciousness is precisely as real as the stars are real, and as their courses, and as all their relations are real. Yet, of course, we cannot undertake to investigate any process such as would enable us to define the natural conditions under which any such superhuman survey of astronomical facts would become psychologically possible.

The acceptance of our natural sciences, as valid interpretations of connections of experience which our form of consciousness forbids us directly to verify, logically presupposes, at every step, that such superhuman forms and unities of consciousness are real. For the facts of science are indefinable except as facts in and for a real experience. But, on the other hand, we can hope for no advance in physical or in psychological knowledge which would enable us to bring these higher forms of consciousness under what we call natural laws. So the superhuman forms of consciousness remain for us also supernatural. *That* they are, we must acknowledge, if any assertion whatever about our world is to be either true or false. For all assertions are made about experience, and about its real connections, and about its systems. But *what* conditions, *what* natural causes, bring such superhuman forms of consciousness into existence we are unable to investigate. For every assertion about nature or about natural laws presupposes that natural facts and laws are real only in so far as they are the objects known to such higher unities of consciousness. The unities in question are themselves no natural objects; while all natural facts are objects for them and are expressions of their meaning.

Thus definite are my reasons for asserting that forms of consciousness superior to our own are real, and that they are all finally united in a single, world-embracing insight, which has also the character of expressing a world-will. Thus definite are also my grounds for calling such higher unities of consciousness both superhuman and supernatural. By the term "The unity of the spirit" I name simply *the unity of meaning which belongs to these superhuman forms of consciousness.* We ourselves partake of this unity, and share it, in so far as, in our lives also, we discover and express, in whatever way our own form of consciousness permits, truth and life that bring us into touch and into harmony with the higher forms of consciousness, that is, with the spirit which, in its wholeness, knows and estimates the world, and which expresses itself in the life of the world.

Thus near are we, in every exercise of our reasonable life, to the superhuman and to the supernatural. Upon the other hand, there is positively no need of magic, or of miracle, or of mysterious promptings from the subconscious, to prove to us the reality of the human and of the supernatural, or to define our reasonable relations with it. And the essential difference between our own type of consciousness and this higher life is a difference of form, and is also a difference of content precisely in so far as its wider and widest span of conscious insight implies that the superhuman type of consciousness possesses a depth of meaning, a completeness of expression, a wealth of facts, a clearness of vision, a successful embodiment of purpose which, in view of the narrowness of our form of consciousness, do not belong to us.

Man needs no miracles to show him the supernatural and the superhuman. You need no signs and wonders, and no psychical research, to prove that the unity of the spirit is a fact in the world. Common-sense tacitly presupposes the reality of the unity of the spirit. Science studies the ways in which its life is expressed in the laws which govern the order of experience. Reason gives us insight into its real being. Loyalty serves it, and repents not of the service. Salvation means our positive harmony with its purpose and with its manifestation.

George Santayana (1863–1952)

The aesthetician and ontologist George Santayana was another contemporary of William James at Harvard. Born in Spain, reared in Boston, and educated in Europe as well as America, Santayana was a brilliant and original thinker as well as an astute interpreter of the thought of others. The present essay was delivered as an address to the Philosophical Union of the University of California at Berkeley in 1911 and published in one of Santayana's many discerning books on American thought and ideas, *Winds of Doctrine* (1913). His other best known study is *Character and Opinion in the United States* (1920).

Santayana's highly individual contribution to the history of ideas is characterized by the conviction that any genuine philosophy "inspires and expresses the life of those who cherish it." Here he uses this insight to good effect as he shows how the empirical "theology" of William James and his pragmatist allies has displaced the genteel philosophy of Transcendentalists like Emerson.

From *Winds of Doctrine* (1913)

The Genteel Tradition in American Philosophy

Ladies and Gentlemen,—The privilege of addressing you to-day is very welcome to me, not merely for the honour of it, which is great, nor for the pleasures of travel, which are many, when it is California that one is visiting for the first time, but also because there is something I have long wanted to say which this occasion seems particularly favourable for saying. America is still a young country, and this part of it is especially so; and it would have been nothing extraordinary if, in this young country, material preoccupations had altogether absorbed people's minds, and they had been too much engrossed in living to reflect upon life, or to have any philosophy. The opposite, however, is the case. Not only have you already found time to philosophise in California, as your society proves, but the eastern colonists from the very beginning were a sophisticated race. As much as in clearing the land and fighting the Indians they were occupied, as they expressed it, in wrestling with the Lord. The country was new, but the race was tried, chastened, and full of solemn memories. It was an old wine in new bottles; and America did not have to wait for its present universities, with their departments of academic philosophy, in order to possess a living philosophy—to have a distinct vision of the universe and definite convictions about human destiny.

Now this situation is a singular and remarkable one, and has many consequences, not all of which are equally fortunate. America is a young country with an old mentality: it has enjoyed the advantages of a child carefully brought up and thoroughly indoctrinated; it has been a wise child. But a wise child, an old head on young shoulders, always has a comic and an unpromising side. The wisdom is a little thin and verbal, not aware of its full meaning and grounds; and physical and emotional growth may be stunted by it, or even deranged. Or when the child is too vigorous for that, he will develop a fresh mentality of his own, out of his observations and actual instincts; and this fresh mentality will interfere with the traditional mentality, and tend to reduce it to something perfunctory, conventional, and perhaps secretly despised. A philosophy is not genuine unless it inspires and expresses the life of those who cherish it. I do not think the hereditary philosophy of America has done much to atrophy the natural activities of the inhabitants; the wise child has not missed the joys of youth or of manhood; but what has happened is that the academic philosophy has grown stale, and that the academic philosophy afterwards developed has caught the stale odour from it. America is not simply, as I said a moment ago, a young country with an old mentality: it is a country with two mentalities, one a survival of the beliefs and standards of the fathers, the other an expression of the instincts, practice, and discoveries of the younger generations. In all the higher things of the mind—in religion, in literature, in the moral emotions—it is the hereditary spirit that still prevails, so much so that Mr. Bernard Shaw finds that America is a hundred years behind the times. The truth is that one-half of the American mind, that not occupied intensely in practical affairs, has remained, I will not say high-and-dry, but slightly becalmed;

it has floated gently in the back-water while, alongside, in invention and industry and social organisation, the other half of the mind was leaping down a sort of Niagara Rapids. This division may be found symbolised in American architecture: a neat reproduction of the colonial mansion—with some modern comforts introduced surreptitiously—stands beside the sky-scraper. The American Will inhabits the sky-scraper; the American Intellect inhabits the colonial mansion. The one is the sphere of the American man; the other, at least predominantly, of the American woman. The one is all aggressive enterprise; the other is all genteel tradition.

Now, with your permission, I should like to analyse more fully how this interesting situation has arisen, how it is qualified, and whither it tends. And in the first place we should remember what, precisely, that philosophy was which the first settlers brought with them into the country. In strictness there was more than one; but we may confine our attention to what I will call Calvinism, since it is on this that the current academic philosophy has been grafted. I do not mean exactly the Calvinism of Calvin, or even of Jonathan Edwards; for in their systems there was much that was not pure philosophy, but rather faith in the externals and history of revelation. Jewish and Christian revelation was interpreted by these men, however, in the spirit of a particular philosophy, which might have arisen under any sky, and been associated with any other religion as well as with Protestant Christianity. In fact, the philosophical principle of Calvinism appears also in the Koran, in Spinoza, and in Cardinal Newman; and persons with no very distinctive Christian belief, like Carlyle or like Professor Royce, may be nevertheless, philosophically, perfect Calvinists. Calvinism, taken in this sense, is an expression of the agonised conscience. It is a view of the world which an agonised conscience readily embraces, if it takes itself seriously, as, being agonised, of course it must. Calvinsim, essentially, asserts three things: that sin exists, that sin is punished, and that it is beautiful that sin should exist to be punished. The heart of the Calvinist is therefore divided between tragic concern at his own miserable condition, and tragic exultation about the universe at large. He oscillates between a profound abasement and a paradoxical elation of the spirit. To be a Calvinist philosophically is to feel a fierce pleasure in the existence of misery, especially of one's own, in that this misery seems to manifest the fact that the Absolute is irresponsible or infinite or holy. Human nature, it feels, is totally depraved: to have the instincts and motives that we necessarily have is a great scandal, and we must suffer for it; but that scandal is requisite, since otherwise the serious importance of being as we ought to be would not have been vindicated.

To those of us who have not an agonised conscience this system may seem fantastic and even unintelligible; yet it is logically and intently thought out from its emotional premises. It can take permanent possession of a deep mind here and there, and under certain conditions it can become epidemic. Imagine, for instance, a small nation with an intense vitality, but on the verge of ruin, ecstatic and distressful, having a strict and minute code of laws, that paints life in sharp and violent chiaroscuro, all pure righteousness and black abominations, and exaggerating the consequences of both perhaps to infinity. Such a people were the Jews after the exile, and again the early Protestants. If such a people is philosophical at all, it will not improbably be Calvinistic. Even in the early American communities many of these conditions were fulfilled. The nation was small and isolated; it lived under pressure and constant trial; it was acquainted with but a small range of goods and evils. Vigilance over conduct and an absolute demand for personal integrity were not merely traditional things, but things that practical sages, like Franklin and Washington, recommended to their countrymen, because they were virtues that justified themselves visibly by their fruits. But soon these happy results themselves helped to relax the pressure of external circumstances, and indirectly the pressure of the agonised conscience within. The nation became numerous; it ceased to be either ecstatic or distressful; the high social morality which on the whole it preserved took another colour; people remained honest and helpful out of good sense and good will rather than out of scrupulous adherence to any fixed principles. They retained their instinct for order, and often created order with surprising quickness; but the sanctity of law, to be obeyed for its own sake, began to escape them; it seemed too unpractical a notion, and not quite serious. In fact, the second and native-born Ameri-

can mentality began to take shape. The sense of sin totally evaporated. Nature, in the words of Emerson, was all beauty and commodity; and while operating on it laboriously, and drawing quick returns, the American began to drink in inspiration from it aesthetically. At the same time, in so broad a continent, he had elbow-room. His neighbours helped more than they hindered him; he wished their number to increase. Good will became the great American virtue; and a passion arose for counting heads, and square miles, and cubic feet, and minutes saved—as if there had been anything to save them for. How strange to the American now that saying of Jonathan Edwards, that men are naturally God's enemies! Yet that is an axiom to any intelligent Calvinist, though the words he uses may be different. If you told the modern American that he is totally depraved, he would think you were joking, as he himself usually is. He is convinced that he always has been, and always will be, victorious and blameless.

Calvinism thus lost its basis in American life. Some emotional natures, indeed, reverted in their religious revivals or private searchings of heart to the sources of the tradition; for any of the radical points of view in philosophy may cease to be prevalent, but none can cease to be possible. Other natures, more sensitive to the moral and literary influences of the world, preferred to abandon parts of their philosophy, hoping thus to reduce the distance which should separate the remainder from real life.

Meantime, if anybody arose with a special sensibility or a technical genius, he was in great straits; not being fed sufficiently by the world, he was driven in upon his own resources. The three American writers whose personal endowment was perhaps the finest—Poe, Hawthorne, and Emerson—had all a certain starved and abstract quality. They could not retail the genteel tradition; they were too keen, too perceptive, and too independent for that. But life offered them little digestible material, nor were they naturally voracious. They were fastidious, and under the circumstances they were starved. Emerson, to be sure, fed on books. There was a great catholicity in his reading; and he showed a fine tact in his comments, and in his way of appropriating what he read. But he read transcendentally, not historically, to learn what he himself felt, not what others might have felt before him. And to feed on books, for a philosopher or a poet, is still to starve. Books can help him to acquire form, or to avoid pitfalls; they cannot supply him with substance, if he is to have any. Therefore the genius of Poe and Hawthorne, and even of Emerson, was employed on a sort of inner play, or digestion of vacancy. It was a refined labour, but it was in danger of being morbid, or tinkling, or self-indulgent. It was a play of intra-mental rhymes. Their mind was like an old music-box, full of tender echoes and quaint fancies. These fancies expressed their personal genius sincerely, as dreams may; but they were arbitrary fancies in comparison with what a real observer would have said in the premises. Their manner, in a word, was subjective. In their own persons they escaped the medioc-

rity of the genteel tradition, but they supplied nothing to supplant it in other minds.

The churches, likewise, although they modified their spirit, had no philosophy to offer save a new emphasis on parts of what Calvinism contained. The theology of Calvin, we must remember, had much in it besides philosophical Calvinism. A Christian tenderness, and a hope of grace for the individual, came to mitigate its sardonic optimism; and it was these evangelical elements that the Calvinistic churches now emphasised, seldom and with blushes referring to hell-fire or infant damnation. Yet philosophic Calvinism, with a theory of life that would perfectly justify hell-fire and infant damnation if they happened to exist, still dominates the traditional metaphysics. It is an ingredient, and the decisive ingredient, in what calls itself idealism. But in order to see just what part Calvinism plays in current idealism, it will be necessary to distinguish the other chief element in that complex system, namely, transcendentalism.

Transcendentalism is the philosophy which the romantic era produced in Germany, and independently, I believe, in America also. Transcendentalism proper, like romanticism, is not any particular set of dogmas about what things exist; it is not a system of the universe regarded as a fact, or as a collection of facts. It is a method, a point of view, from which any world, no matter what it might contain, could be approached by a self-conscious observer. Transcendentalism is systematic subjectivism. It studies the perspectives of knowledge as they radiate from the self; it is a plan of those avenues of inference by which our ideas of things must be reached, if they are to afford any systematic or distant vistas. In other words, transcendentalism is the critical logic of science. Knowledge, it says, has a station, as in a watch-tower; it is always seated here and now, in the self of the moment. The past and the future, things inferred and things conceived, lie around it, painted as upon a panorama. They cannot be lighted up save by some centrifugal ray of attention and present interest, by some active operation of the mind.

This is hardly the occasion for developing or explaining this delicate insight; suffice it to say, lest you should think later that I disparage transcendentalism, that as a method I regard it as correct and, when once suggested, unforgettable. I regard it as the chief contribution made in modern times to speculation. But it is a method only, an attitude we may always assume if we like and that will always be legitimate. It is no answer, and involves no particular answer, to the question: What exists; in what order is what exists produced; what is to exist in the future? This question must be answered by observing the object, and tracing humbly the movement of the object. It cannot be answered at all by harping on the fact that this object, if discovered, must be discovered by somebody, and by somebody who has an interest in discovering it. Yet the Germans who first gained the full transcendental insight were romantic people; they were more or less frankly poets; they were colossal egotists, and wished to make not only their own knowledge but

the whole universe centre about themselves. And full as they were of their romantic isolation and romantic liberty, it occurred to them to imagine that all reality might be a transcendental self and a romantic dreamer like themselves; nay, that it might be just their own transcendental self and their own romantic dreams extended indefinitely. Transcendental logic, the method of discovery for the mind, was to become also the method of evolution in nature and history. Transcendental method, so abused, produced transcendental myth. A conscientious critique of knowledge was turned into a sham system of nature. We must therefore distinguish sharply the transcendental grammar of the intellect, which is significant and potentially correct, from the various transcendental systems of the universe, which are chimeras.

In both its parts, however, transcendentalism had much to recommend it to American philosophers, for the transcendental method appealed to the individualistic and revolutionary temper of their youth, while transcendental myths enabled them to find a new status for their inherited theology, and to give what parts of it they cared to preserve some semblance of philosophical backing. This last was the use to which the transcendental method was put by Kant himself, who first brought it into vogue, before the terrible weapon had got out of hand, and become the instrument of pure romanticism. Kant came, he himself said, to remove knowledge in order to make room for faith, which in his case meant faith in Calvinism. In other words, he applied the transcendental method to matters of fact, reducing them thereby to human ideas, in order to give to the Calvinistic postulates of conscience a metaphysical validity. For Kant had a genteel tradition of his own, which he wished to remove to a place of safety, feeling that the empirical world had become too hot for it; and this place of safety was the region of transcendental myth. I need hardly say how perfectly this expedient suited the needs of philosophers in America, and it is no accident if the influence of Kant soon became dominant here. To embrace this philosophy was regarded as a sign of profound metaphysical insight, although the most mediocre minds found no difficulty in embracing it. In truth it was a sign of having been brought up in the genteel tradition, of feeling it weak, and of wishing to save it.

But the transcendental method, in its way, was also sympathetic to the American mind. It embodied, in a radical form, the spirit of Protestantism as distinguished from its inherited doctrines; it was autonomous, undismayed, calmly revolutionary; it felt that Will was deeper than Intellect; it focussed everything here and now, and asked all things to show their credentials at the bar of the young self, and to prove their value for this latest born moment. These things are truly American; they would be characteristic of any young society with a keen and discursive intelligence, and they are strikingly exemplified in the thought and in the person of Emerson. They constitute what he called self-trust. Self-trust, like other transcendental attitudes, may be expressed in metaphysical fables. The romantic spirit

may imagine itself to be an absolute force, evoking and moulding the plastic world to express its varying moods. But for a pioneer who is actually a world-builder this metaphysical illusion has a partial warrant in historical fact; far more warrant than it could boast of in the fixed and articulated society of Europe, among the moonstruck rebels and sulking poets of the romantic era. Emerson was a shrewd Yankee, by instinct on the winning side; he was a cheery, child-like soul, impervious to the evidence of evil, as of everything that it did not suit his transcendental individuality to appreciate or to notice. More, perhaps, than anybody that has ever lived, he practised the transcendental method in all its purity. He had no system. He opened his eyes on the world every morning with a fresh sincerity, marking how things seemed to him then, or what they suggested to his spontaneous fancy. This fancy, for being spontaneous, was not always novel; it was guided by the habits and training of his mind, which were those of a preacher. Yet he never insisted on his notions so as to turn them into settled dogmas; he felt in his bones that they were myths. Sometimes, indeed, the bad example of other transcendentalists, less true than he to their method, or the pressing questions of unintelligent people, or the instinct we all have to think our ideas final, led him to the very verge of system-making; but he stopped short. Had he made a system out of his notion of compensation, or the over-soul, or spiritual laws, the result would have been as thin and forced as it is in other transcendental systems. But he coveted truth; and he returned to experience, to history, to poetry, to the natural science of his day, for new starting-points and hints toward fresh transcendental musings.

To covet truth is a very distinguished passion. Every philosopher says he is pursuing the truth, but this is seldom the case. As Mr. Bertrand Russell has observed, one reason why philosophers often fail to reach the truth is that often they do not desire to reach it. Those who are genuinely concerned in discovering what happens to be true are rather the men of science, the naturalists, the historians; and ordinarily they discover it, according to their lights. The truths they find are never complete, and are not always important; but they are integral parts of the truth, facts and circumstances that help to fill in the picture, and that no later interpretation can invalidate or afford to contradict. But professional philosophers are usually only apologists: that is, they are absorbed in defending some vested illusion or some eloquent idea. Like lawyers or detectives, they study the case for which they are retained, to see how much evidence or semblance of evidence they can gather for the defence, and how much prejudice they can raise against the witnesses for the prosecution; for they know they are defending prisoners suspected by the world, and perhaps by their own good sense, of falsification. They do not covet truth, but victory and the dispelling of their own doubts. What they defend is some system, that is, some view about the totality of things, of which men are actually ignorant. No system would have

ever been framed if people had been simply interested in knowing what is true, whatever it may be. What produces systems is the interest in maintaining against all comers that some favourite or inherited idea of ours is sufficient and right. A system may contain an account of many things which, in detail, are true enough; but as a system, covering infinite possibilities that neither our experience nor our logic can prejudge, it must be a work of imagination and a piece of human soliloquy. It may be expressive of human experience, it may be poetical; but how should any one who really coveted truth suppose that it was true?

Emerson had no system; and his coveting truth had another exceptional consequence: he was detached, unworldly, contemplative. When he came out of the conventicle or the reform meeting, or out of the rapturous close atmosphere of the lecture-room he heard Nature whispering to him: "Why so hot, little sir?" No doubt the spirit or energy of the world is what is acting in us, as the sea is what rises in every little wave; but it passes through us, and cry out as we may, it will move on. Our privilege is to have perceived it as it moves. Our dignity is not in what we do, but in what we understand. The whole world is doing things. We are turning in that vortex; yet within us is silent observation, the speculative eye before which all passes, which bridges the distances and compares the combatants. On this side of his genius Emerson broke away from all conditions of age or country and represented nothing except intelligence itself.

There was another element in Emerson, curiously combined with transcendentalism, namely, his love and respect for Nature. Nature, for the transcendentalist, is precious because it is his own work, a mirror in which he looks at himself and says (like a poet relishing his own verses), "What a genius I am! Who would have thought there was such stuff in me?" And the philosophical egotist finds in his doctrine a ready explanation of whatever beauty and commodity nature actually has. No wonder, he says to himself, that nature is sympathetic, since I made it. And such a view, one-sided and even fatuous as it may be, undoubtedly sharpens the vision of a poet and a moralist to all that is inspiriting and symbolic in the natural world. Emerson was particularly ingenious and clear-sighted in feeling the spiritual uses of fellowship with the elements. This is something in which all Teutonic poetry is rich and which forms, I think, the most genuine and spontaneous part of modern taste, and especially of American taste. Just as some people are naturally enthralled and refreshed by music, so others are by landscape. Music and landscape make up the spiritual resources of those who cannot or dare not express their unfulfilled ideals in words. Serious poetry, profound religion (Calvinism, for instance), are the joys of an unhappiness that confesses itself; but when a genteel tradition forbids people to confess that they are unhappy, serious poetry and profound religion are closed to them by that; and since human life, in its depths, cannot then express itself openly, imagination is driven for comfort into abstract arts, where human circumstances are lost sight of, and human problems dissolve in a purer medium. The pressure of care is thus relieved, without its quietus being found in intelligence. To understand oneself is the classic form of consolation; to elude oneself is the romantic. In the presence of music or landscape human experience eludes itself; and thus romanticism is the bond between transcendental and naturalistic sentiment. The winds and clouds come to minister to the solitary ego.

Have there been, we may ask, any successful efforts to escape from the genteel tradition, and to express something worth expressing behind its back? This might well not have occurred as yet; but America is so precocious, it has been trained by the genteel tradition to be so wise for its years, that some indications of a truly native philosophy and poetry are already to be found. I might mention the humorists, of whom you here in California have had your share. The humorists, however, only half escape the genteel tradition; their humour would lose its savour if they had wholly escaped it. They point to what contradicts it in the facts; but not in order to abandon the genteel tradition, for they have nothing solid to put in its place. When they point out how ill many facts fit into it, they do not clearly conceive that this militates against the standard, but think it a funny perversity in the facts. Of course, did they earnestly respect the genteel tradition, such an incongruity would seem to them sad, rather than ludicrous. Perhaps the prevalence of humour in America, in and out of season, may be taken as one more evidence that the genteel tradition is present pervasively, but everywhere weak. Similarly in Italy, during the Renaissance, the Catholic tradition could not be banished from the intellect, since there was nothing articulate to take its place; yet its hold on the heart was singularly relaxed. The consequence was that humorists could regale themselves with the foibles of monks and of cardinals, with the credulity of fools, and the bogus miracles of the saints; not intending to deny the theory of the church, but caring for it so little at heart that they could find it infinitely amusing that it should be contradicted in men's lives and that no harm should come of it. So when Mark Twain says, "I was born of poor but dishonest parents," the humour depends on the parody of the genteel Anglo-Saxon convention that it is disreputable to be poor; but to hint at the hollowness of it would not be amusing if it did not remain at bottom one's habitual conviction.

The one American writer who has left the genteel tradition entirely behind is perhaps Walt Whitman. For this reason educated Americans find him rather an unpalatable person, who they sincerely protest ought not to be taken for a representative of their culture; and he certainly should not, because their culture is so genteel and traditional. But the foreigner may sometimes think otherwise, since he is looking for what may have arisen in America to express, not the polite and conventional American mind, but the spirit and the inarticulate principles that animate the community, on which its own genteel mentality seems to sit rather lightly.

When the foreigner opens the pages of Walt Whitman, he thinks that he has come at last upon something representative and original. In Walt Whitman democracy is carried into psychology and morals. The various sights, moods, and emotions are given each one vote; they are declared to be all free and equal, and the innumerable commonplace moments of life are suffered to speak like the others. Those moments formerly reputed great are not excluded, but they are made to march in the ranks with their companions—plain foot-soldiers and servants of the hour. Nor does the refusal to discriminate stop there; we must carry our principle further down, to the animals, to inanimate nature, to the cosmos as a whole. Whitman became a pantheist; but his pantheism, unlike that of the Stoics and of Spinoza, was unintellectual, lazy, and self-indulgent; for he simply felt jovially that everything real was good enough, and that he was good enough himself. In him Behomeia rebelled against the genteel tradition; but the reconstruction that alone can justify revolution did not ensue. His attitude, in principle, was utterly disintegrating; his poetic genius fell back to the lowest level, perhaps, to which it is possible for poetic genius to fall. He reduced his imagination to a passive sensorium for the registering of impressions. No element of construction remained in it, and therefore no element of penetration. But his scope was wide; and his lazy, desultory apprehension was poetical. His work, for the very reason that it is so rudimentary, contains a beginning, or rather many beginnings, that might possibly grow into a noble moral imagination, a worthy filling for the human mind. An American in the nineteenth century who completely disregarded the genteel tradition could hardly have done more.

But there is another distinguished man, lately lost to this country, who has given some rude shocks to this tradition and who, as much as Whitman, may be regarded as representing the genuine, the long silent American mind—I mean William James. He and his brother Henry were as tightly swaddled in the genteel tradition as any infant geniuses could be, for they were born before 1850, and in a Swedenborgian household. Yet they burst those bands almost entirely. The ways in which the two brothers freed themselves, however, are interestingly different. Mr. Henry James has done it by adopting the point of view of the outer world, and by turning the genteel American tradition, as he turns everything else, into a subject-matter for analysis. For him it is a curious habit of mind, intimately comprehended, to be compared with other habits of mind, also well known to him. Thus he has overcome the genteel tradition in the classic way, by understanding it. With William James too this infusion of worldly insight and European sympathies was a potent influence, especially in his earlier days; but the chief source of his liberty was another. It was his personal spontaneity, similar to that of Emerson, and his personal vitality, similar to that of nobody else. Convictions and ideas came to him, so to speak, from the subsoil. He had a prophetic sympathy with the dawning sentiments of the age, with the moods of the dumb majority. His scattered words caught fire in many parts of the world. His way of thinking and feeling represented the true America, and represented in a measure the whole ultra-modern, radical world. Thus he eluded the genteel tradition in the romantic way, by continuing it into its opposite. The romantic mind, glorified in Hegel's dialectic (which is not dialectic at all, but a sort of tragi-comic history of experience), is always rendering its thoughts unrecognisable through the infusion of new insights, and through the insensible transformation of the moral feeling that accompanies them, till at last it has completely reversed its old judgments under cover of expanding them. Thus the genteel tradition was led a merry dance when it fell again into the hands of a genuine and vigorous romanticist like William James. He restored their revolutionary force to its neutralised elements, by picking them out afresh, and emphasising them separately, according to his personal predilections.

For one thing, William James kept his mind and heart wide open to all that might seem, to polite minds, odd, personal, or visionary in religion and philosophy. He gave a sincerely respectful hearing to sentimentalists, mystics, spiritualists, wizards, cranks, quacks, and impostors—for it is hard to draw the line, and James was not willing to draw it prematurely. He thought, with his usual modesty, that any of these might have something to teach him. The lame, the halt, the blind, and those speaking with tongues could come to him with the certainty of finding sympathy; and if they were not healed, at least they were comforted, that a famous professor should take them so seriously; and they began to feel that after all to have only one leg, or one hand, or one eye, or to have three, might be in itself no less beauteous than to have just two, like the stolid majority. Thus William James became the friend and helper of those groping, nervous, half-educated, spiritually disinherited, passionately hungry individuals of which America is full. He became, at the same time, their spokesman and representative before the learned world; and he made it a chief part of his vocation to recast what the learned world has to offer, so that as far as possible it might serve the needs and interests of these people.

Yet the normal practical masculine American, too, had a friend in William James. There is a feeling abroad now, to which biology and Darwinism lend some colour, that theory is simply an instrument for practice, and intelligence merely a help toward material survival. Bears, it is said, have fur and claws, but poor naked man is condemned to be intelligent, or he will perish. This feeling William James embodied in that theory of thought and of truth which he called pragmatism. Intelligence, he thought, is no miraculous, idle faculty, by which we mirror passively any or everything that happens to be true, reduplicating the real world to no purpose. Intelligence has its roots and its issue in the context of events; it is one kind of practical adjustment, an experimental act, a form of vital tension. It does not essentially serve to picture other parts of reality, but to connect

them. This view was not worked out by William James in its psychological and historical details; unfortunately he developed it chiefly in controversy against its opposite, which he called intellectualism, and which he hated with all the hatred of which his kind heart was capable. Intellectualism, as he conceived it, was pure pedantry; it impoverished and verbalised everything, and tied up nature in red tape. Ideas and rules that may have been occasionally useful it put in the place of the full-blooded irrational movement of life which had called them into being; and these abstractions, so soon obsolete, it strove to fix and to worship for ever. Thus all creeds and theories and all formal precepts sink in the estimation of the pragmatist to a local and temporary grammar of action; a grammar that must be changed slowly by time, and may be changed quickly by genius. To know things as a whole, or as they are eternally, if there is anything eternal in them, is not only beyond our powers, but would prove worthless, and perhaps even fatal to our lives. Ideas are not mirrors, they are weapons; their function is to prepare us to meet events, as future experience may unroll them. Those ideas that disappoint us are false ideas; those to which events are true are true themselves.

This may seem a very utilitarian view of the mind; and I confess I think it a partial one, since the logical force of beliefs and ideas, their truth or falsehood as assertions, has been overlooked altogether, or confused with the vital force of the material processes which these ideas express. It is an external view only, which marks the place and conditions of the mind in nature, but neglects its specific essence; as if a jewel were defined as a round hole in a ring. Nevertheless, the more materialistic the pragmatist's theory of the mind is, the more vitalistic his theory of nature will have to become. If the intellect is a device produced in organic bodies to expedite their processes, these organic bodies must have interests and a chosen direction in their life; otherwise their life could not be expedited, nor could anything be useful to it. In other words—and this is a third point at which the philosophy of William James has played havoc with the genteel tradition, while ostensibly defending it—nature must be conceived anthropomorphically and in psychological terms. Its purposes are not to be static harmonies, self-unfolding destinies, the logic of spirit, the spirit of logic, or any other formal method and abstract law; its purposes are to be concrete endeavours, finite efforts of souls living in an environment which they transform and by which they, too, are affected. A spirit, the divine spirit as much as the human, as this new animism conceives it, is a romantic adventurer. Its future is undetermined. Its scope, its duration, and the quality of its life are all contingent. This spirit grows; it buds and sends forth feelers, sounding the depths around for such other centres of force or life as may exist there. It has a vital momentum, but no predetermined goal. It uses its past as a stepping-stone, or rather as a diving-board, but has an absolutely fresh will at each moment to plunge this way or that into the unknown. The universe is an experiment; it is unfinished. It has no ultimate or total nature, because it has no end. It embodies no formula or statable law; any formula is at best a poor abstraction, describing what, in some region and for some time, may be the most striking characteristic of existence; the law is a description *a posteriori* of the habit things have chosen to acquire, and which they may possibly throw off altogether. What a day may bring forth is uncertain; uncertain even to God. Omniscience is impossible; time is real; what had been omniscience hitherto might discover something more to-day. "There shall be news," William James was fond of saying with rapture, quoting from the unpublished poem of an obscure friend, "there shall be news in heaven!" There is almost certainly, he thought, a God now; there may be several gods, who might exist together, or one after the other. We might, by our conspiring sympathies, help to make a new one. Much in us is doubtless immortal; we survive death for some time in a recognisable form; but what our career and transformations may be in the sequel we cannot tell, although we may help to determine them by our daily choices. Observation must be continual if our ideas are to remain true. Eternal vigilance is the price of knowledge; perpetual hazard, perpetual experiment keep quick the edge of life.

This is, so far as I know, a new philosophical vista; it is a conception never before presented, although implied, perhaps, in various quarters, as in Norse and even Greek mythology. It is a vision radically empirical and radically romantic; and as William James himself used to say, the visions and not the arguments of a philosopher are the interesting and influential things about him. William James, rather too generously, attributed this vision to M. Bergson, and regarded him in consequence as a philosopher of the first rank, whose thought was to be one of the turning-points in history. M. Bergson had killed intellectualism. It was his book on creative evolution, said James with humorous emphasis, that had come at last to "*écraser l'infâme*." We may suspect, notwithstanding, that intellectualis, infamous and crushed, will survive the blow; and if the author of the Book of Ecclesiastes were now alive, and heard that there shall be news in heaven, he would doubtless say that there may possibly be news there, but that under the sun there is nothing new—not even radical empiricism or radical romanticism, which from the beginning of the world has been the philosophy of those who as yet had had little experience; for to the blinking little child it is not merely something in the world that is new daily, but everything is new all day.

I am not concerned with the rights and wrongs of that controversy; my point is only that William James, in this genial evolutionary view of the world, has given a rude shock to the genteel tradition. What! The world a gradual improvisation? Creation unpremeditated? God a sort of young poet or struggling artist? William James is an advocate of theism; pragmatism adds one to the evidences of religion; that is excellent. But is not the cool abstract piety of the genteel getting more than it asks for? This empirical naturalistic God is too crude and positive a force; he will work miracles, he will answer prayers, he may inhabit distinct places, and have distinct conditions under which alone he can operate; he is a neighbouring being, whom we can act upon, and rely upon for specific aids, as upon a personal friend, or a physician, or an insurance company. How disconcerting! Is not this new theology a little like superstition? And yet how interesting, how exciting, if it should happen to be true! I am far from wishing to suggest that such a view seems to me more probable than conventional idealism or than Christian orthodoxy. All three are in the region of dramatic system-making and myth to which probabilities are irrelevant. If one man says the moon is sister to the sun, and another that she is his daughter, the question is not which notion is more probable, but whether either of them is at all expressive. The so-called evidences are devised afterwards, when faith and imagination have prejudged the issue. The force of William James's new theology; or romantic cosmology, lies only in this: that it has broken the spell of the genteel tradition, and enticed faith in a new direction, which on second thoughts may prove no less alluring than the old. The important fact is not that the new fancy might possibly be true—who shall know that?—but that it has entered the heart of a leading American to conceive and to cherish it. The genteel tradition cannot be dislodged by these insurrections; there are circles to which it is still congenial, and where it will be preserved. But it has been challenged and (what is perhaps more insidious) it has been discovered. No one need be brow-beaten any longer into accepting it. No one need be afraid, for instance, that his fate is sealed because some young prig may call him a dualist; the pint would call the quart a dualist, if you tried to pour the quart into him. We need not be afraid of being less profound, for being direct and sincere. The intellectual world may be traversed in many directions; the whole has not been surveyed; there is a great career in it open to talent. That is a sort of knell, that tolls the passing of the genteel tradition. Something else is now in the field; something else can appeal to the imagination, and be a thousand times more idealistic than academic idealism, which is often simply a way of white-washing and adoring things as they are. The illegitimate monopoly which the genteel tradition had established over what ought to be assumed and what ought to be hoped for has been broken down by the first-born of the family, by the genius of the race. Henceforth there can hardly be the same peace and the same pleasure in hugging the old proprieties, Hegel will be to the next generation what Sir William Hamilton was to the last. Nothing will have been disproved, but everything will have been abandoned. An honest man has spoken, and the cant of the genteel tradition has become harder for young lips to repeat.

John Jay Chapman
(1862–1933)

John Jay Chapman was little understood by his contemporaries and remains little known today. Yet he was a far-sighted and original if eccentric cultural critic. An Emersonian idealist, Chapman was a man of such intense moral sensibility that, on discovering that he had thrashed an innocent man, he held the offending hand to the fire, burning it so severely that it had to be amputated.

The following is an address delivered by Chapman in 1913 in Coatesville, Pennsylvania. The occasion was the first anniversary of the particularly horrifying lynching of a black man thought to have killed a white police officer. Chapman determined to do penance on behalf of the entire country. Renting a hall in Coatesville, he called a prayer meeting to commemorate the lynching. The citizens of Coatesville were hardly impressed. Only three people attended: a friend Chapman had brought with him from New York, one local who had been sent to see what Chapman was up to, and an old black woman from Boston who happened to be passing through Coatesville. Undeterred by this public indifference and at some risk to his own safety, Chapman went ahead with the address in which he hoped to expose "the unconscious soul of this country."

"Coatesville" (1915)

We are met to commemorate the anniversary of one of the most dreadful crimes in history—not for the purpose of condemning it, but to repent of our share in it. We do not start any agitation with regard to that particular crime. I understand that an attempt to prosecute the chief criminals has been made, and has entirely failed; because the whole community, and in a sense our whole people, are really involved in the guilt. The failure of the prosecution in this case, in all such cases, is only a proof of the magnitude of the guilt, and of the awful fact that everyone shares in it.

I will tell you why I am here; I will tell you what happened to me. When I read in the newspapers of August 14, a year ago, about the burning alive of a human being, and of how a few desperate, fiend-minded men had been permitted to torture a man chained to an iron bedstead, burning alive, thrust back by pitchforks when he struggled out of it, while around it stood hundreds of well-dressed American citizens, both from the vicinity and from afar, coming on foot and in wagons, assembling on telephone call, as if by magic, silent, whether from terror or indifference, fascinated and impotent, hundreds of persons watching this awful sight and making no attempt to stay the wickedness, and no one man among them all who was inspired to risk his life in an atempt to stop it, no one man to name the name of Christ, of humanity, of government! As I read the newspaper accounts of the scene enacted here in Coatesville a year ago, I seemed to get a glimpse into the unconscious soul of this country. I saw a seldom revealed picture of the American heart and of the American nature. I seemed to be looking into the heart of the criminal—a cold thing, an awful thing.

I said to myself, "I shall forget this, we shall all forget it; but it will be there. What I have seen is not an illusion. It is the truth. I have seen death in the heart of this people." For to look at the agony of a fellow-being and remain aloof means death in the heart of the onlooker. Religious fanaticism has sometimes lifted men to the frenzy of such cruelty, political passion has sometimes done it, personal hatred might do it, the excitement of the amphitheater in the degenerate days of Roman luxury could do it. But here an audience chosen by chance in America has stood spellbound through an improvised *auto-da-fé*, irregular, illegal, having no religious significance, not sanctioned by custom, having no immediate provocation, the audience standing by merely in cold dislike.

I saw during one moment something beyond all argument in the depth of its significance. You might call it the paralysis of the nerves about the heart in a people habitually and unconsciously given over to selfish aims, an ignorant people who knew not what spectacle they were providing, or what part they were playing in a judgment-play which history was exhibiting on that day.

No theories about the race problem, no statistics, legislation, or mere educational endeavor, can quite meet the lack which that day revealed in the American people. For what we saw was death. The people stood like blighted things, like ghosts about Acheron, waiting for someone or something to determine their destiny for them.

Whatever life itself is, that thing must be replenished in us. The opposite of hate is love, the opposite of cold is heat; what we need is the love of God and reverence for human nature. For one moment I knew that I had seen our true need; and I was afraid that I should forget it and that I should go about framing arguments and agitations and starting schemes of education, when the need was deeper than education. And I became filled with one idea, that I must not forget what I had seen, and that I must do something to remember it. And I am here to-day chiefly that I may remember that vision. It seems fitting to come to this town where the crime occurred and hold a prayer-meeting, so that our hearts may be turned to God through whom mercy may flow into us.

Let me say one thing more about the whole matter. The subject we are dealing with is not local. The act, to be sure, took place at Coatesville and everyone looked to Coatesville to follow it up. Some months ago I asked a friend who lives not far from here something about this case, and about the expected prosecutions, and he replied to me: "It wasn't in my county," and that made me wonder whose county it was in. And it seemed to be in my county. I live on the Hudson River; but I knew that this great wickedness that happened in Coatesville is not the wickedness of Coatesville nor of to-day. It is the wickedness of all America and of three hundred years—the wick-edness of the slave trade. All of us are tinctured by it. No special place, no special persons, are to blame. A nation cannot practice a course of inhuman crime for three hundred years and then suddenly throw off the effects of it. Less than fifty years ago domestic slavery was ablished among us; and in one way and another the marks of that vice are in our faces. There is no country in Europe where the Coatesville tragedy or anything remotely like it could have been enacted, probably no country in the world.

On the day of the calamity, those people in the automobiles came by the hundred and watched the torture, and passers-by came in a great multitude and watched it—and did nothing. On the next morning the newspapers spread the news and spread the paralysis until the whole country seemed to be helplessly watching this awful murder, as awful as anything ever done on the earth; and the whole of our people seemed to be looking on helplessly, not able to respond, not knowing what to do next. That spectacle has been in my mind.

The trouble has come down to us out of the past. The only reason that slavery is wrong is that it is cruel and makes men cruel and leaves them cruel. Someone may say that you and I cannot repent because we did not do the act. But we are involved in it. We are still looking on. Do you not see that this whole event is merely the last parable, the most vivid, the most terrible illustration that ever was given by man or imagined by a Jewish prophet, of the relation between good and evil in this world, and of the relation of men to one another?

This whole matter has been an historic episode; but it is a part, not only of our national history, but of the personal history of each one of us. With the great disease (slavery) came the climax (the war), and after the climax gradually began the cure, and in the process of cure comes now the knowledge of what the evil was. I say that our need is new life, and that books and resolutions will not save us, but only such disposition in our hearts and souls as will enable the new life, love, force, hope, virtue, which surround us always, to enter into us.

This is the discovery that each man must make for himself—the discovery that what he really stands in need of he cannot get for himself, but must wait till God gives it to him. I have felt the impulse to come here to-day to testify to this truth.

The occasion is not small; the occasion looks back on three centuries and embraces a hemisphere. Yet the occasion is small compared with the truth it leads us to. For this truth touches all ages and affects every soul in the world.

V

Rejections
and Revisions
(1915–1950)

The period between and just after the two world wars was an era of immense confusion, conflict, and creativity. It was a time when for many people old assurances collapsed and new uncertainties emerged, when inherited forms were discarded and new energies released. These developments were greeted variously. Among some, like Christian Biblical Fundamentalists, New Humanists, and Southern Agrarians, these changes inspired fear and loathing and precipitated retreat into one or another of the pieties of the past. Among others, like the writers of the Lost Generation or the followers of John Dewey, these same developments inspired fresh confidence and led to the search for new techniques to cope with the new forms of experience thus discovered and the new kinds of knowledge they brought with them. If the reactionaries looked backward for some stay against all this modern confusion, the radicals looked forward for what they called the essential, the genuine, the authentic. Life seemed to divest itself of illusions during this period—indeed, much of the activity of the period took the form of an attack on illusions—and to ask of its votaries only that they not deceive themselves or others with false hopes, cheap compromises, or easy alternatives. Whether they reacted by attempting to wipe the slate clean of the past and begin all over again or by rejecting all that seemed spurious in the present and revising what still remained usable in the past, they approached the task of reconstructing a New World metaphysics in much the same spirit Herman Melville had allowed his character Pierre to express nearly a century before: "On bold quest, better to sink in boundless deeps than float on vulgar shoals; and give me, ye gods, an utter wreck, if wreck I do."

H. L. Mencken
(1880–1956)

Egotist, iconoclast, and eccentric, H. L. (Henry Louis) Mencken may have done more than any other writer to bring about the cultural and spiritual coming-of-age that occurred in America in the early twentieth century. Mencken's favorite target was "Puritanism" in all its contemporary expressions. That by Puritan Mencken actually meant Victorian, and that by attacking Puritanism Mencken was really zeroing in on "genteel" fastidiousness and modern philistinism, is beside the point. Mencken was not particularly sensitive to historical distinctions, nor were most of his readers. The important thing was that Puritanism provided Mencken with an explanation and cause for everything bloodless, banal, and unreal in American life, and the gusto of his attack provided others with a way of overcoming its legacy. "Puritanism as a Literary Force" was originally published in Mencken's *A Book of Prefaces* (1917).

From "Puritanism as a Literary Force" (1917)

"Calvinism," says Dr. Leon Kellner, in his excellent little history of American literature, "is the natural theology of the disinherited; it never flourished, there-fore, anywhere as it did in the barren hills of Scotland and in the wilds of North America." The learned doctor is here speaking of theology in what may be called its narrow technical sense—that is, as a theory of God. Under Calvinism, in the New World as well as in the Old, it became no more than a luxuriant demonology; even God himself was transformed into a superior sort of devil, ever wary and wholly merciless. That primitive demonology still survives in the barbaric doctrines of the Methodists and Baptists, particularly in the South; but it has been ameliorated, even there, by a growing sense of the divine grace, and so the old God of Plymouth Rock, as practically conceived, is now scarcely worse than the average jail warden or Italian padrone. On the ethical side, however, Calvinism is dying a much harder death, and we are still a long way from the enlightenment. Save where Continental influences have measurably corrupted the Puritan idea—*e.g.,* in such cities as New York, San Francisco and New Orleans,—the prevailing American view of the world and its mysteries is still a moral one, and no other human concern gets half the attention that is endlessly lavished upon the problem of conduct, particularly of the other fellow. It needed no official announcement to define the function and office of the republic as that of an international expert in morals, and the mentor and exemplar of the more backward nations. Within, as well as without, the eternal rapping of knuckles and proclaiming of new austerities goes on. The American, save in moments of conscious and swiftly lamented deviltry, casts up all ponderable values, including even the values of beauty, in terms of right and wrong. He is beyond all things else, a judge and a policeman; he believes firmly that there is a mysterious power in law; he supports and embellishes its operation with a fanatical vigilance.

∿∿∿

All this may be called the Puritan impulse from within. It is, indeed, but a single manifestation of one of the deepest prejudices of a religious and half-cultured people—the prejudice against beauty as a form of debauchery and corruption—the distrust of all ideas that do not fit readily into certain accepted axioms—the belief in the eternal validity of moral concepts—in brief, the whole mental sluggishness of the lower orders of men. But in addition to this internal resistance, there has been laid upon American letters the heavy hand of a Puritan authority from without, and no examination of the history and present condition of our literature could be of any value which did not take it constantly into account, and work out the means of its influence and operation. That authority, as I shall show, transcends both in power and in alertness the natural reactions of the national mind, and is incomparably more potent in combating ideas. It is supported by a body of law that is unmatched in any other country of Christendom, and it is exercised with a fanatical harshness and vigilance that make escape from its operations well nigh impossible. Some of its effects, both direct and indirect, I shall describe later, but before doing so it may be well to trace its genesis and development.

At bottom, of course, it rests upon the inherent Puritanism of the people; it could not survive a year if they were opposed to the principle visible in it. That deep-seated and uncorrupted Puritanism, that conviction of the pervasiveness of sin, of the supreme importance of moral correctness, of the need of savage and inquisitorial laws, has been a dominating force in American life since the very beginning. There has never been any question before the nation, whether political or economic, religious or military, diplomatic or sociological, which did not resolve itself, soon or late, into a purely moral question. Nor has there ever been any surcease of the spiritual eagerness which lay at the bottom of the original Puritan's moral obsession: the American has been, from the very start, a man genuinely interested in the eternal mysteries, and fearful of missing their correct solution. The frank theocracy of the New England colonies had scarcely succumbed to the libertarianism of a godless Crown before there came the Great Awakening of 1734, with its orgies of homiletics and its restoration of talmudism to the first place among polite sciences. The Revolution, of course, brought a set-back: the colonists faced so urgent a need of unity in politics that they declared a sort of *Treuga Dei* in religion, and that truce, armed though it was, left its imprint upon the First Amendment to the Constitution. But immediately the young Republic emerged from the stresses of adolescence, a missionary army took to the field again, and before long the Asbury revival was paling that of White-field, Wesley and Jonathan Edwards, not only in its hortatory violence but also in the length of its lists of slain.

Thereafter, down to the outbreak of the Civil War, the country was rocked again and again by furious attacks upon the devil. On the one hand, this great campaign took a purely theological form, with a hundred new and fantastic creeds as its fruits; on the other hand, it crystallized into the hysterical temperance movement of the 30's and 40's, which penetrated to the very floor of Congress and put "dry" laws upon the statute-books of ten States; and on the third hand, as it were, it established a prudery in speech and thought from which we are yet but half delivered. Such ancient and innocent words as "bitch" and "bastard" disappeared from the American language; Bartlett tells us, indeed, in his "Dictionary of American-isms," that even "bull" was softened to "male cow." This was the Golden Age of euphemism, as it was of euphuism; the worst inventions of the English mid-Victorians were adopted and improved. The word "woman" became a term of opprobrium, verging close upon downright libel; legs became the inimitable "limbs"; the stomach began to run from the "bosom" to the pelvic arch; pantaloons faded into "unmentionables"; the newspapers spun their parts of speech into such gossamer webs as "a statutory offence," "a house of questionable repute" and "an interesting condition." And meanwhile the Good Templars and Sons of Temperance swarmed in the land like a plague of celestial locusts. There was not a hamlet without its

uniformed phalanx, its affecting exhibit of reformed drunkards. The Kentucky Legislature succumbed to a travelling recruiting officer, and two-thirds of the members signed the pledge. The National House of Representatives took recess after recess to hear eminent excoriators of the Rum Demon, and more than a dozen of its members forsook their duties to carry the new gospel to the bucolic heathen—the van-guard, one may note in passing, of the innumerable Chautauquan caravan of later years.

Beneath all this bubbling on the surface, of course, ran the deep and swift undercurrent of anti-slavery feeling—a tide of passion which historians now attempt to account for on economic grounds, but which showed no trace of economic origin while it lasted. Its true quality was moral, devout, ecstatic; it culminated, to change the figure, in a supreme discharge of moral electricity, almost fatal to the nation. The crack of that great spark emptied the jar; the American people forgot all about their pledges and pruderies during the four years of Civil War. The Good Templars, indeed, were never heard of again, and with them into memory went many other singular virtuosi of virtue—for example, the Millerites. But almost before the last smoke of battle cleared away, a renaissance of Puritan ardour began, and by the middle of the 70's it was in full flower. Its high points and flashing lighthouses halt the backward-looking eye; the Moody and Sankey uproar, the triumphal entry of the Salvation Army, the recrudescence of the temperance agitation and its culmination in prohibition, the rise of the Young Men's Christian Association and of the Sunday-school, the almost miraculous growth of the Christian Endeavour movement, the beginnings of the vice crusade, the renewed injection of moral conceptions and rages into party politics (the "crime" of 1873!), the furious preaching of baroque Utopias, the invention of muckraking, the mad, glad war of extermination upon the Mormons, the hysteria over the Breckenridge-Pollard case and other like causes, the enormous multiplication of moral and religious associations, the spread of zoöphilia, the attack upon Mammon, the dawn of the uplift, and last but far from least, comstockery.

In comstockery, if I do not err, the new Puritanism gave a sign of its formal departure from the old, and moral endeavour suffered a general overhauling and tightening of the screws. The difference between the two forms is very well represented by the difference between the program of the half-forgotten Good Templars and the program set forth in the Webb Law of 1913, or by that between the somewhat diffident prudery of the 40's and the astoundingly ferocious and uncompromising vice-crusading of today. In brief, a difference between the *re*nunciation and *de*nunciation, asceticism and Mohammedanism, the hair shirt and the flaming sword. The distinguishing mark of the elder Puritanism, at least after it had attained to the stature of a national philosophy, was its appeal to the individual conscience, its exclusive concern with the elect, its strong flavour of self-accusing. Even the rage against slavery was,

in large measure, an emotion of the mourners' bench. The thing that worried the more ecstatic Abolitionists was their sneaking sense of responsibility, the fear that they themselves were flouting the fire by letting slavery go on. The thirst to punish the concrete slave-owner, as an end in itself, did not appear until opposition had added exasperation to fervour. In most of the earlier harangues against his practice, indeed, you will find a perfect willingness to grant that slave-owner's good faith, and even to compensate him for his property. But the new Puritanism— or, perhaps more accurately, considering the shades of prefixes, the neo-Puritanism—is a frank harking back to the primitive spirit. The original Puritan of the bleak New England coast was not content to flay his own wayward carcass: full satisfaction did not sit upon him until he had jailed a Quaker. That is to say, the sinner who excited his highest zeal and passion was not so much himself as his neighbour; to borrow a term from psychopathology, he was less the masochist than the sadist. And it is that very peculiarity which sets off his descendant of today from the ameliorated Puritan of the era between the Revolution and the Civil War. The new Puritanism is not ascetic, but militant. Its aim is not to lift up saints but to knock down sinners. Its supreme manifestation is the vice crusade, an armed pursuit of helpless outcasts by the whole military and naval forces of the Republic. Its supreme hero is Comstock Himself, with his pious boast that the sinners he jailed during his astounding career, if gathered into one penitential party, would have filled a train of sixty-one coaches, allowing sixty to the coach.

So much for the general trend and tenor of the movement. At the bottom of it, it is plain, there lies that insistent presentation of the idea of sin, that enchantment by concepts of carnality, which has engaged a certain type of man, to the exclusion of all other notions, since the dawn of history. The remote ancestors of our Puritan-Philistines of today are to be met with in the Old Testament and the New, and their nearer grandfathers clamoured against the snares of the flesh in all the councils of the Early Church. Not only Western Christianity has had to reckon with them: they have brothers today among the Mohammedan Sufi and in obscure Buddhist sects, and they were the chief preachers of the Russian Raskol, or Reformation. "The Ironsides of Cromwell and the Puritans of New England," says Heard, in his book on the Russian church, "bear a strong resemblance to the Old Believers." But here, in the main, we have asceticism more than Puritanism, as it is now visible; here the sinner combated is chiefly the one within. How are we to account for the wholesale transvaluation of values that came after the Civil War, the transfer of ire from the Old Adam to the happy rascal across the street, the sinister rise of a new Inquisition in the midst of a growing luxury that even the Puritans themselves succumbed to? The answer is to be sought, it seems to me, in the direction of the Golden Calf—in the direction of the fat fields of our Midlands, the full nets of our lakes and coasts, the factory smoke of our cities—

even in the direction of Wall Street, that devil's chasm. In brief, Puritanism has become bellicose and tyrannical by becoming rich. The will to power has been aroused to a high flame by an increase in the available draught and fuel, as militarism is engendered and nourished by the presence of men and materials. Wealth, discovering its power, has reached out its long arms to grab the distant and innumerable sinner; it has gone down into its deep pockets to pay for his costly pursuit and flaying; it has created the Puritan *entrepreneur,* the daring and imaginative organizer of Puritanism, the baron of moral endeavour, the invincible prophet of new austerities. And, by the same token, it has issued its letters of marque to the Puritan mercenary, the professional hound of heaven, the moral *Junker,* the Comstock, and out of his skill at his trade there has arisen the whole machinery, so complicated and so effective, of the new Holy Office.

ᴑᴑᴑᴑᴑᴑᴑᴑᴑᴑᴑᴑᴑᴑᴑᴑ

Walter Rauschenbusch (1861–1918)

Walter Rauschenbusch was a Baptist clergyman and professor of church history at Rochester Theological Seminary (1897–1918) whose writings helped to create a movement within American

Protestantism which aimed, in the words of one of Rauschenbusch's titles, at *Christianizing the Social Order* (1912). This religious movement for social reform was expressive of liberal currents that swept through the Christian world during the latter half of the nineteenth century and was eventually to arouse the conscience of many Americans outside and inside the churches well into the twentieth century. The present selection is taken from the book whose title gave the movement its name, *A Theology for the Social Gospel* (1917).

From *A Theology for the Social Gospel* (1917)

In the following brief propositions I should like to offer a few suggestions, on behalf of the social gospel, for the theological formulation of the doctrine of the Kingdom. Something like this is needed to give us "a theology for the social gospel."

1. The Kingdom of God is divine in its origin, progress and consummation. It was initiated by Jesus Christ, in whom the prophetic spirit came to its consummation, it is sustained by the Holy Spirit, and it will be brought to its fulfilment by the power of God in his own time. The passive and active resistance of the Kingdom of Evil at every stage of its advance is so great, and the human resources of the Kingdom of God so slender, that no explanation can satisfy a religious mind which does not see the power of God in its movements. The Kingdom of God, therefore, is miraculous all the way, and is the continuous revelation of the power, the righteousness, and the love of God. . . .

2. The Kingdom of God contains the teleology of the Christian religion. It translates theology from the static to the dynamic. It sees, not doctrines or rites to be conserved and perpetuated, but resistance to be overcome and great ends to be achieved. Since the Kingdom of God is the supreme purpose of God, we shall understand the Kingdom so far as we understand God, and we shall understand God so far as we understand his Kingdom. As long as organized sin is in the world, the Kingdom of God is characterized by conflict with evil. But if there were no evil, or after evil has been overcome, the Kingdom of God will still be the end to which God is lifting the race. It is realized not only by redemption, but also by the education of mankind and the revelation of his life within it.

3. Since God is in it, the Kingdom of God is always both present and future. Like God it is in all tenses, eternal in the midst of time. It is the energy of God realizing itself in human life. Its future lies among the mysteries of God. It invites and justifies prophecy, but all prophecy is fallible; it is valuable in so far as it grows out of action for the Kingdom and impels action. No theories about the future of the Kingdom of God are likely to be valuable or true which paralyze or postpone redemptive action on our part. To those who postpone, it is a theory and not a reality. It is for us to see the Kingdom of God as

always coming, always pressing in on the present, always big with possibility, and always inviting immediate action. We walk by faith. Every human life is so placed that it can share with God in the creation of the Kingdom, or can resist and retard its progress. The Kingdom is for each of us the supreme task and the supreme gift of God. By accepting it as a task, we experience it as a gift. By labouring for it we enter into the joy and peace of the Kingdom as our divine fatherland and habitation.

4. Even before Christ, men of God saw the Kingdom of God as the great end to which all divine leadings were pointing. Every idealistic interpretation of the world, religious or philosophical, needs some such conception. Within the Christian religion the idea of the Kingdom gets its distinctive interpretation from Christ. (a) Jesus emancipated the idea of the Kingdom from previous nationalistic limitations and from the debasement of lower religious tendencies, and made it world-wide and spiritual. (b) He made the purpose of salvation essential in it. (c) He imposed his own mind, his personality, his love and holy will on the idea of the Kingdom. (d) He not only foretold it but initiated it by his life and work. . . .

5. The Kingdom of God is humanity organized according to the will of God. Interpreting it through the consciousness of Jesus we may affirm these convictions about the ethical relations within the Kingdom: (a) Since Christ revealed the divine worth of life and personality, and since his salvation seeks the restoration and fulfilment of even the least, it follows that the Kingdom of God, at every stage of human development, tends toward a social order which will best guarantee to all personalities their freest and highest development. This involves the redemption of social life from the cramping influence of religious bigotry, from the repression of self-assertion in the relation of upper and lower classes, and from all forms of slavery in which human beings are treated as mere means to serve the ends of others. (b) Since love is the supreme law of Christ, the Kingdom of God implies a progressive reign of love in human affairs. We can see its advance wherever the free will of love supersedes the use of force and legal coercion as a regulative of the social order. This involves the redemption of society from political autocracies and economic oligarchies; the substitution of redemptive for vindictive penology; the abolition of constraint through hunger as part of the industrial system; and the abolition of war as the supreme expression of hate and the completest cessation of freedom. (c) The highest expression of love is the free surrender of what is truly our own, life, property, and rights. A much lower but perhaps more decisive expression of love is the surrender of any opportunity to exploit men. No social group or organization can claim to be clearly within the Kingdom of God which drains others for its own ease, and resists the effort to abate this fundamental evil. This involves the redemption of society from private property in the natural resources of the earth, and from any condition in industry which makes monopoly profits possible. (d) The reign of love tends toward

the progressive unity of mankind, but with the maintenance of individual liberty and the opportunity of nations to work out their own national peculiarities and ideals.

6. Since the Kingdom is the supreme end of God, it must be the purpose for which the Church exists. The measure in which it fulfils this purpose is also the measure of its spiritual authority and honour. The institutions of the Church, its activities, its worship, and its theology must in the long run be tested by its effectiveness in creating the Kingdom of God. . . .

7. Since the Kingdom is the supreme end, all problems of personal salvation must be reconsidered from the point of view of the Kingdom. It is not sufficient to set the two aims of Christianity side by side. There must be a synthesis, and theology must explain how the two react on each other. The entire redemptive work of Christ must also be reconsidered under this orientation. Early Greek theology saw salvation chiefly as the redemption from ignorance by the revelation of God and from earthliness by the impartation of immortality. It interpreted the work of Christ accordingly, and laid stress on his incarnation and resurrection. Western theology saw salvation mainly as forgiveness of guilt and freedom from punishment. It interpreted the work of Christ accordingly, and laid stress on the death and atonement. If the Kingdom of God was the guiding idea and chief end of Jesus—as we now know it was—we may be sure that every step in His life, including His death, was related to that aim and its realization, and when the idea of the Kingdom of God takes its due place in theology, the work of Christ will have to be interpreted afresh.

8. The Kingdom of God is not confined within the limits of the Church and its activities. It embraces the whole of human life. It is the Christian transfiguration of the social order. The Church is one social institution alongside of the family, the industrial organization of society, and the State. The Kingdom of God is in all these, and realizes itself through them all. During the Middle Ages all society was ruled and guided by the Church. Few of us would want modern life to return to such a condition. Functions which the Church used to perform, have now far outgrown its capacities. The Church is indispensable to the religious education of humanity and to the conservation of religion, but the greatest future awaits religion in the public life of humanity.

Shailer Mathews (1863–1941)

Shailer Mathews was Dean of the Divinity School of the University of Chicago from 1908 to 1933 and was instrumental in developing there the sociohistorical approach to the study of Christianity which came to be associated with "the Chicago school." Viewing the Christian tradition as they would any other religious movement, Mathews and his Chicago colleagues encouraged the study of Christian doctrine in the context of the social and political setting in which it evolved. Walter Rauschenbusch said of Mathews's first book, *The Social Teaching of Jesus* (1897), that it established the biblical basis of the entire Social Gospel movement. In time, however, Mathews's interest in social reform was to give way to an investigation of the nature of modernism itself, which he interpreted as a cultural adaptation of the essence of the Christian faith. Mathews presented this thesis most forcefully in *The Faith of Modernism* (1924), from which the present selection is taken.

From *The Faith of Modernism* (1924)

What then is Modernism? A heresy? An infidelity? A denial of truth? A new religion? So its ecclesiastical opponents have called it. But it is none of these. To describe it is like describing that science which has made our modern intellectual world so creative. It is not a denomination or a theology. *It is the use of the methods of modern science to find, state and use the permanent and central values of inherited orthodoxy in meeting the needs of a modern world.* The needs themselves point the way to formulas. Modernists endeavor to reach beliefs and their application in the same way that chemists or historians reach and apply their conclusions. They do not vote in conventions and do not enforce beliefs by

discipline. Modernism has no Confession. Its theological affirmations are the formulations of results of investigation both of human needs and the Christian religion. The Dogmatist starts with doctrines, the Modernist with the religion that gave rise to doctrines. The Dogmatist relies on conformity through group authority; the Modernist upon inductive method and action in accord with group loyalty.

An examination of the Modernist movement will disclose distinct aspects of these characteristics.

1. The Modernist movement is a phase of the scientific struggle for freedom in thought and belief.

2. Modernists are Christians who accept the results of scientific research as data with which to think religiously.

3. Modernists are Christians who adopt the method of historical and literary science in the study of the Bible and religion.

4. The Modernist Christian believes the Christian religion will help men meet social as well as individual needs.

5. The Modernist is a Christian who believes that the spiritual and moral needs of the world can be met because they are intellectually convinced that Christian attitudes and faiths are consistent with other realities.

6. Modernists as a class are evangelical Christians. That is, they accept Jesus Christ as the revelation of a Savior God.

In brief, then, *the use of scientific, historical, social method in understanding and applying evangelical Christianity to the needs of living persons, is Modernism.* Its interests are not those of theological controversy or appeal to authority. They do not involve the rejection of the supernatural when rightly defined. Modernists believe that they can discover the ideals and directions needed for Christian living by the application of critical and historical methods to the study of the Bible; that they can discover by similar methods the permanent attitudes and convictions of Christians constituting a continuous and developing group; and that these permanent elements will help and inspire the intelligent and sympathetic organization of life under modern conditions. Modernists are thus evangelical Christians who use modern methods to meet modern needs. Confessionalism is the evangelicalism of the dogmatic mind. Modernism is the evangelicalism of the scientific mind.

Robinson Jeffers
(1887–1962)

Robinson Jeffers was born in Pittsburgh, the son of a theological seminary profes-

sor, and educated in Europe, but before he was out of his teens the family moved to California and he eventually settled in Carmel where the neighboring Big Sur country was to provide the setting for much of his poetry. A major portion of his later artistic effort went into the attempt, in the words of the mad preacher in *The Women at Point Sur* (1927), "to uncenter the mind from itself" and redirect human attention to the stark natural world outside consciousness. In a later book *The Double Axe* (1948), Jeffers described his philosophical position as a form of "inhumanism, a shifting of emphasis and significance from man to not-man." "Shine, Perishing Republic" was originally published in *Tamar and Other Poems* (1924). It presents in microcosm Jeffers's uncompromising vision of religious naturalism.

"Shine, Perishing Republic"
(1924)

While this America settles in the
  mould of its vulgarity, heavily
  thickening to empire,
And protest, only a bubble in the
  molten mass, pops and sighs out,
  and the mass hardens,

I sadly smiling remember that the
  flower fades to make fruit, the
  fruit rots to make earth.
Out of the mother; and through the
  spring exultances, ripeness and
  decadence; and home to the
  mother.

You making haste haste on decay: not
　　blameworthy; life is good, be it
　　stubbornly long or suddenly
A mortal splendor: meteors are not
　　needed less than mountains:
　　shine, perishing republic.

But for my children, I would have
　　them keep their distance from the
　　thickening center; corruption
Never has been compulsory, when the
　　cities lie at the monster's feet there
　　are left the mountains.

And boys, be in nothing so moderate
　　as in love of man, a clever servant,
　　insufferable master.
There is the trap that catches noblest
　　spirits, that caught—they say—
　　God, when he walked on earth.

~~~~~~~~~~~~~~~~~~~~~~~~~~~~~~~~

William Carlos Williams (1883–1963)

Writer and poet William Carlos Williams derived greatest strength from his
grasp of the particularity and un-
adorned concreteness—the sheer *this-
ness*—of things. Many of his most
celebrated poems focus on discrete details of perceived reality; a red wheel-
barrow glistening after a rain, the taste
of chilled plums late at night. Yet of all
American poets, none has been more
fascinated by, or even obsessed with,
"the life within the life," as Nathaniel
Hawthorne described it—that nameless

something existing under or shining
through all our misappellations.

　　The following prose selection is from
In the American Grain (1925), a book in
which Williams responds almost directly
to Whitman's challenge, by defining a
metaphysics of the New World experience. In "The Discovery of Kentucky,"
Williams envisions "the life within the
life" as that desire which, for Daniel
Boone as Williams conceives him, found
its appropriate object and complete fulfillment in the spirit of the American
wilderness.

From *In the American Grain* (1925)

The Discovery of Kentucky

There was, thank God, a great voluptu-
ary born to the American settlements
against the niggardliness of the dam-
ming puritanical tradition; one who by
the single logic of his passion, which he
rested on the savage life about him,
destroyed at its spring that spiritually
withering plague. For this he has remained since buried in a miscolored
legend and left for rotten. Far from
dead, however, but full of a rich regenerative violence he remains, when his
history will be carefully reported, for us
who have come after to call upon him.

　　Kentucky, the great wilderness beyond the western edge of the world,
"the dark and bloody ground" of coming years, seemed to the colonists along
the eastern North-American seaboard

as far away, nearly, and as difficult of approach as had the problematical world itself beyond the western ocean to the times prior to Columbus. "A country there was, of this none could doubt who thought at all; but whether land or water, mountain or plain, fertility or barrenness, preponderated; whether it was inhabited by men or beasts, or both or neither, they knew not." But if inhabited by men then it was the savage with whom the settlers had had long since experienced sufficient to make them loth to pry further, for the moment, beyond the securing mountain barrier.

Clinging narrowly to their new foothold, dependent still on sailing vessels for a contact none too swift or certain with "home," the colonists looked with fear to the west. They worked hard and for the most part throve, suffering the material lacks of their exposed condition with intention. But they suffered also privations not even to be estimated, cramping and demeaning for a people used to a world less primitively rigorous. A spirit of insecurity calling upon thrift and self-denial remained their basic mood. Opposed to this lay the forbidden wealth of the Unknown.

Into such an atmosphere, more or less varied, more or less changed for better or worse in minds of different understanding, was born Daniel Boone, the foremost pioneer and frontiersman of his day. A man like none other about him Boone had for the life of his fellow settlers, high or low, no sympathy whatever. Was it his ancestry, full of a rural quietness from placid Dorset or the sober Quaker training of his early asso-ciations that bred the instinct in him, made him ready to take desperate chances with his mind for pleasure? Certainly he was not, as commonly believed, of that riff-raff of hunters and Indian killers among which destiny had thrown him—the man of border foray—a link between the savage and the settler.

His character was not this. Mild and simple hearted, steady, not impulsive in courage—bold and determined, but always rather inclined to defend than attack—he stood immensely above that wretched class of men who are so often the preliminaries of civilization. Boone deliberately chose the peace of solitude, rather than to mingle in the wild wranglings and disputings of the society around him—from whom it was ever his first thought to be escaping—or he would never have penetrated to those secret places where later his name became a talisman.

Three years the junior of George Washington, Boone was taken while still a child from his birthplace on the upper waters of the Schuylkill River near Philadelphia to the then comparatively wild country of western Pennsylvania. Here he grew up. Soon a hunter, even as a boy men stepped back to contemplate with more than ordinary wonder the fearlessness with which he faced the fiercer wild beasts that prowled around. It was the early evidence of his genius. At eighteen, with his love of the woods marked for good, and his disposition for solitude, taciturnity and a hunter's life determined, the family moved again this time from the rapidly settling country of Pennsylvania to the wild Yadkin, a river that takes its rise among the mountains that form the western boundary of North Carolina.

With his arrival on the Yadkin, Daniel Boone married a neighbor's daughter, Rebecca Bryan, and together the young couple left the world behind them. Boone at once traversed the Yadkin Valley at a point still more remote from the seaboard and nearer the mountain; here he placed his cabin. It was a true home to him. Its firelight shone in welcome to the rare stranger who found that riverside. But he was not to remain thus solitary! The lands along the Yadkin attracted the notice of other settlers, and Boone, at thirty, found the smoke of his cabin no longer the only one that floated in that air. These accessions of companionship, however, congenial to the greatest part of mankind, did not suit Boone. He soon became conscious that his time on the Yadkin was limited.

The fields for adventure lay within his reach. The mountains were to be crossed and a new and unexplored country, invested with every beauty, every danger, every incident that could amuse the imagination or quicken action, lay before him, the indefinite world of the future. Along the Clinch River and the Holston River hunting parties pursued their way. As they went, the mysteries of forest life grew more familiar. Boone learned even better than before that neither roof, nor house, nor bed was necessary to existence. There were, of course, many things to urge him on in his natural choice. It was the time just preceding the Revolution. The colonial system of taxation was iniquitous to the last de-gree; this the pioneer could not fathom and would not endure. Such things Boone solved most according to his nature by leaving them behind.

At this point Boone's life may be said really to begin. Facing his first great adventure Boone was now in his best years. His age was thirty-six. He is described by various writers as being five feet ten inches high, robust, clean limbed and athletic, fitted by his habit and temperament, and by his physique, for endurance—a bright eye, and a calm determination in his manner. In 1769, John Finley returned from a hunting trip beyond the mountain. He talked loud and long of the beauty and fertility of the country and Daniel Boone was soon eagerly a listener. It touched the great keynote of his character, and the hour and the man had come.

"It was on the first of May, in the year 1769, that I resigned my domestic happiness for a time and left my family and peaceful habitation on the Yadkin River in North Carolina, to wander through the wilderness of America, in quest of the country of Kentucky, in company with John Finley, John Stewart, Joseph Holden, James Monay, and William Cool. We proceeded successfully and after a long and fatiguing journey through a mountain wilderness, in a westward direction on the seventh day of June following, we found ourselves on Red River, where John Finley had formerly been trading with the Indians, and from the top of an eminence, saw with pleasure the beautiful level of Kentucky."

Thus opens the so-called autobiography, said to have been written down from Boone's dictation, late in his life by one John Filson. But the silly phrases and total disregard for what must have been the rude words of the old hunter serve only, for the most part, to make it a keen disappointment to the interested reader. But now, from everything that is said, all that Boone is known to have put through and willingly suffered during the next two years, there ensued a time of the most enchanting adventure for the still young explorer. For a time the party hunted and enjoyed the country, seeing buffalo "more frequent than I have seen cattle in the settlements, browsing on the leaves of the cane, or cropping the grass on those extensive prairies, . . . abundance of wild beasts of all sorts through this vast forest; and the numbers about the salt springs were amazing." Here the party practised hunting till the twenty-second day of December following.

"On this day John Steward and I had a pleasant ramble; but fortune changed the scene in the close of it. We had passed through a great forest, Nature was here a series of wonders and a fund of delight, and we were diverted with innumerable animals presenting themselves prepetually to our view. In the decline of the day, near the Kentucky River, as we ascended the brow of a small hill, a number of Indians rushed out of a thick cane brake upon us and made us prisoners." Escaping later the two returned to their camp to find it plundered and the others of their party gone.

But now, by one of those determining chances which occur in all great careers Squire Boone, Daniel's brother, who

with another adventurer had set out to get news of the original party if possible, came accidentally upon his brother's camp in the forest. It was a meeting of greatest importance and unbounded joy to Daniel Boone. For a short time there were now four together, but within a month, the man Stewart was killed by Indians while Squire Boone's companion, who had accompanied him upon his quest, either wandered off and was lost or returned by himself to the Colonies. Daniel and Squire were left alone.

"We were then in a dangerous and helpless situation, exposed daily to perils and death amongst the savages and wild beasts—not a white man in the country but ourselves. Thus situated many hundred miles from our families, in the howling wilderness, I believe few would have equally enjoyed the happiness we experienced. We continued not in a state of indolence but hunted every day, and prepared to defend ourselves against the winter's storms. We remained there undisturbed during the winter. . . . On the first day of May, following, my brother returned home to the settlement by himself, for a new recruit of horses and ammunition, leaving me by myself, without bread, salt or sugar, without company of my fellow creatures, or even a horse or a dog.

"I confess I never was under greater necessity of exercising philosophy and fortitude. A few days I passed uncomfortably; The idea of a beloved wife and family, and their anxiety upon the account of my absence, and exposed situation, made sensible impressions on my heart. A thousand dreadful apprehensions presented themselves to my view and had undoubtedly disposed me to melancholy if indulged. One day I undertook a tour through the country, and the diversity and beauty of nature I met with in this charming season expelled every gloom and vexatious thought. Not a breeze shook the most tremulous leaf. I had gained the summit of a commanding ridge, and looking around with astonishing delight, beheld the ample plain, the beauteous tracts below. All things were still; I kindled a fire near a fountain of sweet water and feasted on a loin of a buck which a few hours before I had killed. Night came and the earth seemed to gasp after the hovering moisture——" But only impatience is kindled by the silly language of the asinine chronicler.

But when Filson goes on to declare Boone's loneliness "an uninterrupted scene of sylvan pleasures" it is a little too much to bear. Constant exposure to danger and death, a habitation which he states had been discovered by the savages, the necessity of such stratagems as the resort to the canebrake rather than to take the risk of being found in his cabin, have nothing of sylvan pleasures in them. Boone had too much strong sense to feel anything but patience amidst the scenes of his solitude. And yet, having sounded the depth of forest life, and having considered and weighed all it had to offer, he felt secure enough to brave the perils of an exploring tour. He saw the Ohio, and unquestionably, from the results of this excursion, strengthened his determination to establish himself in such a land of delight.

For three months he was alone. It was an ordeal through which few men could have passed. Certain it is that nothing but a passionate attachment of the most extraordinary intensity could have induced even him to undergo it. If there were perils there was a pleasure keener, which bade him stay on, even in solitude, while his day was lasting. Surely he must have known that it was the great ecstatic moment of his life's affirmation.

By instinct and from the first Boone had run past the difficulties encountered by his fellows in making the New World their own. As ecstasy cannot live without devotion and he who is not given to some earth of basic logic cannot enjoy, so Boone lived to enjoy ecstasy through his single devotion to the wilderness with which he was surrounded. The beauty of a lavish, primitive embrace in savage, wild beast and forest rising above the cramped life about him possessed him wholly. Passionate and thoroughly given he avoided the half logic of stealing from the immense profusion.

Some one must have taken the step. He took it. Not that he settled Kentucky or made a path to the west, not that he defended, suffered, hated and fled, but because of a descent to the ground of his desire was Boone's life important and does it remain still loaded with power,–power to strengthen every form of energy that would be voluptuous, passionate, possessive in that place which he opened. For the problem of the New World was, as every new comer soon found out, an awkward one, on all sides the same: how to replace from the wild land that which, at home, they had scarcely known the Old World meant to them; through difficulty and even brutal hardship to find a ground to take the place of England. They could not do it. They clung, one way or another, to the old, striving the while to pull off pieces to themselves from the fat of the new bounty.

Boone's genius was to recognize the difficulty as neither material nor political but one purely moral and aesthetic. Filled with the wild beauty of the New World to overbrimming so long as he had what he desired, to bathe in, to explore always more deeply, to see, to feel, to touch—his instincts were contented. Sensing a limitless fortune which daring could make his own, he sought only with primal lust to grow close to it, to understand it and to be part of its mysterious movements—like an Indian. And among all the colonists, like an Indian, the ecstasy of complete possession of the new country was his alone. In Kentucky he would stand, a lineal descendant of Columbus on the beach at Santo Domingo, walking up and down with eager eyes while his men were gathering water.

With the sense of an Indian, Boone felt the wild beasts about him as a natural offering. Like a savage he knew that for such as he their destined lives were intended. As an Indian to the wild, without stint or tremor, he offered himself to his world, hunting, killing with a great appetite, taking the lives of the beasts into his quiet, murderous hands as they or their masters, the savages, might take his own, if they were able, without kindling his resentment; as naturally as his own gentle son, his beloved brother, his nearest companions were taken— without his rancor being lifted. Possess-

ing a body at once powerful, compact and capable of tremendous activity and resistance when roused, a clear eye and a deadly aim, taciturn in his demeanor, symmetrical and instinctive in understanding, Boone stood for his race, the affirmation of that wild logic, which in times past had mastered another wilderness and now, renascent, would master this, to prove it potent.

There must be a new wedding. But he saw and only he saw the prototype of it all, the native savage. To Boone the Indian was his greatest master. Not for himself surely to be an Indian, though they eagerly sought to adopt him into their tribes, but the reverse: to be *himself* in a new world, Indianlike. If the land were to be possessed it must be as the Indian possessed it. Boone saw the truth of the Red Man, not an aberrant type, treacherous and anti-white to be feared and exterminated, but as a natural expression of the place, the Indian himself as "right," the flower of his world.

Keen then was the defeat he tasted when, having returned safe to the Colonies after his first ecstatic sojourn, and when after long delay having undertaken to lead a party of forty settlers to the new country, his eldest son, among five others of his own age, was brutally murdered by the savages at the very outset. It was a crushing blow. Although Boone and others argued against it, the expedition turned back and with his sorrowing wife Boone once more took up his homestead on the Yadkin. And this is the mark of his personality, that even for this cruel stroke he held no illwill against the Red Men.

Disappointed in his early hopes and

when through subsequent years of battle against the wild tribes, when through losses and trials of the severest order, he led at last in the establishment of the settlers about the fort and center of Boonesborough, he never wavered for a moment in his clear conception of the Indian as a natural part of a beloved condition, the New World, in which all lived together. Captured or escaping, outwitted by or outwitting the savages, he admired and defended them always, as, implacable and remorseless enemy to the Red Man that he proved, they admired and respected him to the end of his days.

You have bought the land, said an old Indian who acted for his tribe in the transaction which now made Kentucky over to the white man, but you will have trouble to settle it. It proved true. An old lady who had been in the forts was describing the scenes she had witnessed in those times of peril and adventure, and, among other things, remarked that during the first two years of her residence in Kentucky, the most comely sight she beheld, was seeing a young man die in his bed a natural death. She had been familiar with blood, and carnage, and death, but in all those cases the sufferers were the victims of the Indian tomahawk and scalping knife; and that on an occasion when a young man was taken sick and died, after the usual manner of nature, she and the rest of the women sat up all night, gazing upon him as an object of beauty.

It was against his own kind that Boone's lasting resentment was fixed, "those damned Yankees," who took from him, by the chicanery of the law and in his old age, every last acre of the then prosperous homestead he had at last won for himself after years of battle in the new country.

Confirmed in his distrust for his "own kind," in old age homeless and quite ruined, he must turn once more to his early loves, the savage and the wild. Once more a wanderer he struck out through Tennessee for "more elbow-room," determined to leave the young nation which he had helped to establish, definitely behind him. He headed for Spanish territory beyond the Mississippi where the Provincial Governor, having gotten wind of the old hunter's state of mind, was glad to offer him a large tract of land on which to settle. There he lived and died, past ninety, serving his traps as usual.

In the woods he would have an Indian for companion even out of preference to his own sons, and from these men, the Indians, he had the greatest reverence, enjoying always when afield with them the signal honor of disposing them in the order of the hunt.

Too late the American Congress did follow him with some slight recognition. But that was by then to him really a small matter. He had already that which he wanted: the woods and native companions whom, in a written statement of great interest, he defends against all detractors and in that defense establishes himself in clear words: the antagonist of those of his own blood whose alien strength he felt and detested, while his whole soul, with greatest devotion, was given to the New World which he adored and found, in its every expression, the land of heart's desire.

Joseph Wood Krutch (1893–1970)

Joseph Wood Krutch, literary critic and naturalist, served on the editorial staff of *The Nation* and taught literature at Columbia University. In 1929 he published *The Modern Temper,* a probing and influential analysis of the postwar period. In this essay, Krutch asserted that the modern period was witnessing not only the disappearance of God but the death of Man. The death at least of our civilization's faith in Man was being brought about by the new sciences created to study him. The present selection is drawn from the conclusion to *The Modern Temper,* where Krutch describes what he sees as the only antidote to this erosion of belief.

From *The Modern Temper* (1929)

It is not by thought that men live. Life begins in organisms so simple that one may reasonably doubt even their ability to feel, much less think, and animals cling to or fight for it with a determination which we might be inclined to call superhuman if we did not know that a will to live so thoughtless and so unconditional is the attribute of beings rather below than above the human level. All efforts to find a rational justification of life, to declare it worth the living for this reason or that, are, in themselves, a confession of weakness, since life at its strongest never feels the need of any such justification and since the most optimistic philosopher is less optimistic than that man or animal who, his belief that life is good being too immediate to require the interposition of thought, is no philosopher at all.

In view of this fact it is not surprising that the subtlest intellectual contortions of modern metaphysics should fail to establish the existence of satisfactory aims for life when, as a matter of fact, any effort to do so fails as soon as it begins and can only arise as the result of a weakening of that self-justifying vitality which is the source of all life and of all optimism. As soon as thought begins to seek the "ends" or "aims" to which life is subservient it has already confessed its inability to achieve that animal acceptance of life for life's sake which is responsible for the most determined efforts to live and, in one sense, we may say that even the firmest medieval belief in a perfectly concrete salvation after death marks already the beginning of the completest despair, since that belief could not arise before thought had rendered primitive vitality no longer all-sufficient.

The decadent civilizations of the past were not saved by their philosophers but by the influx of simpler peoples who had centuries yet to live before their minds should be ripe for despair. Neither Socrates nor Plato could teach his compatriots any wisdom from which they could draw the strength to compete with the crude energy of their Roman neighbors, and even their thought inevitably declined soon after it has exhausted their vital energy. Nor could these Romans, who flourished longer for the very reason, perhaps, that they had slower and less subtle intellects, live forever; they too were compelled to give way in their time to barbarians innocent alike both of philosophy and of any possible need to call upon it.

The subhuman will to live which is all-sufficient for the animal may be replaced by faith, faith may be replaced by philosophy, and philosophy may attenuate itself until it becomes, like modern metaphysics, a mere game; but each of these developments marks a stage in a progressive enfeeblement of that will to live for the gradual weakening of which it is the function of each to compensate. Vitality calls upon faith for aid, faith turns gradually to philosophy for support, and then philosophy, losing all confidence in its own conclusions, begins to babble of "beneficent fictions" instead of talking about Truth; but each is less confident than what went before and each is, by consequence, less easy to live by. Taken together, they represent the successive and increasingly desperate expedients by means of which man, the ambitious animal, endeavors to postpone the inevitable realization that living is merely a physiological process with only a physiological meaning and that it is most satisfactorily conducted by creatures who never feel the need to attempt to give it any other. But they are at best no more than expedients, and when the last has been exhausted there remains nothing except the possibility that the human species will be revitalized by some race or some class which is capable of beginning all over again.

If modern civilization is decadent then perhaps it will be rejuvenated, but not by the philosophers whose subtlest thoughts are only symptoms of the disease which they are endeavoring to combat. If the future belongs to anybody it belongs to those to whom it has always belonged, to those, that is to say, too absorbed in living to feel the need for thought, and they will come, as the barbarians have always come, absorbed in the processes of life for their own sake, eating without asking if it is worth while to eat, begetting children without asking why they should beget them, and conquering without asking for what purpose they conquer.

Hart Crane
(1899–1933)

Although Hart Crane completed only two books of poetry before his death, he is now regarded as one of the major modern American poets. An enormously talented writer who lacked much formal education, Crane went to school in the turbulent twenties and emerged from that period as perhaps its most authentic visionary.

Crane took upon himself Walt Whitman's heroic attempt to embrace the multitudinousness of America, its terrible oppositions and its appalling beauty. His poetry is a fierce and desperate celebration that steadfastly refuses to concede, as F. Scott Fitzgerald might have put it, that the party's over. Crane's poetry works through daring and often forced conjunctions of images whose relationship is usually more felt than fully understood. The power of this poetry, which Crane held was written according to the logic of metaphor rather than the logic of thought, is almost kinesthetic.

"Proem: To Brooklyn Bridge" is the introduction to Crane's most ambitious work, *The Bridge* (1930). In this epic poem, Crane intended to create what he variously described as "an epic of the modern consciousness" and "a mystical synthesis of 'America.'" Out of images generated by his mediation on figures such as Columbus, Rip Van Winkle, Pocahontas, Edgar Allan Poe, and Walt Whitman, Crane sought to forge his climactic symbol of the bridge spanning past and future, man and nature, death and rebirth, the mundane and the transfigured.

"Proem: To Brooklyn Bridge" (1930)

How many dawns, chill from his
    rippling rest
The seagull's wings shall dip and pivot
    him,
Shedding white rings of tumult,
    building high
Over the chained bay waters Liberty—

Then, with inviolate curve, forsake our
    eyes
As apparitional as sails that cross
Some page of figures to be filed away;
—Till elevators drop us from our
    day . . .

I think of cinemas, panoramic sleights
With multitudes bent toward some
    flashing scene
Never disclosed, but hastened to again,
Foretold to other eyes on the same
    screen;

And Thee, across the harbor,
    silver-paced
As though the sun took step of thee,
    yet left
Some motion ever unspent in thy
    stride,—
Implicitly thy freedom staying thee!
Out of some subway scuttle, cell or loft
A bedlamite speeds to thy parapets,
Tilting there momently, shrill shirt
    ballooning,
A jest falls from the speechless
    caravan.

Down Wall, from girder into street
    noon leaks,
A rip-tooth of the sky's acetylene;
All afternoon the cloud-flown derricks
    turn . . .
Thy cables breathe the North Atlantic
    still.

And obscure as that heaven of the
    Jews,
Thy guerdon . . . Accolade thou dost
    bestow
Of anonymity time cannot raise:
Vibrant reprieve and pardon thou dost
    show.

O harp and altar, of the fury fused,
(How could mere toil align thy
 choiring strings!)
Terrific threshold of the prophet's
 pledge,
Prayer of pariah, and the lover's cry,—

Again the traffic lights that skim thy
 swift
Unfractioned idiom, immaculate sigh
 of stars,
Beading thy path—condense eternity:
And we have seen night lifted in thine
 arms.
Under thy shadow by the piers I
 waited;
Only in darkness is thy shadow clear.
The City's fiery parcels all undone,
Already snow submerges an iron
 year . . .

O Sleepless as the river under thee,
Vaulting the sea, the prairies'
 dreaming sod,
Unto us lowliest sometime sweep,
 descend
And of the curveship lend a myth to
 God.

by the extraordinary use to which they
put traditional religious symbols. He
almost always went behind their contemporary meanings and evoked a
sense of what they originally signified
in experience before their more disturbing connotations were pacified
through incorporation in an inherited
mythological framework.

"Marina" is one of four poems Eliot
originally composed as Christmas greetings (the other poems are "Journey of
the Magi," "A Song for Simeon," and
"Animula"). The title of the poem suggests the moment of joyous reunion
between Shakespeare's Pericles and his
daughter Marina. The moment is
rendered uncertain, however, by the
associations of the Latin epigraph, taken
from Seneca's *Hercules Furens*. In the
incident to which it alludes Hercules,
awakened from a fit of madness, begins
to realize that in his fury he has unwit-
tingly slain all his children. He cries,
"What place is this, what land, what
quarter of the globe?"

<hr>

T. S. Eliot
(1888–1965)

T. S. (Thomas Stearns) Eliot possessed
a rare ability to convey the truth of
spiritual loss as well as recovery, of
religious doubt as well as belief. His
poems in both modes are distinguished

"Marina" (1930)

Quis hic locus, quae
regio, quae mundi plaga?

What seas what shores what grey rocks
 and what islands
What water lapping the bow
And scent of pine and the woodthrush
 singing through the fog
What images return
O my daughter.

Those who sharpen the tooth of the
  dog, meaning
Death
Those who glitter with the glory of the
  hummingbird, meaning
Death
Those who sit in the sty of
  contentment, meaning
Death
Those who suffer the ecstasy of the
  animals, meaning
Death

  Are become unsubstantial, reduced
    by a wind,
A breath of pine, and the woodsong
  fog
By this grace dissolved in place

  What is this face, less clear and
    clearer
The pulse in the arm, less strong and
  stronger—
Given or lent? more distant than stars
  and nearer than the eye

Whispers and small laughter between
  leaves and hurrying feet
Under sleep, where all the waters
  meet.
Bowsprit cracked with ice and paint
  cracked with heat.
I made this, I have forgotten
And remember.
The rigging weak and the canvas
  rotten
Between one June and another
  September.
Made this unknowing, half conscious,
  unknown, my own
The garboard strake leaks, the seams
  need caulking.
This form, this face, this life

Living to live in a world of time
  beyond me; let me
Resign my life for this life, my speech
  for that unspoken,
The awakened, lips parted, the hope,
  the new ships.

  What seas what shores what granite
    islands towards my timbers
And woodthrush calling through the
  fog
My daughter.

Ernest Hemingway (1899–1961)

When "A Clean, Well-Lighted Place" was published in 1933, Ernest Hemingway had long been the spokesman for a disillusioned generation of Americans whose moral and spiritual values had been badly shaken by the experience of the Great War. Frederic Henry, the protagonist of Hemingway's *A Farewell to Arms* (1929), says, "I was always embarrassed by the words sacred, glorious, and sacrifice . . . [and] now for a long time, . . . I had seen nothing sacred, and the things that were glorious had no glory and the sacrifices were like the stockyards at Chicago if nothing was done to the meat except to bury it."

The central figure in "A Clean, Well-Lighted Place" is the old man who is said to have attempted suicide the week before. The drama of the story lies in the different ways in which the two waiters respond to the old man's despair. Their opposite reactions form a kind of moral counterpoint to the theme of hopelessness and its metaphysical dimensions.

"A Clean, Well-Lighted Place" (1933)

It was late and every one had left the café except an old man who sat in the shadow the leaves of the tree made against the electric light. In the day time the street was dusty, but at night the dew settled the dust and the old man liked to sit late because he was deaf and now at night it was quiet and he felt the difference. The two waiters inside the café knew that the old man was a little drunk, and while he was a good client they knew that if he became too drunk he would leave without paying, so they kept watch on him.

"Last week he tried to commit suicide," one waiter said.

"Why?"

"He was in despair."

"What about?"

"Nothing."

"How do you know it was nothing?"

"He has plenty of money."

They sat together at a table that was close against the wall near the door of the café and looked at the terrace where the tables were all empty except where the old man sat in the shadow of the leaves of the tree that moved slightly in the wind. A girl and a soldier went by in the street. The street light shone on the brass number on his collar. The girl wore no head covering and hurried beside him.

"The guard will pick him up," one waiter said.

"What does it matter if he gets what he's after?"

"He had better get off the street now. The guard will get him. They went by five minutes ago."

The old man sitting in the shadow rapped on his saucer with his glass. The younger waiter went over to him.

"What do you want?"

The old man looked at him. "Another brandy," he said.

"You'll be drunk," the waiter said. The old man looked at him. The waiter went away.

"He'll stay all night," he said to his colleague. "I'm sleepy now. I never get into bed before three o'clock. He should have killed himself last week."

The waiter took the brandy bottle and another saucer from the counter inside the café and marched out to the old man's table. He put down the saucer and poured the glass full of brandy.

"You should have killed yourself last week," he said to the deaf man. The old man motioned with his finger. "A little more." he said. The waiter poured on into the glass so that the brandy slopped over and ran down the stem into the top saucer of the pile. "Thank you," the old man said. The waiter took the bottle back inside the café. He sat down at the table with his colleague again.

"He's drunk now," he said.

"He's drunk every night."

"What did he want to kill himself for?"

"How should I know."

"How did he do it?"

"He hung himself with a rope."

"Who cut him down?"

"His niece."

"Why did they do it?"

"Fear for his soul."

"How much money has he got?"

"He's got plenty."

"He must be eighty years old."

"Anyway I should say he was eighty."

"I wish he would go home. I never get to bed before three o'clock. What kind of hour is that to go to bed?"

"He stays up because he likes it."

"He's lonely. I'm not lonely. I have a wife waiting in bed for me."

"He had a wife once too."

"A wife would be no good to him now."

"You can't tell. He might be better with a wife."

"His niece looks after him."

"I know. You said she cut him down."

"I wouldn't want to be that old. An old man is a nasty thing."

"Not always. This old man is clean. He drinks without spilling. Even now, drunk. Look at him."

"I don't want to look at him. I wish he would go home. He has no regard for those who must work."

The old man looked from his glass across the square, then over at the waiters.

"Another brandy," he said, pointing to his glass. The waiter who was in hurry came over.

"Finished," he said, speaking with that omission of syntax stupid people employ when talking to drunken people or foreigners. "No more tonight. Close now."

"Another," said the old man.

"No. Finished." The waiter wiped the edge of the table with a towel and shook his head.

The old man stood up, slowly counted the saucers, took a leather coin purse from his pocket and paid for the drinks, leaving half a peseta tip.

The waiter watched him go down the street, a very old man walking unsteadily but with dignity.

"Why didn't you let him stay and drink?" the unhurried waiter asked. They were putting up the shutters. "It is not half-past two."

"I want to go home to bed."

"What is an hour?"

"More to me than to him."

"An hour is the same."

"You talk like an old man yourself. He can buy a bottle and drink at home."

"It's not the same."

"No, it is not," agreed the waiter with a wife. He did not wish to be unjust. He was only in a hurry.

"And you? You have no fear of going home before your usual hour?"

"Are you trying to insult me?"

"No, hombre, only to make a joke."

"No," the waiter who was in a hurry said, rising from pulling down the metal shutters. "I have confidence. I am all confidence."

"You have youth, confidence, and a job," the older waiter said. "You have everything."

"And what do you lack?"

"Everything but work."

"You have everything I have."

"No. I have never had confidence and I am not young."

"Come on. Stop talking nonsense and lock up."

"I am of those who like to stay late at the café," the older waiter said. "With all those who do not want to go to bed. With all those who need a light for the night."

"I want to go home and into bed."

"We are of two different kinds," the older waiter said. He was now dressed to go home. "It is not only a question of youth and confidence although those things are very beautiful. Each night I am reluctant to close up because there may be some one who needs the café."

"Hombre, there are bodegas open all night long."

"You do not understand. This is a clean and pleasant café. It is well lighted. The light is very good and also, now, there are shadows of the leaves."

"Good night," said the younger waiter.

"Good night," the other said. Turning off the electric light he continued the conversation with himself. It is the light of course but it is necessary that the place be clean and pleasant. You do not want music. Certainly you do not want music. Nor can you stand before a bar with dignity although that is all that is provided for these hours. What did he fear? It was not fear or dread. It was a nothing that he knew too well. It was all a nothing and a man was nothing too. It was only that and light was all it needed and a certain cleanness and order. Some lived in it and never felt it but he knew it all was nada y pues nada y nada y pues nada. Our nada who are in nada, nada be thy name thy kingdom nada thy will be nada in nada as it is in nada. Give us this nada our daily nada and nada us our nada as we nada our nada and nada us not into nada but deliver us from nada; pues nada. Hail nothing full of nothing, nothing is with thee. He smiled and stood before a bar with a shining steam pressure coffee machine.

"What's yours?" asked the barman.

"Nada."

"Otro loco mas," said the barman and turned away.

"A little cup," said the waiter.

The barman poured it for him.

"The light is very bright and pleasant but the bar is unpolished," the waiter said.

The barman looked at him but did not answer. It was too late at night for conversation.

"You want another copita?" the barman asked.

"No, thank you," said the waiter and went out. He disliked bars and bodegas. A clean, well-lighted café was a very different thing. Now, without thinking further, he would go home to his room. He would lie in the bed and finally, with daylight, he would go to sleep. After all, he said to himself, it is probably only insomnia. Many must have it.

John Dewey
(1859–1952)

The American philosopher John Dewey is well known for his contributions to the theory of education and to the application of scientific method to social and political problems. His importance as a religious thinker, however, has been generally overlooked. In "The Construction of the Good," from *The Quest for Certainty* (1929), Dewey describes the modern religious problem as "restoring integration and cooperation between man's beliefs about the world in which he lives and his beliefs about the values and purposes that should direct his conduct." Elsewhere Dewey indicated the source from which the solution to this problem must come:

> Within the flickering inconsequential acts of separate selves dwells a sense of the whole which claims and dignifies them. In its presence we put off mortality and live in the universal. The life of the community in which we live and have our being is the fit symbol of this relationship. The acts in which we express our perception of the ties which bind us to others are its only rites and ceremonies.
>
> *Human Nature and Conduct* (1930)

The following selection is from the one book in which Dewey addressed himself to explicit religious issues, *A Common Faith* (1934).

From *A Common Faith* (1934)

The heart of my point, as far as I shall develop it in this first section, is that there is a difference between religion, *a* religion, and the religious; between anything that may be denoted by a noun substantive and the quality of experience that is designated by an adjective. It is not easy to find a definition of religion in the substantive sense that wins general acceptance. However, in the *Oxford Dictionary* I find the following: "Recognition on the part of man of some unseen higher power as having control of his destiny and as being entitled to obedience, reverence and worship."

This particular definition is less explicit in assertion of the supernatural character of the higher unseen power than are others that might be cited. It is, however, surcharged with implications having their source in ideas connected with the belief in the supernatural, characteristic of historic religions. Let us suppose that one familiar with the history of religions, including those called primitive, compares the definition with the variety of known facts and by means of the comparison sets out to determine just what the definition means. I think he will be struck by three facts that reduce the terms of the definition to such a low common denominator that little meaning is left.

He will note the "unseen powers" referred to have been conceived in a multitude of incompatible ways. Eliminating the differences, nothing is left beyond the bare reference to something unseen and powerful. This has been conceived as the vague and undefined Mana of the Melanesians; the Kami of primitive Shintoism; the fetish of the Africans; spirits, having some human properties, that pervade natural places and animate natural forces; the ultimate and impersonal principle of Buddhism; the unmoved mover of Greek thought; the gods and semi-divine heroes of the Greek and Roman Pantheons; the personal and loving Providence of Christianity, omnipotent, and limited by a corresponding evil power; the arbitrary Will of Moslemism; the supreme legislator and judge of deism. And these are but a few of the outstanding varieties of ways in which the invisible power has been conceived.

There is no greater similarity in the ways in which obedience and reverence have been expressed. There has been worship of animals, of ghosts, of ancestors, phallic worship, as well as of a Being of dread power and of love and wisdom. Reverence has been expressed in the human sacrifices of the Peruvians and Aztecs; the sexual orgies of some Oriental religions; exorcisms and ablutions; the offering of the humble and contrite mind of the Hebrew prophet, the elaborate rituals of the Greek and Roman Churches. Not even sacrifice has been uniform; it is highly sublimated in Protestant denominations and in Moslemism. Where it has existed it has taken all kinds of forms and been directed to a great variety of powers and spirits. It has been used for expiation, for propitiation and for buying special favors. There is no conceivable purpose for which rites have not been employed.

Finally, there is no discernible unity in the moral motivations appealed to and utilized. They have been as far apart as fear of lasting torture, hope of enduring bliss in which sexual enjoyment has sometimes been a conspicuous element; mortification of the flesh and extreme asceticism; prostitution and chastity; wars to extirpate the unbeliever; persecution to convert or punish the unbeliever, and philanthropic zeal; servile acceptance of imposed dogma, along with brotherly love and aspiration for a reign of justice among men.

I have, of course, mentioned only a sparse number of facts which fill volumes in any well-stocked library. It may be asked by those who do not like to look upon the darker side of the history of religions why the darker facts should be brought up. We all know that civilized man has a background of bestiality and superstition and that these elements are still with us. Indeed, have not some religions, including the most influential forms of Christianity, taught that the heart of man is totally corrupt? How could the course of religion in its entire sweep not be marked by practices that are shameful in their cruelty and lustfulness, and by beliefs that are degraded and intellectually incredible? What else than what we find could be expected, in the case of people having little knowledge and no secure method of knowing; with primitive institutions, and with so little control of natural forces that they lived in a constant state of fear?

I gladly admit that historic religions have been relative to the conditions of social culture in which peoples lived. Indeed, what I am concerned with is to press home the logic of this method of disposal of outgrown traits of past religions. Beliefs and practices in a religion that now prevails are by this logic relative to the present state of culture. If so much flexibility has obtained in the past regarding an unseen power, the way it affects human destiny, and the attitudes we are to take toward it, why should it be assumed that change in conception and action has now come to an end? The logic involved in getting rid of inconvenient aspects of past religions compels us to inquire how much in religions now accepted are survivals from outgrown cultures. It compels us to ask what conception of unseen powers and our relations to them would be consonant with the best achievements and aspirations of the present. It demands that in imagination we wipe the slate clean and start afresh by asking what would be the idea of the unseen, of the manner of its control over us and the ways in which reverence and obedience would be manifested, if whatever is basically religious in experience had the opportunity to express itself free from all historic encumbrances.

For we are forced to acknowledge that concretely there is no such thing as religion in the singular. There is only a multitude of religions. "Religion" is a strictly collective term and the collection it stands for is not even of the kind illustrated in textbooks of logic. It has not the unity of a regiment or assembly but that of any miscellaneous aggregate. Attempts to prove the universality prove too much or too little. It is probable that religions have been universal in the sense that all the peoples we know anything about have had *a* religion. But the differences among them are so great and so shocking that any common element that can be extracted is meaningless. The idea that religion is universal proves too little in that the older apologists for Christianity seem to have been better advised than some modern ones in condemning every religion but one as an impostor, as at bottom some kind of demon worship or at any rate a superstitious figment. Choice among religions is imperative, and the necessity for choice leaves nothing of any force in the argument from universality. Moreover, when once we enter upon the road of choice, there is at once presented a possibility not yet generally realized.

For the historic increase of the ethical and ideal content of religions suggests that the process of purification may be carried further. It indicates that further choice is imminent in which certain values and functions in experience may be selected. This possibility is what I had in mind in speaking of the difference between the religious and a religion. I am not proposing a religion, but rather the emancipation of elements and outlooks that may be called religious. For the moment we have a religion, whether that of the Sioux Indian or of Judaism or of Christianity, that moment the ideal factors in experience that may be called religious take on a load that is not inherent in them, a load of current beliefs and of institutional practices that are irrelevant to them.

I can illustrate what I mean by a

common phenomenon in contemporary life. It is widely supposed that a person who does not accept any religion is thereby shown to be a non-religious person. Yet it is conceivable that the present depression in religion is closely connected with the fact that religions now prevent, because of their weight of historic encumbrances, the religious quality of experience from coming to consciousness and finding the expression that is appropriate to present conditions, intellectual and moral. I believe that such is the case. I believe that many persons are so repelled from what exists as a religion by its intellectual and moral implications, that they are not even aware of attitudes in themselves that if they came to fruition would be genuinely religious. I hope that this remark may help make clear what I mean by the distinction between "religion" as a noun substantive and "religious" as adjectival.

To be somewhat more explicit, a religion (and as I have just said there is no such thing as religion in general) always signifies a special body of beliefs and practices having some kind of institutional organization, loose or tight. In contrast, the adjective "religious" denotes nothing in the way of a specifiable entity, either institutional or as a system of beliefs. It does not denote anything to which one can specifically point as one can point to this and that historic religion or existing church. For it does not denote anything that can exist by itself or that can be organized into a particular and distinctive form of existence. It denotes attitudes that may be taken toward every object and every proposed end or ideal.

Before, however, I develop my suggestion that realization of the distinction just made would operate to emancipate the religious quality from encumbrances that now smother or limit it, I must refer to a position that in some respects is similar in words to the position I have taken, but that in fact is a whole world removed from it. I have several times used the phrase "religious elements of experience." Now at present there is much talk, especially in liberal circles, of religious experience as vouching for the authenticity of certain beliefs and the desirability of certain practices, such as particular forms of prayer and worship. It is even asserted that religious experience is the ultimate basis of religion itself. The gulf between this position and that which I have taken is what I am now concerned to point out.

Those who hold to the notion that there is a definite kind of experience which is itself religious, by that very fact make out of it something specific, as a kind of experience that is marked off from experience as æsthetic, scientific, moral, political; from experience as companionship and friendship. But "religious" as a quality of experience signifies something that may belong to all these experiences. It is the polar opposite of some type of experience that can exist by itself. The distinction comes out clearly when it is noted that the concept of this distinct kind of experience is used to validate a belief in some special kind of object and also to justify some special kind of practice.

The discussion may be made more definite by introducing, at this point, a particular illustration of this type of reasoning. A writer says: "I broke down from overwork and soon came to the verge of nervous prostration. One morning after a long and sleepless night ... I resolved to stop drawing upon myself so continuously and begin drawing upon God. I determined to set apart a quiet time every day in which I could relate my life to its ultimate source, regain the consciousness that in God I live, move and have my being. That was thirty years ago. Since then I have had literally not one hour of darkness or despair."

This is an impressive record. I do not doubt its authenticity nor that of the experience related. It illustrates a religious aspect of experience. But it illustrates also the use of that quality to carry a super-imposed load of a particular religion. For having been brought up in the Christian religion, its subject interprets it in the terms of the personal God characteristic of that religion. Taoists, Buddhists, Moslems, persons of no religion including those who reject all supernatural influence and power, have had experiences similar in their effect. . . .

The intent of this discussion is not to deny the genuineness of the result nor its importance in life. It is not, save incidentally, to point out the possibility of a purely naturalistic explanation of the event. My purpose is to indicate what happens when religious experience is already set aside as something *sui generis*. The actual religious quality in the experience described is the *effect*

produced, the better adjustment in life and its conditions, not the manner and cause of its production. The way in which the experience operated, its function, determines its religious value. If the reorientation actually occurs, it, and the sense of security and stability accompanying it, are forces on their own account. It takes place in different persons in a multitude of ways. It is sometimes brought about by a devotion to a cause; sometimes by a passage of poetry that opens a new perspective; sometimes as was the case with Spinoza— deemed an atheist in his day—through philosophical reflection.

~~~

I do not suppose for many minds the dislocation of the religious from a religion is easy to effect. Tradition and custom, especially when emotionally charged, are parts of the habits that have become one with our very being. But the possibility of the transfer is demonstrated by its actuality. Let us then for the moment drop the term "religious," and ask what are the attitudes that lend deep and enduring support to the processes of living. I have, for example, used the words "adjustment" and "orientation." What do they signify?

While the words "accommodation," "adaptation," and "adjustment" are frequently employed as synonyms, attitudes exist that are so different that for the sake of clear thought they should be discriminated. There are conditions we meet that cannot be changed. If they are particular and limited, we modify our own particular attitudes in accordance with them. Thus we accommodate ourselves to changes in weather, to alterations in income when we have no other recourse. When the external conditions are lasting we become inured, habituated, or as the process is now often called, conditioned. The two main traits of this attitude, which I should like to call accommodation, are that it affects *particular* modes of conduct, not the entire self, and that the process is mainly *passive.* It may, however, become general and then it becomes fatalistic resignation or submission. There are other attitudes toward the environment that are also particular but that are more active. We re-act against conditions and endeavor to change them to meet our wants and demands. Plays in a foreign language are "adapted" to meet the needs of an American audience. A house is rebuilt to suit changed conditions of the household; the telephone is invented to serve the demand for speedy communication at a distance; dry soils are irrigated so that they may bear abundant crops. Instead of accommodating ourselves to conditions, we modify conditions so that they will be accommodated to our wants and purposes. This process may be called adaptation.

Now both of these processes are often called by the more general name of adjustment. but there are also changes in ourselves in relation to the world in which we live that are much more inclusive and deep seated. They relate not to this and that want in relation to this and that condition of our surroundings, but pertain to our being in its entirety. Because of their scope, this

modification of ourselves is enduring. It lasts through any amount of vicissitude of circumstances, internal and external. There is a composing and harmonizing of the various elements of our being such that, in spite of changes in the special conditions that surround us, these conditions are also arranged, settled, in relation to use. This attitude includes a note of submission. But it is voluntary, not externally imposed; and as voluntary it is something more than a mere Stoical resolution to endure unperturbed throughout the buffetings of fortune. It is more outgoing, more ready and glad, than the latter attitude, and it is more active than the former. And in calling it voluntary, it is not meant that it depends upon a particular resolve or volition. It is a change *of* will conceived as the organic plenitude of our being, rather than any special change *in* will.

It is the claim of religions that they effect this generic and enduring change in attitude. I should like to turn the statement around and say that whenever this change takes place there is a definitely religious attitude. It is not *a* religion that brings it about, but when it occurs, from whatever cause and by whatever means, there is a religious outlook and function. As I have said before, the doctrinal or intellectual apparatus and the institutional accretions that grow up are, in a strict sense, adventitious to the intrinsic quality of such experiences. For they are affairs of the traditions of the culture with which individuals are inoculated. Mr. Santayana has connected the religious quality of experience with the imaginative, as that is expressed in poetry. "Religion and poetry," he says, "are identical in essence, and differ merely in the way in which they are attached to practical affairs. Poetry is called religion when it intervenes in life, and religion, when it merely supervenes upon life, is seen to be nothing but poetry." The difference between intervening *in* and supervening *upon* is as important as is the identity set forth. Imagination may play upon life or it may enter profoundly into it. As Mr. Santayana puts it, "poetry has a universal and a moral function," for "its highest power lies in its relevance to the ideals and purposes of life." Except as it intervenes, "all observation is observation of brute fact, all discipline is mere repression, until these facts digested and this discipline embodied in humane impulses become the starting point for a creative movement of the imagination, the firm basis for ideal constructions in society, religion, and art."

If I may make a comment upon this penetrating insight of Mr. Santayana, I would say that the difference between imagination that only supervenes and imagination that intervenes is the difference between one that completely interpenetrates all the elements of our being and one that is interwoven with only special and partial factors. There actually occurs extremely little observation of brute facts merely for the sake of the facts, just as there is little discipline that is repression and nothing but repression. Facts are usually observed with reference to some practical end and purpose, and that end is presented only imaginatively. The most repressive discipline has some end in view to which there is at least imputed an ideal quality; otherwise it is purely sadistic. But in such cases of observation and discipline imagination is limited and partial. It does not extend far; it does not permeate deeply and widely.

The connection between imagination and the harmonizing of the self is closer than is usually thought. The idea of a whole, whether of the whole personal being or of the world, is an imaginative, not a literal, idea. The limited world of our observation and reflection becomes the Universe only through imaginative extension. It cannot be apprehended in knowledge nor realized in reflection. Neither observation, thought, nor practical activity can attain that complete unification of the self which is called a whole. The *whole* self is an ideal, an imaginative projection. Hence the idea of thoroughgoing and deep-seated harmonizing of the self with the Universe (as a name for the totality of conditions with which the self is connected) operates only through imagination—which is one reason why this composing of the self is not voluntary in the sense of an act of special volition or resolution. An "adjustment" possesses the will rather than is its express product. Religionists have been right in thinking of it as an influx from sources beyond conscious deliberation and purpose—a fact that helps explain, psychologically, why it has so generally been attributed to a supernatural source and that, perhaps, throws some light upon the reference of it by William James to unconscious factors. And it is pertinent to note that the unification of the self throughout the ceaseless flux of what it does, suffers, and achieves, cannot be attained in terms of itself. The self is always directed toward something beyond itself and so its own unification depends upon the idea of the integration of the shifting scenes of the world into that imaginative totality we call the Universe.

If we apply the conception set forth to the terms of the definition earlier quoted, these terms take on a new significance. An unseen power controlling our destiny becomes the power of an ideal. All possibilities, as possibilities, are ideal in character. The artist, scientist, citizen, parent, as far as they are actuated by the spirit of their callings, are controlled by the unseen. For all endeavor for the better is moved by faith in what is possible, not by adherence to the actual. Nor does this faith depend for its moving power upon intellectual assurance or belief that the things worked for must surely prevail and come into embodied existence. For the authority of the object to determine our attitude and conduct, the right that is given it to claim our allegiance and devotion is based on the intrinsic nature of the ideal. The outcome, given our best endeavor, is not with us. The inherent vice of all intellectual schemes of idealism is that they convert the idealism of action into a system of beliefs about antecedent reality. The character assigned this reality is so different from that which observation and reflection lead to and support that these schemes inevitably glide into alliance with the supernatural.

Any activity pursued in behalf of an ideal end against obstacles and in spite of threats of personal loss because of conviction of its general and enduring value is religious in quality. Many a person, inquirer, artist, philanthropist, citizen, men and women in the humblest walks of life, have achieved, without presumption and without display, such unification of themselves and of their relations to the conditions of existence. It remains to extend their spirit and inspiration to even wider numbers. If I have said anything about religions and religion that seems harsh, I have said those things because of a firm belief that the claim on the part of religions to possess a monopoly of ideals and of the supernatural means by which alone, it is alleged, they can be furthered, stands in the way of the realization of distinctively religious values inherent in natural experience. For that reason, if for no other, I should be sorry if any were misled by the frequency with which I have employed the adjective "religious" to conceive of what I have said as a disguised apology for what have passed as religions. The opposition between religious values as I conceive them and religions is not to be bridged. Just because the release of these values is so important, their identification with the creeds and cults of religions must be dissolved.

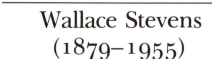

Wallace Stevens (1879–1955)

Wallace Stevens ranks with T. S. Eliot as one of the master poets of the modern period in America. The play of his imagination on the subject of the death of religion brought to birth a kind of religion of the imagination. But the result was not at all a religion of art or cult of aestheticism; it was rather an imagination of the real in what Stevens might have called its more individual aspect.

Marianne Moore, whose aesthetics was like Stevens's in many respects, once suggested that art creates imaginary gardens with real toads in them. This is what the speaker in Stevens's "The Idea of Order at Key West" discovers in the song the girl sings by the sea, and in the way the sea attains intenser being through her song. Stevens believed that all art ministers to the need to break through what he once described as "the man-locked set," to mediate a reality not ourselves. But here poetry does so precisely through the instrumentality of such a set, through the girl's "rage for order." Stevens understands this spiritual paradox perfectly: "In ghostlier demarcations, keener sounds."

"The Idea of Order at Key West" (1935)

She sang beyond the genius of the sea.
The water never formed to mind or voice,
Like a body wholly body, fluttering
Its empty sleeves; and yet its mimic motion
Made constant cry, caused constantly a cry,
That was not ours although we understood,
Inhuman, of the veritable ocean.

The sea was not a mask. No more was she.
The song and water were not medleyed sound
Even if what she sang was what she heard,
Since what she sang was uttered word by word.
It may be that in all her phrases stirred
The grinding water and the gasping wind;
But it was she and not the sea we heard.

For she was the maker of the song she sang.
The ever-hooded, tragic-gestured sea
Was merely a place by which she walked to sing.
Whose spirit is this? we said, because we knew
It was the spirit that we sought and knew
That we should ask this often as she sang.

If it was only the dark voice of the sea
That rose, or even colored by many
    waves;
If it was only the outer voice of sky
And cloud, of the sunken coral
    water-walled,
However clear, it would have been
    deep air,
The heaving speech of air, a summer
    sound
Repeated in a summer without end
And sound alone. But it was more
    than that,
More even than her voice, and ours,
    among
The meaningless plungings of water
    and the wind,
Theatrical distances, bronze shadows
    heaped
On high horizons, mountainous
    atmospheres
Of sky and sea.

       It was her voice that made
The sky acutest at its vanishing.
She measured to the hour its solitude.
She was the single artificer of the
    world
In which she sang. And when she
    sang, the sea,
Whatever self it had, became the self
That was her song, for she was the
    maker. Then we,
As we beheld her striding there alone,
Knew that there never was a world for
    her
Except the one she sang and, singing,
    made.

Ramon Fernandez, tell me, if you
    know,
Why, when the singing ended and we
    turned

Toward the town, tell why the glassy
    lights,
The lights in the fishing boats at
    anchor there,
As the night descended, tilting in the
    air,
Mastered the night and portioned out
    the sea,
Fixing emblazoned zones and fiery
    poles,
Arranging, deepening, enchanting
    night.

Oh! Blessed rage for order, pale
    Ramon,
The maker's rage to order words of
    the sea,
Words of the fragrant portals,
    dimly-starred,
And of ourselves and of our origins,
In ghostlier demarcations, keener
    sounds.

Reinhold Niebuhr
(1892–1971)

Social ethicist, Protestant churchman, and for over thirty years Professor of Applied Christianity at Union Theological Seminary in New York City, Reinhold Niebuhr is most often associated with the neo-orthodox movement in American theology. Neo-orthodoxy joined a Reformed interest in returning to the essentials of "Biblical religion" with a liberal desire to make the Christian message relevant to contemporary life and an active agent for social change. It was an attempt to return to the basic tenets of the Protestant Reformation and at the same time to revive and advance the Social Gospel movement.

Niebuhr's far-reaching influence was in part the result of his many political and social as well as ecclesiastical activities. He was a forceful personality and an eloquent preacher, a vigorous polemicist and a prolific writer. Niebuhr's theology, emphasizing the fallibility of the individual, the selfishness of groups, and the ironies of history, was well suited to the generation raised at the turn of the century and exposed in rapid succession to the spread of industrial capitalism, two world wars, a global depression, and, finally, the threat of nuclear annihilation.

The present selection was originally delivered as a sermon and then revised for publication as a chapter in *Beyond Tragedy* (1937).

From *Beyond Tragedy* (1937)

As Deceivers, Yet True

Among the paradoxes with which St. Paul describes the character, the vicissitudes and the faith of the Christian ministry, the phrase "as deceivers yet true" is particularly intriguing. Following immediately after the phrase "by evil report and good report" it probably defines the evil reports which were circulated about him as charges of deception and dishonesty. This charge is refuted with his "yet true." But the question arises why the charge is admitted before it is refuted. Perhaps this is done merely for the sake of preserving an unbroken line of paradoxical statements. If this be the case, a mere canon of rhetorical style has prompted a very profound statement. For what is true in the Christian religion can be expressed only in symbols which contain a certain degree of provisional and superficial deception. Every apologist of the Christian faith might well, therefore, make the Pauline phrase his own. We do teach the truth by deception. We are deceivers, yet true.

The necessity for the deception is given in the primary characteristic of the Christian world view. Christianity does not believe that the natural, temporal and historical world is self-derived or self-explanatory. It believes that the ground and the fulfilment of existence lie outside of existence, in an eternal and divine will. But it does not hold, as do many forms of dualism, that there is an eternal world separate and distinct from the temporal world. The relation between the temporal and the eternal is dialectical. The eternal is revealed and expressed in the sum total of finite occasions and relationships. He is their ground and they are the creation of His will. But, on the other hand, the finite world is not merely a corrupt emanation from the ideal and eternal. Consequently the relation of time and eternity cannot be expressed in simple rational terms. It can be expressed only in symbolic terms. A rational or logical expression of the relationship invariably leads either to a pantheism in which God and the world are identified, and the temporal in its totality is equated with the eternal; or in which they are separated so that a false supernaturalism emerges, a dualism between an eternal and spiritual world without content and a temporal world without meaning or significance.

I

Before analysing the deceptive symbols which the Christian faith uses to express this dimension of eternity in time, it might be clarifying to recall that artists are forced to use deceptive symbols when they seek to portray two dimensions of space upon the single dimension of a flat canvas. Every picture which suggests depth and perspective draws angles not as they are but as they appear to the eye when it looks into depth. Parallel lines are not drawn as parallel lines but are made to appear as if they converged on the horizon; for so they appear to the eye when it envisages a total perspective. Only the most primitive art and the drawings made by the very small children reveal the mistake of portraying things in their true proportions rather than as they are seen. The necessity of picturing things as they seem rather than as they are, in order to record on one dimension what they are in two dimensions, is a striking analogy, in the field of space, of the problem of religion in the sphere of time.

Time is a succession of events. Yet mere succession is not time. Time has reality only through a meaningful relationship of its successions. Therefore time is real only as it gives successive expressions of principles and powers which lie outside of it. Yet every suggestion of the principle of a process must be expressed in terms of the temporal process, and every idea of the God who is the ground of the world must be expressed in some term taken from the world. The temporal process is like the painter's flat canvas. It is one dimension upon which two dimensions must be recorded. This can be done only by symbols which deceive for the sake of truth.

Great art faces the problem of the two dimensions of time as well as the two dimensions of space. The portrait artist, for instance, is confronted with the necessity of picturing a character. Human personality is more than a succession of moods. The moods of a moment are held together in a unity of thought and feeling, which gives them, however seemingly capricious, a considerable degree of consistency of a character which is never fully expressed in any one particular mood or facial expression. This can be done only by falsifying physiognomic details. Portraiture is an art which can never be sharply distinguished from caricature. A moment of time in a personality can be made to express what transcends the moment of time only if the moment is not recorded accurately. It must be made into a symbol of something beyond itself.

This technique of art explains why art is more closely related to religion than science. Art describes the world not in terms of its exact relationships. It constantly falsifies these relationships, as analysed by science, in order to express their total meaning.

377

II

The Christian religion may be characterised as one which has transmuted primitive religious and artistic myths and symbols without fully rationalising them. Buddhism is much more rational than Christianity. In consequence Buddhism finds the finite and temporal world evil. Spinozism is a more rational version of God and the world than the biblical account; but it finds the world unqualifiedly good and identical with God. In the biblical account the world is good because God created it; but the world is not God. Every Christian myth, in one way or another, expresses both the meaningfulness and the incompleteness of the temporal world, both the majesty of God and his relation to the world.

We are deceivers yet true, when we say that God created the world. Creation is a mythical idea which cannot be fully rationalised. It has therefore been an offence to the philosophers who, with the scientists, have substituted the idea of causality for it. They have sought to explain each subsequent event by a previous cause. Such an explanation of the world leads the more naïve thinkers to a naturalism which regards the world as self-explanatory because every event can be derived from a previous one. The more sophisticated philosophers will at least, with Aristotle, seek for a first cause which gives an original impetus to the whole chain of causation. But such a first cause does not have a living relationship with the events of nature and history. It does not therefore account for the emergence of novelty in each new event. No new fact or event in history is an arbitrary novelty. It is always related to a previous event. But it is a great error to imagine that this relationship completely accounts for the new emergence. In both nature and history each new thing is only one of an infinite number of possibilities which might have emerged at that particular juncture. It is for this reason that, though we can trace a series of causes in retrospect, we can never predict the future with accuracy. There is a profound arbitrariness in every given fact, which rational theories of causation seek to obscure. Thus they regard a given form of animal life as rational because they can trace it historically to another form or relate it in terms of genus and species to other types of life. Yet none of these relationships, whether historical or schematic, can eliminate the profound arbitrariness of the givenness of things.

It is therefore true to account for the meaningfulness of life in terms of the relation of every thing to a creative centre and source of meaning. But the truth of creation can be expressed only in terms which outrage reason. Involved in the idea of creation is the concept of making something out of nothing. The *Shepherd* of Hermas declares "First of all believe that God is one, who created and set in order all things and caused the universe to exist out of nothing." This was the constant reiteration of Christian belief, until in very modern times it was thought possible to substitute the idea of evolutionary causation for the idea of creation. The idea of creation out of nothing is profoundly ultrarational; for human reason can deal only with the stuff of experience, and in experience the previous event and cause are seen, while the creative source of novelty is beyond experience.

The idea of creation relates the ground of existence to existence and is therefore mythical rather than rational. The fact that it is not a rational idea does not make it untrue or deceptive. But since it is not rational it is a temptation to deceptions. Every mythical idea contains a primitive deception and a more ultimate one. The primitive error is to regard the early form in which the myth is stated as authoritative. Thus the Christian religion is always tempted to insist that belief in creation also involves belief in an actual forming of man out of a lump of clay, or in an actual creative activity of six days. It is to this temptation that biblical literalism succumbs. But there is also a more ultimate source of error in the mythical statement of religious belief. That is to regard the relation of each fact and event in history to a Divine Creator as obviating the possibility of an organic relation to other facts and events according to a natural order. By this error, which Etienne Gilson[1] calls "theologism," Christian theology is constantly tempted to deny the significance of the natural order, and to confuse the scientific analysis of its relationships. At the rise of modern thought Malebranche developed a doctrine of "occasionalism" which expressed this error of Christian theology in its most consistent form. But it has been a persistent error

[1] In his *Unity of Philosophical Experience.*

in Christian thought and one which arises naturally out the mythical statement of the idea of creation. The error is analogous to that of certain types of art which completely falsify the natural relations of objects in order to express their ultimate significance.

We are deceivers yet true, when we say that man fell into evil. The story of the fall of man in the Garden of Eden is a primitive myth which modern theology has been glad to disavow, for fear that modern culture might regard belief in it as a proof of the obscurantism of religion. In place of it we have substituted various accounts of the origin and the nature of evil in human life. Most of these accounts, reduced to their essentials, attribute sin to the inertia of nature, or the hypertrophy of impulses, or to the defect of reason (ignorance), and thereby either explicitly or implicitly place their trust in developed reason as the guarantor of goodness. In all of these accounts the essential point in the nature of human evil is missed, namely, that it arises from the very freedom of reason with which man is endowed. Sin is not so much a consequence of natural impulses, which in animal life do not lead to sin, as of the freedom by which man is able to throw the harmonies of nature out of joint. He disturbs the harmony of nature when he centers his life about one particular impulse (sex or the possessive impulse, for instance) or when he tries to make himself, rather than God, the center of existence. This egoism is sin in its quintessential form. It is not a defect of creation but a defect which becomes possible because man has been endowed with a freedom not known in the rest of creation.

The idea of the fall is subject to the error of regarding the primitive myth of the garden, the apple and the serpent, as historically true. But even if this error is not committed, Christian thought is still tempted to regard the fall as an historical occurrence. The fall is not historical. It does not take place in any concrete human act. It is the presupposition of such acts. It deals with an area of human freedom which, when once expressed in terms of an act, is always historically related to a previous act or predisposition. External descriptions of human behaviour are therefore always deterministic. That is the deception into which those are betrayed who seek to avoid the errors of introspection by purely external descriptions of human behaviour. What Christianity means by the idea of the fall can only be known in introspection. The consciousness of sin and the consciousness of God are inextricably involved with each other. Only as the full dimension of human existence is measured, which includes not only the dimension of historical breadth but the dimension of trans-historical freedom, does the idea of the fall of man achieve significance and relevance.

It is interesting to note that Christian theology has usually regarded the fall as an historical occurence, even when it did not accept the primitive myth of the Garden of Eden. It therefore spoke of a perfection before the fall as if that too were an historical era. Even the sophisticated dialectical theology of Barth and his school speaks of the perfection before the fall as historical, and conse-

quently elaborates a doctrine of human sinfulness which approaches, and sometimes surpasses, the extremism of the historic doctrine of total depravity. The perfection before the fall is an ideal possibility which men can comprehend but not realise. The perfection before the fall is, in a sense, the perfection before the act. Thus we are able to conceive of a perfectly disinterested justice; but when we act our own achievements will fall short of this standard. The rationalists always assume that, since men are able to conceive of perfect standards of justice, such standards will be realised as soon as all men become intelligent enough to conceive them. They do not realise that intelligence offers no guarantee of the realisation of a standard, and that the greatest idealists, as well as the most cynical realists or the most ignorant victims of an immediate situation, fall short in their action; nor that such falling short arises not simply from the defect of the mind but from an egoistic corruption of the heart. Self intrudes itself into every ideal, when thought gives place to action. The deceptions to which the idea of the fall give rise are many; and all of them have been the basis of error at some time or other in the history of Christian theology. We are deceivers, yet true in clinging to the idea of the fall as a symbol of the origin and the nature of evil in human life.

III

We are deceivers, yet true, when we affirm that God became man to redeem the world from sin. The idea of eternity entering time is intellectually absurd. This absurdity is proved to the hilt by all the theological dogmas which seek to make it rational. The dogmas which seek to describe the relation of God the Father (the God who does not enter history) and God the son (the God of history) all insist that the Son is equal to the Father and is yet not equal to Him. In the same way all the doctrines of the two natures of Christ assert that he is not less divine for being human and temporal and not less human and temporal for being fully divine. Quite obviously it is impossible to assert that the eternal ground of existence has entered existence and not sacrificed its eternal and unconditioned quality, without outraging every canon of reason. Reason may deal with the conditioned realities of existence in their relationships and it may even point to the fathomless depth of creativity out of which existential forms are born. But it cannot assert that the Divine Creator has come into creation without losing His unconditioned character. The truth that the Word was made flesh outrages all the canons by which truth is usually judged. Yet it is the truth. The whole character of the Christian religion is involved in that affirmation. It asserts that God's word is relevant to human life. It declares that an event in history can be of such a character as to reveal the character of history itself; that without such a revelation the character of history cannot be known. It is not possible to arrive at an understanding of the meaning of life and history without such a revelation. No induction from empirical facts can yield a conclusion about ultimate meaning because every process of induction presupposes some canon and criterion of meaning. That is why metaphysical systems which pretend to arrive at ultimate conclusions about the meaning of life are either covert theologies which unconsciously rationalise some revelation, accepted by faith; or they merely identify rationality with meaning, a procedure which forces them into either pantheism or acosmism. They must either identify the world with God on the supposition that temporal events, fully understood in all their relationships, are transmuted from finiteness and contingency into an unconditioned totality; or they must find the existential world evil in its finiteness because it does not conform in its contingent, existential relationships to a rational idea of unity.

For Christian faith the world is niether perfect nor meaningless. The God who created it also reveals Himself in it. He reveals Himself not only in a general revelation, that is, in the sense that His creation is His revelation; but in a special revelation. A general revelation can only point to the reality of God but not to His particular attributes. A theology which believes only in a general revelation must inevitably culminate in pantheism; because a God who is merely the object of human knowledge and not a subject who communicates with man by His own initiative is something less than God. A knowledge of God which depends only upon a study of the behaviour of the world must inevitably be as flat as the knowledge of any person would be, which depended merely upon the observation of the person's behaviour. The study of human behaviour cannot give a full clue to the meaning of a personality, because there is a depth of freedom in every personality which can only communicate itself in its own "word." That word may be related to an analysis of behaviour and become the principle of interpretation for the analysis. But it is not the consquence of the analysis. Without such a word the picture of any personality would be flat, as the interpretations of the divine which eliminate revelation are flat.

In Christian thought Christ is both the perfect man, "the second Adam" who had restored the perfection of what man was and ought to be; and the Son of God, who transcends all possibilities of human life. It is this idea which theology sought to rationalise in the doctrines of the two natures of Christ. It cannot be rationalised and yet it is a true idea. Human life stands in infinity. Everything it touches turns into infinity. Every moral standard, rigorously analysed, proves to be no permanently valid standard at all short of perfect and infinite love. The only adequate norm of human conduct is love of God and of man, through which all men are perfectly related to each other, because they are all related in terms of perfect obedience and love to the centre and source of their existence. In the same way all evil in human life is derived from an effort to transmute finite values into infinities, to seek infinite power, and infinite wealth and infinite gratification of desire. There is no sharp line between the infinity in man and the infinity beyond man and yet there is a very sharp line. Man always remains a creature and his sin arises from the fact that he is not satisfied to remain so. He seeks to turn creatureliness into infinity; whereas his salvation depends upon subjecting his creaturely weakness to the infinite possibilities of love in human life and the infinite possibilities beyond human life, is thus a true revelation of the total situation in which human life stands. There is every possibility of illusion and deception in this statement of the Christian faith. Men may be deceived by the primitive myth of the Virgin Birth and seek to comprehend as a pure historical fact, what is significant precisely because it points beyond history. Or they may seek to explain the dogma of the Incarnation in terms which will make it an article in a philosophical creed. Such efforts will lead to varied deceptions; but the deceptions cannot destroy the truth of the Incarnation.

Yet the revelation of God in the Incarnation is not of itself the redemption. Christianity believes that Christ died to save men from sin. It has a gospel which contains a crucifixion as well as an incarnation, a cross as well as a manger. This doctrine of the atoning death of the Son of God upon the cross has led to many theological errors, among them to theories of substitutionary atonement which outrage the moral sense. There is in fact no theory of the atonement which is quite as satisfying as the simple statements of the vicarious death of Christ in the Gospels. This may mean that faith is able to sense and appropriate an ultimate truth too deep for human reason. This is the foolishness of God which is wiser than the wisdom of men. The modern world has found not only the theories of atonement but the idea of atonement itself absurd. It rebelled not only against theories of a sacrifice which ransomed man from the devil's clutches or of a sacrifice which appeased the anger of a vindictive divine Father; it regarded the very idea of reconciliation between God and man as absurd.

The reason for this simple rejection of the Christian drama of salvation lies in the modern conception of human nature, rather than in any rejection of the theological absurdities attached to the idea of Christ's atoning death. Modern man does not regard life as tragic. He thinks that history is the record of the progressive triumph of good over evil. He does not recognise the simple but profound truth that man's life remains self-contradictory in its sin, no matter how high human culture rises; that the highest expression of human spirituality, therefore, contains also the subtlest form of human sin. The failure to recognise this fact gives modern culture a non-tragic conception of human history. To recognise this fact, and nothing more, is to reduce human history to simple tragedy. But the basic message of Christian faith is a message of hope in tragedy. It declares that when the Christ, by whom the world was made, enters the world, the world will not receive him. "He came unto his own and his own received him not." Human existence denies its own deepest and most essential nature. That is tragic. But when that fact is understood, when men cease to make the standards of a sinful existence the norms of life but accept its true norm, even though they fail to obey it, their very contrition opens the eyes of faith. This is the Godly sorrow that worketh repentance. Out of this despair hope is born. The hope is simply this: that the contradictions of human existence, which man cannot surmount, are swallowed up in the life of God Himself. The God of Christian faith is not only creator but redeemer. He does not allow human existence to end tragically. He snatches victory from defeat. He is Himself defeated in history but He is also victorious in that defeat.

There are theologies which interpret this article in the Christian creed as if life were really pure tragedy, but for the atoning love of Christ. But the fact is that the atoning death of Christ is the revelation of ultimate reality which may become the principle of interpretation for all human experience. It is not a principle yielded by experience, but it is applicable to experience and validated by it. It is an actual fact that human life, which is always threatened and periodically engulfed by the evil which human sin creates, is also marvellously redeemed by the transmutation of evil into good. This transmutation is not a human but a divine possibility. No man can, by taking thought, turn evil into good. Yet in the total operations of providence in history this transmutation occurs. The Christian faith consequently does not defy the tragic facts of human existence by a single victory over tragedy; nor does it flee the tragedy of temporal existence into a heavenly escape. These forms of the Christian faith are deceptions.

Most profoundly the atonement of Christ is a revelation of what life actually is. It is tragic from the standpoint of human striving. Human striving can do no better than the Roman law and the Hebraic religion, both the highest of their kind, through which the Lord was crucified. Yet this crucifixion becomes the revelation of that in human history which transcends human striving. And without this revelation, that which is beyond tragedy in life could not have been apprehended. Without the cross men are beguiled by what is good in human existence into a false optimism and by what is tragic into despair. The message of the Son of God who dies upon the cross, of a God who transcends history and is yet in history, who condemns and judges sin and yet suffers with and for the sinner, this message is the truth about life. It cannot be stated without deceptions; but the truths which seek to avoid the deceptions are immeasurably less profound. Compared to this Christ who died for men's sins upon the cross, Jesus, the good man who tells all men to be good, is more solidly historical. But he is the bearer of no more than a pale truism.

We are deceivers, yet true, when we declare that Christ will come again at the last judgment, that he who was defeated in history will ultimately triumph over it, will become its judge and the author of its new life. No doctrine of Christianity has led to more deceptions and illusions than the hope of the second coming of Christ. This doctrine has been so frequently appropriated and exploited by sectarian fanatics that the church has been a little ashamed of it. We have made even less of the apocalyptic literature into which Hebraic prophecy culminated and in which Christ was nurtured. The imagery of this literature is so extravagant, and at times so fantastic, that Christian thinkers have been content, on the whole, to leave it alone. Yet the doctrine of Christ's second coming involves all the profoundest characteristics of the Christian religion. It is this doctrine which distinguishes Christianity both from naturalistic utopianism and from Hellenistic otherworldiness. In it the Christian hope of the fulfilment of life is expressed paradoxically and dialectically, holding fast to its essential conception of the relation of time to eternity. History is not regarded as meaningless, as in Greek thought, particularly in later neo-Platonism. For this reason the realm of fulfilment is not above history, in some heaven in which pure form is abstracted from the concrete content of historical existence. The realm of fulfilment is at the end of history. This symbolises that fulfilment both transcends and is relevant to historical forms. The end of history is not a point in history.

The chronological illusion, that it is a point in history, so characteristic of all myths which point to the trans-historical by a symbol of time, is particularly fruitful of error in the doctrine of the second coming. It has led to fantastic sectarian illusions of every type. Yet it is significant that the dispossessed and disinherited have been particularly prone to these illusions, because they were anxious to express the Christian hope of fulfilment in social as well as in individual terms. Sectarian apocalypticism is closely related to modern proletarian radicalism, which is a secularised form of the latter. In both, the individualism of Christian orthodoxy is opposed with conceptions which place the corporate enterprises of mankind, as well as individuals, under an ultimate judgment and under ultimate possibilities of fulfilment. In these secular and apocalyptic illusions the end of time is a point in time beyond which there will be an unconditioned society. But there is truth in the illusions.

The more bourgeois version of this illusory apocalypticism is the idea of progress in which the unconditioned ground of history is explicitly denied, but an unconditioned fulfilment in terms of infinite duration is implicitly affirmed. The Kingdom of God, as the absolute reign of God, is transmuted into a principle of development, immanent in history itself. Against such a conception Christian thought is forced to maintain as rigorous opposition as against dualistic otherworldliness. The ultimate fulfilment of life transcends the possibilities of human history. There is no hope of overcoming the contradictions, in which life stands, in history. But since these contradictions are not the consequence of mere finiteness and temporality, but the fruits of human freedom, they are not overcome merely by translating the temporal into the eternal. Since they persist in all human striving, fulfilment is not a human but a divine contradiction.

Therefore it is Christ who is both the judge of the world and the author of its fulfilment; for Christ is the symbol both of what man ought to be and of what

God is beyond man. In Christ we have a revelation of both the human possibilities which are to be fulfilled and the divine power which will fulfil them. In Christ, too, we have the revelation of the significance of human history and of the ground of its meaning which transcends history.

We are therefore deceivers, yet true, when we insist that the Christ who died on the cross will come again in power and glory, that he will judge the quick and the dead and will establish his Kingdom. We do not believe that the human enterprise will have a tragic conclusion; but the ground of our hope lies not in human capacity but in divine power and mercy, in the character of the ultimate reality, which carries the human enterprise. This hope does not imply that fulfilment means the negation of what is established and developed in human history. Each moment of history stands under the possibility of an ultimate fulfilment. The fulfilment is neither a negation of its essential character nor yet a further development of its own inherent capacities. It is rather a completion of its essence by an annihilation of the contradictions which sin has introduced into human life.

James Agee
(1909–1955)

James Agee was a journalist, essayist, film critic, novelist, and poet. In addition to his brilliant film reviews, he produced two minor literary masterpieces. The first, *Death in the Family,* was a heavily autobiographical novel left unpublished until two years after Agee's death. The second, *Let Us Now Praise Famous Men* (1941), was a journalistic essay on which he collaborated with the photographer Walker Evans. It was originally commissioned by *Fortune* magazine as a series of articles on tenant farming in the South. Agee decided, however, that he could not do justice to the subject under the terms of the assignment, and expanded the project into a kind of religious meditation on the ethics of perception and the dignity of poverty. The following passage conveys a part of what he learned from his attempt to discover and define "the spirit of the place."

From *Let Us Now Praise Famous Men* (1939)

The dead oak and pine, the ground, the dew, the air, the whole realm of what our bodies lay in and our minds in silence wandered, walked in, swam in, watched upon, was delicately fragrant as a paradise, and, like all that is best, was loose, light, casual, totally *actual.* There was, by our minds, our memories, our thoughts and feelings, some combination, some generalizing, some art, and science; but none of the close-kneed priggishness of science, and none of the formalism and straining and lily-gilding

of art. All the length of the body and all its parts and functions were participating, and were being realized and rewarded, inseparable from the mind, identical with it: and all, everything, that the mind touched, was actuality, and all, everything, that the mind touched turned immediately, yet without in the least losing the quality of its total individuality, into joy and truth, or rather, revealed, of its self, truth, which in its very nature was joy, which must be the end of art, of investigation, and of all anyhow human existence.

This situation is possible at any junction of time, space and consciousness: and just as (at least so far as we can know and can be concerned) it is our consciousness alone, in the end, that we have to thank for joy, so too it is our consciousness alone that is defective when we fall short of it. It is curious, and unfortunate, that we find this luck so rarely; that it is so almost purely a matter of chance: yet that, as matters are, becomes inextricably a part of the whole texture of the pleasure: at such time we have knowledge that we are witnessing, taking part in, being, a phenomenon anologous to that shrewd complex of the equations of infinite chance which became, on this early earth, out of lifelessness, life. No doubt we overvalue the difference between life and lifelessness, but there is a certain difference between life and lifelessness, but there is a certain difference, just as, in the situation we are speaking of, a difference is remarkable: the difference between a conjunction of time, place and unconscious consciousness and a conjunction of time, place and conscious consciousness is, so far as we are concerned, the difference between joy and truth and the lack of joy and truth. Unless wonder is nothing in itself, but only a moon which glows only in the mercy of a sense of wonder, and unless the sense of wonder is peculiar to consciousness and is moreover an emotion which, as it matures, consciousness will learn the juvenility of, and discard, or only gratefully refresh itself under the power of as under the power of sleep and the healing vitality of dreams, and all this seems a little more likely than not, the materials which people any intersection of time and place are at all times marvelous, regardless of consciousness: and in either or any case we may do well to question whether there is anything more marvelous or more valuable in the state of being we distinguish as 'life' than in the state of being of a stone, the brainless energy of a star, the diffuse existence of space. Certainly life is valuable; indispensable to all our personal calculations, the very spine of them: but we should realize that life and consciousness are only the special crutches of the living and the conscious, and that in setting as we do so high a value by them we are in a certain degree making a virtue of necessity; are being provincial; are pleading a local cause: like that small Nevada town whose pride, because it is its chiefly discernible exclusive distinction, is in a mineral spring whose water, assisted by salt and pepper, tastes remarkably like chicken soup.

Robert Frost (1874–1963)

Robert Frost is often thought of as a benign nature poet whose re-creation of the rural New England landscape of a bygone era brings solace to a time no longer in touch with the simple pastoral verities. But as Lionel Trilling observed at a celebration honoring Frost on his seventy-fifth brithday, his poetry far more often disturbs than comforts; its disturbing power derives not from the nostaligic evocation of an earlier period made simpler by the absence of contemporary tensions and fears, but from its starkly modern confrontation of the terrible realities within and without us that are inescapable in any age.

In "The Most of It," Frost takes on the legacy of Emerson's conviction that Nature will answer all the questions we put to her, and answer them in a way that accomodates and supports human existence rather than threatening it. Frost's protagonist not only finds his expectations of reality betrayed, he discovers that reality is indeed the realm of the unexpected.

"The Most of It" (1941)

He thought he kept the universe
   alone;
For all the voice in answer he could
   wake

Was but the mocking echo of his own
From some tree-hidden cliff across the
    lake.
Some morning from the
    boulder-broken beach
He would cry out on life, that what it
    wants
Is not its own love back in copy
    speech,
But counter-love, original response.
And nothing ever came of what he
    cried
Unless it was the embodiment that
    crashed
In the cliff's talus on the other side,
And then in the far-distant water
    splashed,
But after a time allowed for it to swim,
Instead of proving human when it
    neared
And someone else additional to him,
As a great buck it powerfully
    appeared,
Pushing the crumpled water up ahead,
And landed pouring like a waterfall,
And stumbled through the rocks with
    horny tread,
And forced the underbrush—and that
    was all.

Marianne Moore
(1887–1972)

Marianne Moore, one of the most devoted craftsmen among modern American poets, was distrustful of what she
once called "consolations of the metaphysical." Yet she still believed, as one of
her best poems is entitled, in a kind of
"Nevertheless." "What Are Years?" was
begun in 1931 but not completed until
1939. In a note to William Rose Benét
and Norman Holmes Pearson, she explained part of its meaning by saying,
"The desperation attendant on moral
fallibility is mitigated for me by admit-
ting that the most willed and resolute
vigilance may lapse, as with the Apostle
Peter's denial that he could be capable
of denial; but that failure, disgrace, and
even death have now and again been
redeemed into inviolateness by a sufficiently transfigured courage."

"What Are Years?" (1941)

    What is our innocence,
what is our guilt? All are
    naked, none is safe. And whence
is courage: the unanswered question,
the resolute doubt—
dumbly calling, deafly listening—that
is misfortune, even death,
      encourages others
      and in its defeat, stirs
    the soul to be strong? He
sees deep and is glad, who
    accedes to mortality
and in his imprisonment rises
upon himself as
the sea in a chasm, struggling to be
free and unable to be,
    in its surrendering
    finds its continuing.

So he who strongly feels
behaves. The very bird,
   grown taller as he sings, steels
his form straight up. Though he is
captive,
his mighty singing
says, satisfaction is a lowly
thing, how pure a thing is joy.
      This is mortality,
      this is eternity.

William Faulkner
(1897–1962)

William Faulkner wrote a series of novels and stories set in the mythical Mississippi county of "Yoknapatawpha." In his Yoknapatawpha saga, which traces the decline of the Old South and the emergence of the New, Faulkner came as close as any American writer before or since to creating a whole fictive universe.

The world of Yoknapatawpha is ordered by a powerful mythology in which the culture of the Old South and its chief representatives are foredoomed. Their destruction is caused by transgressions against the land and the many people who worked it. The privileged few who assumed that the land and those who made it productive were theirs to possess and exploit were guilty of the sin of pride. The arrogance of presuming that one could own land was of a piece with the evil of believing that one could enslave his fellows. The only individuals who succeed in escaping from this diabolical cycle are those who realize that man and Nature, the Negro and the American wilderness, exist not as objects to be dominated and coerced but as resources for self-understanding and moral regeneration.

"The Old People" is one of seven interconnected stories in *Go Down, Moses* (1942). It concerns the initiation of a boy into some of the complex mysteries of this American heritage.

"The Old People" (1942)

1

At first there was nothing. There was the faint, cold, steady rain, the gray and constant light of the late November dawn, with the voices of the hounds converging somewhere in it and toward them. Then Sam Fathers, standing just behind the boy as he had been standing when the boy shot his first running rabbit with his first gun and almost with the first load it ever carried, touched his shoulder and he began to shake, not with any cold. Then the buck was there. He did not come into sight; he was just there, looking not like a ghost but as if all of light were condensed in him and he were the source of it, not only moving in it but disseminating it, already running, seen first as you always see the deer, in that split second after he has already seen you, already slanting away in that first soaring bound, the antlers even in that dim light looking like a small rocking-chair balanced on his head

"Now," Sam Fathers said, "shoot quick, and slow."

The boy did not remember that shot at all. He would live to be eighty, as his father and his father's twin brother and their father in his turn had lived to be, but he would never hear that shot nor remember even the shock of the gun-butt. He didn't even remember what he did with the gun afterward. He was running. Then he was standing over the buck where it lay on the wet earth still in the attitude of speed and not looking at all dead, standing over it shaking and jerking, with Sam Fathers beside him again, extending the knife. "Dont walk up to him in front," Sam said. "If he aint dead, he will cut you all to pieces with his feet. Walk up to him from behind and take him by the horn first, so you can hold his head down until you can jump away. Then slip your other hand down and hook your fingers in his nostrils."

The boy did that—drew the head back and the throat taut and drew Sam Fathers' knife across the throat and Sam stooped and dipped his hands in the hot smoking blood and wiped them back and forth across the boy's face. Then Sam's horn rang in the wet gray woods and again and again; there was a boiling wave of dogs about them, with Tennie's Jim and Boon Hogganbeck whipping them back after each had had a taste of the blood, then the men, the true hunters—Walter Ewell whose rifle never missed, and Major de Spain and old General Compson and the boy's cousin, McCaslin Edmonds, grandson of his father's sister, sixteen years his senior and, since both he and McCaslin were only children and the boy's father had been nearing seventy when he was born, more his brother than his cousin and more his father than either—sitting their horses and looking down at them: at the old man of seventy who had been a negro for two generations now but whose face and bearing were still those of the Chickasaw chief who had been his father; and the white boy of twelve with the prints of the bloody hands on his face, who had nothing to do now but stand straight and not let the trembling show.

"Did he do all right, Sam?" his cousin McCaslin said.

"He done all right," Sam Fathers said.

They were the white boy, marked forever, and the old dark man sired on both sides by savage kings, who had marked him, whose bloody hands had merely formally consecrated him to that which, under the man's tutelage, he had already accepted, humbly and joyfully, with abnegation and with pride too; the hands, the touch, the first worthy blood which he had been found at last worthy to draw, joining him and the man forever, so that the man would continue to live past the boy's seventy years and then eighty years, long after the man himself had entered the earth as chiefs and kings entered it;—the child, not yet a man, whose grandfather had lived in the same country and in almost the same manner as the boy himself would grow up to live, leaving his descendants in the land in his turn as his grandfather had done, and the old man past seventy whose grandfathers had owned the land long before the white men ever saw it and who had vanished from it now with all their kind, what of blood they left behind them running now in another race and for a while even in bondage and now drawing toward the end of its alien and irrevocable course, barren, since Sam Fathers had no children.

His father was Ikkemotubbe himself, who had named himself Doom. Sam told the boy about that—how Ikkemotubbe, old Issetibbeha's sister's son, had run away to New Orleans in his youth and returned seven years later with a French companion calling himself the Chevalier Soeur-Blonde de Vitry, who must have been the Ikkemotubbe of his family too and who was already addressing Ikkemotubbe as *Du Homme;*—returned, came home again, with his foreign Aramis and the quadroon slave woman who was to be Sam's mother, and a gold-laced hat and coat and a wicker wine-hamper containing a litter of month-old puppies and a gold snuff-box filled with a white powder resembling fine sugar. And how he was met at the River landing by three or four companions of his bachelor youth, and while the light of a smoking torch gleamed on the glittering braid of the hat and coat Doom squatted in the mud of the land and took one of the puppies from the hamper and put a pinch of the white powder on its tongue and the puppy died before the one who was holding it could cast it away. And how they returned to the Plantation where Issetibbeha, dead now, had been succeeded by his son, Doom's fat cousin Moketubbe, and the next day Moketubbe's eight-year-old son died suddenly and that afternoon, in the presence of Moketubbe and most of the others (the People, Sam Fathers called them) Doom produced another puppy from the wine-hamper and put a pinch of the white powder on its tongue and Moketubbe abdicated and Doom became in fact The Man which his French friend already called him. And how on the day after that, during the ceremony of accession, Doom pronounced a marriage between the pregnant quadroon and one of the slave men which he had just inherited (that was how Sam Fathers got his name, which in Chickasaw had been Had-Two-Fathers) and two years later sold the man and woman and the child who was his own son to his white neighbor, Carothers McCaslin.

That was seventy years ago. The Sam Fathers whom the boy knew was already sixty—a man not tall, squat rather, almost sedentary, flabby-looking though he actually was not, with hair like a horse's mane which even at seventy showed no trace of white and a face which showed no age until he smiled, whose only visible trace of negro blood was a slight dullness of the hair and the fingernails, and something else which you did notice about the eyes, which you noticed because it was not always there, only in repose and not always then—something not in their shape nor pigment but in their expression, and the boy's cousin McCaslin told him what that was: not the heritage of Ham, not the mark of servitude but of bondage; the knowledge that for a while that part of his blood had been the blood of slaves. "Like an old lion or a bear in a cage," McCaslin said. "He was born in the cage and has been in it all his life; he knows nothing else. Then he smells something. It might be anything, any breeze blowing past anything and then into his nostrils. But here for a second was the hot sand or the cane-brake that he never even saw himself, might not even know if he did see it and probably does know he couldn't hold his own with it if he got back to it. But that's not what he smells then, It was the cage he smelled. He hadn't smelled the cage until that minute. Then the hot sand or the brake blew into his nostrils and blew away, and all he could smell was the cage. That's what makes his eyes look like that."

"Then let him go!" the boy cried. "Let him go!"

His cousin laughed shortly. Then he stopped laughing, making the sound that is. It had never been laughing. "His cage aint McCaslins," he said. "He was a wild man. When he was born, all his blood on both sides, except the little white part, knew things that had been tamed out of our blood so long ago that we have not only forgotten them, we have to live together in herds to protect ourselves from our own sources. He was the direct son not only of a warrior but of a chief. Then he grew up and began to learn things, and all of a sudden one day he found out that he had been betrayed, the blood of the warriors and chiefs had been betrayed. Not by his father," he added quickly. "He probably never held it against old Doom for selling him and his mother into slavery, because he probably believed the damage was already done before then and it was the same warriors' and chiefs' blood

in him and Doom both that was betrayed through the black blood which his mother gave him. Not betrayed by the black blood and not wilfully betrayed by his mother, but betrayed by her all the same, who had bequeathed him not only the blood of slaves but even a little of the very blood which had enslaved it; Himself his own battleground, the scene of his own vanquishment and the mausoleum of his defeat. His cage aint us," McCaslin said. "Did you ever know anybody yet, even your father and Uncle Buddy, that ever told him to do or not do anything that he ever paid any attention to?"

That was true. The boy first remembered him as sitting in the door of the plantation blacksmith-shop, where he sharpened plow-points and mended tools and even did rough carpenter-work when he was not in the woods. And sometimes, even when the woods had not drawn him, even with the shop cluttered with work which the farm waited on, Sam would sit there, doing nothing at all for half a day or a whole one, and no man, neither the boy's father and twin uncle in their day nor his cousin McCaslin after he became practical though not yet titular master, ever to say to him, "I want this finished by sundown" or "why wasn't this done yesterday?" And once each year, in the late fall, in November, the boy would watch the wagon, the hooped canvas top erected now, being loaded—the food, hams and sausage from the smoke-house, coffee and flour and molasses from the commissary, a whole beef killed just last night for the dogs until there would be meat in camp, the crate containing the dogs themselves, then the bedding, the guns, the horns and lanterns and axes, and his cousin McCaslin and Sam Fathers in their hunting clothes would mount to the seat and with Tennie's Jim sitting on the dog-crate they would drive away to Jefferson, to join Major de Spain and General Compson and Boon Hogganbeck and Walter Ewell and go on into the big bottom of the Tallahatchie where the deer and bear were, to be gone two weeks. But before the wagon was even loaded the boy would find that he could watch no longer. He would go away, running almost, to stand behind the corner where he could not see the wagon and nobody could see him, not crying, holding himself rigid except for the trembling, whispering to himself: "Soon now. Soon now. Just three more years" (or two more or one more) "and I will be ten. Then Cass said I can go."

White man's work, when Sam did work. Because he did nothing else: farmed no alloted acres of his own, as the other ex-slaves of old Carothers McCaslin did, performed no field-work for daily wages as the younger and newer negroes did—and the boy never knew just how that had been settled between Sam and old Carothers, or perhaps with old Carothers' twin sons after him. For, although Sam lived among the negroes, in a cabin among the other cabins in the quarters, and consorted with negroes (what of consorting with anyone Sam did after the boy got big enough to walk alone from the house to the blacksmith-shop and then to carry a gun) and dressed like them and talked like them and even

went with them to the negro church now and then, he was still the son of that Chickasaw chief and the negroes knew it. And, it seemed to the boy, not only negroes. Boon Hogganbeck's grandmother had been a Chickasaw woman too, and although the blood had run white since and Boon was a white man, it was not chief's blood. To the boy at least, the difference was apparent immediately you saw Boon and Sam together, and even Boon seemed to know it was there—even Boon, to whom in his tradition it had never occurred that anyone might be better born than himself. A man might be smarter, he admitted that, or richer (luckier, he called it) but not better born. Boon was a mastiff, absolutely faithful, dividing his fidelity equally between Major de Spain and the boy's cousin McCaslin, absolutely dependent for his very bread and dividing that impartially too between Major de Spain and McCaslin, hardy, generous, courageous enough, a slave to all the appetites and almost unratiocinative. In the boy's eyes at least it was Sam Fathers, the negro, who bore himself not only toward his cousin McCaslin and Major de Spain but toward all white men, with gravity and dignity and without servility or recourse to that impenetrable wall of ready and easy mirth which negroes sustain between themselves and white men, bearing himself toward his cousin McCaslin not only as one man to another but as an older man to a younger.

He taught the boy the woods, to hunt, when to shoot and when not to shoot, when to kill and when not to kill, and better, what to do with it afterward.

Then he would talk to the boy, the two of them sitting beneath the close fierce stars on a summer hilltop while they waited for the hounds to bring the fox back within hearing, or beside a fire in the November or December woods while the dogs worked out a coon's trail along the creek, or fireless in the pitch dark and heavy dew of April mornings while they squatted beneath a turkey-roost. The boy would never question him; Sam did not react to questions. The boy would just wait and then listen and Sam would begin, talking about the old days and the People whom he had not had time ever to know and so could not remember (he did not remember ever having seen his father's face), and in place of whom the other race into which his blood had run supplied him with no substitute.

And as he talked about those old times and those dead and vanished men of another race from either that the boy knew, gradually to the boy those old times would cease to be old times and would become a part of the boy's present, not only as if they had happened yesterday but as if they were still happening, the men who walked through them actually walking in breath and air and casting an actual shadow on the earth they had not quitted. And more: as if some of them had not happened yet but would occur tomorrow, until at last it would seem to the boy that he himself had not come into existence yet, that none of his race nor the other subject race which his people had brought with them into the land had come here yet; that although it had been his grandfather's and then his father's

and uncle's and was not his cousin's and someday would be his own land which he and Sam hunted over, their hold upon it actually was as trivial and without reality as the now faded and archaic script in the chancery book in Jefferson which allocated it to them and that it was he, the boy, who was the guest here and Sam Father's voice the mouthpiece of the host.

Until three years ago there had been two of them, the other a full-blood Chickasaw, in a sense even more incredibly lost than Sam Fathers. He called himself Jobaker, as if it were one word. Nobody knew his history at all. He was a hermit, living in a foul little shack at the forks of the creek five miles from the plantation and about that far from any other habitation. He was a market hunter and fisherman and he consorted with nobody, black or white; no negro would even cross his path and no man dared approach his hut except Sam. And perhaps once a month the boy would find them in Sam's shop—two old men squatting on their heels on the dirt floor, talking in a mixture of negroid English and flat hill dialect and now and then a phrase of that old tongue which as time went on and the boy squatted there too listening, he began to learn. Then Jobaker died. That is, nobody had seen him in some time. Then one morning Sam was missing, nobody, not even the boy, knew when nor where, until that night when some negroes hunting in the creek bottom saw the sudden burst of flame and approached. It was Jobaker's hut, but before they got anywhere near it, someone shot at them from the shadows beyond it. It was Sam who fired, but nobody ever found Jobaker's grave.

The next morning, sitting at breakfast with his cousin, the boy saw Sam pass the dining-room window and he remembered then that never in his life before had he seen Sam nearer the house than the blacksmith-shop. He stopped eating even; he sat there and he and his cousin both heard the voices from beyond the pantry door, then the door opened and Sam entered, carrying his hat in his hand but without knocking as anyone else on the place except a house servant would have done, entered just far enough for the door to close behind him and stood looking at neither of them—the Indian face above the nigger clothes, looking at something over their heads or at something not even in the room.

"I want to go," he said. "I want to go to the Big Bottom to live."

"To live?" the boy's cousin said.

"At Major de Spain's and your camp, where you go to hunt," Sam said. "I could take care of it for you all while you aint there. I will build me a little house in the woods, if you rather I didn't stay in the big one."

"What about Isaac here?" his cousin said. "How will you get away from him? Are you going to take him with you?" But still Sam looked at neither of them, standing just inside the room with that face which showed nothing, which showed that he was an old man only when it smiled.

"I want to go," he said. "Let me go."

"Yes," the cousin said quietly. "Of course. I'll fix it with Major de Spain. You want to go soon?"

"I'm going now," Sam said. He went out. And that was all. The boy was nine then; it seemed perfectly natural that nobody, not even his cousin McCaslin, should argue with Sam. Also, since he was nine now, he could understand that Sam could leave him and their days and nights in the woods together without any wrench. He believed that he and Sam both knew that this was not only temporary but that the exigencies of his maturing, of that for which Sam had been training him all his life some day to dedicate himself, required it. They had settled that one night last summer while they listened to the hounds bringing a fox back up the creek valley; now the boy discerned in that very talk under the high, fierce August stars a presage, a warning, of this moment today. "I done taught you all there is of this settled country," Sam said. "You can hunt it good as I can now. You are ready for the Big Bottom now, for bear and deer. Hunter's meat," he said. "Next year you will be ten. You will write your age in two numbers and you will be ready to become a man. Your pa" (Sam always referred to the boy's cousin as his father, establishing even before the boy's orphanhood did that relation between them not of the ward to his guardian and kinsman and chief and head of his blood, but of the child to the man who sired his flesh and his thinking too.) "promised you can go with us then." So the boy could understand Sam's going. But he couldn't understand why now, in March, six months before the moon for hunting.

"If Jobaker's dead like they say," he said, "and Sam hasn't got anybody but us at all kin to him, why does he want to go to the Big Bottom now, when it will be six months before we get there?"

"Maybe that's what he wants," McCaslin said. "Maybe he wants to get away from you a little while."

But that was all right. McCaslin and other grown people often said things like that and he paid no attention to them, just as he paid no attention to Sam saying he wanted to go to the Big Bottom to live. After all, he would have to live there for six months, because there would be no use in going at all if he was going to turn right around and come back. And, as Sam himself had told him, he already knew all about hunting in this settled country that Sam or anybody else could teach him. So it would be all right. Summer, then the bright days after the first frost, then the cold and himself on the wagon with McCaslin this time and the moment would come and he would draw the blood, the big blood which would make him a man, a hunter, and Sam would come back home with them and he too would have outgrown the child's pursuit of rabbits and 'possums. Then he too would make one before the winter fire, talking of the old hunts and the hunts to come as hunters talked.

So Sam departed. He owned so little that could carry it. He walked. He would neither let McCaslin send him in the wagon, nor take a mule to ride. No one saw him go even. He was just gone one morning, the cabin which had never had very much in it, vacant and empty, the shop in which there never had been very much done, standing idle. Then November came at last, and now the boy

made one—himself and his cousin McCaslin and Tennie's Jim, and Major de Spain and General Compson and Walter Ewell and Boon and old Uncle Ash to do the cooking, waiting for them in Jefferson with the other wagon, and the surrey in which he and McCaslin and General Compson and Major de Spain would ride.

Sam was waiting at the camp to meet them. If he was glad to see them, he did not show it. And if, when they broke camp two weeks later to return home, he was sorry to see them go, he did not show that either. Because he did not come back with them. It was only the boy who returned, returning solitary and alone to the settled familiar land, to follow for eleven months the childish business of rabbits and such while he waited to go back, having brought with him, even from his brief first sojourn, an unforgettable sense of the big woods—not a quality dangerous or particularly inimical, but profound, sentient, gigantic and brooding, amid which he had been permitted to go to and fro at will, unscathed, why he knew not, but dwarfed and, until he had drawn honorably blood worthy of being drawn, alien.

Then November, and they would come back. Each morning Sam would take the boy out to the stand allotted him. It would be one of the poorer stands of course, since he was only ten and eleven and twelve and he had never even seen a deer running yet. But they would stand there, Sam a little behind him and without a gun himself, as he had been standing when the boy shot the running rabbit when he was eight years old. They would stand there in the November dawns, and after a while they would hear the dogs. Sometimes the chase would sweep up and past quite close, belling and invisible; once they heard the two heavy reports of Boon Hogganbeck's old gun with which he had never killed anything larger than a squirrel and that sitting, and twice they heard the flat unreverberant clap of Walter Ewell's rifle, following which you did not even wait to hear his horn.

"I'll never get a shot," the boy said. "I'll never kill one."

"Yes you will," Sam said. "You wait. You'll be a hunter. You'll be a man."

But Sam wouldn't come out. They would leave him there. He would come as far as the road where the surrey waited, to take the riding horses back, and that was all. The men would ride the horses and Uncle Ash and Tennie's Jim and the boy would follow in the wagon with Sam, with the camp equipment and the trophies, the meat, the heads, the antlers, the good ones, the wagon winding on among the tremendous gums and cypresses and oaks where no axe save that of the hunter had ever sounded, between the impenetrable walls of cane and brier—the two changing yet constant walls just beyond which the wilderness whose mark he had brought away forever on his spirit even from that first two weeks seemed to lean, stooping a little, watching them and listening, not quite inimical because they were too small, even those such as Walter and Major de Spain and old General Compson who had killed many deer and bear, their sojourn too brief and too harmless to excite to that, but just brooding, secret, tremendous, almost inattentive.

Then they would emerge, they would be out of it, the line as sharp as the demarcation of a doored wall. Suddenly skeleton cotton- and corn-fields would flow away on either hand, gaunt and motionless beneath the gray rain; there would be a house, barns, fences, where the hand of man had clawed for an instant, holding, the wall of the wilderness behind them now, tremendous and still and seemingly impenetrable in the gray and fading light, the very tiny orifice through which they had emerged apparently swallowed up. The surrey would be waiting, his cousin McCaslin and Major de Spain and General Compson and Walter and Boon dismounted beside it. Then Sam would get down from the wagon and mount one of the horses and, with the others on a rope behind him, he would turn back. The boy would watch him for a while against that tall and secret wall, growing smaller and smaller against it, never looking back. Then he would enter it, returning to what the boy believed, and thought that his cousin McCaslin believed, was his loneliness and solitude.

2

So the instant came. He pulled trigger and Sam Fathers marked his face with the hot blood which he had spilled and he ceased to be a child and became a hunter and a man. It was the last day. They broke camp that afternoon and went out, his cousin and Major de Spain and General Compson and Boon on the horses, Walter Ewell and the negroes in the wagon with him and Sam and his hide and antlers. There could have been (and were) other trophies in the wagon. But for him they did not exist, just as for all practical purposes he and Sam Fathers were still alone together as they had been that morning. The wagon wound and jolted between the slow and shifting yet constant walls from beyond and above which the wilderness watched them pass, less than inimical now and never to be inimical again since the buck still and forever leaped, the shaking gun-barrels coming constantly and forever steady at last, crashing, and still out of his instant of immortality the buck sprang, forever immortal;—the wagon jolting and bouncing on, the moment of the buck, the shot, Sam Fathers and himself and the blood with which Sam had marked him forever one with the wilderness which had accepted him since Sam said that he had done all right, when suddenly Sam reined back and stopped the wagon and they all heard the unmistakable and unforgettable sound of a deer breaking cover.

Then Boon shouted from beyond the bend of the trail and while they sat motionless in the halted wagon, Walter and the boy already reaching for their guns, Boon came galloping back, flogging his mule with his hat, his face wild and amazed as he shouted down at them. Then the other riders came around the bend, also spurring.

"Get the dogs!" Boon cried. "Get the dogs! If he had a nub on his head, he had fourteen points! Laying right there by the road in that pawpaw thicket! If I'd a knowed he was there, I could have cut his throat with my pocket knife!"

"Maybe that's why he run," Walter said. "He saw you never had your gun." He was already out of the wagon with his rifle. Then the boy was out too with his gun, and the other riders came up and Boon got off his mule somehow and was scrabbling and clawing among the duffel in the wagon, still shouting, "Get the dogs! Get the dogs!" And it seemed to the boy too that it would take them forever to decide what to do—the old men in whom the blood ran cold and slow, in whom during the intervening years between them and himself the blood had become a different and colder substance from that which ran in him and even in Boon and Walter.

"What about it, Sam?" Major de Spain said. "Could the dogs bring him back?"

"We wont need the dogs," Sam said. "If he dont hear the dogs behind him, he will circle back in here about sundown to bed."

"All right," Major de Spain said. "You boys take the horses. We'll go on out to the road in the wagon and wait there." He and General Compson and McCaslin got into the wagon and Boon and Walter and Sam and the boy mounted the horses and turned back and out of the trail. Sam led them for an hour through the gray and unmarked afternoon whose light was little different from what it had been at dawn and which would become darkness without any graduation between. Then Sam stopped them.

"This is far enough," he said. "He'll be coming upwind, and he dont want to smell the mules." They tied the mounts in a thicket. Sam led them on foot now, unpathed through the markless afternoon, the boy pressing close behind him, the two others, or so it seemed to the boy, on his heels. But they were not. Twice Sam turned his head slightly and spoke back to him across his shoulder, still walking: "You got time. We'll get there fore he does."

So he tried to go slower. He tried deliberately to decelerate the dizzy rushing of time in which the buck which he had not even seen was moving, which it seemed to him must be carrying the buck farther and farther and more and more irretrievably away from them even though there were no dogs behind him now to make him run, even though, according to Sam, he must have completed his circle now and was heading back toward them. They went on; it could have been another hour or twice that or less than half, the boy could not have said. Then they were on a ridge. He had never been in here before and he could not see that it was a ridge. He just knew that the earth had risen slightly because the underbrush had thinned a little, the ground sloping invisibly away toward a dense wall of cane. Sam stopped. "This is it," he said. He spoke to Walter and Boon: "Follow this ridge and you will come to two crossings. You will see the tracks. If he crosses, it will be at one of these three."

Walter looked about for a moment. "I know it," he said. "I've even seen your deer. I was in here last Monday. He aint nothing but a yearling."

"A yearling?" Boon said. He was panting from the walking. His face still looked a little wild. "If the one I saw was any yearling, I'm still in kindergarden."

"Then I must have seen a rabbit," Walter said. "I always heard you quit school altogether two years before the first grade."

Boon glared at Walter. "If you dont want to shoot him, get out of the way," he said. "Set down somewhere. By God, I——"

"Aint nobody going to shoot him standing here," Sam said quietly.

"Sam's right," Walter said. He moved, slanting the worn, silver-colored barrel of his rifle downward to walk with it again. "A little more moving and a little more quiet too. Five miles is still Hogganbeck range, even if we wasn't downwind." They went on. The boy could still hear Boon talking, though presently that ceased too. Then once more he and Sam stood motionless together a tremendous pin oak in a little thicket, and again there was nothing. There was only the soaring and sombre solitude in the dim light, there was the thin murmur of the faint cold rain which had not ceased all day. Then, as if it had waited for them to find their positions and become still, the wilderness breathed again. It seemed to lean inward above them, above himself and Sam and Walter and Boon in their separate lurking-places, tremendous, attentive, impartial and omniscient, the buck moving in it somewhere, not running yet since he had not been pursued, not frightened yet and never fearsome but just alert also as they were alert, perhaps already circling back, perhaps quite near, perhaps conscious also of the eye of the ancient immortal Umpire. Because he was just twelve then, and that morrning something had happened to him: in less than a second he had ceased forever to be the child he was yesterday. Or perhaps that made no difference, perhaps even a city-bred man, let alone a child, could not have understood it; perhaps only a country-bred one could comprehend loving the life he spills. He began to shake again.

"I'm glad it's started now," he whispered. He did not move to speak; only his lips shaped the expiring words: "Then it will be gone when I raise the gun——"

Nor did Sam. "Hush," he said.

"Is he that near?" the boy whispered. "Do you think——"

"Hush," Sam said. So he hushed. But he could not stop the shaking. He did not try, because he knew it would go away when he needed the steadiness—had not Sam Fathers already consecrated and absolved him from weakness and regret too?—not from love and pity for all which lived and ran and then ceased to live in a second in the very midst of splendor and speed, but from weakness and regret. So they stood motionless, breathing deep and quiet and steady. If there had been any sun, it would be near to setting now; there was a condensing, a densifying, of what he had thought was the gray and unchanging light until he realised suddenly that it was his own breathing, his heart, his blood—something, all things, and that Sam Fathers had marked him indeed, not as a mere hunter, but with something Sam had had in his turn of his vanished and forgotten people. He stopped breathing then; there was only his heart, his blood, and in the following silence the wilderness ceased to breathe also, leaning, stooping overhead with its breath held, tremendous and impartial and waiting. Then the shaking stopped too, as he had known it would, and he drew back the two heavy hammers of the gun.

Then it had passed. It was over. The solitude did not breathe again yet; it had merely stopped watching him and was looking somewhere else, even turning its back on him, looking on away up the ridge at another point, and the boy knew as well as if he had seen him that the buck had come to the edge of the cane and had either seen or scented them and faded back into it. But the solitude did not breathe again. It should have suspired again then but it did not. It was still facing, watching, what it had been watching and it was not here, not where he and Sam stood; rigid, not breathing himself, he thought, cried *No! No!*, knowing already that it was too late, thinking with the old despair of two and three years ago: *I'll never get a shot.* Then he heard it—the flat single clap of Walter Ewell's rifle which never missed. Then the mellow sound of the horn came down the ridge and something went out of him and he knew then he had never expected to get the shot at all.

"I reckon that's it," he said. "Walter got him." He had raised the gun slightly without knowing it: He lowered it again and had lowered one of the hammers and was already moving out of the thicket when Sam spoke.

"Wait."

"Wait?" the boy cried. And he would remember that—how he turned upon Sam in the truculence of a boy's grief over the missed opportunity, the missed luck. "What for? Dont you hear that horn?"

And he would remember how Sam was standing. Sam had not moved. He was not tall, squat rather and broad, and the boy had been growing fast for the past year or so and there was not much difference between them in height, yet Sam was looking over the boy's head and up the ridge toward the sound of the horn and the boy knew that Sam did not even see him; that Sam knew he was still there beside him but he did not see the boy. Then the boy saw the buck. It was coming down the ridge, as if it were walking out of the very sound of the horn which related its death. It was not running, it was walking, tremendous, unhurried, slanting and tilting its head to pass the antlers through the undergrowth, and the boy standing with Sam beside him now instead of behind him as Sam always stood, and the gun still partly aimed and one of the hammers still cocked.

Then it saw them. And still it did not begin to run. It just stopped for an instant, taller than any man, looking at them; then its muscles suppled, gathered. It did not even alter its course, not fleeing, not even running, just moving with that winged and effortless ease with which deer move, passing within twenty feet of them, its head high and the eye not proud and not haughty but just full and wild and unafraid, and Sam standing beside the boy now, his right arm raised at full length, palm-outward, speaking in that tongue which the boy had learned from

listening to him and Joe Baker in the blacksmith shop, while up the ridge Walter Ewell's horn was still blowing them in to a dead buck.

"Oleh, Chief," Sam said. "Grandfather."

When they reached Walter, he was standing with his back toward them, quite still, bemused almost, looking down at his feet. He didn't look up at all.

"Come here, Sam," he said quietly. When they reached him he still did not look up, standing above a little spike buck which had still been a fawn last spring. "He was so little I pretty near let him go," Walter said. "But just look at the track he was making. It's pretty near big as a cow's. If there were any more tracks here besides the ones he is laying in, I would swear there was another buck here that I never even saw."

3

It was dark when they reached the road where the surrey waited. It was turning cold, the rain had stopped, and the sky was beginning to blow clear. His cousin and Major de Spain and General Compson had a fire going. "Did you get him?" Major de Spain said.

"Got a good-sized swamp-rabbit with spike horns," Walter said. He slid the little buck down from his mule. The boy's cousin McCaslin looked at it.

"Nobody saw the big one?" he said.

"I dont even believe Boon saw it," Walter said. "He probably jumped somebody's straw cow in that thicket." Boon started cursing, swearing at Walter and at Sam for not getting the dogs in the first place and at the buck and all.

"Never mind," Major de Spain said. "He'll be here for us next fall. Let's get started home."

It was after midnight when they let Walter out at his gate two miles from Jefferson and later still when they took General Compson to his house and then returned to Major de Spain's, where he and McCaslin would spend the rest of the night, since it was still seventeen miles home. It was cold, the sky was clear now; there would be a heavy frost by sunup and the ground was already frozen beneath the horses' feet and the wheels and beneath their own feet as they crossed Major de Spain's yard and entered the house, the warm dark house, feeling their way up the dark stairs until Major de Spain found a candle and lit it, and into the strange room and the big deep bed, the still cold sheets until they began to warm to their bodies and at last the shaking stopped and suddenly he was telling McCaslin about it while McCaslin listened, quietly until he had finished. "You dont believe it," the boy said. "I know you dont——"

"Why not?" McCaslin said. "Think of all that has happened here, on this earth. All the blood hot and strong for living, pleasuring, that has soaked back into it. For grieving and suffering too, of course, but still getting something out of it for all that, getting a lot out of it, because after all you dont have to continue to bear what you believe is suffering; you can always choose to stop that, put an end to that. And even suffering and grieving is better than nothing; there is only one thing worse than not being

alive, and that's shame. But you cant be alive forever, and you always wear out life long before you have exhausted the possibilities of living. And all that must be somewhere; all that could not have been invented and created just to be thrown away. And the earth is shallow; there is not a great deal of it before you come to the rock. And the earth dont want to just keep things, hoard them; it wants to use them again. Look at the seed, the acorns, at what happens even to carrion when you try to bury it: it refuses too, seethes and struggles too until it reaches light and air again, hunting the sun still. And they—" the boy saw his hand in silhouette for a moment against the window beyond which, accustomed to the darkness now, he could see sky where the scoured and icy stars glittered "—they dont want it, need it. Besides, what would it want, itself, knocking around out there, when it never had enough time about the earth as it was, when there is plenty of room about the earth, plenty of places still unchanged from what they were when the blood used and pleasured in them while it was still blood?"

But we want them," the boy said. "We want them too. There is plenty of room for us and them too."

"That's right," McCaslin said. "Suppose they dont have substance, cant cast a shadow——"

"But I saw it!" the boy cried. "I saw him!"

"Steady," McCaslin said. For an instant his hand touched the boy's flank beneath the covers. "Steady. I know you did. So did I. Sam took me in there once after I killed my first deer."

VI
Recoveries
(1950–1980)

F̲ew periods in American history have been more tumultuous and disruptive than the years since World War II. With wars of intervention abroad and massive civil disturbances at home, the menace of thermonuclear destruction from without and the fear of economic collapse from within, the technologically miraculous exploration of outer space and the drug-induced exploitation and destruction of inner space, we have been living in an era marked both by heightened aspirations and by expanded fears, by deeper outrages as well as increased self-indulgence. An earlier time of radical questioning and bold experimentation has given way to a new age polarized by burgeoning cultural narcissism and crippling metaphysical uncertainty. After discovering through the Korean War and the War in Southeast Asia that they cannot simply bend the world to their will, Americans have often found it equally difficult to accept the facts of depleting natural resources and the fragility of the biosphere. After decades of social and economic well-being, Americans have more than ever been tempted to succumb to their own myths of historical entitlement. Now dependent as never before on vast ecosystems and geopolitical systems that will not respond to excessive manipulation, even by the very powerful, Americans find it increasingly difficult and painful to contemplate their own limitations as a culture and a people.

Some have responded to this crisis like spoiled children everywhere, by adopting ever more extreme and callous postures of nationalistic self-assertion. Others have learned to adapt to the present situation with a mixture of political realism and theological resignation. In the absence of any satisfactory vision of American destiny, any absolute image of American order, most contemporary writers and thinkers have been content, in the words David Ignatow wrote as an epigraph for his book *Rescue the Dead*, to "feel along the edges of life/for a way/that will lead to open land."

~~~~~~

Bernard Malamud (1914–   )

Bernard Malamud, for many years professor of language and literature at Bennington College, is one of a number of distinguished contemporary writers whose major concern is the Jewish experience in America. Like many other Jewish artists and intellectuals—Michael Gold, Henry Roth, Delmore Schwartz, and Saul Bellow, to name only a few—Malamud has discovered that America is not only a land of dreams fulfilled but also of promises betrayed; a place of disappointment, failure, oppression, and despair as well as of hope and self-realization. Malamud has exhibited a special ability to portray individuals who are sanctified by suffering. In their great but never merely acquiescent forbearance, as in their deep sympathy for those who share their lot, his vulnerable characters achieve a strange kind of grace.

"The Loan" (1953)

The sweet, the heady smell of Lieb's white bread drew customers in droves long before the loaves were baked. Alert behind the counter, Bessie, Lieb's second wife, discerned a stranger among them, a frail, gnarled man with a hard hat who hung, disjoined, at the edge of the crowd. Though the stranger looked harmless enough among the aggressive purchasers of baked goods, she was at once concerned. Her glance questioned him but he signaled with a deprecatory nod of his hatted head that he would wait—glad to (forever)—though his face glittered with misery. If suffering had marked him, he no longer sought to conceal the sign; the shining was his own—him—now. So he frightened Bessie.

She made quick hash of the customers, and when they, after her annihilating service, were gone, she returned him her stare.

He tipped his hat. "Pardon me—Kobotsky. Is Lieb the baker here?"

"Who Kobotsky?"

"An old friend"—frightening her further.

"From where?"

"From long ago."

"What do you want to see him?"

The question insulted, so Kobotsky was reluctant to say.

As if drawn into the shop by the magic of a voice, the baker, shirtless, appeared from the rear. His pink, fleshy arms had been deep in dough. For a hat he wore jauntily a flour-covered brown paper sack. His peering glasses were dusty with flour, and the inquisitive face white with it so that he resembled a paunchy ghost; but the ghost, through the glasses, was Kobotsky, not he.

"Kobotsky," the baker cried almost with a sob, for it was so many years gone Kobotsky reminded him of, when they were both at least young, and circumstances were—ah, different. Unable, for sentimental reasons, to refrain from

407

smarting tears, he jabbed them away with a thrust of the hand.

Kobotsky removed his hat—he had grown all but bald where Lieb was gray—and patted his flushed forhead with an immaculate handkerchief.

Lieb sprang forward with a stool. "Sit, Kobotsky."

"Not here," Bessie murmured.

"Customers," she explained to Kobotksy. "Soon comes the supper rush."

"Better in the back," nodded Kobotsky.

So that was where they went, happier for the privacy. But it happened that no customers came so Bessie went in to hear.

Kobotsky sat enthroned on a tall stool in a corner of the room, stoop-shouldered, his black coat and hat on, the stiff, gray-veined hands drooping over thin thighs. Lieb, peering through full moons, eased his bones on a flour sack. Besssie lent an attentive ear, but the visitor was dumb. Embarrassed, Lieb did the talking: ah, of old times. The world was new. We were, Kobotsky, young. Do you remember how both together, immigrants out of steerage, we registered in night school?

"Haben, hatte, gehabt." he cackled at the sound of it.

No word from the gaunt one on the stool. Bessie fluttered around an impatient duster. She shot a glance into the shop: empty.

Lieb, acting the life of the party, recited, to cheer his friend: " 'Come,' said the wind to the trees one day, 'Come over the meadow with me and play.' Remember, Kobotsky?"

Bessie sniffed aloud. "Lieb, the bread!"

The baker bounced up, strode over to the gas oven and pulled one of the tiered doors down. Just in time he yanked out the trays of brown breads in hot pans, and set them on the tin-top worktable.

Bessie clucked at the narrow escape.

Lieb peered into the shop. "Customers," he said triumphantly. Flushed, she went in. Kobotsky, with wetted lips, watched her go. Lieb set to work molding the risen dough in a bowl into two trays of pans. Soon the bread was baking, but Bessie was back.

The honey odor of the new loaves distracted Kobotsky. He breathed the sweet fragrance as if this were the first air he was tasting, and even beat his fist against his chest at the delicious smell.

"Oh, my God," he all but wept. "Wonderful."

"With tears," Lieb said humbly, pointing to the large pot of dough.

Kobotsky nodded.

For thirty years, the baker explained, he was never with a penny to his name. One day, out of misery, he had wept into the dough. Thereafter his bread was such it brought customers in from everywhere.

"My cakes they don't like much, but my bread and rolls they run miles to buy."

Kobotsky blew his nose, then peeked into the shop: three customers.

"Lieb"—a whisper.

Despite himself the baker stiffened.

The visitor's eyes swept back to Bessie

out front, then, under raised brows, questioned the baker.

Lieb, however, remained mute.

Kobotsky coughed clear his throat. "Lieb, I need two hundred dollars." His voice broke.

Lieb slowly sank onto the sack. He knew—had known. From the minute of Kobotsky's appearance he had weighed in his thoughts the possibility of this against the remembrance of the lost and bitter hundred, fifteen years ago. Kobotsky swore he had repaid it, Lieb said no. Afterwards a broken friendship. It took years to blot out of the system the memoried outrages.

Kobotsky bowed his head.

At least admit you were wrong, Lieb thought, waiting a cruelly long time.

Kobotsky stared at his crippled hands. Once a cutter of furs, driven by arthritis out of the business.

Lieb gazed too. The button of a truss bit into his belly. Both eyes were cloudy with cataracts. Though the doctor swore he would see after the operation, he feared otherwise.

He sighed. The wrong was in the past. Forgiven: forgiven at the dim sight of him.

"For myself, positively, but she"— Lieb nodded towards the shop—"is a second wife. Everything is in her name." He held up empty hands.

Kobotsky's eyes were shut.

"But I will ask her—" Lieb looked doubtful.

"My wife needs—"

The baker raised a palm. "Don't speak."

"Tell her—"

"Leave it to me."

He seized the broom and circled the room, raising clouds of white dust.

When Bessie, breathless, got back she threw one look at them, and with tightened lips, waited adamant.

Lieb hastily scoured the pots in the iron sink, stored the bread pans under the table and stacked the fragrant loaves. He put one eye to the slot of the oven: baking, all baking.

Facing Bessie, he broke into a sweat so hot it momentarily stunned him.

Kobotsky squirmed atop the stool.

"Bessie," said the baker at last, "this is my old friend."

She nodded gravely.

Kobotsky lifted his hat.

"His mother—God bless her—gave me many times a plate hot soup. Also when I came to this country, for years I ate at his table. His wife is a very fine person—Dora—you will someday meet her—"

Kobotsky softly groaned.

"So why I didn't meet her yet?" Bessie said, after a dozen years, still jealous of the first wife's prerogatives.

"You will."

"Why didn't I?"

"Lieb—" pleaded Kobotsky.

"Because I didn't see her myself fifteen years," Lieb admitted.

"Why not?" she pounced.

Lieb paused. "A mistake."

Kobotsky turned away.

"My fault," said Lieb.

"Because you never go any place," Bessie spat out. "Because you live always in the shop. Because it means nothing to you to have friends."

Lieb solemnly agreed.

"Now she is sick," he announced. "The doctor must operate. This will cost two hundred dollars. I promised Kobotsky—"

Bessie screamed.

Hat in hand, Kobotsky got off the stool.

Pressing palm to her bosom, Bessie lifted her arm to her eyes. She tottered. They both ran forward to catch her but she did not fall. Kobotsky retreated quickly to the stool and Lieb returned to the sink.

Bessie, her face like the inside of a loaf, quietly addressed the visitor. "I have pity for your wife but we can't help you. I am sorry, Mr. Kobotsky, we are poor people, we don't have the money."

"A mistake," Lieb cried, enraged.

Bessie strode over to the shelf and tore out a bill box. She dumped its contents on the table, the papers flying everywhere.

"Bills," she shouted.

Kobotsky hunched his shoulders.

"Bessie, we have in the bank—"

"No—"

"I saw the bankbook."

" So what if you saved a few dollars, so have you got life insurance?"

He made no answer.

"Can you get?" she taunted.

The front door banged. It banged often. The shop was crowded with customers clamoring for bread. Bessie stomped out to wait on them.

In the rear the wounded stirred. Kobotsky, with bony fingers buttoned his overcoat.

"Sit," sighed the baker.

"Lieb, I am sorry—"

Kobotsky sat, his face lit with sadness.

When Bessie finally was rid of the rush, Lieb went into the shop. He spoke to her quietly, almost in a whisper, and she answered as quietly, but it took only a minute to start them quarreling.

Kobotsky slipped off the stool. He went to the sink, wet half his handkerchief and held it to his dry eyes. Folding the damp handkerchief, he thrust it into his overcoat pocket, then took out a small penknife and quickly pared his fingernails.

As he entered the shop, Lieb was pleading with Bessie, reciting the embittered house of his toil, the enduring drudgery. And now that he had a cent to his name, what was there to live for if he could not share it with a dear friend? But Bessie had her back to him.

"Please," Kobotsky said, "don't fight. I will go away now."

Lieb gazed at him in exasperation, Bessie stayed with head averted.

"Yes," Kobotsky sighed, "the money I wanted for Dora, but she is not sick, Lieb, she is dead."

"Ai,", Lieb cried, wringing his hands.

Bessie faced the visitor, pallid.

"Not now," he spoke kindly, "five years ago."

Lieb groaned.

"The money I need for a stone on her grave. She never had a stone. Next Sunday is five years that she is dead and every year I promise her, 'Dora, this year I will give you your stone,' and every year I gave her nothing."

The grave, to his everlasting shame, lay uncovered before all eyes. He had long ago paid a fifty-dollar deposit for a headstone with her name on it in clearly chiseled letters, but had never got the rest of the money. If there wasn't one thing to do with it there was always another: first an operation; the second year he couldn't work, imprisoned again by arthritis; the third a widowed sister lost her only son and the little Kobotsky earned had to help support her; the fourth incapacitated by boils that made him ashamed to walk out into the street. This year he was at least working, but only for just enough to eat and sleep, so Dora still lay without a stone, and for aught he knew he would someday return to the cemetery and find her grave gone.

Tears sprang into the baker's eyes. One gaze at Bessie's face—at the odd looseness of neck and shoulders—told him that she too was moved. Ah, he had won out. She would now say yes, give the money, and they would then all sit down at the table and eat together.

But Bessie, though weeping, shook her head, and before they could guess what, had blurted out the story of her afflictions: how the Bolsheviki came when she was a little girl and dragged her beloved father into the snowy fields without his shoes; the shots scattered the blackbirds in the trees and the snow oozed blood; how, when she was married a year, her husband, a sweet and gentle man, an educated accountant— rare in those days and that place—died of typhus in Warsaw; and how she, abandoned in her grief, years later found sanctuary in the home of an older brother in Germany, who sacrificed his own chances to send her, before the war, to America, and himself ended, with wife and daughter, in one of Hitler's incinerators.

"So I came to America and met here a poor baker, a poor man—who was always in his life poor—without a penny and without enjoyment in his life, and I married him, God knows why, and with my both hands, working day and night, I fixed up for him his piece of business and we make now, after twelve years, a little living. But Lieb is not a healthy man, also with eyes that he needs an operation, and this is not yet everything. Suppose, God forbid, that he died, what will I do alone by myself? Where will I go, where, and who will take care of me if I have nothing?"

The baker, who had ofter heard this tale, munched, as he listened, chunks of white bread.

When she had finished he tossed the shell of a loaf away. Kobotsky, at the end of the story, held his hands over his ears.

Tears streaming from her eyes, Bessie raised her head and suspiciously sniffed the air. Screeching suddenly, she ran into the rear and with a cry wrenched open the oven door. A cloud of smoke billowed out at her. The loaves in the trays were blackened bricks—charred corpses.

Kobotsky and the baker embraced and sighed over their lost youth. They pressed mouths together and parted forever.

Paul Tillich
(1886–1965)

"Religion as a Dimension in Man's Spiritual Life" (1954)

Paul Tillich fled Hitler's Germany after being dimissed from his position as Professor of Philosophy at the University of Frankfurt in 1933. In 1940 he became an American citizen. Holding successive professorships at Union Theological Seminary in New York, Harvard University, and the University of Chicago during the postwar years, Tillich quickly became one of the foremost Protestant theologians in America.

Tillich's writing went in even more directions than he did himself. Ranging easily from depth psychology to systematic theology and from art criticism to social ethics, Tillich brought a new intellectual cosmopolitanism into American religious thinking. He also brought a new existential urgency and a fresh theological candor that enabled him to speak with persuasive force to a generation divided between the desire to believe and the inclination to doubt.

In the following essay, Tillich gives succinct expression to perhaps his best-known idea. Religion, according to Tillich, does not consist of a specific set of creedal affirmations or moral axioms that occupy only one corner of man's spiritual life, but rather constitutes those ultimate concerns that undergird the whole of a person's existence. And our ultimate concern, Tillich believed, "is that which determines our being or not-being."

As soon as one says anything about religion, one is questioned from two sides. Some Christian theologians will ask whether religion is here considered as a creative element of the human spirit rather than as a gift of divine revelation. If one replies that religion is an aspect of man's spiritual life, they will turn away. Then some secular scientists will ask whether religion is to be considered a lasting quality of the human spirit instead of an effect of changing psychological and sociological conditions. And if one answers that religion is a necessary aspect of man's spiritual life, they turn away like the theologians, but in an opposite direction.

This situation shows an almost schizophrenic split in our collective consciousness, a split which threatens our spiritual freedom by driving the contemporary mind into irrational and compulsive affirmations or negations of religion And there is as much compulsive reaction to religion on the scientific side as there is on the religious side.

Those theologians who deny that religion is an element of man's spiritual life have a real point. According to them, the meaning of religion is that man received something which does not come *from* him, but which is given *to* him and may stand against him. They insist that the relation to God is not a human possibility and that God must first relate Himself to man. One could summarize the intention of these theologians in the sentence that religion is not a creation of the human spirit (spirit with a small s) but a gift of the divine Spirit (Spirit with a capital S). Man's spirit, they would continue, is creative with respect to itself and its world, but not with respect to God. With respect to God, man is receptive and only receptive. He has no freedom to relate himself to God. This, they would add, is the meaning of the classical doctrine of the Bondage of the Will as developed by Paul, Augustine, Thomas, Luther, and Calvin. In the face of these witnesses, we certainly ask: Is it then justified to speak of religion as an aspect of the human spirit?

The opposite criticism also has its valid point. It comes from the side of the sciences of man: psychology, sociology, anthropology, and history. They emphasize the infinite diversity of religious ideas and practices, the mythological character of all religious concepts, the existence of many forms of non-religion in individuals and groups. Religion, they say (with the philosopher Comte), is characteristic for a special stage of human development. (the mythological stage), but it has no place in the scientific stage in which we are living. Religion, according to this attitude, is a transitory creation of the human spirit but certainly not an essential quality of it.

If we analyze carefully these two groups of arguments, we discover the surprising fact that although they come from opposite directions, they have something definite in common. Both the theological and the scientific critics of the belief that religion is an aspect of the human spirit define religion as man's relation to divine beings, whose existence the theological critics assert and the scientific critics deny. But it is just this idea of religion which makes any understanding of religion impossible. If you start with the question whether God does or does not exist, you can never reach Him; and if you assert that He does exist, you can reach Him even less than if you assert that He does not exist. A God about whose existence or non-existence you can argue is a thing beside others within the universe of existing things. And the question is quite justified whether such a thing does exist, and the answer is equally justified that it does not exist. It is regrettable that scientists believe that they have refuted religion when they rightly have shown that there is no evidence whatsoever for the assumption that such a being exists. Actually, they have not only not refuted religion, but they have done it a considerable service. They have forced it to reconsider and to restate the meaning of the tremendous word *God*. Unfortunately, many theologians make the same mistake. They begin their message with the assertion that there is a higher being called God, whose authoritative revelations they have received. They are more dangerous for religion than the so-called atheistic scientists. They take the first step on the road which inescapably leads to what is called atheism. Theologians who make of God a highest being who has given some people information about Himself, provoke inescapably the resistance of those who are told they must subject themselves to the authority of this information.

Against both groups of critics we affirm the validity of our subject: religion as an aspect of the human spirit. But, in doing so, we take into consideration the criticisms from both sides and the elements of truth in each of them.

When we say that religion is an aspect of the human spirit, we are saying that if we look at the human spirit from a special point of view, it presents itself to us as religious. What is this view? It is the point of view from which we can look into the depth of man's spiritual life. Relgion is not a special function of man's spiritual life, but it is the dimension of depth in all of its functions. The assertion has far-reaching consequences for the interpretation of religion, and it needs comment on each of the terms used in it.

Religion is not a special function of the human spirit! History tells us the story of how religion goes from one spiritual function to the other to find a home, and is either rejected or swallowed by them. Religion comes to the moral function and knocks at its door, certain that it will be received. Is not the ethical the nearest relative of the religious? How could it be rejected? Indeed, it is not rejected; it is taken in. But it is taken in as a "poor relation" and asked to earn its place in the moral realm by serving morality. It is admitted as long as it helps to create good citizens, good husbands and children, good employees, officials, and soldiers. But the moment in which religion makes claims of its own, it is either silenced or thrown out as superfluous or dangerous for morals.

So religion must look around for another function of man's spiritual life, and it is attracted by the cognitive function. Religion as a special way of knowledge, as mythological imagination or as mystical intuition—this seems to give a home to religion. Again religion is admitted, but as subordinate to pure knowledge, and only for a brief time. Pure knowledge, strengthened by the tremendous success of its scientific work, soon recants its half-hearted acceptance of religion and declares that religion has nothing whatsoever to do with knowledge.

Once more religion is without a home within man's spiritual life. It looks around for another spiritual function to join. And it finds one, namely, the aesthetic function. Why not try to find a place within the artistic creativity of man? religion asks itself, through the mouths of the philosophers of religion. And the artistic realm answers, through the mouths of many artists, past and present, with an enthusiastic affirmative, and invites religion not only to join with it but also to acknowledge that art *is* religion. But now religion hesitates. Does not art express reality, while religion tranforms reality? Is there not an element of unreality even in the greatest work of art? Religion remembers that it has old relations to the moral and the cognitive realms, to the good and to the true, and it resists the temptation to dissolve itself into art.

But now where shall religion turn? The whole field of man's spiritual life is taken, and no section of it is ready to give religion an adequate place. So religion turns to something that accompanies every activity of man and every function of man's spiritual life. We call it feeling. Religion is a feeling: this seems to be the end of the wanderings of religion, and this end is strongly acclaimed by all those who want to have the realms of knowledge and morals free from any religious interference. Religion, if banished to the realm of mere feeling, has ceased to be dangerous for any rational and practical human enterprise. But, we must add, it also has lost its seriousness, its truth, and its ultimate meaning. In the atmosphere of mere subjectivity of feeling without a definite object of emotion, without an ultimate content, religion dies. This also is not the answer to the question of religion as an aspect of the human spirit.

In this situation, without a home, without a place in which to dwell, religion suddenly realized that it does not need such a place, that it does not need to seek for a home. It is at home everywhere, namely, in the depth of all functions of man's spiritual life. Religion is the dimension of depth in all of them. Religion is the aspect of depth in the totality of the human spirit.

What does the metaphor *depth* mean? It means that the religious aspect points to that which is ultimate, infinite, unconditional in man's spiritual life. Religion, in the largest and most basic sense of the word, is ultimate concern. And ultimate concern is manifest in all creative functions of the human spirit. It is manifest in the moral sphere as the unconditional seriousness of the moral demand. Therefore, if someone rejects religion in the name of the moral function of the human spirit, he rejects

religion in the name of religion. Ultimate concern is manifest in the realm of knowledge as the passionate longing for ultimate reality. Therefore, if anyone rejects religion in the name of the cognitive function of the human spirit, he rejects religion in the name of religion. Ultimate concern is manifest in the aesthetic function of the human spirit as the infinite desire to express ultimate meaning. Therefore, if anyone rejects religion in the name of the aesthetic function of the human spirit, he rejects religion in the name of religion. You cannot reject religion with ultimate seriousness, because ultimate seriousness, or the state of being ultimately concerned, is itself religion. Religion is the substance, the ground, and the depth of man's spiritual life. This is the religious aspect of the human spirit.

But now the question arises, what about religion in the narrower and customary sense of the word, be it institutional religion or the religion of personal piety? If religion is present in all functions of the spiritual life, why has mankind developed religion as a special sphere among others, in myth, cult, devotion, and ecclesiastical institutions? The answer is, because of the tragic estrangement of man's spiritual life from its own ground and depth. According to the visionary who has written the last book of the Bible, there will be no temple in the heavenly Jerusalem, for God will be all in all. There will be no secular realm, and for this very reason there will be no religious realm. Religion will be again what it is essentially, the all-determining ground and substance of man's spiritual life.

Religion opens up the depth of man's spiritual life which is usually covered by the dust of our daily life and the noise of our secular work. It gives us the experience of the Holy, of something which is untouchable, awe-inspiring, an ultimate meaning, the source of ultimate courage. This is the glory of what we call religion. But beside its glory lies it shame. It makes itself the ultimate and despises the secular realm. It makes its myths and doctrines, its rites and laws into ultimates and persecutes those who do not subject themselves to it. It forgets that its own existence is a result of man's tragic estrangement from his true being. It forgets its own emergency character.

This is the reason for the passionate reaction of the secular world against religion, a reaction which has tragic consequences for the secular realm itself. For the religious and the secular realm are in the same predicament. Neither of them should be in separation from the other, and both should realize that their very existence as separated is an emergency, that both of them are rooted in religion in the larger sense of the word, in the experience of ultimate concern. To the degree in which this is realized the conflicts between the religious and the secular are overcome, and religion has rediscovered its true place in man's spiritual life, namely, in its depth, out of which it gives substance, ultimate meaning, judgment, and creative courage to all functions of the human spirit.

Richard Wilbur
(1921–   )

Poet, translator, and sometime critic, Richard Wilbur taught for a brief time at Harvard University and Wellesley College before taking up permanent residence at Wesleyan University in 1957. His verse exemplifies the virtues of control, elegance, and sublety of mind. But if his poetry shuns the formless and the indecorous, it is neither stylized nor impersonal. His best poems are lit from within by an imaginative grace that discovers the transcendent in what Wilbur calls "a world of sensible objects."

"Love Calls Us to the Things of This World" (1956)

The eyes open to a cry of pulleys,
And spirited from sleep, the
          astounded soul
Hangs for a moment bodiless and
          simple
As false dawn.
                    Outside the open
          window
The morning air is all awash with
          angels.

Some are in bed-sheets, some are
          in blouses,
Some are in smocks: but truly there
          they are.

Now they are rising together in calm
    swells
Of halcyon feeling, filling whatever
    they wear
With the deep joy of their impersonal
    breathing;

    Now they are flying in place,
        conveying
The terrible speed of their
    omnipresence, moving
And staying like white water; and now
    of a sudden
They swoon down into so rapt a quiet
That nobody seems to be there.
            The soul shrinks

    From all that it is about to
        remember,
From the punctual rape of every
    blessed day,
And cries,
        "Oh, let there be nothing on
    earth but laundry,
Nothing but rosy hands in the rising
    steam
And clear dances done in the sight of
    heaven."

    Yet, as the sun acknowledges
With a warm look the world's hunks,
    and colors,
The soul descends once more in bitter
    love
To accept the waking body, saying
    now
In a changed voice as the man yawns
    and rises,

    "Bring them down from their
        ruddy gallows;
Let there be clean linen for the backs
    of thieves;

Let lovers go fresh and sweet to be
    undone,
And the heaviest nuns walk in a pure
    floating
Of dark habits,
            keeping their difficult
    balance."

H. Richard Niebuhr (1894–1962)

H. Richard Niebuhr, for more than thirty years a professor of theology and Christian ethics at Yale Divinity School, was, like his brother Reinhold Niebuhr, an important Protestant thinker. He was influenced both by the nineteenth-century German theologian, Ernst Troeltsch, who helped him to come to grips with the problem of faith and historical relativism, and by the eighteenth–century American theologian, Jonathan Edwards, who enabled him to reconcile relativism with belief in a soverign God who reveals Himself in terms of the virtue of love. Niebuhr developed his own distinctive theological vision which drew upon, and can be applied to, a variety of American themes and issues. Indeed, much of Niebuhr's thinking dealt specifically with such American problems as voluntarism, pluralism, millennialism, and democracy, and several of his books were devoted to American topics, notably, *The Social Sources of Denominationalism* (1929) and *The King-*

dom of God in America (1937). The present selection is taken from *Radical Monotheism and Western Culture* (1960).

From *Radical Monotheism and Western Culture* (1960)

The Idea of Radical Monotheism

1. *The Social God and the Many Gods*

In ordinary discourse the word "gods" has many meanings. Now we mean by it the powers on which men call for help in time of trouble; now the forces which they summon up in their search for ecstasy; now the realities before which they experience awe and the sense of the holy; now the beings they posit in their speculative efforts to explain the origin and government of things; now the objects of adoration. The question whether religion in which all these attitudes and activities are present is a single movement of the mind and with it the query whether the word "gods" refers to entities of one class, must be left to other contexts. We are concerned now with faith as dependence on a value-center and as loyalty to a cause. Hence when we speak of "gods" we mean the gods of faith, namely, such value-centers and causes.

In this narrowed sense the plural term "gods" seems alone appropriate. The religious and also the political institutions of the West have long been officially monotheistic, so that we do not easily regard ourselves as polytheists, believers in many gods, or as henotheists, loyal to one god among many. Using the word "god" without definition we regard ourselves as either theists or atheists. But if we confine our inquiry to the forms of faith, then it seems more true to say that monotheism as value dependence and as loyalty to One beyond all the many is in constant conflict among us with the two dominant forms: A pluralism that has many objects of devotion and a social faith that has one object, which is, however, only one among many. If by gods we mean the objects of such faith then atheism seems as irreconcilable with human existence as is radical skepticism in the actuality of the things we eat, and breathe, walk upon and bump into. Atheism in this sense is no more a live alternative for us in actual personal existence, than psychological solipsism is in our physical life. To deny the reality of a supernatural being called God is one thing; to live without confidence in some center of value and without loyalty to a cause is another.

The historically and biographically primitive form of faith seems to be the henotheistic, or social, type though it has often been argued that the historic movement is from pluralism to the relative unity of a socialy organized loyalty. Whatever temporal progressions there may be, most frequently in past and present the two forms exist in uneasy rivalry with, and accommodation to, each other. We may begin with henotheism of which the nationalism we previously used to illustrate faith is a characteristic representative. Instead of the nation some smaller social unit—

family or tribe or sectarian community—or a larger one—civilization or humanity—may constitute the center of value and the cause of loyalty. In any case, where such faith prevails the ultimate reference in all answers to questions about the meaning of individual life and about the cause for which one lives, is made, in Bergson's phrase, to some closed society.[1] Such a society may number among its members the dead and the yet unborn as well as the living, supernatural as well as natural existences, animals (totem animals, for instance) as well as men, natural phenomena—wind and sky and thunder—as well as animate beings. But every participant in the group derives his value from his position in the enduring life of the community. Here he is related to an actuality that transcends his own, that continues to be though he ceases to exist. He is dependent on it as it is not dependent on him. And this applies even more to his significance than to his existence. The community is not so much his great good as the source and center of all that is good, including his own value. But the society is also his cause; its continuation, power, and glory are the unifying end of all his actions. The standard by which he judges himself and his deeds, his companions and their actions, by which also he knows himself to be judged, is the standard of loyalty to the community.

Such faith, like any faith, is exhibited not only in religious beliefs and practices but it does manifest itself in these. The sociological analysis of religion is therefore so persuasive because the kind of faith most frequently associated with religion is of the social sort. "The idea of society," says Durkheim, "is the soul of religion." The gods of religion, he maintains—though not without difficulties in view of the protean character of gods—are collective representations. By this he means, first, that they are ideas imposed on individual minds by the group; secondly, and more significantly, that "they not only come from the collective but the things which they express are of a social nature." The reality which "mythologies have represented under so many different forms but which is the universal and eternal objective cause of these sensations *sui generis* out of which religious experience is made, is society." Striking examples of the socially representative character of mythical gods or divine powers are to be found in Vesta, the domestic fire, in Themis, the projection into the cosmos of the social law, in the identification of Osiris with the Egyptian ruler, in the deification of ancestral heroes and Roman emperors. But there are even more significant though less immediately clear illustrations of the expression of social faith in religious mythologies and cults.[2] Hence it is possible to describe many movements in the history of religion by reference to the growth of society from simple and constricted to complex and more inclusive groupings. Though not all religions nor all aspects

[1]In his *The Two Sources of Morality and Religion*, 1932, Henri Bergson described the religion of humanity as that of an open, not closed, society. This interpretation seems highly questionable.

[2]E. Durkheim, *The Elementary Forms of Religious Life*, n.d., pp. 417–19; cf. also F.M. Cornford, *From Religion to Philosophy*, 1912.

of any particular religion are explicable by means of Durkheim's formula, it does have wide applicability because of the prevalence of social faith.

Not only religion, however, indicates the actuality of the henotheism that makes society, usually in the guise of a symbol, the value-center and object of loyalty. This form of faith is expressed with equal frequency in moral behavior: in obedience to written and unwritten social laws, in the sense of merit and of guilt before social authority; in the definitions of good and of right encountered in many a critical analysis of morality. When men's ultimate orientation is in their society, when it is their value-center and cause, then the social mores can make anything right and anything wrong; then indeed conscience is the internalized voice of society or of its representatives. The sociological interpreters of ethics are as persuasive as the sociological interpreters of religion, because for so many human beings, or for all of us at so many times, the implicit or explicit faith that underlies our ethos and ethics is the social faith whose god (value-center and cause) is society itself. From this one source we derive whatever unity there is in our evaluations and our behavior.

Where this faith is dominant art also may have its focus in the society. Hence patriotic art is always popular with its symbolism of the national spirit, with themes taken from the social myth or history, with its enhancement of the glory of national existence.

Henotheistic faith, usually described only as a phenomenon of primitive social life or of childhood, living in the matrix of family, evidently pervades the modern world in the form of nationalism. Its fanatical extremes, encountered in German National Socialism and Italian Fascism, have called to our attention more moderate manifestations in which some polytheism or some movements toward monotheism qualify the central devotion. Nationalism shows its character as a faith whenever national welfare or survival is regarded as the supreme end of life; whenever right and wrong are made dependent on the sovereign will of the nation, however determined; whenever religion and science, education and art, are valued by the measure of their contribution to national existence. By these tests nationalist faith shows its pervasive presence to us in our common life every day in schools and churches no less than in political utterances and policies.

The prevalence of social henotheism may be illustrated, however, also by reference to its nonnationalist versions. Whether or not Marxism is a religion may be disputed, but that it is a faith in the sense in which we are using the term seems very clear. Its ethics is class ethics, its art class art.[3] Its conflict with nationalism in our time is the conflict of one

[3]"Very frequently," said Lenin, "the bourgeoisie makes the charge that we Communists deny all morality.... In what sense do we deny ethics, morals?.... We deny all morality taken from super-human or non-class conceptions. We say that this is a deception, a swindle, a befogging of the minds of the workers and peasants in the interests of the landlords and capitalists. We say that our morality is wholly subordinate to the interests of the class-struggle of the proletariat. We deduce our morality from the facts and needs of the class-struggle of the proletariat." V. I. Lenin, *Religion* (Little Lenin Library, Vol. 7), 1933, pp. 47 f.

social faith with another, though by and large even in the sphere of Communist rule the greater potency of nationalism as a faith has been demonstrated. Another nonnationalist henotheism makes civilization its Alpha and Omega. Though a civilization is a larger community than nation it also remains a closed society; it is always one among many. Where it is the value-center and the cause, then science and religion, art and economics, political and economic institutions, ethos and ethics, are valued as manifestations of the ongoing life of the civilized society or as contributions toward its survival and enhancement. Religious communities, also, that are professedly monotheistic may, as we shall see, revert to a henotheism in which God is the name given to the principle of the religious group itself as a closed society.

The great alternative to henotheism with its relative unification of life is pluralism in faith and polytheism among the gods. Historically and in the contemporary scene such pluralism seems most frequently to follow on the dissolution of social faith. When confidence in nation or other closed society is broken, men who must live by faith take recourse to multiple centers of value and scatter their loyalties among many causes. When the half-gods go the minimal gods arrive. Faith in the social value-center may be dissolved in acids produced in many bitter experiences. Internal conflicts, the recognition that the social loyalties are being used to further the interests of power-seeking individuals or groups; the revelation that the apparently unified society is

without integrity; the rational dissolution of social mythologies; encounters with other societies superior in power or glory; eventually, the breakup of a community or its disappearance into some larger mass—these shatter the confidence that life is worthwhile as lived from and toward the communal center. The natural, perennial faith of men in the society in which they were born—whose authority governed them, whose laws protected them, whose language gave them their logic, which nurtured them in life and by remembrance maintains them in death, for whose sake they reared their children, labored and fought—evermore comes to a cheerless end among large and little, conscious and unconscious treasons, or among natural and political disasters, encountered or foreseen. It is in such a situation that man's other faith, polytheism, never wholly suppressed even in the the midst of his social loyalties, is likely to become dominant.

To be sure, among the most critical and most self-conscious men the dissolution of communal faith may call forth an effort to substitute self for society, to make isolated selfhood both value-center and cause. Epicureanism and existentialism exemplify such an effort. In the former the self seems to seek its center within itself but really finds it in something imposed on the self, the pain-and-pleasure feeling that is the constant accompaniment of conscious existence. On this dual sentiency all that is valuable and disvaluable depends. Pleasurable existence even becomes a kind of cause, since the reasoning self is now required to organize its activities toward the maintenance and enhancement of a pleasurable state of feeling; it is even guilty before itself when it allows itself to be swayed by passion to seek illusory pleasures that are followed by pain. Moreover, this sad philosophy of life is overshadowed at all times by the inescapable realities of pain and of death. If pleasure makes life worth living, pain makes it not only valueless but disvaluable, while the death of the self is the end of all transient value and disvalue. Existentialism is a more robust assertion of faith seeking a center in the self and a cause projected by a self. In its most radical form it has man making himself "man in order to be God" and "losing himself in order that the self-cause may exist."[4] Such extreme existentialism seems to represent the dying effort of the self to maintain itself by faith—but now by faith in nothing. Its confidence is not the confidence *in* the self but *of* a self, and it is confidence in nothing; its cause is not the self but the self projecting itself toward nothing.

Epicureanism and existentialism look like ghostly survivals of faith among men who, forsaken by the gods, continue to hold on to life. The more common alternative to communal confidence and loyalty appears in that less radical egoism in which an unintegrated, diffuse self-system depends for its meanings on many centers and gives its partial loyalties to many interests. This is polytheism whatever mythology accompany the pluralistic faith. In it a break has occurred between the centers

[4]Jean-Paul Sartre, *Being and Nothingness,* 1956, p. 626.

of values and the causes which for henotheism were one. Now men look for their worth to various beings, human and superhuman, who value them or from whom by effort they can extract some recognition of value. The old sense that the self is important because it is and exists as part of one enduring community is replaced by the feeling that it is justified in living only insofar as it can prove its worth. In time when supernatural beings are thought to regard the actions of men, value dependence becomes a frantic effort to satisfy these gods that the believer is worthy of their attention. When there are no supernatural beings in one's world then the proof of worth must be offered to other humans, to the prestige persons in one's environment. These become the centers of valuation. Their presence is supplemented by beings to whom the self looks for unmerited recognition. The need to be valued for one's own sake rather than for one's achievements may manifest itself in restless searching for transient lovers; it may also appear in the cultivation of a piety that looks to the Deity or deities of established religion for love while it scarcely thinks of them as causes requiring loyalty. Within Christendom Jesus as the lover of the soul, a kind heavenly Father, a comforting Holy Spirit, a compassionate Virgin, may play roles in such piety that are hard to distinguish religiously, morally, or psychologically, from the roles of guardian spirits in other societies. They are looked to for assurance of worth, while the self continues to pursue interests of many sorts and gives its fragmented loyalty to many causes.

For as the sources of value are many in polytheism so are the causes. These, however, are no longer realities requiring unified fidelity; they have become interests that from moment to moment attract vagrant potencies resident in the mind and body. To be sure, their objective nature may be posited; they may be given semipersonal names, such as Truth, Beauty, Justice, Peace, Love, Goodness, Pleasure. A kind of theology or mythology of such gods may even be developed which maintains that these "Values" have being and power apart from all human desiring; that they exercise claims upon men. Or it may be argued that nothing objective is present, that values are projections; that the basis of science is curiosity, of art the urge to make, of politics and morality the will to power. More commonly the question about the ontological status of such gods is avoided by naturalistic as well as by supernaturalistic polytheists. They move simply and uncritically from service of the lares and penates of the home to devotion to the public welfare, to participation in the worship of established religion, to concern for the increase of knowledge, to nurture of the arts.

The pluralism of the gods has its counterpart in the pluralism of self and society. What is valuable in the self is not its being in wholeness or selfhood but the activities, the knowing, creating, loving, worshiping, and directing that issue from it. It has become a bundle of functions tied together by the fibers of the body and the brain. So also the society is an assemblage of associations devoted to many partial interests, held together in meaningful unity by no common derivation from a value-center and by no loyalty to an inclusive cause.

Some thirty years ago Walter Lippmann described the situation of pluralistic modern man in words even more applicable today. "Each ideal is supreme within a sphere of its own. There is no point of reference outside which can determine the relative value of competing ideals. The modern man desires health, he desires money, he desires power, beauty, love, truth, but which of them he shall desire the most since he cannot pursue them all to their logical conclusions, he no longer has any means of deciding. His impulses are no longer part of one attitude toward life; his ideals are no longer in a hierarchy under one lordly ideal. They have become differentiated. They are free and they are incommensurable."[5] Polytheism of this sort is no peculiarly modern problem. It has appeared in every period of human history in which social faith has been shattered.

2. Radical Monotheism

There is a third form of human faith with which we are acquainted in the West, more as hope than as datum, more perhaps as a possibility than as an actuality, yet also as an actuality that has modified at certain emergent periods our natural social faith and our polytheism. In all the times and areas of our Western history this faith has struggled with its rivals, without becoming triumphant save in passing moments and in the clarified intervals of personal exis-

[5]*Preface to Morals*, 1929, p. 111.

tence. We look back longingly at times to some past age when, we think, confidence in the One God was the pervasive faith of men; for instance, to early Christianity, or to the church society of the Middle Ages, or to early Protestantism, or to Puritan New England, or to the pious nineteenth century. But when we study these periods we invariably find in them a mixture of the faith in the One God with social faith and polytheism; and when we examine our longings we often discover that what we yearn for is the security of the closed society with its social confidence and social loyalty. It is very questionable, despite many protestations to the contrary, despite the prevalence of self-pity among some modern men because "God is dead," that anyone has ever yearned for radical faith in the One God.

We shall call this third form of faith radical monotheism.[6] We must try to describe it formally, in abstract fashion, though the form does not appear in our history or in our contemporary life otherwise than as embodied and expressed in the concreteness of communal and personal, of religious and moral existence.

For radical monotheism the value-center is neither closed society nor the principle of such a society but the principle of being itself; its reference is

[6]The term "radical monotheism" is suggested by Rudolf Bultmann's definition of the ethics of Jesus as "radical obedience," by Erik Peterson's book *Der Monotheismus als Politisches Problem,* and by the definition liberal theology offered of prophetic religion as "ethical monotheism." Each of these definitions seem to be somewhat inaccurate yet each is helpful as a pointer.

to no one reality among the many but to One beyond all the many, whence all the many derive their being, and by participation in which they exist. As faith, it is reliance on the source of all being for significance of the self and of all that exists. It is the assurance that because I am, I am valued, and because you are, you are beloved, and because whatever is has being, therefore it is worthy of love. It is the confidence that whatever is, is good, because it exists as one thing among the many which all have their origin and their being, in the One—the principle of being which is also the principle of value. In Him we live and move and have our being not only as existent but as worthy of existence and worthy in existence. It is not a relation to any finite, natural or supernatural, value-center that confers value on self and some of its companions in being, but it is value relation to the One to whom all being is related. Monotheism is less than radical if it makes a distinction between the principle of being and the principle of value; so that while all being is acknowledged as absolutely dependent for existence on the One, only some beings are valued as having worth for it; or if, speaking in religious language, the Creator and the God of grace are not identified.

Radical monotheism is not in the first instance a theory about being and then a faith, as though the faith orientation toward the principle of being as value-center needed to be preceded by an ontology that established the unity of the realm of being and its source in a single power beyond it. It is not at all evident that the One beyond the many, whether made known in revelation or always present to man in hiddenness, is principle of being before it is principle of value. Believing man does not say first, "I believe in a creative principle." and then, "I believe that the principle is gracious, that is, good toward what issues from it." He rather says, "I believe in God the Father, Almighty Maker of heaven and earth." This is a primary statement, a point of departure and not a deduction. In it the principle of being is identified with the principle of value and the principle of value with the principle of being.[7] Neither is it evident, despite our intellectualist bias toward identifying ourselves with our reason, that the self is more itself as reasoning self than as faithful self, concerned about value. It is the "I" that reasons and the "I" that believes; it is present in its believing as in its reasoning. Yet the believing self must reason; there is always a reasoning in faith so that rational efforts to understand the One beyond the many are characteristic of radical monotheism. Only, the orientation of faith toward the One does not wait on the development of theory.

As faith reliance, radical monotheism depends absolutely and assuredly for the worth of the self on the same principle by which it has being; and since that principle is the same by which

[7] I use the terms "principle of being" and "principle of value" in distinction from the terms "highest being" and "highest value," or "Being" and "the Good," because the principle of being is not immediately to be identified with being nor the principle of value with value. As many theologians have undertaken to say, God is beyond being; they ought also to say that he is beyond value. That by reference to which all things have their value is not itself a value in the primary sense.

all things exist it accepts the value of whatever is. As faith loyalty, it is directed toward the principle and the realm of being as the cause for the sake of which it lives. Such loyalty on the one hand is claimed by the greatness and inclusiveness of the objective cause; on the other hand it is given in commitment, since loyalty is the response of a self and not the compulsive reaction of a thing. The cause also has a certain duality. On the one hand it is the principle of being itself; on the other, it is the realm of being. Whether to emphasize the one or the other may be unimportant, since the principle of being has a cause, namely, the realm of being, so that loyalty to the principle of being must include loyalty to its cause; loyalty to the realm of being, on the other hand, implies keeping faith with the principle by virtue of which it is, and is one realm.

The counterpart, then, of universal faith assurance is universal loyalty. Such universal loyalty cannot be loyalty to loyalty, as Royce would have it, but is loyalty to all existents as bound together by a loyalty that is not only resident in them but transcends them. It is not only their loyalty to each other that makes them one realm of being, but the loyalty that comes from beyond them, that originates and maintains them in their particularity and their unity. Hence universal loyalty expresses itself as loyalty to each particular existent in the community of being and to the universal community. Universal loyalty does not express itself as loyalty to the loyal but to whatever is; not as reverence for the reverent but as reverence for being;

not as the affirmation of world affirmers but as world affirmation. Such loyalty gives form to morality, since all moral laws and ends receive their form, though not their immediate content, from the form of faith reliance and faith loyalty. Love of the neighbor is required in every morality formed by a faith; but in polytheistic faith the neighbor is defined as the one who is near me in my interest group, *when* he is near me in that passing association. In henotheistic social faith my neighbor is my fellow in the closed society. Hence in both instances the counterpart of the law of neighbor-love is the requirement to hate the enemy. But in radical monotheism my neighbor is my companion in being; though he is my enemy in some less than universal context the requirement is to love him. To give to everyone his due is required in every context; but what is due to him depends on the relation in which he is known to stand.

All moral laws receive a universal form in the context of radically monotheistic faith and it is an evidence of the influence of radical faith that all our mores are haunted by the presence to the conscience of a universal form of those laws that for the most part we interpret in pluralistic and closed-society fashion. To such a universal form testimony is offered by Kant's categorical imperative, by the intuitions of universal equity and universal benevolence that Clarke and Sidgwick cannot escape, by the *prima facie* rightness of promise-keeping that Ross contends for. It is one thing to maintain that the universal form is given with reason or conscience itself; it is another thing to point out that where the universal form of moral law is acknowledged the actuality of a universal community and the claim of a universal cause have also been recognized.

The meaning of radical monotheism may be further clarified if we compare it with some of the nonradical, mixed forms of faith in which it seems to appear in disguised or broken fashion. Something like monotheism is present in henotheism at those points in personal or social life where a closed society fills the whole horizon of experience, where it is in fact not yet a closed society because everything that comes into view is a part of it. But as soon as in-group and out-group are distinguished and as soon as the contingency of the society, as not self-existent but as cast into existence, is brought to consciousness, such embryonic radical monotheism is put to the test. Though the possibility of a movement toward conscious radical monotheism may be present in such a moment, the apparently invariable process in human history at such points leads toward closed-society faith or toward polytheism or toward both.

The religion of humanity has been proclaimed by many critics of the little faiths in little gods which they find represented in the religious or national communities of their time. So far as there is protest here against forms of faith in which some men assure themselves of a special value because of their relation to a special god and in which they practice an exclusive loyalty that does not extend beyond the household of faith, we must regard such protest as movement toward universal faith assurance and faith loyalty. So Henri Bergson's critique of the defensive ethics and religion of closed societies, and his espousal of the aspiring religion and morals of open society, seem to move toward monotheism. But when he defines the open society as humanity, this aspiring religion and morality reveal themselves as merely the prelude to a new defensive and closed-society faith; so it was also with Comte's religion of humanity. Nothing human is alien to the believer in humanity and he is alien to no other human; but mankind for him remains alien in a world that contains so many other powers besides itself; and all these existents, whatever their mode of being, are alien to it. Be they worlds, or ideas, or ideals, or microbes, they derive their value only from man, and mankind's meaning depends on itself. And where does this faith find the integrating loyalty that makes the human community one? Mankind does not find the unifying center within itself any more than any individual person does. The religion of humanism, starting as protest against the doubtful assurance and the partial loyalties of closed societies, ends with an enlarged but yet dubious and partial closed-society faith. It remains a kind of henotheism.

Again naturalism, insofar as it expresses a faith, as it often does, is intelligible to us as a movement of protest against exclusive loyalties and dubious assurances of value. Most frequently the faith it seeks to live by is humanistic but sometimes it sees man as significant because of his participation in a more than human community, the world of nature. Whether this reality whence he derives his being is regarded as implicitly purposive, moving toward unspecified good ends in wonderful progression, or whether it be regarded aesthetically as marvellous in its unity of the diverse, or whether it be otherwise conceived as unified, still it is from nature that man derives his meaning. Nothing natural is alien to him and he is alien to nothing natural. Moreover, nature becomes an object of loyalty, a cause. To understand nature through science, not because its forces can so be made serviceable to man, but because nature is there and is remarkable; to find out its "laws" and willingly to accept and conform to them; to make explicit its implicit purposes—this becomes man's purpose in naturalistic faith. As a faith it is more inclusive than even humanism. But it is also a closed-society faith and not a radical monotheism. Being is greater in extent than nature as is indicated by the place naturalism must accord to ideals that attract and compel men, which, it believes, somehow emerge out of nature yet are not actual in it.[8] In such naturalism the conflict of radical monotheism with henotheism comes to appearance, yet naturalism remains henotheistic in its refusal even to entertain the possibility that there are provinces of being not accessible to its special methods of understanding, in its reduction of all value to value-in-relation-to-nature. Into its faith loyalty an element of polytheism also intrudes, expressed in the manifoldness of ideals to be served.

[8]See for instance John Dewey's *A Common Faith*, 1934, esp. Chap. II. In writing this section I have also had in mind the unacknowledged role that the ideal of human liberty plays in Spinoza's *Ethics*.

More inclusive than humanism, less so than naturalism, is Albert Schweitzer's faith, so far as this is expressed in his writings rather than in his action; for in this case the confession of a life lived is greater than the confession in words. "Reverence for life" means that life is the value-center; whatever lives is good and to be reverenced because it participates in life and is the creation of life. Life is the value-center rather than the value; living beings call forth reverence because they are functions of the will-to-live. Reverence for life is also the expression of a loyalty that goes out to the whole realm of the living and every member of it. The man who has consciously found his ground in the unconscious will-to-live "feels a compulsion," writes Schweitzer, "to give to every will-to-live the same reverence for life that he gives to his own. He experiences that other life in his own. He accepts as being good: to preserve life, to promote life, to raise to its highest value life which is capable of development; and as being evil: to destroy life, to injure life, to repress life which is capable of development. This is the absolute, fundamental principle of the moral."[9] One notes the protest in Schweitzer's assertion of faith against all closed systems, including humanism. But he is not asserting a radically monotheistic faith. This is the henotheism of the community of the living which excludes from the realm of value all that is not alive; and from the sphere of loyalty all beings that are not endowed with that biological will-to-live I find within myself. A

[9]*Out of My Life and Thought*, 1933, pp. 186–88.

radical monotheism would include reverence for the dead, and that not simply because they were once alive; it would include also reverence for beings, inorganic perhaps, perhaps ideal, that though not living claim the wondering and not exploitative attention of us other creatures that have the will-to-live.

All such ways of faith seem, at least as protests, to be movements in the direction of radical monotheism. Yet they all fall short of the radical expression; each excludes some realm of being from the sphere of value; each is claimed by a cause less inclusive than the realm of being in its wholeness.

Radical monotheism dethrones all absolutes short of the principle of being itself. At the same time it reverences every relative existent. Its two great mottoes are: "I am the Lord thy God; thou shalt have no other gods before me" and "Whatever is, is good."

~~~~~~~~~~~~~~~~~~~~~~~~~~~~

James Wright
(1927–1980)

James Wright, poet and translator, first began to write in the philosophical, discursive mode of earlier moderns like Edwin Arlington Robinson and Robert Frost. In his later work, however, he has created a more open, less formal style in which images take on a life of their own. His most recent poetry is divided between political subjects and the immanent regenerative possibilities of the world of nature. His best poems seem to work by a process that is wholly without artifice as well as deeply religious. Even when they begin as narratives and move through assertions, as in "The Blessing," they end with epiphanies, incandescent moments of revelation. The mystery is not so much in the place one arrives as in how one got there.

"A Blessing" (1961)

Just off the highway to Rochester,
    Minnesota,
Twilight bounds softly forth on the
    grass.
And the eyes of those two Indian
    ponies
Darken with kindness.
They have come gladly out of the
    willows
To welcome my friend and me.
We step over the barbed wire into the
    pasture
Where they have been grazing all day,
    alone.
They ripple tensely, they can hardly
    contain their happiness
That we have come.
They bow shyly as wet swans. They
    love each other.
There is no loneliness like theirs.
At home once more,
They begin munching the young tufts
    of spring in the darkness.
I would lilke to hold the slenderer one
    in my arms,
For she has walked over to me

And nuzzled my left hand.
She is black and white,
Her mane falls wild on her forehead,
And the light breeze moves me to
    caress her long ear
That is delicate as the skin over a girl's
    wrist.
Suddenly I realize
That if I stepped out of my body I
    would break
Into blossom.

James Baldwin
(1924–   )

James Baldwin, novelist, playwright, essayist, is one of the foremost literary spokesmen for the black experience in America and one of the most gifted of contemporary writers. The following selection comes from "Down at the Cross" in *The Fire Next Time* and was originally published as "Letter from a Region in My Mind" in *The New Yorker*. This essay was written during the years of the civil rights struggle and accurately prophesies the increasing militancy and violence of that movement. Baldwin's essay transcends its historical moment, however, because it gives effective expression to structures of feeling and patterns of response typical of the experience of generations of black people in America. Baldwin's subject is a variant of what W. E. B. DuBois first defined as the double consciousness of black Americans. His purpose is not only to dramatize its effects but to portray the way religion provided a way of coping with them.

From *The Fire Next Time* (1963)

I underwent, during the summer that I became fourteen, a prolonged religious crisis. I use the word "religious" in the common, and arbitrary, sense, meaning that I then discovered God, His saints and angels, and His blazing Hell. And since I had been born in a Christian nation, I accepted this Deity as the only one. I supposed Him to exist only within the walls of a church—in fact, of *our* church—and I also supposed that God and safety were synonymous. The word "safety" brings us to the real meaning of the word "religious" as we use it. Therefore, to state it in another, more accurate way, I became, during my fourteenth year, for the first time in my life, afraid—afraid of the evil within me and afraid of the evil without. What I saw around me that summer in Harlem was what I had always seen; nothing had changed. But now, without any warning, the whores and pimps and racketeers on the Avenue had become a personal menace. It had not before occurred to me that I could become one of them, but now I realized that we had been produced by the same circumstances. Many of my comrades were clearly headed for the Avenue, and my father said that I was headed that way, too. My friends began to drink and smoke, and embarked—at first avid, then groaning—on their sexual careers. Girls, only slightly older than I was, who sang in the choir or taught Sunday school, the children of holy parents, underwent, before my eyes, their incredible metamorphosis, of which the most bewildering aspect was not their budding breasts or their rounding behinds but something deeper and more subtle, in their eyes, their heat, their odor, and the inflection of their voices. Like the strangers on the Avenue, they became, in the twinkling of an eye, unutterably different and fantastically *present*. Owing to the way I had been raised, the abrupt discomfort that all this aroused in me and the fact that I had no idea what my voice or my mind or my body was likely to do next caused me to consider myself one of the most depraved people on earth. Matters were not helped by the fact that these holy girls seemed rather to enjoy my terrified lapses, our grim, guilty, tormented experiments, which were at once as chill and joyless as the Russian steppes and hotter, by far, than all the fires of Hell.

Yet there was something deeper than these changes, and less definable, that frightened me. It was real in both the boys and the girls, but it was, somehow, more vivid in the boys. In the case of the girls, one watched them turning into matrons before they had become women. They began to manifest a curious and really rather terrifying single-mindedness. It is hard to say exactly how this was conveyed: something implacable in the set of the lips, something farseeing (seeing what?) in the eyes, some new and crushing determination in the walk, something peremptory in the voice. They did not tease us, the boys, any more; they reprimanded us sharply, saying, "You better be thinking about your soul!" For the girls also saw the evidence on the Avenue, knew what the price would be, for them, of one misstep, knew that they had to be protected and that we were the only protection there was. They understood that they must act as God's decoys, saving the souls of the boys for Jesus and binding the bodies of the boys in marriage. For this was the beginning of our burning time, and "It is better," said St. Paul—who elsewhere, with a most unusual and stunning exactness, described himself as a "wretched man"— "to marry than to burn." And I began to feel in the boys a curious, wary, bewildered despair, as though they were now settling in for the long, hard winter of life. I did not know then what it was that I was reacting to; I put it to myself that they were letting themselves go. In the same way that the girls were destined to gain as much weight as their mothers, the boys, it was clear, would rise no higher than their fathers. School began to reveal itself, therefore, as a child's game that one could not win, and boys dropped out of school and went to work. My father wanted me to do the same. I refused, even though I no longer had any illusions about what an education could do for me; I had already encountered too many college-graduate handymen. My friends were now "downtown," busy as they put it, "fighting the man." They began to care

less about the way they looked, the way they dressed, the things they did; presently, one found them in twos and threes and fours, in a hallway, sharing a jug of wine or a bottle of whiskey, talking, cursing, fighting, sometimes weeping: lost, and unable to say what it was that oppressed them, except that they knew it was "the man"—the white man. And there seemed to be no way whatever to remove this cloud that stood between them and the sun, between them and love and life and power, between them and whatever it was that they wanted. One did not have to be very bright to realize how little one could do to change one's situation; one did not have to be abnormally sensitive to be worn down to a cutting edge by the incessant and gratuitous humiliation and danger one encountered every working day, all day long. The humiliation did not apply merely to working days, or workers; I was thirteen and was crossing Fifth Avenue on my way to the Forty-second Street library, and the cop in the middle of the street muttered as I passed him, "Why don't you niggers stay uptown where you belong?" When I was ten, and didn't look, certainly, any older, two policemen amused themselves with me by frisking me, making comic (and terrifying) speculations concerning my ancestry and probably sexual prowess, and for good measure, leaving me flat on my back in one of Harlem's empty lots. Just before and then during the Second World War, many of my friends fled into the service, all to be changed there, and rarely for the beter, many to be ruined, and many to die. Others fled to other states and cities—that is, to other ghettos. Some went on wine or whiskey or the needle, and are still on it. And others, like me, fled into the church.

For the wages of sin were visible everywhere, in every wine-stained and urine-splashed hallway, in every clanging ambulance bell, in every scar on the faces of the pimps and their whores, in every helpless, newborn baby being brought into this danger, in every knife and pistol fight on the Avenue, and in every disastrous bulletin: a cousin, mother of six, suddenly gone mad, the children parcelled out here and there; an indestructible aunt rewarded for years of hard labor by a slow, agonizing death in a terrible small room; someone's bright son blown into eternity by his own hand; another turned robber and carried off to jail. It was a summer of dreadful speculations and discoveries, of which these were not the worst. Crime became real, for example—for the first time—not a possibility but as *the* possibility. One would never defeat one's circumstances by working and saving one's pennies; one would never, by working, acquire that many pennies, and besides, the social treatment accorded even the most successful Negroes proved that one needed, in order to be free, something more than a bank account. One needed a handle, a lever, a means of inspiring fear. It was absolutely clear that the police would whip you and take you in as long as they could get away with it, and that everyone else—housewives, taxi-drivers, elevator boys, dishwashers, bartenders, lawyers, judges, doctors, and grocers—would never, by the operation of any

generous human feeling, cease to use you as an outlet for his frustrations and hostilities. Neither civilized reason nor Christian love would cause any of those people to treat you as they presumably wanted to be treated; only the fear of your power to retaliate would cause them to do that, or to seem to do it, which was (and is) good enough. There appears to be a vast amount of confusion on this point, but I do not know many Negroes who are eager to be "accepted" by white people, still less to be loved by them; they, the blacks, simply don't wish to be beaten over the head by the whites every instant of our brief passage on this planet. White people in this country will have quite enough to do in learning how to accept and love themselves and each other, and when they have achieved this—which will not be tomorrow and may very well be never—the Negro problem will no longer exist, for it will no longer be needed.

People more advantageously placed than we in Harlem were, and are, will no doubt find the psychology and the view of human nature sketched above dismal and shocking in the extreme. But the Negro's experience of the white world cannot possibly create in him any respect for the standards by which the white world claims to live. His own condition is overwhelming proof that white people do not live by these standards. Negro servants have been smuggling odds and ends out of white homes for generations, and white people have been delighted to have them do it, because it has assuaged a dim guilt and testified to the intrinsic superiority of white people. Even the most doltish and servile Negro could scarcely fail to be impressed by the disparity between his situation and that of the people for whom he worked; Negroes who were neither doltish nor servile did not feel that they were doing anything wrong when they robbed white people. In spite of the Puritan-Yankee equation of virtue with well-being, Negroes had excellent reasons for doubting that money was made or kept by any very striking adherence to the Christian virtues; it certainly did not work that way for black Christians. In any case, white people, who had robbed black people of their liberty and who profited by this theft every hour that they lived, had no moral ground on which to stand. They had the judges, the juries, the shotguns, the law—in a word, power. But it was a criminal power, to be feared but not respected, and to be outwitted in any way whatever. And those virtues preached but not practiced by the white world were merely another means of holding Negroes in subjection.

It turned out, then, that summer, that the moral barriers that I had supposed to exist between me and the dangers of a criminal career were so tenuous as to be nearly non-existent. I certainly could not discover any principled reason for not becoming a criminal, and it is not my poor, God-fearing parents who are to be indicted for the lack but this society. I was icily determined—more determined, really, than I then knew—never to make my peace with the ghetto but to die and go to Hell before I would let any white man spit on me, before I would accept my "place" in this repub-

lic. I did not intend to allow the white people of this country to tell me who I was, and limit me that way, and polish me off that way. And yet, of course, at the same time, I *was* being spat on and defined and described and limited, and could have been polished off with no effort whatever. Every Negro boy—in my situation during those years, at least—who reaches this point realizes, at once, profoundly, because he wants to live, that he stands in great peril and must find, with speed, a "thing," a gimmick, to lift him out, to start him on his way. *And it does not matter what the gimmick is.* It was this last realization that terrified me and—since it revealed that the door opened on so many dangers—helped to hurl me into the church. And, by an unforeseeable paradox, it was my career in the church that turned out, precisely, to be my gimmick.

For when I tried to assess my capabilities, I realized that I had almost none. In order to achieve the life I wanted, I had been dealt, it seemed to me, the worst possible hand. I could not become a prizefighter—many of us tried but very few succeeded. I could not sing. I could not dance. I had been well conditioned by the world in which I grew up, so I did not yet dare take the idea of becoming a writer seriously. The only other possibility seemed to involve my becoming one of the sordid people on the Avenue, who were not really as sordid as I then imagined but who frightened me terribly, both because I did not want to live that life and because of what they made me feel. Everything inflamed me, and that was bad enough, but I myself had also become a source of fire and temptation. I had been far too well raised, alas, to suppose that any of the extremely explicit overtures made to me that summer, sometimes by boys and girls but also, more alarmingly, by older men and women, had anything to do with my attractiveness. On the contrary, since the Harlem idea of seduction is, to put it mildly, blunt, whatever these people saw in me merely confirmed my sense of my depravity.

It is certainly sad that the awakening of one's senses should lead to such a merciless judgment of oneself—to say nothing of the time and anguish one spends in the effort to arrive at any other—but it is also inevitable that a literal attempt to mortify the flesh should be made among black people like those with whom I grew up. Negroes in this country—and Negroes do not, strictly or legally speaking, exist in any other—are taught really to despise themselves from the moment their eyes open on the world. This world is white and they are black. White people hold the power, which means that they are superior to blacks (intrinsically, that is: God decreed it so), and the world has innumerable ways of making this difference known and felt and feared. Long before the Negro child perceives this difference, and even longer before he understands it, he has begun to react to it, he has begun to be controlled by it. Every effort made by the child's elders to prepare him for a fate from which they cannot protect him causes him secretly, in terror, to begin to await, without knowing that he is doing so, his mysterious and inexorable punishment. He must be "good" not only in order to

please his parents and not only to avoid being punished by them; behind their authority stands another, nameless and impersonal, infinitely harder to please, and bottomlessly cruel. And this filters into the chid's consciousness through his parents' tone of voice as he is being exhorted, punished, or loved; in the sudden, uncontrollable note of fear heard in his mother's or his father's voice when he has strayed beyond some particular boundary. He does not know what the boundary is, and he can get no explanation of it, which is frightening enough, but the fear he hears in the voices of his elders is more frightening still. The fear that I heard in my father's voice, for example, when he realized that I really *believed* I could do anything a white boy could do, and had every intention of proving it, was not at all like the fear I heard when one of us was ill or had fallen down the stairs or strayed too far from the house. It was another fear, a fear that the child, in challenging the white world's assumptions, was putting himself in the path of destruction. A child cannot, thank Heaven, know how vast and how merciless is the nature of power, with what unbelievable cruelty people treat each other. He reacts to the fear in his parents' voices because his parents hold up the world for him and he has no protection without them. I defended myself, as I imagined, against the fear my father made me feel by remembering that he was very old-fashioned. Also, I prided myself on the fact that I already knew how to outwit him. To defend oneself against a fear is simply to insure that one will, one day, by conquered by it; fears must be faced.

As for one's wits, it is just not true that one can live by them—not, that is, if one wishes really to live. That summer, in any case, all the fears with which I had grown up, and which are now a part of me and controlled my vision of the world, rose up like a wall between the world and me, and drove me into the church.

As I look back, everything I did seems curiously deliberate, though it certainly did not seem deliberate then. For example, I did not join the church of which my father was a member and in which he preached. My best friend in school, who attended a different church, had already "surrendered his life to the Lord," and he was very anxious about my soul's salvation. (I wasn't, but any human attention was better than none.) One Saturday afternoon, he took me to his church. There were no services that day, and the church was empty, except for some women cleaning and some other women praying. My friend took me into the back room to meet his pastor—a woman. There she sat, in her robes, smiling, an extremely proud and handsome woman, with Africa, Europe, and the America of the American Indian blended in her face. She was perhaps forty-five or fifty at this time, and in our world she was a very celebrated woman. My friend was about to introduce me when she looked at me and smiled and said, "Whose little boy are you?" Now this, unbelievably, was precisely the phrase used by pimps and racketeers on the Avenue when they suggested, both humorously and intensely, that I "hang out" with them. Perhaps part of the terror they had caused me to feel came from the fact that I unquestionably wanted to be *somebody's* little boy. I was so frightened, and at the mercy of so many conundrums, that inevitably, that summer, *someone* would have taken me over; one doesn't, in Harlem, long remain standing on any auction block. It was my good luck—perhaps—that I found myself in the church racket instead of some other, and surrendered to a spiritual seduction long before I came to any carnal knowledge. For when the pastor asked me, with that marvellous smile, "Whose little boy are you?" my heart replied at once, "Why, yours."

The summer wore on, and things got worse. I became more guilty and more frightened, and kept all this bottled up inside me, and naturally, inescapably, one night, when this woman had finished preaching, everything came roaring, screaming, crying out, and I fell to the ground before the altar. It was the strangest sensation I have ever had in my life—up to that time, or since. I had not known that it was going to happen, or that it could happen. One moment I was on my feet, singing and clapping and, at the same time, working out in my head the plot of a play I was working on then; the next moment, with no transition, no sense of falling, I was on my back, with the lights beating down into my face and all the vertical saints above me. I did not know what I was doing down so low, or how I had got there. And the anguish that filled me cannot be described. It moved in me like one of those floods that devastate countries, tearing everything down, tearing children from their parents and lovers from each other, and making everythng an unrecognizable waste. All I really remember is the pain, the unspeakable pain; it was as though I were yelling up to Heaven and Heaven would not hear me. And if Heaven would not hear me, if love could not descend from Heaven—to wash me, to make me clean—then utter disaster was my portion. Yes, it does indeed mean something—something unspeakable—to be born, in a white country, an Anglo-Teutonic, antisexual country, black. You very soon, without knowing it, give up all hope of communion. Black people, mainly, look down or look up but do not look at each other, not at you, and white people, mainly, look away. And the universe is simply a sounding drum; there is no way, no way whatever, so it seemed then and has sometimes seemed since, to get through a life, to love your wife and children, or your friends, or your mother and father, or to be loved. The universe, which is not merely the stars and the moon and the planets, flowers, grass, and trees, but *other people,* has evolved no terms for your existence, has made no room for you, and if love will not swing wide the gates, no other power will or can. And if one despairs— as who has not?—of human love, God's love alone is left. But God—and I felt this even then, so long ago, on that tremendous floor, unwillingly—is white. And if His love was so great, and if He loved all His children, why were we the blacks, cast down so far? Why? In spite of all I said thereafter, I found no answer on the floor—not *that* answer, anyway—and I was on the floor all night. Over me, to bring me "through,"

the saints sang and rejoiced and prayed. And in the morning, when they raised me, they told me that I was "saved."

Well, indeed I was, in a way, for I was utterly drained and exhausted, and released, for the first time, from all my guilty torment. I was aware then only of my relief. For many years, I could not ask myself why human relief had to be achieved in a fashion at once so pagan and so desperate—in a fashion at once so unspeakably old and so unutterably new. And by the time I was able to ask myself this question, I was also able to see that the principles governing the rites and customs of the churches in which I grew up did not differ from the principles governing the rites and customs of other churches, white. The principles were Blindness, Loneliness, and Terror, the first principle necessarily and actively cultivated in order to deny the two others. I would love to believe that the principles were Faith, Hope, and Charity, but this is clearly not so for most Christians, or for what we call the Christian world.

<hr />

Malcolm X
(1925–1965)

The Autobiography of Malcolm X was completed barely a year before Malcolm X was shot and killed while addressing a rally. He clearly envisioned such a possibility and his book was written in part to repudiate violence as a solution to the problem of racism. *The Autobiography of Malcolm X* is already an American classic, not only because it is a powerful narrative of an extraordinary life, but because it depicts that life as following certain American patterns and supporting a variety of distinctive American values. *The Autobiography* traces Malcolm X's journey from obscurity to fame, from solitude to society, from provinciality to cosmopolitanism, and from estrangement to cautious accommodation, and embraces in its own terms such inherited American values as the importance of self-improvement, the need for self-criticism, the moral responsibility for public service, and the spiritual significance of human brotherhood.

Malcolm X's "Letter from Mecca" was written toward the end of his personal odyssey. It serves at least as a partial summary of what he learned on his torturous pilgrimage from the dark ghetto of American racism to the holy City of Islam.

From *The Autobiography of Malcolm X* (1964)

I have reflected since that the letter I finally sat down to compose had been subconsciously shaping itself in my mind.

The *color-blindness* of the Muslim world's religious society and the *color-blindness* of the Muslim world's human society: these two influences had each

day been making a greater impact, and an increasing persuasion against my previous way of thinking.

The first letter was, of course, to my wife, Betty. I never had a moment's question that Betty, after initial amazement, would change her thinking to join mine. I had known a thousand reassurances that Betty's faith in me was total. I knew that she would see what I had seen—that in the land of Muhammad and the land of Abraham, I had been blessed by Allah with a new insight into the true religion of Islam, and a better understanding of America's entire racial dilemma.

After the letter to my wife, I wrote next essentially the same letter to my sister Ella. And I knew where Ella would stand. She had been saving to make the pilgrimage to Mecca herself.

I wrote to Dr. Shawarbi, whose belief in my sincerity had enabled me to get a passport to Mecca.

All through the night, I copied similar long letters for others who were very close to me. Among them was Elijah Muhammad's son Wallace Muhammad, who had expressed to me his conviction that the only possible salvation for the Nation of Islam would be its accepting and projecting a better understanding of Orthodox Islam.

And I wrote to my loyal assistants at my newly formed Muslim Mosque, Inc. in Harlem, with a note appended, asking that my letter be duplicated and distributed to the press.

I knew that when my letter became public knowledge back in America, many would be astounded—loved ones, friends, and enemies alike. And no less astounded would be millions whom I did not know—who had gained during my twelve years with Elijah Muhammad a "hate" image of Malcolm X.

Even I was myself astounded. But there was precedent in my life for this letter. My whole life had been a chronology of—*changes.*

Here is what I wrote . . . from my heart:

"Never have I witnessed such sincere hospitality and the overwhelming spirit of true brotherhood as is practiced by people of all colors and races here in this Ancient Holy Land, the home of Abraham, Muhammad, and all the other prophets of the Holy Scriptures. For the past week, I have been utterly speechless and spellbound by the graciousness I see displayed all around me by people *of all colors.*

"I have been blessed to visit the Holy City of Mecca. I have made my seven circuits around the Ka'ba, led by a young *Mutawaf* named Muhammad. I drank water from the well of Zem Zem. I ran seven times back and forth between the hills of Mt. Al-Safa and Al-Marwah. I have prayed in the ancient city of Mina, and I have prayed on Mt. Arafat.

"There were tens of thousands of pilgrims, from all over the world. They were of all colors, from blue-eyed blonds to black-skinned Africans. But we were all participating in the same ritual, displaying a spirit of unity and brotherhood that my experiences in America had led me to believe never could exist between the white and the non-white.

"America needs to understand Islam, because this is the one religion that erases from its society the race problem. Throughout my travels in the Muslim world, I have met, talked to, and even eaten with people who in America would have been considered 'white'— but the 'white' attitude was removed from their minds by the religion of Islam. I have never before seen *sincere* and *true* brotherhood practiced by all colors together, irrespective of their color.

"You may be shocked by these worlds coming from me. But on this pilgrimage, what I have seen, and experienced, has forced me to *re-arrange* much of my thought-patterns previously held, and to *toss aside* some of my previous conclusions. This was not too difficult for me. Despite my firm convictions, I have been always a man who tries to face facts, and to accept the reality of life as new experience and new knowledge unfolds it. I have always kept an open mind, which is necessary to the flexibility that must go hand in hand with every form of intelligent search for truth.

"During the past eleven days here in the Muslim world, I have eaten from the same plate, drunk from the same glass, and slept in the same bed (or on the same rug)—while praying to the *same* God—with fellow Muslims, whose eyes were the bluest of blue, whose hair was the blondest of blond, and whose skin was the whitest of white. An in the *words* and in the *actions* and in the *deeds* of the 'white' Muslims, I felt the same sincerity that I felt among the black African Muslims of Nigeria, Sudan, and Ghana.

"We were *truly* all the same (brothers)—because their belief in one God had removed the 'white' from their *minds,* the 'white' from their *behavior,* and the 'white' from their *attitude.*

"I could see from this, that perhaps if white Americans could accept the Oneness of God, then perhaps, too they could accept *in reality* the Oneness of Man—and cease to measure, and hinder, and harm others in terms of their 'differences' in color.

"With racism plaguing America like an incurable cancer, the so-called 'Christian' white American heart should be more receptive to a proven solution to such a destructive problem. Perhaps it could be in time to save America from imminent disaster—the same destruction brought upon Germany by racism that eventually destroyed the Germans themselves.

"Each hour here in the Holy Land enables me to have greater spiritual insights into what is happening in America between black and white. The American Negro never can be blamed for his racial animosities—he is only reacting to four hundred years of the conscious racism of the American whites. But as racism leads America up the suicide path, I do believe, from the experiences that I have had with them, that the whites of the younger generation, in the colleges and universities, will see the handwriting on the wall and many of them will turn to the *spiritual* path of *truth*—the only way left to America to ward off the disaster that racism inevitably must lead to.

"Never have I been so highly hon-ored. Never have I been made to feel more humble and unworthy. Who would believe the blessings that have been heaped upon an *American Negro?* A few nights ago, a man who would be called in America a 'white' man, a United Nations diplomat, an ambassa-dor, a companion of kings, gave me *his* hotel suite, *his* bed. By this man, His Excellency Prince Faisal, who rules this Holy Land, was made aware of my presence here in Jedda. The very next morning, Prince Faisal's son, in person, informed me that by the will and decree of his esteemed father I was to be a State Guest.

"The Deputy Chief of Protocol him-self took me before the Hajj Court. His Holiness Sheikh Muhammad Harkon himself okayed my visit to Mecca. His Holiness gave me two books on Islam, with his personal seal and autograph, and he told me that he prayed that I would be a successful preacher of Islam in America. A car, a driver, and a guide, have been placed at my disposal, mak-ing it possible for me to travel about this Holy Land almost at will. The govern-ment provides air-conditioned quarters and servants in each city that I visit. Never would I have even thought of dreaming that I would ever be a recipi-ent of such honors—honors that in America would be bestowed upon a King—not a Negro.

"All Praise is due to Allah, the Lord of all the Worlds.

"Sincerely,

"El-Hajj Malik El-Shabazz
"(Malcom X)"

Theodore Roethke (1908–1963)

Theodore Roethke was a major modern American poet for whom recognition came slowly except among his fellow poets. The natural world was his principle subject, and its immanent powers of creation and re-creation provided his principal theme. He gave expression to this theme in his exploration of such strange things as "the lives on a leaf," "squirmers in bogs," and the snuff-laden breath of the three ancient ladies who had worked in his father's greenhouse. Roethke was drawn to the most elemental forms of existence, vegetable as well as animal—what another contemporary American poet, Stanley Kunitz, called "news of the root."

Most of Roethke's poetry concentrates on the miracle of growth, the restoration of life, yet he knew times of "Dolor," as he titled one poem—moments of blackness. "The Abyss" records one such moment, but here, as in many of Roethke's longer poems, the focus is not so much on the experience itself as on the movements of the poet's mind, fitfully attempting to grasp and absorb its own agonized rebirth from the darkness of despair.

"The Abyss" (1964)

I

Is the stair here?
Where's the stair?
'The stair's right there,
But it goes nowhere.'

And the abyss? the abyss?
The abyss you can't miss:
It's right where you are—
A step down the stair.

Each time ever
There always is
Noon of failure,
Part of a house.

In the middle of,
Around a cloud,
On top a thistle
The wind's slowing.

II

I have been spoken to variously
But heard little.
My inward witness is dismayed
By my unguarded mouth.
I have taken, too often, the dangerous
      path,
The vague, the arid,
Neither in nor out of this life.

Among us, who is holy?
What speech abides?
I hear the noise of the wall.
They have declared themselves,
Those who despise the dove.

Be with me, Whitman, maker of
      catalogues:
For the world invades me again,

440

And once more the tongues begin
    babbling.
And the terrible hunger for objects
    quails me:
The sill trembles.
And there on the blind
A furred caterpillar crawls down a
    string.
My symbol!
For I have moved closer to death,
    lived with death;
For like a nurse he sat with me for
    weeks, a sly surly attendant,
Watching my hands, wary.
Who sent him away?
I'm no longer a bird dipping a beak
    into rippling water
But a mole winding through earth,
A night-fishing otter.

III

Too much reality can be a dazzle, a
    surfeit;
Too close immediacy an exhaustion:
As when the door swings open in a
    florist's storeroom—
The rush of smells strikes like a cold
    fire, the throat freezes,
And we turn back to the heat of
    August,
Chastened.

So the abyss—
The slippery cold heights,
After the blinding misery,
The climbing, the endless turning,
Strike like a fire,
A terrible violence of creation,
A flash into the burning heart of the
    abominable;
Yet if we wait, unafraid, beyond the
    fearful instant,

The burning lake turns into a forest
    pool,
The fire subsides into rings of water,
A sunlit silence.

IV

How can I dream except beyond this
    life?
Can I outleap the sea—
The edge of all the land, the final sea?
I envy the tendrils, their eyeless seeking,
The child's hand reaching into the
    coiled smilax,
And I obey the wind at my back
Bringing me home from the twilight
    fishing.

In this, my half-rest,
Knowing slows for a moment,
And not–knowing enters, silent,
Bearing being itself,
And the fire dances
To the stream's
Flowing.

Do we move toward God, or merely
    another condition?
By the salt waves I hear a river's
    undersong,
In a place of mottled clouds, a thin
    mist morning and evening.
I rock between dark and dark,
My soul nearly my own,
My dead selves singing.
And I embrace this calm—
Such quiet under the small leaves!—
Near the stem, whiter at root,
A luminous stillness.

The shade speaks slowly:
'Adore and draw near.
Who knows this—
Knows all.'

V

I thirst by day. I watch by night.
I receive! I have been received!
I hear the flowers drinking in their
    light,
I have taken counsel of the crab and
    the sea-urchin,
I recall the falling of small waters,
The stream slipping beneath the mossy
    logs,
Winding down to the stretch of
    irregular sand,
The great logs piled like matchsticks.

I am most immoderately married:
The Lord God has taken my heaviness
    away;
I have merged, like the bird, with the
    bright air,
And my thought flies to the place by
    the bo-tree.

Being, not doing, is my first joy.

Richard Rubenstein
(1924–   )

Richard Rubenstein is a Jewish thinker
and professor of religion most of whose
work has been devoted to understanding the causes and significance of the
Holocaust. His first book, *After Auschwitz*
(1966), dealt with the problems for
traiditional religious belief created by
the Holocaust, and Rubenstein was
quickly, if somewhat mistakenly, associated with the radical Death-of-God

movement in contemporary theology.
Although he shared the conviction that
contemporary history rendered orthodox views of God obsolete and belief in
God virtually impossible, he nevertheless maintained that this actually
strengthened the case for many of the
institutions and functions of traditional
Judaism.

Since that time, Rubenstein has, in his
autobiography, *Power Struggle* (1974),
repudiated his earlier ideas concerning
the integrity and meaningfulness of
traditional Judaism. The present selection, however, is from "The Making of a
Rabbi," a chapter of *After Auschwitz*.

From *After Auschwitz* (1966)

"The Making of a Rabbi"

I can remember distinctly the objective
issues which brought about my disen-
chantment with classical Reform and my
eventual turning to a more traditional
Judaism. By the fall of 1944, the facts
about the Nazi death camps had become
generally known. Reports of the capture
of the camp at Madjdanek, Poland, with
its huge piles of ownerless shoes, left an
indelible impression upon me. I read
about Madjdanek at about the same
time I was preparing to serve as a
student rabbi for the High Holy days in
Tupelo, Mississippi.

The revelation of the death camps
caused me to reject the whole optimistic
theology of liberal religion. People
weren't getting any better, nor did I
believe they ever would. The evil rooted

in human nature would never entirely disappear. Like the plague in Albert Camus's novel, radical evil might lie dormant for long periods but it remained forever capable of disrupting the pathetically weak fragments of reason and decency with which men have constructed their fragile civilization. My generation might add to the treasury of knowledge, but it was incapable of adding significantly to humanity's store of goodness. Each generation had to confront the choice between good and evil unaided by those who went before.

The death camps spelled the end of my optimism concerning the human condition. Though twenty years have passed, I see little reason to alter my pessimism. I regarded the camps and Nazism as far more than a sport of history. They revealed the full potentiality of the demonic as a permanent aspect of human nature. I was all the more shaken because I began to recognize that the difference between the Germans and other men was not very great. Given similar conditions of political and social stress, most of us could commit very terrible crimes. Moral nihilism had, in any event, been one of the deepest strains in my nature. I had struggled to overcome it from childhood, but the anarchic creature of infantile desire within me had never been put to death. During my years at the Hebrew Union College, it had been suppressed by the regnant liberal optimism. The discovery of the Nazi camps again demonstrated its potency to me. The polite, optimistic religion of a prosperous middle class hardly offered much hope against the deep

strains of disorder I saw in the world and in myself.

The shock of the extermination camps was paralleled by the shock of realization of the degree to which both the occupied peoples and even the Allies had, to a degree, cooperated in or assented to the Nazi holocaust. I began to understand the relationship between the Christian theology of history and the deep and abiding hatred of the Jew in the Occident. When the death camps were followed by Britain's refusal to permit the entry of the survivors into Palestine, I came to understand the inadequacy of any definition of Jewish life which rested on religious confession alone. Perhaps the healthiest aspect of my understanding of the ethnic aspect of Jewish life was that I could now see myself and the Jews of eastern Europe as united by ties of common fate and psychology. I had become and remain unimpressed with American Jewish life as a special case.

At about the same time, I became enormously impressed with the Jewish concept of *galuth* or exile. Objectively the destruction of European Jewry and the attempt to establish a new Jewish nation were both expressions of *galuth* as the abiding condition of Jewish life. Liberal Judaism had rejected the notion. Since the war liberal Jewish thinkers have re-examined *galuth* as a meaningful religious category. At the time, many Jewish religious liberals were convinced that we lived in the best of times, in spite of the recent setback, a conviction I found impossible to sustain. I especially remember the blindness with which some of the leaders opposed the establishment of the State of Israel. They insisted that Europe's Jews had an obligation to re-establish themselves and contribute to the liberalism and democracy of their native lands.

The notion of *galuth* seemed to make a great deal of sense both psychologically and existentially. Even in America, I felt that Jews would remain in *galuth* to an extent. *Galuth* had long ceased to be only a Jewish fact. Modern literature is replete with protagonists in real or psychological exile: Kafka's Joseph K., Mann's Joseph, Camus's Mersault, Sartre's Antoine Rocquentin, Melville's Ahab are a few who come to mind. Neither as a Jew nor as an intellectual would I ever entirely be "in," but then who would be? Existence is exile. We are all superfluous men, whether we know it or not. I was surprised that "old fashioned," "unenlightened," traditional Judaism was more directly on target in its description of both the Jewish and the human condition than was "liberal," "progressive," "modern" Judaism. I began to wonder whether I could in good conscience remain tied to a liberal prayerbook and system of worship which so falsified the human condition by its unwarranted optimism.

Exile expresses theologically much the same reality which underlies the concept of alienation in contemporary social science. It has remained a cornerstone of my religious and psychological perspective. At the level of Jewish-Christian relations, I progressively gave up real hope that the Jew could ever feel entirely at home in the gentile world. This may sound harsher than it is meant to be. There are countless gentiles who

have experienced a similar alienation, though it does have a special quality for Jews. We are destined to be strangers and wanderers upon the earth to the end of days. Even the State of Israel cannot escape this destiny, being the Jewish nation in a gentile world. Abraham's destiny would never depart from his progeny.

I also turned to the question of *geulah* or redemption, which is the other side of the coin of exile. Classical Reform Judaism was convinced that the Messiah had already come in the form of German and American enlightenment. As one reads the social and intellectual history of the late nineteenth century, one realizes how hopelessly out of touch the Reformers were. Important social forces were preparing a northern European racial tribalism which would effectively isolate all Jews. My pessimistic reading of twentieth-century Jewish history made me ask the age-old Jewish question, "When will the Messiah come? When will redemption begin?" My real concern was not about a personal Messiah but about the dream of the redemptive alteration of the human condition.

I was very much drawn to the insights of the Jewish mystics on this issue. In the years following the expulsion of the Jewish community from Spain in 1492, Jewish mystics were agonized by a problem similar to the one which had seized our times. The catastrophic destruction of Spanish Jewry made the problems of exile and redemption central to them; the end of European Jewry had made exile and redemption central to me.

The insights of Rabbi Isaac Luria of Safed, Palestine (d. 1572), and his followers have been especially helpful. They saw existence itself as alienation. Even God the Creator could exist only through an act of self-alienation. In their system, the first creative act was self-diminution, *tsimtsum*, of the absolutely simple Ground of existence into Himself, leaving thereby a space for the created world. According to Luria, the primal act of creation was one in which that which was All, and therefore no discrete limited thing, withdrew into Himself so that both He and the created world could be limited and defined by each other. This accorded strangely with my earliest nihilism which saw nothingness as the origin and destiny of all things. I saw God as the Holy Nothingness. I had exchanged my atheistic nihilism for a mystical nihilism. To be all that there is, as God was in the beginning and will be in the end, is equivalent to being, so to speak, absolutely nothing. In the beginning, God dwelt in the womb of his own omnipotent nothingness. The first act of creation was an act of self-estrangement whereby the revealed God, in contrast to the primordial hidden ground, and the created world came into existence.

Since the world came into existence, so to speak, out of God's nothingness, all conscious existence is beset by a conflict between the desire for survival, identity, and individual self-maintenance and the yearning to return to its source in God's nothingness. Redemption is return; existence is exile. We purchase identity at the price of estrangement. We know who we are only insofar as we know who we are not. We both crave and fear redemption because its reward and its price are the

same: disappearance of the individual into the Source whence he came. This mystical doctrine is not unlike Freud's secularized version of the same conflict in his late work *Beyond the Pleasure Principle*. Freud posited a lifelong conflict between our instinct for life and our yearning to return to the quiescence which preceded our existence. Freud used the metaphor of the *eros-thanatos* conflict. The mystics tended to see the very same conflict in terms of the polarities of the maintenance of the self and the return to the Source. I tended to regard both the mystics and Freud as utilizing different symbolic systems to point to a common reality.

I was particularly struck by the remark a later mystic, Rav Schneur Zalman of Ladi (d. 1813), is reputed to have made. Interrupting his prayers, he declared, "I do not want Your paradise. I do not want Your world to come. I want You and You only."

Eternal separation is eternal exile. The Rav of Ladi yearned ultimately to return. He also knew, insofar as it is given to any human being to know, what it was he was returning to. Shortly before his death he asked his grandson, "Do you see anything?" The boy was astonished. The Rav then said, "All I can see is the Holy Nothingness which gives life to the world."

Life is exile. Evil, pain, suffering can be ended only by ending life. The Jewish situation, like so many Jewish gestures, exaggerates what is common to all men. The Jewish people remain in exile awaiting the redeeming Messiah. The conflict with Christianity is strongest at this point. The good news of the

Church is that the Messiah has come, bringing with him actual or potential redemption. There is sadness in the Jewish rejection of the Christian claim. It rests upon a tragic wisdom which asserts the inevitability of pain and evil, along with real moments of joy and fulfillment, as long as life continues. By asserting that the Messiah will come, the Jewish community was also saying of any given *actual era* that his redemption has yet to begin.

There are many Jewish speculations concerning the time of the coming of the Messiah. Isaac Bashevis Singer, the contemporary novelist, has, I believe, penetrated to the heart of the mystical meaning of the hour of the Messiah at the very end of his novel *The Family Moskat*. As Hitler's armies approach the gates of Warsaw, bringing the final destruction of European Jewry with them, one of Singer's characters affirms that the Messiah will come speedily. This affirmation of faith is greeted with astonishment, whereupon Hertz Yanovar clarifies his assertion: "Death is the Messiah. That is the real truth."

Only death perfects life and ends its problems. God can redeem only by slaying. We have nothing to hope for beyond what we are capable of creating in the time we have allotted to us. Of course, this leaves room for much doing and much creating. Nevertheless, in the final analysis all things crumble away into the nothingness which is at the begining and end of creation.

If existence is ultimately devoid of hope and God offers us absolutely nothing, why bother with religion at all? I must confess that at a significant level I have much sympathy with the contemporary "death of God" Protestant theologians, though many of their concerns are specifically rooted in the ethos of Christianity, which has had to grapple with the meaning of the death of God involved in the crucifixion of Jesus. The question, "Why religion?" probably is meaningless. There are men and women devoid of all illusion who nevertheless regard withdrawal from the religious community as unthinkable. I am one of them. The decision to partake of the life of a community rests upon forces within the psyche which have little to do with rational argument. There is absolutely no reason for those who can do without religion to bother. At a certain tribal level, religion is inescapable in the United States. Our identities are shaped by the religious groups into which we are born. Our religions are less what we profess than what we inherit. There are Protestant, Catholic, and Jewish atheists. Jewish "death of God" theology is very different from its Christian counterpart. At the level of religious philosophy, Jewish and Christian radical theologians make similar denials. Their life styles inevitably reflect the communities they come from. Was it not Santayana who declared that there is no God but Mary is his mother? Nowhere in America can one find abstract men who are Americans without any other qualification.

Inheritance may influence personal identity. It does not necessarily compel religious commitment or affiliation. Undoubtedly the need for a community of manageable proportions to which one can belong and in which one is welcome has had a lot to do with the proliferation of churches and synagogues in middle-class America. For me, another need determined my affiliation. Like the Polish Jew in the East European *Shtetl,* the tribesman in an African tribe untouched by "civilization," and the Spanish peasant, I cannot dispense with the institution through which I can dramatize, make meaningful, and share the decisive moments of my life. For me that institution is the synagogue; for all men it is the religious community they have inherited. Of course there is something absurd and irrational about this. I did not choose to be Jewish. It has been one of the givens of my nature, but no religious institution other than the synagogue is psychologically and culturally appropriate for my need to celebrate and share the decisive moments of existence. These moments include birth, puberty, marriage, temporary or permanent infirmity, the marking of time irretrievably past, the rearing of children, the need to express and find catharsis for feelings of guilt, the need for personal renewal, and the feeling of awe and wonder which overcomes me when I think about God's nothingness as the ultimate source and the final end.

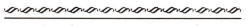

Schubert M. Ogden (1928–   )

Schubert M. Ogden is a Christian theologian usually associated with the "pro-cess" philosophy exemplified by the work of Alfred North Whitehead and Charles Hartshorne, and Ogden's second book, *The Reality of God* (1966), clearly shows their influence. His first book, however, *Christ Without Myth* (1961), an analysis of the theology of Rudolf Bultmann, revealed an existentialist side to his thought, and his more recent work, including the following selection, shows a strong affinity to aspects of American pragmatism. This appears in his method as well as in his conclusions. "How Does God Function in Human Life?" was published in somewhat different form in the journal *Christianity and Crisis* (May 15, 1967).

From "How Does God Function in Human Life?" (1967)

This is a complex and difficult question which cannot be easily answered. But it is also an important question which Christian theology cannot ignore or evade. If certain theologians at the moment seem to have forgotten this, there are sensitive unbelievers who are quite capable of reminding them of their task.

Michael Harrington, for example, has recently given some "radical advice" to "radical religionists." The "new reformation will not be accomplished," he suggests, "on the basis of that irreligious adage, 'If you can't lick 'em, join 'em.' The Church will not regain its vitality—

if that is to happen—by simply being hipper than thou. It must, to be sure, fight for the earthly implication of the heavenly values it affirms; it can never again divorce God from the Negroes, the poor, those dying in war and the rest of humanity. But over and above that witness to the temporal meetings of the eternal, there must be the assertion of the eternal itself. And, amid all the showmanship and swinging theology, this is what I miss."

Harrington's point is simply the truism that theologians, as he puts it, "still have an obligation to talk about their old theological hero, God." But if this obligaion is to be met in an age like ours, it will only be by speaking of God's function in human life. To talk about God today is to try, at least, to answer such questions as these: What is the relevance of God? Granted that God is real, in what way does he make a difference? How can we so relate to God that he can be said to be significant in our lives?

These questions all ask how *God himself* functions in human life. But there is a somewhat different question often asked today that needs to be kept in mind. This is the question, How does the *word "God"* function in human language, in which our life and experience are somehow represented? I mention this because I propose to approach the question expressed in the title by speaking, first, to this second question. I can offer as a reason for this only that it seems to me as good a way as any to clarify the original question. If God has any function in our life, if he in any way makes a difference to us, is relevant to us, or has significance for us, this must be because the word "God" when properly used serves to designate something that our experience discloses to be in some way real, relevant, functional, or significant. Let us ask, then, how the word "God" properly functions.

I begin by simply stating some points of fundamental importance. In my judgment, it is necessary to challenge the popular positivistic assumption that human experience is exhausted by the external sense perception of which science and history in their different ways are the critical analysis and reflection. Man, I believe, also enjoys an internal nonsensuous awareness of his own existence and of the existence of his fellow creatures as finite-free parts of an infinite and encompassing whole. Indeed, this second kind of experience is fundamental to the other kind, to our external sense perception. Presupposed by all my sense experience and the judgments arising from it is what I call the certainty of existence—the certainty that I exist as the subject of my experience and that I exist together with others, fellow creatures like myself, with whom I am related and on whose actions I am dependent, even as they are thus related and dependent with respect to me. And no less fundamental is the certainty that both I and my fellow creatures exist within, and, therefore, as parts of, an all-inclusive whole, that circumambient reality which is our primal source and final end, whence we come and whither we go.

I hold that this complex experience of existence—of myself, others, and the whole—is the experience out of which all religious language arises and in terms of which it must be understood. In this sense, all religious language, including the word "God," is *existential* language, the language in which we express and refer to our own existence as selves related to others and to the whole.

It is important to bear in mind that this fundamental certainty of existence has a richness or thickness that the word "existence" may not adequately convey. My experience of myself, others, and the whole is not simply the experience *that* we are, in some neutral or nonevaluative sense—as mere facts, so to speak—but is always, precisely as the experience of existence, an experience of worth, of value, of meaning, of significance. In experiencing my own existence in relation to others and the whole, the essence of my experience is *the sense of worth*—of my own worth for myself and others, of their worth for themselves and me, and of our common worth for the whole and its worth for all of us.

Thus the foundational certainty underlying all of my experience is not only that I am together with others in the whole, but that what I am and what they are is significant, makes a difference, is worthwhile. This certainty that I am and that what I am is significant or worthwhile is what I call basic confidence in the worth of life. It is, I hold, the primal faith which is constitutive of our very lives as human beings and which, therefore, is in the proper sense the "common faith" of mankind. To exist as a man at all is to exist as one who shares in this common faith, because every attempt to deny or controvert it presupposes it. I cannot question the worth of life without presupposing the worth of questioning and therefore the worth of the life by which alone such questioning can be done. In the same way, to look for evidence against the claim that life is worthwhile assumes not only that there is or can be such evidence, but that it is worth while spending one's time and energy to try to find it. As a matter of fact, even suicide, as the intentional act of taking one's own life, does not entail so much a denial of life's worth as an affirmation of it. I can hardly choose to end my life unless I assume that doing so is not merely pointless but is somehow significant or makes a difference.

I recognize that these points can all be questioned and both require and deserve fuller elaboration and defense than I have provided. But I must now simply assume them and infer what seems to me the proper use or function of the word "God."

I submit that the use of this word is to refer to the objective ground in reality itself of what I have called basic confidence in the worth of life. It lies in the nature of this basic confidence to affirm that the real whole of which we experience ourselves and others to be parts is such as to be worthy of , and thus itself to evoke in us, this very confidence. The word "God" serves to designate whatever it is about this experienced whole that calls forth and justifies our original and inalienable trust in life's worth. Thus the meaning of the word may be appropriately paraphrased in the words once proposed by William James: "You can dismiss certain kinds of fear," namely, the kinds of fear that sometimes overtake you and drive you to ask why your life is, after all, worth living. It follows that to be free of such fear by existing in this trust is one and the same with affirming the reality of God.

∞·∞·∞

If this analysis of how the word "God" properly functions is correct, we should now be able to give something in the way of an answer to our original question of how God himself functions in human life. The function of God, quite simply, is to make the whole venture of human life worthwhile and to call forth in each of us our abiding confidence in life's worth. The relevance of God, then, is that he and he alone provides the ultimate justification for giving ourselves fully and freely to the tasks of human existence, to knowing and doing, feeling and loving, with all their terrors and all their joys. Or, to speak to yet another of the ways of expressing our question, the difference God's reality makes in our life is that he and he alone enables our life itself really to make a difference—to contribute not only to the life of others which likewise makes no abiding difference if taken solely in itself, but also to his own strictly universal and everlasting life, to which each life makes an imperishable difference, and in which, therefore, all lives find their ultimate justification.

Finally, if we ask how we can relate to God so that he can be significant in our lives, the answer seems clear: we can thus relate to him only by abandoning ourselves to him and to him alone as our final *raison d'être*. Instead of compromising our basic confidence by resting it in part in ourselves or in others, we are to look to God's love alone as providing our ultimate justification. The reward of such radical trust is just that emphasized in the statement of William James cited earlier—namely, that we can then dismiss certain kinds of fear: we are then released from all anxiety as to the ultimate worth of our lives. But this is to say that God functions in our lives to set us free—both free *from* ourselves and others as in any way ultimate conditions of a meaningful existence, and free *for* ourselves and others as the proper objects of the love whereby our returning love for God himself can alone be fully realized.

It will be recognized that, in thus speaking to our original question, I have presupposed not only the foregoing philosophical analysis, but also the answer to the question historically given by Christian faith and theology. I have spoken of God's function in our lives as it is given to those who orient themselves to the decisive importance of Jesus Christ to understand that function. But, if as we saw from our earlier analysis, the meaning of the word "God" is what ultimately makes our life worth living, must we not concede that whatever functions for a particular person or community to make his or its life worthwhile is, in effect, God for that person or community? And must we not go on to concede that the word "God" no longer has the unique referent intended by Christian faith—that there are in fact "many gods," as many, indeed, as there are different ways of understanding what it is that makes our life worth living?

The answer to both questions, clearly, must be affirmative. It is necessary to say—as Luther, for one, did say—that faith and God belong together, so that whatever a man looks to as the ultimate reason for his existence, the final ground of its meaning or worth, is in a way his God—whether this be the only true God, or rather country and Yale, or health, reputation, and success. And this implies that the word "God" does in a sense have many referents, contingently on the alternative understandings of their basic confidence by which men can live and to which they can give expression in their various religions and ideologies. As a matter of fact, it is only by saying precisely this that we can give any clear meaning to what Scripture means by atheism, namely, *idolatry.*

But here I would introduce two cautions. First, there is (or at least may be) a difference between the understanding of existence by which a person in fact lives and the understanding of himself of which he is reflectively aware or to which he gives explicit expression. Not everyone who professes to believe in God as revealed by Jesus Christ has authentic faith in that God; and, just as important, some who expressly deny faith in that God may nevertheless actually understand themselves as related to him, rather than to the other gods they explicitly affirm. Then, second, even the deepest and most serious form of atheism—namely, the denial of God by my actual existence and not merely by what I think or say—even this atheism of the heart is never simply the absence of faith in the one true God. The popular idea that the godless man,

or the idolater, trusts only in his idol and in no way trusts in the true God revealed to Christian faith, cannot be sustained consistently with Christian faith itself. Scripture makes unmistakably plain that the idolater is always the adulterer, the one who adulterates the unqualified confidence he owes to God alone by resting it in part in something alongside of God—whether himself or one or more of his fellow creatures. Because the God in whom Christian faith believes is "the Father Almighty, Maker of heaven and earth, and of all things visible and invisible," it knows that no man can be utterly without faith in that God, even if the mode of his faith be the inauthentic mode of idolatry.

The point of these brief remarks about idolatry is this: from the standpoint of Christian faith, the mark of every idolatry or atheism, whether practical or theoretical, whether of the heart or of the mind, is that it fails to set man free. Instead of enabling him so to understand his basic confidence in the worth of life that he is at once free *for* and free *from* himself and others in a radical way, all atheistic or idolatrous self-understandings condemn man to some form of bondage, whether of the heart or of the mind—or both. If one believes, say, that his life is worthwhile only on condition that he enjoys at least three-score-and-ten years of uninterrupted good health and pleasure, he is not free to live as and when he is met with a destiny of illness and pain. Or, to take an example of the cramping effects of a theoretical atheism, if one claims that the only statements that are cognitively meaningful are those which can be falsified by sense perception, he is not free to consider religious, moral, and aesthetic statements on their own terms, but must dump all of them in the great wastebasket labeled "emotive language" and engage in colossal feats of explaining away.

But no less clear is the response of Christian faith to the presence of genuine freedom, whether of the heart or of the mind, wherever it encounters such freedom. Because faith knows that the God revealed to it is the great emancipator of mankind—not only of Christians, but of *every child of man*—it cannot but note the presence and working of that God wherever men are free and are engaged in the one task worthy of men: the task of witnessing by word and deed to the great movement of emancipation which is how God functions in human life.

Norman Mailer
(1923–   )

Norman Mailer has been embroiled in controversy ever since the publication of his first novel, *The Naked and the Dead* (1948). Regarded by some as the foremost writer of our time, and dismissed by others as a literary hipster who got lost, in his own words, "on that uncharted journey into the rebellious imperatives of the self" ("The White Negro"), Mailer has turned in recent years from fiction to journalism, or, better, to

a kind of fictionalized journalism or journalistic fiction. Mailer has used this mode in *The Armies of the Night: History as a Novel, The Novel as History* (1968) and *Of a Fire on the Moon* (1970) to produce two central cultural documents of the contemporary period.

The present selection is taken from the conclusion of *The Armies of the Night,* Mailer's treatment of the antiwar protest march on the Pentagon that took place in the fall of 1967. The reaction to the war in Southeast Asia profoundly challenged many of the assumptions of the prevailing cultural metaphysics and rekindled the desire to find a replacement for it. Perhaps no contemporary writer has more vigorously enlisted himself in that quest for a new New World metaphysics than Norman Mailer.

From *The Armies of the Night* (1968)

The End of the Rite

When the count was made, there proved to be one thousand arrests. It was not a small number; it was not an enormous number—it was certainly a respectable number to be arrested over thirty-two hours in protest of a war. Six hundred had charges pressed. The others were taken to the back of the Pentagon, photographed, and driven away in buses to be released on the street. Of the six hundred arrested, no felony charges for assault were brought in, indeed only a dozen were charged with assault, only two went to trial, and both were acquitted.

Yes, the end seemed to have come, and the immediate beneficiary of the March could be nobody other than the President of the United States. Lyndon Johnson made a point to have his picture taken Saturday sitting at a table on the White House lawn with Hubert Humphrey, Dean Rusk, and Orville Freeman. The caption informed that he had spent the day in work. Headlines on Monday: "LBJ Hits Peaceniks." He had sent a memorandum to Defense Secretary McNamara and Attorney General Clark. "I know that all Americans share my pride in the man in uniform and the civilian law enforcement personnel for their outstanding performance in the nation's capital during the last two days. They performed with restraint, firmness and professional skill. Their actions stand in sharp contrast to the irresponsible acts of violence and lawlessness by many of the demonstrators."

The press was, in the aftermath, antagonistic to the March. Some measure of the condemnation and the abuse can be indicated by quoting Reston of the *Times* who was not immoderate in his reaction. Nor untypical.

> It is difficult to report publicly the ugly and vulgar provocation of many of the militants. They spat on some of the soldiers in the front line at the Pentagon and goaded them with the most vicious personal slander.
>
> Many of the signs carried by a small number of the militants, and many of the lines in the theatrical performances put on by the hippies, are too obscene to print. In view of this underside of the

protest, many officials here are surprised that there was not much more violence.

The rest of the stories went about that way.

Emphasis was put on every rock thrown, and a count was made of the windows broken. (There were, however, only a few.) But there was no specific mention of The Wedge. Indeed, stories quickly disappeared. No features nor follow-up a few days later. In six weeks, when an attempt was made in New York to close down the draft induction centers, it seemed that public sentiment had turned sharply against resistance. The Negro riots had made the nation afraid of lawlessness. Lyndon Johnson stood ten percentage points higher in the popularity polls—he had ridden the wave of revulsion in America against demonstrators who spit in the face of U.S. troops—when it came to sensing new waves of public opinion, LBJ was the legendary surfboarder of them all.

It probably did not matter. Ever since he had been in office, the popularity of LBJ had kept going up on the basis of his ability to ride every favorable wave, and had kept going down on the unwillingness of the war in Vietnam to fulfill the promises his Administration was making. So his popularity would go up and down again. There would be many to hope it did not go up in the last week before election. In the demonstrations in New York in December against the draft centers, Teague was arrested for carrying a knife—to anyone who had listened to his verbal militancy in jail it seemed altogether likely that a knife was not his weapon, and he had been framed. And a month later, Dr. Spock, and Coffin, and Marcus Raskin, and Michael Ferber, and Mitch Goodman were indicted by a grand jury for advocating resistance to the draft law. Such advocacy was a felony—their sentences, if guilty, could run to five years.

Mitch Goodman called a meeting at Town Hall. Five hundred and sixty people (including Allen Ginsberg, Noam Chomsky, and Mailer) signed statements implicating themselves legally to aid and abet draft resisters. Macdonald, Lowell, and Paul Goodman had already signed such statements. They could now all receive the same sentence. So the weekend in Washington which had begun with a phone call from Mitch Goodman gave promise of ending in Harrisburg or Leavenworth.

But probably it was in Occoquan and the jail in Washington, D.C., that the March ended. In the week following, prisoners who had chosen to remain, refused in many ways to cooperate, obstructed prison work, went on strikes. Some were put in solitary. A group from the Quaker Farm in Voluntown, Connecticut, practiced noncooperation in prison. Among them were veterans of a sleep-in of twenty pacifists at the Pentagon in the spring before. Now, led by Gary Rader, Erica Enzer, Irene Johnson, and Suzanne Moore, some of them refused to eat or drink and were fed intravenously. Several men at the D.C. jail would not wear prison clothing. Stripped of their own, naked, they were thrown in the Hole. There they lived in cells so small that not all could lie down at once to sleep. For a day they lay naked on the floor, for many days naked with blankets and mattress on the floor. For many days they did not eat nor drink water. Dehydration brought them near to madness.

Here was the last of the rite of passage, "the chinook salmon . . . nosing up the impossible stone," here was the thin source of the stream—these naked Quakers on the cold floor of a dark isolation cell in D.C. jail, wandering down the hours in the fever of dehydration, the cells of the brain contracting to the crystals of their thought, essence of one thought so close to the essence of another—all separations of water gone—that madness is near, madness can now be no more than the acceleration of thought.

Did they pray, these Quakers, for forgiveness of the nation? Did they pray with tears in their eyes in those blind cells with visions of a long column of Vietnamese dead, Vietnamese walking a column of flame, eyes on fire, nose on fire, mouth speaking flame, did they pray, "O Lord, forgive our people for they do not know, O Lord, find a little forgiveness for America in the puny reaches of our small suffering, O Lord, let these hours count on the scale as some small penance for the sins of the nation, let this great nation crying in the flame of its own gangrene be absolved for one tithe of its great sins by the penance of these minutes, O Lord, bring more suffering upon me that the sins of our soldiers in Vietnam be not utterly unforgiven—they are too young to be damned forever."

The prayers are as Catholic as they are Quaker, and no one will know if they were ever made, for the men who might have made them were perhaps too far out on fever and shivering and thirst to recollect, and there are places no history can reach. But if the end of the March took place in the isolation in which these last pacifists suffered naked in freezing cells, and gave up prayers for penance, then who was to say they were not saints? And who to say that the sins of America were not by their witness a tithe remitted?

Whole crisis of Christianity in America that the military heroes were on one side, and the unnamed saints on the other! Let the bugle blow. The death of America rides in on the smog. America—the land where a new kind of man was born from the idea that God was present in every man not only as compassion but as power, and so the country belonged to the people; for the will of the people—if the locks of their life could be given the art to turn—was then the will of God. Great and dangerous idea! If the locks did not turn, then the will of the people was the will of the Devil. Who by now could know where was what? Liars controlled the locks.

Brood on that country who expresses our will. She is America, once a beauty of magnificence unparalled, now a beauty with a leprous skin. She is heavy with child—no one knows if legitimate—and languishes in a dungeon whose walls are never seen. Now the first contractions of fearsome labor begin—it will go on: no doctor exists to tell the hour. It is only known that false labor is not likely on her now, no, she will probably give birth, and to what?— the most fearsome totalitarianism the

world has ever known? or can she, poor giant, tormented lovely girl, deliver a babe of a new world brave and tender, artful and wild? Rush to the locks. God writhes in his bonds. Rush to the locks. Deliver us from our curse. For we must end on the road to that mystery where courage, death, and the dream of love give promise of sleep.

~~~~~~~~~~~~~~~~~~

Henry G. Bugbee (1915–   )

Henry G. Bugbee is a philosopher very much after the manner of Thoreau. This likeness to Thoreau, however, is deceptive. It is not a simple matter of making the experience of Nature one of his principle subjects of reflection; Bugbee's affinity with Thoreau is also revealed in the way he turns thinking itself to experiential account. He practices the art of what the French existentialist Gabriel Marcel once termed "recuperative reflection," a kind of inquiry which seeks to bring us once again into the presence of those things we cannot possibly not know and remain human.

Henry G. Bugbee is the author of *The Inward Morning* (1953), one of those rare and beautiful chronicles of self-exploration which, like Thoreau's *Walden*, burrows beneath of the platitudes of thought and convention into the subsoil of truth, or into what Bugbee calls "certitude," to those things which cannot play us false. The present essay represents another journey downward toward bedrock, and was originally published under an abbriviated title as "Wilderness in America" in the *Journal of the American Academy of Religion.*

"Wilderness in America" (1974)

During recent months my reflections on wilderness have been worked and re-worked through participation in hearings concerning the disposition of areas and rivers in the Northwest which might still be conceived wild. Attending to the testimony of hundreds, and attempting to formulate my own, I have strained to discern both the actual significance wilderness may hold for us in manifold ways and, more deeply, to ponder anew the potential significance it might yet hold within the shaping of our destiny as a people.

These hearings themselves have brought out a wracking incongruity of relatively recent origin: When Thoreau wrote "that in Wildness is the preservation of the World," he surely was not thinking of Wildness as being yarded and bounded in specified preserves. Yet more and more, of course, we have been forced to conceive wilderness lands under the rubric of conservation.

The deliberateness of Thoreau's West-ward Walking was not that of an excursion into an area *set aside* to remain in its natural state. The "West" he signified did not remain by a man's decree, subject to regulations aimed at preserving it from human onslaught, or to quotas of scheduled access. "The unexplored forests and meadows" but for which he thought "our village life would stagnate" still sufficiently abounded *matter-of-factly* to obviate their holding tenure under the aegis of planning and deliberate disposition. Thus the re-creative tonic of wild-ness was not about to be bottled and labeled as a recreational resource. And matter-of-factness in the style of human venturing amidst wild places was not yet massively invaded by self-conscious searching for "the wilderness experience," even though eulogies of natural beauty and sublimity were popular among the cultivated.

Most widely, in Thoreau's time, the appeal was to venturesomeness, to set-ting out anew, to a break with conventions in which life might have been constrained if not falisified, to exploration and discovery rich in promise of new beginnings and firmer foundations, to a testing of mettle in which a man might find himself and inherit a dignity proper to him. Wilderness offered invitation and opportunity for active undertaking on which the person might thrive and even communities might be founded. Its call was that of a rallying of men to enterprise, to work that might befit them, to a life to be instituted in conscious affirmation and not one merely acquiesced in as a matter of course.

Whatever one may say of the significance wilderness thus formerly assumed in this country, or of what came of response to its appeal to active engagement, we may note that its significance lay squarely in the mainstream of men's lives; and if not directly so with many, at least sufficiently so to become widely acknowledged and traditionalized in such a vein.

With the advance of the technological era and of bureaucratic management of human affairs, what is now left of *de facto* wilderness areas still does present itself to some within the attenuated heritage of the wilderness tradition in America as continuous with human enterprise. The formerly seismic passion seems to linger strongest with those whose life's work is carried out in closest proximity to wilderness lands—"the back country," as it were. Out of their understanding of themselves in their work, these people tend to avow as an inalienable right the accessibility of the land to human enterprise and livelihood. And I think that to them the denial of this assumed right goes far deeper than an economic threat. One suspects that to them this denial seems maddeningly frivolous, an offense to manliness, and a contradiction of the significance which the land assumes at the center of a lived working relationship with it. You will perceive I am not talking about corporate interests or calculating exploitation, but about an attitude to be discerned in the passionate voices raised by individual persons close to the land—*against* the setting aside of wilderness sanctuaries subject to restrictions. However numerous or few these persons may be, it seems worth pondering the basic question they propound: the dilemma concerning wilderness in our time. If one respects their attestation that the land is to be truly met in the mainstream of life and accordingly warrants unilateral accessibility of the land to human enterprise, one knows full well the attrition of what remains "undeveloped" to be expected under the ever-mounting demand for diminishing resources. This land too will be made captive to the dogma of multiple *use,* and those who cling so fiercely to keeping the land in the ambience of man's work in the world will awaken one day to their own irretrievable loss: the source of their very passion. Yet alternatively, in setting wilderness areas aside as inviolate, does one not inadvertently attenuate their very significance by removing them from the mainstream of life? Already in the very speaking surrounding that alternative, even among its fervent advocates, one may sense contradiction of the matter-of-factness but for which we will fail to "stand right fronting and face to face to a fact"—in Thoreau's sense. As he warns, indeed,

> Very few men speak of Nature . . . with any truth. They overstep her modesty, somehow or other, and confer no favor. They do not speak a good word for her. The surliness with which the woodchopper speaks of his woods, handling them as indifferently as his axe, is better than the mealy-mouthed enthusiasm of the lover of Nature. Better that the primrose by the river's brim be a yellow primrose, and nothing more, than that it be something else.

Yes, discretion in speaking is called for. Perhaps discretion would *preclude* trying to "speak a good word for Nature." Yet wilderness may bear upon the possibility of discretion in speech—even upon the speaking carried on afar, in the far-flung sprawl of cities upon the land. From of old, in traditions vastly antedating that of the enterprising spirit in which our American forebears tended to respond to the land, a more deeply heeding attentiveness in the wilderness found sponsorship therein for a speaking that might yet hold for us commanding resonance—such speaking as one may hear, for example, in the Voice from the Whirlwind, on which Melville's ear was trained.

Speaking is potentiated in a listening through which we find ourselves addressed. From of old, genuinely destinate speech, awakening speech, seems to have come forth bred of the address in which wilderness played no small or accidental part. The very silence, the solitude, and the infinite manifestness of the place being germane to the speaking that might be called for—especially in those junctures of the lives of peoples from which men were singled out *in withdrawing to that distance* on the mainstream of life from which they might recollect themselves and submit to being placed in radical question. There, in turn, they knew themselves to receive life anew—as given them. With all this, which no man made, given in foreverness—the measure of our hours, of the generations of mankind—in ancestral memory and progeniture.

Wilderness, it would seem, may lie closer to the whence of speaking than to the thematization of a speaking about. And deeper, then, than enterprise may fathom the significance thereof. For it would be in the abeyance of enterprise that one might find, might heed, the primordial address of the place in which the potential of speech may be trued and renewed.

If wilderness may yet speak to us and place us as respondents in the ambience of respect for the wild—for Nature as primordial—it must be liberated from ultimate subsumption to human enterprise. That is, its voice will be heard anew only as we come in decisive forbearance into its presence. Attentive listening, active receptivity, candor of spirit are the mood of the place. Or, as Kant might say: disinterested interest. I suggest wilderness is not to be understood as a place appropriated to human interests or to a special human interest. Its fundamental gift lies in a qualification of disinterestedness with which human interest requires to be informed. But for such qualification we tend to lapse into a wallow of anthropocentricity and suppose ourselves to be titular on the face of the Earth. Such was the supposition our Indian forebears simply could not understand: How could we assume a *proprietary right* over the land? What, indeed, could that mean? How could that which bears sacred power to man be obliterated in that capacity by an absolutized claim to exert a power of disposition over it?

Even for the Indian, when he lived so unobtrusively upon the land which owned him, wilderness seems to have afforded a measure of dialectical interplay with daily life—as an ultimate place of withdrawal, of purification, of fasting, of vigil, and of prayer. There if anywhere he might find himself addressed in a manner decisive at once for his own life and that of his people. His withdrawal, his removal from others into solitude, marked a suspension of normal pursuits and a bringing of the manifold of his cares into closer proximity with that sovereign spirit to which he felt himself to belong: gatherer of the world of fellow creatures and sustainer of the ancestral voices which might speak to him again; source of those promptings from which his whole life might take on direction more appropriate to it and which his own intentions and daily endeavors might have tended to dissipate, to inhibit, or to misconstrue. The dialectical interplay between such wilderness placement and the mainstream placement of everyday life was implicitly appreciated as something fundamental and not to be intruded upon by other members of the community. Correspondingly there was nothing ostentatious about either the withdrawal or the return. Others could understand what such a thing might mean and the discretion it would presuppose. The community carried wilderness in its heart and wilderness spoke to men in their solitude as bearers of the community as well. Even for the Indian, living in the immediacy and constancy of wilderness, it seems to have called for some measure of placement in withdrawal from everyday life. One might speak of this as a kind of sabbatical placement relative to the currency of everyday pursuits. Of course in everyday life, too, and seasonally as well, rituals of mindfulness, of acknowledgment, kept faith with the deliverances of solitude.

In the Indian cultures of former times, most salient for our consideration is the tradition of reverence and respect in which the land was received and acknowledged. Can it be that this is the vein in which wilderness requires of us that it be understood? And may it be that even the wilderness left to us is itself our vestigial hope of being instructed in such a vein? If so, by inverse proportion the need of the instruction increases as the opportunity for it decreases. And the opportunity decreases by reason of the want of instruction. To the extent that we may be far down the road of such a progression, it would follow that the potential significance of wilderness in American life may be as critical as obliviousness to it may be prevalent.

The pervasive culture seems to be in dialectical *contrariety* to a wilderness ethos. Technology may be the mechanical embodiment—the vehicle—of that culture, seemingly endowed with overwhelming autonomy. Yet the language of the culture betrays the underlying human stance: the claimant's stance, speaking in terms of want and use, resources at our disposal, the exertion of control, the projection of goals, and the humanly conferred status of "values." The language itself is programmed and consumerized, accomplishing a packaging and marketing of meaning in banalized form. A "processing" of meaning has tended to supplant responsibility for meaning, and human communication has become a problem to which techniques of solution are sought. Feeling, having become subjectivized, is one thing, and thought, having become objectivized, is another—rendering thoughtful commitment an anomaly hardly to be recognized, let alone carried out. Yet everywhere rights are asserted and demands are pressed, and accountability has become a watchword of the day. Responsibility is chiefly what one insists upon from others, and quantitative measurement of how they are measuring up would get us down to brass tacks. For oneself there is the central possibility of a life of one's own to do with as one pleases, in exchange for an abstract concession that others are like-minded about this and will expect not to be interfered with in the right they likewise claim to jurisdiction over their own lives. And isn't property, too, the embodiment of that claim? Indeed it is a propriety claim, through and through.

What, then, of lands not owned by private and corporate interests? They come under public ownership and the mediation of government jurisdiction. In the aspect of property, nonetheless, they are subsumed under right of use. One has the right to use public land as he pleases so long as his exercise of that right does not conflict with that of other users. The values for the sake of which a person uses such land remain his own business; let him use it for what he gets out of it. Some get aesthetic values. Some get economic values. Some get recreational values. Some get religious values. Some get wilderness values. That's the package. And the public buys it so long as human uses and value-profits are kept equitably distributed, and the resources made use of are not getting scarce. While the uses and corresponding values remain the business of those concerned in them, the disposi-

tion of the public land requires a neutral managerial stance in arbitrating to accommodate competing uses and values. The weighting of uses and values is to be adjudicated and according to the numbers of their respective adherents and advocates. And what if a comparatively few were to claim large tracts as appropriate to their peculiar use and values at the expense of excluding a host of others with their uses and values? Where interest confers status on the land, what a high-handed lockout that would be. In such terms the keeping of wilderness would seem tantamount to an arbitrary transferral of public property to the status of the private property of a very few—even if unspecified—persons. A selfish, self-appointed elite, no doubt, who want the land all to themselves. In an age when the very resources on which our way of life depends are in shrinking supply and increasing demand, is someone going to have the temerity to pose *wilderness* as a scarce resource? Why, the very category of resource commits one by implication to development of it, and to pose wilderness as a resource implying the contrary would carry contradiction to the point of perversity indeed. Such is the embarrassment of the Forest Service when called upon to manage land by leaving it alone, a *reductio ad absurdum* and emasculation, it would seem, of this managerial agency. No, it would be difficult for this agency of ours to represent us in a capacity other than that of handmaiden of development. Even to enforce a measure of restraint in this capacity has often placed it at odds with the thrust of a "culture of values," for which economic development is the underlying and the dominant carrier of our orientation and destiny, setting the very categories of our thought and speech.

Of what significance, then, can wilderness be—in dialectical *contrariety* with such a culture? Well, it can give the lie to it. It can extend, now and then, its elemental emissaries to shores, to suburbs, to the folks downriver, to throngs in airports, to the passengers of balked transports, to the breadbasket of America, to swaying buildings and empty streets. In pelting downpours, the reach of sky, the weathering willy-nilly impartial to all, the crawling of ants, the cry of gulls and caw of crows, the rankness of weeds, the silence of snow. Perhaps too in occasional revels Dionysus comes, and the wild is revived in the human frame, the fibres of life plucked to the wild strain. The stirring of barnyard fowl to their migrating kin. God save us, then, 'ere there be life in us yet. May we struggle the birth of tongues of our own and derive our words as we use them from the wild stock. And we may yet believe "that a tide rises and falls behind every man which can float the British Empire like a chip, if he should ever harbor it in his mind." Our very dreams might suggest the hidden bulk of the wild which is immolated by our day. And the culture *contrary* to the wild may prove after all, though cloying, to be made of feeble stuff, able to pass itself off only in our waking sleep; some pantomime of life, a common dream, mumbled in unison by an endless crowd.

Need the awakening be rude? Or might it be graced by some gentleness and simplicity? That would seem to depend on each one, who must determine in his heart whether he will be party to claiming ownership of life, thus to remain the slave of consumption, rigidified in the conflicts of control, anxiously demanding, stultified in imagination, and ungenerous toward life itself. Not just in getting and spending, but in passing time, too, there is fostered the sense of the world running out, tending into vacuousness, a deathly trend. Apocalyptic visions only dramatize the sense of the affair.

A more radical reckoning and a more thoughtful way seem to be gaining upon us, if even in spite of ourselves. The revulsions of younger people are telling signs. They clearly do not subscribe to the propertied life. They seem prepared to do with less without feeling deprived. The quality of lived relationships concerns them far more than the setting and achieving of goals of accomplishment. And it is above all among the young that a new sense of the land seems to be gathering force. They can understand what it might mean to renounce the titular stance in relation with the land. When they speak at these wilderness hearings, as so many of them have, they speak almost univocally of places and creatures having claim upon us to be recognized in their own right. Their plea is not to appropriate a few pristine places to themselves but, here and there, to acknowledge what is thus given us in a manner appropriate to it, with gratitude, with forbearance, with respect, in a more liberal frame of mind akin to sacrifice. For them wilderness is the stronghold of a new ethos upon the land, working in dialectical *complementarity* with the full range of the relationships and activities in which we may stand.

Yet, how could it be that a place might hold such force? Only, it would seem, in some radical way—positioning us, as it were, with respect to our involvement in reality, as a matter to be resolved. No doubt our situation is always implicitly a metaphysical affair. But wilderness, to the extent that it will not permit one to take one's surroundings for granted, is a place which will not let one off the metaphysical hook. At the same time it establishes us in such decisively lived relationship with our surroundings that it precludes subsumption of the lived relationship to any depictive representation of how we are situated in relation to our surroundings, for example in ecological terms. We are not there as seen by ourselves, as parts within a whole. No, we are there as on the spot with respect to the meaning of what we behold. How does nature speak to our concern? That is the question. And the relationship is one of participation in what occurs, the presencing of heaven-and-earth and of all that abounds therein. One is brought to realize one is held within the embrace of what is proffered in its being proffered. No behind or beyond the things themselves. Therefore no understanding of their presencing in the mode of a comprehension of it. From within the lived relationship in which the presencing occurs must arise the *sense* of the occurrent, if at all. The givens of life are laid down. The foundations of the world are laid. Things are in place and stand firm.

Beings stand forth on their own. They do not ask our leave. They invite mutuality. That measure of trust. If one agrees to live with them, rather than summarily to reduce them to the service of intention. In contrast with the subordination of attention to intention, to be intent in attending is to give heed, and therein the perceived may work evocatively, to cumulative effect. Together, the perceived and perceiver enter into the working of the world: things in their meaning as responded to, taking shape. In wilderness the partnership of man and nature dawns on our surmise—prior to all undertaking and use to which nature may lend. The partnership seems to be a dialogic affair, in which we are charged with responsibility in the way things come to mean, having been placed in that way. Even as the things of the place command attention in the presencing of the world they are discovered to us from within the depth of responsiveness in confirmation of our mutuality with them. Reflexively we acknowledge ourselves in promisory relation with the given, even as the given warrants our full attention. A two-fold authorization, or sponsorship, of the pledging of ourselves in the relationship seems to obtain: At once salient in attention, there is the initiative of the reach of nature as given—primordially given—yet given at the same time in a receiving of the given reflexively sponsored from within a depth underlying our own ability to respond. Thus nature jumps with the responsive soul on the strength of a power imparted in unison to both. Its grace is twofold and affords the foundation of respect, which is in turn at once respect for beings as given in attention and—reflexively—self-respect. In this fashion we are ordained in responsible relationship with beings given into our keeping in the very presencing of the world. The mystery of this, it would seem, can only deepen, and with its deepening enhance the sense the world might make. But one is charged to make good on that sense, and in the mainstream of human destiny within which its implications require to be worked out—within the full gamut of ambiguities, of perplexities, and of anguish that prevail in the received world. Primordial placement again and again requires to be worked out in the flux of our historical and communal placement, in our shared participation in the lived world. But what has been found meaningful asks to be shared in the lived world, in a bringing forth in consciousness, in a speaking it both sponsors and calls for, in a finding of embodiment. True solitude is as a wellspring of communal life; its return affords measure of what has become of communal life, perhaps most closely in the dissipation of one's own resolutions, the forgetting of one's whence and whitherto. For wilderness puts our standard of living to the test. What can stand to the mutuality of man and nature can be affirmed in the relations between men. What cannot stands to exposure as scurf. And without respect for nature man cannot stand, not even in the mutual regard of men. For it is in coming to know fellow creatures as such that respect for them can obtain as warranted and upheld. One's fellow men as well come to one in solitude, for how else should one come forth to greet them, knowingly, and by way of confirmation of that in which we share?

Neither the proportion of time one may spend there nor the numbers for whom it figures in direct encounter would seem indicative of the potential significance of wilderness for the quality of human life. If its instruction goes deep its implications are lifelong, and only with long discipline, it seems, does one commence to fathom the instruction received. That discipline may well be as intensely an affair of embodiment as it can become one of reflection. The sea and the land we walk are prolongations of the task. Again and again it is as if one first gets the feel of the matter simply in movement and the coursing of breath and blood, the working of a frame of mind, a dispositon sent in quest of forms appropriate to its explicitation and the realization of what is asking to be born. Incipient gestures are fledged in fumbling speech, fragile-winged and fleeting. But permission is granted to participate in the world, and nature invites it. To breathe, to walk, to sleep, to rise, to eat and to drink; to talk. In all these, of our daily doing, the style of nature may qualify our life—with some measure of primordial simplicity, so unobtrusively withal as to escape notice quite. That nature is with us more surely than we know seems sure. Out of a very piety of the body some places might be kept sacred to us. They will bless the lands in which we dwell. But nothing can bless us apart from being acknowledged in its own right.

Robert Lowell
(1917–1977)

Robert Lowell is widely regarded as one of the most gifted poets of his generation. A writer of immense talent, Lowell was always enlarging the scope of his art and colonizing new spiritual territory. Lowell possessed an extraordinary ability to place himself at the cultural and historical center of things both by feeling the casualties of our past as personal tribulations and by turning private agonies into representative forms of public experience. Lowell's sensibility was religious even after his verse lost its gnarled, theological edge. Where in his earlier poetry he engrafted a severe and violent Roman Catholicism to the aesthetics of a literary formalist, in his later work he developed the more informal, if still tensed, voice of a latterday New England Puritan who addresses moral and spiritual problems in terms of great personal as well as political immediacy.

"Thanks-Offering for Recovery" (1977)

The airy, going house grows small
tonight and soft enough to be
　　crumpled up
like a handkerchief in my hand.

Here with you by this hotbed of coals,
I am the *homme sensuel,* free
to turn my back on the lamp, and
　　work.
Something has been taken off,
a wooden winter shadow—
goodbye nothing. I give thanks,
　　thanks—
thanks too for this small
Brazilian *ex voto,* this primitive head
sent me across the Atlantic by my
　　friend . . .
a corkweight thing,
to be offered *Deo gratias* in church
on recovering from head-injury or
　　migraine—
now mercifully delivered in my hands,
though shelved awhile unnoticing and
　　unnoticed.
Free of the unshakable terror that
　　made me write . . .
I pick it up, a head holy and unholy,
tonsured or damaged,
with gross black charcoaled brows and
　　stern eyes
frowning as if they had seen the
　　splendor
times past counting . . . unspoiled,
solemn as a child is serious—
light balsa wood the color of my skin.
It is all childcraft, especially
its shallow, chiseled ears,
crudely healed scars lumped out
to listen to itself, perhaps, not knowing
it was made to be given up.
Goodbye nothing. Blockhead,
I would take you to church,
if any church would take you . . .
This winter, I thought
I was created to be given away.

BT-81-0964